D0671418

THE CAROLINAS & GEORGIA

18th Edition

Where to Stay and Eat
for All Budgets

Must-See Sights
and Local Secrets

Ratings You Can Trust

Fodor's Travel Publications   New York, Toronto, London, Sydney, Auckland
www.fodors.com

FODOR'S THE CAROLINAS & GEORGIA

Editors: Salwa Jabado *(lead project editor)*, Doug Stallings

Editorial Contributors: Jess Moss
Writers: Christine Anderson, Liz Biro, Mary Erskine, Michele Foust, Amber Nimocks, Lan Sluder, Eileen Robinson Smith, Christine Van Dusen

Production Editor: Astrid deRidder
Maps & Illustrations: David Lindroth, Ed Jacobus, *cartographers*; Bob Blake, Rebecca Baer, *map editors;* William Wu, *information graphics*
Design: Fabrizio La Rocca, *creative director*; Guido Caroti, Siobhan O'Hare, *art directors*; Tina Malaney, Chie Ushio, Ann McBride, Jessica Walsh, *designers*; Melanie Marin, *senior picture editor*
Cover Photo: Parris Island, South Carolina: Eric Horan
Production Manager: Amanda Bullock

COPYRIGHT

Copyright © 2009 by Fodor's Travel, a division of Random House, Inc.

Fodor's is a registered trademark of Random House, Inc.

All rights reserved. Published in the United States by Fodor's Travel, a division of Random House, Inc., and simultaneously in Canada by Random House of Canada, Limited, Toronto. Distributed by Random House, Inc., New York.

No maps, illustrations, or other portions of this book may be reproduced in any form without written permission from the publisher.

18th Edition

ISBN 978–1–4000–0808–7

ISSN 1525–5832

SPECIAL SALES

This book is available at special discounts for bulk purchases for sales promotions or premiums. Special editions, including personalized covers, excerpts of existing books, and corporate imprints, can be created in large quantities for special needs. For more information, write to Special Markets/Premium Sales, 1745 Broadway, MD 6-2, New York, New York 10019, or e-mail specialmarkets@randomhouse.com.

AN IMPORTANT TIP & AN INVITATION

Although all prices, opening times, and other details in this book are based on information supplied to us at press time, changes occur all the time in the travel world, and Fodor's cannot accept responsibility for facts that become outdated or for inadvertent errors or omissions. So **always confirm information when it matters**, especially if you're making a detour to visit a specific place. Your experiences—positive and negative— matter to us. If we have missed or misstated something, **please write to us.** We follow up on all suggestions. Contact the The Carolinas & Georgia editor at editors@fodors.com or c/o Fodor's at 1745 Broadway, New York, NY 10019.

PRINTED IN THE UNITED STATES OF AMERICA

10 9 8 7 6 5 4 3 2

Be a Fodor's Correspondent

Your opinion matters. It matters to us. It matters to your fellow Fodor's travelers, too. And we'd like to hear it. In fact, we need to hear it.

When you share your experiences and opinions, you become an active member of the Fodor's community. That means we'll not only use your feedback to make our books better, but we'll publish your names and comments whenever possible. Throughout our guides, look for "Word of Mouth," excerpts of your unvarnished feedback.

Here's how you can help improve Fodor's for all of us.

Tell us when we're right. We rely on local writers to give you an insider's perspective. But our writers and staff editors—who are the best in the business—depend on you. Your positive feedback is a vote to renew our recommendations for the next edition.

Tell us when we're wrong. We're proud that we update most of our guides every year. But we're not perfect. Things change. Hotels cut services. Museums change hours. Charming cafés lose charm. If our writer didn't quite capture the essence of a place, tell us how you'd do it differently. If any of our descriptions are inaccurate or inadequate, we'll incorporate your changes in the next edition and will correct factual errors at fodors.com immediately.

Tell us what to include. You probably have had fantastic travel experiences that aren't yet in Fodor's. Why not share them with a community of like-minded travelers? Maybe you chanced upon a beach or bistro or B&B that you don't want to keep to yourself. Tell us why we should include it. And share your discoveries and experiences with everyone directly at fodors.com. Your input may lead us to add a new listing or highlight a place we cover with a "Highly Recommended" star or with our highest rating, "Fodor's Choice."

Give us your opinion instantly at our feedback center at www.fodors.com/feedback. You may also e-mail editors@fodors.com with the subject line "The Carolinas & Georgia Editor." Or send your nominations, comments, and complaints by mail to The Carolinas & Georgia Editor, Fodor's, 1745 Broadway, New York, NY 10019.

You and travelers like you are the heart of the Fodor's community. Make our community richer by sharing your experiences. Be a Fodor's correspondent.

Happy Traveling!

Tim Jarrell, Publisher

CONTENTS

ABOUT THIS BOOK

OUR RATINGS

Sometimes you find terrific travel experiences and sometimes they just find you. But usually the burden is on you to select the right combination of experiences. That's where our ratings come in.

As travelers we've all discovered a place so wonderful that its worthiness is obvious. And sometimes that place is so unique that superlatives don't do it justice: you just have to be there to know. These sights, properties, and experiences get our highest rating, **Fodor's Choice**, indicated by orange stars throughout this book.

Black stars highlight sights and properties we deem **Highly Recommended**, places that our writers, editors, and readers praise again and again for consistency and excellence.

By default, there's another category: any place we include in this book is by definition worth your time, unless we say otherwise. And we will.

Disagree with any of our choices? Care to nominate a place or suggest that we rate one more highly? Visit our feedback center at www.fodors.com/feedback.

BUDGET WELL

Hotel and restaurant price categories from ¢ to $$$$ are defined in the opening pages of each chapter. For attractions, we always give standard adult admission fees; reductions are usually available for children, students, and senior citizens. Want to pay with plastic? **AE, D, DC, MC, V** following restaurant and hotel listings indicate whether American Express, Discover, Diner's Club, MasterCard, and Visa are accepted.

RESTAURANTS

Unless we state otherwise, restaurants are open for lunch and dinner daily. We mention dress only when there's a specific requirement and reservations only when they're essential or not accepted—it's always best to book ahead.

HOTELS

Hotels have private bath, phone, TV, and air-conditioning unless we specify otherwise. They may operate on the Continental Plan (CP, with a Continental breakfast), Breakfast Plan (BP, with a full breakfast), or Modified American Plan (MAP, with breakfast and dinner). We always list facilities but not whether you'll be charged an extra fee to use them, so when

pricing accommodations, find out what's included.

Many Listings
★   Fodor's Choice
★   Highly recommended
⊠   Physical address
♣   Directions
🕮   Mailing address
☎   Telephone
🖷   Fax
⊕   On the Web
✎   E-mail
🖃   Admission fee
☉   Open/closed times
Ⓜ   Metro stations
🚃   Credit cards

Hotels & Restaurants
🏨   Hotel
🛏   Number of rooms
⚲   Facilities
🍽   Meal plans
✗   Restaurant
🕮   Reservations
🚭   Smoking
🍷   BYOB
✗🏨   Hotel with restaurant that warrants a visit

Outdoors
🏌   Golf
⛺   Camping

Other
☺   Family-friendly
⇨   See also
⊠   Branch address
☞   Take note

Experience the Carolinas & Georgia

WORD OF MOUTH

"My favorite beach getaway is Jekyll Island. Used to go to Hilton Head many years ago but hate the traffic and crowds. Jekyll is very small, very quiet and a lovely island. . . . We like to swim, fish, go crabbing, ride bikes, walk on the beach, etc. . . . If you load the car with groceries and rent a place, it's very economical. We love it!!"

—minimn

WHAT'S WHERE

The following numbers refer to chapters in the book.

2 The North Carolina Coast. Nothing in the region compares with the Outer Banks. This thin band of barrier islands with wind-twisted oaks and gnarled pines has some of the best beaches on the East Coast.

3 The Piedmont & the Sandhills, NC. The New South comes alive in three major metropolitan centers—Charlotte, the Triad, and the Triangle. Shopping, dining, and nightlife abound, and sports get top billing here, from college football games to NASCAR races.

4 The North Carolina Mountains. Western North Carolina is home to more than 1½-million acres of stupendous vertical scenery. In addition to opportunities for outdoor adventures, visitors will find edgy art galleries and sophisticated eateries in Asheville. The nation's largest private residence, the Biltmore House, sits nearby.

5 Great Smoky Mountains National Park. Nine million visitors annually can't be wrong; while the Smokies is the most visited of the national parks, there is more than enough beauty and deserted woodland on the 276,000 acres of the North Carolina side for peaceful communion with nature.

6 Myrtle Beach & the Grand Strand, SC. South Carolina's Grand Strand, a 60-mi-long expanse of white sandy beach, offers varied pleasures: the quiet refuge of Pawleys Island and its sometimes shabby, sometimes elegant summer homes; Brookgreen Gardens, with its magnificent sculptures and landscaped grounds; 120-plus golf courses; and the bustle of Myrtle Beach.

7 Charleston, SC. Charleston anchors the Lowcountry in high style. The harbor town's past, dating to 1670, is evident in cobblestone streets, antebellum mansions and plantations, and Gullah accents. It also hosts the renowned Spoleto performing arts festival.

8 Hilton Head, SC, & the Lowcountry. The coastal lowlands feature picturesque landscapes of coastal forests and wide-open marshes, undisturbed beaches, and fishing villages with quaint waterfront areas. Farther south, Hilton Head Island is home to more than 25 world-class golf courses and even more resorts, hotels, and top restaurants.

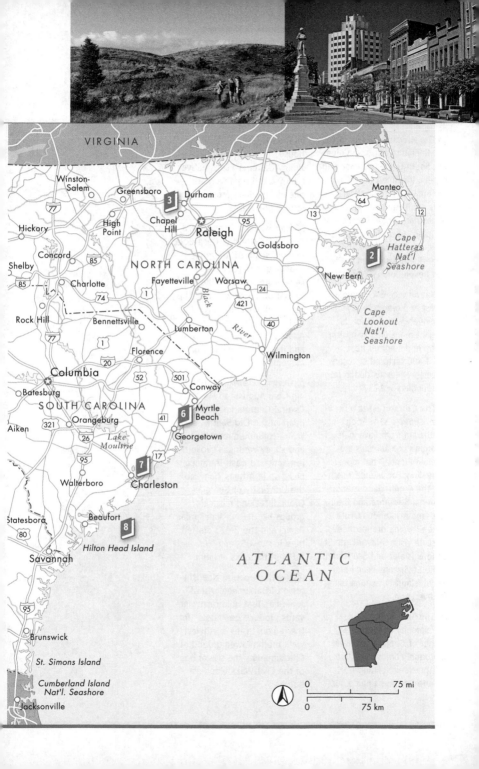

VIRGINIA

NORTH CAROLINA

Winston-Salem
Greensboro
Durham
Chapel Hill
Raleigh
Goldsboro
Manteo
Cape Hatteras Nat'l Seashore
High Point
Hickory
Concord
Charlotte
Fayetteville
Warsaw
New Bern
Shelby
Rock Hill
Bennettsville
Lumberton
Wilmington
Cape Lookout Nat'l Seashore
Black River
Florence
Columbia
Batesburg
SOUTH CAROLINA
Orangeburg
Conway
Myrtle Beach
Georgetown
Aiken
Lake Moultrie
Charleston
Walterboro
Beaufort
Hilton Head Island
Statesboro
Savannah
ATLANTIC OCEAN
Brunswick
St. Simons Island
Cumberland Island Nat'l. Seashore
Jacksonville

0   75 mi
0   75 km

WHAT'S WHERE

9 The Midlands & Upstate, SC. Radiating out from Columbia, South Carolina's engaging capital, the small towns of the area have their claims to fame: Aiken is a national equestrian center; Camden is the place to go for well-priced antiques; Greenwood and Abbeville are steeped in Civil and Revolutionary War history.

10 Savannah, GA. Georgia's oldest and grandest city, Savannah is known for its elegant mansions, Spanish moss, and summer heat. It has 1,400 restored or reconstructed buildings dating from its founding in 1733.

11 The Coastal Isles & the Okefenokee, GA. Stretching southward from Savannah, Georgia's coastal isles are "almost Florida," but more appealing. For wildlife watchers, the Cumberland Island National Seashore and the wild and mysterious Okefenokee Swamp are must-sees. Upscale visitors favor Little St. Simons Island and Sea Island, while St. Simons Island and Jekyll Island have something for everyone.

12 Southwest Georgia. The serenity of this quiet corner of Georgia has been thoroughly enjoyed by two U.S. presidents. Franklin Delano Roosevelt had a summer home, "The Little White House," in Warm Springs. Jimmy Carter, a Plains native, returned to begin work as one of America's most active former presidents.

13 Atlanta, GA. The Georgia Aquarium, World of Coca-Cola, High Museum of Art, great shopping, and restaurants keep visitors busy in the capital of the New South. The Martin Luther King Jr. National Historic Site brings to life Atlanta's racially divided past and its ties to the civil rights movement.

14 Central Georgia. Stretching from Augusta to Macon, Central Georgia lies at the heart of the Old South. White-columned mansions and shady verandas evoke a romanticized past. The pace picks up in Athens, home to the University of Georgia. Groundbreaking musical groups like R.E.M., Widespread Panic, and the B-52's started here in the '80s and '90s, and Athens still rocks at night.

15 North Georgia. Near the town of Dahlonega, site of America's first gold rush, vineyards produce new "gold" for the region. In the northwest, walk the hallowed ground of Chickamauga, the site of one of the Civil War's bloodiest battles.

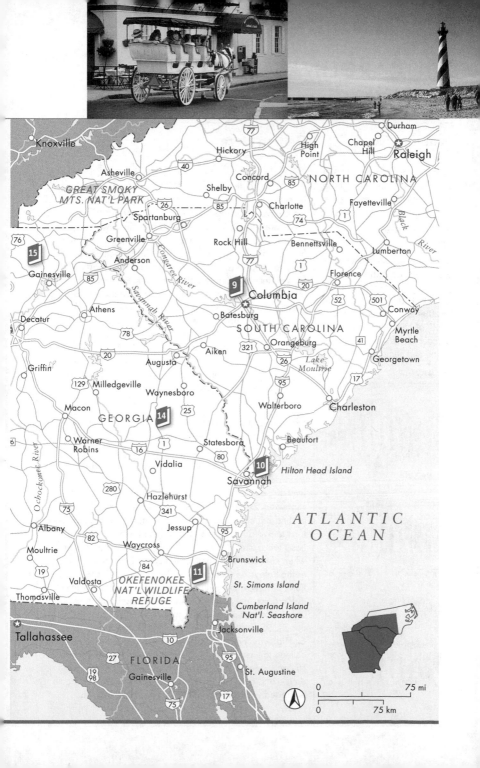

Knoxville

Durham

Chapel
Hill
High
Point

Raleigh

Hickory

Asheville

NORTH CAROLINA

GREAT SMOKY
MTS. NAT'L PARK

Concord

Shelby

Spartanburg

Charlotte

Fayetteville

Greenville

15

Anderson

Rock Hill

Bennettsville

Lumberton

Gainesville

9

Columbia

Florence

Conway

Decatur

Athens

Batesburg

SOUTH CAROLINA

Myrtle
Beach

Griffin

Aiken

Orangeburg

Georgetown

Augusta

Lake
Moultrie

Milledgeville

Waynesboro

Charleston

Macon

GEORGIA **14**

Walterboro

Warner
Robins

Statesboro

Beaufort

Vidalia

Savannah

10

Hilton Head Island

Hazlehurst

ATLANTIC
OCEAN

Albany

Jessup

Moultrie

Waycross

Brunswick

Valdosta

11

St. Simons Island

Thomasville

OKEFENOKEE
NAT'L WILDLIFE
REFUGE

Cumberland Island
Nat'l. Seashore

Jacksonville

Tallahassee

FLORIDA

Gainesville

St. Augustine

0   75 mi

0   75 km

THE CAROLINAS & GEORGIA PLANNER

When to Go

Spring is the best time to see the Carolinas and Georgia in bloom. Fall can bring spectacular foliage in the mountains.

CLIMATE

Spring and fall daytime temperatures are delightful—bring a jacket at night. Summer can be hot and humid. In winter, mild weather is punctuated by brief bouts of cold. Short afternoon thunderstorms are common in spring and summer.

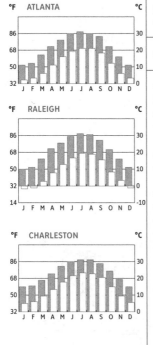

Getting Here

Due to the sheer number of flights into Hartsfield-Jackson Atlanta International Airport (ATL) it's often the most logical, if hectic, choice for the region. Flying here means navigating a crowded airport and Atlanta's notorious traffic snarls. If you are staying in Atlanta, especially in downtown, Midtown, or Buckhead, consider taking the MARTA train from the airport to your hotel. The Charlotte-Douglas International Airport (CLT) in North Carolina is a good option for travelers heading to both Carolinas. Raleigh-Durham International Airport (RDU) is located in the heart of the state, making it convenient for the eastern and central areas of North Carolina. The Asheville Regional Airport (AVL) provides access to the mountains and adjoining areas. The Piedmont Triad International Airport (GSO) serves Greensboro, Winston-Salem, and High Point. For links to these airports, the airlines that serve them, and more, go to ⊕ *www.airlineandairportlinks.com.*

Getting Around

Once in the region, major highways—such as Interstates 75, 85, 20, 40, and 95 lead to major cities and many other destinations. For beachgoers, the route to hit is Highway 17, along the Grand Strand. In the mid-Carolinas, Highways 27 and 77 are important connectors. Especially around big cities such as Charlotte and Atlanta, plan your trips to avoid rush hours. If staying in town, check with hosts for expected road conditions, even on the weekends when concerts, ball games, and special events can cause traffic delays. In Georgia, the Department of Transportation's ⊕ *www.georgia-navigator.com* provides real-time traffic data, including trip times and construction and accident information on major highways statewide. Myrtle Beach, SC, is likely to feel the effect of travelers jamming in on Highway 17 on holiday weekends. Sports fans rush into college towns such as Clemson, NC; Athens, GA; Chapel Hill and Raleigh, NC; and Atlanta, GA during big game days—and in the South every game is a big game. Come equipped with directions, atlases, or a GPS system.

1

With Kids

Try these sights around the Carolinas and Georgia for guaranteed family fun.

WET AND WILD

NASCAR's slick **Lowe's Motor Speedway** in Charlotte, NC, holds up to 167,000 fans on race days. On non-race days, racetrack tours—including a drive around the track—are available.

Atlanta's **Georgia Aquarium** is the largest in the world, with sea creatures in 8 million gallons of water.

The **Kangaroo Conservation Center** in Dawsonville, GA, is home to the largest gathering of the hopping critters outside Australia. A bonus is the center's avid focus on the environment.

BACK TO THE FUTURE

Guides in native costume at the **Oconaluftee Indian Village** will take you back 225 years with demonstrations of weaving, hunting techniques, and canoe construction. The nearby **Museum of the Cherokee Indian** contains artifacts and displays that cover 12,000 years. Both are near Cherokee, NC, and the entrance to the Great Smoky Mountains National Park.

Flash forward a few thousand years and visit the **Wright Brothers National Memorial**, south of Kitty Hawk, NC. Stand right on the spot where the Ohio bicyclists first took flight on December 17, 1903, and examine a replica of their Flyer.

HANDS-ON ADVENTURES

Along the way to major attractions, take side trips to spots guaranteed to please. **EdVenture Children's Museum** in Columbia, SC, is nothing but hands-on fun, from science experiments to anchoring a real newscast.

Myrtle Beach is awash with activities guaranteed to bring smiles—and squeals—from the **Family Kingdom Amusement Park** to **Myrtle Waves**, the state's largest water park.

DO NOTHING

Collect shells on the beach during a stroll on **Pawleys Island**, NC. Stalk bears, deer, and elk in the **Smoky Mountains**. Splash through the Fountain of Rings at **Atlanta's Centennial Olympic Park**. Just remember to bring sunscreen, bug repellent, and a change of clothes!

Southernisms

Use this knowledge of Southernisms and Southern culture while navigating around.

FOOD & DRINK

Sweet tea, made by dissolving cupfuls of sugar in hot tea and adding ice, is the aptly named universal beverage of the South.

Very Southern restaurants offer **meat-and-three** menus. Think of it as a cafeteria: your choice of a meat or fish main accompanied by three vegetable sides, which almost always include mac and cheese. Yup, it's a veggie in the South.

Whenever possible, order **angel biscuits,** so light they float on air, and smother them with butter and honey or sausage gravy.

Boiled peanuts, usually found at road-side stands, are nothing like their roasted Virginia cousins. They're served hot, salty, and packed in juice and are a real taste of the South—if an acquired one.

TALK PURTY

"Fixing to" find a store that carries postcards? Ask the clerk, but don't be startled if the reply is: "sure don't." That's not said to be "ugly," or ill mannered, but to be polite, Southern style.

Even in their disdain, Southerners show a certain grace, couching insults or pity in phrases like "poor thing" and "bless your heart."

TOP EXPERIENCES

Play top Southern chef

Comfort-food junkies may not learn how to make creamy mac and cheese, Southern fried chicken, or gooey butter cake while they're at **The Lady & Sons** restaurant in Savannah, Georgia, but they sure can enjoy tasting all of Paula Deen's favorites. And while Momma may be busy taping her television shows or writing a cookbook, customers might also get the chance to meet sons Jamie or Bobby while they're buttering their biscuits.

Learn secrets from the vintners

On Georgia's Wine Trail, oenophiles can taste their fill of award-winning wines, walk among the vineyards, admire outstanding views, and learn secrets about the grapes from the vintners themselves. From vintners David Harris at **BlackStock Winery** near Dahlonega and John Ezzard at **Tiger Mountain Vineyards**, near Clayton, the information flows as easily as the fine wines.

Hit a hole-in-one like the pros

The Southeast is known for its outstanding golf courses. While no one but members can play the **Augusta National Golf Course**, longtime home of the Masters Tournament, the hundreds of courses in the region provide ample opportunities to get in some practice and play Tiger Woods wannabes. And while Augusta National closed sales for tournament badges in 2000, a limited number of practice-round tickets are available. Applications must be filed by mid-July for the next year's tournament. Lucky winners are notified in early September for the next year's round.

Swim or dive with the fishes

Make a splash at the **Georgia Aquarium** by becoming part of a new educational program allowing a limited number of land-lubbers to pay for a swim or dive in the Ocean Voyager's 6.3-million-gallon tank. They cavort with fish including zebra and whale sharks, schools of tarpon, cownose rays, and many more ocean creatures.

Touch the clouds

By car or by trail, check out the clouds and gorgeous scenery at the tip-top of North and South Carolina and Georgia. And don't forget to bring a camera to record the visit! Taking top honors is **Mount Mitchell**, near Burnsville, NC, the highest point east of the Mississippi at 6,686 feet. **Sassafras Mountain**, with an elevation of 3,560 feet, is located in northwestern South Carolina. In Georgia, **Brasstown Bald** near Hiawassee claims the honor at 4,784 feet.

Live like royalty for a day

Tour the luxurious **Biltmore Estate** chateau and grounds, taste the homegrown wine, and enjoy a meal at one of the estate's restaurants. You can even stay the night on the 8,000-acre property at the **Inn on Biltmore Estate**. A visit during the holiday season means sparkling Biltmore decorations, special events, and live music. Another memorable Asheville, NC, splurge is spending the night at the legendary **Grove Park Inn**, enjoying a fine dinner, drinks, and music in front of the massive fireplace in the lobby. Wake up to pampering at the 40,000-square-foot spa, featuring swimming and mineral pools, waterfalls, and hot tubs. It's been named one of the country's finest spas.

Take a hike—all the way to Maine

The **Appalachian National Scenic Trail**, known to hikers as the AT, begins at Springer Mountain in Georgia and meanders 2,175 mi north to Maine. Walkers, day hikers, or backpackers can catch por-

tions of the trail in parks and at highways that cross it. Hiking is especially spectacular in the spring, when wildflowers bloom, and fall, when the leaves paint the mountains red, orange, and yellow. The South's hiking areas are among the most remote and strenuous on the trail—for anything but a short hike, prepare ahead. If you're just looking for a great photo op featuring a massive AT engraved rock, head to Dicks Creek Gap, on U.S. 76 near Clayton, GA.

Drive like a demon

Richard Petty Driving Experience participants can drive a NASCAR Sprint Cup–style stock car at speeds as fast as 155 mph around the Lowe's Motor Speedway track, or they can choose to go along for a ride with an instructor at speeds as high as 165 mph. Laps allowed 'round the track vary from three to 80, depending on the package selected. The adventure is a hands-on inside look at the sport, from the driver's perspective. For many fans, it's a lifelong dream fulfilled. Reservations are recommended for driving, but last-minute chances are available if you have a valid driver's license and are able to drive a four-speed manual transmission.

Chill out at the beach

Whether the beach means shag music, tacky T-shirts, and water parks, which you'll find in ample supply at South Carolina's **Myrtle Beach**, or quiet days spent contemplating one of the most beautiful shorelines, looking for dolphin, and shell collecting on Georgia's **Jekyll Island**, the Carolinas-Georgia coast has universal appeal. Treat yourself to a truly Southern experience and rent a cottage—or grand home—right on the shorefor a vacation retreat.

Southern shopping spree

Southerners know how to look gorgeous in the most humid weather and to dress their homes to dispense the grandest Southern hospitality. That takes great shopping experience and demand for quality. Check out upscale **King Street** in Charleston, SC, for Saks Fifth Avenue, Bob Ellis Shoe Store, and Ann Taylor, as well as antiques and specialty shops aplenty. **Phipps Plaza** and **Lenox Square** in Atlanta, GA, are quintessential shopping destinations. And conveniently, the two sit catty-corner on Peachtree Road. **Concord Mills** in Charlotte, NC, keeps shoppers more than satisfied with Bass Pro Shops Outdoor World, Polo Ralph Lauren Factory Store, Bose Factory Outlet, NASCAR SpeedPark, Anne Klein Outlet, and Brooks Brothers. **North Georgia Premium Outlets** offers Restoration Hardware, Ann Taylor, Burberry, Coach, and many more.

Time travel to the Antebellum South

While the Yankees occupied the small mill town of Roswell, GA, in 1864 and burned its cotton and woolen mills, they spared its antebellum mansions, mill workers' homes, and churches on their trek toward the battle of Atlanta. Today visitors tour a 640-acre historic district. Highlights are three historic homes open daily: **Bulloch Hall**, where Teddy Roosevelt's mother was married; **Barrington Hall**, a stunning Greek Revival home; and the **Archibald Smith Plantation**, once part of a 300-acre cotton farm. Catch weekend ghost tours featuring tales of haunted houses. While you're there, enjoy fine dining, art galleries, boutiques, and antiques shops.

QUINTESSENTIAL CAROLINAS & GEORGIA

Serious BBQ

Barbecue is one of the most revered traditions in the region. Eating barbecue is a social event—from church lunches to July 4 parties to family get-togethers. Even at restaurants, customers often share long tables filled most often with pork barbecue (served chopped, sliced or pulled from the bone), white bread or buns, never-ending glasses of sweet tea, and extra sauce. Locals are fiercely loyal to their favorite 'cue haunts and their favorite sauces. Visitors quickly learn that while most sauces are based on ketchup, mustard, vinegar, and hot peppers, there are exceptions. On the coast in all three states, but especially in eastern North Carolina, barbecue is served with a flavorful mixture of vinegar, spices, and hot peppers. Central South Carolina is known for its mustard barbecue. Richer sauces containing ketchup, molasses, and onion show up in the mountains.

The Big Game

It's hard not to feel like a local surrounded by thousands of sports fans yelling, screaming, or, in the case of Georgia Bulldog boosters, barking for their favorite college teams. During football season a party atmosphere takes over the entire region, when cars festooned with colorful flags, decals, and bumper stickers stream toward the stadiums. But all the action doesn't take place in fall: basketball is also legendary, with powerhouse teams playing in packed arenas in all three states. Even for games featuring famous rivals—the University of South Carolina and Clemson, the University of North Carolina and North Carolina State University, and the University of Georgia and Georgia Tech—tickets are generally available.

If you want to get a sense of contemporary culture in the Carolinas and Georgia, and indulge in some of the region's pleasures, start by getting familiar with the rituals of daily life. These are a few highlights—things visitors can take part in with relative ease.

On the Waterfront

The blue ribbons of rivers, creeks, and streams do more than decorate the green landscape of the Carolinas and Georgia. They're among the region's most popular destinations for outdoor enthusiasts. Jet Skis and pontoon boats can be found on the glass-smooth lakes, and canoes and kayaks are great for exploring mysterious swamps hung with Spanish moss. In the mountains, roaring rapids promise a wild ride for white-water rafters, and quieter stretches are perfect for a lazy afternoon in an inner tube. And anglers won't be disappointed, either. Children here don't just learn how to fish; they set crab traps with chicken necks and maneuver nets to bring home a mess of shrimp. The ocean is never far away, and more remote shores such as Kitty Hawk and Ocracoke Island offer peace and privacy.

Southern Sounds

Bluegrass, blues, and gospel music all trace their lineage to the Carolinas and Georgia. Although each genre has a distinctive sound, they were all nurtured in the homes, churches, and social clubs of the region, where they were passed on to future generations. Hear this distinctive music today at pickin' parlors—where the competition can get fierce—and at local music festivals, county fairs, and in concert halls. Seek out Southern sounds— and some of the South's best barbecue— at Swallow at the Hollow in Roswell, just outside Atlanta. For a modern take, head to college towns like Athens, Georgia; Chapel Hill, North Carolina; and Columbia, South Carolina; where bands such as Hootie and the Blowfish, Ben Folds Five, and the B-52's got their start. And for fans of hip-hop and R&B, Atlanta is the place to gear up for great entertainment.

IF YOU LIKE

Southern Dining

Although Southerners still thrive on meat-and-three menus, cooking with fresh regional foods and herbs has also caught on in the South.

Savannah cook Paula Deen has reintroduced America to traditional Southern fare through her wildly successful **Lady and Sons** restaurant in Savannah, GA, and her cooking shows on the Food Network.

On your way into the Greek Revival mansion that houses Savannah's **Elizabeth on 37th,** you might see the staff snipping the herbs that flavor the remarkable dishes.

Mama Dip, aka Mildred Edna Cotton Council, opened her Chapel Hill, NC, restaurant in 1976, and serves up traditional Southern fare. To-go picnics include fried chicken, potato and pasta salads, pickles, and pecan tarts, all tucked inside a wicker basket.

Elsewhere in Georgia, Summerland Farm grows organic herbs and produce for use in Anne Quatrano and Clifford Harrison's award-winning Atlanta restaurant **Bacchanalia.** Quinones at Bacchanalia, another Quatrano and Harrison restaurant, emphasizes Southern cuisine.

Contemporary cuisine with a Southern twist—think okra rellenos and spicy green-tomato soup with crab and country ham—is the star of the show at **Magnolia Grill,** a Durham, NC hot spot.

Chef Bob Waggoner offers up buttermilk-fried oysters with deviled-egg dressing; confit with dirty grits; and pan-seared catfish with fried shrimp and grits at his **Charleston Grill** in South Carolina.

Golfing

One of the best reasons to visit the Carolinas and Georgia is that the mild climate allows play all year. Even better, the scenery is as good as the game. Courses abound in the area, but having the chance to play the most honored links during high seasons—spring and fall—can be a bigger challenge than getting a hole-in-one. Resorts and country clubs offer first choice of tee times to guests. If any times are left open, it is possible to get reservations.

Golf legend Bobby Jones called this resort "the St. Andrews of United States golf." The site of more championships than any other golf resort in the country, **Pinehurst,** in North Carolina, is consistently ranked among the best in the world. Among its eight courses, the Donald Ross–designed Number Two is considered the masterpiece.

Offering views of the ocean from all 18 holes, Kiawah Island Golf Resort's **Ocean Course** winds through salt marshes and seaside forests filled with wildlife, including the occasional alligator. This South Carolina course has one of most dramatic last holes in golf.

In the shadow of the Harbor Town Lighthouse, Hilton Head Island's **Harbour Town Golf Links** is devilishly difficult. Although deceptively short by today's standards, South Carolina's top course leaves no room for error.

Often called the "granddaddy of golf," **Pine Lakes Country Club** has long been a landmark in Myrtle Beach, SC. The columned clubhouse, resembling an antebellum mansion, was built in 1927.

Grand Gardens

The temperate climate in the Carolinas and Georgia, combined with the huge diversity of flora in the region, makes this area a draw for garden lovers.

Henry Middleton, president of the First Continental Congress, began the lush, semitropical gardens of Charleston, South Carolina's **Middleton Place and Magnolia Plantation and Gardens** in 1741. Restoration of the gardens began during World War I, and today they are among the most beautiful in the world, ablaze with camellias, azaleas, roses, and magnolias. Also in the area is one of America's oldest gardens, **Magnolia Plantation and Gardens**, first planted in the mid-1680s. Among the sights here are the **Barbados Tropical Garden** with plants native to the Caribbean and a **Biblical Garden** with many trees and flowers with connections to the Bible.

Two outstanding gardens are located in Asheville, NC. The 434-acre **North Carolina Arboretum** was established in 1986 as a part of the University of North Carolina. Here you can find a quilt garden, with plantings patterned after the designs found on local quilts. The castle-like grandeur of the **Biltmore Estate**, the country's largest private residence, has gorgeous grounds designed by Frederick Law Olmsted of New York City's Central Park fame.

The superb **Calloway Gardens** are part of a resort, but that shouldn't dissuade a visit to this outstanding spot in Pine Mountain, Georgia. **Overlook Garden** has some 700 varieties of azaleas, and the **Azalea Bowl** has 3,400 hybrid azaleas plants that should not to be missed in the spring.

Civil War History

The Civil War forever changed the character of the South, particularly the bastions of plantation life in the Carolinas and Georgia. In the many museums in the region, period furnishings offer a glimpse into antebellum life, and heart-wrenching letters tell of the toll the war took on families—rich and poor—and photographs show the hardships suffered by slaves.

A huge painting that encircles the viewer inside the **Atlanta Cyclorama & Civil War Museum** depicts the 1864 Battle of Atlanta in detail. Inside the museum there's an impressive collection of period weapons, uniforms, maps, and photographs.

The site of one of the Civil War's worst conflicts, Chickamauga battlefield saw almost 35,000 soldiers killed or injured during a three-day struggle in September of 1863. North Georgia's **Chickamauga & Chattanooga National Military Park and Visitor Center** offers a glimpse into the strategies used by both sides during the campaign. Visitors can take a 7-mi driving tour to see many of the 700 monuments and historical markers.

Although it was built to protect Charleston after the War of 1812, **Fort Sumter** became a symbol of Southern resistance after it became the site of the first battle of the Civil War. The first shots were fired here on April 12, 1861.

Near Charleston, **Drayton Hall** is the only plantation along Ashley River Road not destroyed during Gen. William Tecumseh Sherman's march through South Carolina.

GREAT ITINERARIES

SALT & SAND: THE BEACHES OF THE CAROLINAS & GEORGIA

The coastline of the Carolinas and Georgia runs for more than 600 mi and includes some of the superlative stretches of sand on the East Coast. If you're looking for the perfect beach vacation, visit one or more of the top beaches below.

Cumberland Island, GA

John F. Kennedy Jr. and Carolyn Bessette's barefoot wedding put Cumberland Island on the map. You won't forget the sight of wild horses running along the pristine beaches, high sand dunes, and lovely stretches of marsh. If your budget allows, stay at the island's only public lodging, the century-old Greyfield Inn.

Jekyll Island, GA

Jekyll Island was once the winter playground of the Rockefellers, Morgans, and Vanderbilts. For a taste of the millionaire's lifestyle, bunk at the 1886 Jekyll Island Club Hotel and drive around the island to see many of the sprawling "cottages" that were summer getaways for wealthy families a century ago.

Sapelo Island, GA

Sapelo Island's beaches are uncrowded and undeveloped, but the real reason to visit here is to glimpse the unique culture of the Geechee, direct descendents of slaves who speak a blend of English and West African languages. After a 30-minute ferry ride through the marshes, a local guide leads visitors on a fascinating tour.

Savannah & Tybee Island, GA

Stay in one of the lovely bed-and-breakfast inns of Savannah. Hit the 1950s-vintage beach resort of Tybee Island, about 18 mi east of downtown, for some beach time.

Hilton Head Island, SC

Best known for chic boutiques and outlet malls, trend-setting restaurants, and world-class golf resorts, Hilton Head Island also has a network of trails that let visitors explore this enclave off the South Carolina coast on foot, by bike, or at the lovely Sea Pines Resort.

Charleston, SC

Charleston delivers both the sand and salt and the chance to stroll by and visit outstanding historic homes. To fully appreciate Charleston's charms, you'll want to stay in a B&B or small inn. For a quick dip, Folly Beach and the Isle of Palms are a short drive away.

Myrtle Beach & the Grand Strand, SC

Myrtle Beach's carnival-like strip of mini-golf, mega water parks, T-shirt shops, and bars is part of the appeal of this family-friendly city. If you're looking for a quieter time, head farther south on the Grand Strand to Pawleys Island and Georgetown.

Ocracoke Island, NC

The island is basically one long beach, with nearly 16 mi of undeveloped national seashore. Don't miss the Ocracoke Lighthouse, the oldest operating lighthouse on the East Coast.

Hatteras Island, NC

Hatteras Island, a 33-mi-long narrow ribbon of sandy national seashore, is dotted with seven small villages. You can explore two historic lighthouses or go birding at the Pea Island National Wildlife Refuge.

CHARLOTTE: HUB-AND-SPOKE ITINERARIES

Charlotte, NC, is a fascinating and diverse city, and its central location makes it ideal as a hub for a series of several-day itineraries throughout the Carolinas and Georgia. Pick and choose from these great trips after seeing the sights in Charlotte.

Two days: Charlotte, NC

Charlotte, already the home of **Lowe's Motor Speedway** and the heart of NASCAR racing nationwide, is revving up for even more racing fever as the **NASCAR Hall of Fame** complex roars to completion early in 2010. Charlotte has lots to offer non-NASCAR fans as well. The **Mint Museum of Art** specializes in American and European paintings, as well as African and pre-Columbian art. And a ticket stub from the museum earns free admission to the **Mint Museum of Craft + Design**, a major American craft museum. Young visitors will happily spend time with the bugs and butterflies at the **Charlotte Nature Museum** that is affiliated with **Discovery Place**, a complex filled with an IMAX theater, a rain forest, and aquariums. And, the funky **North Davidson Arts District** lures shoppers and gawkers alike.

Getting Here: Fly into the Charlotte Douglas International Airport (CLT). While staying in Charlotte, consider using the Charlotte Area Transportation System, with its light rail, buses, and trolleys.

GREAT ITINERARIES

Three days: Asheville & Cherokee, NC
Asheville's beautiful mountain views, blooming arts and culture scene, cosmopolitan but funky downtown area, and lively restaurant and entertainment choices make it a great place to visit and one of the most livable cities in the country. While it is the home of the largest number of art deco buildings in the southeast outside Miami Beach, the city is best known for the French Renaissance chateau, the **Biltmore Estate**. The largest private residence in the country, with 250 rooms and extensive gardens, was constructed for George Vanderbilt in the 1890s. It's memorable to visit the home and gardens in warmer months, but the Christmas candlelight tours are spectacular. After taking in the sights of Asheville, spend a day in Cherokee at the **Oconaluftee Indian Village** and the **Great Smoky Mountains National Park**. You can learn about Native American culture and history, hike, take in the scenic views, and spot wildlife.

Getting Here: Drive about two hours northwest of Charlotte (try to avoid driving at rush hour) via I–85, U.S. 321, and I–40 to Asheville. Leaving Asheville, drive about one hour via I–40 and U.S. 19 to Cherokee.

Three days: Atlanta, GA
Atlanta may be hundreds of miles from the ocean, but travelers can come eye-to-eye with thousands of sea creatures at the **Georgia Aquarium**. A few visitors can even sign up to swim or dive with the fish (advance reservations are necessary). Right next door is the new **World of Coke**, offering the chance to learn about the city's hometown beverage. Amidst Atlanta's massive skyscrapers and high-rise condos are also some of the most beautiful parks in the Southeast—including the **Atlanta Botanical Garden** and **Centennial Olympic Park**. Children will be delighted with stops at the **Center for Puppetry Arts** and **Imagine It! The Children's Museum of Atlanta**. And while Atlanta may at first epitomize the New South—with its gleaming buildings and traffic jams—echoes from the past reverberate. Don't miss a stop at the **Ebenezer Baptist Church** and especially the **Birth Home of Martin Luther King Jr.** (sign up for limited same-day tickets early in the morning). Learn about the Civil War at the **Cyclorama**, the **Atlanta History Center**, and in small towns nearby, such as Marietta, Kennesaw, and Roswell, featuring museums and antebellum homes.

Getting Here: Take I–85 from Charlotte to Atlanta; it's about a four hour drive. Plan to avoid the gridlock that is Atlanta's rush hour.

Three days: Myrtle Beach & the Grand Strand, SC
Myrtle Beach, the showpiece of the 60-mi Grand Strand, explodes with visitors each summer seeking everything from amusement parks and nightlife to seafood restaurants and bargain shopping. Children can't wait to arrive at **Family Kingdom Amusement Park; Myrtle Waves**, South Carolina's water park behemoth; and the **IMAX Discovery Theater**. Golfers relish making choices between more than 120 golf courses, some designed by the game's top

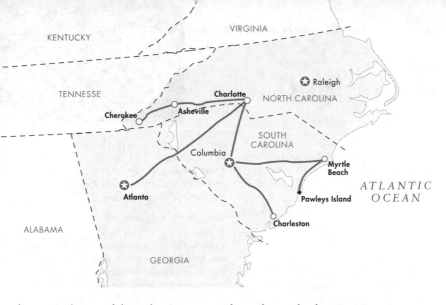

players. And none of that takes into consideration the miles of beach for walking, biking, shelling, surfing, sunbathing, and swimming. Nearby **Brookgreen Gardens**, the nation's oldest sculpture garden, is an oasis from the sometimes-frenetic energy along Myrtle Beach's Kings Highway, Ocean Boulevard, and Restaurant Row. For a bit more peace and quiet, travel slightly south to charming **Pawleys Island**, with its shabby-chic reputation, relaxed shopping areas, and beautiful beach. Lucky shell seekers will spot a Pawleys Island shell at low tide.

Getting Here: The three-hour trip from Charlotte to Myrtle Beach threads through North and South Carolina byways and federal highways, with no stretch longer than 44 miles. A site-to-site Internet map or GPS system is extremely helpful. It's a 35-minute trip from Myrtle Beach to Pawleys Island on U.S. 17 South.

Three days: Charleston, SC
Charleston is one of the most charming—and thoroughly Southern—cities in the Southeast. Historic buildings line the streets. There are over 2,000 in the downtown area alone. Some restored homes, such as the **Nathaniel Russell House**, are open to the public, and give the best firsthand view of life in the South in the early 1800s. After getting a close-up view of the city, head to the **Battery** for picturesque views of the striking mansions and the busy port. Then travel farther away to visit **Boone Hall Plantation and Garden** for a look at plantation life—from the mansion to the slave cabins. Charlestonians love the arts as much as history. Museums and art galleries fill the city—and it hosts the annual **Spoleto Festival USA** performing arts spectacle for more than two weeks in May and June.

Getting Here: The 3½-hour drive from Charlotte to Charleston is a direct route. Take I–77 South, and then merge onto I–26 East outside Columbia, SC.

TOP ATTRACTIONS

Cataloochee Cove, NC
In 1934 more than 1,200 residents of Cataloochee Cove had to abandon their town after the land became part of the Great Smoky Mountains National Park. Of their 200 buildings, only about a dozen remain, but they provide a fascinating look into the past.

Biltmore Estate, NC
The largest private home in the United States, much of the luxurious Biltmore Estate and gardens is open to the public. The French Renaissance chateau was built in the 1890s. Its ornate 250 rooms are filled with exquisite art and antiques collected by the Vanderbilts. The 8,000 acres of property include 75 acres of landscaped grounds and gardens.

Blue Ridge Parkway, NC
Connecting the Great Smoky Mountains in North Carolina and Shenandoah National Park in Virginia is one of America's most scenic roadways. You can relax and enjoy the view on the meandering 469 mi road, 252 mi of which are in North Carolina, and stop at more than 250 scenic overlooks.

Brookgreen Gardens, SC
This idyllic sculpture garden, the oldest in America, showcases 550 pieces of American sculpture in outstanding outdoor garden galleries. On display is sculpture by Daniel Chester French, Frederic Remington, and Anna Hyatt Huntington, among others. It's kid-friendly too: their Lowcountry zoo has everything from alligators to otters.

Spoleto Festival USA, SC
The best of the performing arts in one of the country's most glorious cities, Spoleto transforms elegant Charleston into an entertainment paradise for more than two weeks each May and June. Dance, opera, theater, and music events—from symphony to rap—have been filling churches, auditoriums, and open-air sites since the festival began in 1977.

The Georgia Aquarium
Breathtaking beluga whales and whale sharks, the largest fish on the globe, are naturals at the world's largest aquarium. Pass through the 100-foot long underwater tunnel and see thousands of saltwater fish, from sharks to whip rays. The 8-million-gallon aquarium also has sea lions, otters, penguins, and a coral reef with tropical fish.

MLK National Historic District, GA
Make the poignant pilgrimage to Sweet Auburn in Atlanta to visit the King Center and learn about the civil rights movement and Dr. King's role in it. His tomb and that of his wife, Coretta Scott King, are here as well as a number of his personal effects. Take a guided tour of the modest home where King was born and then visit Ebenezer Baptist Church, where members of the King family preached for three generations.

Chickamauga & Chattanooga National Military Park, GA
The Civil War profoundly changed the nation, but little evidence of the war remains. At Chickamauga, 9,000 acres of battlefield have been preserved and enhanced to honor more than 34,000 Union and Confederate soldiers who were killed or injured there in one of the Civil War's bloodiest battles. Over 700 historical markers and monuments chronicle events that took place here in September 1863.

ON THE CALENDAR

WINTER	
December	Held in early December, Atlanta's **Children's Christmas Parade** benefiting Children's Healthcare of Atlanta is one of the Southeast's premiere Christmas traditions, attracting about 300,000 spectators. Highlights include marching bands, antique autos, floats, giant balloons, and more. Santa himself provides the grand finale. Winston-Salem's **Old Salem Christmas**, re-creates a traditional Moravian Christmas early in December.
January	In Atlanta, **Martin Luther King Jr. Week** is celebrated midmonth with lectures, exhibits, and rallies.
February	On the third weekend of the month, Asheville, NC, hosts the annual **National Arts and Crafts Conference** at the Grove Park Inn. Chapel Hill stages the **Carolina Jazz Festival,** usually at the end of the month. The weekend of lectures, concerts, and jam sessions includes many free events.
SPRING	
March	Spring is celebrated with a mid-month **International Cherry Blossom Festival** in Macon, GA. The city is covered with pink-and-white blooms, since its streets are lined with more than 300,000 trees. South Carolina's **SpringFest,** held on Hilton Head Island, takes place during the entire month. The **Annual Reenactment of the Battle of Guilford Courthouse** takes place the weekend nearest the battle date, March 15, in Greensboro, NC. Savannah has one of the country's most spirited celebrations of **St. Patrick's Day.** It should, as it has marked the day since 1813. Aiken, SC, is home to the **Aiken Triple Crown,** which includes thoroughbred races, steeplechases, and polo matches. It's held on three consecutive Saturdays in March.
April	Wilmington, NC, has been holding the **North Carolina Azalea Festival** since 1948, usually in early April. In early to mid-April the **Masters Golf Tournament** attracts thousands of ticketed spectators to the Augusta National Golf Club.

ON THE CALENDAR

		The Biltmore Estate in Asheville, NC, hosts the **Festival of Flowers** in early April to late May. This breathtaking display has more than 50,000 tulips, hundreds of varieties of azaleas, and plenty of pink-and-white dogwood and cherry trees.
		In Wilkesboro, NC, **MerleFest,** usually the last weekend in the month, is a celebration of the late musician Merle Watson and Appalachian music. Come to hear some great bluegrass picking.
	May	Held over Memorial Day weekend in Anderson, SC, **Freedom Weekend Aloft** is one of the country's largest hot-air balloon rallies.
		In South Carolina, Beaufort's **Gullah Festival,** held on the weekend before Memorial Day, highlights the fine arts, customs, language, and dress of Lowcountry African-Americans.
		For more than two weeks in May and June, Charleston's **Spoleto Festival USA** is one of the world's biggest arts festivals. Some of the best-known names in music and theater perform in music halls, auditoriums, theaters, and even outdoor spaces.
SUMMER		Summer gets under way in early June at the **Sun Fun Festival** at Myrtle Beach.
	June	The **Virginia-Highland Summerfest,** held in early June, brings top-notch art, music, food, and family events to this popular Atlanta neighborhood.
		Western North Carolina's **Brevard Music Center Institute & Festival,** which takes place mid-June to early August, showcases everything from chamber music to opera.
		Held over a Friday–Sunday in June, the **Atlanta Pride Festival** is one of the largest gay-pride events in the country, attracting 300,000 people to a parade, concerts, and a marketplace.
	July	The renowned **American Dance Festival** is held in early July in Durham, NC.
		Clog and figure dancing are part of the **Shindig on the Green,** held in Asheville from early July to early September. These concerts of bluegrass and string band music start "along about sundown."

		The last two weeks of the month, **Folkmoot USA** brings folk music and dance to Waynesville, NC.
		The last weekend of July, Asheville's **Bele Chere** is the largest free street festival in the Southeast, with lots of music, crafts, and food.
	August	August music festivals include the **Mountain Dance & Folk Festival**, held annually since 1928, which begins the first weekend in the month in Asheville.
		The **Beach Music Festival** is held mid-month on Jekyll Island, GA.
		In late August or early September, the **North Carolina Apple Festival** brings bushels of these red, yellow, and green orbs to Hendersonville.
FALL	October	A parade of pigs marks North Carolina's **Lexington Barbecue Festival**, held in mid-October. Don't ask for barbecue sauce here. Locals call it "dip," and it's made with a special blend of vinegar, ketchup, salt, and pepper.
		Raleigh's **North Carolina State Fair** and Columbia's **South Carolina State Fair** are both held mid-month.
		The annual **Stone Mountain Highland Games**, a celebration of Scottish heritage, is held the third weekend of the month at Georgia's Stone Mountain Park.
	November	Asheville's **Christmas at Biltmore Estate,** held early November to early January, features candlelight tours of the mansion, decorated with dozens of Christmas trees, hundreds of poinsettias and wreaths.
		The **Tanglewood Festival of Lights,** in Winston-Salem, is one of the country's most spectacular displays of Christmas lights. It runs from November 15 to January 1.
		Fantasy in Lights is an outdoor sound and light display at Callaway Gardens in Pine Mountain, GA. The highlight is a 5-mi-long roadway lined with 8 million twinkling lights. The festival begins in mid-November and runs through late December.

The North Carolina Coast

WORD OF MOUTH

"My family has annually gone to Corolla since I was four (I'm now 18). I really love the town. It's very family-friendly and a short drive to other popular towns in OBX. Even if you stay on the sound side, you can walk to the beach in minutes. Pretty much anywhere you stay in Corolla guarantees you access to the restaurants and shops in the center of town."

—caitpre

"Make time for a drive to Morehead City and the Sanitary Restaurant (classic NC institution). Think great seafood, wild ponies, pretty boats, and the flash of the lighthouse in the night sky."

—travelhappyfamily

Updated by
Liz Biro

NORTH CAROLINA'S 300-PLUS MI OF coastline are fronted by a continuous series of fragile barrier islands. Broad rivers lead inland from the sounds, along which port cities have grown. Lighthouses, dunes, and vacation homes (often built by out-of-staters) dot the water's edge. There are battle sites from the American Revolution and the Civil War, elegant golf links, and kitschy putt-putt courses. Aquariums, fishing charters, and museum outreach programs put you up close and personal with the seashore critters. North Carolina's small towns (mostly of 1,000 to 3,000 people) offer genuine warmth and hospitality.

The coast is generally divided into three broad sections that include islands, shoreline, and coastal plains: the Outer Banks (Corolla south through Ocracoke, including Roanoke Island), the Crystal Coast (Core and Bogue Banks, Beaufort, Morehead City, and the inland river city of New Bern), and the greater Cape Fear region (Wrightsville Beach through the Brunswick County islands, including Wilmington). The Outer Banks are visible from space: th a thin, delicate tracing of white are the barrier islands, which form a buffer between the Atlantic Ocean and the mainland.

Although other states' coasts have turned into wall-to-wall hotels and condominiums, much of North Carolina's coast belongs to the North Carolina Division of Parks and Recreation. This arrangement keeps much of the coast accessible to the public for exploration, athletic activities, picnicking, and camping. Still, property values have skyrocketed as summer residents' dream houses continually replace generations-old beach cottages.

Some of the coast closes during midwinter, but even the colder season is a special time to visit. You can escape both crowds and peak prices but still enjoy seafood, beaches, and museums. Whether you're seeking peace or adventure, you can find it on the coast.

ORIENTATION & PLANNING

GETTING ORIENTED

You could pick a destination and stick to it, but touring the entire Carolina coast is doable in a few days, especially during spring and fall when traffic is lighter. Drive here from nearby locales or fly into airports at Wilmington, New Bern, Myrtle Beach, SC, or Norfolk, VA, then rent a car. A car is essential for navigating the coast here, as little public transportation is available. State-operated vehicle ferries and smaller private ferries run between islands and provide an enjoyable, relaxing tour. Boat touring is another option. Dozens of marinas line the shore and the Intracoastal Waterway runs the length of the North Carolina Coast.

The Outer Banks. Long stretches of wild beach are intermingled with small towns on this ribbon of sand. The north end is a tourist mecca of shops, resorts, restaurants, beach cottages, and historic sites. Quiet

TOP REASONS TO GO

Water, water everywhere: Surfers delight in Cape Hatteras's mighty waves. Kayakers and boaters prefer the Crystal Coast's sleepy estuaries and rippling inlets. Beach strollers love Ocracoke's remote, unspoiled shore. The landscape variety lets you choose your own adventure, whether it's boating, trekking, sunning, or simply observing.

Pirate lore and hidden booty: The Graveyard of the Atlantic is littered with shipwrecks, many of them popular dive sights. See artifacts from what researchers believe was Blackbeard's flagship, *Queen Anne's Revenge*. The booty—cannon balls, gold nuggets, and nautical instruments—is displayed at Beaufort's North Carolina Maritime Museum.

Lighting the darkness: North Carolina's seven lighthouses have individual personalities, from the masculine elegance of Currituck's brick facade to the iconic spiral of Hatteras. You'll want to take time to see them all.

The Lost Colony: In a mystery for the ages, 90 settlers, including the first European baby born in the New World, disappeared without a trace. Their story is presented both in historical context and dramatic entertainment in Manteo.

Don't skimp on the shrimp: You can get fresh seafood of every variety fixed in practically every method—fried, grilled, stuffed, blackened, sautéed, pasta-ed, kebabed, or even raw. And since you're on vacation, the calories don't count, right?

villages and open, undeveloped beach mark the south end where travelers often hear nothing but surf and shorebirds. With just one two-lane road stretching the length of the Outer Banks, locals speak of mile markers instead of street numbers.

Cape Hatteras National Seashore. With challenging waves, myriad fish, and the mighty Cape Hatteras lighthouse anchoring the south end, this wide-open beach is a surfer's playground, an angler's dream, and a history buff's treasure.

The Crystal Coast & New Bern. History here ranges from Colonial sites to the birthplace of Pepsi, while extensive ocean, sound, and river fronts please boaters, anglers, water-sports lovers, and those who just want to relax on a big Southern porch with a glass of sweet tea.

Wilmington & the Cape Fear Coast. Part cosmopolitan, part old-fashioned Southern charm, the Cape Fear region has attracted people from all over the world since explorers first landed here in the early 1500s. You can still cast a line off an old wooden pier or spend the day roaming art galleries and wine bars.

THE NORTH CAROLINA COAST PLANNER

WHEN TO GO

North Carolina's coast shines in spring (April and May) and fall (September and October), when the weather is most temperate and the water reasonably warm. Traveling during these times means you can avoid the long lines and higher prices associated with peak tourist season.

GETTING HERE & AROUND

BY AIR The closest large, commercial airports to the Outer Banks are Raleigh-Durham, a 5-hour drive, and Norfolk International in Virginia, a 1½-hour drive. Craven County Regional Airport in New Bern has charter service and car rentals available. Wilmington International Airport serves the Cape Fear Coast.

Barrier Island Aviation provides charter service between the Dare County Regional Airport and major cities along the East Coast, as does Flightline Aviation, which flies into the First Flight depot, at the Wright Memorial in Kill Devil Hills. US Airways Express and Delta fly into Craven County Regional Airport in New Bern. US Airways, Delta, and Allegiant serve Wilmington International Airport.

BY BOAT & FERRY Seagoing folks travel the Intracoastal Waterway through the Outer Banks and the Albemarle region. Boats may dock at just over 400 marinas, including Db City Marina in Elizabeth City, Manteo Waterfront Marina, and National Park Service Silver Lake Marina, in Ocracoke. From Ocracoke, car ferries take off to Hatteras Island, Cedar Island, and the mainland's Swan Quarter. You need to reserve some ferries by calling the NC Department of Transportation's ferry division.

The Intracoastal Waterway provides access to many Central Coast destinations, including Beaufort, Morehead City, and Emerald Isle. The region has more than 70 marinas, among them Beaufort Town Docks and the Morehead City Yacht Basin. New Bern can be reached via the Neuse River from Pamlico Sound. Several marinas are available here, including the Sheraton Grand Marina. You can dock for the day (but not overnight) at the public docks of Union Point Park.

The Wilmington area has public marinas at Carolina Beach State Park and Wrightsville Beach, and a number of hotels provide docking facilities for guests. A state-run car ferry connects Fort Fisher, south of Kure Beach, with Southport on the coast. For information about the state-run ferry system and its schedules and costs, call the North Carolina Department of Transportation's ferry information line. ■TIP➜ ⊕ *NCwaterways.com* **provides an online listing of hundreds of marinas and boating services as well as information about bridge schedules, tide tables, and waterway issues.**

BY CAR On the one hand, navigation in the Outer Banks is a snap because there's only one road—Route 12. On the other, traffic can make that single road two lanes of pure frustration on a rainy midsummer day when everyone is looking for something besides sunbathing. Low-lying areas of the highway are also prone to flooding.

Highways into the other areas along the coast—U.S. 158 into Kitty Hawk and Nags Head; U.S. 64/264 around Nags Head and Manteo; Interstate 40, which can take you from Wilmington all the way to Las Vegas or California if you desire, or Raleigh if you're catching a plane; and U.S. Highway 17, which services Wilmington and New Bern—run smoothly during all but weekday rush hours and the busiest days of high season.

Driving on the beaches is occasionally allowed in designated areas, and permits are sometimes required. The strictly enforced speed limit on the beaches is 25 mph, and pedestrians always have the right of way. Driving on sand can be tricky, so be careful.

BY TAXI Beach Cabs, based in Nags Head, runs 24-hour service from Norfolk to Ocracoke and towns in between. The Connection is a shuttle service with passenger vans large enough to handle families, camping gear, surfboards, and bikes. It's a bargain at $155 from Norfolk to Nags Head. The Outer Banks Limousine Service, headquartered in Nags Head, serves the entire area and Norfolk International Airport and runs around the clock; getting to the airport in a sedan costs about $175 from Nags Head.

ESSENTIALS **Air Contacts Dare County Regional Airport** (⊠ *410 Airport Rd., Manteo* ☎ *252/475-5570* ⊕ *www.fly2mqi.com*). **Norfolk International** (⊠ *2200 Norview Ave.* ☎ *757/857-3351* ⊕ *www.norfolkairport.com*). **Wilmington International Airport** (⊠ *1740 Airport Blvd.* ☎ *910/341-4125* ⊕ *www.flyilm.com*). **Allegiant Air** (☎ *702/505-8888* ⊕ *www.allegiantair.com*). **Flightline Aviation** (☎ *252/338-5347* ⊕ *www.flightlineair.com*). **Delta** (☎ *800/221-1212* ⊕ *www.delta.com*). **Barrier Island Aviation** (☎ *252/473-4247* 🖷 *www.barrierislandaviation.com*). **US Airways Express** (☎ *800/428-4322* ⊕ *www.usair.com*).

Boat & Ferry Contacts Beaufort Town Docks (☎ *252/728-2053*). **Carolina Beach State Park** (☎ *910/458-7770*). **Cedar Island Ferry Terminal** (☎ *252/225-3551 or 800/856-0343*). **Db City Marina in Elizabeth City** (☎ *252/338-2886*). **Manteo Waterfront Marina** (☎ *252/305-4800*). **Morehead City Yacht Basin** (☎ *252/726-6862*). **National Park Service Silver Lake Marina** (☎ *252/928-5111*). **North Carolina Department of Transportation Ferry Information** (☎ *800/293-3779*). **Outer Banks Ferry Service** (☎ *252/728-4129*). **Sheraton Grand Marina** (☎ *252/514-2574*). **Union Point Park** (☎ *252/639-2900*). **Wrightsville Beach Marina** (☎ *910/256-6666*). **NCwaterways.com** (☎ *252/728-2144*).

Taxi Contacts Beach Cabs (☎ *252/441-2500*). **The Connection** (☎ *252/449-2777* ⊕ *www.calltheconnection.com*). **Outer Banks Limousine Service** (☎ *252/256-1343* ⊕ *www.outerbankslimousine.com*).

Visitor Information National Park Service's Group Headquarters (⊠ *1401 National Park Dr., Manteo* ☎ *252/473-2111* ⊕ *www.nps.gov/caha*). **National Park Service Superintendent** (⊠ *1401 National Park Dr, Manteo*).

ABOUT THE RESTAURANTS

Raw bars serve oysters and clams on the half shell; seafood houses sell each day's local catch, be it tuna, wahoo, mahi, mackerel, shrimp, or blue crabs. This is, after all, the coast, though highly trained chefs are settling in the region and increasingly diversifying menus. Fish dishes—

broiled, fried, grilled, or steamed—are listed alongside entrées fusing Asian, European, and Latin flavors with traditional Southern ingredients such as black-eyed peas.

Expect up to hour-long waits at many restaurants during summer and festival periods. Many places don't accept reservations. Restaurant hours are frequently reduced in winter, and some restaurants in remote beach communities close for a month or more. Only the most upscale, pricey restaurants call for a tie; usually a collared shirt will do. Casual dress (shorts and polo shirts) is acceptable in most restaurants.

ABOUT THE HOTELS
Hundreds of rental properties are available. Small beach cottages can be had, but increasingly, so-called "sand castles," large multistory homes, suit large groups. Motels and hotels clustered all along the Outer Banks are still the more affordable way to go.

Throughout the coast, the main choices are cottages, condos, and waterfront resorts. Chain hotels have outlets here, too, but you can also opt to stay at a surprising number of small, family-run lodgings. You might also consider one of many quaint bed-and-breakfasts often filled with antiques and managed by accommodating hosts. Always ask about special packages (price breaks on multiple-night stays) and off-season rates.

WHAT IT COSTS					
	¢	$	$$	$$$	$$$$
Restaurant	under $10	$10–$14	$15–$19	$20–$24	over $24
Hotel	under $100	$100–$150	$151–$200	$201–$250	over $250

Restaurant prices are for a main course at dinner. Hotel prices are for two people in a standard double room in high season.

PLANNING YOUR TIME
The North Carolina coast is a string of beach and inland towns each with its own character. Pick one and plan day trips from there. Boisterous Nags Head and Wilmington provide dining, shopping, and nightlife, but they are also short drives from quite beaches, dense woodlands, and historic landmarks. Beaufort's Colonial air is a brief private ferry ride away from barrier islands where wild horses roam. Just an hour inland are New Bern's vibrant downtown and historic Tryon Palace and gardens. In summer, on secondary roads and some major highways you're bound to pass fresh seafood and produce stands.

THE OUTER BANKS

North Carolina's Outer Banks stretch from the Virginia state line south to Cape Lookout. Think of the OBX (a shorthand used on popular bumper stickers) as a series of stepping stones in the Atlantic Ocean. Throughout history the treacherous waters surrounding these islands have been the nemesis of shipping, gaining them the nickname "Grave-

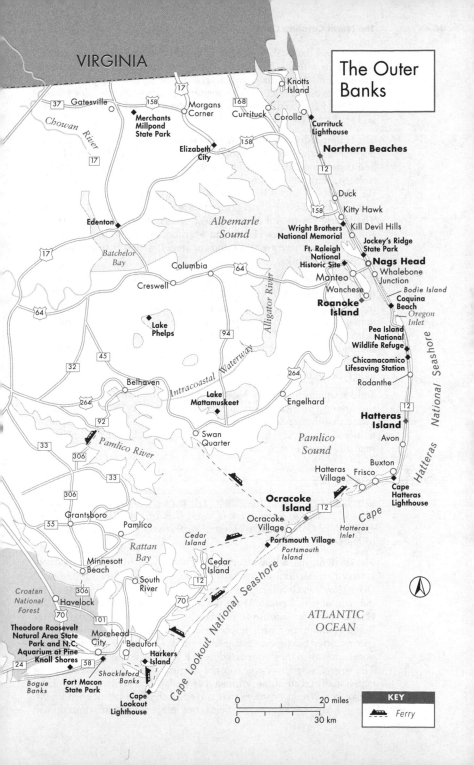

yard of the Atlantic." A network of lighthouses and lifesaving stations, which grew around the need to protect seagoing craft, attracts curious travelers, just as the many submerged wrecks attract scuba divers. The islands' coves and inlets, which sheltered pirates—the notorious Blackbeard lived and died here—now give refuge to anglers, bird-watchers, and sunbathers.

The region is divided into four coastal sections: the Northern Beaches, beginning with Corolla, followed by Roanoke Island, Hatteras Island, and then Ocracoke Island. For many years the Outer Banks remained isolated, with only a few hardy commercial fishing families. Today the islands are linked by bridges and ferries, and much of the area is included in the Cape Hatteras and Cape Lookout national seashores. The largest towns are also the most colorfully named: Kitty Hawk, Kill Devil Hills, Nags Head, and Manteo. Vacation rentals here are omnipresent—there are thousands of weekly rental cottages available on the Outer Banks.

You can travel the region from the south end by taking a car ferry from Cedar Island to Ocracoke Island or from the north end. Driving the 120-mi stretch of Route 12 from Corolla to Ocracoke can be managed in a day, but be sure to allow plenty of time in summer for delays due to heavy traffic, for ferry waiting times, and for exploring the undeveloped beaches, historic lighthouses, and interesting beach communities along the way. Mile markers (MM) indicate addresses all along the Outer Banks.

Sudden squalls frequently blow up on the Outer Banks in summer, and the Atlantic hurricane season runs from June 1 to November 30. Be aware that during major storms and hurricanes, evacuations are mandatory and roads and bridges become clogged with traffic following the blue-and-white evacuation-route signs.

NORTHERN BEACHES

Corolla: 91 mi south of Norfolk, VA, via U.S. 17, U.S. 158, and Rte. 12; 230 mi east of Raleigh via U.S. 64, U.S. 17, and Rte. 12. Duck: 16 mi south of Corolla. Kitty Hawk: 19 mi south of Corolla, 7 mi south of Duck.

The small northern beach settlements of Corolla and Duck are largely seasonal, residential enclaves full of summer rental condominiums. Drive slowly in Corolla: here freely wandering wild horses always have the right of way. Upscale Duck has lots of restaurants and shops. Kitty Hawk, with a few thousand permanent residents, is among the quieter beach communities with fewer rental accommodations. Given these communities' contiguous nature and similar looks, the uninitiated may not realize when they've crossed from Kitty Hawk into Kill Devil Hills. The towns' respective roles in the drama of the first powered flight occasionally create some confusion as well. When arriving at the Outer Banks, the Wright brothers first stayed in the then-remote fishing village of Kitty Hawk, but their flight took place some 4 mi south on Kill

Devil Hill, a gargantuan sand dune where today the Wright Brothers National Memorial stands.

GETTING HERE & AROUND
Most people drive to the northern beaches via U.S. 17, 64, and 264, which all link to the local U.S. 158 and Rte. 12. Some commercial and charter flights are available from nearby airports. Plan your time wisely, as heavy traffic can lead to long travel delays in summer. Marked paths and wide shoulders accommodate bikers and walkers. Guided tours are available, too. Still, a car is essential for getting around on your own time.

ESSENTIALS
Visitor Information Aycock Brown Welcome Center (⊠ *5230 North Croatan Highway MM 1, Kitty Hawk* ☎ *877/629–4386*).

EXPLORING
The **Currituck Beach Lighthouse** is the northernmost lighthouse on the Outer Banks. Except in high winds or thunderstorms, you can climb 214 steps to the top. Completed in 1875 of around 1 million bricks, the lighthouse is unpainted. ⊠ *1101 Corolla Village Rd., Rte. 12, north of Whalehead club sign, Corolla* ☎ *252/453–8152* ⊕ *www.currituck-beachlight.com* ⊡ *$7* ⊙ *Easter–Thanksgiving, daily 9–5.*

The Whalehead Club is a 21,000-square-foot monument to gracious living. Built between 1922 and 1925 as the private residence of a Northern couple taken with the area's reputation for waterfowl hunting, the home was given its current name by the second owner. After having been abandoned, sold, and vandalized, it was restored by a team of specialists and is listed on the National Register of Historic Places. A floral motif is carried throughout the art-nouveau home in Tiffany lamps with flower detailing and mahogany woodwork carved with water lilies. ⊠ *1100 Club Way, Currituck Heritage Park, off Rte. 12, Corolla* ☎ *252/453–9040* ⊕ *www.whaleheadclub.com* ⊡ *$7* ⊙ *9–5 daily.*

⟳
★ The **Wright Brothers National Memorial,** a 60-foot granite monument that resembles the tail of an airplane, stands as a tribute to Wilbur and Orville Wright. The two bicycle mechanics from Ohio took to the air here on December 17, 1903. You can see a replica of the *Flyer* and stand on the spot where it made four takeoffs and landings, the longest flight a distance of 852 feet. Exhibits and an informative talk by a National Park Service ranger bring the event to life. The Wrights had to bring in the unassembled airplane by boat, along with all their food and supplies for building a camp. They made four trips to the site beginning in 1900. The First Flight is commemorated annually. ⊠ *1401 National Park Dr., off U.S. 158 between MM 7 and MM 8, 5 mi south of Kitty Hawk, Kill Devil Hills* ☎ *252/441–7430* ⊕ *www.nps.gov/wrbr* ⊡ *$4* ⊙ *Sept.–May, daily 9–5; June–Aug., daily 9–6.*

OFF THE BEATEN PATH

Merchants Millpond State Park. A man-made millpond built in 1811 and ancient Lassiter Swamp combine to form one of the state's rarest ecosystems. Cypress and gum trees hung with Spanish moss reach out of the still, dark waters that are ideal for canoeing. ■ **TIP**➔ Rent a canoe

MINI-KITSCH

There seems to be an unspoken competition among miniature golf courses here to come up with the most outrageous themes and outlandish decor. Trams that resemble old mining trains roll through manmade caves and under waterfalls. Stocks await unruly pirates, and giant giraffes hide in bushy corners. It's all in good fun, and putt-putt provides great family entertainment. Many facilities also have snack grills, arcades, and batting cages. Here are some of our favorites:

Lost Treasure Golf (✉ *976 Salter Path Rd., Salter Path* ☎ *252/247–3024*).

Carolina Beach Jungle Mini Golf (✉ *906 Lake Park Blvd., Carolina Beach* ☎ *910/458–8888*).

Lost Treasure Golf (✉ *1600 N. Croatan Hwy., Kill Devil Hills* ☎ *252/480–0142*).

or go fishing or hiking. Campsites are also available. A visitor center is scheduled to open in 2009. The park is on the mainland, 80 mi northwest of Kitty Hawk. ✉ *71 U.S. 158E, Gatesville* ☎ *252/357–1191* ⊕ *www.ncparks.gov/visit/parks/memi/main.php* ☑ *Free* ⊙ *June–Aug., daily 8 AM–9 PM; March, Apr., May,, Sept., and Oct., daily 8–8; ; Nov.–Feb., daily 8–6.*

WHERE TO EAT

$$–$$$
SEAFOOD
★

✕ **Blue Point Bar & Grill.** This upscale spot with an enclosed porch overlooking Currituck Sound is as busy as a diner and as boldly colorful—with a red, black, and chrome interior. The menu mixes Southern style with local seafood, including the ever-popular she-crab soup, a thick and rich concoction made with cream, sherry, herbs, Old Bay seasoning, and, of course, crab roe. Lunch is served Tuesday–Sunday. ✉ *1240 Duck Rd., Duck* ☎ *252/261–8090* ⊕ *www.thebluepoint.com* 🗎 *AE, MC, V.*

$$$$
ECLECTIC

✕ **Elizabeth's Café & Winery.** This small bistro evokes big-time romance even though it's in a shopping center. Choose to eat in the French-country dining room or in the stone grotto. À la carte and fixed menus change to reflect the day's market purchases, whether it's rack of lamb, Angus beef tenderloin, or the freshest vegetables for the Vegetarian du Jour dish. The restaurant's wine list has been written about in the *Wine Spectator,* and Elizabeth's has more than 1,600 bottles for sale. ✉ *Scarborough Faire Shopping Village, 1177 Duck Rd., #11, Duck* ☎ *252/261–6145* ⊕ *www.elizabethscafe.com* ⌲ *Reservations essential* 🗎 *AE, DC, MC, V* ⊙ *No lunch.*

$$$–$$$$
ITALIAN

✕ **Nicoletta's Italian Café.** White linen tablecloths, flowers, and a view of the Currituck Beach Lighthouse mean atmosphere with a capital A. For more than a decade, Nicoletta's has been known for fresh seafood and southern Italian pasta dishes, and owner Pasquale Anzalone carries on the tradition. Off-season hours may vary. ✉ *106 Corolla Light Town Center, Rte. 12, Corolla* ☎ *252/453–4004* 🗎 *MC, V* ⊙ *No lunch.*

CLOSE UP

First in Flight

December 17, 1903, was a cold and windy day on the Outer Banks, but Wilbur and Orville Wright took little notice. The slightly built brothers from Ohio were undertaking an excellent adventure. With Orville at the controls, Wilbur running alongside, and the men of the nearby Lifesaving Service stations acting as ground crew, the fragile *Wright Flyer* lifted off from the Kill Devil Hills dune near Kitty Hawk and flew 120 feet in 12 seconds.

John Daniels, an Outer Banker, photographed the instant the world forever changed: a heavier-than-air machine was used to achieve controlled, sustained flight with a pilot aboard. To prove they were not accidental aviators, the Wrights took two flights each that day, and in Wilbur's second attempt, he flew 852 feet in 59 seconds.

Others were attempting—and dying in the attempt of—powered flight as the Wright brothers opened their Dayton bicycle-repair shop in 1892. Using information on aerodynamics from the Smithsonian Institution and observation of birds in flight, they began experimenting using a box kite roughly shaped like a biplane and a makeshift wind tunnel. The strong, steady winds drew them to the then-remote Outer Banks, where they could test their next phase, manned glider flights, in privacy. In time, they added power to the three-axis control they developed and eventually solved the problems of mechanical flight, lift, and propulsion that had vexed scientists for hundreds of years.

Their success is honored at the Wright Brothers National Memorial in Kill Devil Hills and by the North Carolina boast emblazoned on millions of license plates: FIRST IN FLIGHT.

WHERE TO STAY

$$$–$$$$
★
Advice 5¢. A roof with varied pitches and eaves tops this contemporary steely blue-gray beach house with white trim and multipane windows rising from the sandy dunes. Although the name is light-hearted, Advice 5¢ is very serious about guest care. Beds in each room are dressed with crisp, colorful linens. All rooms have private decks, ceiling fans, and baths stocked with thick cotton towels. The suite has a whirlpool bath, sitting area, and cable TV. You have use of the tennis courts, swimming pool, and the beach access at Sea Pines, a nearby resort. From the North Beach area you can easily walk to downtown shops and restaurants. **Pros:** on-site massage therapy; quiet and secluded but walking distance to commercial area. **Cons:** no ocean view. ⊠*111 Scarborough La., Duck* ☎*252/255–1050 or 800/238–4235* ⊕*www.advice5.com* ⇨*4 rooms, 1 suite* ⌂*In-room: no phone. In-hotel: restaurant, no-smoking rooms* ▤*MC, V* ⊙*Closed mid-Nov.–mid-Mar.* ⏀*BP.*

$$$–$$$$
The Inn at Corolla Light. The inn is a part of the Corolla Light Resort and sits along Currituck Sound, about 10 mi from Duck. The ocean, ¼ mi away, is easily accessed via bikes or open-air trolley service. Even the smaller rooms feel big thanks to the generous use of richly toned fabrics, large beds, and windows with views of the garden, pool, or sound. A special treat are the off-road tours for the inn's guests to the secluded

spot where the area's wild horses are now confined. **Pros:** lots of resort amenities available; some rooms have fireplaces for cozy or romantic fall and winter vacations. **Cons:** you'll have walk several blocks to the ocean; there is a $45 fee for reservation changes made prior to seven days of arrival. ⊠1066 Ocean Trail, Corolla ☎252/453–3340 or 800/215–0772 ⊕www.corolla-inn.com ⇆30 rooms, 13 suites ⌂In-room: kitchen (some), refrigerator, DVD. In-hotel: tennis courts, pools, gym, bicycles, no-smoking rooms ▤D, MC, V ⎟◎⎟BP.

$$$$ ⊡**The Sanderling Resort & Spa.** Located on a remote beach 5 mi north
★ of Duck, the Sanderling is a fine place to be pampered, go swimming, or go for a stroll. The three inn buildings and villas recently underwent a multimillion-dollar refurbishment; they feature the mellow look of classic Carolina beach cottages with warm tones, wood furniture, and chenille lounge chairs. A 3-mi nature trail winds through the adjacent Pine Island Bird Sanctuary, and the concierge can help arrange kayak tours and other activities. The elegant, dinner-only Left Bank restaurant ($$$$) has a wall of windows overlooking Currituck Sound. The resort-casual Lifesaving Station ($$–$$$), in a restored 1899 lifesaving station, serves breakfast, lunch, and dinner and includes a second-floor lounge. **Pros:** on-site spa; natural surroundings; plush robes in every room. **Cons:** king-size beds only; maximum of two guests per room unless otherwise authorized; third-person room charges for guests 17 and older. ⊠1461 Duck Rd., Duck ☎252/261–4111 or 800/701–4111 ⊕www.sanderlinginn.com ⇆88 rooms, 5 villas ⌂In room: refrigerator, DVD (some), Wi-Fi. In-hotel: 2 restaurants, room service, bar, pool, gym, spa, laundry service ▤AE, D, MC, V ⎟◎⎟BP.

NAGS HEAD

9 mi south of Kitty Hawk.

It's widely accepted that Nags Head got its name because pirates would tie lanterns around the necks of their horses to lure merchant ships onto the shoals hoping to wreck them and profit from the cargo. Dubious citizenry aside, Nags Head was established in the 1830s as North Carolina's first tourist haven.

The town—one of the largest on the Outer Banks, yet still with a population of only about 3,000 people—lies between the Atlantic Ocean and Pamlico Sound, along and between U.S. 158 ("the bypass") and Route 12 ("the beach road" or Virginia Dare Trail). Both roads are congested in the high season, and the entire area is commercialized. Many lodgings, whether they're dated cottages, shingled older houses, or sprawling new homes with plenty of bells and whistles, are available through the area's plentiful vacation rentals. Numerous restaurants, motels, hotels, shops, and entertainment opportunities keep the town hopping day and night.

Nags Head has 11 mi of beach with 40 public access points from Route 12, some with paved parking and some with restrooms and showers. ■ TIP➜It's easy to overlook the flagpoles stationed along many area beaches; but if there's a red flag flying from one of them, it means the water

is too rough even for wading. These are not a suggestion—ignoring them can mean hefty fines.

GETTING HERE & AROUND

From the east, arrive by car on U.S. 64/264 or from the north on U.S. 17 and U.S. 158. Although many people cycle and walk on designated paths, most exploring requires a car.

ESSENTIALS

Visitor Information Whalebone Welcome Center (⊠ *2 N.C. 12 Highway MM 17, Nags Head* ☎ *877/441–6644*).

EXPLORING

The first North Carolina Historic Shipwreck Site, the 175-foot **USS** *Huron,* lies in 20 feet of water off the Nags Head Pier and is a favorite with scuba divers. The iron-hulled ship sank in a November storm in 1877, taking all but a handful of her 124-man crew with her. ⊠ *Offshore between MM 11 and MM 12.*

Jockey's Ridge State Park has 426 acres that encompass the tallest sand dune on the East Coast (about 80 to 100 feet). Walk along the 384-foot boardwalk from the visitor center to the edge of the dune. The climb to the top is a challenge; nevertheless, it's a popular spot for hang gliding, kite flying, and sand boarding. You can also explore an estuary, a museum, and several trails through the park. In summer, join the free Sunset on the Ridge program: watch the sun disappear while you sit on the dunes and learn about their local legends and history. Covered footwear is a wise choice here, as the loose sand gets quite hot in the summer months. ⊠ *U.S. 158, MM 12* ☎ *252/441–7132* ⊕ *www.jockeysridgestatepark.com* 🎫 *Free* ☉ *Daily 8–sunset.*

Coquina Beach, in the Cape Hatteras National Seashore, is considered by locals to be the loveliest beach in the Outer Banks. The wide-beam ribs of the shipwreck *Laura Barnes* rest in the dunes here. Driven onto the Outer Banks by a nor'easter in 1921, she ran aground north of this location; the entire crew survived. The wreck was moved to Coquina Beach in 1973 and displayed behind ropes, but subsequent hurricanes have scattered the remains and covered them with sand, making it difficult to discern. Free parking, public changing rooms, showers, and picnic shelters are available. ⊠ *Off Rte. 12, MM 26, 8 mi south of U.S. 158.*

OFF THE BEATEN PATH

Lake Phelps At 16,600 acres, Lake Phelps, a part of Pettigrew State Park, is a Carolina Bay 5 mi across and about 4 feet deep that has long been considered a treasure by boaters and anglers. In 1985 researchers began to prize it for other reasons. Discovered underneath the sand in the beautifully clear water were ancient American Indian artifacts, including 30 dugout canoes, one of which dates back some 4,400 years. Two are displayed in Pettigrew Park. The park also includes a boat ramp, canoe launch, fishing pier, and camping sites. ⊠ *2252 Lake Shore Rd., 56 mi east of Nags Head via I–64, Creswell* ☎ *252/797–4475.*

WHERE TO EAT

$$$–$$$$
SEAFOOD
★
✗**Basnight's Lone Cedar Café.** Hearts were broken when this 25-year-old restaurant, owned by powerful North Carolina Senator Marc Basnight and family, burned in 2007, but the new contemporary setting with simple pine tables and a huge glass-walled wine rack in the main dining room is sleeker and larger than the original. Big windows all around allow everyone a chance to see the osprey mother and chicks

---

SIFTING ECOLOGY

The vegetation on the sand dunes is practically all that's keeping them from blowing away in the wind. Dune conservation is very serious for the survival of the beaches, and the vegetation also provides shelter to turtles, rabbits, snakes, and other wildlife. Please don't disturb it!

---

that nest on a waterfront piling outside. North Carolina produce and seafood are the stars here. Soft-shell crabs in season come from an on-site shedding facility, and a stunning, extensive herb garden provides fresh seasoning. Beef, chicken, pork, and pastas are also on the menu. ✉*Nags Head–Manteo Causeway, 7623 S. Virginia Dare Trail* ☎*252/441–5405* ⊕*www.lonecedarcafe.com* ⚑*Reservations not accepted* ⊟*D, MC, V* ☾*Closed Jan.*

$$$–$$$$
SEAFOOD
Fodor'sChoice
★
✗**Owens' Restaurant.** A classic clapboard cottage with pine paneling hosts this half-century-old restaurant that has been in the same family and location since 1946. Stick with the seafood or beef, at which the kitchen staff excels. Miss O's crab cakes are ever-popular, as is the filet mignon topped with lump crabmeat and asparagus with béarnaise sauce. Pecan-encrusted sea scallops are plump and tender. The 16-layer lemon and chocolate cakes are delicious. In summer arrive early and expect to wait. The brass-and-glass Station Keeper's Lounge has entertainment Thursday, Friday, and Saturday nights in summer. ✉*U.S. 158, MM 16.5, 7114 S. Virginia Dare Trail* ☎*252/441–7309* ⊕*www.owensrestaurant.com* ⚑*Reservations not accepted* ⊟*AE, D, MC, V* ☾*Closed Jan. and Feb. No lunch.*

$$$–$$$$
AMERICAN
☾
✗**Penguin Isle Soundside Bar & Grille.** The views from Penguin Isle's main and gazebo dining rooms on Roanoke Sound are panoramic and seductive. The decor is muted as if not to detract from what you're seeing or tasting. Though especially busy in summer, the dining experience here is never uncomfortable, as tables are well spaced. For dinner there's a little of everything: beef tenderloin, yellowfin tuna, grilled chicken piccata, as well as options for the kids, who especially love the shrimp feast and seafood smorgasbord Sunday and Monday nights. ✉*U.S. 158, MM 15.5, 6708 S. Croatan Highway* ☎*252/441–2637* ⊕*www.penguinisle.com* ⊟*AE, D, MC, V* ☾*Closed Jan. and Feb.*

$$–$$$
SEAFOOD
✗**Pier House Restaurant.** The restaurant is literally *on* the crooked, rickety Nags Head Fishing Pier, and if you catch and clean your own fish, the chef will cook it to your liking. If fishing was bad, no worries; the restaurant has a homestyle American menu including seafood and breakfast. ✉*3335 S. Virginia Dare Trail, U.S. 158, MM 12* ☎*252/441–4200* ⚑*Reservations not accepted* ⊟*D, MC, V* ☾*Closed Thanksgiving–Easter. No dinner Oct.–Easter.*

$$$ ✗**RV's Sugar Creek.** If fiery red sunsets and marinated tuna entice you,
SEAFOOD this is the place for you. It's where locals come to eat, drink, and take
in serene views of Roanoke Sound. Portions of everything—from clam
chowder to barbecued shrimp to crab cakes and tuna—are huge. You
can also get steak, ribs, and chicken. The marvelous turtle cake, with
chocolate, pecans, and caramel, is a dieter's nightmare. There's a lit-
tle pier outside and an attached outdoor gazebo where you can get
a drink. The causeway is between Nags Head and Roanoke Island.
✉*Nags Head–Manteo Causeway, MM 16.5, 7340 S. Virginia Dare
Trail* ☎*252/441–4963* ⊕*www.rvssugarcreek.com* ⌁*Reservations not
accepted* ▤*MC, V* ⊗*Call for off-season hours.*

¢–$ ✗**Sam & Omie's.** This no-nonsense niche is named after two fishermen
SEAFOOD who were father and son. Opened in 1937, it's one of the oldest restau-
rants on the Outer Banks. Fishing illustrations hang on the walls, and
country music plays in the background. It's open daily 7 to 10, serving
every imaginable kind of seafood, and then some. Try the fine marinated
tuna steak, Cajun tuna bites, or frothy crab-and-asparagus soup. You
might catch owner Carol Sykes munching fresh peach cake with pecans
if you call in July, and the chef has been using the same recipe for the
she-crab soup for 22 years. Locals love breakfast here. ■TIP➜**Die-hard
fans claim that Sam & Omie's serves the best oysters on the beach.** ✉*U.S.
158, MM 16.5, 7228 Virginia Dare Trail* ☎*252/441–7366* ⊕*www.
samandomies.net* ⌁*Reservations not accepted* ▤*D, MC, V* ⊗*Closed
Dec.–Feb.*

WHERE TO STAY

$$–$$$ ⊡**First Colony Inn.** Stand on the verandas that encircle this old, three-
Fodor'sChoice story, cedar-shingle inn and admire the ocean views. Two rooms have
★ wet bars and kitchenettes; others have four-poster or canopy beds,
handcrafted armoires, and English antiques. All rooms contain extras,
such as heated towel bars. The story of this landmark's near demoli-
tion, its rescue, and the move to the present site is told in framed photo-
graphs, letters, and news accounts lining the sunny dining room. In fall
and winter, Nature Conservancy birding weekends include excursions
to the Pea Island Wildlife Refuge. **Pros:** homey accommodations feel like
grandma's house; some in-room hot tubs. **Cons:** you'll have to cross a
road to get to the beach; no elevator. ✉*6720 S. Virginia Dare Trail, U.S.
158 MM 16* ☎*252/441–2343 or 800/368–9390* ⊕*www.firstcolonyinn.
com* ⇆*26 rooms* ⌂*In-room: kitchen (some), refrigerator. In-hotel: res-
taurant, pool, no-smoking rooms* ▤*AE, D, MC, V* ⏀|*BP.*

$$–$$$ ⊡**The Nags Head Inn.** Being an independent property, not a chain, is
ↄ not the only thing that makes this motel stand out—the blocky, white
stucco exterior with blue accents is in sharp contrast with the cottages
that surround it. The five-story hotel has basic, tidy rooms right on the
beach. Ask for an oceanside room to get a balcony. The inn is espe-
cially family-friendly: kids under 12 stay free, and cribs and cots are
available for $10 extra. **Pros:** shaded parking; on the beach. **Cons:** no
breakfast; a small, no-frills lobby. ✉*Rte. 12, MM 14, 4701 S. Virginia
Dare Trail* ☎*252/441–0454 or 800/327–8881* ⊕*www.nagsheadinn.
com* ⇆*100 rooms* ⌂*In-room: refrigerator. In-hotel: pool, spa, no-
smoking rooms* ▤*AE, D, MC, V* ⊗*Closed late Nov.–Dec.*

BEACH CAMPING

Camping is permitted in four designated areas along the Cape Hatteras National Seashore. These campgrounds have spaces for tents, trailers, and motor homes. All camping at Cape Lookout National Seashore is primitive, and allowed only from mid-April through mid-October. Be sure to take extra-long tent stakes for sand, and don't forget insect repellent. All sites are available on a first-come, first-served basis, except Ocracoke, where reservations are accepted. For information about private campgrounds, contact the Dare County Tourist Bureau.

Contacts Cape Hatteras National Seashore (✉ *1401 National Park Dr., Manteo* ☎ *252/473–2111* ⊕ *www.nps.gov/caha*). **Cape Lookout National Seashore** (✉ *131 Charles St., Harkers Island* ☎ *252/728–2250* ⊕ *www.nps.gov/calo*). **Dare County Tourist Bureau** (☎ *252/473–2138 or 800/446–6262* ⊕ *www.outerbanks.org*).

SPORTS & THE OUTDOORS

Outer Banks Boarding Company (✉ *103 E. Morning View Pl., U.S. 158, MM 11* ☎ *252/441–1939*) rents surfboards and gives private lessons; it also has a retail shop.

Nags Head Golf Links (✉ *5615 S. Seachase Dr., off Rte. 12, MM 15* ☎ *252/441–8073 or 800/851–9404*) has a par-71, 18-hole course with sound views and challenging coastal winds.

Outer Banks Dive Center (✉ *3917 S. Croatan Hwy.* ☎ *252/449–8349*) has equipment rental, diving instruction, guided offshore charters, and leads off-the-beach dives to shipwrecks.

SHOPPING

For 35 years, Gallery Row has been a small cluster of art-related businesses that sell everything from beach crafts to oil paintings and from piggy banks to diamond earrings. **Morales Art Gallery** (✉ *107 E. Gallery Row* ☎ *252/441–6484 or 800/635–6035*) is the fine-arts store that started it all. Most of the gallery owners live on-site.

The **Tanger Outlet Center** (✉ *U.S. 158 bypass, MM 16* ☎ *252/441–5634 or 800/720–6747* ⊕ *www.tangeroutlets.com*) has two dozen stores—including Bass, Coach, Gap Outlet, and Polo Ralph Lauren—selling designer clothes, shoes, casual attire, books, sunglasses, and more.

ROANOKE ISLAND

10 mi southwest of Nags Head.

On a hot July day in 1587, 117 men, women, and children left their boat and set foot on Roanoke Island to form the first permanent English settlement in the New World. Three years later, when a fleet with supplies from England landed, the settlers had disappeared without a trace, leaving a mystery that continues to baffle historians. Much of the 12-mi-long island, which lies between the Outer Banks and the mainland, remains wild. Of the island's two towns, Wanchese is the fishing village, and Manteo is more tourist-oriented, with sights related to the island's history, as well as an aquarium.

GETTING HERE & AROUND

From the east, drive to the island on U.S. 64/264; from the Outer Banks, follow U.S. 158 to U.S. 64/264. Although Manteo's main drag and downtown waterfront have sidewalks, a car is useful for visiting the town's various sites. Charter flights are available at Dare County Regional Airport.

ESSENTIALS

Visitor Information **Outer Banks Welcome Center on Roanoke Island** (⊠ *1 Visitors Center Circle, Manteo* ☎ *877/629–4386*).

EXPLORING

☼ A history, educational, and cultural-arts complex, **Roanoke Island Festival Park** sits on the waterfront in Manteo. Costumed interpreters conduct tours of the 69-foot ship, *Elizabeth II,* a representation of a 16th-century vessel. The complex also has an interactive museum and shop, a recreated 16th-century settlement site, a fossil pit, plays, concerts, arts-and-crafts exhibitions, and special programs. ⊠ *Waterfront, off Budleigh St., Manteo* ☎ *252/475–1500, 252/475–1506 for event hotline* ⊕ *www.roanokeisland.com* ⊠ *$8* ☉ *Nov.–Dec. and Feb.–Mar., daily 9–5; Apr.–Oct., daily 9–6.*

★ The lush **Elizabethan Gardens** are a 10-acre re-creation of 16th-century English gardens, established as an elaborate memorial to the first English colonists. Walk through the brick and wrought-iron entrance to see antique statuary, wildflowers, rose gardens, and a sunken garden, all sponsored by the Garden Club of North Carolina. The gatehouse, designed in the style of a 16th-century orangery, serves as a reception center and gift and plant shop. ■TIP➜ **Many weddings are held in one tranquil garden or another.** ⊠ *1411 National Park Dr., 3 mi north of downtown Manteo* ☎ *252/473–3234* ⊕ *www.elizabethangardens.org* ⊠ *$8* ☉ *Dec.–Feb., daily 10–4; Mar. and Nov., daily 9–5; Apr., May, Sept., and Oct., daily 9–6; June–Aug., Sun.–Fri. 9–8, Sat. 9–7.*

★ **Fort Raleigh National Historic Site** is a restoration of the original 1585
☼ earthworks that mark the beginning of English-colonial history in America. ■TIP➜ **Be sure to see the orientation film and then take a guided tour of the fort.** A nature trail through the 513-acre grounds leads to an outlook over Albemarle Sound. Native American and Civil War history is also preserved here. *The Lost Colony* (⊠ *1409 U.S. 64/264, 27954* ☎ *252/473–3414 or 800/488–5012* ⊕ *www.thelostcolony.org* ⊠ *$16*), Pulitzer Prize–winner Paul Green's drama, was written in 1937 to mark the 350th birthday of Virginia Dare. Except from 1942 to 1947, it has played every summer since in Fort Raleigh National Historic Site's Waterside Theatre. It reenacts the story of the first colonists, who settled here in 1587 and mysteriously vanished. Cast alumni include Andy Griffith and Lynn Redgrave. Reservations are essential. ⊠ *1401 National Park Dr., off U.S. 64/264, 3 mi north of downtown*

Manteo ☎*252/473–5772* ⊕*www.
nps.gov/fora* ✉*Free* ⊙*Sept.–May,
daily 9–5; June–Aug., daily 9–6.*

☾ The **North Carolina Aquarium at Roanoke Island,** overlooking Croatan Sound, occupies 68,000 square feet of space. There are touch tanks, but *The Graveyard of the Atlantic* is the centerpiece exhibit. It's a 285,000-gallon ocean tank containing the re-created remains of the USS *Monitor,* sunk off Hatteras Island. The aquarium hosts a slew of activities and field trips, from feeding fish to learning about medicinal aquatic plants to kids' workshops. ✉*374 Airport Rd., off U.S. 64, 3 mi northeast of Manteo* ☎*252/473– 3493, 866/332–3475 for aquarium, 252/473–3494 for educational programs* ⊕*www.ncaquariums.com* ✉*$8* ⊙*Daily 9–5.*

WHERE TO EAT

¢–$ ✕**Big Al's Soda Fountain and Grill.** Burgers, blue-plate specials, seafood,
AMERICAN and ice-cream confections dominate the menu at this fun place with '50s decor, Coca-Cola memorabilia, a game room, and dance floor. Breakfast is served year-round, but there's an all-you-can-eat breakfast buffet daily from June to August and on weekends in the off-season. ✉*100 Patty La., U.S. 64/264, Manteo* ☎*252/473–5570* ⊕*www. themefifty.com* ▭*MC, V, D.*

$$–$$$ ✕**Full Moon Café.** Colorful stained-glass panels hang in the large front
AMERICAN windows of this wonderfully cheerful bistro renovated from a gas sta-
★ tion. The herbed hummus with roasted pita is fantastic, as are the fat crab cakes and baked crab-dip appetizer. The kitchen uses fresh local seafood and never deep fries the catch. Other choices include salads, veggie wraps, Cuban-style enchiladas, burgers of all kinds, Angus beef, and a dozen innovative and hearty sandwiches. Light eaters beware: even the Waldorf salad comes with a million pecans and apples; expect lots of cheese on any dish that includes it. ■**TIP**➜ **The café also serves specialty cocktails and maintains a thoughtfully selected wine list.** ✉*207 Queen Elizabeth Ave., Manteo* ☎*252/473–6666* ⊕*www.thefullmoon-cafe.com* ▭*AE, D, MC, V.*

¢ ✕**Magnolia Grille.** Freddy and Pam Ortega, cheerful New York trans-
AMERICAN plants, run the immensely popular restaurant on Manteo's downtown waterfront. The place is hopping, even at breakfast; lunch gets the over-flow from nearby Festival Park. ■**TIP**➜ **If it's too busy, get takeout and savor your sandwich by the waterfront.** You can choose from char-grilled chili cheeseburgers, quesadillas, salads, assorted sandwiches including a fried oyster sandwich, and hearty chicken dishes; some dishes are intended—and others can be modified—for vegetarians. ✉*408 Queen*

Elizabeth Ave., Manteo ☎*252/475–9877* ☰*AE, D, MC, V* ⊘*No dinner Sun. and Mon.*

WHERE TO STAY

$–$$ 🖼**Island House of Wanchese.** Roy and Jeanne Green purchased the circa-1900 house in 1991 and updated it, turning it into a B&B, but they retained the original wood flooring and wavy glass windows. The wraparound porch is glassed in so you can sit and see the lovely gardens without interference from bugs. Rooms are decorated with antiques, hope chests, and handmade quilts. The resident innkeepers provide evening turndown service; complimentary beach chairs, towels, and umbrellas; a freezer for your catch; and a full breakfast. **Pros:** lots of quirky antique trinkets on display; serene setting; cozy gardens. **Cons:** far from business and beach districts; common rooms and some guest rooms are a little dark; no kids allowed unless approved by owners. ⊠*104 Old Wharf Rd., Wanchese* ☎*252/473–5619* ⊕*www.islandhouse-bb.com* ⇝*3 rooms, 1 suite* ♿*In-hotel: no-smoking rooms* ☰*AE, D, MC, V* ⨌*BP.*

¢–$ 🖼**Scarborough Inn.** Two stories of wraparound porches surround the Scarborough, which is modeled after a turn-of-the-20th-century inn. Outside each room are benches and rocking chairs; inside, each is decorated differently, with family heirlooms as well as modern conveniences, like coffeemakers. Room refrigerators come stocked with ready-made, packaged breakfast items. The property is within walking distance of popular shops and restaurants and about 5 mi from the beach. **Pros:** nicely groomed garden areas; B&B feel at a good price. **Cons:** located on a busy road; small lobby; innkeeper may step out and lock front office. ⊠*524 U.S. 64/264, Manteo* ☎*252/473–3979* ⊕*www.scarborough-inn.com* ⇝*14 rooms* ♿*In-room: refrigerator. In-hotel: no-smoking rooms* ☰*AE, D, MC, V* ⨌*EP.*

$$$–$$$$ 🖼 **Tranquil House Inn.** This charming 19th-century-style inn sits water-
★ front, a few steps from shops, restaurants, and the Roanoke Island Fes-
☾ tival Park. The individually decorated rooms have classic, clean lines and muted colors; some have comfy sitting areas. Complimentary wine and cheese are served in the evening. The popular restaurant, 1587 ($$$$), is known for its chop-house-style cuts and inventive entrées, such as pan-roasted, chipotle-spiced duck breast and grilled tuna over spicy Thai noodles. **Pros:** easy walking distance from shops and restaurants; complimentary evening wine reception; child-friendly. **Cons:** located on a busy commercial waterfront; small, cramped lobby; no elevator. ⊠*405 Queen Elizabeth Ave., Box 2045, Manteo* ☎*252/473–1404 or 800/458–7069* ⊕*www.1587.com* ⇝*25 rooms* ♿*In-hotel: restaurant, bicycles no-smoking rooms* ☰*AE, D, MC, V* ⨌*BP.*

SPORTS & THE OUTDOORS

Oregon Inlet Fishing Center (⊠*98 Rte. 12, north end of Oregon Inlet Bridge* ☎*252/441–6301 or 800/272–5199*) is a full-service marina that leads fishing excursions and has supplies such as bait, tackle, ice, and fuel for the fisherman. The National Park Service maintains an adjacent boat launch.

Pirates Cove Yacht Club and Marina
(✉ *2000 Sailfish Dr., Manteo* ☎ *252/
473–3906 or 800/367–4728*) has a
deep-water, charter dock. Internet
access is available in the store. Amenities include a restaurant, a kiddy
pool and playground, a fitness center, and tennis courts.

SHOPPING

Manteo Booksellers (✉ *105 Sir Walter Raleigh St., Manteo* ☎ *252/473–
1221 or 866/473–1222* ⊕ *www.
manteobooksellers.com*) stocks an
admirable collection of books on
the Outer Banks, cuisine, history,
nature, lighthouses, shipwrecks,
folklore, and related fiction. Local
author readings are frequent. The
children's section is quite large, too.

> **GONE FISHING**
>
> When you're considering charter-
> ing a boat, in addition to asking
> the price, find out the answer to
> these questions: How long will
> you actually be fishing once the
> travel time is factored out? Where
> will you go, and for what will
> you be fishing? Will they supply
> the rods and tackle? How many
> people are required for a trip? Will
> there be other fishing parties on
> board? Are food and drinks pro-
> vided? Will they clean the catch
> and ice it down?

CAPE HATTERAS NATIONAL SEASHORE

Longtime visitors to the Outer Banks have seen how development
changes these once unspoiled barrier islands, so it's nice to know
that the 70-mi stretch of the Cape Hatteras National Seashore will
remain protected. Its pristine beaches, set aside as the first national
seashore in 1953, stretch from the southern outskirts of Nags Head to
Ocracoke Inlet, encompassing three narrow islands: Bodie, Hatteras,
and Ocracoke.

Some of the best fishing and surfing on the East Coast are in these
waters, which also are ideal for other sports such as windsurfing, diving, and boating. Parking is allowed only in designated areas. Fishing
piers are in Rodanthe, Avon, and Frisco.

With 300 mi of coastline, there are plenty of beaches that don't have
lifeguards on duty. ■**TIP→ To identify beaches with trained staff, contact the Ocean Rescue in the town, or if you're in a National Park, the Park
Service.**

BODIE ISLAND

7 mi south of Nags Head.

Natives pronounce it "Bah-dy" not "Bow-dy," which harkens back to
the days when this corner of the Graveyard of the Atlantic was known
as "Bodies Island" because of all the dead seafarers who washed onto
the shores. The island remains mostly barren, but the boardwalks and
observation decks on its marshes offer excellent opportunities to watch
wading birds and to kayak or canoe through the inlets.

GETTING HERE & AROUND

From the north, reach Bodie Island via U.S. 158. From the east, take U.S. 64/264 to U.S. 158. South of the Outer Banks, U.S. 70 leads to Rte. 12 but requires a couple of ferry rides. Some commercial and charter flights are available from nearby airports. Tour buses visit major sites, but a car is necessary to travel around freely.

ESSENTIALS

Visitor Information Whalebone Welcome Center (⊠ *2 N.C. 12 Highway MM 17, Nags Head* ☎ *877/441–6644*).

EXPLORING

Bodie Island Lighthouse designer Dexter Stetson is also the brains behind the Cape Hatteras lighthouse, which explains why the two look so much alike. Bodie, with its fat (22 feet tall) black-and-white horizontal stripes, stands 156 feet tall and is capped by a black cast-iron lantern. It's actually the third lighthouse to guard this area of the coast. The first, built in 1847, was simply abandoned because of its shoddy construction. A second, build in 1859, was blown up in 1861 by retreating Confederate soldiers because they feared it would be used as a Yankee observation tower. The current lighthouse was completed in 1872, and is in the midst of a two-part renovation that won't be complete until 2009. ■TIP➔ Only the lower level, keeper's house, and museum can be toured. ⊠ *1401 National Park Dr.* ☎ *252/473–2111 or 252/441–5711* ⊕ *www.nps.gov/caha/bdlh.htm* ✉ *Free* ⊙ *Memorial Day–Labor Day, daily 9–6; Labor Day–Thanksgiving, daily 9–5.*

HATTERAS ISLAND

15 mi south of Nags Head

The Herbert C. Bonner Bridge arches for 3 mi over Oregon Inlet and carries traffic to Hatteras Island, a 42-mi-long curved ribbon of sand jutting out into the Atlantic Ocean. At its most distant point (Cape Hatteras), Hatteras is 25 mi from the mainland. About 85% of the island belongs to Cape Hatteras National Seashore, and the remainder is privately owned in seven small, quaint villages strung along Route 12, the island's fragile lifeline to points north. Among its nicknames, Hatteras is known as the blue marlin (or billfish) capital of the world. The fishing's so great here because the Continental Shelf is 40 mi offshore, and its current, combined with the nearby Gulf Stream and Deep West Boundary Current, create an unparalleled fish habitat. The total population of the towns—Rodanthe, Waves, Salvo, Avon, Buxton, Frisco, and Hatteras Village—is around 4,000.

GETTING HERE & AROUND

From the north, reach Hatteras Island via U.S. 158. From the east, take U.S. 64/264 to U.S. 158. South of the Outer Banks, U.S. 70 leads to Rte. 12 and requires a couple of ferry rides. Some commercial and charter flights are available from nearby airports.

ESSENTIALS

Hatteras Welcome Center (⊠ *57190 Kohler Rd, Hatteras Village* ☎ *252/986–2203* ⊕ *www.outerbanks.org*).

EXPLORING

Pea Island National Wildlife Refuge is made up of more than 5,800 acres of marsh on the Atlantic Flyway. To bird-watchers' delight more than 365 species have been sighted from its observation platforms and spotting scopes and by visitors who venture into the refuge. Pea Island is home to threatened peregrine falcons, piping plovers, and tundra swans, which winter here. A visitor center on Route 12 has an information display and maps of the two trails. ■TIP→ **Remember to douse yourself in bug spray, especially in spring.** Guided canoe tours are available for a fee. ⊠*Pea Island Refuge Headquarters, Rte. 12, 5 mi south of Oregon Inlet* ☎*252/987–2394* ⊕*www.fws.gov/peaisland* ⊠*Free* ⊗*June–Aug., daily 9–5; Mar.–May and Sept.–Nov., daily 9–4; Dec.–Feb., hrs vary, call ahead.*

The restored 1911 **Chicamacomico Lifesaving Station** (pronounced "chik-a-ma-*com*-i-co") is now a museum that tells the story of the brave people who manned 29 stations that once lined the Outer Banks. These were the precursors to today's Coast Guard, with staff who rescued people and animals from seacraft in distress. Living-history reenactments are performed June through August. ⊠*23645 N.C. Hwy 12 at MM 39.5, Rodanthe* ☎*252/987–1552* ⊕*www.chicamacomico.net* ⊠*$6* ⊗*Mid-Apr.–Nov., weekdays noon–5.*

★ **Cape Hatteras Lighthouse** was the first lighthouse built in the region,
♻ authorized by Congress in 1794 to help prevent shipwrecks. The original structure was lost to erosion and Civil War damage; this 1870 replacement is, at 208 feet, the tallest brick lighthouse in the world. Endangered by the sea, in 1999 the lighthouse was actually raised and rolled some 2,900 feet inland to its present location. A visitor center is located near the base of the lighthouse. In summer the principal keeper's quarters are open for viewing, and you can climb the lighthouse's 257 steps (12 stories) to the viewing balcony. ■TIP→ **Children under 42 inches in height aren't allowed in the lighthouse.** Offshore lay the remains of the USS *Monitor,* a Confederate ironclad ship that sank in 1862. ⊠*Off Rte. 12, 30 mi south of Rodanthe, Buxton* ☎*252/995–4474* ⊕*www.nps.gov/caha* ⊠*Visitor center and keeper's quarters free, lighthouse tower $6* ⊗*Visitor center and keeper's quarters: daily 9–5. Lighthouse tower: Apr.–mid-Oct., daily 10–5.*

A nationally recognized collection of Native American artifacts fills the **Frisco Native American Museum & Natural History Center.** Galleries display native art from across the United States as well as relics from the first inhabitants of Hatteras Island. The museum has been designated as a North Carolina Environmental Education Center. Several acres of nature trails wind through a maritime forest, and a pavilion overlooks a salt marsh. ⊠*Rte. 12, 53536 N.C. Hwy 12 Frisco* ☎*252/995–4440* ⊕*www.nativeamericanmuseum.org* ⊠*$5* ⊗*Tues.–Sun. 11–5, Mon. by appointment. Call ahead for winter hours.*

To the Lighthouse

Sooner or later while visiting the coast, you come within sight of one of the "mighty seven": a North Carolina lighthouse. These beacons were once tended by service keepers. But one by one they've been automated and transferred to the Coast Guard, the National Park Service, or a nonprofit organization.

The last major lighthouse constructed is the first you reach traveling from north to south: Currituck Beach Lighthouse (162 feet, 1875) is an unpainted redbrick tower. Bodie Island Lighthouse (165 feet, 1872) is covered in broad horizontal black-and-white stripes.

Cape Hatteras Lighthouse is famous as America's tallest brick lighthouse (208 feet, 1870) and for having been relocated 2,900 feet inland in 1999. Ocracoke Lighthouse (77 feet, 1817), rebuilt after a fire in 1823, is the second-oldest lighthouse in the United States still in continuous service. The bright white exterior was once achieved with a whitewash blend of unslaked lime, glue, rice, salt, and powdered fish.

Cape Lookout Lighthouse (169 feet, 1859) is painted with distinctive black-and-white diamonds—black facing north and south, white facing east and west. Bald Head Island Lighthouse (90 feet, 1817), nicknamed "Old Baldy," is south of Southport; visitors can climb 112 steps to the top of its octagonal weathered gray tower. Far to the south, Oak Island Lighthouse (169 feet, 1958) is the U.S.'s youngest lighthouse and has the last manually operated light in the world. But it lacks the elegance of its older siblings: the completely cylindrical tower has three broad horizontal stripes—black, white, and gray, and its beacon is so bright and hot that workman have to wear protective clothing when working on it.

WHERE TO STAY & EAT

$$–$$$
SEAFOOD
✕ **Breakwater.** Fat Daddy crab cakes, rolled in potato chips then fried and served with pineapple jalapeño salsa is one of the more creative signature dishes. You also get more standard seafood options, such as shrimp fried or broiled with white wine and butter. The restaurant sits atop Oden's Dock. Given the casual nature of life here, Breakwater stands out with tables dressed in white linen. The dining room is a bit small, but waiting for a table in comfortable chairs on the deck overlooking Pamlico Sound is not a chore. ⊠ *Waterfront, Rte. 12, Hatteras Village* ☎ *252/986–2733* ⊕ *www.odensdock.com* ⊟ *AE, D, MC, V* ⊘ *Closed Sun.–Wed. Labor Day–Memorial Day. No lunch.*

$$–$$$
AMERICAN
✕ **The Captain's Table.** South of the entrance for the Cape Hatteras Lighthouse, this place is popular for its well-prepared food and homey manner. In addition to offering the usual seafood, the menu has pork barbecue, chicken, and beef. It's also a popular breakfast spot. ⊠ *Rte. 12, Buxton* ☎ *252/995–5988* ⊟ *MC, V* ⊘ *Closed Dec.–early Apr. No lunch.*

$–$$
▥ **Sea Gull Motel.** The 1950s-era, family-operated Sea Gull was renovated in 2004 with comfort in mind. Adjacent cottage properties, each of which sleeps up to six, rent ($$$$) by the week during high season. The 15 rooms, about 50 yards from the beach, all have at least a mini-refrigerator and microwave; a two-bedroom suite with a full

kitchen is also available. Ask about corner room No. 116 with ocean views on two sides. **Pros:** quiet setting; oceanfront pool; family-friendly. **Cons:** remote location; no breakfast; no Wi-Fi. ⌧ *56883 N.C. Hwy 12, between MM 70 and 71, Hatteras Village* ☎*252/986–2550* ⊕*www. seagullhatteras.com* ⇴*15 rooms, 1 suite, 2 cottages* ⌂*In-room: kitchen (some), refrigerator, Internet. In-hotel: pool, beachfront, no-smoking rooms* ▭*D, MC, V.*

OCRACOKE ISLAND

Ocracoke Village: 15 mi southwest of Hatteras Village.

Fewer than 1,000 people live on this, the last inhabited island in the Outer Banks, which can be reached only by water or air. The village itself is in the widest part of the island, around a harbor called Silver Lake. Man-dredged canals form the landscape of a smaller residential area called Oyster Creek.

Centuries ago, however, Ocracoke was the stomping ground of Edward Teach, the pirate known as Blackbeard. A major treasure cache from 1718 is still rumored to be hidden somewhere on the island. Fort Ocracoke was a short-lived Confederate stronghold that was abandoned in August 1861 and blown up by Union forces a month later.

Although the island remains a destination for people seeking peace and quiet, they can be hard to find during the summer season, when tourists and boaters swamp the place. About 90% of Ocracoke is part of Cape Hatteras National Seashore; the island is on the Atlantic Flyway for many migrating land and water birds. A free ferry leaves hourly from Hatteras Island and arrives 40 minutes later; toll ferries connect with the mainland at Swan Quarter (2½ hours) and at Cedar Island (2 hours and 25 minutes). Reserve well in advance.

GETTING HERE & AROUND

The only way to reach Ocracoke Island is by private boat or ferry. State car ferries land at either end of the island and depart as late as 10 PM to Cedar Island and midnight to Hatteras Island. Only one road, Rte.12, traverses the island. Quiet streets shoot off to the left and right at the south end. Lots of cyclists come to Ocracoke, and many inns have bikes guests may use, but be careful when biking Rte. 12 from one end of the island to the other in summer; traffic can be heavy, and there are no designated bike paths along the highway.

ESSENTIALS

Visitor Information National Park Service Visitor Center (⌧ *Rte. 12, Ocracoke Island* ☎*252/928–4531).*

EXPLORING

Ocracoke Island **beaches** are among the least populated and most beautiful on the Cape Hatteras National Seashore. Four public access areas have parking as well as off-road vehicle access. ⌧*Off Rte. 12, .*

Look out from the **Ocracoke Pony Pen** observation platform at the descendants of the Banker Ponies that roamed wild before the island came under the jurisdiction of Cape Hatteras National Seashore. The Park Service took over management of the ponies in 1960 and has helped maintain the population of about 30 animals; the wild herd once numbered nearly 500. All the animals you see today were born in captivity and are fed and kept on a 180-acre range. Legends abound about the arrival of the island's Banker Ponies. Some believe they made their way to the island after the abandonment of Roanoke's Lost Colony. Others believe they were left by early Spanish explorers or swam to shore following the sinking of the *Black Squall,* a ship carrying circus performers. ⊠*Rte. 12, 6 mi southwest of Hatteras-Ocracoke ferry landing.*

Ocracoke Preservation Society Museum, run by the local preservation society, contains photographs and artifacts illustrating the island's lifestyle and history. "Porch talk" lectures, presentations, and folk stories are regular summer events. The National Park Service visitor center is nearby. ⊠*Silver Lake Rd., off Rte. 12 and beside Cedar Island ferry dock, Ocracoke Village* ☎*252/928–7375* ⊕*www.ocracokepreservation.org* ⊠*Free* ☉*June–Aug., weekdays 10–5, Sat. 11–4, closed Sun.; Easter–May and Sept.–Nov., Mon.–Sat. 11–4.*

Built in 1823, **Ocracoke Lighthouse** is the second-oldest operating lighthouse in the U.S. (Sandy Hook, New Jersey, has the oldest). It was first fueled by whale oil, then kerosene, and finally electricity. ■**TIP→ The squat whitewashed structure, 77 feet, 5 inches tall, is unfortunately not open to the public for climbing, but the base is open between Memorial Day and Labor Day. The lighthouse is a photographer's dream.** ⊠*Off Rte. 12, Live Oak Rd., Ocracoke Village* ⊕*www.nps.gov/caha/ocracokelh.htm.*

On May 11, 1942, the HMS *Bedfordshire,* an armed British trawler on loan to the United States, was torpedoed by a German U-boat and sank with all 37 hands lost off the coast of Ocracoke Island. The men were buried on Ocracoke in a corner of the community graveyard. Each year the Queen of England remembers this loss by sending a British flag, via a personal envoy, to the tiny, nicely landscaped **British Cemetery,** which is tended by Ocracoke Coast Guard Station personnel. The wreck was discovered in 1980 and some artifacts were recovered. It's still frequented by divers. ⊠*Off Rte. 12, British Cemetery Rd., Ocracoke Village* ☎*252/926–9171.*

OFF THE BEATEN PATH

Mattamuskeet National Wildlife Refuge. Hyde County's Lake Mattamuskeet is the largest natural lake in North Carolina. Fed only by rainwater and runoff, the lake is 3 feet below sea level. Although it's been drained for farmland, the reclaimed lake is the centerpiece of a 50,000-acre wildlife refuge that echoes with the calls of some 800 bird species. ⊠*38 Mattamuskeet Rd., 2½-hr ferry ride and 15-min drive from Ocracoke Island, Swan Quarter* ☎*252/926–4021, 800/345–1665 for ferry* ⊕*www.mattamuskeet.org.*

WHERE TO EAT

$$–$$$
SEAFOOD
✕ **Back Porch Restaurant.** Seafood is the star here, naturally, but there are notable beef and chicken dishes, including pecan-crusted chicken breast in bourbon sauce and spinach, tofu, and chickpea curry. You have the

choice of enjoying your meal indoors or on a screened porch. Enjoy the respectable wine list in the wine bar. ✉*110 Back Rd., Ocracoke* ☎*252/928–6401* 🍴*MC, V* ⊗*No lunch.*

$$–$$$ ✕**The Pelican Restaurant and Patio Bar.** This 19th-century harborfront
SEAFOOD home in a grove of twisted oak trees has a patio next to an outdoor bar: many people take a seat here and don't leave for a long while. Jumbo shrimp stuffed with cream cheese and jalapeño peppers and lump crab cakes are two of the most requested food items. "Shrimp Hour," which is really two hours every day (3 to 5), draws crowds because large steamed shrimp sell for 15¢ each. The Pelican also serves breakfast—cereal, egg dishes, biscuits with homemade jelly, and corned beef hash—until 11 AM. Acoustic music plays at times during the off-season but seven nights a week in summer. ✉*305 Irvin Garrish Hwy., Ocracoke* ☎*252/928–7431* 🍴*AE, D, MC, V.*

WHERE TO STAY

$$ 🏨**Island Inn and Dining Room.** This white-clapboard inn on the National Register of Historic Places was built as a private lodge back in 1901. It's starting to show its age a bit, but is full of Outer Banks character. The rooms in the modern wing are good for families. The large rooms in the Crow's Nest, on the third floor, have cathedral ceilings and look out over the island. One- and two-bedroom villas ($$$$) with full kitchens, living rooms, and laundry facilities are also available. **Pros:** quiet taste of old Ocracoke; spectacular views from the Crow's Nest; walking distance to shops and restaurants; heated pool. **Cons:** starting to show its age; no-frills rooms and some with no television. ✉*Lighthouse Rd. and Rte. 12, Box 9* ☎*252/928–4351, 877/456–3466* ⊕*www.ocracokeislandinn.com* ⤙*28 rooms, 4 villas* ⏃*In-room: no TV (some). In-hotel: pool, no-smoking rooms* 🍴*AE, MC, V.*

¢–$ 🏨**Sand Dollar Motel.** The Sand Dollar is small and unassuming, but well run. A garden and a walkway to a secluded swimming pool give this motel a sense of privacy. It's on a quiet residential street two blocks from Route 12 and the village center. Manager Roger Garrish, an Ocracoke native, is a great source of island information. **Pros:** picnic area with grill; free Wi-Fi; walking distance to shops, restaurants and historic sites. **Cons:** small rooms, no breakfast. ✉*70 Sand Dollar Rd.* ☎*252/928–5571 or 866/928–5571* ⊕*www.ocracokeisland.com/sand_dollar_motel.htm* ⤙*12 rooms, 1 apartment, 1 cottage* ⏃*In-room: kitchen (some), refrigerator, Wi-Fi. In-hotel: pool, no-smoking rooms* 🍴*AE, D, MC, V* ⊗*Closed Dec.–Mar.*

SHOPPING

In 1920 Albert Styron set up **Styron's General Store** (✉*Lighthouse Rd.* ☎*252/928–2609*) in Ocracoke; three generations later, the store is a place to pick up not dry goods and fishing equipment but souvenirs and gifts. An old, red Coca-Cola cooler today holds big jars of nickel candy.

CAPE LOOKOUT NATIONAL SEASHORE

Southwest of Ocracoke Island via Cedar Island.

Extending for 55 mi from Portsmouth Island to Shackleford Banks, Cape Lookout National Seashore includes 28,400 acres of uninhabited land and marsh. The remote, sandy islands are linked to the mainland by private ferries. Loggerhead sea turtles, which have been placed on the federal list of threatened and endangered species, nest here. To the south, wild ponies roam Shackleford Banks. Four-wheel-drive vehicles are allowed on the beach, and primitive camping is allowed. There are primitive cabins (with and without electricity, no linens or utensils) with bunk beds. Ferry service is available from Harkers Island to the Cape Lookout Lighthouse area, from Davis to Shingle Point, from Atlantic to an area north of Drum Inlet, and from Ocracoke Village to Portsmouth Village.

GETTING HERE & AROUND

The park's various islands are accessible by boat only. Various private ferries run back and forth to the island, and a list of authorized ferry services can be found at the park's Web site: ⊕ *www.nps.gov/calo/ planyourvisit/ferry.htm.*

ESSENTIALS

Visitor Information Cape Lookout Visitor Center (✉ *131 Charles St., Harkers Island* ☎ *252/728–2250* ⊕ *www.nps.gov/calo*).

EXPLORING

The **Cape Lookout visitor center** is on Harkers Island at the end of U.S. 70 East near a private ferry terminal. ✉ *U.S. 70 E, Harkers Island, 131 Charles St.* ☎ *252/728–2250 for visitor center, 252/729–2791, 252/241–6783, 225–4261 for cabins* 🖃 *Park free, ferry ride $10–$30 or up to $300 for vehicles,* ⊕ *www.nps.gov/calo/planyourvisit/ferry. htm for authorized private ferry service* ☉ *Visitor center daily 9–5.*

Portsmouth Village was inhabited from 1753 until the early 1970s. At its peak in 1860, the census listed 685 permanent residents. It was a "lightering" town, where ships heavy with cargo had to unload to smaller boats that could navigate the shallow Ocracoke Inlet. But the Civil War and the dredging of a deeper inlet at Hatteras were the beginning of the end for Portsmouth. By 1956 there were 17 inhabitants; the last two left in 1971. Today the public can tour the visitor center, the one-room schoolhouse, the post office and general store, the Methodist church, and the turn-of-the-20th-century Life Saving Station (a multiroom Coast Guard station). The walking trails can be difficult because of standing water, sandy soil, and mosquitoes. Public restrooms are not abundant; bring your own food and water. ✉ *Portsmouth Island,* ⊹ *Take ferry from Ocracoke* ☎ *252/728–2250 for ferry* ⊕ *www.nps. gov/calo or www.friendsofportsmouthisland.com* 🖃 *Free* ☉ *Visitor center and buildings Apr.–Nov.*

When the original red-and-white-stripe 1812 lighthouse proved too short and unstable, the 1859 **Cape Lookout Lighthouse** was built to replace it. This 169-foot lighthouse withstood retreating Confederate troops' attempts to blow it up to keep it out of Union hands (they stole the lens instead). With its white-and-black diamond markings, the beacon continues to function as a navigational aid. A small museum inside the visitor center on Harkers Island tells the story of the lighthouse from its first incarnation in 1812. From there you must take a ferry to get to the lighthouse. The tower is undergoing renovation and is open infrequently. ⊠ *Core Banks* ☎*252/728–2250 for updates on lighthouse renovations* ⊕*www.nps.ov/calo* ⊠*Free.*

THE CRYSTAL COAST & NEW BERN

Carteret County, with nearly 80 mi of ocean coastline, is known as the Crystal Coast. It's composed of the south-facing beaches along the barrier island Bogue Banks (Atlantic Beach, Pine Knoll Shores, Indian Beach, Salter Path, and Emerald Isle), three major mainland townships (Morehead City, Beaufort, and Newport), and a series of small, unincorporated "down-east" communities traversed by a portion of U.S. 70, designated a Scenic Byway.

Neighboring Craven County—which contains New Bern, a good chunk of the 157,000-acre Croatan National Forest, and Cherry Point, the world's largest Marine Corps–air station—is by turns genteel and historic, modern and commercialized, rural and wild. Golfers, boaters, and a growing number of retirees find the area a haven.

BEAUFORT

20 mi west of Harkers Island–Cape Lookout ferry; 150 mi southeast of Raleigh.

There's a feeling of having stepped back in time in the small seaport with a bustling boardwalk; residents take great pride in the city's restored public buildings and homes—and in their homes' histories, which sometimes include tales of sea captains and pirates. Established in 1713, the third-oldest town in North Carolina was named for Henry Somerset, duke of Beaufort, and it's hard to miss the English influence here. Streets, at least those in the historic district, are named after British royalty and colonial leaders.

GETTING HERE & AROUND

Beaufort is near the far eastern end of U.S. 70, which links to U.S. 17. The town has a small airstrip, but no commercial flights. For boaters, it's located along the Intracoastal Waterway, and downtown docks are available. The closest major airport is in New Bern. The town is a perfect park-and-stroll location, with historic sites, museums, and a retail center all within walking distance of each other.

ESSENTIALS

Visitor Information Beaufort Historic Site Visitor Center (⊠*130 Turner St., Beaufort* ☎*252/728–5225*).

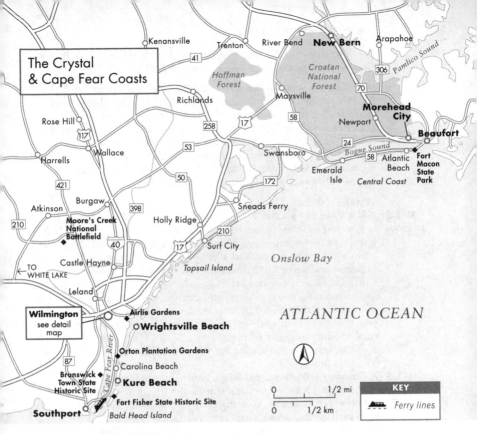

The Crystal & Cape Fear Coasts

Kenansville Trenton River Bend **New Bern** Arapahoe
41
Hoffman
Forest
Croatan
National
Forest
Pamlico Sound
306
Maysville
70
Richlands
Rose Hill
58
Newport
Morehead City
258 17
117
Beaufort
Wallace
53
24
Swansboro
Bogue Sound
58 Atlantic Fort
Beach Macon
State
Park
Harrells
Emerald
Isle
Central Coast
421
50
172
Burgaw
Atkinson
398
Sneads Ferry
210
Moore's Creek National Battlefield
Holly Ridge
210
40
Castle Hayne
17 Surf City
TO
WHITE LAKE
Topsail Island
Onslow Bay
Leland

Wilmington see detail map
Airlie Gardens
○**Wrightsville Beach**

ATLANTIC OCEAN

87
●**Orton Plantation Gardens**
○Carolina Beach
Brunswick Town State Historic Site
●**Kure Beach**
Southport ▲ **Fort Fisher State Historic Site**
Bald Head Island

0   1/2 mi
0   1/2 km

KEY
🚤 Ferry lines

EXPLORING

Today the town still has a strong connection with the sea—everything from motorized dinghies to graceful sailboats to fabulous yachts from around the world anchor here. Boat rides of all types—dolphin watches, dinner cruises, lighthouse excursions, party jaunts, and scenic harbor tours—are available for a fee. Restaurants and shops line the waterfront. Also on the harbor is the private Duke University Marine Laboratory, with the National Science Foundation's huge research vessel, the *Cape Hatteras,* moored out back.

The **Beaufort Historic Site,** in the center of town, consists of 10 buildings dating from 1778 to 1859, eight of which have been restored, including the 1796 **Carteret County Courthouse** and the 1859 **Apothecary Shop and Doctor's Office.** Don't miss the **Old Burying Grounds** (1709), where Otway Burns, a privateer in the War of 1812, is buried under his ship's cannon; a nine-year-old girl who died at sea is buried in a rum keg; and an English soldier saluting the king is buried upright in his grave. The required tours, either on an English-style double-decker bus or by guided walk, depart from the visitor center. ⊠*130 Turner St.* ☎*252/728–5225 or 800/575–7483* ⊕*www.beauforthistoricsite. org* 🎫*$8 tour* ⊙*Mon.–Sat., walking tours at 10, 11:30, 1, and 3:30.*

Bus tour: Apr.–Oct., Mon., Wed., Fri., and Sat. at 11 and 1:30. Burying Ground tour: June–Sept., Tues.–Thurs. at 2:30.

★ **North Carolina Maritime Museum** documents the state's seafaring history.
☾ An exhibit about the infamous pirate Blackbeard includes artifacts recovered from the discovery of his flagship, *Queen Anne's Revenge,* near Beaufort Inlet. Other exhibits focus on local fossils and duck decoys. The associated **Watercraft Center,** across the street, has lectures on boat-building and stargazing, birding treks, and fossil hunting tours. ⊠*315 Front St.* ☎*252/728–7317* ⊕*www.ncmaritime.org* ▭*Free* ☾ *Weekdays 9–5, Sat. 10–5, Sun. 1–5.*

WHERE TO EAT

$$–$$$
AMERICAN

✕**Blue Moon Bistro.** Chef Kyle Swain, a Beaufort native, returned home to put into use the lessons he learned apprenticing at some of North Carolina's top restaurants. He pairs classical French technique with creative presentations such as shrimp and grits seasoned with a touch of lemon and served in a martini glass. Specials include grilled tuna with succotash risotto and local vegetables. Though the emphasis is on local seafood, a meat, poultry, and interesting vegetarian dish is usually among the entrées. The restaurant occupies the 1827 Dill House, which has been dressed up with oak woodwork, wainscoting, and suns and moons made of pressed tin. ⊠*119 Queen St.* ☎*252/728–5800* ⊕*www.bluemoonbistro.biz* ▭*AE, D, MC, V* ☾*Closed Sun. and Mon. No lunch.*

$$–$$$
CONTEMPORARY
☾

✕**Clawson's 1905 Restaurant & Pub.** Housed in what was a general store in the early 1900s, Clawson's is stuffed with memorabilia. ■**TIP➔It gets crowded in summer, so arrive early for both lunch and dinner.** Hearty food such as ribs, steaks, pasta, and local seafood are part of the attraction. The pub has a large selection of North Carolina microbrews. ⊠*425 Front St.* ☎*252/728–2133* ⊕*www.clawsonsrestaurant.com* ▭*D, MC, V* ☾*Closed Sun. Labor Day–Memorial Day.*

$$–$$$
SEAFOOD

✕**The Net House.** Once upon a time, the Net House, a long, low-slung building with few windows, was just that—a place where fishing nets were made, repaired, and stored. Today people, not fishing gear, occupy every corner of the building, which is divided into dining rooms with walls of weathered pine. Hungry diners spill onto the sidewalk waiting to get into this family-owned restaurant to sample specialties such as steamed shellfish and broiled or lightly battered and fried oysters, shrimp, and other seafood. Locals tout the clam chowder, broiled grouper Dijon, and key lime pie for good reason. Call in the off-season to make sure it's open; hours vary. ⊠*133 Turner St.* ☎*252/728–2002* ⚏*Reservations not accepted* ▭*MC, V.*

$$–$$$
SEAFOOD

✕**The Spouter Inn.** Dining at a shaded table on the Spouter's deck overlooking Beaufort Harbor and Taylor's Creek is one of life's treats. Boats glide by, you see a wild horse or two on Carrot Island just across the way, and a waiter appears with a cool drink and plate of shrimp caught that day. The prime rib and steak are popular alternatives to seafood. The attached bakery produces all kinds of cakes and pies: the banana-cream crepe may make you forget all other desserts for a while. Sunday brunch choices include quiche, omelets, and eggs Benedict with crab

CLOSE UP

North Carolina's Pirates

North Carolina's coast was a magnet for marauding sea dogs during the Golden Age of Piracy, a period in the first quarter of the 18th century. Among those who visited was Stede Bonnet, the so-called "gentleman pirate." For this successful owner of a sugar plantation, piracy seemed the result of a midlife crisis. He should have stayed on the farm: he was cheated by Blackbeard, captured by authorities, and hanged in 1718.

Anne Bonny was the Irish illegitimate daughter of a lawyer. Married at 16 to a small-time pirate, she fell in love with "Calico Jack" Rackham, and the two ran away together and put together a pirate crew. In 1720 they were attacked and most of the scalliwags were too drunk to defend themselves; Rackham was sentenced to be hanged; Bonny claimed she was pregnant and was eventually pardoned. She disappeared from history before the age of 25.

Of course, the most notorious buccaneer of them all was Blackbeard, whose two-year reign of terror began in 1716. He cultivated fear by strapping on six pistols and six knives, tying his luxuriant beard into pigtails and, legend has it, tucking lighted matches into it during battle.

A polygamist with at least 12 wives, Blackbeard attacked ships in the Caribbean and settlements along the coasts of Virginia and the Carolinas. At least three of his ships sank in North Carolina's waters; archaeologists are studying artifacts from what is likely the flagship, *Queen Anne's Revenge*, which ran aground on a sandbar near Beaufort Inlet in May 1718.

The following November a seafaring posse caught Blackbeard in one of his favorite playgrounds, Ocracoke Inlet. The pirate was decapitated and his head was hung from one of the conquering ships. Blackbeard's other lost ships and his reputedly fabulous treasure are still being sought today.

2

cakes. There's indoor seating as well. ⊠*218 Front St.* ☎*252/728–5190* ⊕*www.thespouterinn.com* ⊟*AE, MC, V* ⊗*Closed Mon. Labor Day–Memorial Day. Closed Jan.*

WHERE TO STAY

¢–$ **Captain's Quarters Bed & Biscuit.** Richard (Capt. Dick) and Ruby (Miss Ruby) Collins, and their daughter Polly, welcome guests with an enthusiasm that is as genuine as their passion for Beaufort and Carteret County, an area Dick first came to know during his years as a Navy pilot in World War II. Each morning, along with a weather report, the captain serves breakfast, which includes fresh biscuits his wife and daughter make from an old family recipe. Antiques, most of them family heirlooms, fill the 19th-century home that the family restored. Reading material and reading lights are just two of the thoughtful touches you'll find. **Pros:** quiet home; a large white wraparound porch with a sky-blue ceiling has cozy rockers; the innkeeper is a great source of sea stories; major historic sites across the street. **Cons:** located on a busy street; common rooms can be a little warm in summer. ⊠*315 Ann St.* ☎*252/728–7711 or 800/659–7111* ⊕*www.captainsquarters. us* ⇨*3 rooms* ♿*In-room: no phone, no TV. In-hotel: restaurant, no* *kids under 10, no-smoking rooms* ▭*MC, V* 🍽*BP.*

$ **The County Home B&B.** Billed as something between a country inn and a bed-and-breakfast, the inn was once a publicly funded poorhouse like those that existed in America before the days of welfare and Social Security. Renovated in 1996, the inn is listed on the National Register of Historic Places. Rooms are bright and cozy, each with a private entrance. Breakfast baskets containing bagels, muffins, juice, and a local newspaper are delivered to your door each morning. **Pros:** private baths in each room; large porch with rockers; pets allowed. **Cons:** located just over a mile from the historic downtown area, but on a route too busy for pedestrians; no communal dining room. ✉*299 N.C. Hwy. 101* ☎*252/728–4611* 🌐*www.countyhomeb-b.com* *10 rooms* *In room: Wi-Fi, refrigerator. In hotel: bicycles* ▭*MC, V.*

$–$$ **Pecan Tree Inn.** Local lore has it that when the 1866 Queen Anne building with gingerbread trim was converted from a Masonic Lodge and schoolhouse to a private home, it was the first in Beaufort to have gas lighting, indoor plumbing, and a telephone. Today technological amenities include Wi-Fi and cable television. Innkeepers Dave and Allison DuBuisson haven't forgotten, however, the things that make for gracious living. Rooms have lush floral fabrics and rugs, as well as antiques. Fresh-baked bread and pastries are part of every breakfast. A 5,000-square-foot flower-and-herb garden displays 1,000 plant species. **Pros:** quiet location; friendly hosts; close to two of the area's best restaurants. **Cons:** no elevator; small children are not allowed. ✉*116 Queen St.* ☎*252/728–6733 or 800/728–7871* 🌐*www.pecantree.com* *7 rooms* *In-room: Wi-Fi. In-hotel: restaurant, no kids under 10, no-smoking rooms* ▭*AE, D, MC, V* 🍽*BP.*

OUR CASA IS YOUR CASA

Vacation rentals, booked primarily through agencies, are increasingly popular, as properties are available to meet almost every taste and budget. If you're looking for a rental home, two of our favorite local agencies are:

Intracoastal Realty (☎*910/256-3780 or 800/346-2463* 🌐*www.intracoastalrentals.com*). **Midgett Realty** (☎*252/986-2841 or 800/527-2903* 🌐*www.midgettrealty.com*).

MOREHEAD CITY

3 mi west of Beaufort via U.S. 70.

The quiet commercial waterfront at Morehead City is dotted with restaurants and shops that have put new life in its old buildings. The largest town on the Crystal Coast, it hosts a state port and charter fishing arena. It's also home to sizeable marine research facilities for the National Oceanic and Atmospheric Administration, the University of North Carolina at Chapel Hill, and North Carolina State University.

Arendell Street (U.S. 70) is Morehead City's main drag. Running parallel to the waterfront, it and some side streets contain the Fish Walk, a series of colorful sculptures in clay relief depicting indigenous fish and other types of sea life as well as gift shops, restaurants, and the Crystal Coast Tourism Authority.

Outside the city, you can fish, swim, picnic, and hike at Fort Macon State Park. Route 58 passes through all the beach communities on Bogue Banks, a barrier island across Bogue Sound from Morehead City. There are a number of popular family beaches, including Atlantic Beach and Emerald Isle. Points of public access along the shoreline are marked by orange-and-blue signs. Lifeguards monitor only a few beaches.

GETTING HERE & AROUND
Morehead City is near the far east end of U.S. 70. A small regional airport is in nearby Beaufort and a commercial airport about an hour away in New Bern. There is no public bus service in this busy town; a car is essential.

ESSENTIALS
Visitor Information **Crystal Coast Visitor Center** (⊠ *3409 Arendell St., Morehead City* ☎ *877/206-0929* ⊠ *263 Rte. 58, Cape Carteret* ☎ *252/393-3100* ⊕ *www. sunnync.com*).

EXPLORING
The North Carolina Seafood Festival, on the first weekend in October, is much anticipated and heavily attended; it has celebrated the Central Coast's fishing and seafood heritage for 22 years. A chef's tent features special seafood preparations, and fresh North Carolina seafood may be purchased on the festival grounds. There are also arts-and-crafts vendors as well as all sorts of food, live entertainment, rides, and a blessing of the fishing fleet. ■**TIP→ If you've never tried alligator, here's your chance.** ⊠ *Waterfront, 907-B Arendell St.* ☎ *252/726-6273* ⊕ *www. ncseafoodfestival.org.*

The History Place has a large artifact collection, which reflects the history of Carteret County and the Cape Lookout region from Native American through modern times. There's also a gift shop, tea room, and a public research library with a notable genealogy collection. ⊠ *1008 Arendell St.* ☎ *252/247-7533* ⊕ *www.thehistoryplace.org* ⊠ *Free* ⊙ *Tues.–Sat. 10–4.*

★ The centerpiece of **Fort Macon State Park** is the 1834 pentagon-shape for-
⟳ tress used first to protect the coast against foreign invaders and pirates, then against Yankees during the Civil War. You can explore on your own or take a guided tour. The 365-acre park set in a maritime forest also offers picnicking areas, hiking trails, a mile-long beachfront with a large bathhouse and refreshments, and summer concerts. Rangers offer a wide selection of nature talks and walks, including Civil War weapons demonstrations, bird or butterfly hikes, and beach explorations. Follow the boardwalk over the dunes to the beach, which, due to strong currents, has lifeguards on duty June through Labor Day from 10 to 5:45. A bathhouse locker costs $4. ⊠ *East end of Rte. 58, Bogue Banks, 3 mi south of Morehead City, 2300 E. Fort Macon Road, Atlantic Beach* ☎ *252/726-3775* ⊕ *www.ncparks.gov/visit/ parks/foma/main.php* ⊠ *Free* ⊙ *Fort: daily 9–5:30. Grounds: Mar., Apr., May, Sept., and Oct. daily 8–7; June–Aug., daily 8–8.*

Fodor'sChoice
★
☺

The **North Carolina Aquarium at Pine Knoll Shores.** A recent $25 million renovation tripled the facility's size. Exhibits include a touch pool with live horseshoe crabs; river otters; and a 306,000-gallon, 64-foot-long Living Shipwreck of a German submarine sunk off the North Carolina coast in 1942. There's a large selection of programs, walks, and excursions. You can take a nighttime stroll on the beach looking for loggerhead turtles or kayak the Theodore Roosevelt Natural Area. Kids will love seeing the aquarium menagerie getting fed or spending a night at a slumber party in front of the Living Shipwreck exhibit. ☎252/247–4003, 866/294–3477 for activities ✉U.S. 58, Atlantic Beach, 1 Roosevelt Blvd. ⊕www.ncaquariums.com ✉$8 ☉Daily 9–5.

WHERE TO EAT

$$–$$$
ECLECTIC
★

✕**Bistro by the Sea.** An atrium in the bar is decorated as a grape arbor, which says a lot about the importance of wines to the dining experience here. The stonework and stucco exterior hint at the Mediterranean style within, but the cuisine defies any particular theme. Beef, chicken, and seafood all share space on the menu—but the flavor is as likely to be Asian as Italian. Don't miss the tuna sushi served the same day it is caught. There's a vodka and piano bar as well as a cigar patio. ✉4031 Arendell St. ☎252/247–2777 ⊕www.bistro-by-the-sea.com ▤AE, D, MC, V ☉Closed Sun. and Mon. No lunch.

$$$
SEAFOOD

✕**Chefs 105.** Named for its street address in a 1929 Gulf Oil Corp. warehouse, this casual restaurant has a hip feel. Chef Andy Hopper, of Chicago's Spiaggia Cafe fame, is busy in the kitchen with rustic takes on fresh local seafood and meats. Smoked gouda seasons the creamy crab dip, and fire-grilled ahi tuna is served with ginger cucumber salad, mango slaw, and seaweed salad. Grab a chicken salad wrap or yellow fin tuna salad melt for lunch. ■TIP→The second-story deck has particularly nice views. ✉105 S. 7th St. ☎252/240–1105 ⊕www.chefs505.com/chefs105.htm ▤AE, D, MC, V.

$$ $$$
SEAFOOD
★
☺

✕**Sanitary Fish Market.** In 1938, when the Sanitary was founded, many fish houses were ill kept. The owners wanted to signal that theirs was different; clean, simple, and generous are still the bywords at this waterfront place where diners sit at long wooden tables. It can get busy (waits of an hour) and noisy (the restaurant seats 600), but people from around the world (their photos, many celebrities among them, line the walls) gush about the seafood and don't mind the fine-dining prices with the no-frills atmosphere. Have seafood prepared almost any way you want it—steamed, fried, grilled, or broiled. The two-course Deluxe Shore dinner has, among other things, shrimp, oysters, crabs, and fish. Hush puppies and coleslaw come with every meal. ✉501 Evans St. ☎252/247–3111 ⊕www.sanitaryfishmarket.com ▤AE, D, MC, V ☉Closed mid-Dec. and Jan.

WHERE TO STAY

$$
☺

🖭**Windjammer Inn.** What you get here is straightforward—a comfortable, large room with a private balcony, an ocean view, and easy access to the beach. The five-story glass elevator sets the inn apart from typical beach lodging. There's a two-night minimum stay on summer weekends; great off-season rates. **Pros:** outdoor Jacuzzi; all rooms are oceanfront; beach is right outside the door and feels private. **Cons:** small lobby; no breakfast. ✉*103 Salter Path Rd., Atlantic Beach* ☎*252/247–7123 or 800/233–6466* ⊕*www.windjammerinn.com* ⇌*46 rooms* △*In-room: refrigerator. In-hotel: pool, no-smoking rooms* ⊟*AE, D, MC, V* ⊚|*EP.*

SPORTS & THE OUTDOORS

Two wreck sites popular for scuba diving are the former German gunship *Schurz*, seized by the United States and sunk following a collision in 1918, and the *Papoose*, a 412-foot tanker sunk by a German torpedo in 1942, which is now inhabited by docile sand sharks. **Olympus Dive Center** (✉*713 Shepard St.* ☎*252/726–9432* ⊕*www.olympusdiving.com*) has two dive boats and offers full- and half-day charters, special charters for divers seeking decompression certification., equipment rental, and lessons. ■**TIP**➜ **In addition to wreck excursions, it sponsors photography dives, spearfishing charters, and shark expeditions.**

SHOPPING

The oldest continuously operating curb market in North Carolina, **Carteret County Curb Market** (✉*13th and Evans Sts., Morehead City* ☎*252/222–6359*) is open each Saturday from May to Labor Day from 7:30 AM to 11:30 AM. It's the place to find everything from flowers to flounder, locally grown vegetables, fresh seafood, baked goods of all descriptions, and a variety of North Carolina crafts.

Dee Gee's Gifts & Books (✉*508 Evans St., Morehead City* ☎*252/726–3314 or 800/333–4337*) offers a wide variety of books with regional interest and frequently holds book signings by local authors. This is also the place to look for North Carolina crafts, cards, gifts, candy, nautical charts, and art.

NEW BERN

36 mi northeast of Morehead City via U.S. 70.

This city of 23,500 was founded in 1710 by a Swiss nobleman who named it after his home: Bern, Switzerland. Since "bern" means "bear" in German, black bears are the mascot of New Bern, peering from carvings, the city's seal, and town souvenirs. New Bern boasted the state's first printing press in 1749, the first newspaper in 1751, and the first publicly funded school in 1764. For nearly 30 years it was also the state capital until it moved to Raleigh in 1792. George Washington even slept in New Bern . . . *twice.* In 1898 New Bern cemented its place in pop-culture history when pharmacist Caleb Bradham mixed up a digestive aid that would become known as Pepsi-Cola.

Today New Bern has a 20-block historic district that includes more than 150 significant buildings, some 50 of which are on the National Register. The diverse architecture covers colonial, Georgian, Federal, Greek Revival, and Victorian styles. Since 1979 more than $70 million has been spent preserving and revitalizing the downtown area, now a pleasant mix of shops, restaurants, and museums. Sailors and sun seekers enjoy the area, too, as the Neuse and Trent rivers are perfect for such activities as waterskiing and crabbing. The town has eight marinas, and, if water sports aren't your thing, five public or semipublic golf courses.

GETTING HERE & AROUND

The east–west U.S. 70 and north–south U.S. 17 intersect at New Bern, allowing highway access from all directions. The city also has a medium-sized airport offering commercial flights. Most of the walking is done downtown, but you'll need a car to maneuver the city.

ESSENTIALS

Visitor Information Craven County Convention and Visitors Bureau (⊠ *203 S. Front St., New Bern* ☎ *252/637–1551* ⊕ *www.visitnewbern.com*).

Air Contact Craven County Regional Airport (⊠ *U.S. 70, 200 Terminal Dr., New Bern* ☎ *252/638–8591* ⊕ *www.newbernairport.com*).

EXPLORING

Fodor'sChoice
★
The reconstructed **Tryon Palace,** an elegant 1770 Georgian building, was the colonial capitol and originally the home of Royal Governor William Tryon. The palace burned to the ground in 1798, and it wasn't until 1952 that a seven-year, $3.5-million effort to rebuild it took place. Today only the stable and one basement wall are original; but the structure and furnishings are so authentic—reconstructed from architect plans, maps, and letters—that 82% of the books in the library are the same titles as were there 200 years ago. It's furnished with English and American antiques corresponding to Governor Tryon's inventory. The stately **John Wright Stanly House** (circa 1783), the **George W. Dixon House** (circa 1830), the **Robert Hay House** (circa 1805), and the **New Bern Academy** (circa 1809) are all part of the 13-acre Tryon Palace complex. You can also stroll through the 18th-century formal gardens, which bloom year round but are especially popular during spring tulip and fall mum seasons. ⊠ *610 Pollock St.* ☎ *252/514–4900 or 800/767–1560* ⊕ *www.tryonpalace.org* ⊞ *Guided tours of garden, kitchen, office, and stables $8; tour of all buildings and gardens and good for two days $15* ⊙ *Mon.–Sat. 9–5, Sun. 1–5.*

In honor of the soda's 100th anniversary, the local bottling company opened the **Birthplace of Pepsi-Cola** in the same corner store where teacher-turned-pharmacist Caleb Bradham brewed his first batch of "Brad's Drink." He later renamed it Pepsi-Cola, began marketing the syrup to other soda fountains, and a conglomerate was born. This old-fashioned pharmacy shop feels like a museum, with its reproduction of Bradham's fountain and exhibits of memorabilia and gift items. ⊠ *256 Middle St.* ☎ *252/636–5898* ⊕ *www.pepsistore.com* ⊙ *Mon.–Thurs. and Sat. 10–6, Fri. 10–8, Sun. 12–4.*

WHERE TO EAT

$–$$
AMERICAN
★
♺
✕**Captain Ratty's Seafood & Steakhouse.** The storefront of this local favorite is draped in fish netting and colorful pennants listing the names of patrons' boats. Sandwiches and generous salads are popular lunch items; seafood and steaks are the prime choices for evening meals. The price of oysters depends on whether you do the shucking or have the

Ratty's staff do it for you. Kid's menus, takeout, and delivery are available. The upstairs bar features live entertainment Thursday through Saturday, and an outdoor rooftop bar provides a bird's-eye view of downtown. ⊠ *202 Middle St.* ☎ *252/633–2088* ⊕ *www.captainrattys. com* ⊟ *MC, V.*

$$–$$$
AMERICAN
✗**The Chelsea.** This two-story restored 1912 structure, originally the second drugstore of the pharmacist who invented Pepsi-Cola, retains some fine architectural details, such as its tin ceiling. It's a magnet for weekday business lunches and weekenders looking for a quick sandwich (including wraps, pitas, and burgers) or large salad. Not just a lunch spot, the entrées include shrimp and grits and Southern osso buco, a roasted pork shank in red wine sauce with capers and fire-roasted tomatoes. The bar is well stocked, and Pepsi products are, as might be expected, the nonalcoholic drinks of choice. ⊠ *335 Middle St.* ☎ *252/637–5469* ⊕ *www.thechelsea.com* ⊟ *AE, D, MC, V.*

¢
AMERICAN
☼
✗**Cow Cafe.** New Bern's only "4-hoof" restaurant, everything is "moolicious" at this black-and-white spotted café from the nearby Maola Milk and Ice Cream Company. Cows rule here, which make children squeal with delight. Every gift, toy and corner has something to do with the animals. Most popular, however, is the ice cream in flavors named Moonilla, Udder Pecan, Wild Mooberry Cheesecake. Apart from the ice cream, sandwiches, hot dogs, and "cowsadillas" are served. ⊠ *319 Middle St.* ☎ *252/672–9269* ⊴ *Reservations not accepted* ⊟ *MC, V*

$$$–$$$$
STEAK
☼
✗**The Flame.** The considerate staff at this woodsy steak house with furnishings vaguely reminiscent of the Victorian era help make dinners special. Steak, grilled shrimp, and teriyaki chicken are all good bets, much of which you can watch the chef cook at an open grilling station. All-you-can-eat crab legs are served on Thursday. Sunday brunch with fried turkey and seafood Newburg (crab and shrimp in a cream sherry sauce topped with bread crumbs) is popular. Legend has it that the restaurant's colorful murals of old New Bern scenes were painted by local artist and oenophile William Taglieri, who accepted wine as payment for his work. ⊠ *2303 Neuse Blvd.* ☎ *252/633–0262* ⊕ *www.the-flamerestaurant.com* ⊟ *AE, D, MC, V* ☯ *No dinner Sun. No lunch.*

¢–$
AMERICAN
✗**Pollock Street Deli.** Good-size crowds gather in the tiny rooms of this historic-district Colonial house—and at its sidewalk tables—for classic deli treats (the Reuben is renowned; the chicken salad a winner) and Sunday brunch (consider eggs Benedict). Service can be leisurely, but it's also friendly and the walls covered with funky comics and license plates from all over the world provide ample distraction. ⊠ *208 Pollock St.* ☎ *252/637–2480* ⊟ *AE, MC, V* ☯ *No dinner Sat.–Thurs.*

WHERE TO STAY

¢–$
⊞**Hanna House.** Camille and Joe Klotz moved here from "up North" and renovated the Rudolph Ulrich House (circa 1896), incorporating the latest in plumbing and bath fixtures into antiques-filled rooms. In so doing, they made a home not just for themselves, but for other visitors to this river city. Regulars return again and again to the small B&B, where lush robes hang in closets. Breakfast, with customized coffee blend, is served at the time of your preference, and may include eggs Florentine with hollandaise sauce, apple pancakes, or poached gray

trout in rémoulade sauce. **Pros:** a short walk from downtown shops and a riverfront park; recently renovated; special breakfast requests taken. **Cons:** no pets allowed; no small children; no phones or televisions in rooms. ⊠*218 Pollock St.* ☎*252/635–3209 or 866/830–4371* ⊕*www.hannahousenc.net* ☞*5 rooms* ⚭*In-room: no phone, no TV. In-hotel: restaurant, no kids under 12, no-smoking rooms* ⊟*AE, MC, V* ⫶⊙⫶*BP.*

$–$$ ⛫ **Harmony House Inn.** This old 8,000-square-foot home has a curious
★ past—at one point, two brothers sawed the house in half to install a large Victorian staircase. Today the house is 9 feet wider, and you sleep in spacious rooms that lodged Yankee soldiers during the Civil War. Crafty wreaths, quilts, and embroidery complement the mix of antiques and reproductions in guest rooms. Wine and cheese are served in the evening. **Pros:** on a quiet downtown side street; easy walking distance to shops, restaurants, and the waterfront park; whirlpool baths in some suites. **Cons:** no elevator; no pets allowed; smoking permitted on front porch. ⊠*215 Pollock St.* ☎*252/636–3810 or 800/636–3113* ⊕*www.harmonyhouseinn.com* ☞*7 rooms, 3 suites* ⚭*In-hotel: restaurant, no-smoking rooms* ⊟*D, MC, V* ⫶⊙⫶*BP.*

¢ ⛫ **New Berne House.** Just around the corner from Tryon Palace, owner Barbara Pappas has turned the three floors of a 1922 brick house into a tasteful, albeit eclectic, showcase for her collections. Breakfast is served on vintage dishes, books fill built-in shelves, art covers the walls, and a funky set of hats hangs on the second-floor landing. One bedroom has a brass bed that was reportedly not only saved from a brothel fire in 1897, but was also once owned by U.S. Senator Barry Goldwater. Pappas, soft-spoken and genial, keeps a refrigerator stocked with drinks. Her popular mystery weekends (advance reservations a must) involve scavenging the town's nearby historic district for clues. **Pros:** innkeeper is knowledgeable about the local area and its history; off-street parking. **Cons:** located on a busy highway; innkeeper not always on-site; no pets allowed. ⊠*709 Broad St.* ☎*252/636–2250 or 866/782–8301* ⊕*www.newbernehouse.com* ☞*7 rooms* ⚭*In-room: no phone, no TV. In-hotel: no-smoking rooms* ⊟*MC, V* ⫶⊙⫶*BP.*

$$–$$$ ⛫ **Sheraton New Bern.** At the confluence of the Neuse and Trent rivers, this Sheraton—with marina facilities—is actually two properties in one. A hotel has guest rooms overlooking the Trent River, and rooms at the inn have either waterfront or city views. **Pros:** recently renovated lobby is sleek and cool; away from downtown bustle; lovely dock. **Cons:** no complimentary breakfast; staff can be a little scattered. ⊠*100 Middle St.* ☎*252/638–3585 or 888/326–3745* ⊕*www.sheraton.com/newbern* ☞*171 rooms* ⚭*In-room: refrigerator (some), Wi-Fi. In-hotel: restaurant, room service, pool, no-smoking rooms* ⊟*AE, D, DC, MC, V.*

SHOPPING

The success of the downtown revitalization process is obvious in the variety of businesses in these old buildings. **Art of the Wild** (⊠*218 Middle St.* ☎*252/638–8806*) features wildlife sculptures carved from wood, stone, horn, and driftwood as well as other gifts and prints. **Bear Essentials** (⊠*309 Middle St.* ☎*252/637–6663*) specializes in earth-friendly products ranging from cosmetics to lotions. A selection of 100% organic cotton baby clothes and women's wear made from hemp is also sold. **The Four C's** (✉*252 Middle St.* ☎*252/636–3285*) is the Coastal Casual Clothing Co. and the best place to pick out sportswear and camping gear. **Fraser's Wine & Cheese Gourmet Shoppe** (✉*210 Middle St.* ☎*252/634–2580*), a specialty food shop, has an enviable international wine selection and imported chocolates. Regional and national artists of every genre are represented at **Carolina Creations** (✉*317A Pollock St.* ☎*252/633–4369*) art gallery and gift shop. You can find blown glass, pottery, jewelry, wood carvings, and all manner of paintings and prints.

WILMINGTON & THE CAPE FEAR COAST

The greater Cape Fear region stretches from Topsail Island north of Wilmington south to Southport. The Cape Fear River Basin begins in the Piedmont region and meanders several hundred miles before spilling into the Atlantic Ocean about 30 mi south of downtown Wilmington.

Miles and miles of sand stretch northward to the Outer Banks and southward to South Carolina. The beaches offer activities from fishing to sunbathing to scuba diving, and the towns here have a choice of accommodations. Approximately 100 points of public access along the shoreline are marked by orange-and-blue signs.

First settled in 1729, Wilmington is one of two deepwater ports in the state. It also has a 300-block historic district and a picturesque riverfront listed on the National Register of Historic Places. South of Wilmington there are three distinct island communities that are an easy day trip: Wrightsville Beach, Kure (pronounced "*cure*-ee") Beach, and Carolina Beach. Southport, which sits along the west side of the Cape Fear River's mouth, has a revitalized waterfront, shaded streets, grand homes, and year-round golf. Such is the personality of the region that it has something for artists, sportspeople, history buffs, naturalists, shoppers, sunbathers, and filmmakers alike. EUE/Screen Gems Studios, the largest full-service motion-picture facility in the United States east of California, is headquartered in Wilmington.

WILMINGTON

89 mi southwest of New Bern via U.S. 17 and 117; 130 mi south of Raleigh via I–40.

The city's long history, including its part in the American Revolution, is revealed in sights downtown and in the surrounding area. The Cotton Exchange and Water Street Market are old buildings now used as shopping and entertainment centers. *Henrietta II,* a paddle-wheeler similar to those that plied the waters of the Cape Fear River, has been put into service as a tourist vessel. Wilmington, also a college town, hosts special annual events such as the Azalea Festival, North Carolina Jazz Festival, Christmas candlelight tours, and fishing tournaments.

GETTING HERE & AROUND

Wilmington is at the crossroads of U.S. 17 and the I–40 terminus. Commercial flights land at Wilmington International Airport. The downtown historic district along the riverfront is very walkable. As you move away from this immediate area, however, a car becomes necessary for visits to places such as the Cameron Art Museum, Airlie Gardens, and the USS *North Carolina* Battleship Memorial. In summer the major thoroughfare can be fairly busy, so allow more time than the distance would indicate. Route 132, the main north–south road through town, continues south where I–40 leaves off. U.S. 76 runs from downtown east to Wrightsville Beach; U.S. 421 goes south to Carolina and Kure beaches.

ESSENTIALS

Visitor Information Cape Fear Coast Convention and Visitors Bureau (✉ *24 N. 3rd St., Wilmington* ☎ *910/341–4030 or 800/406–2356* ⊕ *www.cape-fear.nc.us*).

EXPLORING

TOP ATTRACTIONS

2 Burgwin-Wright Museum House. The house General Cornwallis used as his headquarters in April 1781 was built in 1770 on the foundations of a jail. After a fine, furnished restoration, this colonial gentleman's town house was turned into a museum that includes seven distinct period gardens. ✉ *224 Market St., Downtown* ☎ *910/762–0570* ✑ *$10* ☉ *Tues.–Sat. 10–4.*

1 Cape Fear Museum of History and Science. Trace the natural, cultural, and social history of the lower Cape Fear region from its beginnings to the present. One exhibit follows the youth of one of Wilmington's most famous native sons, basketball superstar Michael Jordan. Another is about the fossilized skeleton of an ancient (1.5 million years old), giant (20 feet long, 6,000 pounds) sloth discovered in 1991 during the construction of a Wilmington retention pond. ✉ *814 Market St., Downtown* ☎ *910/798–4350* ⊕ *www.capefearmuseum.com* ✑ *$5* ☉ *Late May–early Sept., Mon.–Sat. 9–5, Sun. 1–5; mid-Sept.–mid-May, Tues.–Sat. 9–5, Sun. 1–5.*

4 Cotton Exchange. In an area along the Cape Fear River that has flourished as a trading center since pre–Civil War days stands a shopping mall in a rambling renovated warehouse, once headquarters of the largest cotton exporter in the world. There are also several restaurants on-site. ✉ *321 N. Front St., Downtown* ☎ *910/343–9896* ⊕ *www. shopcottonexchange.com* ☉ *Mon.–Sat. 10–5:30, Sun. 1–5.*

Haunted Wilmington Tours. Give yourself chills even on a sultry night. Choose between the Ghost Walk of Old Wilmington—with its stories of privateers, murderers, and unmarked graves—or the Haunted Pub Crawl, where you wash down tales of madmen and saucy wenches with Dutch courage (must be 21). ✉ *Tours depart from riverfront at Market and Water Sts., Downtown* ☎ *910/794–1866* ⊕ *www.hauntedwilmington.com* ✑ *$12, ghost walk; $15 pub crawl, drinks not included.*

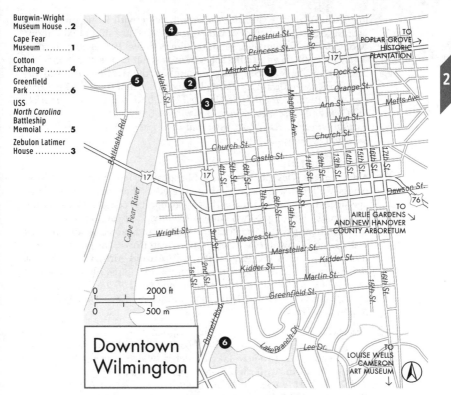

Downtown
Wilmington

Louise Wells Cameron Art Museum. The museum, formerly known as the St. John's Museum of Art, is dedicated to the fine art and crafts of North Carolina from the 18th to the 20th centuries. Its permanent collection, contained in a sleek 40,000-square-foot facility, includes originals by Mary Cassatt, master potter Ben Owen, and folk artist Clyde Jones. On the 10-acre grounds are restored Confederate defense mounds built during a battle in the waning days of the Civil War. ⊠*3201 S. 17th St., 4 mi south of downtown, South Metro* ☎*910/395–5999* ⊕*www.cameronartmuseum.com* ⊡*$7* ⊗ *Tues., Fri., Sat. and Sun. 11–5, Thurs. 11–9.*

**OFF THE
BEATEN
PATH**

Moore's Creek National Battlefield. American patriots not only ambushed charging Loyalists on this site on February 27, 1776, but they also seized the equivalent of $1 million in British sterling. The battle is reenacted on the anniversary each year. An interpretive trail lines the battlefield and there are exhibits in the visitor center. The 85-acre park is also a wildlife habitat. ⊠*40 Patriots Hall Dr., 20 mi northwest of Wilmington on Rte. 210, Currie* ☎*910/283–5591* ⊕*www.nps.gov/mocr* ⊡*Free* ⊗*Daily 9–5.*

⑤ **USS *North Carolina* Battleship Memorial.** Take a self-guided tour of a ship that participated in every major naval offensive in the Pacific during World War II. Exploring the floating city, with living quarters, a post office, chapel, laundry, and even an ice-cream shop, takes about two hours. A 10-minute orientation film is shown throughout the day. ■ TIP→ **A climb down into the ship's interior is not for the claustrophobic.** The ship can be reached by car or by taking the river taxi from Riverfront Park, Memorial Day through Labor Day, at a cost of $4 per person. ⊠ *1 Battleship Rd., junction of U.S. 74/76 and U.S. 17 and 421, west bank of Cape Fear River, Downtown* ☎ *910/251–5797* ⊕ *www. battleshipnc.com* ⊠ *$12* ⊙ *Memorial Day–Labor Day, daily 8–8; early Sept. to late May, daily 8–5.*

WORTH NOTING

★ **Airlie Gardens.** Designed first as a European-style garden showcasing plants in all four seasons, Airlie has suffered its share of hurricane damage since it was built in the early 1900s, but has come back each time and is now owned by New Hanover County. There are 67 acres in this lush Southern garden—azaleas, magnolias, and camellias abound—as well as two freshwater lakes that attract waterfowl. The greatest specimen of them all is the gargantuan 450-year-old Airlie Oak. The last tickets for the day are sold one hour before closing. ⊠ *300 Airlie Rd., 8 mi east of downtown via U.S. 76, Midtown* ☎ *910/798–7700* ⊕ *www. airliegardens.org* ⊠ *$5* ⊙ *Mid-Mar.–late Dec., Tues.–Sun. 9–5, mid-Mar.–May, Thurs.–Sat. 9–7.*

❻ Greenfield Park. Come here for picnic spots, bike paths, nature trails, playgrounds, tennis courts, a skateboard park, and canoe and paddleboat rentals on a 150-acre lake bordered by cypress trees laden with Spanish moss. In April the 250-acre park is ablaze with azaleas. ⊠ *S. 3rd St., U.S. 421, 1 mi south of downtown, South Metro* ☎ *910/341–7852* ⊠ *Free* ⊙ *Daily 6 AM–11 PM.*

New Hanover County Arboretum. Lose yourself in numerous natural exhibits, among dozens of varieties of shade-loving camellias. There are magnolia and patio gardens, a salt-spray garden, and a children's garden with a maze. ⊠ *6206 Oleander Dr., 6 mi east of downtown via U.S. 76, Midtown* ☎ *910/452–6393* ⊕ *www.arboretumnhc.org* ⊠ *Free* ⊙ *Daily dawn–dusk.*

Poplar Grove Historic Plantation. Take a tour of what was once the first major peanut farm in North Carolina, the 1850 Greek Revival manor house, and its outbuildings. You can also see blacksmith and weaving demonstrations as well as farm animals (goats, sheep, horses, rabbits, and chickens). The site also includes the 67-acre Abbey Nature Preserve. ⊠ *10200 U.S. 17, 9 mi northeast of downtown, North Metro* ☎ *910/686–9518* ⊕ *www.poplargrove.com* ⊠ *Guided tours $8* ⊙ *Mid-Feb.–mid-Dec., Mon.–Sat. 9–5, Sun. noon–5.*

OFF THE
BEATEN
PATH

White Lake. The white, sandy bottom at this Carolina bay in Bladen County is clearly visible. Because the lake has no currents, tides, or hidden depressions, it has a reputation as the "nation's safest beach." Although White Lake has only 500 year-round residents, the lake draws 200,000 people each summer because of its swimming, boating, wake boarding, jet skiing, and waterskiing opportunities. Other attractions include an amusement park and tent and RV–camping accommodations. ⊠*1879 Lake Dr., 58 mi northwest of Wilmington via U.S. 74 and Rte. 87, White Lake* ☎*910/862–4800* ⊕*www.whitelakenc.com.*

❸ Zebulon Latimer House. Built in 1852 in the Italianate style, this home museum, with thousands of Victorian items in its collection, is a reminder of opulent antebellum living. The Lower Cape Fear Historical Society is based here; it leads two-hour, 12-block guided walking tours of the downtown historic district. ⊠*126 S. 3rd St., Downtown* ☎*910/762–0492* ⊕*www.latimerhouse.org* ⊠*$10* ☉*Weekdays 10–4, Sat. noon–5.*

> **WATCH THOSE RAYS!**
>
> It's tempting to overdo it your first day at the beach, but be careful to avoid a sunburn that could ruin the remainder of your vacation. Apply sunscreen at least 15 minutes before you go out since it takes a little while for sunscreens to start working. Carry a hat, sunglasses, and a long-sleeved cover up. Gradually increase your exposure over a period of days. And remember, the water vapor in clouds magnifies the sun's rays—you can get a nasty burn in weather so overcast you didn't need sunglasses.

WHERE TO EAT

$-$$
FRENCH
✕**Caprice Bistro.** White-lace curtains at the windows, tables dressed in white, and plain white plates serve as an unobtrusive backdrop for the food here, which is all French, all the time. Chef Thierry is proud of his "solid bistro cooking"—onion soup, *pommes frites* (fries) served with aioli, classic steak au poivre, and crisped duck confit. The wine list has American labels as well as French. Although there's no smoking allowed downstairs, you can smoke at the art-filled bar after 10 PM; it stays open until 2 AM. ⊠*10 Market St., Downtown* ☎*910/815–0810* ⊕*www.capricebistro.com* ⊟*AE, MC, V* ☉*No lunch.*

$
SEAFOOD
✕**Catch.** A Wilmington native, chef/owner Keith Rhodes knows where to find fresh, local seafood and how to cook it so that the flavor is not trumped by other ingredients. Asian and Southern influences dictate the menu at this tiny, casual lunchtime venue that is sometimes open for dinner. Curried almonds give crunch to hickory smoked shrimp salad, and blackened mahi is served with maple-cinnamon sweet potatoes. Locals love the fried seafood platters of shrimp, flounder, and oysters, or some combination of the three. Arrive early to grab a seat, as lots of downtown professionals lunch here. ⊠*215 Princess St.* ☎*910/762–2841* ⌕*Reservations not accepted* ⊟*MC, V* ☉*No dinner most nights.*

¢-$
SOUTHWESTERN
✕**K38 Baja Grill.** Named for a popular surfers' point break in Baja, Mexico, where some friends once shared memorable roadside fish tacos, the K38 menu heavily references Baja culinary traditions. You won't find Americanized Mexican fare here. Standard Mexican dishes feature seafood, such as the tacos with crisp beer-battered fish. Chicken and beef are also available. The restaurant also has two nearby outposts— Tower 7 at Wrightsville Beach and K38 Baja Grill in north Wilmington. ⊠*5410 Oleander Dr., Midtown* ☎*910/395–6040* ⊟*AE, D,*

MC, V. ✉*Porter's Neck Shopping Center, 8211 Market Street, North Wilmington* ☎*910/686–8211* ▭*AE, D, MC, V* ✉*4 N. Lumina Ave., Wrightsville Beach* ☎*910/256–8585* ▭*AE, D, MC, V.*

$–$$
AMERICAN
✕**Water Street Restaurant & Sidewalk Café.** A restored two-story brick waterfront warehouse dating from 1835 holds a contemporary restaurant and outdoor café with an impressive wine list of more than 50 labels. Incredibly tender grilled free-range chicken is topped with zesty gremolata. Housemade apple-sage sausage patties perch atop fluffy cheese grits with a Tabasco bite. Crisp shoestring fries are irresistible, and seafood chowder is made daily on the premises. Sidewalk and balcony diners are right on the waterfront, making sunset a nice time to linger over cheesy crab dip and a glass of wine. ▪**TIP→There's live music most nights, including a popular jazz Sunday brunch.** ✉*5 Water St., Downtown* ☎*910/343–0042* ⊕*www.5southwaterstreet.com* ▭*AE, MC, V.*

WHERE TO STAY

$$$–$$$$
🏨**Graystone Inn.** Less B&B than elegant country manor, Graystone is downtown, but feels as quiet and remote as the countryside. The turn-of-the-20th-century home was built by the widow of a successful merchant, and she wasted no expense when it came to architectural detail—it's rich with ceiling coffers, columns, moldings, fireplaces, and other decorative touches. A covered veranda is inviting even if the weather doesn't cooperate for a stroll through the gardens. Bedrooms are stately and comfortable without being overdone. Suite bathrooms are unusually modern and roomy. Continental breakfast items are available for those who can't make the 8:30 to 9 cooked meal. **Pros:** luxurious lobby; considerate touches like umbrellas at the door; spacious rooms. **Cons:** on a busy street; smoking is permitted on outdoor, verandas; "proper attire" required in common areas—that means clean shoes, neat shirts, and no swimsuits; no red wine allowed. ✉*100 S. 3rd St., Downtown* ☎*910/763–2000 or 888/763–4773* ⊕*www.graystoneinn.com* ✎*6 rooms, 3 suites* ♨*In-room: Wi-Fi. In-hotel: restaurant, no kids under 12* ▭*AE, D, MC, V* ⧖*BP.*

¢–$
🏨**Jameson Inn.** Midway between downtown Wilmington and Wrightsville Beach, this small hotel with large rooms offers all the comforts of home, including recliners in some rooms. Across the street from a Target-anchored shopping center, there are plenty of restaurant choices within walking distance. Jameson's deluxe continental breakfast includes make-your-own Belgian waffles. **Pros:** pet-friendly, near two key thoroughfares, walking distance to shopping and chain restaurants. **Cons:** small bathrooms, far from the downtown historic district, surrounded by congested roads. ✉*5102 Dunlea Ct., Market* ☎*910/452–5660 or 800/526–3766* ⊕*www.jamesoninns.com* ✎*67 rooms* ♨*In-room: refrigerator (some), Wi-Fi. In-hotel: pool, gym, some pets allowed, no-smoking rooms* ▭*AE, D, MC, V* ⧖*BP.*

$$–$$$
★
🏨**The Wilmingtonian.** Members of the entertainment industry often frequent the Wilmingtonian. Luxurious suites each have a different theme—classic movies, nautical heritage, country French, and so on. Rooms are spread throughout four buildings set in gardens, including a convent. ▪**TIP→ Request ground-floor accommodations if stairs are a**

problem; there are no elevators. Pros: walking distance to downtown business district; private courtyard; celebrity spottings. **Cons:** no break-fast; near noisy downtown nightclubs. ☒*101 S. 2nd St., Downtown* ☎*910/343–1800 or 800/525–0909* ⊕*www.thewilmingtonian.com* ⤳*40 suites* ⅙*In-room: kitchen (some), refrigerator, Wi-Fi. In-hotel: restaurant, laundry facilities, some pets allowed, no-smoking rooms* ☰*AE, D, MC, V.*

NIGHTLIFE & THE ARTS

The city has its own symphony orchestra, oratorio society, civic ballet, community theater, and concert association. The North Carolina Symphony makes four appearances here each year. The old riverfront area, with its restaurants and nightclubs, strolling couples, and horse-drawn carriages, really jumps on weekend nights.

Cape Fear Blues Festival (☎*910/350–8822* ⊕*www.capefearblues.org*), held for three days in July, culminates in an all-day blues jam. There are also concerts in nightclubs and on paddle wheelers, and festival parties and workshops.

Level 5 at City Stage (☒*21 S. Front St., Downtown* ☎*910/342–0272* ⊕*www.citystageatlevel5.com*) . Part bar, part theater, Level 5 is all entertainment. At the top of an old Masonic temple, the facility includes a 250-seat venue for offbeat productions and comedy troupes as well as a rooftop bar with live music.

Since 1979 the **North Carolina Jazz Festival** (☎*910/350–0250*) ⊕*www.capefearjazz.com*) has heated up a chilly February weekend with nightly sets in the Hilton Wilmington Riverside. World-famous musicians perform in a variety of styles, such as swing and Dixieland.

Campy, good fun is the order of the night at **Rum Runners: Dueling Piano Bar** (☒*21 N. Front St., Downtown* ☎*910/815–3846* ⊕*www.rumrunnersusa.com*), a 6,000-square-foot tiki bar where embarrassingly fruit-filled punches and margaritas are mandatory. When the dueling pianists take the stage and demand you sing along to hits from the past 40 years, you just have to go with the flow.

Thalian Hall Center for the Performing Arts (☒*310 Chestnut St., Downtown* ☎*910/343–3664 or 800/523–2820*), a restored opera house in continuous use since 1858, hosts dozens of theater, dance, stand-up comedy, cinema society, and musical performances each year.

SPORTS & THE OUTDOORS

Wrecks such as the World War II oil tanker *John D. Gill,* sunk by Germans in 1942 on her second-ever voyage, make for exciting scuba diving off the Cape Fear Coast. **Aquatic Safaris** (☒*6800-1A Wrightsville Ave., Wilmington* ☎*910/392–4386* ⊕*www.aquaticsafaris.com*) leads trips to see the wrecks and rents scuba equipment.

From April through December, **Cape Fear Riverboats, Inc.** (☒*101 S. Water St., Downtown* ☎*910/343–1611 or 800/676–0162* ⊕*www.cfrboats.com*) runs several types of cruises aboard a three-deck,

156-foot riverboat, the *Henrietta III,* which departs from docks at Water and Dock streets.

WRIGHTSVILLE BEACH

12 mi east of Wilmington.

Wrightsville Beach is a small (5-mi-long), upscale, quiet island community. Many beach houses have been in the same families for generations. Increasingly, however, they're being razed in favor of striking contemporary homes.

The beaches are havens for serious sunning, swimming, surfing, and surf fishing, and the beach patrol is vigilant about keeping ATVs, glass containers, alcohol, pets, and bonfires off the sands. In summer, when the population skyrockets, parking can be a problem if you don't arrive early, and towing is enforced.

GETTING HERE & AROUND

A short drive from Wilmington, Wrightsville Beach is a good day-trip destination. U.S. 74/76 is the only road access to this small, friendly town. In town you can walk and bike or boat on the Intracoastal Waterway.

ESSENTIALS

Visitor Information Wrightsville Beach Visitor Center (⊠ *305 Salisbury St., Wrightsville Beach* ☎ *910/256–8116*).

WHERE TO EAT

¢–$

AMERICAN

★

✕**Causeway Café.** Sipping coffee supplied by the efficient staff, patrons waiting to be seated contemplate what to order this time—malted pancakes? Eggs Benedict? A country ham sandwich? Cinnamon-raisin-sourdough French toast? Shrimp and grits? Though the lunch menu is perfectly respectable, breakfast (served all day) is what packs 'em in at Causeway, which is less than ¼ mi from the bridge separating Wilmington from Wrightsville Beach Island. ⊠ *114 Causeway Dr.* ☎ *910/256–3730* ⚒ *Reservations not accepted* ▤ *No credit cards* ⊘ *No dinner.*

$–$$

SEAFOOD

✕**South Beach Grill.** Tight parking on a cramped lot doesn't deter diners from this lively, casual restaurant that suits families as well as singles. The fried seafood is good, but the chef shows off with crab-crusted mahi, five spice-rubbed yellowfin tuna, and the eggplant and shrimp stack with tasso ham, roasted red peppers, and boursin-asiago cheese sauce. Beef, pork, chicken, steak, and vegetarian options please landlubbers. ⊠ *100 S. Lumina Ave.* ☎ *910/256–4646* ⊕ *www.southbeach-grillwb.com* ▤ *V, MC, D.*

WHERE TO STAY

$$$–$$$$

▥**Holiday Inn SunSpree Resort Wrightsville Beach.** If you like to be pampered, this is the only place on Wrightsville Beach to fit the bill—but you'll pay a premium for the amenities. Supervised children's activities (ages four to 12) give mom and dad a chance to sneak away, perhaps for a massage. The rooms are standard, although the ocean views are anything but; don't overlook the third-floor oceanview terrace. The restaurant is missable, but live music on the terrace (Thursday through Sunday in summer) is a nice end to the day. **Pros:** activities for kids; indoor and outdoor pools; steps away from the beach. **Cons:** expensive rates; mediocre restaurant. ✉*1706 N. Lumina Ave.* ☎*910/256–2231 or 877/330–5050* ⊕*www.wrightsville.sunspreeresorts.com* ⇆*184 rooms, 8 suites* ⚷*In-room: refrigerator, Internet, Wi-Fi. In-hotel: restaurant, bar, pools, gym, children's programs (ages 4–12), laundry facilities, no-smoking rooms* ⊟*AE, D, MC, V.*

$$–$$$ ⊡**Silver Gull Motel.** This 37-year beach mainstay might be showing its age a little, but the rooms are clean and reasonably priced, and the kitchens were renovated in 2006. The location, right next to Johnny Mercer Pier, is terrific. Movie fans should ask for No. 326, where scenes from *Divine Secrets of the Ya-Ya Sisterhood* were filmed. **Pros:** good oceanfront value; next door to a classic wooden fishing pier; shaded parking. **Cons:** no breakfast; no-frills decor. ✉*20 E. Salisbury St.* ☎*910/256–3728 or 800/842–8894* ⇆*32 rooms* ⚷*In-room: refrigerator, Wi-Fi* ⊟*AE, D, MC, V.*

KURE BEACH

17 mi southwest of Wrightsville Beach; 21 mi southwest of Wilmington via U.S. 421.

A resort community with rocketing construction, Kure Beach contains Fort Fisher State Historic Site and one of North Carolina's three aquariums. In some places twisted live oaks still grow behind the dunes. The community has miles of beaches; public access points are marked by orange-and-blue signs. ■**TIP→A stroll down the boardwalk, lighted at night, is the romantic cap to an evening.**

GETTING HERE & AROUND
Drive to Kure Beach on U.S. 421 or take the ferry from Rte. 211 in Southport. Once at the beach, you'll want a car to get up and down the island, although some people walk and bike along the narrow main highway.

ESSENTIALS
Visitor Information Pleasure Island Visitor Center(✉*1121 N. Lake Park Blvd., Carolina Beach* ☎*910/458-8434*).

EXPLORING
Fort Fisher State Historic Site marks one of the South's largest and most important earthworks fortifications from the Civil War, so tough it was known as the Southern Gibraltar. A reconstructed battery, Civil War relics, and artifacts from sunken blockade runners are on-site. The fort is part of the Fort Fisher Recreation Area, with 4 mi of undeveloped beach. It's also known for its underwater archaeology sites. At least two guided tours are available daily. ✉*U.S. 421, Kure Beach* ☎*910/458-5538* ⊕*www.nchistoricsites.org/fisher* ⊡*Free* ☉*Apr.– Sept., Mon.–Sat. 9–5, Sun. 1–5; Oct.–Mar., Tues.–Sat. 10–4.*

♻ The oceanfront **North Carolina Aquarium at Fort Fisher** features a 235,000-gallon saltwater tank that's home to sharks, stingrays, moray eels, and other fish from nearby waters. Twice a day, scuba divers enter the multistory tank and answer questions from the onlookers. New exhibits feature creatures of the deep from every undersea corner of the earth. There's a touch tank, a tank with glowing jellyfish, and alligator and turtle ponds. ⊠ *900 Loggerhead Rd., off U.S. 421, Kure Beach* ☎ *866/301–3476* ⊕ *www.ncaquariums.com* ⊠ *$8* ⊙ *Daily 9–5.*

Carolina Beach, a town established in 1857, has an old-fashioned boardwalk undergoing revitalization. A semi-open arcade features vintage games, and a doughnut shop still fries its rounds daily. Bars and marinas line a central business district. Its popularity with young people once earned it the nickname "Pleasure Island," but affluent families snapping up waterfront property are changing the demographics. Fishing is a major activity, and anglers can test their skill on the pier, in the surf, and on deep-sea charter excursions. You can also take a nightly party cruise. ⊠ *3 mi northeast of Kure Beach via U.S. 421 .*

WHERE TO STAY & EAT

$$–$$$
SEAFOOD
ⓒ

✗ **Big Daddy's.** You can't miss this 30-year-old institution—the huge sign sits next to the only stoplight in town. Inside, the enormity continues: three noisy, dimly lighted dining areas seat nearly 500 people. The menu is substantial; although some chicken, steak, and prime rib are listed, seafood stars. It comes prepared almost any way you could want it, and portions are large. An all-you-can-eat salad bar is equally filling. The gift shop at the entrance, which sells beach kitsch and candy, is a magnet for children. ⊠ *202 K Ave., Kure Beach* ☎ *910/458–8622* ⊟ *AE, D, MC, V* ⊙ *Closed late Nov.–Feb.*

$$–$$$
SEAFOOD

✗ **Shuckin' Shack.** The front doors of this main-drag raw bar are wide open even in wintertime, giving the casual restaurant a backyard-oyster-roast feel. Servers are efficient; the crowd fun, with locals reminiscing over the newspaper clippings that plaster the bar. Shorts and jeans rule the scene, and bottled beer is de rigueur. Fat, salty local oysters are served fall and winter; shrimp and clams year round. For munchies try deep-fried jalapeño coins, jumbo buffalo wings, and hushpuppies with a sweet edge. ⊠ *6 N. Lake Park Blvd., Carolina Beach* ☎ *910/458–7380* ⚑ *Reservations not accepted* ⊟ *V, MC*

$$–$$$

⌂ **Beacon House Inn.** Back in the 1950s, these pine-panel rooms were a boarding house, and Beacon House is filled with reminders of those days. In the morning enjoy a full Southern breakfast and borrow towels before heading across the street for a day at the beach. The rooms aren't particularly large, but all except one have an en-suite bathroom, and suite bathrooms are luxurious, with a hot tub or multihead shower. Three cottages with full kitchens give families—and pet owners—a vacation alternative. **Pros:** quiet; off the main drag; close to the beach. **Cons:** can be difficult to find; pets are only allowed in two of the cottages and you have to pay a fee; breakfast not included with cottages; children under 12 are only allowed in the cottages. ⊠ *715 Carolina Beach Ave. N, Carolina Beach* ☎ *910/458–6244 or 877/232–2666* ⊕ *www.beaconhouseinnb-b.com* ⚑ *5 rooms (4 with bath), 2 suites, 3 cottages* ⚐ *In-room: Wi-Fi. In-hotel: no kids under 12 (some), some pets allowed, no-smoking rooms* ⊟ *D, MC, V* ⊙ *BP.*

SOUTHPORT

10 mi southwest of Kure Beach via U.S. 421 and ferry; 30 mi south of Wilmington via Rte. 133.

This small town, which sits quietly at the mouth of the Cape Fear River, is listed on the National Register of Historic Places. An increasingly desirable retirement spot, Southport retains its village charm and character. Stately and distinctive homes, antiques stores, gift shops, and restaurants line streets that veer to accommodate ancient oak trees. The town, portrayed in Robert Ruark's novel *The Old Man and the Boy,* is ideal for walking; it's also popular with moviemakers—*Crimes of the Heart* was filmed here.

GETTING HERE & AROUND

From U.S. 17, Rtes. 211 and 133 both land in Southport. A state car ferry arrives every 45 minutes from Kure Beach to the north. Once downtown, you can park your car and walk or bike all over the waterfront area. Commercial airports are located at nearby Wilmington and Myrtle Beach, SC.

ESSENTIALS

Visitor Information **Southport Visitor Center**(⊠ *113 W. Moore St.* ☎ *910/457–7927*).

EXPLORING

If you're approaching the town from Kure Beach and Fort Fisher via U.S. 421, the **Southport–Fort Fisher Ferry,** a state-operated car ferry, provides a river ride between Old Federal Point at the tip of the spit and the mainland. Old Baldy Lighthouse on Bald Head Island is seen en route, as well as the Oak Island Lighthouse and the ruins of the Price's Creek Lighthouse—in fact, this is the only point in the United States where you can see three lighthouses at the same time. It's best to arrive early (30 minutes before ferry departure), as it's first-come, first-served. ☎ *910/457–6942 or 800/368–8969* ⊕ *www.ncferry.org* ⊠ *$5 per car, one-way* ☉ *Call for schedule.*

WHERE TO STAY & EAT

¢   ✗ **Trolly Stop.** An institution in the Cape Fear region (there are also loca-
AMERICAN   tions in Wrightsville Beach, Carolina Beach, and Wilmington), this long, narrow hot-dog joint is known for a unique selection of wieners, all with individual names. The North Carolina comes with chili, slaw, and mustard, and the Surfer Dog is topped with bacon bits and cheese. For the health conscious, there are also vegetarian or fat-free dogs and other sandwiches. ⊠ *111 S. Howe St.* ☎ *910/457–7017* ▤ *No credit cards.*

$ ▦ **Bald Head Island Resort.** Reached by ferry from Southport, this entire
★   island bills itself as a resort. It's a self-contained, carless community,
☼   complete with a grocery store, restaurants, two inns, and ample rental properties from shingled cottages to luxury homes. You can explore the semitropical island on foot, by bicycle, or in a golf cart. Climb to the top of the quaint "Old Baldy" lighthouse, watch the loggerhead turtles, or take a guided tour through the maritime forest. The entire island will gather for a concert or to watch a movie projected on the 1817-era

lighthouse. The 20-minute ferry ride costs $15 per person round-trip; for most of the year, it leaves Southport on the hour and BHI on the half hour. Discounted tickets are available for same-day trips originating on the island. Advance reservations are necessary for the ferry and resort. **Pros:** friendly small-town feel; remote and exclusive; lots of natural areas; children's programs. **Cons:** island is accessible only by ferry; no cars allowed on the island; activities at the island's recreation clubs are not available to all accommodations. ⊠ *Bald Head Island,* ☎ *910/457–5000, 800/432–7368, 910/457–5003 for ferry reservations* ⊕ *www.baldheadisland.com* ⊃ *195 condos, villas, and cottages; 25 rooms in 2 B&Bs* �&In-room: kitchen. In-hotel: 5 restaurants, golf course, tennis courts, pool, bicycles, children's programs (ages 4–17), no-smoking rooms *⊟AE, MC, V.*

**OFF THE
BEATEN
PATH**

Thirteen miles north of Southport, the house at **Orton Plantation Gardens** is not open to the public, but the 20 acres of beautiful, comprehensive gardens, begun in 1910, are great for strolling. The former rice plantation holds magnolias, ancient oaks, and all kinds of ornamental plants; the grounds are also a refuge for waterfowl. Thirty-five movies have had scenes shot here. Visitors can buy plants and seeds from the extensive greenhouses. ⊠ *9149 Orton Rd. SE, off Rte. 133* ☎ *910/371–6851* ⊕ *www.ortongardens.com* ⊠ *$9* ⊗ *Mar.–Aug., daily 8–6; Sept.–Nov., daily 10–5.*

At **Brunswick Town State Historic Site** you can explore the excavations of a colonial town, see the Civil War earthworks Fort Anderson, and have a picnic. Special events include reenactments of Civil War encampments. ⊠ *8884 St. Phillip's Rd., off Rte. 133* ☎ *910/371–6613* ⊕ *www.ah.dcr. state.nc.us/sections/hs* ⊠ *Free* ⊗ *Tues.–Sat. 9–5.*

The Piedmont & the Sandhills, NC

WORD OF MOUTH

"The Triangle area in general is great—three hours from mountains and 2½ from the beach . . . great food, travel, weather, art, sports (colleges are dominant), parks, university/college stuff (lectures, etc.), outdoor recreation. There is no shortage of stuff to do. Plus, you get that Southern hospitality. People are so friendly and helpful. You can't go wrong."

—jspence

Updated
by Amber
Nimocks

THE GENTLY ROLLING HILLS OF the Piedmont make up the central third of North Carolina. This region, wedged between the mountains and the coastal plain, gradually rises from 300 to 1,500 feet above sea level. Long ridges, meandering rivers, and large human-made lakes characterize the area, the most heavily developed region of the state. The Piedmont includes North Carolina's three major metropolitan centers—Charlotte, the Triad, and the Triangle. For the sake of verbal convenience, North Carolinians group six of the area's urban centers into two threesomes: the Triad and the Triangle. The Triad is short for Greensboro, Winston-Salem, and High Point; the Triangle refers to the shape traced by Raleigh, Durham, and Chapel Hill, in the center of which sits Research Triangle Park—a renowned complex of international companies and public and private research facilities. These urban centers have brought world-class museums, shopping, sophisticated restaurants, and professional sporting venues to the region. And one of the beauties of the Piedmont's cities—including Charlotte, which has the state's most dramatic skyline—is that they're characterized by canopies of hardwoods and pines.

South of the Piedmont is the Sandhills region, famous for its clay and its grass: the pottery made by generations of craftsmen and the golf courses that attract players from all over the world. Although there's not much sightseeing here, vacationers can relax in the lap of luxury in some of the state's best resorts.

ORIENTATION & PLANNING

GETTING ORIENTED

North Carolina's dramatic mountains and beaches tend to overshadow the state's Piedmont and Sandhills regions. However, visitors who take the time to experience the woodlands and hills that grace the heart of the state will find themselves enchanted by the same sturdy beauty that has nurtured generations of intellectuals and artists, from early 20th-century wit O. Henry to the modern master of dark humor David Sedaris.

The Triangle. Since the region is home to Duke University, North Carolina State University, and the University of North Carolina at Chapel Hill, life in the Triangle revolves around basketball and higher education. Leafy campuses offer architectural delights, and the surrounding communities reflect the universities' progressive spirits with a vibrant farm-to-table food scene and a passion for learning and the arts.

The Triad. A legacy of devotion to craft and faith is woven into the fabric of the Triad communities. History comes to life here in the restored Moravian village of Old Salem, and the furniture-making traditions of the Piedmont thrive at High Point's International Home Furnishings Market. Theater fans can take in performances at Winston-Salem's North Carolina School of the Arts and its biannual National Black

TOP REASONS TO GO

Raleigh museums: More than a dozen museums and historical sites—several within an easy walk of one another—cover every aspect of North Carolina life, from its prehistoric roots to its arts achievements and sports heroes.

Old Salem: Costumed guides fill this quaint restored village in the heart of Winston-Salem, founded by the Moravians in the mid-18th century.

Seagrove: This Sandhills community has been renowned for its pottery for two centuries. A dozen or more potters provide the wares, from charmingly ugly face jugs to mugs, plates, and other treasures.

College sports: Home to four of the original Atlantic Coast Conference teams—Duke University, North Carolina State University, University of North Carolina at Chapel Hill, and Wake Forest University—even visitors to the region have to pick sides.

Wineries: North Carolina has more than 70 wineries, and many of the finest are in the Piedmont. Sample a few fine vintages in their tasting rooms.

Theater Festival and at High Point's North Carolina Shakespeare Festival.

Charlotte. The Queen City's contemporary facade dazzles, and its skyline gleams with the most impressive modern architecture in the state. Alongside fans cheering the NFL's Carolina Panthers and hipsters hitting the city's sleek nightspots in this New South metropolis, you'll find traditional Southern hospitality and a lot of good eating inspired by regions around the world.

The Sandhills. Quieter than the neighboring Piedmont communities, the Sandhills boasts Pinehurst, a quaint village that happens to be one of the world's most cherished golf destinations. Fort Bragg, home to the Army's storied 82nd Airborne Division, the North Carolina Zoo, and the vast Seagrove pottery district also draw visitors to the region.

THE PIEDMONT & THE SANDHILLS PLANNER

WHEN TO GO

North Carolina's Piedmont and Sandhills regions shine particularly in spring (April and May) and fall (September and October), when the weather is most temperate and the trees and flowers burst with color.

GETTING HERE & AROUND

BY AIR The Raleigh-Durham International Airport (RDU), off Interstate 40 between the two cities, is served by most major airlines. RDU Airport Taxi Service provides taxi service from the airport.

Charlotte-Douglas International Airport (CLT), served by most major airlines, is west of Charlotte off Interstate 85. From the airport, taxis charge a set fee to designated zones; the cost is $13 to $21 (plus $2 for each additional passenger) to most destinations in Charlotte. Airport vans are approximately $8 per person. Just west of Greensboro, the

Piedmont Triad International Airport (PTI) is off Route 68 north from Interstate 40; it's served by Allegiant Air, American Eagle, Continental Express, Delta, Northwest, United, and US Airways. Taxi service to and from PTI is provided by Piedmont Triad Airport Transportation.

BY BUS Capital Area Transit is Raleigh's public transport system, Chapel Hill Transit serves Chapel Hill and Carrboro, and Durham Area Transit Authority is Durham's intracity bus system. The fare for the Raleigh and Durham systems is $1. Chapel Hill Transit is free.

The Triangle Transit Authority, which links downtown Raleigh with Cary, Research Triangle Park, Durham, and Chapel Hill, runs weekdays except major holidays. Rates start at $2.

BY CAR While it's possible to use buses and trains for travel within the Piedmont and Sandhills, they're usually not convenient or fast. Interstates 40, 85, and 77, as well as several U.S. and state highways, offer easy access to most of the region's destinations. Traffic is an issue in the metropolitan areas during morning and evening rush hours, but it is light compared to conditions in larger U.S. cities.

U.S. 1 runs north–south through the Sandhills and the Triangle and is the recommended route from the Raleigh-Durham area to Southern Pines.

Charlotte is a transportation hub; Interstate 77 comes in from Columbia, South Carolina, to the south, and then continues north to Virginia, intersecting Interstate 40 on the way. Interstate 85 arrives from Greenville, South Carolina, to the southwest, and then goes northeast to meet Interstate 40 in Greensboro. From the Triangle Interstate 85 continues northeast and merges with Interstate 95 in Petersburg, Virginia.

Greensboro and Winston-Salem are on Interstate 40, which runs east–west through North Carolina. From the east Interstate 40 and Interstate 85 combine coming into the Triad, but in Greensboro, Interstate 85 splits off to go southwest to Charlotte. High Point is off a business bypass of Interstate 85 southwest of Greensboro.

U.S. 1 runs north–south through the Triangle and links to Interstate 85 going northeast. U.S. 64, which makes an east–west traverse across the Triangle, continues eastward all the way to the Outer Banks. Interstate 95 runs northeast–southwest to the east of the Triangle and the Sandhills, crossing U.S. 64 and Interstate 40, from Virginia to South Carolina.

BY TAXI Taxis and airport vans service all the area towns and airports and are an alternative to renting a car if you don't plan on doing a lot of sightseeing. Reputable companies include Blue Bird Taxi in Greensboro, Central Piedmont Transportation in Winston-Salem, and Crown Cab and Yellow Cab in Charlotte.

BY TRAIN From Charlotte, there's daily service to Washington, D.C., Atlanta, and points beyond, as well as daily service to the Triangle cities of Raleigh, Durham, and Cary. In Greensboro, Amtrak's *Crescent* stops in before continuing from New York to New Orleans (or vice versa).

And the *Carolinian* also stops in Greensboro as it goes from Charlotte to Raleigh and then north to Baltimore, Washington, and New York. The in-state *Piedmont* connects nine cities—including Greensboro—between Raleigh and Charlotte each day.

Both southbound and northbound Amtrak trains—one daily in each direction—stop in Southern Pines.

TOUR INFORMATION On Lake Norman, near Charlotte, the *Catawba Queen* paddle wheeler gives lunch and dinner cruises and tours and the *Lady of the Lake*, a 90-foot yacht, offers dinner cruises.

3

ESSENTIALS **Air Contacts Charlotte-Douglas International Airport** (*CLT* ✉ *5501 Josh Birmingham Pkwy., Airport/Coliseum, Charlotte* ☎ *704/359-4013* ⊕ *www.charlotteairport.com*). **Piedmont Triad International Airport** (*PTI* ✉ *6451 Bryan Blvd., Greensboro* ☎ *336/665-5666* ⊕ *www.flyfrompti.com*). **PTI Airport Transportation** (✉ *6415 Bryan Blvd., Greensboro* ☎ *336/668-9808*). **Raleigh-Durham International Airport** (*RDU* ✉ *1600 Terminal Blvd., Morrisville* ☎ *919/840-2123* ⊕ *www.rdu.com*). **RDU Airport Taxi Service** (✉ *1600 Terminal Blvd. Raleigh-Durham* ☎ *919/840-7277*).

Bus Contacts Capital Area Transit (☎ *919/833-5701* ⊕ *www.raleighnc.gov/transit*). **Chapel Hill Transit** (☎ *919/968-2769* ⊕ *www.townofchapelhill.org*). **Durham Area Transit Authority** (☎ *919/683-3282* ⊕ *www.durhamnc.gov*). **Triangle Transit Authority** (☎ *919/549-9999* ⊕ *www.ridetta.org*).

Taxi Contacts Blue Bird Taxi (✉ *1205 W. Bessemer Ave., Suite 208 Greensboro* ☎ *336/272-5112*). **Central Piedmont Transportation** (✉ *6415 Bryan Blvd. Greensboro* ☎ *336/668-9808*). **Crown Cab** (✉ *1541 St. George Pl., Charlotte* ☎ *704/334-6666*). **Yellow Cab** (✉ *4257 Golf Acres Dr., Charlotte* ☎ *704/332-6161*).

Train Contacts Amtrak (☎ *800/872-7245* ⊕ *www.amtrak.com*).

Tour Contacts *Catawba Queen* and *Lady of the Lake* (✉ *1459 River Hwy., Mooresville* ☎ *704/663-2628* ⊕ *www.queenslanding.com*).

ABOUT THE RESTAURANTS

In the Piedmont it's as easy to grab a bagel, empanada, or spanakopita as a biscuit. The region is still the home of barbecue: wood-fired, pit-cooked, chopped or sliced pork traditionally served with coleslaw and hush puppies. Southern dishes such as catfish, fried green tomatoes, grits, collard greens, fried chicken, sweet potatoes, and pecan pie are also favorites. ■**TIP→** **You'll label yourself a tourist if you pick at your grits, fail to order sweet tea, or ask for the gravy on the side.**

ABOUT THE HOTELS

Accommodations in the Piedmont include everything from roadside motels to sprawling resorts to lovely bed-and-breakfasts. Most major chains are represented, and some offer great weekend packages with perks like theater tickets. During the International Home Furnishings Show, held in spring and fall in High Point, tens of thousands of people descend on the region, making hotel rooms almost impossible to find. May is graduation time for the region's colleges and universities. If you're planning on visiting the Triangle during these peak times, book accommodations well in advance.

Most lodging options in the Sandhills fall into the resort category; pricing plans and options are multitudinous and can be confusing. Many of the prices quoted are for golf packages. However, there are some chain motels in Southern Pines as well numerous B&Bs. The high seasons for golf, which bring the most expensive lodging rates, are from mid-March to mid-May and from mid-September to mid-November.

WHAT IT COSTS					
	¢	$	$$	$$$	$$$$
Restaurants	under $10	$10–$14	$15–$19	$20–$24	over $24
Hotels	under $100	$100–$150	$151–$200	$201–$250	over $250

Restaurant prices are for a main course at dinner. Hotel prices are for two people in a standard double room in high season.

PLANNING YOUR TIME

Because the areas within the Piedmont are fairly compact, it makes sense to tackle them one at a time. Downtown Raleigh, with its expanding array of restaurants and hotels, makes a good base for exploring Durham and Chapel Hill on day trips. Take on Charlotte and the Triad separately. In Charlotte, Uptown is centrally located and provides plenty of entertainment, dining, and lodging within walking distance. The Sandhills, which covers the area from Asheboro southeast to Fayetteville, is more diverse and a bit more cumbersome. Staying in one of the luxurious resorts in Southern Pines or Pinehurst would put you close to the pottery region of Seagrove. Give yourself more driving time when exploring this part of the state.

THE TRIANGLE

The cities of Raleigh, Durham, and Chapel Hill are known collectively as the Triangle, with Raleigh to the east, Durham to the north, Chapel Hill to the west, and, in the center, Research Triangle Park—a cluster of public and private research facilities set in 6,800 acres of lake-dotted pineland—attracts scientists, academics, and businesspeople from all over the world. Throughout the Triangle, an area that has been characterized as "trees, tees, and PhDs," politics and basketball are always hot topics. The NCAA basketball championship has traded hands among the area's three major universities.

RALEIGH

85 mi east of Greensboro; 143 mi northeast of Charlotte.

Raleigh is Old South and New South, down-home and upscale, all in one. Named for Sir Walter Raleigh, who established the first English colony on the coast in 1585, it's the state capital and one of the country's fastest growing cities. Many of the state's largest and best muse-

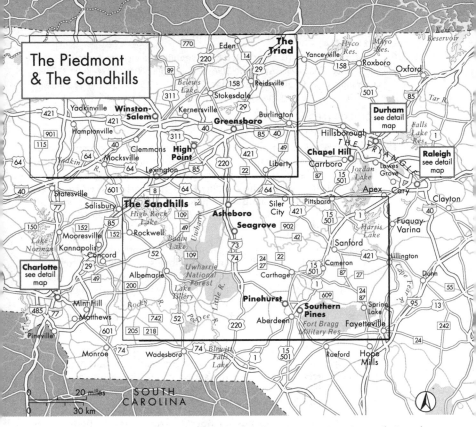

The Piedmont & The Sandhills

ums are here, as are North Carolina State University and six other universities and colleges.

GETTING HERE & AROUND

Like Washington, D.C., Raleigh has a highway that loops around the city. The terms "Inner Beltline" and "Outer Beltline" refer to your direction: The Inner Beltline runs clockwise; the Outer Beltline runs counterclockwise. Don't confuse the Outer Beltline with the Outer Loop, which refers to Interstate 540.

If you come by train or bus, you'll step off in Raleigh's Warehouse District, a developing area of cool clubs and restaurants a few blocks west of downtown. RDU International is a 15-minute cab ride, depending on rush-hour traffic, from downtown. Buses and taxis serve all parts of the city, including the suburbs.

You can board a trolley run by **Historic Raleigh Trolley Tours** (☎919/857–4364) for a narrated hour-long tour of historic Raleigh. Between March and December, the trolley runs Saturday at 10 and 11 AM and 12, 1:30 and 2:30 PM. Although the tour starts and ends at Mordecai Historic Park, you can hop aboard at any stop along the route, including the State Capital Bicentennial Plaza, the Joel Lane House, and City Market. The cost is $8 per person.

ESSENTIALS

Visitor Information Greater Raleigh Convention and Visitors Bureau (⊠ *Bank of America Bldg., 421 Fayetteville St. Mall, Suite 1505* ☎ *919/834–5900* ⊕ *www. raleighcvb.org*). **Capital Area Visitor Services** (⊠ *5 E. Edenton St., Raleigh* ☎ *919/807–7950* ⊕ *ncmuseumofhistory.org/vs/index.html*).

EXPLORING

TOP ATTRACTIONS

⑧ Artspace. A nonprofit visual-arts center, Artspace offers open studios where the artists are happy to talk to you about their work. The gift shop showcases the work of the resident artists. ■ TIP→**The place bustles with visitors during the monthly First Friday art walk, when galleries and museums throughout the city host public receptions to show off new work.** ⊠ *201 E. Davie St., Downtown* ☎ *919/821–2787* ⊕ *www. artspacenc.org* ⊠ *Free* ⊘ *Tues.–Sat. 10–6.*

⑦ City Market. Specialty shops, art galleries, restaurants, and a small farmers' market are found in this cluster of cobblestone streets. A free trolley shuttles between City Market and other downtown restaurant and nightlife locations from 5:30 PM to 11:30 PM Thursday through Saturday. ⊠ *Martin and Blount Sts., Downtown* ☎ *919/821–1350* ⊘ *Most stores Mon.–Sat. 10–5:30; most restaurants Mon.–Sat. 7 AM–1 AM, Sun. 11:30–10.*

③ Executive Mansion. Since 1891, this 37,500-square-foot brick Queen Anne–style structure with elaborate gingerbread trim and manicured lawns has been the home of the state's governors. Reservations for tours must be made at least two weeks in advance. ⊠ *200 N. Blount St., Downtown* ☎ *919/807–7948* ⊠ *Free.*

⑨ Marbles Kids Museum Two museums merged to create this 84,000-square-foot cathedral of play and learning. Everything is hands-on, so your little one is free to fill a shopping cart in the marketplace, don a fireman's hat, clamber through the cab of a city bus, scale the crow's nest of a three-story pirate ship, or splash in numerous water stations. Older children can don costumes in a backstage dressing room and make a big entrance on a child-size stage, play chess with two-foot pawns, perform simple science experiments or create Web pages with their pictures on them. The wide-open design of the space and its architectural details, including a suspension bridge and a courtyard with a 6-foot marble fountain give adults something to look at as well. There's also an IMAX theater. ⊠ *201 E. Hargett St., Downtown* ☎ *919/834–4040* ⊕ *www.marbleskidsmuseum. org* ⊠ *Museum $5; museum and IMAX $9.50–$12.95* ⊘ *Tues.–Sat. 9–5, Sun. noon–5.*

⑤ North Carolina Museum of History. Founded in 1898, the museum is now in a state-of-the-art facility on Bicentennial Plaza. It houses the N.C. Sports Hall of Fame, which displays memorabilia from 260

HOOFING IT

It's easy to get around downtown Raleigh, as the streets are laid out in an orderly grid around the State Capitol. A good place for a stroll is the Oakwood Historic District, a 19th-century neighborhood with dozens of restored homes.

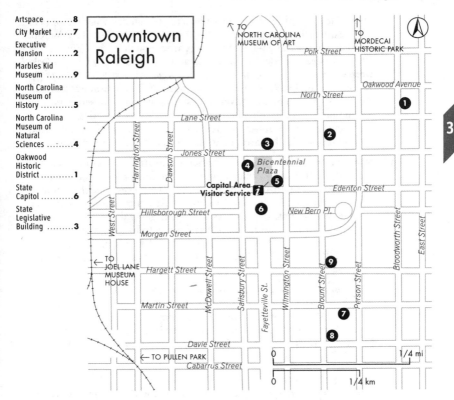

Downtown Raleigh

inductees, from college heroes to pro superstars to Olympic contenders. You can see Richard Petty's race car, Arnold Palmer's Ryder cup golf bag, and Harlem Globetrotter Meadowlark Lemon's uniforms. ■TIP→The Capital Area Visitor Services, in the museum's lobby, is a great place to plan your downtown itinerary, pick up brochures, or arrange area tours. ⊠5 E. Edenton St., Downtown ☎919/807–7900 ⊕www.ncmuseumofhistory.org ⊠Free ⊗Mon.–Sat. 9–5, Sun. noon–5.

❹ ★ ℃ North Carolina Museum of Natural Sciences. At 200,000 square feet, this museum is the largest of its kind in the Southeast. Exhibits and dioramas celebrate the incredible diversity of species in the state's various regions. There are enough live animals and insects—including butterflies, hummingbirds, snakes, and a two-toed sloth—to qualify as a small zoo. One display contains rare whale skeletons. The pièce de résistance, however, is the "Terror of the South" exhibit, featuring the dinosaur skeleton of "Acro," a giant carnivore that lived in the region 110 million years ago. ⊠11 W. Jones St., Downtown ☎919/733–7450 or 877/462–8724 ⊕www.naturalsciences.org ⊠Free ⊗Mon.–Sat. 9–5, Sun. noon–5.

❶ Oakwood Historic District. Several architectural styles—though the Victorian structures are especially notable—can be found in this tree-shaded

19th-century neighborhood. Brochures for self-guided walking tours of the area, which encompasses 20 blocks bordered by Person, Edenton, Franklin, and Watauga–Linden streets, are available at the Capital Area Visitor Services on Edenton Street. Adjacent to historic Oakwood is **Oakwood Cemetery** (⊠*701 Oakwood Ave., Downtown* ☎*919/832–6077*). Established in 1869, it's the resting place of 2,800 Confederate soldiers, Civil War generals, governors, and numerous U.S. senators. The grounds are carefully cultivated and feature willows, towering oaks, and crepe myrtles. The House of Memory next to the Confederate burial ground recalls North Carolinians' involvement in the U.S. military.

6 **State Capitol.** This beautifully preserved example of Greek Revival architecture from 1840 once housed all the functions of state government. Today it's part museum, part executive offices. Under its domed rotunda, the capitol contains a copy of Antonio Canova's statue of George Washington depicted as a Roman general with tunic, tight-fitting body armor, and a short cape. Guided tours are given Saturdays starting at 11 AM and 2 PM. ⊠*Capitol Sq., 1 E. Edenton St., Downtown* ☎*919/733–4994* ⊕*www.ah.dcr.state.nc.us* ▣*Free* ☉ *Weekdays 8–5, Sat. 10–4, Sun. 1–4.*

3 **State Legislative Building.** One block north of the State Capitol, this complex hums with lawmakers and lobbyists when the legislature is in session. It's fun to watch from the gallery. A free guided tour is also available through Capital Area Visitor Services. ⊠*Salisbury and Jones Sts., Downtown* ☎*919/733–7928* ▣*Free* ☉ *Weekdays 8–5, Sat. 9–5, Sun. 1–5.*

WORTH NOTING
The city is spread out, so a car is necessary for visits to museums and parks beyond downtown.

Ava Gardner Museum. In the hometown of the legendary movie star is this museum with an extensive collection of memorabilia tracing her life from childhood on the farm to Hollywood glory days. It's about 30 mi southeast of Raleigh in downtown Smithfield. ⊠*325 E. Market St., Smithfield* ☎*919/934–5830* ⊕*www.avagardner.org* ▣*$6* ☉*Mon.–Sat. 9–5, Sun. 1–5.*

Joel Lane Museum House. Dating to the 1760s, the oldest dwelling in Raleigh was the home of Joel Lane, known as the "father of Raleigh" because he once owned the property on which the capital city grew. Costumed docents lead tours of the restored house and beautiful period gardens. ⊠*728 W. Hargett St., at St. Mary's St., Downtown* ☎*919/833–3431* ⊕*www.joellane.org* ▣*$5* ☉*Mar.–mid-Dec., Wed.–Fri. 10–2, Sat. 1–4.*

Mordecai Historic Park. You can see the Mordecai family's Greek Revival plantation home and other historically significant structures that have been moved onto the 2-acre property, including the house where President Andrew Johnson was born in 1808. Moses Mordecai, a well-respected lawyer, married two granddaughters of Joel Lane, the "Father of Raleigh." Mordecai's descendants lived in the house until 1964. There are guided tours hourly from 10 to 3 Tuesday to Saturday, and from 1 to 3 on Sunday. ■TIP→The historical figure's name is pronounced MOR-de-key. Using a long "i" will mark you as a newcomer immediately. ⊠*1 Mimosa St., at Wake Forest Rd., Downtown* ☎*919/857–4364* ⊕*www.raleighnc.gov/mordecai* ⊠*Free; guided tour $5* ⊗*Tues.–Sat. 1 hr after sunrise–1 hr before sunset.*

WORD OF MOUTH

"Angus Barn would be the place. No reservations and on graduation weekend expect to wait for hours, along with EVERYone else. It is good. You can order drinks in the courtyard, and they may even bring appetizers to appease the wait."

—Gretchen

★ **North Carolina Museum of Art.** On the west side of Raleigh, the NCMA houses 5,000 years of artistic heritage, including one of the nation's largest collections of Jewish ceremonial art. The museum hosts touring exhibitions of works by such artists as Caravaggio and Rodin. There are tours at 1:30 Tuesday to Sunday. A 164-acre park featuring nine monumental works of art, which visitors can view on foot or by bike, adjoins the museum. The in-house restaurant, Blue Ridge, looks out on mammoth modernistic sculptures that, when viewed from above, spell the words PICTURE THIS. ⊠*2110 Blue Ridge Rd., Northwest/Airport* ☎*919/839–6262* ⊕*www.ncartmuseum.org* ⊠*Free* ⊗*Tues.–Thurs. and Sat. 9–5, Fri. 9–9, Sun. 10–5.*

☺ **Pullen Park.** Attracting more than 1 million visitors annually, the park near North Carolina State University draws folks who come to ride the train, the paddleboats, or the 1911 Dentzel carousel. You can swim in a large indoor aquatic center, play a game of tennis, or, if the timing is right, see a summer play at the Theater in the Park. ⊠*520 Ashe Ave., University* ☎*919/831–6468 or 919/831–6640* ⊠*Free* ⊗*Mar., Mon.–Sat. 10–5:30, Sun. 1–5:30; Apr., weekdays 10–5:30, Sat. 10–6:30, Sun. 1–6:30; May–Aug., weekdays 10–6:30, Sat. 10–7:30, Sun. 1–7:30; Sept. and Oct. weekdays 10–4, Sat. 10–6:30, Sun. 1:30–6:30; Nov., Fri. and Sat. 10–5, Sun. 1–5.*

WHERE TO EAT

$$$$
STEAK
✗**Angus Barn.** A huge rustic barn houses this local institution. The dimly lighted, always-busy restaurant is known for its steaks, baby back ribs, prime rib, fresh seafood, and an 85-page wine and beer list. The clubby Wild Turkey Lounge is an after-work destination for Research Triangle Park workers and travelers who just landed at RDU International. A wine cellar, an outdoor pavilion that seats 350, and a teaching kitchen where chef Walter Royal shows off his Iron Chef skills, are well suited for larger gatherings. The oversize desserts are freshly made; on your way out, you can purchase pies at a small stand near the front door. ⊠*4901 Glenwood Ave., Northwest/Airport* ☎*919/781–2444* ⊕*www.angusbarn.com* ⊟*AE, D, MC, V* ⊗*No lunch.*

¢
SOUTHERN
✗**Big Ed's City Market Restaurant.** This place was founded by Big Ed Watkins, who claims some of the recipes were handed down from his great-grandfather, a Confederate mess sergeant. Southern cooking doesn't get much more traditional than this place; make sure you indulge in

the biscuits. The restaurant is filled with antique farm implements and political memorabilia, including snapshots of presidential candidates who have stopped by. Every Saturday morning a Dixieland band plays. ✉ *220 Wolfe St., City Market, Downtown* ☎ *919/836–9909* ⚠ *Reservations not accepted* ▤ *AE, D, MC, V* ⊗ *Closed Sun. No dinner.*

$$
ECLECTIC

✕ **Enoteca Vin.** As the French–Italian name indicates, wine takes center stage at this sophisticated but unpretentious restaurant. The sleek interior—part of the old Pine State Creamery—consists of warm maple, stainless steel, and exposed brick. The eclectic menu emphasizes organic ingredients that are local (flounder, goat cheese) and seasonal (okra, peaches), complemented by food-friendly wines from all over the world. The ever-changing Sunday brunch menu might include French toast with fresh strawberries or shrimp with goat cheese, papaya, avocado, and cherry tomatoes in a red-pepper vinaigrette. ✉ *410 Glenwood Ave., Suite 350, Downtown* ☎ *919/834–3070* ⊕ *www. enotecavin.com* ▤ *AE, MC, V* ⊗ *Closed Mon. No lunch.*

$$$$
MODERN
SOUTHERN
Fodor's Choice
★

✕ **Herons.** Set in the sleek new Umstead hotel, Herons offers a seasonally changing locally grown menu of lighthearted takes on traditional Southern dishes as well as international fare. Among the highlights are a haute interpretation of biscuits and gravy—a fluffy, chive-studded buttermilk biscuit in a creamy porcini sauce with lightly battered pan-fried foie gras—and a roasted rack of lamb with mint-basil pesto and baby vegetables. The well-timed service, expansive wine list, and subtle spotlighting are all designed to make every diner a star for the night. ✉ *100 Woodland Pond Rd. Northwest/Airport* ☎ *919/447–4200* ▤ *AE, DC, D, MC, V.*

$$–$$$
AMERICAN

✕ **Irregardless Café.** This café's menu—a combination of dishes for meat eaters as well as vegetarians and vegans—changes daily. You might find chicken breast coated with crushed cashews and marinated in a lemon-tahini dressing, for example, or mushroom ravioli in a smoked tomato cream sauce. Salads are amply portioned, and the breads, soups, and yogurts are made on the premises. There's live music every night, and dancing on Saturday and brunch on Sunday spice things up. The blond wood, brightly hued contemporary art, sunny dining areas, and well-spaced tables all add to the relaxing vibe. The restaurant is midway between North Carolina State University and downtown. ✉ *901 W. Morgan St., University* ☎ *919/833–8898* ⊕ *www.irregardlesscafe.com* ▤ *AE, D, MC, V* ⊗ *No lunch Sat. No dinner Sun. Closed Mon.*

$$$
ECLECTIC
★

✕ **Margaux's.** Eclectic is the best way to describe the cuisine at this North Raleigh fixture. The menu changes daily and might include peppercorn-crusted beef fillet with crispy fried oysters or phyllo-wrapped salmon with Brie, cranberry jam, and asparagus. A stone fireplace warms the room in winter, and modern sculpture stands and hangs here, there, and everywhere. ✉ *Brennan Station Shopping Center, 8111 Creedmoor Rd., North Hills* ☎ *919/846–9846* ⊕ *www.margauxsrestaurant. com* ▤ *AE, D, MC, V.*

$$$$
AMERICAN
★

✕ **Second Empire.** Wood paneling, muted lighting, and well-spaced tables make for a calming and elegant dining experience in this restored 1879 historic house. The menu, which changes seasonally, has a regional flavor; the food is intricately styled so that colors, textures, and tastes fuse. For an entrée you might order pan-roasted sea scallops served with grits and applewood-smoked bacon, or five-spiced duck confit with green lentils and orzo. A brick tavern on the lower level has a less expensive menu that includes braised lamb shank and grilled trout. ⊠ *330 Hillsborough St., Downtown* ☎ *919/829–3663* ⊕ *www.second-empire.com* ⊟ *AE, D, MC, V* ⊘ *Closed Sun. No lunch.*

WHERE TO STAY

$ 🏨 **North Raleigh Hilton.** This freshly renovated hotel is a favorite spot for corporate meetings. Large rooms invite you to kick back on the sofa for some TV or soak in the extra-deep tub, but if you need to work, the ergonomic desk chair is quite accommodating. Lofton's Cafe is open for breakfast, and the Skybox Grill & Bar has several dozen flat-screen televisions so fans won't miss a second of the action. The fitness center has exercise bikes, treadmills, and a whirlpool. **Pros:** newly redone rooms are comfortable, and the hotel is close to I–440; a free airport shuttle is available between 6 AM and 10 PM. **Cons:** busy location makes getting in and out of the hotel at rush-hour tough. ⊠ *3415 Wake Forest Rd., North Hills* ☎ *919/872–2323 or 800/445–8667* ⊕ *www.hilton.com* 🛏 *338 rooms, 7 suites* ⊙ *In-room: Internet, Wi-Fi. In-hotel: restaurant, room service, bars, pool, gym, laundry service* ⊟ *AE, D, MC, V.*

$$ 🏨 **Oakwood Inn.** This 1871 Victorian B&B, one of the first to be built in what is now the Oakwood Historic District, is listed on the National Register of Historic Places. Each of the individually decorated guest rooms has a working fireplace. Rosewood antiques fill one room; another has a queen-size sleigh bed as its centerpiece. Wine and sweets are always on hand, so guests can enjoy refreshments on the front porch overlooking a yard filled with irises and star magnolias. Walkers may find themselves drawn to the nearby Krispy Kreme; as the sweet scent of doughnuts cooking fills the morning air. **Pros:** fans of Victorian architecture can get their fill of sights on a morning walk through the neighborhood. **Cons:** Victorian decor dominates the interior, so this would be a poor fit for fans of sleek, modern surroundings. ⊠ *411 N. Bloodworth St., Downtown* ☎ *919/832–9712 or 800/267–9712* ⊕ *www.oakwoodinnbb.com* 🛏 *6 rooms* ⊙ *In-room: Wi-Fi.* ⊟ *AE, D, MC, V* �🍽BP.*

$$$$ 🏨 **The Raleigh Marriott City Center.** The 17-story hotel, built to complement the city's new convention center, opened in summer 2008. Rooms are decorated in earth tones and feature halogen lights and prints of local architecture. In-room desks swivel away from the wall, allowing guests to work and watch plasma screen TV at the same time. Bedside clock radios feature iPod docks. Views are good from every side, showing off either expanses of urban greenery or the city's skyline and convention center. The lobby is a wide, welcoming space that flows into the large bar, done in polished hardwood and marble. The hotel is served by Posta Tuscan Grille, run by Italian brothers. **Pros:** downtown location puts you within walking distance of restaurants, bars, museums, and some historic sites. **Cons:** pricier than the chain hotels farther from the city center. ⊠ *500 Fayetteville St., Downtown* ☎ *919/833-1120* ⊕ *www.marriott.com* 🛏 *390 rooms, 10 suites* ⊙ *In room: DVD, Internet, Wi-Fi. In-hotel: restaurant, bar, pool, gym, laundry facilities,*

Taking Your 'Cue

Want a guaranteed one-word conversation starter in any gathering of North Carolinians? Say "barbecue." Barbecue has been called "the most Southern meal of all." But just as there are myriad Southern accents, there are many types of barbecue. Understanding the distinctions is key to understanding a culinary and cultural phenomenon in North Carolina, where barbecue begins with pork (banish all thoughts of beef) and is not so much a verb as a noun (that is, a dish or an event known as a pig-pickin').

The state's barbecue tradition, variously linked to the cooking techniques of Native Americans, African slaves, and Scottish-Irish settlers, has been immortalized in song, prose, poetry, and the electronic media. So revered is the moist and tangy meat that it has inspired place names such as Barbecue Presbyterian Church, which rises beside Barbecue Creek in the Piedmont's Harnett County. Versions of it are served in eateries ranging from top-drawer to lunch counter, though many argue the most authentic barbecue is found in small-town cinder-block restaurants with on-site smokehouses.

And right there is the, ah, meat of the matter: taste. The method of cooking the meat and the ingredients of the sauce that coats it spark a passion that cuts across lines of age, class, and race. One hundred years or more of tradition have dictated that either whole hogs or shoulders be slow-roasted over a wood or charcoal fire to imbue the meat with an appropriate smoky flavor. Over the past few decades, however, an increasing number of barbecuers have switched to cleaner propane flames.

The real fault line, though, is geography. In eastern North Carolina (that's east of Interstate 95) the entire hog is cooked and the meat is "pulled" (off the bone) or coarsely chopped and then heavily seasoned with a vinegar-and-pepper-based sauce. This concoction, whose exact ingredients are jealously guarded by each owner, has a definite kick. West of Interstate 85, the meat, which usually includes just the pork shoulders, can be sliced or chopped. It's then mixed with a somewhat sweeter sauce made of vinegar, ketchup, brown sugar, and perhaps Worcestershire sauce. Serving as a buffer between these two regions is the Research Triangle area, where you'll find both types of barbecue.

No matter where North Carolinians stand on the barbecue debate, both sides agree that the line of good taste has to be drawn somewhere. In this case, it's at the mustardy sauce used in the state just south of the border.

laundry service, Internet terminal, Wi-Fi, parking (paid), no-smoking rooms ▤D, DC, MC, V.

$$ ⊞**Raleigh Marriott Crabtree Valley.** Fresh floral arrangements adorn the elegant public rooms of one of the city's most comfortable hotels. The guest rooms have nice touches like extra-thick mattresses covered with 300-thread-count linens and cozy down comforters. You can dine in the Crabtree Grill and in Quinn's at 4500, a lounge that serves light fare. **Pros:** some of the best shopping in the Triangle is right across the street at Crabtree Valley Mall; there is a free airport shuttle between 6 AM

and 10 PM. **Cons:** traffic from the mall can be an issue ✉*4500 Marriott Dr., U.S. 70 near Crabtree Valley Mall, University* ☎*919/781–7000 or 800/909–8289* ⊕*www.marriotthotels.com/rdunc* ⬅*371 rooms, 5 suites* ⌂*In-hotel: 2 restaurants, bar, pool, gym, laundry service, Wi-Fi* ▤*AE, D, MC, V.*

$$$$
Fodor'sChoice
★

⊡ **The Umstead.** A few exits from RDU International, the Umstead's modern design and wooded landscape make it feel light-years away from the traffic on I–40. The hotel, which opened in 2007, incorporates signature North Carolina elements, including paintings and oversized ceramic works by local artists, floor-to-ceiling windows that bring the 3-acre lake and towering long-leaf pine trees into the decor, and, at the hotel's bar, a by-the-glass wine list with more than two dozen offerings from North Carolina vineyards. Limestone and granite bathrooms, sumptuous beds with 330-count sheets, flat-screen plasma televisions with DVDs and CD players, and balconies with lake views heighten the sense of escape. Hotel guests can use the spa facilities or simply relax in a cabana by the vanishing-edge pool. **Pros:** luxurious hotel with restaurant, bar, and spa meets almost every traveler's needs. **Cons:** its location is convenient to the airport, but it's not within walking distance of downtown or attractions. ✉*100 Woodland Pond Rd., Northwest/ Airport* ☎*919/447-4000 or 866/877-4141* ⊕*www.theumstead.com* ⬅*123 rooms, 27 suites* ⌂*In room: safe, DVD, Wi-Fi. In hotel: restaurant, room service, bar, pool, gym, spa, laundry service, some pets allowed, no-smoking rooms.* ▤*AE, DC, D, MC, V.*

NIGHTLIFE & THE ARTS

THE ARTS The **Progress Energy Center for the Performing Arts** (✉*2 E. South St., Downtown* ☎*919/831–6011* ⊕*www.raleighconvention.com/pe.html*) has several different performance spaces. The 2,277-seat **Memorial Auditorium** (☎*919/831–6061*) is home to the North Carolina Theatre and the nationally acclaimed Carolina Ballet. The 1,700-seat **Meymandi Concert Hall** hosts the North Carolina Symphony. The 600-seat **Fletcher Opera Theater** provides a showcase for the A. J. Fletcher Opera Institute. The 170-seat **Kennedy Theater** stages shows by smaller, more alternative theater groups.

The **Time Warner Cable Music Pavilion at Walnut Creek** (✉*3801 Rock Quarry Rd., Southeast Metro* ☎*919/831–6666* ⊕*www.livenation. com/raleigh*) accommodates 20,000 fans. Headliners at this amphitheater range from Nine Inch Nails to Counting Crows to Chicago.

NIGHTLIFE The **Berkeley Café** (✉*217 W. Martin St., Downtown* ☎*919/821–0777*) hosts live music, including rock and roll, metal, and electronic. **Goodnight's Comedy Club** (✉*861 W. Morgan St., University* ☎*919/828–5233*) combines dinner with a night of laughs. Past performers include Jerry Seinfeld, Chris Rock, and Ellen DeGeneres. Faces of early-20th-century newsboys stare out from a 20-foot photo mural covering one wall at **The Raleigh Times Bar**, a 1906 newspaper office that's been artfully restored as a gastropub. The bar features a great selection of Belgian beers and thoughtful wine and cocktail lists. (✉*14 E. Hargett St., Downtown* ☎*919/833–0999*).

SPORTS & THE OUTDOORS

BASKETBALL   Raleigh's Atlantic Coast Conference entry is the North Carolina State University **Wolfpack** (☎919/865 1510 ⊕www.gopack.com). The team plays basketball in the RBC Center, also home to the Carolina Hurricanes.

GOLF   **Hedingham Golf Club.** Designed by architect David Postlethwait, this semiprivate course has water hazards on eight holes. Watch out for hole 9, where a large pond affects your play three times. ⊠4801 Harbour Towne Dr. ☎919/250–3030 ⊕www.hedingham.org ↡18 holes. 6609 yds. Par 71. Green Fee: $20–$39 ⌒Facilities: Golf carts, golf academy/lessons.

Lochmere Golf Club. Designed by Carolina PGA Hall of Famer Gary Hamm, this course meanders through the tree-lined links, challenging players with several different types of water hazards. A tiered green makes Hole 3 a difficult par 3. ⊠2511 Kildaire Farm Rd., Cary ☎919/851–0611 ⊕www.lochmere.com ↡18 holes. 6136 yds. Par 71. Green Fee: $20–$49 ⌒Facilities: Driving range, putting green, golf carts, rental clubs, pro shop, golf academy/lessons, restaurant.

Neuse Golf Club. About 20 minutes from downtown Raleigh, this semiprivate course feels far from the city's hustle and bustle. The 1993 John LaFoy–designed course follows the Neuse River and is characterized by rolling fairways and rock outcroppings. ⊠918 Birkdale Dr., Clayton ☎919/550–0550 ⊕www.neusegolf.com ↡18 holes. 7010 yds. Par 72. Green Fee: $40–$60 ⌒Facilities: Driving range, putting green, rental clubs, pro shop, golf academy/lessons.

HOCKEY   The NHL's Stanley Cup-winning **Carolina Hurricanes** (⊠RBC Center, 1400 Edwards Mill Rd., Northwest/Airport ☎919/861–2323 or 866/645–2263) play in the 18,800-seat RBC Center.

SHOPPING

SHOPPING CENTERS   Raleigh's first shopping center, **Cameron Village Shopping Center** (⊠1900 Cameron St., Cameron Village ☎919/821–1350) is an upscale assemblage of boutiques and restaurants. The **Triangle Town Center** (⊠5959 Triangle Town Blvd., North Raleigh ☎919/792–2222) contains some 165 stores, including Abercrombie & Fitch, Coldwater Creek, Lindt Chocolates, Saks Fifth Avenue, and Williams-Sonoma.

ANTIQUES   The merchandise changes daily at **Pirates Chest Fine Antiques and Interiors** (⊠Cameron Village Shopping Center, 2050 Clark Ave. ☎919/833–8227), where 32 dealers stock the 21,000-square-foot floor.

FOOD   Open year-round, the 60-acre **State Farmers' Market** (⊠1201 Agriculture St., Southwest Metro ☎919/733–7417) is the place to go for locally grown fruits and vegetables, flowers and plants, and North Carolina crafts. The cavernous down-home restaurant is a great place to grab a bite.

DURHAM

23 mi northwest of Raleigh.

Although its image as a tobacco town lingers, Durham is now also known for the medical facilities and research centers associated with the city's prestigious Duke University. With more than 20,000 employees, Duke is the largest employer in this city of 188,000, and residents and visitors alike can take advantage of the lectures, art activities, and sports events associated with the university. Durham has more than a dozen historic sites, including several of North Carolina's 38 National Historic Landmarks.

GETTING HERE & AROUND

Durham's city center has grown rather haphazardly around its universities and commercial districts in the past 100 years. One-way streets and roads that change names can make navigation tricky. Using Durham Freeway, aka Highway 147 as a guide helps. This thoroughfare bisects the city diagonally, connecting Interstates 85 and 40, and most places of interest can be reached via its exits.

ESSENTIALS

Visitor Information Durham Convention and Visitors Bureau (⊠ *101 E. Morgan St.* ☎ *919/687–0288 or 800/446–8604* ⊕ *www.durham-nc.com*).

EXPLORING

7 Bennett Place State Historic Site. In April 1865 Confederate General Joseph E. Johnston surrendered to U.S. General William T. Sherman in this house, 17 days after Lee's surrender to Grant at Appomattox. The two generals then set forth the terms for a "permanent peace" between the South and the North. Live historical events are held throughout the year; demonstrating how Civil War soldiers drilled, lived in camps, got their mail, and received medical care. ⊠ *4409 Bennett Memorial Rd., Downtown* ☎ *919/383–4345* ⊕ *www.nchistoricsites.org/bennett/bennett.htm* ⊠ *Free* ☉ *Tues.–Sat. 9–5.*

3 Brightleaf Square (⊠ *Main and Gregson Sts., Duke University* ☎ *919/682–9229*), in the former Watts and Yuille warehouses, is named for the tobacco that once filled these buildings. The two long buildings—filled with stores like James Kennedy Antiques, Offbeat Music, Shiki Pottery, and Wentworth and Leggett Rare Books and Prints—sandwich an attractive brick courtyard.

5 Duke Chapel. A Gothic-style gem
★ built in the early 1930s, this chapel

> **WORD OF MOUTH**
>
> "There is a beautiful 'mall' area next to the Durham Bulls ballpark, where there is usually live music on Friday evenings from 6–8 PM. There is also often music at Brightleaf Square—where a number of restaurants have outdoor patios you can sit and eat and listen. Durham has the exquisite Duke Gardens adjoining the campus of Duke. One of our favorite historic sites is the Bennett Place Farm (where the biggest surrender in the Civil War occurred)."
>
> —uhoh_busted

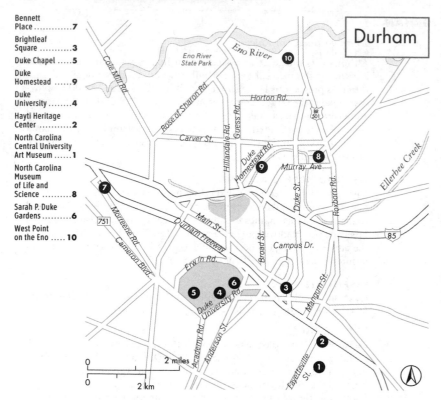

is the centerpiece of Duke University. Modeled after England's Canterbury Cathedral, it has a 210-foot-tall bell tower. Weekly services are held here Sunday at 11 AM. ■TIP→The chapel is a popular wedding spot, so check the Web site for tour availability before going on Saturday. ⊠*Chapel Dr., West Campus, Duke University* ☎*919/681–1704* ⊕*www.chapel.duke.edu* ☉*Sept.–May, daily 8* AM–10 PM; *June–Aug., daily 8–8.*

9 **Duke Homestead.** Washington Duke, patriarch of the now famous Duke family, moved into this house in 1852. It wasn't until he heard how the Union soldiers were enjoying smoking his tobacco that he decided to market his "golden weed." Explore the family's humble beginnings at this State Historic Site, which includes the first ramshackle "factory" as well the world's largest spittoon collection. Guided tours demonstrate early manufacturing processes; the visitor center exhibits early tobacco advertising. ⊠*2828 Duke Homestead Rd., Downtown* ☎*919/477–5498* ⊕*www.ah.dcr.state.nc.us* ⊠*Free* ☉*Tues.–Sat. 9–5.*

4 **Duke University.** A stroll along the tree-lined streets of this campus, founded in 1924, is a lovely way to spend a few hours. The university, known for its Georgian and Gothic Revival architecture, encompasses 525 acres in the heart of Durham. A highlight of any visit is the **Nasher**

Museum of Art (✉ *2001 Campus Dr., Duke University* ☎ *919/684–5135* ⊕ *www.nasher.duke.edu*), which displays African, American, European, and Latin American artwork from various eras. The collection includes works by Rodin, Picasso, and Matisse. Tours of the campus, available during the academic year, can be arranged in advance. ✉ *Office of Special Events, Smith Warehouse, 114 Buchannan Blvd.* ☎ *919/684–3710* ⊕ *www.duke.edu.*

❷ **Hayti Heritage Center.** One of Durham's oldest ecclesiastical structures, St. Joseph's AME Church, houses this center for African-American art and culture. In addition to exhibitions of traditional and contemporary art by local, regional, and national artists, the center hosts events like the Bull Durham Blues Festival and the Black Diaspora Film Festival. ✉ *804 Old Fayetteville St., Downtown* ☎ *919/683–1709* ⊕ *www.hayti.org* 🎫 *Free* ⊙ *Weekdays 9–7:30, Sat. 10–3.*

> **GLASS HALF FULL**
>
> They've stood up to 75 years of inclement weather, including barrages by hurricanes Hazel and Fran. But when Duke Chapel's 77 stained-glass windows—the largest measuring 17 by 38 feet—began to weaken, steps had to be taken. The painstaking restoration is being carried out one window at a time by German-born Dieter Goldkuhle, an artisan who has saved the windows in many houses of worship, including in Washington's National Cathedral. In the meantime, you'll see a bit of scaffolding both inside and outside of Duke Chapel.

❶ **North Carolina Central University Art Museum.** African-American art is showcased at the 1910 North Carolina Central University, the first publicly supported liberal-arts college for African-Americans. The permanent collection includes 19th-century masterpieces and 20th-century works created during the Harlem Renaissance; also on display is artwork by students and local artists. ✉ *Lawson St., between fine arts and music buildings, South/NCCU* ☎ *919/530–6211* ⊕ *www.nccu.edu/art-museum/* 🎫 *Free* ⊙ *Tues.–Fri. 9–4:30, Sun. 2–5.*

❽ **North Carolina Museum of Life and Science.** Here you can ride in a flying ★ machine, sail a radio-controlled boat on an outdoor pond, view arti-☾ facts from space missions, and ride a train through a wildlife sanctuary. The nature center contains such animals as black bears, red wolves, and lemurs. The three-story Magic Wings Butterfly House lets you walk among tropical species in a rain-forest conservatory. In the Insectarium you can see and hear live insects under high magnification and amplification. ✉ *433 Murray Ave., off I–85, Downtown* ☎ *919/220–5429* ⊕ *www.ncmls.org* 🎫 *Museum $10.85, train ride $2* ⊙ *Mon.–Sat. 10–5, Sun. noon–5. Closed Mon. Sept.-Dec.*

❻ **Sarah P. Duke Gardens.** A wisteria-draped gazebo and a Japanese garden ★ with a lily pond teeming with fat goldfish are a few of the highlights of these 55 acres in Duke University's West Campus. More than 5 mi of pathways meander through formal plantings and woodlands. The Terrace Café serves lunch Monday through Friday and brunch Saturday and Sunday. ✉ *426 Anderson St. at Campus Dr., West Campus, Duke*

University ☎*919/684–3698* ⊕*www.hr.duke.edu/dukegardens* ⊠*Free* ☉ *Daily 8–dusk.*

❿ **West Point on the Eno.** In a city park on the banks of the Eno River you'll find a restored mill dating from 1778—one of 32 that once dotted the area. Also on site are a 19th-century Greek Revival farmhouse that was occupied by John Cabe McCown, the onetime owner of the mill, and a museum that showcases early-20th-century photographer Hugh Mangum's pictures of the surrounding area. The park is the site of an annual three-day folk festival held each year near July 4; musicians, artists, and craftspeople come from around the region. ⊠*5101 N. Roxboro Rd., U.S. 501N, North Metro* ☎*919/471–1623* ⊠*Free* ☉ *Park daily 8–dark; buildings weekends 1–5.*

WHERE TO EAT

$$$
ECLECTIC

✗**George's Garage.** This restaurant defies pigeonholing. It's part nouvelle restaurant, part prepared-food market, part bar, and part bakery—all in a cavernous, pumped-up room. Fresh fish and Mediterranean fare are specialties, but you can also dine on grilled chicken, pork, lamb, and beef. Live entertainment and dancing make this a popular after-hours hangout. Don't miss brunch every Sunday. ⊠*737 9th St., Downtown* ☎*919/286–1431* ⊟*AE, D, MC, V.*

$–$$
SEAFOOD

✗**Kemp's Seafood House.** Everything about Kemp's is big, especially the platters of shrimp, stuffed crab, and flounder. This counter-service hot spot serves seafood cooked in a variety of ways, but the specialty of the house is calabash style, lightly battered and fried. Hush puppies and sweet tea round out the experience. ⊠*115 Page Point Circle, Southeast Metro* ☎*919/957–7155* ⚠*Reservations not accepted* ⊟*AE, D, MC, V.*

$$$–$$$$
MODERN
SOUTHERN
Fodor'sChoice
★

✗**Magnolia Grill.** This bistro is consistently one of the area's finest, most innovative places to dine. The food created by chef-owners Ben and Karen Barker is as eye-catching as the art on the walls. The daily menu, which maintains a Southern sensibility, may include spicy green-tomato soup with crab and country ham or striped bass with oyster stew. ⊠*1002 9th St., Downtown* ☎*919/286–3609* ⊟*AE, MC, V* ☉ *Closed Sun. and Mon. No lunch.*

$$
MODERN
SOUTHERN
★

✗**Watts Grocery.** When slow food enthusiasts say "eat local," this is what they mean. The menu of dressed-up Southern dishes at Watts Grocery, which reflects both the chef's Southern roots and her French training, relies on the freshest seasonal ingredients and locally raised meats. The smooth and savory meat terrines served with homemade pickles, and the grilled pork tenderloin over corn pudding are standouts on the summer menu. The decor is stylish but understated with comfortable banquettes and local artwork. Sunday brunch draws a crowd with dishes like andouille sausage and stewed chilies Benedict, and a toasted pimento cheese sandwich with local tomatoes and bacon. ⊠*1116 Broad St., Trinity Park* ☎*919/416–5040* ⊟*AE, MC, V* ☉ *Closed Mon.*

3

WHERE TO STAY

$$–$$$ 📷**Arrowhead Inn.** Brick chimneys and tall Doric columns distinguish this Federal Revival plantation situated on 6 acres dotted with 200-year-old magnolias. Antiques and working fireplaces in every room create a cozy environment, and the whirlpool tubs and steam showers in many rooms lend an air of luxury. **Pros:** comfortable inn offers suites and roomy cottages. **Cons:** it's a bit removed from the city center. ✉*106 Mason Rd., North Metro* ☎*919/477–8430 or 800/528–2207* ⊕*www.arrowheadinn.com* ➥*7 rooms, 1 cabin, 1 cottage* ♿*In-room: Wi-Fi.* 🖅*AE, D, MC, V* ⦿*BP.*

$–$$ 📷**Blooming Garden Inn.** With its yellow exterior, this B&B is literally and figuratively a bright spot in the Holloway Historic District. Inside, the inn explodes with color and warmth, thanks to exuberant hosts Dolly and Frank Pokrass. Your gourmet breakfast might be walnut crepes with ricotta cheese and warm raspberry sauce. At the Holly House, a restored Victorian home across the street, the Pokrasses accommodate extended stays. **Pros:** great location near downtown; highly-regarded service. **Cons:** quiet setting may be too sedate for those seeking nightlife action. ✉*513 Holloway St., Downtown* ☎*919/687–0801 or 888/687–0801* ⊕*www.bloominggardeninn.com* ➥*3 rooms, 2 suites* ♿*In-room: Internet, Wi-Fi.* 🖅*AE, D, MC, V* ⦿*BP.*

$–$$ 📷**Durham Marriott at the Convention Center.** Given this nine-story hotel's excellent downtown location, the rates here are reasonable. Several fountains run through the lobby entrance, and the rooms are spacious and well appointed. Guests have access to the YMCA across the street. **Pros:** located near plenty of sights. **Cons:** not a whole lot of frills. ✉*201 Foster St., Downtown* ☎*919/768–6000* ⊕*www.marriotthotels.com* ➥*185 rooms, 2 suites* ♿*In-room: safe, Internet, Wi-Fi. In-hotel: restaurant, room service, bar, laundry service* 🖅*AE, D, MC, V.*

$$$$ 📷**Washington Duke Inn & Golf Club.** On the campus of Duke University, ★   this luxurious hotel evokes the feeling of an English country inn. Guest rooms with plaid bedspreads and creamy wall coverings overlook either a park or a Robert Trent Jones and Rees Jones–designed golf course. On display in the public rooms are memorabilia belonging to the Duke family, for whom the hotel and university are named. At the quietly sophisticated Fairview restaurant ($$$$)you can dine on poached tiger shrimp and mango cocktail sauce followed by prosciutto-wrapped monkfish with goat-cheese grits. **Pros:** well appointed and service-oriented; luxury travelers will feel right at home. **Cons:** the stately setting may make you feel like you need to mind your p's and q's. ✉*3001 Cameron Blvd., Duke University* ☎*919/490–0999 or 800/443–3853* ⊕*www.washingtondukeinn.com* ➥*271 rooms, 42 suites* ♿*In-room: Internet, Wi-Fi. In-hotel: restaurant, room service, bar, golf course, tennis courts, pool, gym, laundry service* 🖅*AE, D, MC, V.*

NIGHTLIFE & THE ARTS

THE ARTS   Performances that are part of the internationally known **American Dance Festival** (☎*919/684–6402* ⊕*www.americandancefestival.org*), held annually in June and July, take place at various locations around town.

The Beaux-Arts **Carolina Theatre** (✉ *309 W. Morgan St., Downtown* ☎ *919/560–3030* ⊕ *www.carolinatheatre.org*), dating from 1926, hosts classical, jazz, and rock concerts, as well as April's Full Frame Film Festival and August's North Carolina Gay and Lesbian Film Festival. **ManBites Dog Theater** (✉ *703 Foster St., Downtown* ☎ *919/682–3343* ⊕ *www.manbitesdogtheater.org*) performs edgy, socially conscious plays.

NIGHTLIFE **The American Tobacco Complex**, adjacent to the Durham Bulls Athletic Park, houses offices, bars and restaurants in a series of beautifully refurbished warehouses left over from the city's cigarette-rolling past. Free summer concerts are staged on a central lawn, in the shadow of a freshly painted Lucky Strike water tower. A new performing arts center hosting touring Broadway shows was on track to open in December 2008. ✉ *318 Blackwell St., Downtown* ☎ *919/433–1566* ⊕ *www.americantobaccohistoricdistrict.com.*

With 19 beers on tap, the **James Joyce Irish Pub** (✉ *912 W. Main St., Downtown* ☎ *919/683–3022*) is a popular meeting place. Live musical acts perform at 10 PM on Friday and Saturday.

SPORTS & THE OUTDOORS

BASEBALL The **Durham Bulls** (✉ *Durham Bulls Athletic Park, 409 Blackwell St., North Metro* ☎ *919/687–6500* ⊕ *www.dbulls.com*), a tradition since 1902, were immortalized in the hit 1988 movie *Bull Durham*. This AAA affiliate of the Tampa Bay Devil Rays plays in the $16 million 10,000-seat Durham Bulls Athletic Park.

BASKETBALL Durham's Atlantic Coast Conference team is Duke's **Blue Devils** (☎ *919/681–2583* ⊕ *www.goduke.com*), which plays its home games at the 8,800-seater Cameron Indoor Stadium.

GOLF **Duke University Golf Club.** Twice host of the NCAA men's championship, this course was designed in 1955 by the legendary Robert Trent Jones; his son, Rees Jones, completed a renovation of the links in 1994. The whopping 442-yard par 4 on Hole 18 separates serious players from duffers. ✉ *3001 Cameron Blvd., at Science Dr.* ☎ *919/490–0999 or 800/443–3853* ⊕ *www.washingtondukeinn.com/golfclub.html* ⚑ *18 holes. 6868 yds. Par 72. Green Fee: $30–$100* ⛳ *Facilities: Driving range, golf carts, rental clubs, pro shop, golf academy/lessons, restaurant, bar.*

Hillandale Golf Course. The oldest course in the area, Hillandale was designed by the incomparable architect Donald Ross, but was redesigned by George Cobb following the course's move in 1960. The pro shop is consistently named one of the best in the country. The course, with a couple of doglegs and a slew of water hazards, gives even experienced golfers a strategic workout. ✉ *1600 Hillandale Rd.* ☎ *919/286–4211* ⊕ *www.hillandalegolf.com* ⚑ *Reservations essential* ⚑ *18 holes. 6339 yds. Par 71. Green Fee: $20–$44* ⛳ *Facilities: Driving range, golf carts, rental clubs, pro shop, golf academy/lessons, restaurant, bar.*

SHOPPING

SHOPPING
CENTERS
Durham's funky **9th Street** (⊠*9th St. at Markham Ave., West Durham* ☎*919/572–8808*) is lined with shops and restaurants. The **Streets of Southpoint Mall** (⊠*6910 Fayetteville Rd., off I–40, Southeast Metro* ☎*919/572–8808*) dominates Durham's shopping scene with its village look, restaurants, movie theaters, and upward of 150 stores, including Nordstrom and Restoration Hardware.

CRAFTS
One World Market (⊠*811 9th St., Duke University* ☎*919/286–2457*) holds 2,000 square feet of unique, affordable arts and crafts collected from around the world, from home accessories to children's toys. As a nonprofit enterprise, the market sells crafts from fair trade vendors, which aim to provide artisans in developing countries a living wage,

FOOD
Parker and Otis (⊠*112 S. Duke St., Downtown* ☎*919/683–3200*) stocks local produce and specialty foods as well as international spices, wines, chocolates, teas, coffees, and scads of candy. Gourmet breakfast and lunch dishes are served until 7 PM. Gift baskets can be shipped all over the country and internationally.

CHAPEL HILL

28 mi northwest of Raleigh; 12 mi southwest of Durham.

Chapel Hill may be the smallest city in the Triangle, but its reputation as a seat of learning looms large. This is the home of the nation's first state university, the University of North Carolina, which opened its doors in 1795. Despite the large number of students and retirees, Chapel Hill retains the feel of a quiet village. Franklin Street, with its interesting mix of trendy bars, tasty eateries, and oddball stores, has always been the heart of downtown Chapel Hill.

GETTING HERE & AROUND

Chapel Hill is a wonderful place to walk around, and a terrible place to park a car. Find a parking space in one of the lots along Rosemary Street, one block off Franklin, and give yourself a chance to enjoy the Carolina blue skies. Start at the Old Well on Cameron Avenue and wander through campus, or eat, sip and shop your way down Franklin Street, beginning at the Old Post Office, heading west to Carrboro.

ESSENTIALS

Visitor Information Chapel Hill/Orange County Visitors Bureau (⊠*501 W. Franklin St., Chapel Hill* ☎*919/968–2060* ⊕ *www.visitchapelhill.org*).

EXPLORING

Franklin Street runs along the northern edge of the **University of North Carolina** campus, which is filled with oak-shaded courtyards and stately old buildings. The **Ackland Art Museum** (⊠*Columbia and Franklin Sts., University* ☎*919/966–5736* ⊕*www.ackland.org*) showcases one of the Southeast's strongest collections of Asian art, plus an outstanding selection of drawings, prints, and photographs as well as old-master paintings and sculptures. The **Louis Round Wilson Library** (⊠*Polk Pl., between E. Cameron Ave. and South Rd., University* ☎*919/962–0114*

⊕*www.lib.unc.edu/wilson*) houses the largest single collection of state literature in the nation.

Morehead Planetarium and Science Center where the original Apollo astronauts trained, is one of the largest in the country. You can see planetarium shows, science demonstrations, and exhibits for children and adults. ⊠*250 E. Franklin St., University* ☎*919/962–1236* ⊕*www. moreheadplanetarium.org* ⊠*$6* ⊙*Open daily; hrs vary by season. Call or check Web site before visiting.*

The **North Carolina Botanical Garden,** south of downtown, has the largest collection of native plants in the Southeast. Nature trails wind through a 300-acre Piedmont forest. The herb garden and carnivorous-plant collection are impressive. A new visitor education center is slated to open in summer 2009. ⊠*Totten Center, Old Mason Farm Rd., South Metro* ☎*919/962–0522* ⊕*www.ncbg.unc.edu* ⊠*Free* ⊙*Weekdays 8–5; March–Oct., Sat. 9–6, Sun. 1–6; Nov.–Feb., Sat. 9–5, Sun. 1–5.*

WHERE TO EAT

$$–$$$
SOUTHERN
★
✕**Crook's Corner.** In business since 1982, this small restaurant has been an exemplar of Southern chic. The menu, which changes nightly, highlights local produce and regional specialties such as green-pepper chicken with hoppin' john (black-eyed peas), crab gumbo, buttermilk pie, and honeysuckle sorbet. A wall of bamboo and a waterfall fountain make the patio a delightful alfresco experience (it's heated for wintertime dining). Look for the faded pink pig atop the building. ⊠*610 W. Franklin St., Downtown* ☎*919/929–7643* ⊟*AE, D, MC, V* ⊙*Closed Mon. No lunch.*

¢–$
SOUTHERN
★
✕**Mama Dip's Country Kitchen.** In Chapel Hill, Mildred Edna Cotton Council—better known as Mama Dip—is just about as famous as Michael Jordan. That's because she and her eponymous restaurant, which serves authentic home-style Southern meals in a roomy but simple setting, have been on the scene since the early '60s. Everything from chicken and dumplings, ribs, and country ham to fish, beef, salads, a mess of fresh vegetables, and melt-in-your-mouth buttermilk biscuits appear on the lengthy menu. ■**TIP→ Mama Dip's two cookbooks explain her famed "dump cooking" method and offer up more than 450 recipes.** ⊠*408 W. Rosemary St., Downtown* ☎*919/942–5837* ⊟*MC, V.*

¢–$
PIZZA
✕**Pepper's Pizza.** Local kids have been eating—and working—at this Franklin Street institution for more than 20 years, Handmade crusts and fresh toppings, which range from artichoke hearts to Eastern North Carolina-style barbecue, distinguish the pies. The sleek interior, complemented by a local artist's mural of musicians born in the state, contributes to a casual atmosphere suited for students, parents, and children as long as they don't mind the music being a bit loud. ⊠*117 E. Franklin St., University* ☎*919/967–7766* ⚠*No reservations.* ⊟*AE, D, MC, V.*

$$
AMERICAN
✕**Weathervane Café.** This 30-year-old eatery, tucked into an expansive fine-foods shop, uses those top-notch ingredients for such dishes as mustard-glaze salmon and goat-cheese risotto. There's plenty of comfortable seating around the open kitchen, but the spacious courtyard, filled with plants and fountains, is why people stand in line. The all-day

CLOSE UP

Piedmont Gardens

Exploring the gorgeous gardens in North Carolina's Piedmont is a year-round pleasure. For starters, there are lots of them, and they are diverse in size, style, and plant life. Many offer the charm of surprise, as they can be found in little-known places as well as open but unlikely spaces. From April until the first frost in November, for example, wildflowers offer dazzling bursts of color along the roads. Here's a sample of the state's signature gardens, regional treasures, and smaller gardens of note:

Asheboro: In the Uwharrie Mountains are the city of Asheboro and the **North Carolina Zoo** (⊠ *4401 Zoo Pkwy.* ☎ *336/879-7000 or 800/488-0444* ⊕ *www.nczoo.org*), home not just to creatures great and small, but also botanicals from the Arctic to the tropics.

Belmont: The **Daniel Stowe Botanical Garden** (⊠ *6500 S. New Hope Rd., 13 mi west of Charlotte* ☎ *704/825-4490* ⊕ *www.dsbg.org*) is known for its painterly display of colors in a vast perennial garden, wildflower meadow, Canal Garden, an orchid conservatory, and other themed areas.

Charlotte: At the **Wing Haven Garden & Bird Sanctuary** (⊠ *248 Ridgewood Ave.,* ☎ *704/331-0664* ⊕ *www. winghavengardens.com*), 4 acres of formal gardens in one of the city's most exclusive neighborhoods create a serene environment for feathered visitors and others.

Fayetteville: Cape Fear Botanical Garden (⊠ *536 N. Eastern Blvd., 45 mi east of Aberdeen* ☎ *910/486-0221* ⊕ *www.capefearbg.org*), spanning 79-acres at the confluence of the Cape Fear River and Cross Creek, boasts 2,000 varieties of ornamental plants, an old-growth forest, a heritage garden, and separate gardens dedicated to daylilies, camellias, and hostas.

Greensboro: Sandwiched between two busy roads, the **Bicentennial Gardens & Bog Garden** (⊠ *Hobbs Rd. and Starmount Farms Dr.,* ☎ *336/373-2199* ⊕ *www.greensborobeautiful.org*) flourish almost despite themselves. The garden beds are carefully tended, especially compared to the nearby bog, whose natural setting includes wooden walkways over water and wetlands.

Raleigh: JC Raulston Arboretum at North Carolina State University (⊠ *4415 Beryl Rd.* ☎ *919/515-3132* ⊕ *www.ncsu.edu/jcraulstonarboretum*) is primarily a working, research, and teaching garden; it has the most diverse collection of hardy temperate-zone plants in the southeastern United States, a white garden, a 450-foot-long perennial border, and more.

Sunday brunch is a big draw; French toast stuffed with mascarpone and strawberries is popular, as are poached eggs and crabmeat on a buttermilk biscuit. ⊠ *Eastgate Shopping Center, 201 S. Estes Dr., North Metro* ☎ *919/929-9466* ▭ *AE, D, MC, V.*

WHERE TO STAY

$$$$ 🛏 **Fearrington House Country Inn.** A member of the prestigious Relais
★ & Châteaux group, this inn sits on a 200-year-old farm that has been remade to resemble a country village. "Oreo" cows (Belted Galways

that are black on the ends, white in the middle) roam the pasture near the entrance. Carefully chosen antiques, English-pine furnishings, and oversize tubs fill the inn's modern guest rooms, which overlook a courtyard and the gardens. Some suites have a whirlpool or fireplace. The prix-fixe restaurant ($$$$) serves contemporary cuisine, including seared scallops with parsnip puree, black trumpet mushrooms, salsify, and blood-orange butter. Guests can choose a full English breakfast or homemade granola. The hotel is in Pittsboro, 8 mi south of Chapel Hill. **Pros:** feels like a country inn but with up-to-date luxuries. **Cons:** the setting, while pristine, can feel a bit contrived. ⌧*2000 Fearrington Village Center, Pittsboro* ☎*919/542–2121* ⊕*www.fearringtonhouse. com* ⊃*35 rooms, 8 suites* ⌂*In-room: Wi-Fi. In-hotel: 2 restaurants, tennis courts, pool, laundry service* ⊟*AE, MC, V* ❙❍❙*BP.*

$$$–$$$$ ▦ **The Franklin Hotel.** A boutique hotel minutes from UNC's campus,
Fodor'sChoice The Franklin has helped sustain a renaissance on Franklin Street's west
★ end since it opened in 2007. Its posh amenities, including marble bathrooms, in-room spa services, iPod docks, a pillow menu, and on-site parking (truly a luxury in Chapel Hill), lend an air of sophistication, while the understated elegant design of the building blends with the neighborhood's village aesthetic. Guests can people-watch from room balconies or mingle with the after-work crowd at Roberts, the cushy ground floor bar and patio. Service is spot-on, from the friendly hosts behind the counter to the well-versed bartender. The setting and the luxury combine to make guests feel at once part of the college scene but also far-removed from their everyday lives. **Pros:** high-tech in-room facilities include iPod docks and flat-screen TVs. **Cons:** Franklin Street location can get noisy when the campus is buzzing with students. ⌧*311 W. Franklin St., University* ☎*919/442–9000* ⊕ *www.franklin-hotelnc.com* ⊃*67 rooms, 7 suites* ⌂*In room: Wi-Fi. In hotel: restaurant, room service, bar, gym, spa* ⊟*AE, D, MC, V.*

$$$ ▦ **Siena Hotel.** Sam and Susan Longiotti's love for Italy has carried over to their posh European-style hotel. The lobby and rooms have imported carved-wood furniture, along with fabrics and artwork that conjure up the Italian Renaissance. The public areas are filled with plush furniture grouped for conversation. Tuscan cuisine is the hallmark of Il Palio Ristorante ($$$–$$$$), open for breakfast, lunch, and dinner. Entrées include grilled shiitake mushroom and herb-stuffed ostrich fillet and spaghetti squash primavera. **Pros:** the setting is elegant and close to shopping at Eastgate Mall. **Cons:** pricey Il Palio may not be your best bet; adventurous eaters should explore West Franklin Street and Carrboro for dining options. ⌧*1505 E. Franklin St., North Metro* ☎*919/929–4000 or 800/223–7379* ⊕*www.sienahotel. com* ⊃*67 rooms, 12 suites* ⌂*In-room: Wi-Fi. In-hotel: restaurant, room service, bar, laundry service* ⊟*AE, MC, V* ❙❍❙ *BP.*

NIGHTLIFE & THE ARTS

THE ARTS The University of North Carolina's **Dean E. Smith Center** (⌧*Skipper Bowles Dr., University* ☎*919/962–2296 or 800/722–4335* ⊕*tarheelblue.cstv.com*) hosts not only basketball games, but also concerts and other special events.

The **Playmakers Repertory Company** (⊠ *Country Club Rd., University* ☎*919/962–7529* ⊕*www.playmakersrep.org*), a professional theater company, performs in the Paul Green Theatre.

NIGHTLIFE The Chapel Hill area is the place to hear live rock and alternative bands. The stalwart of the club scene is the dark and funky **Cat's Cradle** (⊠*300 E. Main St., Carrboro* ☎*919/967–9053*), which has nightly entertainment primarily from local and regional bands. The **West End Wine Bar** (⊠*450 W. Franklin St., Downtown* ☎*919/967–7599*) attracts a more affluent crowd with its comprehensive wine list (more than 100 by the glass), dinner menu, and rooftop patio. The downstairs speakeasy-style Cellar has three pool tables, eight draft beers, and a 1,200-song jukebox.

SPORTS & THE OUTDOORS

BASKETBALL The University of North Carolina's **Tar Heels** (☎*919/962–2296 or 800/722–4335* ⊕*tarheelblue.cstv.com*) are Chapel Hill's Atlantic Coast Conference team. They play in the Dean E. Smith Student Activities Center, commonly known as the "Dean Dome."

GOLF **UNC Finley Golf Course.** This public golf course was designed by golf legend Tom Fazio, who gave the links wide fairways and fast greens. ⊠*Finley Golf Course Rd.* ☎*919/962–2349* ⊕*www.uncfinley.com* ⅄*18 holes. 6231 yds. Par 72. Green Fee: $47–$80* ☞*Facilities: Driving range, putting green, golf carts, pro shop, golf academy/lessons, restaurant.*

SHOPPING

SHOPPING CENTERS Minutes from downtown, the lively **Eastgate Shopping Center** (⊠*E. Franklin St. at U.S. 15/501 bypass, North Metro*) sells everything from antiques to wine. **Fearrington Village** (⊠*2000 Fearrington Village Center, Pittsboro* ☎*919/542–4000*), 8 mi south of Chapel Hill on U.S. 15/501 in Pittsboro, has upscale shops selling art, garden items, handmade jewelry, and more.

BOOKS At the independent **McIntyre's Bookstore** (⊠*Fearrington Village, 2000 Fearrington Village Center, Pittsboro* ☎*919/542–3030*) you can read by the fire in one of the cozy rooms. McIntyre's has a big selection of mysteries, as well as gardening and cookbooks. The store also hosts some 125 readings throughout the year.

FOOD **A Southern Season** (⊠*Eastgate Shopping Center, 201 S. Estes Dr., North Metro* ☎*919/929–7133 or 800/253–3663*) stocks a dazzling variety of items for the kitchen, from classic recipe books to the latest gadgets. Many of the foods, such as barbecue sauces, peanuts, and hams, are regional specialties. Custom gift baskets can be sent anywhere in the world.

THE TRIAD

Although they share geography and the major arteries of the region, and claim rich histories as well as institutions of higher learning, the Triad's leading cities have very distinct personalities. Greensboro, to the

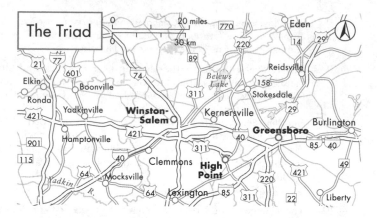

east, bustles as a center of commerce. Smaller Winston-Salem, to the west, may catch you by surprise with its eclectic arts scene. High Point, to the south, has managed to fuse the simplicity of Quaker forebearers with its role as a world-class furniture market.

GREENSBORO

96 mi northeast of Charlotte; 26 mi east of Winston-Salem; 58 mi west of Durham.

The Gate City earned its nickname when it became a railway hub in the 1840s, becoming so important in transporting textiles that many of the mills moved to town. Today the textile industry isn't what it used to be, and Greensboro, with the third largest population in the state, has diversified into insurance, banking, and other industries. Commerce aside, the complex history—of soldiers and protestors, of writers and journalists—makes Greensboro an enriching place to visit.

The diversity of Greensboro's museums and historic sites ranges from hands-on children's exhibits to meticulously explained rare collections to open fields where your imagination has to create the scene. The city also has a thriving arts community, with college, community, or professional theater most weekends, as well as small galleries that showcase local and regional artists. With six colleges and universities, Greensboro also plays host to a diverse selection of seminars and lectures by both celebrities and educators.

GETTING HERE & AROUND

Interstates 40 and 85 diverge just to the northeast of Greensboro, which means getting here is quite easy. Navigating the city is easy, too, especially in the booming and walkable downtown

ESSENTIALS

Visitor Information Greensboro Area Convention and Visitors Bureau (✉ *2200 Pinecroft Rd., Suite 200* ☎ *336/274–2282* ⊕ *www.greensboronc.org*).

EXPLORING

Guilford Courthouse National Military Park, established in 1917, has more than 200 acres with wooded hiking trails. It memorializes one of the earliest events in the area's recorded history and a pivotal moment in the life of the colonies. On March 15, 1781, the Battle of Guilford Courthouse so weakened British troops that they surrendered seven months later at Yorktown. ✉*2332 New Garden Rd., Northwest Metro* ☏*336/288–1776* ⊕*www.nps.gov/ guco* ☐*Free* ⊘*Daily 8:30–5.*

> ### OH, HENRY!
>
> It's easy to overlook a three-piece sculpture celebrating writer O. Henry. Before adopting his pen name, William Sydney Porter spent his youth in Greensboro. The life-size sculpture, on the corner of North Elm and Bellemeade streets, depicts the writer, his faithful dog, and a huge bronze book revealing some of his most famous characters.

Tannenbaum Historic Park, near Guilford Courthouse National Military Park, draws you into the life of early settlers. Among the buildings you'll find here is the restored 19th-century Hoskins House. Exhibits in the Colonial Heritage Center provide a hands-on history lesson. The park has one of the country's most outstanding collections of original colonial settlement maps. ✉*2200 New Garden Rd., Northwest Metro* ☏*336/545–5315* ⊕*www.greensboro-nc.gov/departments/parks/facilities/tannenbaum* ☐*Free* ⊘*Tues.–Sat. 9–4.*

☺ You can roam through a room filled with dinosaurs, learn about gems and minerals, and see the lemurs and other creatures at the **Natural Science Center of Greensboro.** A planetarium, a petting zoo, and a herpetarium are on the premises. Animal Discovery, a 22-acre science museum-zoological garden is on the grounds. ✉*4301 Lawndale Dr., Northwest Metro* ☏*336/288–3769* ⊕*www.natsci.org* ☐*Center $6, planetarium $2* ⊘*Mon.–Sat. 9–5, Sun. 12:30–5. Animal Discovery Mon.–Sat. 10–4, Sun. 12:30–4.*

☺ Home to the offices of 15 art, dance, music, and theater organizations, the **Greensboro Cultural Center at Festival Park** also has four small art galleries, a studio theater, an outdoor amphitheater, a sculpture garden, and a restaurant with outdoor seating. Green Hill's **ArtQuest** (☏*336/333–7460* ⊕*www.greenhillcenter.org*) is North Carolina's first hands-on art gallery for children. ✉*200 N. Davie St., Downtown* ☏*336/373–2712* ☐*$5* ⊘*Mon. 9:30–12:30, Tues.–Sat 12:30–5.*

☺ Exhibits and activities at the **Greensboro Children's Museum** are designed for children under 12. They can tour an airplane cockpit, explore a fire truck or police car, scale a climbing wall, create a craft out of recycled materials, or learn about buildings in the construction zone. ■TIP➔ **Admission is reduced to $3 Friday 5–8 and Sunday 1–5.** ✉*220 N. Church St., Downtown* ☏*336/574–2898* ⊕*www.gcmuseum.com* ☐*$6* ⊘*Early Sept.–late May, Tues.–Sat. 9–5, Sun. 1–5; late May–early Sept., Tues.–Thurs. 9–5, Fri. 9–8, Sat. 9–5, Sun. 1–5.*

Elm Street, with its turn-of-the-20th-century architecture, is the heart of **Old Greensborough** (✉*Elm St., between Market and Lee Sts., Downtown*

⊕*www.downtowngreensboro.net*). Listed on the National Register of Historic Places, it has become one of Greensboro's most vibrant areas, with lively galleries, trendy nightspots, and interesting boutiques and antiques shops. "Friday After Five" brings weekly live music to the district in summer. ■TIP→If you need to get online, there's even wireless Internet access throughout the area.

The elegant **Blandwood Mansion**, home of former governor John Motley Morehead, is considered the prototype of the Italian-villa architecture that swept the country during the mid-19th century. Noted architect Alexander Jackson Davis designed the house, which has a stucco exterior and towers and still contains many of its original furnishings. ⊠*447 W. Washington St., Downtown* ☎*336/272–5003* ⊕*www.blandwood.org* ⊠*$5* ☉*Tours Tues.–Sat. 11–2, Sun. 2–5.*

> ### MAKING HISTORY
>
> On February 1, 1960, four young black men from North Carolina A&T State University walked into the Woolworth's on Elm Street and did the unthinkable—they sat down at the white section of the segregated lunch counter. Although refused service, they stayed. And when they left, others took their place. Within two months, the concept of sit-ins had spread to more than 50 other cities. Woolworth's is slated to become the **International Civil Rights Center and Museum** (⊠*301 N. Elm St., Downtown* ☎*336/274–9199 or 800/748–7116* ⊕*www.sitinmovement.org*).

On the campus of the University of North Carolina at Greensboro, the **Weatherspoon Art Museum** consists of six galleries and a sculpture garden. It's known for its permanent collection, which includes lithographs and bronzes by Henri Matisse, and for its changing exhibitions of 20th-century American art. ⊠*Tate and Spring Garden Sts., University* ☎*336/334–5770* ⊕*weatherspoon.uncg.edu* ⊠*Free* ☉*Tues., Wed., and Fri. 10–5, Thurs. 10–9, weekends 1–5.*

WHERE TO EAT

$–$$
ITALIAN
✗**Bianca's.** Four- and five-course meals offer a lot of bang for the buck at this Italian-style eatery. But you can still impress your date, as it has been consistently voted the city's most romantic restaurant. Paneled walls painted cream, royal-blue window treatments, and twinkling white lights set the mood. Ample portions abound; the pork chops are as popular as some of the pastas. The wine list is extensive. ⊠*1901 Spring Garden St., Coliseum* ☎*336/273–8114* ▭*AE, D, MC, V* ☉*No lunch. Closed Sun.*

$$–$$$
AMERICAN
✗**Liberty Oak.** Liberty Oak's move to its current address several years ago helped spearhead revitalization efforts downtown. The upscale but reasonably priced restaurant changes its menu weekly. Whether you try the flakey croissant sandwiches served at lunch or the grilled pork chops topped with a demi-glace of dried pear, sherry vinegar, and bourbon that are offered at dinner, your taste buds—and your wallet—are going to thank you. ⊠*100–D W. Washington St., Downtown* ☎*336/273–7057* ▭*AE, D, MC, V.*

3

¢–$
ASIAN

╳**Pho Hien Vuong.** Don't be fooled by the appearance of this storefront restaurant decorated with a few items that speak to the owners' Vietnamese and Thai ancestry. There's nothing unassuming about the food. The flavors and textures of the dishes are excellent, permeating everything from the hot-and-sour shrimp soup to the vegetable curry to the sliced grilled pork. If you want the food to have extra kick, request it "hot." ☒ *4109-A Spring Garden St., Downtown* ☎ *336/294–5551* ▤ *D, MC, V.*

WHERE TO STAY

$$

▦**Biltmore Greensboro Hotel.** In the heart of the central business district, the Biltmore has an old-world, slightly faded feel, with 16-foot ceilings, a cage elevator, and a lobby with walnut-panel walls and a fireplace. Some guest rooms have Victorian-era or Victorian-reproduction furniture and electric candle sconces. **Pros:** fans of old hotels will find the setting appealing. **Cons:** travelers who prefer sleek surroundings should go elsewhere. ☒ *111 W. Washington St., Downtown* ☎ *336/272–3474 or 800/332–0303* ➻ *24 rooms, 2 suites* ⌂ *In-room: refrigerator, Wi-Fi. In-hotel: room service* ▤ *AE, D, MC, V* ❘◎❘ *BP.*

$$$–$$$$
★

▦**O. Henry Hotel.** This boutique hotel, named for the renowned author who grew up in Greensboro, evokes turn-of-the-20th-century luxury with lots of wood paneling, leather sofas, and mohair club chairs. Particularly nice are the oversize rooms, which have soaring ceilings ringed by crown molding. The equally large bathrooms have separate showers and tubs. A complimentary breakfast buffet is served in a sunny pavilion overlooking a small garden. For lunch or dinner, grab a table in the courtyard of the Green Valley Grill ($–$$), a European-style restaurant with a wood-fired oven. **Pros:** historic property offers nostalgic setting with modern comforts. **Cons:** some room views are of unattractive commercial properties, so ask for a scenic view if you want one. ☒ *624 Green Valley Rd., Friendly* ☎ *336/854–2000 or 800/965–8259* ⊕ *www.o.henryhotel.com* ➻ *121 rooms, 10 suites* ⌂ *In-room: safe, refrigerator, Internet, Wi-Fi. In-hotel: restaurant, room service, pool, laundry service.* ▤ *AE, D, MC, V* ❘◎❘ *BP.*

$

▦**Sheraton Greensboro Hotel at Four Seasons.** It's no surprise that business travelers dominate this place, because it's adjacent to the convention center. Accommodations are a notch above standard. It's convenient to major thoroughfares and to the Four Seasons Town Centre, an enormous three-story mall. **Pros:** there is a lot do without ever leaving the hotel-mall complex. **Cons:** hotel is geared to conventioneers, so individuals seeking a quiet getaway may feel overwhelmed by large crowds. ☒ *3121 High Point Rd., West Metro* ☎ *336/292–9161 or 800/242–6556* ⊕ *www.sheratongreensboro.com* ➻ *910 rooms, 80 suites* ⌂ *In-room: Internet, Wi-Fi. In-hotel: 3 restaurants, room service, bars, pools, gym, laundry facilities, laundry service* ▤ *AE, D, DC, MC, V.*

NIGHTLIFE & THE ARTS

THE ARTS

The **Broach Theatre** (☒ *520-C S. Elm St., Downtown* ☎ *336/378–9300* ⊕ *www.broachtheatre.org*) stages six professional shows each year in the Old Greensborough historic district. It specializes in little-known comedy gems. **Triad Stage** (☒ *232 S. Elm St., Downtown* ☎ *336/274–*

0067 ⊕*www.triadstage.org*) is a professional company that mixes classic and original plays.

The 1927 **Carolina Theatre** (⊠*310 S. Greene St., Downtown* ☎*336/333–2605* ⊕*www.carolinatheatre.com*) serves as one of the city's principal performing-arts centers, showcasing dance, music, films, and plays. The vast **Greensboro Coliseum Complex** (⊠*1921 W. Lee St.* ☎*336/373–7474* ⊕*www.greensborocoliseum.com*) hosts arts and entertainment events throughout the year. The Greensboro Symphony and the Greensboro Opera Company perform here.

The **Eastern Music Festival** (⊠*200 N. Davie St., Downtown* ☎*336/333–7450 or 877/833–6753* ⊕*www.easternmusicfestival.org*), whose guests have included Billy Joel, André Watts, and Wynton Marsalis, brings a month of more than four dozen classical-music concerts to Greensboro's Guilford College and music venues throughout the city beginning in late June.

NIGHTLIFE The **Blind Tiger** (⊠*2115 Walker Ave., Coliseum* ☎*336/272–9888*), a Greensboro institution, is one of the best places in the Triad to hear live music. The schedule includes mostly rock and blues, with a bit of alternative thrown in for good measure. **Natty Greene's Pub & Brewing Company** (⊠*345 S. Elm St., Downtown* ☎*336/274–1373*) has 10 of its own beers on tap, from a pale ale to a stout. The food isn't imaginative, but the potato chips are made on the premises. Upstairs is a noisy sports bar with pool tables and smallish TVs. There's patio seating in nice weather.

SPORTS & THE OUTDOORS

GOLF **Bryan Park & Golf Club.** These two public courses, 6 mi north of Greensboro, have 36 holes of great golf. The Players Course, designed by Rees Jones in 1988, reopened after a major renovation in 2006; it features 79 bunkers and eight water hazards. Jones outdid himself on the lovely 1990 Champions Course, in which seven holes hug Lake Townsend. ⊠*6275 Bryan Park Rd., Browns Summit* ☎*336/375–2200* ⊕*www. bryanpark.com* ⌨*2 18-hole courses. Players: 6600 yds. Champions: 6853 yds. Players: Par 72. Champions: Par 72. Green Fee: $42–$54* ✐*Facilities: Driving range, golf carts, pro shop, golf academy/lessons, restaurant.*

Grandover Resort & Conference Center. Greensboro's only resort hotel tempts you with 36 holes on the East and West courses, designed by golf architects David Graham and Gary Panks. Golf packages are available; the deluxe package includes dinner for two at the resort's Di Valletta Restaurant. The resort is parallel to Interstate 85, but it's set so deep into 1,500 acres, you'll never think about the traffic. ⊠*1000 Club Rd.* ☎*336/294–1800* ⊕*www.grandoverresort.com* ⌨*2 18-hole courses. East: 6600 yds. West: 6,300 yds. East: Par 72. West: Par 72. Green Fee: $75* ✐*Facilities: Driving range, putting green, golf carts, pull carts, caddies, rental clubs, pro shop, golf academy/lessons, restaurant, bar.*

Greensboro National Golf Club. The clubhouse is known for its hot dogs, so you know this course lacks the pretense of others in the area. Called "a golf course for guys who like golf courses," the Don and Mark Charles–designed public links features wide fairways, expansive greens, and layouts that are challenging without resorting to blind spots and other trickery. ⊠ *330 Niblick Dr., Summerfield* ☎ *336/342–1113* ⊕ *www.greensboronatl.com* ⚑ *18 holes. 6417 yds. Par 72. Green Fee: $35–$40* ☞ *Facilities: Driving range, golf carts, restaurant, bar.*

SHOPPING

Replacements, Ltd (⊠ *I–85/I–40 at Mt. Hope Church Rd., Exit 132* ☎ *800/737–5223*), between Greensboro and Burlington, is the world's largest retailer of discontinued and active china, crystal, flatware, and collectibles. It stocks more than 12 million pieces in 286,000 patterns. The cavernous showroom is open 9 to 7 daily, and free tours begin every half hour between 9:30 and 6:30.

WINSTON-SALEM

26 mi west of Greensboro; 81 mi north of Charlotte.

Two historical areas—Old Salem and Bethabara—are welcome reminders of the hard-working Moravians who founded the area in the mid-18th century. With its Williamsburg-like period reconstruction (and tasty, tasty cookies), Old Salem in particular shouldn't be missed even if you have only an afternoon to spend in the Twin Cities.

With two world-class art museums, a symphony orchestra, a film festival, the internationally respected North Carolina School of the Arts, and the biannual National Black Theatre Festival, there's plenty for visitors to do within the city limits.

GETTING HERE & AROUND

Easily accessed by Interstate 40, Winston-Salem is laid out in an orderly grid. Parts of the city are great for walking, especially Old Salem and the neighborhoods surrounding it. Parking near most sights is not a problem.

ESSENTIALS

Visitor Information Winston-Salem Convention and Visitors Bureau (⊡ *Box 1409, 27102* ☎ *336/728–4200* ⊕ *www.visitwinstonsalem.com*).

EXPLORING

Fodor'sChoice ★ Founded in 1766 as a backcountry trading center, **Old Salem Museum & Gardens** is one of the nation's most well-documented colonial sites. This living-history museum, a few blocks from downtown Winston-Salem, is filled with dozens of original and reconstructed buildings. Costumed guides explain household activities common in the late-18th and early-19th century Moravian communities. Tours include a stop by the 1861 St. Philip's Church, the state's oldest-standing African-American church. Old Salem also has a toy museum, a children's museum, and a restaurant. ■ TIP→ Don't miss the "world's largest coffeepot," a 12-foot-tall vessel built by Julius Mickey in 1858 to advertise his tinsmith shop. Having survived two car-coffeepot collisions, it was moved to its present location at the edge of Old Salem in 1959. ✉*600 S. Main St., Old Salem* ☎*336/721–7300 or 888/653–7253* ⊕*www.oldsalem.org* 🎫*$21, includes admission to Museum of Early Southern Decorative Arts* ⊙*Mon.–Sat. 9:30–4:30, Sun. 1–5.*

NEED A BREAK?

No trip to the Old Salem Museum & Gardens is complete without a trip to the **Winkler Bakery** (✉*525 S. Main St.* ☎*336/721–7302*), where you can buy bread and pillowy sugar cakes baked in the traditional brick ovens. Moravian ginger cookies, paper-thin and dense with spice, are the traditional treat, although they also come in lemon, sugar, pumpkin spice, and key lime flavors.

★ The **Museum of Early Southern Decorative Arts,** on the southern edge of Old Salem, is the only museum dedicated to the decorative arts of the early South. Two dozen intricately detailed period rooms and seven galleries showcase the furniture, painting, ceramics, and metalware used through 1820. The bookstore carries hard-to-find books on Southern culture and history. ✉*924 S. Main St., Old Salem* ☎*336/721–7360 or 888/653–7253* ⊕*www.mesda.org* 🎫*$21, includes admission to Old Salem Museum & Gardens* ⊙*Mon.–Sat. 9:30–5, Sun. 1:30–5. Jan.– Feb., closed Mon.*

☾ The **SciWorks** complex has 45,000 square feet of interactive and hands-on exhibits. There's also a 120-seat planetarium and a 15-acre environmental park with barnyard animals and paved walking trails. ✉*400 W. Hanes Mill Rd., North Metro* ☎*336/767–6730* ⊕*www.sciworks.org* 🎫*$10* ⊙*Labor Day–May, weekdays 10–4, Sat. 11–5; June 1–Labor Day, Mon.–Sat. 10–5.*

☾ In a wooded 180-acre wildlife preserve, **Historic Bethabara Park** was the site of the first Moravian settlement in North Carolina. The 1753 community—whose name means "house of passage"—was never intended to be permanent. It fell into decline after Salem's completion. You can tour restored buildings, such as the 1788 Gemeinhaus congregation house, or wander the colonial and medicinal gardens. God's Acre, the first colony cemetery, is a short walk away. Children love the reconstructed fort from the French and Indian War. Brochures for self-guided walking tours are available year-round at the visitor center. ✉*2147 Bethabara Rd., University* ☎*336/924–8191* ⊕*www.bethabarapark. org* 🎫*$2* ⊙*Apr.–Dec., Tues.–Fri. 10:30–4:30, weekends 1:30–4:30.*

The **Reynolda House Museum of American Art** was the home of Katharine Smith Reynolds and her husband Richard Joshua Reynolds, founder of the R. J. Reynolds Tobacco Company. Their 1917 home is filled with paintings, prints, and sculptures by such artists as Thomas Eakins, Frederic Church, and Georgia O'Keeffe. There's also a costume collection, as well as clothing and toys used by the Reynolds children. The museum is next to **Reynolda Village,** a collection of shops, restaurants, and gardens that fill the estate's original outer buildings. ✉*2250 Reynolda Rd., University* ☎*336/758–5150 or 888/663–1149* ⊕*www.reynoldahouse.org* 🎫*$10* ⊙*Tues.–Sat. 9:30–4:30, Sun. 1:30–4:30.*

On land once claimed for Queen Elizabeth by Sir Walter Raleigh is **Tanglewood Park,** open to the public for golfing, boating, hiking, fishing, horseback riding, and swimming. The Tanglewood Festival of Lights, the largest holiday-lights festival in the Southeast, runs from mid-November to early January every year. ⊠ *U.S. 158 off I–40, Clemmons* ☎ *336/778–6300* ⊕ *www. forsyth.cc/tanglewood* ⊠ *$2 per car* ⊙ *Daily dawn–dusk.*

WHERE TO EAT

¢–$
GREEK

✕ **Grecian Corner.** In a white building with blue trim, this Greek eatery has been dishing up gyros and chicken and pork souvlakia since 1970. Patrons, from workers at the nearby hospital to soccer moms, appreciate the friendly service and ample portions of moussaka, spanakopita, and salads, plus more familiar fare like hamburgers and pizza. The wine list includes Greek reds and whites. ⊠ *1st St. at Cloverdale Ave., Downtown* ☎ *336/722–6937* ▭ *No credit cards* ⊙ *Closed Sun.*

$$$–$$$$
MODERN
SOUTHERN

✕ **Noble's Grille.** New Southern flavors with European accents are key to the menu. Typical entrées, grilled or roasted over the omnipresent oak-and-hickory fire, include jumbo shrimp and milled grits with bacon, wood grilled tuna with herbed white beans and pan-seared Carolina Amber Jack. The dining room, with tall windows and track lighting, has a view of the grill. ⊠ *380 Knollwood St., Thruway* ☎ *336/777–8477* ▭ *AE, D, MC, V.*

$–$$
AMERICAN

✕ **Old Salem Tavern Dining Room.** The costumed staff happily details the varied lunch and dinner menus, from which you might order traditional Moravian bratwurst or chicken pie. You can also opt for something more innovative, such as lobster-crab cakes or fillet of beef with brandied green peppercorns. In warmer months drinks are served under the arbor, and outdoor seating draws diners to the covered back porch. ⊠ *736 S. Main St., Old Salem* ☎ *336/748–8585* ▭ *AE, MC, V.*

WHERE TO STAY

$–$$
★

🛏 **Brookstown Inn.** Handmade quilts, tubs big enough for two, and evening cookies and milk in the parlor are just a few of the amenities at this lovely lodging. The rooms, with their exposed rafters, high ceilings, and brick walls, retain the character of the original 1837 textile mill. The graffiti wall, where young female factory workers left their mark, has been carefully preserved. Each guest also gets a ticket for a complimentary glass of wine at the nearby Meridian restaurant. **Pros:** historic setting is unique. **Cons:** it may not be as posh as newer hotels. ⊠ *200 Brookstown Ave., Old Salem* ☎ *336/725–1120 or 800/845–4262* ⊕ *www.brookstowninn.com* ⋑ *40 rooms, 31 suites* ♿ *In-room: Wi-Fi. In-hotel: gym* ▭ *AE, D, MC, V* ⊙∣ *BP.*

BARN TO BE WILD

As you're driving through the Piedmont, you'll notice two-story wood structures in various states of disrepair. The differences in architecture are subtle, but fascinating: a wide tin awning, a small overhang, a roof patched together as abstract art. These are tobacco barns, where tobacco was hung to be "cured." Although most have been left to fall apart, some have been transformed into workshops, studios, garages, or even small apartments.

3

North Carolina's Wineries

Bet you didn't know that North Carolina was home to the nation's first cultivated grape. French explorer Giovanni de Verazzano took note of the "big white grape" he found in the Cape Fear River valley in 1524. Two centuries later, settlers were cultivating these "scuppernongs." Most of North Carolina's 25 wineries were closed by Prohibition. But wineries are making a robust comeback. Today there are around 75 wineries in the state, many of them located in the Piedmont.

Benjamin Vineyards & Winery (✉ *6516 Whitney Road, Graham* ☎ *336/376–1080* ⊕ *www.benjamin-vineyards.com*) uses an 1840 recipe to make scuppernong wine. **Black Wolf Vineyards** (✉ *283 Vineyard La., Dobson* ☎ *336/374–2532* ⊕ *www. blackwolfvineyards.com*) is also home to the Wolf's Lair Restaurant. **Buck Shoals Vineyard** (✉ *6121 Vintner Way, Hamptonville* ☎ *336/468–9274* ⊕ *www.buckshoalsvineyard.com*) produces Merlot, Pinot Grigio, Syrah, and other wines. An award-winning Riesling is a highlight of **Chatham Hill Winery** (✉ *3800 Gateway Centre Blvd., St. 310, Morrisville* ☎ *800/808–6768* ⊕ *www.chathamhillwine. com*). **Childress Vineyards** (✉ *1000 Childress Vineyards Road, Lexington* ☎ *336/236-9463* ⊕ *www.childress-vineyards.com*), founded by a former NASCAR driver, makes some of the best red wines in the South, including Syrah and Cabernet Sauvignon.

At **Dennis Vineyards** (✉ *24043 Endy Rd., Albemarle* ☎ *800/230–1743* ⊕ *www.dennisvineyards.com*), father and son turned a hobby into a profession. **Grove Winery** (✉ *7360 Brooks Bridge Rd., Gibsonville* ☎ *336/584–4060* ⊕ *www.grove-winery.com*) grows grapes like the French-American hybrid Traminette and Cabernet Franc. After honeymooning in France, Michael and Amy Helton started **Hanover Park Vineyard** (✉ *1927 Courtney-Huntsville Rd., Yadkinville* ☎ *336/463–2875* ⊕ *www. hanoverparkwines.com*). **Laurel Gray Vineyards** (✉ *5726 Old Hwy. 21, Hamptonville* ☎ *336/468–8463* ⊕ *www.laurelgray.com*) plant grapes on land owned by the same family for 10 generations. **McRitchie Winery & Ciderworks** (✉ *315 Thurmond PO Road, Thurmond* ☎ *336/874–3003* ⊕ *www.mcritchiewine.com*) is one of the newest and most accomplished vineyards in the state.

Raffaldini Vineyards (✉ *450 Groce Rd., Ronda* ☎ *336/835–9463* ⊕ *www. raffaldini.com*) has an Italian villa-style tasting room with stunning views of the Blue Ridge Mountains. **RagApple Lassie Vineyards & Winery** (✉ *3724 Rockford Rd., Boonville* ☎ *336/367–6000* ⊕ *www.ragapplelassie.com*) is named for the owner's pet cow from childhood. **Shelton** (✉ *286 Cabernet Ln., Dobson* ☎ *336/366-4724* ⊕ *www. sheltonvineyards.com*) produces award-winning Riesling and stages a popular summer concert series in the amphitheater at the vineyard.

Westbend Vineyards led the state's wine-making renaissance by planting European grapes 30 years ago. (✉ *5394 Williams Rd., Lewisville* ☎ *336/945–5032* ⊕ *www.westbend-vineyards.com*). **The Winery at Iron Gate Farm** (✉ *2540 Lynch Store Rd., Mebane* ☎ *919/304–9463* ⊕ *www. irongatevineyards.com*) makes the well-regarded Pack House Red, a blend whose name recalls the property's former life as a tobacco farm.

3

$-$$ 🏠 **Henry F. Shaffner House.** Accessible to downtown, this B&B is a favorite with business travelers and honeymooners. The rooms in the restored turn-of-the-20th-century house are meticulously furnished in Victorian elegance. Rates include evening wine and cheese. **Pros:** personalized service of a B&B right in downtown. **Cons:** hotel is near a highway, so traffic noise might be a bother. ✉*150 S. Marshall St., Old Salem* ☎*336/777–0052 or 800/952–2256* ⊕*www.shaffnerhouse.com* ⇨*7 rooms, 2 suites* ⌂*In-hotel: restaurant* ▭*AE, MC, V* ⌾*BP.*

$$–$$$ 🏠 **Marriott Winston-Salem.** This hotel is part of Twin City Quarter, a shopping and dining area in downtown Winston-Salem. There are plenty of restaurants nearby, as well as WS Prime, a steak house with a 150-bottle wine list that's right in the hotel. The location, adjacent to the Benton Convention Center, makes this hotel an ideal destination for business travelers. The rooms have down pillows and premium bedding. **Pros:** it's an easy walk to the arts district and jazz clubs. **Cons:** not overly luxurious. ✉*425 N. Cherry St., Downtown* ☎*336/725–3500 or 877/888–9762* ⊕*www.marriott.com* ⇨*309 rooms, 6 suites* ⌂*In-room: Internet, Wi-Fi. In-hotel: restaurant, pool, laundry facilities, laundry service* ▭*AE, D, MC, V.*

NIGHTLIFE & THE ARTS

THE ARTS   Many North Carolina School of the Arts musical and dramatic performances are held at the **Stevens Center** (✉*405 W. 4th St., Downtown* ☎*336/721–1945*), a restored 1929 movie palace.

Every other August, the North Carolina Black Repertory Company hosts the **National Black Theatre Festival** (✉*610 Coliseum Dr., University* ☎*336/723–2266* ⊕*www.nbtf.org*). This weeklong showcase of African-American arts attracts tens of thousands of people to venues all over the city. The next festival is scheduled for 2009.

NIGHTLIFE   The **Garage** (✉*110 W. 7th St., Downtown* ☎*336/777–1127*) offers up two or three performances a week from mostly regional talent. In the heart of downtown, the **Speakeasy** (✉*410 W. 4th St., Downtown* ☎*336/722–6555*) is the kind of place where live jazz spills out into the street. The menu includes bar food staples as well as sushi. Performances begin at 8.

SPORTS & THE OUTDOORS

BASKETBALL   Winston-Salem's Atlantic Coast Conference entry is the Wake Forest University **Demon Deacons** (☎*336/758–3322 or 888/758–3322* ⊕*wakeforestsports.cstv.com*). The team plays in Lawrence Joel Veterans Memorial Coliseum.

GOLF   **Reynolds Park Golf Course.** This is the elder statesman of local links: a public course designed by Ellis Maples, which opened in 1940. The final hole tests any player's stamina with a 425-yard fairway that ends on an elevated green. ✉*2931 Reynolds Park Rd.* ☎*336/650–7660* 📠*336/650–7664* ⛳*18 holes. 6320 yds. Par 71. Green Fee: $20–$31* ⌥*Facilities: Driving range, putting green, golf carts, pro shop.*

Tanglewood Park Golf Club. In addition to Tanglewood Park's Reynolds Course, there's the Championship Course, which was long home to the

Vantage Championship. Both courses were designed by Robert Trent Jones in the mid-'50s, and both feature pine-lined fairways (narrower on the Reynolds course) and lakes that come into play several times. ⊠*U.S. 158 off I–40, Clemmons* ☎*336/778–6320* ⊕*www.forsyth.cc/ tanglewood* ⅃*3 18-hole courses. Reynolds: 6068 yds. Championship: 6638 yds. Reynolds: Par 72. Championship: Par 72. Green Fee: $20– $47* ⌒*Facilities: 2 driving ranges, golf carts, pro shop.*

SHOPPING

ANTIQUES **Farmstead Antiques** (⊠*120 Farmstead La., Mocksville* ☎*336/998– 3139*) is housed in a former dairy barn about 15 mi southwest of Winston-Salem, just off I–40 at exit 174. It carries antiques, furniture, and decorative objects from the South as well as from England and France.

CRAFTS Contemporary and traditional works from more than 350 craftspeople fill the **Piedmont Craftsmen's Shop & Gallery** (⊠*601 N. Trade St., Downtown* ☎*336/725–1516* ⊕*www.piedmontcraftsmen.org*). The organization has held an annual fair in November for 45 years.

▌ **Bob Timberlake Gallery.** North Carolina's most successful artist is best OFF THE known for his landscapes of the rural South, especially his native BEATEN Lexington. Many of his original paintings, done in a highly detailed PATH "American Realist" style, are exhibited in this gallery about 20 mi from Winston-Salem. You'll also find his personal collections: canoes, decoys, quilts. ⊠*1714 E. Center St. Extension, Exit 94 off I–85, Lexington* ☎*800/244–0095* ⊕*www.bobtimberlake.com* ⊠*Free* ☉*Mon.– Sat. 10–5.*

HIGH POINT

18 mi southeast of Winston-Salem; 76 mi northeast of Charlotte; 20 mi southwest of Greensboro.

High Point earned its name by simple geography: it was the highest point on the railroad line between Goldsboro and Charlotte. Nowadays the city's biannual high point is hosting the International Home Furnishings Market, the largest wholesale furniture trade show in the world. Each spring and fall for a week or more, so many people flood the town that its population of 93,000 nearly doubles. The city is also the home of the North Carolina Shakespeare Festival.

GETTING HERE & AROUND
High Point is one of the Piedmont's smaller cities, with very little traffic. Navigating it by car is fairly simple, and if you happen to get turned around, friendly folks are ready to offer help with directions

ESSENTIALS
Visitor Information **High Point Convention and Visitors Bureau** (⊠*300 S. Main St.* ☎*336/884–5255* ⊕*www.highpoint.org*).

EXPLORING

The **High Point Museum & Historical Park,** focusing on Piedmont history and Quaker heritage, lets you wander through the 1786 Haley House and the 1801 Hoggatt House. Exhibits highlight furniture, pottery, communication, transportation, and military artifacts. Tours of the buildings, conducted by costumed staff, are available weekends. Ever wonder about candle-dipping and writing with a quill? You can try these and other activities here. ⊠*1859 E. Lexington Ave.* ☎*336/885–1859* ⊕*www.highpointmuseum.org* ⊠*Free* ⊙*Museum: Tues.–Sat. 10–4:30, Sun. 1–4:30; Park: Sat. 10–4, Sun. 1–4.*

ᕐ The **Doll & Miniature Museum of High Point** houses a collection of more than 2,500 dolls, costumes, miniatures, and dollhouses. Highlights include 125 Shirley Temple dolls and an extensive crèche with figures dating back to 1490. ⊠*101 W. Green Dr.* ☎*336/885–3655* ⊠*$5* ⊙*Mon.–Fri. 10–4, Sat. 9–4, Sun. 1–4; Closed Mon. Nov.–March.*

In the 1920s a building shaped like an 18th-century chest of drawers was constructed to call attention to the city's standing as the "furniture capital of the world." The **World's Largest Chest of Drawers** (⊠*508 N. Hamilton St.*) rises 40 feet high; dangling from one drawer are two 6-foot-long socks meant to symbolize the city's hosiery industry. The building now houses the offices for the High Point Jaycees.

A few miles northwest of High Point is the **Mendenhall Plantation,** a well-preserved example of 19th-century domestic architecture. As Quakers, the Mendenhalls opposed slavery, and here you can find one of the few surviving false-bottom wagons, used to help slaves escape to freedom on the Underground Railroad. ■TIP➔**Come in July, when kids can learn how to make a corn-husk doll or design a quilt square during the Village Fair.** ⊠*603 W. Main St., Jamestown* ☎*336/454–3819* ⊕*www.mendenhallplantation.org* ⊠*$2* ⊙ *Tues.–Fri. 11–3, Sat. 1–4, Sun. 2–4. Closed Mon.*

WHERE TO STAY & EAT

$$$–$$$$
AMERICAN
★
✗**J. Basul Noble.** Locals hold this place in high esteem, and it's easy to see why. It's architecturally dramatic, with 10-foot-tall pillars, a pyramid-shape glass ceiling, and a river-rock wall. The menu includes creative dishes like spit-roasted chicken with cheddar-cheese grits or pan-seared halibut with truffles and pork belly. You could make a meal out of the fine breads (baked daily on the premises) and desserts. A bistro menu is served in the bar area, and brunch is offered on Sunday. ⊠*101 S. Main St.* ☎*336/889–3354* ▭*AE, D, MC, V.*

$–$$
STEAK
✗**Liberty Steakhouse & Brewery.** With a melting pot of a menu, Liberty's offers food ranging from New England to New Orleans and from the South to the Southwest. Steaks, seafood, salads, and soups are all amply represented. The on-site brewery offers up internationally influenced stouts, lagers, and ales. ⊠*Oak Hollow Mall, 914 Mall Loop Rd.* ☎*336/882–4677* ▭*AE, D, MC, V.*

$–$$
▦**Radisson Hotel High Point.** The central location makes this chain hotel a favorite with people arriving for weekend shopping trips. Guest rooms are standard, but each suite is outfitted with furniture from the

different manufacturers in the area. Room rates can more than double during the International Home Furnishing Shows. **Pros:** close to popular furniture shops. **Cons:** decor is dated. ⊠*135 S. Main St.* ☎*336/889–8888* ⊕*www.radisson.com* ✍*239 rooms, 13 suites* ⬧*In-room: refrigerator, Internet, Wi-Fi. In-hotel: restaurant, bar, pool, gym* ▤*AE, D, MC, V.*

PLANNING AHEAD

If your visit to High Point coincides with the International Home Furnishings Show, make dinner reservations as far ahead as possible. Well-regarded restaurants in town—and neighboring towns, too—book far in advance.

NIGHTLIFE & THE ARTS

Headquartered in the High Point Theatre is the **North Carolina Shakespeare Festival** (⊠*High Point Theatre, 220 E. Commerce Ave.* ☎*336/887–3001* ⊕*www.ncshakes.org*). The professional troupe, founded in 1977, performs two of the Bard's plays in September and October and *A Christmas Carol* in December.

SPORTS & THE OUTDOORS

GOLF **Oak Hollow.** The Pete Dye–designed public course makes use of its lakeside position by including peninsula greens and an island tee on the par 4 sixth hole. ⊠*3400 N. Centennial St.* ☎*336/883–3260* ⊕*www.oakhollowgc.com* 🏌*18 holes. 6564 yds. Par 72. Green Fee: $27–$36* ✐*Facilities: Driving range, golf carts, pro shop, golf academy/lessons, restaurant.*

HIKING The 376-acre **Piedmont Environmental Center** (⊠*1220 Penny Rd.* ☎*336/883–8531* ⊕*www.piedmontenvironmental.com*) has 11 mi of hiking trails and a 10-mi paved greenway adjacent to City Lake Park.

SHOPPING

Solo and group shows rotate through the three exhibition spaces of the **Theatre Art Galleries** (⊠*220 E. Commerce Ave.* ☎*336/887–2137* ⊕*www.tagart.org*), in the same building as the High Point Theatre.

CHARLOTTE

Although it dates from Revolutionary War times (it's named for King George III's wife), Charlotte is definitely part of the New South. Uptown Charlotte has broad streets and a skyline of gleaming skyscrapers. It also has some fashionable historic neighborhoods that are noted for their architecture and their winding, tree-shaded streets. Public art—such as the sculptures at the four corners of Trade and Tryon streets—is increasingly displayed in the city. Erected at Independence Square, the sculptures symbolize Charlotte's roots and aspirations: a gold miner (commerce), a mill worker (the city's textile heritage), a railroad builder (transportation), and a mother holding her baby aloft (the future).

Heavy development has created some typical urban problems. Outdated road systems in this metropolis make traffic a nightmare during rush hours, and virtually all the city's restaurants are packed on weekends. But the locals' Southern courtesy is contagious, and people still love the laid-back pleasures of jogging, picnicking, and sunning in Freedom Park.

GETTING HERE & AROUND

Charlotte is a driver's town, but a new light rail system has made going sans car a much more palatable option for commuters and visitors. The LYNX blue line is clean and fast, and runs from Uptown Charlotte, through the convention center, to I–485. Check for routes and schedules at ⊕*www.charmeck.org/departments/cats/lynx.*

You'll be able to walk around Uptown and the historic Fourth Ward.

ESSENTIALS

Visitor Information **Visit Charlotte/Main Street Charlotte** (✉ *330 S. Tryon St., Uptown* ☎ *704/331–2700* ⊕ *www.charlottesgotalot.com*).

UPTOWN CHARLOTTE

Uptown Charlotte is ideal for walking. The city was laid out in four wards around Independence Square, at Trade and Tryon streets. The Square, as it is known, is the center of the Uptown area.

EXPLORING

② **Bank of America Corporate Center.** Architecture fans should make time for a trip to see one of the city's most striking buildings. The Cesar Pelli–designed structure rises 60 stories to a crownlike top. The main attractions are three monumental lobby frescoes by world-renowned Ben Long, whose themes are making/building, chaos/creativity, and planning/knowledge. Also in the tower are the **North Carolina Blumenthal Performing Arts Center** and the restaurants, shops, and exhibition space of **Founders Hall.** ✉ *100 N. Tryon St., Uptown.*

⑤ **Discovery Place.** Allow at least two hours for the **aquariums,** the three-
★ story **rain forest,** and the **IMAX Dome Theater.** A ham-radio room, a
☺ puppet theater, and plenty of hands-on science experiments are other highlights. Check the schedule for special exhibits. ✉ *301 N. Tryon St., Uptown* ☎ *704/372–6261 or 800/935–0553* ⊕ *www.discoveryplace. org* 🖅 *$10* ☉ *Labor Day–May, weekdays 9–5, Sat. 10–6, Sun. 12:30–6; June–Labor Day, Mon.–Sat. 10–6, Sun. 12:30–6.*

③ **Fourth Ward.** Charlotte's popular old neighborhood began as a political subsection created for electoral purposes in the mid-1800s. The architecture and sensibility of this quiet, homespun neighborhood provide a glimpse of life in a less hectic time. A brochure includes 18 places of historic interest.

④ **Levine Museum of the New South.** With its 8,000-square-foot centerpiece exhibit "Cotton Fields to Skyscrapers: Charlotte and the Carolina Piedmont in the New South" as a jumping-off point, this museum offers a comprehensive interpretation of post–Civil War Southern history. Interactive exhibits and different "environments"—a tenant farmer's house, an African-American hospital, a bustling street scene—bring to

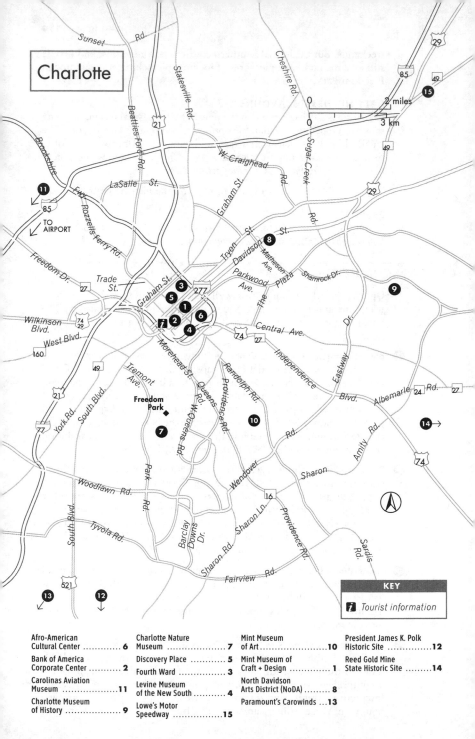

Charlotte

TO AIRPORT

Freedom Park

KEY

i Tourist information

life the history of the region. ■TIP➔ **Admission is free on Sunday.** ✉*200 E. 7th St., Uptown* 🕿*704/333–1887* ⊕*www.museumofthenewsouth. org* ✎*$6* ⊙*Mon.–Sat. 10–5, Sun. noon–5.*

 Mint Museum of Craft + Design. This museum is a showplace for contemporary crafts. In addition to the 16,000-square-foot gallery, with its spectacular 40-foot-tall glass wall, the permanent collections of ceramics, glass, fiber, metal, and wood make this one of the country's major crafts museums. ■TIP➔ **Use your ticket stub from the crafts museum for free same-day the Mint Museum of Art.** ✉*220 N. Tryon St., Uptown* 🕿*704/337–2000* ⊕*www.mintmuseum.org* ✎*$6* ⊙*Tues.–Sat. 10–5, Sun. noon–5.*

Fodor'sChoice ★

3

GREATER CHARLOTTE

Farther afield lie many of Charlotte's most interesting sights, from gardens to museums. You can reach the ones listed below by car or by city bus; for visits elsewhere a car is essential.

EXPLORING
TOP ATTRACTIONS

6 **Afro-American Cultural Center.** In a 1911 house of worship, this is a showcase for art, music, drama, and dance. ■TIP➔ **Come on Sunday, when admission is free.** ✉*401 N. Myers St., Uptown* 🕿*704/374–1565* ⊕*www. aacc-charlotte.org* ✎*$5; free Sun.* ⊙*Tues.–Sat. 10–5, Sun. 1–5.*

9 **Charlotte Museum of History.** Built in 1774, this stone building is the oldest dwelling in the county. Hezekiah Alexander and his wife Mary reared 10 children in this house and farmed the land. Seasonal events commemorate the early days. Permanent and rotating exhibits in the museum span 300 years of southern Piedmont history. ■TIP➔ **Admission is free on Sunday.** ✉*3500 Shamrock Dr., East Charlotte/Merchandise Mart* 🕿*704/568–1774* ⊕*www.charlottemuseum.org* ✎*Tues.–Sat. $6; Sun. free* ⊙*Tues.–Sat. 10–5, Sun. 1–5.*

7 **Charlotte Nature Museum.** You'll find a butterfly pavilion, bugs galore, live animals, nature trails, a puppet theater, and hands-on exhibits just for children at this museum affiliated with Discovery Place. ✉*1658 Sterling Ave., next to Freedom Park, Uptown* 🕿*704/372–0471* ⊕*www. discoveryplace.org* ✎*$4* ⊙*Weekdays 9–5, Sat. 10–5, Sun. 1–5.*

 Lowe's Motor Speedway. This state-of-the-art facility, holding 167,000 fans, is considered the heart of NASCAR. An estimated 90% of driving teams live within 50 mi. Hosting more than 350 events each year, this is one of the busiest sports venues in the United States. Racing season runs April to November, and tours are offered on non-race days. The Speedway Club, an upscale restaurant, is on the premises. ■TIP➔ **When there's a race, the population of Concord can jump from 60,000 to more than 250,000. Make sure you book your lodging well in advance.** ✉*5555 Concord Pkwy. S, northeast of Charlotte, Concord* 🕿*704/455–3200 or 800/455–3267* ⊕*www.lowesmotorspeedway.com.*

★ If you want to indulge the driver in you, you can take lessons through the **Richard Petty Driving Experience** (☎ *704/455–9443 ⊕www.1800bepetty. com*). You can drive a NASCAR-style stock car at speeds up to 155 mph around the Lowe's track. If you want the thrill of the ride without being in the driver's seat, you can ride with an instructor and go up to 165 mph. Classes are available throughout the year, though only when there's no event at Lowe's Motor Speedway. Prices vary, but start at $400 for eight laps around the track. ■**TIP→You must have a valid driver's license and be able to drive a manual (stick shift) transmission car to drive, and you'll need to reserve ahead of time.**

Slated to open in early 2010, the 50,000-square-foot **NASCAR Hall of Fame** will celebrate the only sport born in North Carolina. Visitors will be able to watch films on NASCAR history, see cars that ran the speedways, view changing exhibits, and experience simulations of what racing is like for NASCAR drivers and crews. It will also serve as the ceremony site for the legends inducted into the Hall. ⊠*Martin Luther King Blvd. and Brevard St., Uptown ⊕www.nascarhall.com* .

⑩ **Mint Museum of Art.** Built in 1836 as the first U.S. Mint, this building
★ has been a home for art since 1936. Among the holdings in its impressive permanent collections are American and European paintings, furniture, and decorative arts; African, pre-Columbian, and Spanish-colonial art; porcelain and pottery; and regional crafts and historic costumes. ■**TIP→Your ticket stub gets you free admission to downtown's Mint Museum of Craft + Design.** ⊠*2730 Randolph Rd., East Charlotte/ Merchandise Mart* ☎*704/337–2000 ⊕www.mintmuseum.org* ✉*$6* ☉*Tues. 10–9, Wed.–Sat. 10–5, Sun. noon–5.*

⑧ **North Davidson Arts District.** Charlotte's answer to SoHo or TriBeCa is NoDa, a neighborhood as funky as Uptown is elegant. Creative energy flows through the reclaimed textile mill and mill houses, cottages, and commercial spaces of this north Charlotte neighborhood, where you'll find both the kooky and the conformist—artists, musicians, and dancers; street vendors; and restaurateurs—sharing space.

A 1945 movie palace called the Astor Theater has been given new life as the 700-seat **Neighborhood Theatre** (⊠*511 E. 36th St. 28205* ☎*704/358–9298 ⊕www.neighborhoodtheatre.com*), hosting concerts by the likes of the Indigo Girls, Little Feat, and the Nitty Gritty Dirt Band. On the first and third Friday of every month an evening "gallery crawl" is held from 6 to 9:30 through the exhibition spaces of NoDa. The **Center of the Earth Gallery** (⊠*3204 N. Davidson St.* ☎*704/375– 5756 ⊕www.centeroftheearth.com*) displays contemporary art from 50 regional and national painters, sculptors, and craftspeople. The **Smelly Cat Coffeehouse** (⊠*514 E. 36th St.* ☎*704/374–9656*) is a tiny place with a big choice of pastries. **The Dog Bar** (⊠*3307 N. Davidson St.* ☎*704/370–3595*) is a neighborhood tavern where pooches are welcome (and their birthdays are celebrated). Live music plays five nights a week in the **Evening Muse** (⊠*3227 N. Davidson St.* ☎*704/376–3737 ⊕www.theeveningmuse.com*)

WORTH NOTING

Historic sites, a speedway, and a theme park provide plenty to explore beyond the city.

⑪ **Carolinas Aviation Museum.** At the Charlotte-Douglas International Airport, the museum has a collection of 50 major aircraft, including a working DC-3 and a F-14D Super TomCat. ✉*4108 Minuteman Way* ☎*704/359–8442* ⊕*www.carolinasaviation.org* ◪*$8* ⏱*Tues.–Fri. 10–4, Sat. 10–5, Sun. 1–5.*

⑬ **Paramount's Carowinds.** This 100-acre amusement park, 15 mi from Charlotte, has dozens of rides and attractions. Costumed movie and TV characters greet visitors. Star entertainers and touring shows perform at the Paladium Amphitheatre and in Carowinds Theatre. ✉*14523 Carowinds Blvd., off I–77 at Carowinds Blvd., South Charlotte/Pineville* ☎*704/588–2600 or 800/888–4386* ⊕*www.carowinds. com* ◪*$45* ⏱*Late Mar.–May and mid-Aug.–early Oct., weekends; June–mid-Aug., daily. Park opens at 9; closing hrs vary.*

⑫ **President James K. Polk State Historic Site.** A state historic site 10 mi south of Charlotte marks the humble birthplace and childhood home of the 11th U.S. president. Guided tours of the log cabins (replicas of the originals) show what life was like for settlers back in 1795. ✉*12031 Lancaster Hwy., Pineville* ☎*704/889–7145* ⊕*www.polk.nchistoric-sites.org* ◪*Free* ⏱*Tues.–Sat. 9–5.*

⑭ **Reed Gold Mine State Historic Site.** This historic site, about 22 mi east of Charlotte, is where America's first documented gold rush began, following Conrad Reed's discovery of a 17-pound nugget in 1799. Forty-minute guided underground tours of the gold mine are available, as well as seasonal gold panning, walking trails, and a stamp mill. ✉*9621 Reed Mine Rd., north of Rte. 24/27, Midland* ☎*704/721–4653* ⊕*www. reedmine.com* ◪*Free* ⏱ *Tues.–Sat. 9–5.*

WHERE TO EAT

$–$$ ✕**300 East.** The gentrified neighborhood in which this casual spot resides
ECLECTIC   doesn't lack for charming older houses. Even so, 300 East makes its
★   mark, and not just because of its brightly hued signage. The bold contemporary menu—pork tenderloin with banana-mango salsa and saffron rice, for instance, or penne with duck and lobster—attracts a hip and eclectic bunch. Choose a table in one of the private dining nooks and crannies, or outside on the open-air patio. Here people-watching is as much fun as eating. ✉*300 East Blvd., SouthPark* ☎*704/332–6507* ▭*AE, D, MC, V.*

$$$–$$$$ ✕**Bentley's on 27.** Where to look? To one side is the city skyline, viewed
FRENCH   from the 27th floor. To the other is the impressive display at the *gueridon,* a French cooking cart. The food itself is elegant in its simplicity: a salad of baby greens, shallots, pearl tomatoes, and a champagne vinaigrette dressing, for instance, or a filet mignon with roasted potatoes, pearl onions, wild mushrooms, spinach leaf, and red wine reduction, grilled asparagus, baby carrots, roasted pears, and blue-cheese risotto. You'd close your eyes to savor the taste, but then you'd miss the

view. ✉ *Charlotte Plaza, 201 S. College St., Uptown* ☎ *704/343–9201* ⊟ *AE, MC, V.*

¢–$
AMERICAN

✕ **Landmark Diner.** This spacious and informal diner is a cut above most other inexpensive restaurants, and it's open until 1 AM on weeknights, 4 AM Friday and Saturday and midnight Sunday. The chef's salad with grilled chicken is a must, as is chicken Sorrento made with sautéed artichokes, spinach, and sun-dried tomatoes. For dessert there's chocolate-cream pie. ✉ *4429 Central Ave., East Charlotte/Merchandise Mart* ☎ *704/532–1153* ⊟ *AE, MC, V.*

$$–$$$
LATIN
AMERICAN

✕ **Latorre's.** The emphasis at this downtown eatery is on the heat, color, and flavor of Latin America. Art splashed with vibrant shades of mango, lemon, and papaya complements exposed-brick walls and hardwood floors. Live salsa and merengue is the perfect backdrop for the likes of orange-and-cumin-encrusted salmon over black-bean rice cakes, and tender grilled *chimichurri* (a piquant Argentinian herb sauce) flank steak served with tortillas and three salsas. On weekends the place is open for dancing until 2:30 AM. ✉ *118 W. 5th St., Uptown* ☎ *704/377–4448* ⊟ *AE, MC, V* ☉ *Closed Sun.*

$$$
MEDITERRANEAN
★

✕ **M5.** It would be easy for a place so hip and beautiful to skimp on the food, but M5 pays as much attention to the cuisine as it does to its chic club-like setting. Ricotta gnocchi starters are pillow-soft and pungent, and the paella with roasted jumbo prawns offers a real depth of flavor. Servers are attentive and knowledgeable, which is a big help when navigating the vast wine list, replete with interesting Mediterranean choices. The spacious patio, in a corner of the posh SouthPark mall complex is a see-and-be-seen affair in warm weather, but don't let the people-watching distract you from the food. It's the real deal. ✉ *4310 Sharon Road, Suite W01, SouthPark* ☎ *704/909-5500* ⊟ *AE, MC, V* ☉ *Closed Mon.*

¢
SOUTHERN
Fodor's Choice
★

✕ **Mert's Heart and Soul.** Talk about the New South. Business executives and arts patrons make their way to Mert's—named for Myrtle, a favorite customer with a sunny disposition. Owners James and Renee Bezzelle serve large portions of Low Country and Gullah staples, such as fried chicken with greens, macaroni and cheese, and corn bread. Lowcountry specialties include shrimp-and-salmon omelets and red beans and rice. Buckwheat and sweet-potato pancakes draw a weekend brunch crowd. ✉ *214 N. College St., Uptown* ☎ *704/342–4222* ⊟ *AE, MC, V* ☉ *No dinner Mon. and Tues.*

¢
SOUTHERN

✕ **Price's Chicken Coop.** If you want to know where the locals eat, just follow the scent of oil to this storefront institution in the historic South End neighborhood, just across I–277 from Uptown. The place isn't much to look at, but that's OK because the food is to-go only. And the chicken is the reason to go—and go again and again. A light crispy coating cuddles succulent meat so juicy you'll begin to understand that there is indeed an art to running a deep fryer. Take some back to your hotel in Uptown and make everyone on the elevator jealous with the scent of Southern-fried goodness. ✉ *1614 Camden Road, South End* ☎ *704/333-9866* ⚅ *Reservations not accepted* ⊟ *No credit cards* ☉ *Closed Sun. and Mon.*

$$–$$$ ✕ **Providence Café.** The signature purple awnings lead you to this lively
ECLECTIC café. New dishes, many with subtle Asian influences, are introduced
every spring and fall, but the menu always includes options for meat
eaters as well as vegetarian. Delicious focaccia is baked daily on the
premises. It's a great place for Sunday brunch, and on Wednesday and
Thursday evening there's often live jazz. ✉*110 Perrin Pl., SouthPark*
☎*704/376–2008* ⊕*www.providencecafe.com* ⊟*AE, MC, V.*

WHERE TO STAY

3

$$$–$$$$ 🏨 **Ballantyne Resort Hotel.** Nestled on 2,000 acres, Ballantyne is a stately
structure, with towering two-story windows in the lobby that make a
strong impression. Even if you check in expecting a vacation filled with
golf and tennis, you might find you can barely budge from the spa. The
spacious guest rooms have classic furniture and color schemes of gold,
cream, and sage. You can choose a sunset view or golf view. The Lodge,
designed for corporate retreats, has a great room with a fireplace and
a porch with rocking chairs. **Pros:** luxury defined. **Cons:** not conve-
nient for exploring city center. ✉*10000 Ballantyne Commons Pkwy.,
South Charlotte* ☎*704/248–4000 or 866/248–4824* ⊕*www.ballan-
tyneresort.com* ⬂*200 rooms, 14 suites* ⚙*In-room: Internet, Wi-Fi.
In-hotel: 2 restaurants, room service, bar, golf course, tennis courts,
pool, gym, spa, laundry service* ⊟*AE, D, MC, V.*

¢ 🏨 **Best Western Sterling Inn.** This economy option has an upscale sen-
sibility, with large and tasteful rooms with oversize beds and coffee-
makers. The inn is near Interstates 77 and 85 and Charlote Douglas
International Airport. **Pros:** great location for those traveling by car or
plane. **Cons:** can be a little noisy. ✉*242 E. Woodlawn Rd., Airport/
Coliseum* ☎*704/525–5454* ⬂*100 rooms* ⚙*In-room: refrigerator. In-
hotel: gym, laundry service* ⊟*AE, D, MC, V* ⛉*BP.*

¢ 🏨 **Econo Lodge Lake Norman.** This motel for the budget-minded is north
of Charlotte on Interstate 77, within 3 mi of Lake Norman and David-
son College. All rooms have refrigerators and coffeemakers, and a
gym is right across the street. **Pros:** great value. **Cons:** don't expect
luxury. ✉*20740 Torrence Chapel Rd., Cornelius* ☎*704/892–3500
or 800/848–9751* ⊕*www.choicehotels.com* ⬂*90 rooms* ⚙*In-room:
refrigerator, Wi-Fi. In-hotel: pool, laundry facilities.* ⊟*AE, D, MC,
V* ⛉*BP.*

$$$ 🏨 **Hilton Charlotte Center City.** In the financial district, this hotel sits across
the street from the Charlotte Convention Center. The wood-panel
lobby, with marble floors and a sweeping staircase, is impressive. Guest
rooms are large and comfortable, if unimaginatively decorated. Each
has a nice view of the city. **Pros:** great for convention-goers; YMCA on
the premises. **Cons:** some rooms have only showers, so unless you ask,
you might not get a bathtub. ✉*222 E. 3rd St., Uptown* ☎*704/377–
1500 or 800/445–8667* ⊕*www.charlottecentercity.hilton.com* ⬂*401
rooms, 25 suites* ⚙*In-room: Internet, Wi-Fi. In-hotel: restaurant, room
service, bar, pool, gym, laundry service* ⊟*AE, D, MC, V* ⛉*BP.*

$–$$ 🏨 **Omni Charlotte Hotel.** This 16-story hotel is in the heart of downtown,
within walking distance of the convention center as well as many arts

and sports venues. An escalator whisks you to the OverStreet Mall, where you'll find shops, restaurants, and a lounge. Many guest rooms have glass walls overlooking the city skyline. Satin hangers and rainfall showers are among the ways a guest feels pampered. You can also request a "Get Fit" room with a portable treadmill. **Pros:** location and amenities are great for downtown. **Cons:** busy setting might be too much for some travelers. ⊠*132 E. Trade St., Uptown* ☎*704/377–0400 or 800/843–6664* ⊕*www.omnicharlotte.com* ↩*374 rooms, 33 suites* ⚷*In-room: Internet, Wi-Fi. In-hotel: restaurant, bar, pool, laundry service* ▤*AE, D, MC, V.*

$–$$ ⛭**Westin Charlotte.** The Westin Charlotte is a study in modern comfort. The vast medallion chandelier in the lobby is as striking as the hotel's gleaming green-glass facade. Rooms feature ultra-comfy beds and roomy showers in marble bathrooms as well as stunning views of the city. The concierges know the area well, from where the best touring Broadway shows are to where to find baby supplies in a pinch. A stop for the new LYNX light rail is just outside the hotel door. Both service and comfort are delivered at very high levels. **Pros:** helpful staff and beautiful surroundings; in-room spa services. **Cons:** parking in the on-site deck is not included in room rate. ⊠*601 S. College St., Uptown* ☎*704/375–2600* ⊕*www.westin.com/charlotte* ↩*700 rooms* ⚷*In room: Internet. In hotel: restaurant, room service, bar, gym, pool, laundry service, parking (paid)* ▤*AE, D, MC, V.*

BED-AND-BREAKFASTS

$$$–$$$$ ⛭**Duke Mansion.** Coming up the boxwood-lined drive of the Duke Mansion feels like going back in time. The well-preserved property was once home to Duke University benefactor James Buchanan Duke. The inn, which changed hands many times since Duke's death, is now run by a nonprofit organization. Some of the rooms have original fixtures, including bathtubs and vanities. Spacious sleeping-porch balconies overlook the well-maintained grounds. Modern amenities include flat-screen TVs, comfortable beds, and cozy robes. In the morning, a full breakfast is served in the dining room. Staying at the Duke Mansion seems more like borrowing a wealthy friend's estate than spending a night in a hotel. **Pros:** guests get a real sense of history and a neighborhood feel. **Cons:** older bathroom fixtures do not perform to modern standards. ⊠*400 Hermitage Road, Myers Park* ☎*704/714–4400* ⊕*www.dukemansion.com* ↩*20 rooms* ⚷*In-room: Wi-Fi* ▤*MC, V.*

$–$$ ⛭**Morehead Inn.** Built in 1917, this grand Colonial Revival home is in the Dilworth neighborhood. Wedding parties and family reunions frequently reserve the entire estate. Rooms are filled with period antiques, including several with impressive four-poster beds. **Pros:** cozy and historic. **Cons:** it is a popular spot for weddings and parties, so it can be noisy. ⊠*1122 E. Morehead St., SouthPark* ☎*704/376–3357 or 888/667–3432* ⊕*www.moreheadinn.com* ↩*12 rooms* ⚷*In-room: Wi-Fi. In-hotel: room service, bicycles* ▤*AE, DC, MC, V* ⏹*BP.*

CAMPING

Lake Norman State Park (⊠*159 Inland Sea La., Troutman* ☎*704/ 528–6350*) is ideal for hiking and water sports. More than 32 sites have tent pads, picnic tables, and grills. Group camp sites for up to 25 people have picnic tables and a fire ring. Near Charlotte, 56 campsites— 36 for tents, 13 for RVs, and seven rentable tents—can be found at **McDowell Nature Center and Preserve** (⊠*15222 York Rd., South Charlotte/Pineville* ☎*704/583–1284*). The campground also has a new bathhouse.

> **WORD OF MOUTH**
>
> "We flew into Charlotte and visited all the race shops in the area and Lowe's Motor Speedway. If you go during a time they aren't racing, you can tour the track (big highlight of our trip)."
>
> —Buffy9297

NIGHTLIFE & THE ARTS

THE ARTS

With the 2,100-seat Belk Theatre, the **North Carolina Blumenthal Performing Arts Center** (⊠*130 N. Tryon St., Uptown* ☎*704/372–1000* ⊕*www.performingartsctr.org*) houses several resident companies, such as the Charlotte Symphony Orchestra, North Carolina Dance Theatre, and Opera Carolina. At Paramount's Carowinds, the **Paladium Amphitheater** (⊠*14523 Carowinds Blvd., South Charlotte/Pineville* ☎*704/588–2600 or 800/888–4386* ⊕*www.paramountparks.com*) presents family-friendly acts spring to fall. The **Verizon Wireless Amphitheater** (⊠*707 Pavilion Blvd., Speedway* ☎*704/549–5555* ⊕*www.verizonwireless-amphitheater.com*) spotlights big-name concerts—Norah Jones, Tim McGraw, Melissa Etheridge—spring through fall.

NIGHTLIFE

In business since 1973, the **Double Door Inn** (⊠*1218 Charlottetown Ave., Uptown* ☎*704/376–1446*) is a staple of the national blues circuit. Eric Clapton, Junior Walker, and Stevie Ray Vaughn are among the legends who've played at this laid-back venue. **Ri Ra** (⊠*208 N. Tryon St., Uptown* ☎*704/333–5554*), Gaelic for "uproar," serves up traditional food, ale, and, on Thursday to Sunday night, live music.

SPORTS & THE OUTDOORS

AUTO RACING

NASCAR races, such as May's Coca-Cola 600, draw huge crowds at the **Lowe's Motor Speedway** (⊠*5555 Concord Pkwy. S, northeast of Charlotte, Concord* ☎*704/455–3200 or 800/455–3267* ⊕*www.lowesmotorspeedway.com*). ⇨ *See Greater Charlotte's Top Attractions above for more details.*

BOATING

Inlets on Lake Norman are ideal for canoeing. You can rent canoes, rowboats, and paddleboats for $5 for the first hour and $3 for each additional hour from the **North Carolina Division of Parks and Recreation** (☎ *704/528–6350 ⊕www.ils.unc.edu/parkproject/visit/lano/do.html*).

FISHING

You can find good fishing in Charlotte's neighboring lakes and streams. A license can be bought at local bait-and-tackle shops or over the phone from the **North Carolina Wildlife Commission** (☎ *888/248–6834 ⊕www. ncwildlife.org*). A 10-day, out-of-state license is $10, or $20 if you want to fish for mountain trout. Game fish in Lake Norman waters include crappie, bluegill, and yellow perch, as well as striped, largemouth, and white bass.

FOOTBALL

The National Football League's **Carolina Panthers** (✉ *800 S. Mint St., Airport/Coliseum* ☎ *704/358–7800 ⊕www.panthers.com*) play from August through December—and hopefully into the post-season play-offs as well—in the 73,000-seat Bank of America Stadium.

GOLF

Larkhaven Golf Club. The oldest public course in Charlotte, Larkhaven opened in 1958. Mature trees have narrowed the fairways, and there's a 60-foot elevation drop on Hole 9, a par 3. ✉ *4801 Camp Stewart Rd.* ☎ *704/545–4653 ⊕www.larkhavengolf.com* ⚑ *18 holes. 6328 yds. Par 72. Green Fee: $30–$42$32-$45* ⚲ *Facilities: Golf carts, pro shop.*

Paradise Valley Golf Center. This short course is perfect for players without much time, as a round usually takes just an hour. But don't let that fool you: this course can challenge the best of them. Unique elements include two island tees. There's also a miniature golf course called the Lost Duffer set in a 19th-century mining town. ✉ *110 Barton Creek Dr.* ☎ *704/548–1808 ⊕ www.charlottepublicgolf.com/paradise-valley. php* ⚑ *18 holes. 1264 yds. Par 54. Green Fee: $8–$17* ⚲ *Facilities: Golf carts.*

Woodbridge Golf Links. This semiprivate course is lovely to look at and challenging to play. You have to be careful with the water hazards; there are water features on 13 holes. ✉ *7107 Highland Creek Pkwy.* ☎ *704/875–9000 ⊕www.highlandcreekgolfclub.com* ⚑ *18 holes. 6520 yds. Par 72. Green Fee: $49–$69* ⚲ *Facilities: Driving range, putting green, golf carts, pro shop, restaurant, bar.*

SHOPPING

Charlotte is the largest retail center in the Carolinas. Most stores are in suburban malls; villages and towns in outlying areas have shops selling regional specialties.

SHOPPING MALLS

Two-story **Carolina Place Mall** (✉ *11025 Carolina Place Pkwy., off I–485, South Charlotte/Pineville* ☎ *704/543–9300*) is on the interstate. Destination shopping has been raised to an art form at **Concord Mills** (✉ *8111 Concord Mills Blvd., off I–85, Concord* ☎ *704/979–5000*), which sells hundreds of brand names and discounted designer labels. Look for stores carrying Ralph Lauren, Louis Vitton, Burburry, and OshKosh B'Gosh. **SouthPark Mall** (✉ *4400 Sharon Rd., SouthPark* ☎ *704/364–4411*) has such high-end stores as Tiffany & Co., Montblanc, Coach, and Hermes.

3

SPECIALTY STORES

ANTIQUES The nearby towns of Waxhaw, Pineville, and Matthews are the best places to find antiques. You can find a good selection of antiques and collectibles at the sprawling **Metrolina Expo** (✉ *7100 N. Statesville Rd., off I–77, North Charlotte/Lake Norman* ☎ *704/596–4643*) on the first weekend of the month.

FOOD The **Charlotte Regional Farmers Market** (✉ *1801 Yorkmount Rd., Airport/ Coliseum* ☎ *704/357–1269*) sells produce, eggs, plants, and crafts.

THE SANDHILLS

Because of their sandy soil—they were once Atlantic beaches—the Sandhills weren't of much use to early farmers, most of whom switched to lumbering and making turpentine for a livelihood. Since the turn of the 20th century, however, this area, with its vast pine forests and lakes, has proved ideal for golf, tennis, and horse farms. A panel of experts assembled by *Golf Digest* magazine has named the region one of the top three golfing destinations in the world. First-class resorts are centered around the region's 40 championship golf courses, which have seen their share of PGA tournaments. Public and private tennis courts abound, and dozens of equestrian events are held each year, including professional steeplechase and harness racing.

The Highland Scots who settled the area left a rich heritage perpetuated through festivals and gatherings. In colonial times English potters were attracted to the rich clay deposits in the soil, and today their descendants and others turn out beautiful wares sold in more than 40 local shops.

SOUTHERN PINES

104 mi east of Charlotte; 71 mi southwest of Raleigh.

The center of the Sandhills, Southern Pines is a good place to begin exploring the region. The three-block Cameron Historical District, once the end of the line for the Raleigh-Augusta Railroad, is now a thriving antiques center. You'll find a dozen shops lining Carthage Street.

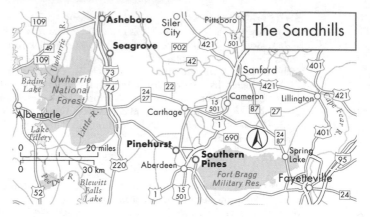

GETTING HERE & AROUND

Southern Pines is easy to reach from the Triangle in the east via U.S. 1. From Charlotte the route is a bit more roundabout and involves driving southeast on U.S. 74 then heading north on U.S. 1. Once you've arrived, you will find Southern Pines to be laid out in a neat grid with Broad Street at the center.

ESSENTIALS

Visitor Information Pinehurst/Southern Pines/Aberdeen Area Convention and Visitors Bureau (⊠ *1480 U.S. 15/501, Box 2270, Southern Pines* ☎ *910/692–3330* ⊕ *www.homeofgolf.com*).

EXPLORING

Sandhills Horticultural Gardens has a wetland area that can be observed from elevated boardwalks. It's part of a 32-acre series of gardens showcasing roses, fruits and vegetables, herbs, conifers, hollies, a formal English garden, pools, and a waterfall. ⊠ *Sandhills Community College, 2200 Airport Rd., Pinehurst* ☎ *910/695–3964 or 800/338–3944* ⊕ *www.sandhills.cc.nc.us/lsg/hort.html* ☜ *Free* ⊙ *Daily sunrise–sunset.*

OFF THE BEATEN PATH

House in the Horseshoe. The two-story 1772 home 10 mi from Carthage earned its name because it was built in a bend of Deep River, the cotton plantation home of Gov. Benjamin Williams. In a late Revolutionary War battle in 1781, David Fanning's Tories defeated Philip Alston's Whigs in the colonial era's equivalent of a hail of gunfire. You can still view the bullet holes from the skirmish today. ⊠ *324 Alston House Rd., Sanford* ☎ *910/947–2051* ⊕ *www.nchistoricsites.org/horsesho* ☜ *Free* ⊙ *Tues.–Sat. 9–5.*

The 1820 **Shaw House** is typical of the sturdy homes built by the Scottish families who settled the region. It serves as headquarters for the Moore County Historical Association. Two other restored cabins, both of which date to the 1700s, help illustrate the lives of early settlers. ⊠ *S.W. Broad St. and Morganton Rd.* ☎ *910/692–2051* ⊕ *www.moorehistory.com* ☜ *Free* ⊙ *Tues.–Fri. 1–4.*

Weymouth Woods Sandhills Nature Preserve, on the eastern outskirts of town, is a 900-acre wildlife preserve with 4 mi of hiking trails. A staff naturalist will answer your questions about the beaver pond and other interesting sights. ⊠ *1024 N. Fort Bragg Rd., off U.S. 1* ☎ *910/692–2167* ⊕ *www.ncparks.net* ☜ *Free* ⊗ *Apr.–Oct., daily 8–8; Nov.–Mar., daily 8–6.*

OFF THE BEATEN PATH

3

Cameron. The town of Cameron, with a historic district on the National Register of Historic Places, has pockets that haven't changed all that much since the 19th century. This is the place to shop for antiques: approximately 60 antiques dealers operate out of 13 stores. Most shops are open Tuesday through Saturday 10 to 5, Sunday 1 to 5. The town holds antiques fairs with about 350 antique dealers twice a year on the first Saturday in October and May. ⊠ *Off U.S. 1, 12 mi north of Southern Pines* ☎ *910/245–7001 for information on antiques shops* ⊕ *www.antiquesofcameron.com.*

WHERE TO EAT

$$$–$$$$
STEAK
✕ **Lob Steer Inn.** Salad and dessert bars complement generous broiled seafood and prime-rib dinners at this casual, dimly lighted steak house. As you'd expect from the name, the surf and turf is a good bet. ⊠ *U.S. 1* ☎ *910/692–3503* ⊟ *AE, MC, V* ⊗ *No lunch.*

¢–$
AMERICAN
✕ **Sweet Basil.** This cozy corner café is run by a family whose considerable expertise is plain to see: lots of homemade breads, hefty loaded sandwiches, and lush salads. Special treats are the soups—especially the flavorful ginger-carrot and red-pepper varieties—and decadent desserts. ■ TIP→ Make sure to arrive early to avoid the lunch rush. ⊠ *134 N.W. Broad St.* ☎ *910/693–1487* ⊟ *MC, V* ⊗ *Closed Mon. and Sun. No dinner.*

WHERE TO STAY

$$$
⌨ **Mid Pines Inn & Golf Club.** In a building dating from 1921, this resort is the sibling of Pine Needles Lodge. On the premises is a Georgian-style clubhouse and a golf course designed by Donald Ross that has hosted numerous tournaments. The spacious rooms are filled with authentic antiques and good copies. Seven private villas with kitchenettes are also available. **Pros:** elegant historic setting has loads of charm. **Cons:** not a good fit for those who need modern decor and up-to-the-minute amenities. ⊠ *1010 Midland Rd.* ☎ *910/692–2114 or 800/323–2114* ⊕ *www.pineneedles-midpines.com* ⇆ *103 rooms, 7 villas* ⌂ *In-room: Wi-Fi. In-hotel: restaurants, bar, golf course, tennis courts, pool, gym* ⊟ *AE, D, MC, V* ⏍ *MAP.*

$$$$
⌨ **Pine Needles Lodge & Golf Club.** One of the bonuses of staying at this resort is the chance to meet Peggy Kirk Bell, a champion golfer who built the place with her late husband. The club, known for its excellent golf course, has hosted the U.S. Women's Open. The rooms are done in a rustic chalet style; many have exposed beams, pine paneling, and fireplaces. Private lodges with four bedrooms are great for families. **Pros:** rustic inn is a bit more relaxed than some of its neighbors. **Cons:** if you're looking for the ultimate luxury experience, this one probably isn't for you. ⊠ *1005 Midland Rd.* ☎ *910/692–7111 or 800/747–7272* ⊕ *www.pineneedles-midpines.com* ⇆ *78 rooms* ⌂ *In-room: Internet,*

Wi-Fi. In-hotel: restaurant, bar, golf course, tennis courts, pool, gym, bicycles ⊟*AE, MC, V* ⫶⊙⫶*MAP.*

SPORTS & THE OUTDOORS

GOLF **Club at Longleaf.** Photos from 30 years ago reveal how this golf course was built on the site of a steeplechase. Some elements of the horse track still can be spotted on Holes 1, 8, and 9. ⊠*10 N. Knoll Rd.* ☎*910/692–6100* ⊕*www.longleafgolf.com* ⛳*18 holes. 6098 yds. Par 71. Green Fee: $39–$90* ☞*Facilities: Driving range, putting green, pitching area, golf carts, pro shop, restaurant.*

Mid Pines Golf Club. This course, designed in 1921 by Donald Ross, has been completely restored. This course is shorter than at the Pine Needles Golf Club, but its hillier terrain means it provides an ample challenge. ⊠*1010 Midland Rd.* ☎*910/692–2114 or 800/323–2114* ⊕*www.pineneedles-midpines.com* ⛳*18 holes. 6528 yds. Par 72. Green Fee: $105–$180* ☞*Facilities: Driving range, putting green, pitching area, golf carts, rental clubs, pro shop, golf academy/lessons, restaurant, bar.*

Pine Needles Golf Club. A 2005 renovation restored the course to its original Donald Ross design featuring long line greens. The par-5 Hole 10 presents a particular challenge, with a sand trap along the inside curve of a dogleg. ⊠*1005 Midland Rd.* ☎*910/692–8611 or 800/747–7272* ⊕*www.pineneedles-midpines.com* ⛳*18 holes. 7015 yds. Par 71. Green Fee: $120–$195* ☞*Facilities: Driving range, putting green, pitching area, practice course, golf carts, pull carts, pro shop, golf academy/lessons, restaurant, bar.*

Talamore at Pinehurst. Now you can answer that age-old question, "Do llamas make good caddies?" The answer, as even the lowliest duffer at this course knows, is yes. They won't cough when you're putting, either. Architect Rees Jones probably didn't predict the presence of llamas here, but since their feet don't harm the grass, he probably wishes someone had thought of it sooner. ⊠*1595 Midland Rd.* ☎*910/692–5884 or 800/552–6292* ⊕*www.talamoregolfresort.com* ⛳*18 holes. 6025 yds. Par 71. Green Fee: $79–$129* ☞*Facilities: Driving range, rental clubs, rental carts, restaurant.*

SHOPPING

Regional authors read from their works at the **Country Bookshop** (⊠*140 N.W. Broad St. 28387* ☎*910/692–3211*). The store, in the historic downtown district, stocks a lot of everything, including books by Southern authors and children's books and puzzles.

PINEHURST

6 mi west of Southern Pines.

Pinehurst is a New England–style village with quiet, shaded streets and immaculately kept homes ranging from massive Victorians to tiny cottages. It was laid out in the late 1800s in a wagon-wheel pattern by landscape genius Frederick Law Olmsted, who also designed New York

City's Central Park. Annie Oakley lived here for a number of years, and while she was here headed the local gun club. Today Pinehurst is renowned for its golf courses.

GETTING HERE & AROUND

A manicured traffic circle directs travelers coming from five directions to the village center and resorts. Golf courses line the five-mile stretch of N.C. 22 (aka Midland Road) between Southern Pines and Pinehurst. The community's namesake resort is just east of the village center.

EXPLORING

The **Tufts Archives** recount the founding of Pinehurst in the letters, pictures, and news clippings, dating from 1895, of James Walker Tufts, who once served as president of the United States Golf Association. Pinehurst owes its origins to Tufts, who chose this area to build a health resort. ⊠ *Given Memorial Library, 150 Cherokee Rd.* ☎910/295–6022 or 910/295–3642 ⊠ *Free* ⊘ *Weekdays 9:30–5, Sat. 9:30–12:30.*

WHERE TO EAT

¢ ✕**Players Sports Café.** This casual spot is *the* place to meet for breakfast,
AMERICAN soups, sandwiches, and pizza. It's in the shop-filled Theater Building in the heart of the village. ⊠*100 W. Village Green* ☎910/215-9000 ⚠*Reservations not accepted* ▭AE, D, MC, V

$$–$$$ ✕**Theo's Taverna.** Behind some shops facing Chinquapin Road you'll
MEDITERRANEAN find this authentic taverna. It's as sunny as the Greek countryside from which owner Elias Dalitsouris hails. Fresh flowers, brightly colored artwork, vaulted ceilings, lots of windows, and outdoor seating on a garden patio draw diners; the made-from-scratch food, including breads and desserts, keeps them coming back. Seafood, lamb, paella, and Kobe beef are the specialties of the house. Wash it all down with strong Greek coffee served in traditional small cups. ⊠*140 Chinquapin Rd. 28370*☎*910/295–0780* ▭*AE, MC, V* ⊘*Closed Sun.*

WHERE TO STAY

$$$–$$$$ ☷**The Carolina.** In business since 1901, this stately hotel has never lost
Fodor'sChoice its turn-of-the-20th-century charm. Civilized pleasures await in the
★ spacious public rooms and elegantly traditional accommodations, on the rocker-lined wide verandas, and amid the gardens. You can tee off on one of eight golf courses or relax in the spa, with warm, dark wood accented by a moss-green-and-cream color scheme. The 45-room Manor Inn has the feel of a B&B; guests have access to all the resort facilities, including the formal Carolina Dining Room, with an eclectic menu. **Pros:** historic setting combined with attentive service and luxurious amenities make staying at the Carolina a special experience. **Cons:** the resort is geared to golfers and spa-goers with deep pockets, so bring plenty of cash. ⊠*1 Carolina Vista Dr.* ☎*910/295–6811 or 800/487–4653* ⊕*www.pinehurst.com* ➾*222 rooms, 89 condos* ⚠*In-room: Internet. In-hotel: 2 restaurants, room service, bar, golf courses, tennis courts, pools, gym, spa, water sports, bicycles, Wi-Fi, children's programs (ages 3–12)* ▭*AE, D, DC, MC, V.*

$$$–$$$$ ☷**The Holly Inn.** The first in the village, the Holly has crown molding, elegant lighting, and other architectural features that recall the 1890s.

Luxuries include silk-covered hangers, embroidered robes, and afternoon sandwiches, cookies, and iced tea. The menu at the 1895 Grille, the restaurant, changes seasonally and serves a semi-formal breakfast and dinner. Inventive entrées include Parmesan-roasted chicken breast, Dijon-and-herb-crusted lamb, and veal tenderloin. Jackets are required at the restaurant. The more casual Tavern, known for its caramelized five-onion soup, has a pub atmosphere and a patio. **Pros:** historic inn is beautiful and a bit less imposing than its sister property. **Cons:** folks looking for the ultimate Pinehurst experience might prefer staying closer to the golf course. ⊠*155 Cherokee Rd.* ☎*910/295–6811 or 800/487–4653* ⊕*www.pinehurst.com* ⇨*78 rooms, 7 suites* ⋒*In-room: Internet. In-hotel: 2 restaurants, room service, bar, golf courses, tennis courts, pool, Wi-Fi* ⊟*AE, D, DC, MC, V* ¶⊙*MAP.*

$–$$ 🔲**Magnolia Inn.** This 112-year-old inn, once just a hangout for golfing buddies, now draws a more diverse crowd after being tastefully decorated with unusual antiques. Bathrooms have original fixtures such as claw-foot tubs. The inn's dining rooms, with their butter-yellow walls and fireplaces, are cozy. The regional menu includes shrimp and grits and blackened North Carolina catfish as well as sea bass and filet mignon. There's also an English-style pub. **Pros:** cozy and historic, and the food is well regarded. **Cons:** older bathrooms may not be up to some travelers' standards. ⊠*65 Magnolia Rd.* ☎*910/295–6900 or 800/526–5562* ⊕*www.themagnoliainn.com* ⇨*11 rooms* ⋒*In-hotel: restaurant* ⊟*AE, MC, V* ¶⊙*BP.*

¢–$ 🔲**Pine Crest Inn.** Chintz and mahogany fill the rooms of this slightly faded gem. The chefs whip up meals reminiscent of Sunday supper: homemade soups, fresh fish dishes, and the house specialty, a 22-ounce pork chop. Mr. B's Lounge is one of the liveliest nightspots in town. Guests have golf and tennis privileges at local clubs. **Pros:** restaurant gets high marks, and the bar's casual atmosphere is a contrast to the more formal settings at most area hotels. **Cons:** nonsmokers note that smoking is allowed in the bar; if you want a large room, request one, as some are small. ⊠*50 Dogwood Rd., Box 879* ☎*910/295–6121 or 800/371–2545* ⊕*www.pinecrestinnpinehurst.com* ⇨*40 rooms* ⋒*In-hotel: restaurant, bar* ⊟*AE, D, MC, V* ¶⊙*MAP.*

SPORTS & THE OUTDOORS

GOLF   **Pinehurst Resort.** Pinehurst has been the site of more championships than any other golf resort in the country. The eight courses—unfortunately known by their numbers—can bring a tear to a golfer's eye with their beauty. The courses range from the first, designed in 1898 by Donald Ross, to the most recent, designed in 1996 by Tom Fazio to mark the resort's centennial. The hilly terrain of Course Seven, completely renovated in 2003, makes it especially tough. ⊠*1 Carolina Vista Dr.* ☎*910/235–8125 or 800/487–4653* ⊕*www.pinehurst.com* ⚐*8 18-hole courses. Average of 6600 yds. Par 70–72. Green Fee: $89–$410* ⚘*Facilities: Driving range, putting green, pitching area, golf carts, caddies, rental clubs, pro shop, golf academy/lessons, restaurant, bar.*

Pit Golf Links. Designed by Pinehurst native Dan F. Maples, this course runs through 230 acres of an abandoned sand quarry. ✉ *410 Pit Link La., Hwy. 5* ☎*910/944–1600 or 800/574–4653* ⊕*www.pitgolf.com* ⚑*18 holes. 7007 yds. Par 72. Green Fee: $64–$119* ☞*Facilities: Driving range, putting green, pitching area, golf carts, pro shop, golf academy/ lessons, restaurant, bar.*

TENNIS The **Lawn and Tennis Club of North Carolina** (✉*1 Merrywood Pl.* ☎*910/692–7270*) has seven clay courts and a swimming pool.

3

SEAGROVE

★ *35 mi northwest of Pinehurst.*

Potters, some of whom are carrying on traditions that have been in their families for generations and others who are newer to the art, handcraft mugs, bowls, pitchers, platters, vases, and clay "face jugs" in the Seagrove area. Some of the work of local artisans is exhibited in national museums, including the Smithsonian. More than 90 potteries are scattered along and off Route 705 and U.S. 220. The annual Seagrove Pottery Festival, held in November, is always a much-anticipated event.

GETTING HERE & AROUND

A chance to meander is part of the Seagrove area's draw. If you're coming from Charlotte, take N.C. 49 or Interstate 85 east to U.S. 64, Take U.S. 64 east to U.S. 220 and follow U.S. 220 south to the town of Seagrove and the North Carolina Pottery Center, which is a good starting point. From the Triangle, take U.S. 64 west, then U.S. 220 south. No matter where you come from, you'll see signs directing you to potteries before you reach the town of Seagrove. Stop, check them out and see where the traveler's spirit leads.

EXPLORING

★ The **North Carolina Pottery Center** exhibits pottery from all around the state. You can pick up maps of the various studios around the area. ✉*250 East Ave., 27341* ☎*336/873–8430* ⊕*www.ncpotterycenter. com* ✉*$2* ☉*Tues.–Sat. 10–4.*

ASHEBORO

13 mi north of Seagrove; 23 mi south of Greensboro.

Asheboro, the seat of Randolph County, sits in the Uwharrie National Forest, which is popular with those who like hiking, biking, and horseback riding. At 500 million years old, the Uwharries are the oldest mountain range in North America. This part of the southern Piedmont is a lovely place to view scenery and visit crafts shops.

GETTING HERE & AROUND

U.S. 220 and U.S. 64 intersect just south of Asheboro, providing easy access from all directions. The N.C. Zoo, the area's most popular attraction, is southeast of town. To reach it, follow U.S. 220 south and go east on N.C. 159.

ESSENTIALS

Visitor Information Randolph County Tourism Development Authority (⊠ *222 Sunset Ave., Suite 108, Asheboro* ☎ *800/626-2672* ⊕ *www.visitrandol-phcounty.com*).

EXPLORING

★ The 1,500-acre **North Carolina Zoo,**
☺ home to more than 1,100 animals representing more than 250 species, was the first zoo in the country designed from the get-go as a natural-habitat facility. It includes more than five miles of walking trails. The park includes the 300-acre African pavilion, which features the new Watani Grasslands elephant exhibit, a 200-acre North American habitat with polar bears and grizzlies, and an interactive kids zone. ■ TIP➔ **This is a massive park, so take advantage of the tram that connects the various areas.** ⊠ *4401 Zoo Pkwy.* ☎ *336/879-7000 or 800/488-0444* ⊕ *www.nczoo.org* 🎟 *$10* ⊙ *Apr.–Sept., daily 9–5; Oct.–Mar., daily 9–4.*

> ### WORD OF MOUTH
>
> "One word about the Asheboro zoo—it isn't like the Bronx Zoo or the National Zoo, if that's what you're used to. In Asheboro, many of the animals have large habitats, so it's quite possible that the animals will be hanging out in a part of their habitat that makes them a little more difficult (and occasionally, almost impossible) to see. It's much more humane to the animals, but it can make for a surprising viewing experience, if you were expecting the animal to be in a 10' x 10' cage in front of you at all times."
>
> —kgh8m

OFF THE BEATEN PATH

Town Creek Indian Mound Historic Site. About 30 mi south of Asheboro, this historic site is a glimpse into North Carolina's pre-Columbian past. A self-guided tour takes you through reconstructions of buildings that belonged to the Pee Dee people. Guided tours are available on weekends or by appointment. Excavations of the site began in 1937 and are still in progress. ⊠ *509 Town Creek Mound Rd., Mt. Gilead* ☎ *910/439-6802* ⊕ *www.nchistoricsites.org/town* 🎟 *Free* ⊙ *Tues.–Sat. 9–5, Sun. 1–5.*

The North Carolina Mountains

WORD OF MOUTH

"My favorite time [in the mountains] is late April through May. You can always hit rain during the spring, but the crowds are much less, flowers are starting to bloom and the waterfalls are at their best. We always try to go during the week (avoiding the crowded weekends). The fall is definitely the prettiest and probably best weather-wise . . ."

—maj

By Lan Sluder   **THE MAJESTIC PEAKS, MEADOWS, BALDS,** and valleys of the Appalachian, Blue Ridge, and Great Smoky Mountains epitomize the western corner of North Carolina. The Great Smoky Mountains National Park, national forests, handmade-crafts centers, Asheville's eclectic and sophisticated pleasures, the astonishing Biltmore Estate, and the Blue Ridge Parkway are the area's main draws, providing prime opportunities for shopping, skiing, hiking, bicycling, camping, fishing, canoeing, and just taking in the views.

The city of Asheville is one of the stops on the counterculture trail and a center of the New Age movement, as well as being a popular retirement area. Its restaurants regularly make the TV food show circuit. Thanks to their monied seasonal residents and long histories as resorts, even smaller towns like Highlands, Cashiers, Flat Rock, and Hendersonville are surprisingly sophisticated, boasting restaurants with daring chefs and professional summer theater. In the High Country, where summer temperatures are as much as 15 degrees cooler than in the flatlands, and where snow skiing is a major draw in winter, affluent retirees and hip young entrepreneurs bring a panache to even the most rural enclaves.

Some of the most important arts and culture movements of the 20th century, including abstract Impressionist painting and the Beat movement, had roots just east of Asheville, at Black Mountain College, where in the 1930s and 1940s the notables included famed artists Josef Albers, Willem de Kooning, and Robert Motherwell, dancemeisters John Cage and Merce Cunningham, thinker Buckminster Fuller, architect Walter Gropius, and writers Charles Olson and Paul Goodman.

ORIENTATION & PLANNING

GETTING ORIENTED

The buzz about the North Carolina mountains dates back to the early 19th century, when wealthy Lowcountry planters flocked to the highlands to escape the summer heat. Today visitors still come here to enjoy the cool, green mountains and all the activities they provide—hiking, camping, fishing, boating, and just marveling at the scenery. Asheville, the hub of the mountain region, is one of the biggest small cities you'll ever visit, with the artsy élan and dynamic downtown of a much larger burg.

Asheville. Set in a valley surrounded by the highest mountains in Eastern America, Asheville is a base for exploring the region, but it is also a destination unto itself. Here you can tour America's largest home and discover why Asheville has a national reputation for its arts, crafts, and music scenes. Coffee houses, brewpubs, sidewalk cafés, boutiques, antiques shops, clubs, and galleries are everywhere in the city's art deco downtown. Just a short drive away are inviting small mountain towns, mile-high vistas that will take your breath away, and enough high-energy outdoor fun to keep your heart rate way up.

TOP REASONS TO GO

Biltmore Estate: The 250-room Biltmore House, modeled after the great Renaissance châteaus of the Loire Valley in France, is the largest private home in America. The 8,000-acre estate, with extensive gardens, deluxe hotel, and restaurants, is the most-visited attraction in North Carolina.

Blue Ridge Parkway: This winding two-lane road, which ends at the edge of the Great Smokies and shows off the highest mountains in eastern America, is the most scenic drive in the South.

Asheville: Hip, artsy, sometimes funky, with scores of restaurants and active nightlife, Asheville is one of America's coolest places to live, and visit.

Engaging small towns: You could easily fall in love with the charm, style, and Southern hospitality of Black Mountain, Blowing Rock, Brevard, and Hendersonville, to name a few.

Mountain arts and crafts: The mountains are a center of handmade art and crafts, with more than 4,000 working craftspeople. Two nationally noted crafts schools—the Penland School of Crafts and John C. Campbell Folk School—are also in the region.

4

The High Country. The High Country is the snow skiing area of the mountains. Boone, Beech Mountain (the highest-elevation incorporated community east of the Mississippi River), Blowing Rock, and Seven Devils together have four ski resorts. Summers here are noticeably cooler than elsewhere in the Southeast, and the mountain scenery notably dramatic.

The Southern Mountains. The Southern Mountains is comprised of towns in North Carolina south of Asheville, including Hendersonville, Flat Rock, Brevard, and also the chic enclaves of Lake Toxaway, Cashiers, and Highlands. These towns are diverse in terms of size, elevation, and attractiveness. If they have anything in common, it is high real estate prices and a reputation as summer getaways for well-to-do flatlanders.

THE NORTH CAROLINA MOUNTAINS PLANNER

WHEN TO GO

Western North Carolina is a four-season destination. Dates for high season vary from hotel to hotel, but generally it's from Memorial Day through early November. It's most difficult to get a hotel reservation, especially on weekends, in October, which is peak leaf-peeping time. Mid-June to mid-August draws a lot of families, since kids are out of school. Around ski resorts, winter, especially the Christmas season and the months of January and February, is prime time; elsewhere, these winter months are dead, and some hotels are closed.

GETTING HERE & AROUND

BY AIR Asheville Regional Airport (AVL), one of the most pleasant and most modern airports in the South, is served by Delta Connection, Continental Express, Northwest, and US Airways Express. Most of the flights are in one-class regional jets. In 2005 the airport completed a

$20-million expansion and improvement project, and additional major improvements were made in 2007–2008. There are nonstop flights to and from Atlanta, Charlotte, Cincinnati, Detroit, Houston, Minneapolis, and Newark. US Airways Express serves the Hickory Airport (HKY), about 40 mi from Blowing Rock.

BY CAR Interstate 40 runs east–west through Asheville. Interstate 26 runs from Charleston, South Carolina, to Asheville and, partly on a temporary route, continues northwest into Tennessee. Interstate 240 forms a perimeter around the city. U.S. 19/23 is a major north and west route. The Blue Ridge Parkway runs northeast from Great Smoky Mountains National Park to Shenandoah National Park in Virginia, passing Cherokee, Asheville, and the High Country. U.S. 221 runs north to the Virginia border through Blowing Rock and Boone and intersects Interstate 40 at Marion. U.S. 321 intersects Interstate 40 at Hickory and heads to Blowing Rock and Boone.

ESSENTIALS **Airport Information Asheville Regional Airport** (*AVL* ✉ *708 Airport Rd., Fletcher* ☎ *828/684–2226* ⊕ *www.flyavl.com*). **Hickory Airport** (*HKY* ✉ *3101 9th Ave. Dr. NW* ☎ *828/323–7408* ⊕ *www.hickorygov.com/airport*).

Visitor Information North Carolina High Country Host (✉ *1701 Blowing Rock Rd., Boone* ☎ *828/264–1299 or 800/438–7500* ⊕ *www.visitboonenc.com*).

ABOUT THE RESTAURANTS

You can still get traditional mountain food, served family-style, at inns around the region. Increasingly, though, mountain cooks are offering more sophisticated fare. Asheville chefs, trained at leading culinary programs, are creating innovative dishes. At many places the emphasis is on "slow food"—made with locally grown, often organic, ingredients. You can find nearly every world cuisine somewhere in the region, from Thai to Jamaican to northern Indian.

ABOUT THE HOTELS

Around the mountains, at least in the larger cities and towns such as Asheville, Hendersonville, and Boone, you can find the usual chain motels and hotels. For more of a local flavor, look at the many mountain lodges and country inns, some with just a few rooms with simple comforts, others with upmarket amenities like tennis courts, golf courses, and spas. Bed-and-breakfasts bloom in the mountains like wildflowers, and there are literally scores of B&Bs in the region; Asheville alone has more than three dozen. The mountains also have a few large resorts, of which the Grove Park Inn in Asheville is the prime example. Visiting in the off-season can save you a third or more on hotel rates.

WHAT IT COSTS					
	¢	$	$$	$$$	$$$$
Restaurant	under $10	$10–$14	$15–$19	$20–$24	over $24
Hotel	under $100	$100–$150	$151–$200	$201–$250	over $250

Restaurant prices are for a main course at dinner. Hotel prices are for two people in a standard double room in high season.

PLANNING YOUR TIME

The Asheville area makes a convenient base for day visits to Hendersonville, Brevard, and even Cashiers and Highlands. Of course, if you want to see these areas more completely, you're better off spending the night in one or several of these Southern Mountains towns. Likewise, it's easy to make day trips to the Great Smoky Mountain National Park from Asheville. The Oconaluftee entrance to the Smokies is only an hour and 15 minutes' drive from downtown Asheville. But, if you want to spend several days or longer in the Smokies you'll be better off staying in the park or at one of the small towns at the edge of it, such as Bryson City or Waynesville. ⇨ *For more information about the park, see Chapter 5: Great Smoky Mountains National Park.* The High Country is too far away for a comfortable day visit from Asheville, especially considering the winding mountain roads and possible weather conditions (snow in winter and fog almost anytime). To explore the High Country in detail, you'll want to make your headquarters in the appealing college town of Boone or one of the other towns nearby, such as Blowing Rock or Banner Elk.

4

ASHEVILLE

Asheville is the hippest city in the South. At least that's the claim of Asheville's fans, who are legion. Visitors flock to Asheville to experience the arts and culture scene, which rivals that of Santa Fe, and to experience the city's blossoming downtown, with its myriad restaurants, coffeehouses, museums, galleries, bookstores, antiques shops, and boutiques.

Named "the best place to live" by many books and magazines, Asheville is also the destination for retirees escaping the cold North, or of "halfbacks," those who moved to Florida but who are now coming half the way back to the North. Old downtown buildings have been converted to upmarket condos for these affluent retirees, and, despite the housing slowdown, new residential developments are springing up south, east, and west of town. As a result of this influx, Asheville has a much more cosmopolitan population than most cities of its size (70,000 people in the city, about 400,000 in the metro area).

Asheville has a diversity you won't find in many cities in the South. There's a thriving gay community, many aging hippies, and young alternative-lifestyle seekers. People for the Ethical Treatment of Animals (PETA) has named Asheville the most vegetarian-friendly city in America.

The city really comes alive at night, with the restaurants, sidewalk cafés, and coffeehouses; so visit after dark to see the city at its best. Especially on warm summer weekends, Pack Square, Biltmore Avenue, Haywood Street, Wall Street, and Battery Park Avenue are busy until well after midnight.

GETTING HERE & AROUND

From the east and west, the main route to Asheville is I-40. The most scenic route to Asheville is via the Blue Ridge Parkway, which meanders between Shenandoah National Park in Virginia and the Great Smoky

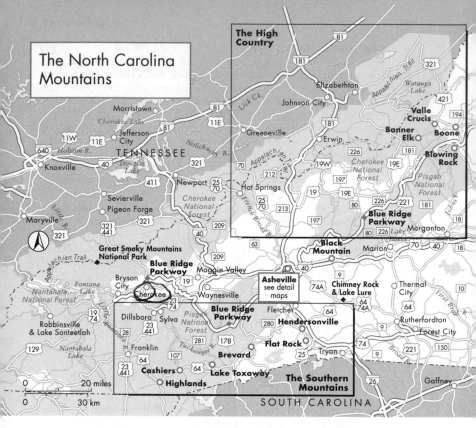

Mountains National Park near Cherokee, NC. I–240 forms a freeway perimeter around Asheville, and Pack Square is the center of the city.

While a car is virtually a necessity to explore Asheville thoroughly, the city does have a metropolitan bus system with 24 routes radiating from the Transit Center in downtown. Asheville also has a sightseeing trolley service; tickets are available at the Asheville Convention and Visitors Bureau. Asheville is highly walkable, and the best way to see downtown is on foot.

ESSENTIALS

Visitor Information Asheville Convention and Visitors Bureau (✉ *36 Montford Ave., Box 1010* ☎ *828/258–6101 or 888/247–9811* ⊕ *www.exploreasheville.com*).

DOWNTOWN ASHEVILLE

A city of neighborhoods, Asheville rewards careful exploration, especially on foot. You can break up your sightseeing with stops at the more than 50 restaurants in downtown alone, and at any of hundreds of unique shops.

Downtown Asheville has the largest extant collection of art deco buildings in the Southeast outside of Miami Beach, most notably the S&W

Cafeteria (1929), Ash... ...st Baptist Church
(1927), an... ...nown for its archi-
...neo-Georgian; the
...of St. Lawrence
...y known as Old
...e.

Cherokee
51 mi west of Asheville
Blue Ridge Parkway
Medicine Man Crafts
_Q144?_

...se–head archi-
...chitect Rafael
...d in 1908. It
...k and poly-
...Catalan-style
...042 ☎ Free

❷

...ntain Col-
r. ...e develop-
m. ...d literary
in ...t lifetime
...henberg,
Jo... ...us, and Franz Kline;
dai... ...ian John Cage; filmmaker Arthur
Pen... ...nth Noland, Charles Olson, and Robert Creeley.
A m... ...um and gallery dedicated to the history of the radical college
occupies a small space in downtown Asheville. It puts on occasional
exhibits and publishes material about the college. Call ahead to find out
what's currently happening. ✉ _54 Broadway, Downtown_ ☎ _828/299–
9306_ ⊕ _www.blackmountaincollege.org_ ✉ _Varies, depending on the
exhibit; usually $5–$10_ ⊙ _Wed.–Sat. noon–4._

❺ **Grove Arcade Public Market.** When it opened in 1929, the Grove Arcade
was trumpeted as "the most elegant building in America" by its builder,
W. E. Grove, the man also responsible for the Grove Park Inn. With the
coming of the Great Depression and World War II, the Grove Arcade
evolved into a dowdy government building. In late 2002 its polished
limestone elegance was restored, and it reopened as a public market
patterned in some ways after Pike Place Market in Seattle. The market covers a full city block and has about 50 locally owned stores and
restaurants, along with apartments and office space. A new Arts &
Heritage Gallery features interactive exhibits and regional crafts and
music. The building is an architectural wonder, with gargoyles galore,
and well worth a visit even if you don't shop or dine here. ✉ _1 Page
Ave., Downtown_ ☎ _828/252–7799_ ⊕ _www.grovearcade.com_ ✉ _Free_
⊙ _Mon.–Sat. 10–6, Sun. noon–5; store hrs vary._

❶ **Pack Place Education, Arts & Science Center.** This 92,000-square-foot complex in downtown Asheville houses the **Asheville Art Museum, Colburn Earth Science Museum, Health Adventure,** and **Diana Wortham
Theatre.** The **YMI Cultural Center,** also maintained by Pack Place,
and focusing on the history of African-Americans in western North
Carolina, is across the street. The Health Adventure has 11 galler-

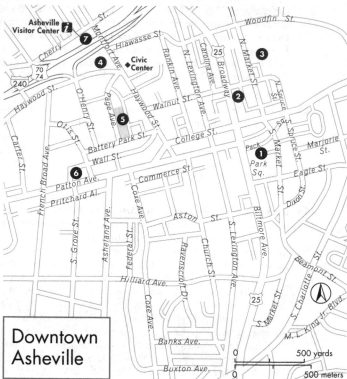

Downtown
Asheville

ies with hands-on exhibits, all of interest to children. The Asheville Art Museum stages major exhibits several times a year, with some highlighting regional artists. The Colburn Earth Science Museum displays local gems and minerals. The intimate 500-seat Diana Wortham Theatre hosts musical concerts and dance and theater performances year-round. ⊠*2 S. Pack Sq., Downtown* ☎*828/257–4500* ⊕*www. packplace.org* ⊠*Art museum $6, Health Adventure $8.50, earth science museum $4, YMI Cultural Center $5* ☉*Tues.–Sat. 10–5, Sun. 1–5 (art museum open until 8 Fri.).*

❸ **Thomas Wolfe Memorial.** Asheville's most famous son, novelist Thomas
Fodor'sChoice Wolfe (1900–38), grew up in a 29-room Queen Anne–style home that
★ his mother ran as a boardinghouse. The house, a state historic site, was badly damaged in a 1998 fire (a still-unsolved case of arson); it reopened in mid-2004 following a painstaking $2.4 million renovation. Though about one-fourth of the furniture and artifacts were lost in the fire, the house—memorialized as "Dixieland" in Wolfe's novel *Look Homeward, Angel*—has been restored to its original 1916 condition, including a light canary yellow paint on the exterior. You'll find a visitor center and many displays, and there are guided tours of the house and heirloom gardens. The admission, at only a dollar, is one of the

best bargains in town. ✉*52 Market St., Downtown* ☎*828/253–8304* ⊕*www.wolfememorial.com* ☜*$1* ⊙*Tues.–Sat. 9–5, Sun. 1–5.*

WORTH NOTING

7 **Asheville Historic Trolley Tour.** A motorized trolley bus takes you to the main points of interest around Asheville, including the Grove Park Inn, Biltmore Village, the Thomas Wolfe Memorial, the Montford area, the River Arts District, and Pack Square and downtown. You can buy tickets and board the trolley at the Asheville Convention and Visitors Bureau and get on or off at any stop on this 80-minute narrated tour. Reservations are available but usually aren't necessary. Ghost Tours on Saturday nights at 7:30 from March to November explore Asheville's supernatural side. It will take you past spooky sights like as the notorious murder site at Battery Park and phantoms on Church Street ✉*Asheville Convention and Visitors Bureau, 36 Montford Ave.* ☎*888/667–3600* ⊕*www.ashevilletrolleytours.com* ☜*$19; ghost tours, $20.*

6 **National Climatic Data Center (NCDC).** The world's largest active archive of global weather data, the National Climatic Data Center provides weather data to researchers all over the world. The NCDC gathers and maintains weather data from some 10,000 weather stations around the U.S., and some of its historical data goes back over 200 years. Users of the data range from large engineering firms planning energy-efficient development to individuals planning a retirement move. ■**TIP→ At present, only group tours of the center are available, and must be arranged in advance.** ✉*Federal Plaza, 151 Patton Ave., Downtown* ☎*828/271–4800* (for group tours, 828/271–4203) ⊕*www.ncdc.noaa.gov* ☜*Free* ⊙*Weekdays 8–4:30.*

GREATER ASHEVILLE

North Asheville, the historic Montford section (home to more than a dozen B&Bs), and the Grove Park neighborhood all have fine Victorian-era homes, including many remarkable Queen Anne houses. Biltmore Village, across from the entrance to the Biltmore Estate, was constructed at the time that Biltmore House was being built, and is now predominantly an area of retail boutiques and galleries. The River District, along the French Broad River, is an up-and-coming arts area, with many studios and lofts. Across the river, West Asheville has suddenly become the hottest part of the city, with its main artery, Haywood Road, sporting new restaurants, edgy stores, and popular clubs, though much of West Asheville retains its low-key, slightly scruffy, 1950s ambience.

TOP ATTRACTIONS

Fodor's Choice ★ **Biltmore Estate.** Built in the 1890s as the private home of George Vanderbilt, the astonishing 250-room French-Renaissance château is America's largest private residence. (Some of Vanderbilt's descendants still live on the estate, but the bulk of the home and grounds are open to visitors.) Richard Morris Hunt designed it, and Frederick Law Olmsted landscaped the original 125,000-acre estate (now 8,000 acres), which faces Biltmore Village. It took 1,000 workers five years to complete the gargantuan project. On view are the priceless antiques and art collected by the Vanderbilts, including notable paintings by Renoir and John Singer Sargent, along with 75 acres of gardens and formally landscaped grounds. You can also see the state-of-the-art winery and an 1890s-era farm, River Bend. Candlelight tours of the house are offered at Christmastime. Also on the grounds are a deluxe hotel, five restaurants open to the public, and an equestrian center. Each year in August, Biltmore Estate hosts music concerts with nationally known entertainers such as B.B. King and REO Speedwagon. Biltmore House's fourth floor, whose rooms are now open to the public, includes an observatory with sweeping views of the surrounding landscape, an architectural model room housing Hunt's 1889 model of the house, and servants' bedrooms and meeting hall, so you can see how the staff lived. Most people tour the house on their own, but guided tours are available ($15 additional). Note that there are a lot of stairs to climb, but much of the house is accessible for guests in wheelchairs or with limited mobility. ■TIP→ **If possible, avoid visiting on weekends during fall color season and the weeks between Thanksgiving and Christmas, when crowds are at their largest. Save by booking online rather than buying at the gate.** Saturday admission prices are higher than weekday rates, but, if you come back, the second visit in two days is only $10. The best deal is the annual pass, allowing unlimited admission for a year and costing only about twice as much as a one-day admission. ⌧ *Exit 50 off I–40, South Metro* ☎ *828/255–1700 or 800/411–3812* ⊕ *www.biltmore.com* ⌧ *$47, Sun.–Fri.; $51, Sat.; $59 flex ticket for any day of the year; $99 unlimited visit annual pass; $15 extra for guided group tours of the house; $150 extra for premium tour with personal guide and visits to areas not normally open to the public.* ⊙ *Admission gate and reception and ticket center: Jan.–Mar., daily 9–4; Apr.–Oct., daily 8:30–5; Nov.–Dec. 8:30–8.*

Biltmore Village. Across from the Biltmore Estate, Biltmore Village is a highly walkable collection of restored English village–style houses, now mostly shops and galleries. Badly flooded in 2004, with many buildings damaged and shops closed, the Village has come back to life, with nearly all shops now reopened. Of particular note is **All Souls Cathedral**, one of the most beautiful churches in America. It was designed by Richard Morris Hunt following the traditional Norman cross plan and opened in 1896. ⌧ *3 Angle St., South Metro* ☎ *828/274–2681* ⌧ *Free* ⊙ *Daily, hrs vary.*

CLOSE UP

Biltmore Boasts

The Biltmore Estate is North Carolina's leading tourist attraction and boasts many superlatives. Biltmore Estate:

■ Is the largest private home in America, with 250 rooms in 175,000 square feet of living space.

■ Is America's most-visited historic house, followed by Mount Vernon, Hearst Castle, and Graceland, with more than 1 million visitors annually.

■ Has appeared in over a dozen movies, including *The Swan* (1956), *Richie Rich* (1994), *Forrest Gump* (1994), *Patch Adams* (1998), and *Hannibal* (2001).

■ Has been visited by U.S. Presidents William McKinley, Woodrow Wilson, and Richard Nixon.

■ Had many innovations rarely seen at the time, including fire alarms, elevators, an intercom system, and centrally controlled clocks.

■ Has its own bowling alley, 70,000-gallon indoor swimming pool, 10,000-volume library, and fully equipped gym.

■ Has more than 1,600 employees, making it one of Asheville's largest private employers.

4

Fodor'sChoice **North Carolina Arboretum.** Part of the original Biltmore Estate, these 434 acres completed Frederick Law Olmsted's dream of creating a world-class arboretum in the western part of North Carolina. Highlights include southern Appalachian flora in stunning settings, such as the Blue Ridge Quilt Garden, with bedding plants arranged in patterns reminiscent of Appalachian quilts, and sculptures set among the gardens. An extensive network of trails is available for walking or mountain biking. A bonsai exhibit features miniature versions of many native trees. The 16,000-square-foot Baker Exhibit Center, which opened in late 2007, hosts traveling exhibits on art, science, and history. ■TIP→**For an unusual view of the arboretum, try the Segway tour, where you can glide through the forest for two hours on the gyroscopically controlled "Human Transporter" invented by Dean Kamen.** The cost ($45 weekdays, $55 Saturdays) includes training on the Segway. Riders must be at least 18 years old and weigh between 80 and 250 pounds. Tours are at 10 and 2 Monday–Saturday. ⊠ *100 Frederick Law Olmsted Way, 10 mi southwest of downtown Asheville, at Blue Ridge Pkwy. (MM 393), near I–26 and I–40, South Metro* ☎ *828/665–2492* ⊕ *www.ncarboretum. org* ⊠ *$6 per car parking fee; free Tues.* ☉ *Visitor education center: Mon.–Sat. 9–5, Sun. noon–5. Gardens and grounds: Apr.–Oct., daily 8* AM*–9* PM*; Nov.–Mar., daily 8* AM*–7* PM.

WNC Farmers Market. The highest-volume farmers' market in North Carolina is a great place to buy local jams, jellies, honey, stone-ground grits and cornmeal, and, in season, local fruits and vegetables. In spring look for ramps, a wild cousin of the onion with a very strong odor. A wholesale section below the main retail section (both are open to all) offers produce in bulk. ⊠ *570 Brevard Rd., 5 mi southwest of downtown Asheville, off I–40, South Metro* ☎ *828/253–1691* ⊠ *Free* ☉ *Apr.–Oct., daily 8–6; Nov.–Mar., daily 8–5.*

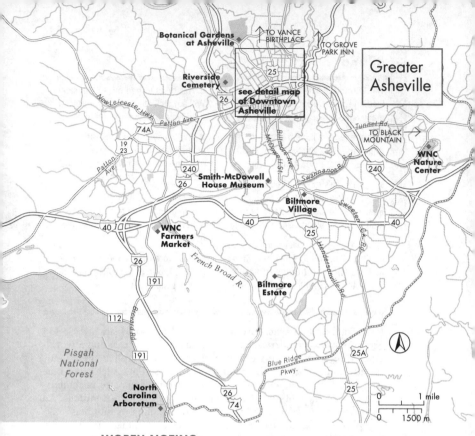

WORTH NOTING

Asheville Urban Trail. This 1.7-mi walk developed by the City of Asheville has about 30 "stations," with plaques marking places of historical or architectural interest. The self-guided tour begins at Pack Place Education, Arts & Science Center. ■**TIP**➔To enhance your walking experience, rent an audio guide at the Asheville Art Museum, which is part of the Pack Place complex. From April to November, guided group tours leaving from park Place are usually scheduled at 10:30 and 3 on Saturday, weather permitting. ⊠*2 S. Pack Sq., at Pack Place, Asheville Art Museum* ☎*828/258–0710* ⊕*www.urbantrails.net* ☞*Audio guide $5, tour $5.*

Botanical Gardens at Asheville. Adjoining the University of North Carolina at Asheville campus, this 10-acre site has walking trails and displays of native plants, including a bog with carnivorous plants such as Venus flytraps, pitcher plants, and sundew. ■**TIP**➔It's a fine place for a picnic, and not far from the busy downtown. ⊠*151 Weaver Blvd., at Broadway, 2 mi north of downtown Asheville, North Metro* ☎*828/252–5190* ⊕*www.ashevillebotanicalgardens.org* ☞*Free* ☉*Daily dawn–dusk.*

★ **Grove Park Inn.** This large resort overlooking Asheville is well worth a visit even if you don't stay here, as eight U.S. presidents have. The oldest section was built in 1912–13 using huge, locally mined granite stones, some weighing 10,000 pounds. It was modeled after the grand railroad hotels in the American West. Inside there's the largest collection of Arts and Crafts furniture in the world. On the grounds are two small but interesting museums. The **North Carolina Homespun Museum** (⊕*www.grovewood.com/homespun_museum.php*) tells the story of a training school established by the Vanderbilt family (of Biltmore Estate fame) to revive interest in native crafts. A collection of antique cars assembled by a local car dealer is the main feature of the **Estes-Winn Memorial Automobile Museum** (⊕*www.grovewood.com/car_museum.php*). Grovewood Gallery, also on the resort grounds in a 1917 English-style cottage, showcases the work of some 500 craftspeople and artists. ■**TIP**→If you visit in the cooler months, be sure to warm yourself in front of the two enormous stone fireplaces in the inn's lobby. ⊠*290 Macon Ave., North Metro* ☎*800/438–5800 or 828/252–2711* ⊕*www.groveparkinn.com* ✆*Free* ⊙*Hotel daily 24 hrs; Homespun Museum and Estes-Winn Automobile Museum Apr.–Dec., Mon.–Sat 10–5, Sun. 11–5.*

Riverside Cemetery. Authors Thomas Wolfe and O. Henry are buried here, along with about 13,000 others, including some of Asheville's most prominent citizens. The 87-acre cemetery, overlooking the French Broad River in the historic Montford area, has flower gardens and ancient oaks and poplars. ■**TIP**→ Take the drive through the cemetery, where signs direct you to the graves of noted people. ⊠*Birch St. off Pearson Dr., North Metro* ☎*828/258–8480.*

Smith-McDowell House Museum. This is the oldest surviving brick house in Asheville, dating from 1840. The grounds were designed by Frederick Law Olmsted in 1900. The interior has much of the house's original Greek Revival woodwork, and restored rooms date from 1840 to 1900. Exhibits in the gallery focus on Asheville's early history. On the grounds is the Buncombe County Civil War Memorial, listing the names of the 551 soldiers from Buncombe County who died in the war. From mid-November to early January the house has Victorian Christmas displays, and it also hosts the campy Aluminum Christmas Tree Museum, a collection of pop-culture trees from the 1950s and '60s. ⊠*283 Victoria Rd., East Metro* ☎*828/253–9231* ⊕*www.wnchistory. org* ✆*$7 Jan.–Nov., $10 Dec.* ⊙*Thurs.–Sat. 10–4; extended hours during Christmas season.*

Vance Birthplace. A reconstructed pioneer cabin and outbuildings mark the childhood home of Zebulon Vance, three-time governor of North Carolina and United States senator from 1879 to 1894. You can tour the site, which is representative of more prosperous mountain homesteads during the early 19th century. ⊠*911 Reems Creek Rd., 13 mi north of downtown Asheville, North Metro* ☎*828/645–6706* ✆*Free* ⊙*Apr.–Oct., Tues.–Sat. 9–5; Nov.–Mar., Tues.–Sat. 10–4.*

☼ **WNC Nature Center.** On a 42-acre Natural Heritage site, the WNC Nature Center is one of the region's most popular attractions for kids. It's basically a zoo focusing on animals native to the region, with cougars, bobcats, black bears, white-tailed deer, gray and red wolves, and

Carolina Arts & Crafts

A century ago, as young George Vanderbilt prepared to build a retreat in then-bucolic Asheville, he and an architect traveled the French countryside, looking at 16th-century Loire Valley châteaus for inspiration. Craftspeople labored to create the resulting Biltmore Mansion, including its unlikely gargoyles and grotesques.

The lesson is, when it comes to arts and crafts in western North Carolina, expect the unexpected. Sometimes handmade treasures are found out in the open: more than 85 crafts fairs are held annually throughout the region. The best source of information is *The Craft Heritage Trails of Western North Carolina.* Widely available in local bookstores, it gives details on more than 500 crafts studios, shops, and galleries.

More than 4,000 people in this region earn part or all of their living from crafts. Many can be found "around the bend" and in homes tucked back in forested hollows. They patiently coax form from clay and wood and metal, and they are usually happy to talk about what they do—so explore. Interesting roads that are off the map can lead to workshops.

In the beginning, practical function was behind all the quilting, weaving, woodworking, and pottery making. But by the late 19th century, missionaries, social workers, and women of means—Frances Goodrich and Edith Vanderbilt among them—began to recognize that these things of day-to-day life contained artistry. Today utility and aesthetics have melded. From furnaces in Mitchell and Yancey counties comes art glass prized by collectors and dealers worldwide. Many glassblowers perfected their

métier at the prestigious **Penland School of Crafts,** whose courses also include printmaking, wood, drawing, clay, and fibers. Another well-known crafts school is **John C. Campbell Folk School,** in Brasstown in the far western tip of the state.

Here are several other good places to begin your crafts search:

The **Craft Fair of the Southern Highlands,** the largest crafts event in the Southeast, is held in mid-July and again in October in the Asheville Civic Center. In the tiny village of Crossnore, a rock cottage houses the **Crossnore School's Weaving Room** (⊠ *U.S. 221* ☎ *828/733–4660).* Patterns used by the early settlers of the Appalachians are favored here; however, the materials are modern easy-care rayon, synthetics, cotton, wool, and linen. The **Folk Art Center** (⊠ *Blue Ridge Pkwy., MM 382* ☎ *828/298–7298),* puts on quilt, woodworking, pottery, and other crafts shows and demonstrations. This is an excellent place to purchase very high quality (and expensive) traditional crafts, such as quilts, baskets, and pottery. On the Cherokee Reservation, elders pass on the secrets of finger weaving, wood carving, and mask and beaded jewelry making. Their work, found in shops such as **Medicine Man Crafts** (⊠ *U.S. 441,* ☎ *828/497–2202)* in downtown Cherokee, is a connective thread to a time predating the United States by thousands of years.

gray and red foxes in natural-like settings. The center also has an excellent area on native reptiles and amphibians, plus a petting zoo. ☒ *75 Gashes Creek Rd., East Metro* ☎ *828/298–5600* ⊕ *www.wildwnc.org* ☜ *$7* ⊙ *Daily 10–5.*

WHERE TO EAT

Because of the large number of visitors to Asheville and the many upscale retirees who've moved here, the city has a dining scene that's much more vibrant and varied than its size would suggest. You'll find everything from Greek to Vietnamese, Moroccan to Southern soul food, and barbecue to sushi. Asheville has more vegetarian restaurants per capita than any other city, and there are coffeehouses on many corners.

DOWNTOWN

$$$
SEAFOOD
✕ **Bistro 1896.** Bistro 1896 (in a building on Pack Square dating from that year) focuses on seafood but also offers other dishes. Start with oysters on the half shell, so fresh you can smell the salt air, or fried calamari, then jump to seafood-stuffed salmon or sesame-encrusted tuna. The bistro look comes from the period photos on the walls and glass-top tables with fresh flowers. On Sunday there's a brunch with a build-it-yourself Bloody Mary bar. Sidewalk seating lets you take in the street performers on bustling Pack Square. ☒ *7 Pack Sq., Downtown* ☎ *828/251–1300* ⊟ *AE, MC, V.*

¢
ASIAN
✕ **Doc Chey's.** "Peace, love, and noodles" is the theme at this outpost of an Atlanta noodle house, with Vietnamese, Thai, Japanese, and Chinese noodle bowls and rice plates served fast, cheap, and tasty. It's always packed. ☒ *37 Biltmore Ave., Downtown* ☎ *828/252–8220* ⊟ *AE, MC, V.*

$
SOUTHERN
✕ **Early Girl Eatery.** Named after an early-maturing tomato variety, Early Girl Eatery is casually Southern, with a cheerfully chic twist. A wall of south-facing windows provides wonderful light most of the day. No white tablecloths here: you eat on brown butcher paper. The dinner menu runs to items like seared duck breast with collard greens. At breakfast, choose huge stacks of buttermilk pancakes or Creole catfish and stone-ground grits. ☒ *8 Wall St. Ave., Downtown* ☎ *828/259–9592* ⊟ *MC, V.*

$
ECLECTIC
★
✕ **Greenlife.** Asheville's wildly popular organic and natural foods grocery is *the* place to stock up on healthful, delicious picnic supplies. In addition to groceries, Greenlife has an extensive prepared food and takeout section, featuring a variety of soups of the day (including several vegan soups), hot lunch items, fresh sushi, and made-to-order sandwiches on organic breads. Greenlife also has the friendliest employees in town. ☒ *70 Merrimon Ave., Downtown* ☎ *828/254–5440* ⊟ *MC, V*

¢–$
VEGETARIAN
✕ **Laughing Seed Café.** You'll get more than brown rice and beans at this vegetarian eatery, with a bold mural on one wall and a bar. The extensive menu ranges from fruit drinks to sandwiches and pizzas to dinner specialties influenced by the flavors of India, Thailand, Mexico, and Morocco. Fruits and vegetables come from local organic farms during the growing season. Breads are baked daily on premises. There's outdoor dining on charming Wall Street. ☒ *40 Wall St., Downtown* ☎ *828/252–3445* ⊟ *AE, D, MC, V* ⊙ *Closed Tues.*

$$$$
MODERN
SOUTHERN

✕**The Market Place.** Clean lines, neutral colors, and brushed-steel mobiles create a sophisticated style at one of Asheville's longest-lived fine-dining establishments. (It opened in 1979.) The food offers refreshing twists on ingredients indigenous to the mountains, such as game and trout, and the South in general. Possible entrées are pan-seared red trout with corn fritters and squash slaw, and wood-grilled pork chop with sautéed greens, herbed quinoa, and strawberry-ginger compote. Iron gates open onto an exterior courtyard and dining patio. On the casual side of the restaurant, Bar 100 offers a bar menu of snacks and lighter dishes, all made with ingredients from within 100 mi of Asheville. ⊠ *20 Wall St., Downtown* ☎ *828/252–4162* ⚒ *Reservations essential* ▤ *AE, MC, V* ☽ *Closed Sun. No lunch.*

$–$$
INDIAN
★

✕**Mela Indian Restaurant.** Mela opened in 2005 and quickly established itself as the best Indian restaurant in the city. Rather than specialize in one type of Indian cuisine, it offers dishes from across the country. The tandoori dishes (chicken, salmon, or lamb) are especially delicious. Entrées are served with basmati rice, lentil stew, and *papadum* (lentil wafers). Portions are large, making this one of the best values downtown. The space is unexpectedly modern, with rough tile walls and a high ceiling, though accented with woodwork, doors, and furnishings from India. ⊠ *70 N. Lexington, Downtown* ☎ *828/225–8880* ▤ *AE, D, MC, V.*

¢
EASTERN
EUROPEAN

✕**Old Europe.** The Hungarian owners, Zoltan and Melinda Vetro, bring a European sensibility to this immensely popular pastry shop and coffeehouse. It's often jammed; the crowd spills over to the courtyard, slurping coffee—served with a piece of chocolate—and liqueurs and downing delicious tortes, cakes, and other European pastries. Although full meals are served, you're better off sticking to the desserts and coffees. There's live entertainment on weekends, in a nightclub upstairs. ⊠ *41 N. Lexington Ave., Downtown* ☎ *828/252–0001* ▤ *MC, V.*

¢–$
LATIN-
AMERICAN

✕**Salsa's.** In an expanded space with a slightly retro-hippie look, you'll find spicy and highly creative Mexican and Caribbean fare in huge portions. Pan-fried fish tacos, roast pumpkin empanadas, and organic chicken enchiladas are among the recommended entrées. ⊠ *6 Patton Ave., Downtown* ☎ *828/252–9805* ▤ *AE, D, MC, V* ☽ *Closed Sun.*

$–$$
SOUTHERN
☺

✕**Tupelo Honey Café.** Hello, darlin'! This is the place for down-home Southern cooking with an uptown twist. Owner Sharon Schott delivers a lot more than grits, with dishes like seared salmon with corn bread, and hormone-free pork chop with mashed sweet potatoes. Breakfast is served anytime, and there is a jar of tupelo honey available on every table. The atmosphere is loud and a little funky, and there's often a line. Kids are welcome; they can entertain themselves by drawing on the paper tablecloths. ⊠ *12 College St., Downtown* ☎ *828/255–4863* ⚒ *Reservations not accepted* ▤ *AE, MC, V* ☽ *Closed Mon. No lunch Fri. and Sat.*

$$–$$$
SPANISH
★

✕**Zambras.** Sophisticated tapas selections, such as grilled scallops with parsnip-potato gratin, prosciutto-wrapped medjool dates with goat cheese, pan-seared local trout with hazelnuts and oranges, and steamed mussels make this one of the most interesting restaurants in the mountains. There are also several varieties of paella and other dishes, many influenced by the cuisine of Mediterranean Spain and North Africa, and a wine list featuring unusual Spanish wines and sherries. Voluptuous Moorish colors and live gypsy music (and belly dancers on weekends) lend an exotic air. ⊠*85 Walnut St., Downtown* ☎*828/232–1060* ⚘*Reservations essential* ☰*AE, D, MC, V* ⊗*No lunch.*

GREATER ASHEVILLE

$–$$
BARBECUE

✕ **12 Bones Smokehouse.** You'll recognize this spot by the long line of customers snaking out the door. Open only weekdays 11 to 4, the wait to place your order is often a half hour. True to the barbecue joint ethos, with concrete floors and old Formica-top tables, 12 Bones has no atmosphere. What it does have is the smokiest baby back ribs you've ever tasted, and delicious sides including collard greens, corn pudding, and "mashed sweet taters." The crowd ranges from hippie potters from the River District art-studio types to downtown suits—the staff will call you "Sweetie." ⊠*5 Riverside Dr., River District* ☎*828/253–4499* ☰*MC, V* ⊗*Closed weekends. No dinner.*

$–$$
PIZZA

✕ **Asheville Pizza and Brewing Company.** Locally known as the "Brew 'n View," this funky brewery-cum-eatery-cum-movie theater is extremely popular. Grab a microbrew beer and a pizza with portobello mushrooms and fresh spinach, and watch *Pink Floyd The Wall* from the comfort of a sofa in the recently redone theater. ⊠*675 Merrimon Ave., North Metro* ☎*828/254–1281* ☰*MC, V.*

$$$$
CONTINENTAL
Fodor'sChoice
★

✕ **Gabrielle's.** From the moment you're met at the door, offered an ice-cold martini, and invited to stroll the lovely Victorian gardens while your table is readied, you suspect that dinner at Gabrielle's is going to be one of your best dining experience in the mountains—and chances are it will be. The best does come at a price, however. The five-course tasting menu, which changes frequently, is $79, or $139 with paired wines. The somewhat less expensive (around $60) prix-fixe menu has items such as wild Alaskan halibut dusted with fennel pollen, served with local foraged mushrooms and grilled ramps (a wild onion-like vegetable) and rack of Kurabuto pork with heirloom corn hominy. The near-perfect service and the setting in an elegant, art-filled 19th-century cherry-panel space, with piano music in the background, make for a memorable splurge. Executive chef Perry Hendrix, stolen away by Robert Redford when Redford was filming in Asheville a few years ago, returned to Gabrielle's in 2008. ⊠*87 Richmond Hill Dr., at Richmond Hill Inn, North Metro* ☎*828/252–7313 or 800/545–9238* ⚘*Reservations essential* ☰*AE, MC, V* ⊗*Dinner Wed.–Sun. No lunch.*

¢–$
AMERICAN

✕ **Sunny Point Café and Bakery.** In a restored storefront in up-and-coming West Asheville, Sunny Point lives up to its name with bright, cheerful decor. It's a good spot for breakfast, where free-range pork sausage shares the menu with granola, herbed potatoes, and some of the biggest biscuits in town. Now open for dinner, it experiments a little at this meal, with dishes like chicken-fried tofu. In good weather the best tables are outside on the patio. ⊠*626 Haywood Rd., West Metro* ☎*828/252–0055* ☰*MC, V* ⊗*Closed Sun. and Mon.*

CLOSE UP

Mountain Brews

Microbreweries have replaced moonshine stills in the North Carolina mountains. At last count, there were at least seven microbreweries in the Asheville area.

The **Asheville Brews Cruise** (☎ 828/545–5181) takes microbrew aficionados on tours of several local breweries, complete with tastings, for $39 per person (four person minimum). **Asheville Brewing Co.** (✉ 675 Merrimon Ave., Asheville ☎ 828/254–1281) creates well-crafted brews in a converted movie theater near UNC–Asheville and serves them, along with pizzas and sandwiches, in its brewpub. You can enjoy a second-run movie ($3) and your favorite beer in the theater. **French Broad Brewing Company** (✉ 101 Fairview Rd., Asheville ☎ 828/277–0222) is a microbrewery that creates lagers and specialty ales. The on-site tasting room also has tours and live music many nights. **Green Man Brewing Co.** (✉ 95 Patton Ave., Asheville ☎ 828/252–5445)

is the brewing arm of Jack of the Wood, a Celtic-style pub that serves Green Man's English-style ales.

At **Heinzelmannchen Brewery** (✉ 545 Mill St., Sylva ☎ 828/631–4466?), German-born brewermaster-Dieter Kuhn does light German ales in downtown Sylva. **Highland Brewing Company** (✉ 12 Old Charlotte Hwy., Ste. H, Asheville ☎ 828/299–3370), is one of the oldest (established in 1994) and largest (capacity of 20,000 barrels annually) microbreweries in the region. Its best-selling product is Gaelic Ale, a deep amber, malty ale. **Pisgah Brewing Company** (✉ 150 Eastside Business Park, Black Mountain ☎ 828/669–2491) brews certified organic beers, including the rich, dark, Belgian-influenced Cosmos. **Wedge Brewing Co.** (✉ 151 Roberts St., Asheville ☎ 828/279–6393), new in 2008, is in the River Arts District and brews Iron Rail India Pale Ale, named after the railroad tracks that run by its location, and other artisan beers.

BILTMORE VILLAGE

$$$–$$$$
FRENCH

✕**Fig Bistro.** Fig many be tiny in size, with only around 15 tables, but it's big in creativity. Most dishes are at least vaguely French, as the chef trained in France. The menu changes frequently, but the scallops, cod, snapper, and other seafood are a delight. When available, the duck—grilled with a sweet potato puree, as a confit salad, or in pâté mousse—is also terrific. Fig has a true bistro ambience, with hardwood floors, pressed-tin ceilings, black chairs, a near floor-to-ceiling wall of windows (though the view is of a commercial street), and exposed brick. In good weather, there's seating in an outdoor courtyard. Light drinkers can order half glasses of wine. ✉ 18 Brook St., Biltmore Village ☎ 828/277–0889 ☐ AE, D, MC, V ⊘ Closed Sun.

$$$
MEDITERRANEAN
★

✕**Rezaz.** With abstract art displayed on the cinnamon- and apricot-color walls and waiters dressed in black rushing around pouring wine, you'd never know this sophisticated Mediterranean restaurant is in the site of a former hardware store. Try the veal osso bucco milanese or the aborio-crusted sea scallops. There are daily specials, such as goat-cheese ravioli on Monday and seared ahi tuna on Friday. You enter the restaurant through Enoteca, Rezaz's wine bar, which serves panini

CAFFEINATED ASHEVILLE

Given Asheville's artsy sensibilities, it shouldn't come as a surprise that the city has a flourishing café scene.

City Bakery Café (⌖ 60 Biltmore Ave. ☎ 828/254-4426) has so-so coffee but great European-style breads, in about 20 varieties, made from organic flours. **Clingman Ave. Coffee and Catering Co** (⌖ 242 Clingman Ave. ☎ 828/253-2177) is in the River District, near many pottery and other art-and-crafts studios. **Dripolator** (⌖ 144 Biltmore Ave. ☎ 828/252-0021) serves Fair Trade coffees and attracts a mixed crowd

of alternative younger folks and businesspeople. **Green Sage** (⌖ 5 Broadway St. ☎ 828/252-4450), new in 2008, features organic and natural food and beverages (including local beers and wines) produced or processed in the area; delicious breakfasts are served all day. **Malaprop's Café** (⌖ 55 Haywood St. ☎ 828/254-6734) is associated with a first-rate downtown independent bookstore. **Mountain Java** (⌖ 870 Merrimon Ave. ☎ 828/255-3881) has a drive-through for a cuppa joe to go.

4

sandwiches, antipasti, and other less-expensive fare in a casual setting. ⌖ 28 Hendersonville Rd., Biltmore Village ☎ 828/277-1510 ⊟ AE, MC, V ⊘ Closed Sun.

WHERE TO STAY

The Asheville area has a nice mix of B&Bs, motels, and small owner-operated inns. There are more than three dozen B&Bs, one of the largest concentrations in the South. Most are in the Montford area near downtown and the Grove Park area north in the city. At least eight B&Bs in the area promote themselves as gay-owned and actively seek gay and lesbian guests, and an equal number advertise that they are gay-friendly. More than 100 chain motel properties are dotted around the metropolitan area, with large clusters on Tunnel Road near the Asheville Mall, on U.S. Highway 25 and Biltmore Avenue near the Biltmore Estate, and southwest near Biltmore Square Mall. Also, you'll find inns and boutique hotels, both downtown and around the city. In rural areas around the city are a few lodges and cabin colonies.

DOWNTOWN

$$$-$$$$ ⌖ **Haywood Park Hotel.** Location is the main draw of this downtown hotel, which was once a department store. Once ensconced in a suite here, you're within walking distance of many of Asheville's shops, restaurants, and galleries. The lobby has golden oak woodwork accented with gleaming brass. The suites are spacious, with baths done in Spanish marble. The long-popular Flying Frog Café, with an astonishingly eclectic menu—mixing French, Indian, and German cuisine—is in the hotel. There's a small shopping galleria in the atrium, and a very popular sidewalk café. **Pros:** great central downtown location; expansive suites. **Cons:** limited parking (valet); somewhat outdated decor in rooms and lobby; service sometimes spotty; no pool. ⌖ 1 Battery Park Ave., Downtown ☎ 828/252-2522 or 800/228-2522 ⊕ www.

haywoodpark.com ⇨*33 suites* ⵊ*In-room: safe (some), refrigerator, Wi-Fi. In-hotel: restaurant, room service, bar, gym, laundry service, no-smoking rooms* ☰*AE, D, DC, MC, V* ⑩❘*BP.*

NORTH METRO

$$$–$$$$ ⊡ **1900 Inn on Montford.** Guests are pampered at this Arts and Crafts–
Fodor'sChoice style B&B, where most rooms have whirlpool baths, some have big-
★ screen plasma TVs, and all have fireplaces. There are lots of nooks and corners in the expansive public spaces for snuggling up with a book. The inn has a social hour every evening. Innkeepers Ron and Lynn Carlson say that the Cloisters—a 1,300-square-foot suite in their carriage house out back—is the largest suite in Asheville. Younger children are discouraged in the main house. **Pros:** well-run and deluxe B&B; antiques but also modern amenities. **Cons:** not for families with small children. ⊠*296 Montford Ave., North Metro* ☎*828/254–9569 or 800/254–9569* ⊕*www.innonmontford.com* ⇨*5 rooms, 3 suites* ⵊ*In-room: refrigerator (some), DVD, Internet, Wi-Fi. In-hotel: Wi-Fi, no kids under 12, no-smoking rooms* ☰*AE, D, MC, V* ⑩❘*BP.*

$$$–$$$$ ⊡**Albemarle Inn.** Famed Hungarian composer Béla Bartók lived here
★ in the early 1940s, creating his Third Piano Concerto, the "Asheville Concerto." You can stay in his room on the third floor, although Juliet's Chamber, with its private balcony overlooking lovely gardens, may appeal more to modern Romeos. Owners Cathy and Larry Sklar left their jobs as lawyers in Connecticut in order to turn this 1907 Greek Revival mansion in a quiet North Asheville residential area into one of the top B&Bs in the region. Some rooms have working fireplaces and canopied beds. Gourmet breakfasts are prepared by the inn's chef. **Pros:** delightfully upscale B&B; lovely residential neighborhood; excellent breakfasts. **Cons:** old-fashioned claw foot tubs in some rooms make showering difficult. ⊠*86 Edgemont Rd., 1 mi north of I–240, North Metro* ☎*828/255–0027 or 800/621–7435* ⊕*www.albemarleinn.com* ⇨*10 rooms, 1 suite* ⵊ*In-room: Wi-Fi. In-hotel: no kids under 12, no-smoking rooms* ☰*D, MC, V* ⑩❘*BP.*

$$$–$$$$ ⊡**Black Walnut Inn.** The Biltmore House supervising architect Richard Sharp Smith built this 1899 home in Asheville's Montford section. Today it's a B&B on the National Register of Historic Places. Most of the rooms—all redone in 2004 by owners Peter and Lori White—have working fireplaces. Parts of the 2000 movie *28 Days* were filmed here. (The star, Sandra Bullock, stayed in the Dogwood Room.) **Pros:** a gem of a B&B; charming antiques-filled house; excellent breakfast and afternoon wine and appetizer hour included. **Cons:** grounds are not large, with only a small garden. ⊠*288 Montford Ave., North Metro* ☎*828/254–3878 or 800/381–3878* ⊕*www.blackwalnut.com* ⇨*6 rooms, 1 cottage* ⵊ*In-room: VCR. In-hotel: Wi-Fi, no-smoking rooms* ☰*D, MC, V* ⑩❘*BP.*

$$$$ ⊡**Grove Park Inn Resort & Spa.** Asheville's premier large resort is an
★ imposing granite edifice that dates from 1913 and has panoramic views of the Blue Ridge Mountains. Henry Ford, F. Scott Fitzgerald (who stayed in room 441), and Michael Jordan, as well as eight U.S. presidents from Woodrow Wilson to George H. W. Bush, have stayed here. It's furnished with oak antiques in the Arts and Crafts style, and

CLOSE UP

Arts & Crafts Movement

The Arts and Crafts Movement was an international movement of the late 19th and early 20th century that emphasized local and natural materials, craftsmanship, and a strong horizontal line in architecture and furniture. Inspired by the writings of British art critic John Ruskin, the Arts and Crafts or American Craftsman style romanticized the role of the craftsperson and rebelled against the mass production of the Industrial Age. Prominent examples of Craftsman style include the furniture and other decorative arts of Gustav Stickley, first presented in his magazine, *The Craftsman*; the Roycroft community in Ohio, founded by Elbert Hubbard; the Prairie School of architect Frank Lloyd Wright; and the bungalow style of houses popularized in California. At its height between 1880 and 1910, the Arts and Crafts Movement flourished in Asheville. The Grove Park Inn's construction was heavily influenced by Arts and Crafts principles, and today the resort hotel has one of the largest collections of Arts and Crafts furniture in the world. Several hundred Asheville bungalows were also built in the Arts and Crafts style. Today, the influence of the Arts and Crafts Movement remains strong in the Asheville area, reflected in the large number of working craft studios in the region.

the lobby fireplaces are as big as cars. Four restaurants offer plenty of choices. The spa is one of the finest in the country. As the hotel's main focus is on group meetings, alas, sometimes individual guests get short shrift. Rooms in the original section are mostly smaller but have more character than those in the newer additions. **Pros:** imposing historic hotel; wonderful setting; magnificent mountain views; first-rate spa and golf course. **Cons:** individual guests sometimes play second fiddle to large group meetings. ✉ *290 Macon Ave., North Metro* ☎ *828/252–2711 or 800/438–5800* ⊕ *www.groveparkinn.com* ⟳ *498 rooms, 12 suites* ⚷ *In-room: Internet, Wi-Fi. In-hotel: 4 restaurants, bars, golf course, tennis courts, pools, gym, spa, laundry service, Wi-Fi, no-smoking rooms* ▤ *AE, D, DC, MC, V* ❚⦾❚ *EP.*

$$$–$$$$
Fodor'sChoice
★ ▦ **Richmond Hill Inn.** Once a private residence, this elegant Victorian mansion is on the National Register of Historic Places. Many rooms in the mansion are furnished with canopy beds, Victorian sofas, and other antiques, while the more modern cottages have contemporary pine poster beds. Although Richmond Hill does not enjoy the panoramic views of Asheville's other top hotels, and the immediate neighborhood is not exactly upscale, the 46-acre grounds are stunning, with ever-changing gardens. Its dinner restaurant, Gabrielle's, is one of the best in the region. **Pros:** outstanding historic inn; beautiful grounds; excellent service. **Cons:** location isn't ideal; lacks stunning mountain views; no pool. ✉ *87 Richmond Hill Dr., North Metro* ☎ *828/252–7313 or 888/742–4536* ⊕ *www.richmondhillinn.com* ⟳ *24 rooms, 3 suites, 9 cottages* ⚷ *In-room: Internet. In-hotel: 2 restaurants, no-smoking rooms* ▤ *AE, MC, V* ❚⦾❚ *BP* ⊗ *Closed Jan.*

$$–$$$
★ ▦ **The Lion and the Rose.** One of the characters in Thomas Wolfe's *Look Homeward, Angel* lived in this house, an 1898 Queen Anne–Georgian

in the historic Montford Park area near downtown. It couldn't have looked any better then than it does now. A special detail is a 6-foot Palladian-style stained-glass window at the top of oak stairs. Innkeepers Jim and Linda Palmer keep the heirloom gardens and five guest rooms looking gorgeous. The landscaping around the house is striking. For snacks and wine, guests have 24-hour access to a a well-stocked pantry. For the most privacy, choose the Craig-Toms suite, which occupies the entire third floor. **Pros:** comfortable small B&B; impressively landscaped grounds; good value. **Cons:** as at all the B&Bs in Montford, it's a bit of a walk to downtown. ⊠*276 Montford Ave., North Metro* ☎*828/255–6546 or 800/546–6988* ⊕*www.lion-rose.com* ➪*4 rooms, 1 suite* ⚷*In-room: refrigerator (some), DVD, Wi-Fi. In-hotel: Wi-Fi, no kids under 12, no-smoking rooms* ⊟*D, MC, V* ⱓ*BP.*

SOUTH METRO

$$$–$$$$ 🏨**Bohemian Hotel.** You can't stay any closer to the Biltmore Estate than at this hotel, unless you are on the Estate grounds. New in late 2008, the Bohemian is steps from the Estate's main gate, and close to all the shops and restaurants in Biltmore Village. The down side is that this is a congested area, with frequent delays due to a nearby train track crossing on Biltmore Avenue; you'll need the hotel's valet parking. The Tudor style of the hotel is designed to blend with the architecture of Biltmore Village, though some say it reminds them of Hogwarts school in the Harry Potter movies and novels. Spacious rooms have sumptuous velvet fabrics, antique mirrors, and plasma TV. **Pros:** new upscale hotel; at Biltmore Estate gate, near Biltmore Village. **Cons:** located in a congested area with heavy traffic. ⊠*11 Boston Way, South Metro* ☎*828/505–2949* ⊕*www.bohemianhotelasheville.com* ➪*104 rooms* ⚷*In-room: refrigerator (some), Wi-Fi. In-hotel: restaurant, bar, gym, spa, Wi-Fi, no-smoking rooms* ⊟*AE, D, MC, V.*

$$$$ 🏨**Inn on Biltmore Estate.** Many people who visit the Biltmore mansion
Fodor's Choice   long to stay overnight; if you're one of them, your wish is granted in
★   the form of this posh hilltop property. The hotel mimics the look of Biltmore House with natural stone and copper. French manor houses inspired the interior. Nice touches include afternoon tea in the library. The dining room, reserved for hotel guests only, is bookended by large windows with mountain views and a massive fireplace. Menus deftly blend local and international ingredients. Available packages include admission to Biltmore Estate for the length of your stay and free shuttles to all parts of the estate. **Pros:** deluxe hotel on Biltmore Estate grounds; exclusive restaurant; top-notch service. **Cons:** very expensive; atmosphere can be a bit formal. ⊠*Biltmore Estate, Exit 50 off I–40, South Metro* ☎*800/922–0084* ⊕*www.biltmore.com/inn* ➪*204 rooms, 9 suites* ⚷*In-room: refrigerator (some), Internet, Wi-Fi. In-hotel: restaurant, room service, bar, pool, spa, gym, bicycles, Wi-Fi, no-smoking rooms* ⊟*AE, D, DC, MC, V* ⱓ*EP.*

$$$–$$$$ 🏨**The Residences at Biltmore.** Located not far from the gates of Bilt-
★   more Estate, these suites-style accommodations are some of the most luxe in Asheville. Studio and one-bedroom condo apartments (some two- and three-bedroom units are available), tastefully decorated with Arts and Crafts touches, have fully equipped kitchens with granite

countertops and stainless-steel appliances, stacked stone gas fireplaces, hardwood floors, wall-mounted flat-screen TVs, and washers and dryers. Most units have whirlpool baths. **Pros:** luxury suites with fully equipped kitchens; convenient location near both Biltmore Estate and downtown Asheville; well-managed with helpful staff. **Cons:** on-site restaurant planned but not yet open; a bit of a hike to restaurants in Biltmore Village. ⊠ *700 Biltmore Ave., South Metro* ☎ *828/350–8000 or 866/433–5594* ⊕ *www.residencesatbiltmore.com* ⟜ *55 suites* ⚒ *In-room: kitchen, DVD, Wi-Fi. In-hotel: pool, gym, Wi-Fi, no-smoking rooms* ⊟ *AE, D, MC, V*

NEARBY ASHEVILLE

$$$–$$$$ 🖭 **Pisgah View Ranch.** Saddle up! In the same family since 1790, this 2,000-acre dude ranch may suit you if you're looking for a rural mountain experience and a family atmosphere, with plenty of ranch-style food, homey activities like square dancing and cookouts, and unlimited horseback riding. Cottages, which vary considerably in size and appeal, are functional rather than fancy. On an all-inclusive basis, with all meals and activities including horseback riding, rates are $320 per day double occupancy ($220 without the horseback riding) plus 11% tax and 15% gratuity. Camping and RV sites also available. **Pros:** beautiful mountain setting on 2,000 acres; ride horses to your heart's content on miles of riding trails; filling country food served family-style. **Cons:** simple cabin accommodations are far from deluxe; may be too "Andy Griffith" for some. ⊠ *70 Pisgah View Ranch Rd., 16 mi west of Asheville, Candler* ☎ *828/667–9100 or 866/252–8361* ⊕ *www.pisgahviewranch.net* ⟜ *39 cottages* ⚒ *In-room: no phone, no TV (some). In-hotel: restaurant, pool* ⊟ *D, MC, V* ⊙ *Closed Nov.–Apr.* ⦿ *AI.*

$$ 🖭 **Sourwood Inn.** Two miles from the Blue Ridge Parkway, down
★ a narrow winding road, sits one of the most stunning small inns in the mountains. The inn is constructed of stone and cedar, in the Arts and Crafts style. Twelve large rooms each have a real wood-burning fireplace, a bathtub with a view (there's also a separate shower), and French doors that open onto a private balcony. ■**TIP**➜**Unfortunately, the inn doesn't have air-conditioning. Even at 3,000 feet it can be a little warm at times in summer.** Sassafras Cabin is a private retreat about 100 yards from the inn. **Pros:** stunning mountainside setting; handsome rooms; bathrooms with views. **Cons:** requires a 20-minute drive to get to downtown Asheville and to restaurants; no air-conditioning. ⊠ *810 Elk Mountain Scenic Hwy.* ☎ *828/255–0690* ⊕ *www.sourwoodinn. com* ⟜ *12 rooms, 1 cabin* ⚒ *In-room: no a/c, no phone, no TV (some). In-hotel: restaurant, no-smoking rooms* ⊟ *AE, MC, V* ⊙ *Closed Jan. and weekdays in Feb.* ⦿ *BP.*

NIGHTLIFE & THE ARTS

For the latest information on nightlife, arts, and entertainment in the Asheville area, get a copy of *Take 5*, an entertainment tabloid in Friday's *Asheville Citizen-Times* or the weekly free newspaper, *Mountain Express*.

THE ARTS

The Asheville area has about 40 theaters and theater companies. Asheville also has a vibrant art and crafts gallery scene, with about two dozen galleries. Most of the galleries are within a block or two of Pack Square, while some, especially working studios, are in the River District. Biltmore Village also has several galleries.

One of the oldest community theater groups in the country, **Asheville Community Theatre** (⊠ *35 E. Walnut St., Downtown* ☎ *828/254–1320*) stages professional plays year-round in its own theater building. The biggest art gallery in town, with 14,000 square feet of exhibit space, **Blue Spiral 1** (⊠ *38 Biltmore Ave., Downtown* ☎ *800/291–2513*) has about 30 exhibits of sculpture, paintings, and photographs each year.

In the Pack Place complex, the 500-seat **Diana Wortham Theatre** (⊠ *2 S. Pack Sq., Downtown* ☎ *828/257–4530*) is home to more than 100 musical and theatrical events each year. As the headquarters of the prestigious Southern Highland Craft Guild, the **Folk Art Center** (⊠ *Blue Ridge Pkwy., MM 382* ☎ *828/298–7298*), regularly puts on exceptional quilt, woodworking, pottery, and other crafts shows and demonstrations. This is a top spot to purchase very high quality (and expensive) traditional crafts, such as quilts, baskets, and pottery. In a 1928 landmark building decorated with polychrome terra-cotta tile, **Kress Emporium**(⊠ *19 Patton Ave., Downtown* ☎ *828/281–2252*) is a place for more than 75 craftspeople to show and sell their crafts. The space is not air-conditioned and can be hot in summer. Owned by arts entrepreneur John Cram, **New Morning Gallery** (⊠ *7 Boston Way. Biltmore Village* ☎ *828/274–2831 or 800/933–4438*) has 12,000 square feet of exhibit space, focusing on more popular ceramics, garden art, jewelry, furniture, and art glass. In a tiny, 99-seat theater, **North Carolina Stage Company** (⊠ *33 Haywood St., Downtown* ☎ *828/350–9090*) is a professional company that puts on edgy, contemporary plays. With professional summer theater that often celebrates mountain culture, **Southern Appalachian Repertory Theatre (SART)** (⊠ *Owen Hall, Mars Hill College* ☎ *828/689–1239*) produces plays such as William Gregg and Perry Deane Young's *Mountain of Hope,* about the 1835 controversy over whether or not Mt. Mitchell is the highest peak east of the Rockies. In a 1938 building that housed a five-and-dime, **Woolworth Walk** (⊠ *25 Haywood St., Downtown* ☎ *828/254–9234*) features the work of 150 crafts artists in 20,000 square feet of exhibit space on two levels, and there's even a soda fountain, built to resemble the original Woolworth luncheonette.

The 2,400-seat **Thomas Wolfe Auditorium** (⊠ *87 Haywood St., Downtown* ☎ *828/259–5736*), in the Asheville Civic Center, hosts larger events including traveling Broadway shows and performances of the Asheville Symphony. The Civic Center, which is showing its age, is looking at a $140 million expansion to include a new performing-arts theater.

NIGHTLIFE

More than a restaurant, more than a movie theater, **Asheville Pizza and Brewing Company** (⊠*675 Merrimon Ave.* ☏*828/254–1281*), also called Brew 'n' View, is a wildly popular place to catch a flick while lounging on a sofa, drinking a microbrew, and scarfing a veggie pizza. In a renovated downtown appliance store, the ever-popular **Barley's Taproom** (⊠*42 Biltmore Ave.* ☏*828/255–0504*) has live bluegrass and Americana music three or four nights a week. The bar downstairs has about two dozen microbrew beers on draft, and you can play pool and darts upstairs in the Billiard Room. Billed as a "listening room," **Grey Eagle** (⊠*185 Clingman Ave.* ☏*828/232–5800*), in the River Arts District area, features popular local and regional bands four or five nights a week, with contra dancing on some other nights.

The camp decor at **Club Hairspray** (⊠*38 N. French Broad Ave.* ☏*828/258–2027*) will make you feel like you're back in 1961, though the music is contemporary. The crowd is diverse but predominately gay. **The Orange Peel Social Aid and Pleasure Club** (⊠*101 Biltmore Ave.* ☏*828/225–5851*) is far and away the number one nightspot in downtown Asheville. Bob Dylan, Hootie and the Blowfish, and Steve Winwood have played here in an intimate, smoke-free setting for audiences of up to 950. In 2008 *Rolling Stone* named it one of the top five rock clubs in the U.S. For smaller events, it also has a great dance floor, with springy wood slats.

Asheville's best-known gay and lesbian club, **Scandals** (⊠*11 Grove St.* ☏*828/252–2838*), has a lively dance floor and drag shows on weekends. In a 1913 downtown building, the jazz and blues club **Tressa's** (⊠*28 Broadway* ☏*828/254–7072*) is nominally private, but lets nonmembers in for a small cover charge. There's a quieter, no-smoking room upstairs. In happening West Asheville, the smoke-free **Westville Pub** (⊠*777 Haywood Rd.* ☏*828/225–9782*) has about 50 different beers on the menu, and a different band plays nearly every night.

SPORTS & THE OUTDOORS

BASEBALL

A Class A farm team of the Colorado Rockies, the **Asheville Tourists** (⊠*McCormick Pl., off Biltmore Ave.* ☏*828/258–0428*) play April to early September at historic McCormick Field, which opened in 1924. McCormick Field appears briefly in the 1987 movie *Bull Durham,* starring Kevin Costner and Susan Sarandon. Many well-traveled baseball fans consider McCormick Field one of the most appealing minor league stadiums in the country.

GOLF

Asheville Municipal Golf Course (⊠*226 Fairway Dr.* ☏*828/298–1867*), is a par-72, 18-hole public municipal course designed by Donald Ross. Affordable fees start at $30. **Broadmoor** (⊠*101 French Broad La., Fletcher* ☏*828/687–1500*), 15 mi south of Asheville, is a public Scottish-style links course, playing to 7,111 yards, par 72. **Apple Valley at Colony Lake Lure Golf Resort** (⊠*201 Blvd. of the Mountains, Lake Lure*

☎ *828/625–2888 or 800/260–1040*), 25 mi from Asheville, has two 18-hole, par-72 courses known for their beauty.

Grove Park Inn Resort (✉ *290 Macon Ave.* ☎ *828/252–2711 Ext. 1012 or 800/438–5800*) has a par-70 course that's more than 100 years old. You can play the course ($85 if you start after 2 PM) even if you're not a guest at the hotel. **Southern Tee** (✉ *111 Howard Gap Rd., Fletcher* ☎ *828/687–7273*) is an 18-hole, par-3 course with attractive rates— $22 with cart even on weekends in peak season.

HORSEBACK RIDING

Cataloochee Ranch (✉ *119 Ranch Rd., Maggie Valley* ☎ *828/926–1401 or 800/868–1401*) allows riders to explore the property's mile-high vistas on horseback. Trail rides are offered by stables throughout the region between April and November, including **Pisgah View Ranch** (✉ *Pisgah View Ranch Rd., Candler* ☎ *828/667–9100*), where you can gallop through the wooded mountainside.

LLAMA TREKS

Avalon Llama Trek (✉ *450 Old Buckeye Cove Rd., Swannanoa* ☎ *828/299–7155*) leads llama trips on the lush trails of the Pisgah National Forest.

SKIING

In addition to having outstanding skiing, **Cataloochee Resort** (✉ *Rte. 1, Maggie Valley* ☎ *828/926–0285 or 800/768–0285*) hosts lots of different activities for the whole family. **Fairfield-Sapphire Valley** (✉ *4000 U.S. 64W, Sapphire Valley* ☎ *828/743–3441 or 800/533–8268*) offers basic skiing despite minimal snowfall. You can "Ski the Wolf" at **Wolf Ridge Ski Resort** (✉ *578 Valley View Cir., Mars Hill* ☎ *828/689–4111 or 800/817–4111*), which has night skiing and excellent snowmaking capabilities.

SHOPPING

Biltmore Village (✉ *Hendersonville Rd.,* ☎ *828/274–5570*), across from the Biltmore Estate, is a cluster of specialty shops, restaurants, galleries, and hotels in an early-20th-century-English-hamlet style. You'll find everything from children's books to music, antiques, and wearable art. **New Morning Gallery,** a jewelry, crafts, and art gallery at 7 Boston Way attracts customers from all over the Southeast.

Shopping is excellent all over **Downtown Asheville,** with at least 200 stores, including about 30 art galleries and over a dozen antiques shops. Several streets, notably **Biltmore Avenue, Lexington Avenue,** and **Wall Street** are lined with small, independently owned stores.

The **Grove Arcade Public Market** (✉ *1 Page Ave., Downtown* ☎ *828/252–7799*), one of America's first indoor shopping centers, originally opened in 1929. The remarkable building, which covers an entire city block, was totally redone and reopened in 2002 as a collection of some 50 local specialty shops and restaurants.

Grovewood Gallery at the Homespun Shops (✉ *111 Grovewood Rd.* ☎ *828/253–7651*), adjacent to the Grove Park Inn and established by

Mrs. George Vanderbilt, sells furniture and contemporary and traditionally crafted woven goods made on the premises.

SIDE TRIPS FROM ASHEVILLE

BLACK MOUNTAIN

16 mi east of Asheville via I–40.

Black Mountain is a small town that has played a disproportionately large role in American cultural history, because it's the site of Black Mountain College. For 20 years in the middle of the 20th century, from its founding in 1933 to its closing in 1953, Black Mountain College was one of the world's leading centers for experimental art, literature, architecture, and dance, with a list of faculty and students that reads like a *Who's Who* of American arts and letters.

On a different front, Black Mountain is also the home of evangelist Billy Graham. The Graham organization maintains a training center near Black Mountain, and there are several large church-related conference centers in the area, including Ridgecrest, Montreat, and Blue Ridge Assembly. Downtown Black Mountain is small and quaint, with a collection of little shops and several B&Bs.

Fodor's Choice
★
Originally housed in rented quarters at nearby Blue Ridge Assembly, in 1941 **Black Mountain College** moved across the valley to its own campus at Lake Eden, where it remained until it closed in 1953. The school's buildings were originally designed by the Bauhaus architects Walter Gropius and Marcel Breuer, but at the start of World War II the college turned to an American architect, Lawrence Kocher, and several intriguing buildings resulted, including one known as "The Ship," which still stands, with murals by Breuer. Among the students who enrolled at Black Mountain College in the 1940s were Arthur Penn, Kenneth Noland, Robert Rauschenberg, and James Leo Herlihy. Today the site is a privately owned 550-acre summer camp for boys. ■ TIP→ **Although the site of Black Mountain College usually is closed to the public, during the Lake Eden Festival, a music and arts festival in mid-May and mid-October, you can visit the grounds, either on a one-day pass or for weekend camping.** Other times of the year you can rent a cabin on the grounds for overnight stays. The Ship building and other campus buildings are viewable from Lake Eden Road. There's a small museum devoted to Black Mountain College in Asheville. ⊠ *375 Lake Eden Rd., 5 mi west of Black Mountain* ☎ *828/686–3885.*

WHERE TO STAY & EAT

¢–$
AMERICAN
✕ **Verandah Café.** With its gingham curtains and checkered tablecloths, the atmosphere is cozy and small-townish, and the food is unpretentious and tasty at this popular café in the heart of downtown Black Mountain. The grilled cheese sandwich with fresh tomato is a winner. ⊠ *119 Cherry St.* ☎ *828/669–8864* ▤ *MC, V* ⊘ *Closed Sun.*

$-$$ 🏠 **Red Rocker Inn.** A dozen red rocking chairs line the front porch of this inn in a quiet residential area two blocks from downtown. Your room (some are on the small side and most are ready for an update) may have a golf theme (the Pinehurst Room) or skylights, a fireplace, and a claw-foot tub (the Garrett Room). The restaurant ($$$–$$$$) is open to the public for breakfast and dinner by reservation. At dinner you'll enjoy heaping portions of Southern food, served by candlelight. **Pros:** pleasant small inn; in charming small town; filling Southern breakfasts. **Cons:** smallish rooms; not much public space; could use some updating. ⊠*136 N. Dougherty St.* ☎*888/669–5991 or 828/669–5991* ⊕*www.redrockerinn.com* ⥤*17 rooms* ⚿*In-room: safe, no TV. In-hotel: restaurant, no-smoking rooms* ▤*MC, V* ❑|*BP.*

SPORTS & THE OUTDOORS

GOLF   Black Mountain doesn't have the plethora of golf courses that some other mountain towns do, but **Black Mountain Golf Course** (⊠*Black Mountain,* ☎*828/669–2710*), a par-72, 6,215-yard public course, boasts the longest par 6 in the country, the 747-yard 17th hole.

SHOPPING

Part authentic small-town hardware store and part gift shop, **Town Hardware & General Store** (⊠*103 W. State St.,* ☎*828/669–7723*) sells hard-to-find tools like scythes and push plows, along with cast-iron cookware, Case knives, and Radio Flyer red wagons.

THE HIGH COUNTRY

Here you'll find the highest, steepest, coldest, snowiest, windiest, and, some say, friendliest parts of the mountains. The High Country has not only the tallest mountains east of the Rockies, but the highest average elevation in all of eastern America. With temperatures 10 to 15 degrees cooler than in the foothills and flatlands, even folks from Asheville come to the High Country in the summer to cool down.

Unlike the rest of the mountains, winter is the peak season in much of the High Country. The reason? The white stuff. Towns like Boone, Blowing Rock, and Banner Elk have boomed in the 40 years since the introduction of snowmaking equipment, and the ski resorts of Beach Mountain, Sugar Mountain, and Appalachian Ski Mountain attract skiers, snowboarders, and snow-tubers from all over the Southeast. A magnificent scenic road, the Blue Ridge Parkway is a highlight of this region.

BLUE RIDGE PARKWAY

Entrance 2 mi east of Asheville, off I–40 and at many other points.

The Blue Ridge Parkway's 252 mi within North Carolina wind down the High Country through Asheville, ending near the entrance of Great Smoky Mountains National Park. Highlights on and near the parkway include Mt. Mitchell, the highest mountain peak east of the Rockies, Grandfather Mountain, and Mt. Pisgah. Although in this section we list

Literary Mountain Lions

They may not be able to go home again, but many famous writers have made their homes in the North Carolina Mountains. The one most closely associated with the terrain is Thomas Wolfe (1900–38), author of *Look Homeward, Angel,* who was born and buried in Asheville. His contemporary F. Scott Fitzgerald visited Asheville and environs frequently in the 1930s, staying for long periods at the Grove Park Inn and at other hotels in the area. Fitzgerald's wife, Zelda, an author and artist in her own right, died in a 1948 fire at Highland Hospital, then a psychiatric facility in North Asheville.

William Sydney Porter, who under the pen name O. Henry, wrote "The Ransom of Red Chief," "The Gift of the Magi," and many other stories, married into an Asheville-area family and is buried in Asheville at Riverside Cemetery. Carl Sandburg, Pulitzer Prize–winning poet and biographer of Lincoln, spent the last 22 years of his life on a farm in Flat Rock. A younger generation of poets, including Jonathan Williams, Robert Creeley, Joel Oppenheimer, Robert Duncan, and Charles Olson, made names for themselves at Black Mountain College, an avant-garde hotbed during the 1940s and early 1950s.

More recently, Jan Karon, Elizabeth Daniels Squire, and Sharyn McCrumb have set popular mystery series in the area. Novelist Charles Frazier, born in Asheville in 1950, made Cold Mountain, in the Shining Rock Wilderness of the Pisgah National Forest, the setting (and the title) for his million-selling Civil War drama. The mountain can be viewed from the Blue Ridge Parkway at mile marker 412. The movie, however, was filmed in Romania. Enka-Candler native Wayne Caldwell writes eloquently of the people of the Cataloochee section of what is now the Great Smokies in his 2007 novel, *Cataloochee.* In several books, Canton native and former North Carolina poet laureate Fred Chappell paints powerful images of his hometown and its odiferous paper mill. Novelist Anne Tyler (*The Accidental Tourist*) spent her early years in the small town of Celo, near Mt. Mitchell, and Marjorie Rawlings wrote her classic novel, *The Yearling,* in Banner Elk.

4

sights and lodging that are close to the parkway, nearly all the towns and cities along the parkway route offer accommodations, dining, and sightseeing. In particular, Boone, Blowing Rock, Burnsville, Asheville, Waynesville, Brevard, and Cherokee, are all near popular entrances to the parkway.

GETTING HERE & AROUND

The Parkway connects Shenandoah National Park near Waynesboro, VA (mile marker 0) with Great Smoky Mountains National Park near Cherokee (mile marker 469). Entrances to the Parkway are located at many points along I–40 and I–26 as well as along other major highways. In North Carolina, Asheville and Boone are the largest cities along the way.

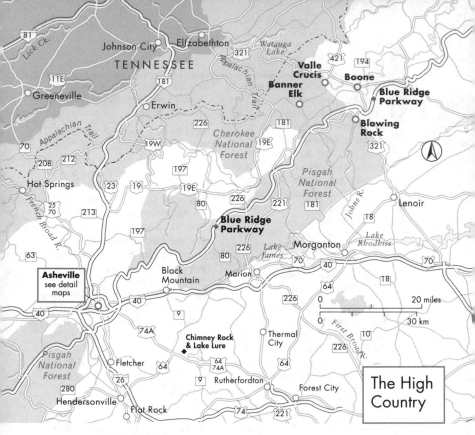

EXPLORING

The beautiful **Blue Ridge Parkway (BRP)** gently winds through mountains and meadows and crosses mountain streams for more than 469 mi on its way from Cherokee, North Carolina, to Waynesboro, Virginia, connecting the Great Smoky Mountains and Shenandoah national parks. With elevations ranging from 649 to 6,047 feet, and with more than 250 scenic lookout points, it is truly one of the most beautiful drives in North America. Admission to the Parkway is free. No commercial vehicles are allowed, and the entire parkway is free of billboards, although in a few places residential or commercial development encroaches close to the road. The parkway, which has a maximum speed limit of 45 mph, is generally open year-round but often closes during inclement weather. In winter, sections can be closed for weeks at a time due to snow, and even in good weather fog and clouds occasionally make driving difficult. Maps and information are available at visitor centers along the highway. Mile markers (MM) identify points of interest and indicate the distance from the parkway's starting point in Virginia. A new Park headquarters and visitor center near Asheville at mile marker 384 opened in late 2007. It has a "green roof" with plants growing on it. ■TIP→ Gas up before you get on the Parkway. Although there are no gas stations on the Parkway itself, you'll find stations at intersecting highways near Parkway exits. ⌧*Superintendent, Blue Ridge Pkwy.,*

199 Hemphill Knob Rd., Asheville
☎*828/298–0398* ⊕*www.nps.gov/
blri* ✉*Free.*

Craggy Gardens at mile marker 364.6, at 5,500 to 6,000 feet, has some of the parkway's most colorful displays of rhododendrons, usually in June. You can also hike trails and picnic here. ✉*MM 364.6* ☎*828/298–0398* ✉*Free.*

⟳ At **Emerald Village** you can tour an underground mine or dig for gems of your own. ✉*331 McKinney Mine Rd. at BRP, MM 334, Little Switzerland* ☎*828/765–6463 or 877/389–4653* ⊕*www.emeraldvillage.com* ✉*Mine $5, gem bucket $3–$100* ☺*May–Oct., weekdays 9–5, weekends 9–6; Apr., daily 10–4.*

The **Folk Art Center** displays and sells authentic mountain crafts made by members of the Southern Highland Craft Guild. Demonstrations are held frequently. ■ TIP→ **This is one of the best places in the region to buy high-quality crafts.** ✉*BRP, MM 382 at Asheville* ☎*828/298–7928* ☺*Jan.–Mar., daily 9–5; Apr.–Dec., daily 9–6.*

Just off the parkway at mile marker 305, **Grandfather Mountain** soars to 6,000 feet and is famous for its Mile-High Swinging Bridge, a 228-foot-long bridge that sways over a 1,000-foot drop into the Linville Valley. The **Natural History Museum** has exhibits on native minerals, flora and fauna, and pioneer life. The annual **Singing on the Mountain,** in June, is an opportunity to hear old-time gospel music and preaching, and the **Highland Games** in July bring together Scottish clans from all over North America for athletic events and Highland dancing. The owner of Grandfather Mountain, Hugh Morton, was a noted nature photographer; he died in 2006 at age 86. ✉*BRP and U.S. 221, Linville* ☎*828/733–4337 or 800/468–7325* ⊕*www.grandfather.com* ✉*$14* ☺*Apr.–mid-Nov., daily 8–dusk; mid-Nov.–Mar., daily 8–5.*

Green spaces along the parkway include **Julian Price Park,** which has hiking, canoeing on a mountain lake, trout fishing, and camping. ✉*MM 295–MM 298.1.*

⟳ **Linville Caverns** are the only caverns in the Carolinas. They go 2,000 feet beneath Humpback Mountain and have a year-round temperature of 51°F. North of Asheville, exit the parkway at mile marker 317.4 and turn left onto U.S. 221. ✉*U.S. 221, between Linville and Marion* ☎*828/756–4171* ⊕*www.linvillecaverns.com* ✉*$6* ☺*June–early Sept., daily 9–6; Apr., May, and mid-Sept.–Oct., daily 9–5; Nov. and Mar., daily 9–4:30; closed Dec.-Feb.*

From the **Linville Falls Visitor Center** a ½-mi hike leads to one of North Carolina's most photographed waterfalls. The easy trail winds through evergreens and rhododendrons to overlooks with views of the series of cascades tumbling into Linville Gorge. There are also a campground and a picnic area. ⊠ *Rte. 1, MM 316.3, Linville* ☎*828/765–1045.*

The **Moses H. Cone Park** has a turn-of-the-20th-century manor house that's now the **Parkway Craft Center.** The center sells fine work by area craftspeople. ⊠*MM 292.7–MM 295* ☎*828/295–7938* ☉*Mar. 15–Nov. 30, daily 9–5.*

Mt. Mitchell State Park includes the highest mountain peak east of the Rockies, Mt. Mitchell at 6,684 feet. The summit was named after Elisha Mitchell, who died from a fall while trying to prove the mountain's true height. At the 1,855-acre park you can climb an observation tower and get food at a restaurant. Keep an eye on the weather here, as high winds and snow can occur at almost any time, occasionally even in summer. The lowest temperature ever recorded in North Carolina was at Mt. Mitchell on Jan. 21, 1985: -34°F. Clouds obscure the views here for at least parts of eight days out of 10. ⊠*2388 NC Hwy. 128, MM 355, Burnsville* ☎*828/675–4611* ☜*Free.*

Mt. Pisgah, at 5,721 feet one of the most easily recognized peaks due to the television tower installed there in the 1950s, has walking trails, an amphitheater where nature programs are given most evenings June through October, a campground, inn, picnic area, and small grocery. The nearby area called **Graveyard Fields** is popular for blueberry picking in July. In 1992 a snowstorm in *May* dropped more than 5 feet of snow here. ⊠*Blue Ridge Pkwy., MM 408.6* ☎*828/648–2664 campground.*

☾ **Museum of North Carolina Minerals** at mile marker 331 has hands-on displays about gold, copper, kaolin, and other minerals found nearby. The museum was recently renovated. ⊠*MM 331 at U.S. 226* ☎*828/765–2761* ☜*Free* ☉*Daily 9–5.*

WHERE TO STAY

$$$$ ⌂**Eseeola Lodge at Linville Golf Club.** Built by Harvard professor Wil-
★ liams James in 1891 and rebuilt in 1936 after a fire, this lakeside lodge, best described as dressed-up rustic, sits 3,800 feet above sea level and is one sure way to beat summer's heat. Golf is a passion here, on the Donald Ross-designed course, but the diversions are many. All rooms overlook the manicured grounds and gardens. Rich chestnut paneling and stonework grace the public areas. Entrées at the restaurant ($$$$) may include free-range chicken and rainbow trout; jacket and tie are required at dinner. **Pros:** upscale lodge on championship golf course. **Cons:** a bit too much like a country club for some tastes. ⊠*175 Linville Ave., off U.S. 221, Linville* ☎*828/733–4311 or 800/742–6717* ⊕*www.eseeola.com* ⇖*19 rooms, 5 suites, 1 cottage* ♿*In-hotel: restaurant, bar, golf course, tennis courts, pool, gym, spa, no-smoking rooms* ⊟*AE, MC, V* ☉*Closed late Oct.–mid-May* ⌺*MAP.*

$$ ⌂ **Little Switzerland Inn.** Families cozy up in the lobby of this old mountain inn, which dates to 1910, to play Monopoly or just doze over a book. The staff is cheerful, and you have a choice of comfy lodge rooms (without a/c) or bigger, brighter rooms in newer buildings. A "motorcycle lodge" is an eight-room cabin ($65 double) with parking for your bike. The Swiss theme is carried through to the Chalet restaurant

($–$$) and there are ice-cream and sweets shops on the grounds. **Pros:** unpretentious lodge near parkway, good value. **Cons:** some rooms need upgrading and updating. ⊠*MM 334 at Hwy. 226A, Little Switzerland* ☎*828/765–2153 or 800/654–4026* ⊕*www.switzerlandinn.com* ➟*59 rooms, 5 cottages* ⅏*In-room: no a/c (some), no phone (some). In-hotel: restaurant, tennis courts, pool, Wi-Fi, no-smoking rooms* ▤*MC, V* ⊘*Closed Nov.–mid-Apr.* ⏉*BP.*

$–$$ ▦**Pisgah Inn.** This inn, run by a park-service concessionaire, has motel-like rooms of no distinction, but the setting, at almost 1 mi high right on the parkway, is spectacular. Rooms have small porches or balconies with rocking chairs. Although an inn has been on this site since 1919, most of the present structures were built in 1964. Some rooms were renovated in 2008. The restaurant has great views to the west and offers mountain trout, along with burgers and other standard fare. **Pros:** unbeatable setting a mile high on a mountaintop with 30-mi views; good value; on-site restaurant. **Cons:** motel-like rooms; remote setting; often fully booked months in advance. ⊠*MM 408, Waynesville* ☎*828/235–8228* ⊕*www.pisgahinn.com* ➟*51 rooms* ⅏*In-room: no a/c, refrigerator (some). In-hotel: restaurant, no-smoking rooms* ▤*MC, V* ⊘*Closed Nov.–late Mar.*

SPORTS & THE OUTDOORS

HIKING More than 100 trails lead off the Blue Ridge Parkway, from easy strolls to strenuous hikes. For more information on parkway trails, contact the **National Park Service Blue Ridge Parkway office** (☎*828/298–0398* ⊕*www.nps.gov/blri*). Another good source is *Walking the Blue Ridge: A Guide to the Trails of the Blue Ridge Parkway,* by Leonard Adkins, available at most parkway visitor center gift shops. The **Bluff Mountain Trail,** at Doughton Park (MM 238.5), is a moderately strenuous 7½-mi trail winding through forests, pastures, and valleys, and along the mountainside. Moses H. Cone Park's (MM 292.7) **Figure 8 Trail** is an easy and beautiful trail that the Cone family designed for their morning walks. The ½-mi loop winds through a tunnel of rhododendrons and a hardwood forest. Those who tackle the strenuous, ½-mi **Waterrock Knob Trail** (MM 451.2), near the south end of the parkway, will be rewarded with spectacular views from the 6,400-foot-high Waterrock Knob summit.

ROCK CLIMBING One of the most challenging climbs in the country is the **Linville Gorge** (⊠*MM 317* ☎*828/652–2144*), often called "the Grand Canyon of North Carolina." Permits are available from the district forest ranger's office in Nebo or from the Linville Falls Texaco station on U.S. 221.

SKIING **Moses H. Cone Park** (☎*828/295–7591*) is known for its cross-country skiing trails. On the Blue Ridge Parkway, **Roan Mountain** (☎*615/772–3303*), open daily during the winter, is famous for its deep powder. Tours and equipment are available from **High Country Ski Shop** (☎*828/733–2008*) in Pineola on U.S. 221.

BLOWING ROCK

86 mi northeast of Asheville; 93 mi west of Winston-Salem.

Blowing Rock, a draw for mountain visitors since the 1880s, has retained the flavor of a quiet New England village, with stone walls and buildings with wood shakes or bark siding. About 1,000 people are permanent residents of this town at a 4,000-foot elevation, but the population swells each summer. On summer afternoons it seems as if most of the town's population is sitting on benches in the town park. To ensure that the town would remain rural, the community banded together to prohibit large hotels and motels. Blowing Rock is the inspiration for the small town in resident Jan Karon's novels about country life in the fictional town of Mitford. To get here from the Blue Ridge Parkway, take U.S. 221/321 to just north of the entrance to Moses H. Cone Park.

The **Blowing Rock** looms over the Johns River Gorge. If you throw your hat over the sheer precipice, it may blow back to you, should the wind gods be playful. The story goes that a Cherokee man and a Chickasaw maiden fell in love. Torn between his tribe and his love, he jumped from the cliff, but she prayed to the Great Spirit, and he was blown safely back to her. ⊠ *Off U.S. 321* ☎ *828/295–7111* ⊕ *www.blowingrock. org* ≅ *$6* ⊗ *June–Oct., daily 8–8; Jan.–Mar., daily 8:30–5; Apr., daily 8:30–6; May, daily 8:30–7; Nov. and Dec., daily 9–5.*

The **Tweetsie Railroad** is a popular Wild West theme park built into the side of a mountain and centered on a steam locomotive beset by robbers. A petting zoo, carnival amusements, gem panning, shows, and concessions, all mostly of interest to young children, are also here. Several of the attractions are at the top of the mountain and can be reached on foot or by ski lift. ⊠ *U.S. 321/221, off Blue Ridge Pkwy. at MM 291* ☎ *828/264–9061 or 800/526–5740* ⊕ *www.tweetsie-railroad.com* ≅ *$30 (children 3-12, $22)* ⊗ *Early May and Sept.–Oct., Fri.–Sun. 9–6; mid-May–late Aug., daily 9–6; closed Dec.–Apr.*

WHERE TO STAY & EAT

¢–$ ✕ **Canyons.** The long-range view from the deck of Canyons is so dra-
SOUTHWESTERN matic that owner Bart Conway put a live minicam on the restaurant's Web site. While oohing over the mountain scenery, or eyeing the funky artwork on the walls inside, you can munch on fresh-made tortilla chips, chimichangas, veggie burritos, or a classic drive-in burger slathered with chili and slaw. On most days the restaurant is the busiest one in town. There's live entertainment Thursday to Sunday nights and a Sunday brunch. ⊠ *8960 U.S. 321 Bypass* ☎ *828/295–7661* ⊟ *AE, D, MC, V.*

$–$$ ⬚ **Alpine Village Inn.** This motel in the heart of Blowing Rock harks back to a simpler time. Rooms are neat and attractive in a homey way. Owners Rudy and Lynn Cutrera have decorated them with antiques, quilts, even flowers on holidays. They were renovated in 2005. Room refrigerators are available, and morning coffee is served. **Pros:** cheerful little motel; near downtown shops and restaurants; good value. **Cons:** small rooms; don't expect luxury. ⊠ *297 Sunset Dr.* ☎ *828/295-7206* ⊕ *www.alpine-*

village-inn.com ➷*17 rooms* ☌*In-room: refrigerator (some). In-hotel: no-smoking rooms* ▤*D, MC, V* ⊙*Closed Jan.–mid-Apr.*

$$$–$$$$ ⌷**Chetola Resort.** This inn and condo resort, named for the Cherokee word meaning "haven of rest," grew out of an early-20th-century stone-and-wood lodge. The original building now houses the resort's restaurant and meeting rooms and is adjacent to the 1988 lodge. Many guest rooms in the lodge have private balconies facing either the mountains, a small lake, or both. The Bob Timberlake Inn is a more upscale lodge within a lodge. Condominiums are spread among the hills, and the 87-acre property adjoins Moses H. Cone Park, with hiking trails and riding facilities. **Pros:** variety of accommodations from condos to motel-like rooms to upscale lodge rooms. **Cons:** no golf on premises, some units need upgrading. ⊠*N. Main St., Box 17, ½ mi north of BRP via U.S. 321* ☏*828/295–5500 or 800/243–8652* ⊕*www.chetola.com* ➷*45 rooms, 5 suites, 62 condominiums* ☌*In-room: safe (some), kitchen (some), refrigerator (some), DVD (some). In-hotel: 2 restaurants, bar, tennis courts, pool, gym, bicycles, laundry facilities, no kids under 21 (at Bob Timberlake Inn), no-smoking rooms* ▤*AE, D, MC, V.*

$$$–$$$$ ⌷**Hound Ears Club.** This alpine inn and golf resort on 750 acres overlooking Grandfather Mountain and a lush golf course designed by George Cobb (green fees are $90, plus $22 cart fee) offers amenities such as a swimming pool secluded in a natural grotto and comfortable, well-kept rooms dressed in Waverly print fabrics. The main lodge, with a Scottish theme down to red-and-green plaid carpet, has only four rooms. Condos and cottages are also available for rent. The dining room is open only to guests and members; reservations are required, as are a jacket and tie for dinner. **Pros:** golf, golf, and more golf; stunning mountain views. **Cons:** some may not like dress code for dinner. ⊠*328 Shulls Mill Rd., off Rte. 105, Blowing Rock* ☏*828/963–4321* ⊕*www.houndears.com* ➷*28 rooms* ☌*In-hotel: restaurant, golf course, tennis courts, pool, gym, no-smoking rooms* ▤*AE, MC, V* ⏻*BP.*

$$$–$$$$ ⌷**Inn at Ragged Gardens.** With a grand stone staircase in the entry hall, colorful gardens, richly toned chestnut paneling, and the chestnut-bark siding found on many older homes in the High Country, it's no wonder that this manor-style house in the heart of Blowing Rock gets rave reviews. You're likely to appreciate the attention to detail: the European and American antiques blended with contemporary art and the all-hours butler's pantry. All rooms have fireplaces, and some have private balconies. A two-night minimum is required on weekends. The Best Cellar restaurant (entrées $18–$35), which relocated here after a fire in its original location, is excellent. **Pros:** historic old inn; within walking distance of Blowing Rock shops and restaurants. **Cons:** if you're on the first floor, you may hear guests on floor above. ⊠*203 Sunset Dr.* ☏*828/295–9703* ⊕*www.ragged-gardens.com* ➷*6 rooms, 5 suites* ☌*In-hotel: restaurant, no kids under 13, no-smoking rooms* ▤*MC, V* ⏻*BP.*

$$$$ ⌷**Westglow Spa.** If you want to get buff, lose weight, and be pampered at a beautiful mountain estate, and if money is no object, Westglow Spa may be your cup of herbal tea. Housed in an elegant 1916 mansion on 20 acres, once the home of 19th-century impressionist painter Elliott

Daingerfield, the health resort spares nothing for its few, select guests. The fitness center is packed with the latest workout machines, health gizmos, spa facilities, and an indoor pool with a stunning view of the mountains. Spa packages start at $576 per person, double occupancy. Meals, emphasizing low-fat and high-fiber items, are served in the Elliott restaurant in the manor house. **Pros:** rejuvenate yourself in luxury surroundings; complete health spa facilities; healthful meals. **Cons:** very expensive. ⊠*2845 U.S. 221 S* ☎*828/295–4463 or 800/562–0807* ⊕*www.westglow.com* ⇆*8 rooms, 2 cottages* ⚷*In-room: Wi-Fi In-hotel: restaurant, tennis court, pool, spa, no kids under 16, no-smoking rooms* ☰*AE, MC, V* ⊙*EP*

SPORTS & THE OUTDOORS

RAFTING   You can go white-water rafting on Wilson Creek or the Nolichucky or Wautaga rivers with **High Mountain Expeditions** (⊠*1380 Hwy. 105 S, Boone* ☎*828/264–7368 or 800/262–9036).*

SKIING   There's downhill skiing and snowboarding at **Appalachian Ski Mountain** (⊠*940 Ski Mountain Rd., Boone* ☎*828/295–7828 or 800/322–2373).*

SHOPPING

Bolick Pottery (⊠*Martin House, Main St., Blowing Rock* ☎*828/295–3862),* sells mountain crafts and pottery handcrafted by Glenn and Lula Bolick, fifth-generation potters.

BOONE

8 mi north of Blowing Rock.

Boone, at the convergence of three major highways—U.S. 321, U.S. 421, and Route 105—is a fast-growing college town, home to Appalachian State University (ASU) and its 16,000 students. Suburban sprawl has arrived, especially along U.S. 321 with its clusters of fast-food restaurants, chain motels, and a small mall, the only enclosed mall in the High Country. Closer to ASU, however, you get more of the college-town vibe, with organic-food stores and boutiques. The town was named for frontiersman Daniel Boone, whose family moved to the area when Daniel was 15. Restaurants here serve only wine and beer, not mixed drinks.

On 6 acres adjacent to the Horn in the West amphitheater, **Daniel Boone Native Gardens** highlights local plants and trees in a setting of quiet beauty. The wrought-iron gate to the gardens was a gift of Daniel Boone VI, a direct descendant of the pioneer. ⊠*651 Horn in the West Dr., .25 mi off U.S. 321,* ☎*828/264–6390* ⊡*$2* ⊙*May–Oct. 9–6*

WHERE TO STAY & EAT

$ ✕**Dan'l Boone Inn Restaurant.** Near Appalachian State University, in a
★   former hospital surrounded by a picket fence and flowers, Dan'l Boone
AMERICAN   offers old-fashioned food served family style. Warning: the portions of fried chicken, country-style steak, ham, mashed potatoes, scrambled eggs, bacon, and breads (to name a few) are extremely generous. Lunch or dinner, including beverage and dessert, is a bargain at $15.95, and

breakfast is $8.95. (You can't get breakfast on weekdays.) There's usually a line waiting to get in. The kitchen and part of the restaurant were renovated in mid-2006. ⊠*130 Hardin St.,* ☏*828/264–8657* ▭*No credit cards* ⊘*Breakfast Sat.–Sun. only; no lunch weekdays, Jan.–Apr.*

$$–$$$ ★ ⌦**Lovill House Inn.** This restored two-story country farmhouse once housed the law offices of Captain Edward Francis Lovill, a decorated Confederate officer and a founding trustee of what became Appalachian State University. Built in 1875 and featuring unusual details such as wormy chestnut woodwork, the inn occupies 11 wooded acres in a quiet area just west of downtown. On the grounds are a picnic area, gardens, and a stream with a waterfall. Some rooms have antique iron bedsteads or sleigh beds and fireplaces. Every evening owners Scott and Anne Peecook host a social hour. **Pros:** well-run B&B; charming rooms (some with fireplaces); delicious breakfasts. **Cons:** no air-conditioning in rooms in main house. ⊠*404 Old Bristol Rd.,* ☏*828/264–4204 or 800/849–9466* ⊕*www.lovillhouseinn.com* ⇨*6 rooms* ⌕*In-room: no a/c (some), Wi-Fi. In-hotel: Wi-Fi, no kids under 12, no-smoking rooms* ▭*MC, V* ⌶⊙⌶*BP.*

NIGHTLIFE & THE ARTS

Horn in the West, a project of the Southern Appalachian Historical Association, is an outdoor drama that traces the story of the lives of Daniel Boone and other pioneers, as well as the Cherokee, during the American Revolution. ⊠*Amphitheater at 591 Horn in the West Dr., off U.S. 321,* ☏*828/264–2120* ⊠*$18* ⊙*Performances mid-June–mid-Aug., Tues.–Sun. at 8* PM.

A part of Appalachian State University, and expanded in 2004 with new gallery space and a 135-seat lecture hall, the **Turchin Center for the Visual Arts** (⊠*423 W. King St.* ☏*828/262–3017*) is the largest visual-arts center in the High Country, with regular exhibitions of regional as well as national and international art.

SPORTS & THE OUTDOORS

CANOEING &
RAFTING

Near Boone and Blowing Rock, the New River, a federally designated Wild and Scenic River (Class I and II rapids) provides excitement for canoeists and rafters, as do the Watauga River, Wilson Creek, and the Toe River. One outfitter is **Wahoo's Adventures** (☏*828/262–5774 or 800/444–7238*).

GOLF

The High Country has many challenging courses. **Boone Golf Club** (⊠*433 Fairway Dr.* ☏*828/264–8760*) is a good par-71 public course for the whole family. Green fee $22–$44, plus $15 for a cart. **Hound Ears Club** (⊠*Rte. 105, 328 Shulls Mill Rd. Blowing Rock* ☏*828/963–4312*) has a par-72 18-hole course with great mountain views. Green fee $90. **Linville Golf Club** (⊠*83 Roseboro Rd., Linville* ☏*828/733–4363*), 17 mi from Boone, has a par-72 Donald Ross–designed course. This private course is open to guests at Eseeola Lodge. Green fee, including cart, is $115.

VALLE CRUCIS

5 mi south of Boone.

This tiny mountain town has the state's first rural historic district; vintage stores line the downtown streets.

Everything from ribbons and overalls to yard art and cookware is sold in the original **Mast General Store** (⊠*Rte. 194* ☎*828/963–6511*). Built in 1882, the store has plank floors worn to a soft sheen and an active old-timey post office. You can take a shopping break by sipping bottled soda pop while sitting in a rocking chair on the store's back porch. For more shopping, an annex is just down the road.

WHERE TO STAY

$$$–$$$$
★
Mast Farm Inn. You can turn back the clock and still enjoy modern amenities at this charming pastoral inn, built in the 1800s and now on the National Register of Historic Places. Rooms are in the farmhouse or in log cottages. The restaurant (reservations essential) uses locally and organically grown vegetables to enhance its innovative uptown menu. Organic gardening demonstrations are held in the inn's gardens. **Pros:** delightful country inn; personalized service; amazing food. **Cons:** a little off the beaten path. ⊠*2543 Broadstone Rd., Box 704* ☎*828/963–5857 or 888/963–5857* ⊕*www.mastfarminn.com* ⇆*7 rooms, 7 cottages* ⚭*In-hotel: restaurant, no-smoking rooms* ⊟*AE, D, MC, V* ⃝*BP.*

SHOPPING

If you're looking for a mountain painting, stop by **Gallery Alta Vista** (⊠*2839 Broadstone Rd.* ☎*828/963–5247*), which features the work of some 200 artists, many from western North Carolina. If shopping wears you out, you can overnight here, because the gallery is also a B&B.

BANNER ELK

6 mi southwest of Valle Crucis; 11 mi southwest of Boone.

Banner Elk is a ski-resort town, which bills itself as the "highest town in the East," surrounded by the lofty peaks of Grandfather, Hanging Rock, Beech, and Sugar mountains. The massively ugly condo tower you'll see on top of Little Sugar Mountain (not a part of the Sugar Mountain ski resort) is the only scar on the scenic beauty of the area. At least something good came of the monstrosity—it so outraged local residents that it prompted the passing of a ridge line law preventing such mountaintop development.

OFF THE BEATEN PATH
Land of Oz (⊠*2669 Beech Mountain Pkwy., Beech Mountain* ☎*828/387–2000* ⊕*www.emeraldmtn.com*). You're not in Kansas anymore, Toto—you're in Beech Mountain. From 1970 to 1980 this High Country town had its own Land of Oz, a theme park devoted to re-creating Frank Baum's famous Emerald City. In its first year the park attracted 400,000 visitors, making it one of the leading tourist attractions in the state. Changing tastes and economic problems led to its demise,

MOUNTAIN FOOD

Traditional mountain cooking is rib-sticking fare, intended for people who work hard on the farm all day. It dates to a time when the biggest meal of the day was dinner, taken at noon, and the food was heavy: country ham with red-eye gravy, pan-fried chicken, and vegetables from the garden such as half-runner beans seasoned with fatback, creamed sweet corn, and new potatoes. With it came cat-head biscuits (so called because of their size), fresh-churned butter, sourwood honey (light-color honey from sourwood trees that bloom in late spring), and tall glasses of springwater and buttermilk. Some the more unusual mountain dishes, only rarely available at local restaurants, include ramps (a smelly cousin of the onion) with eggs; baked groundhog; bear meat (prepared as a roast or stew); creases or creasie greens (a salad of wild wintercress); leather-britches (beans dried in the pod and boiled with salt pork); and sweet dried-apple pie.

and it sat vacant for another decade, until 1990, when a 440-acre housing development called Emerald Mountain was developed on the site. Most of Oz's Emerald City is now gone, but Dorothy's farm was restored and the Yellow Brick Road patched. Now **Emerald Mountain Development** sells homesites and offers resort rentals. (You can rent what's purported to be Dorothy's House, a three-bedroom, one-bath farmhouse, for $135 to $165 a night, depending on the season.) One weekend a year, usually in early October, the public is invited to visit what remains of the Land of Oz theme park at the Autumn at Oz Party. Munchkins welcome.

WHERE TO STAY

$$$ **Banner Elk Inn Bed & Breakfast and Cottages.** Here, less than ½ mi from Banner Elk's only stoplight, you have the choice of either traditional B&B rooms in a restored 1912 farmhouse or spacious cottages with kitchens. The newly constructed Bark House has two bedrooms, fully equipped kitchen, a stone fireplace, and 19-foot cathedral ceiling. Even if you opt for the Bark House or one of pewter-gray cottages at the back of the main house, you can get a full B&B breakfast on weekends, or a continental breakfast weekdays. Owner Beverly Lait also offers several vacation rental houses nearby. **Pros:** variety of accommodations from rooms in historic house to new cottages, full breakfasts on weekends. **Cons:** a little away from center of town. ⊠ *407 Main St. E* ☎ *828/898–6223 or 800/295–7851* ⊕ *www.bannerelkinn.com* ⇆ *6 rooms, 4 cottages* ⌂ *In-room: no a/c (some), kitchen (some), no TV (some), Wi-Fi (some).* ☐ *MC, V* ⍿ *BP.*

SPORTS & THE OUTDOORS

CANOEING & RAFTING   **Edge of the World Outfitters** (⊠ *Rte. 184,* ☎ *828/898–9550 or 800/789–3343*) offers white-water rafting, rappelling, canoeing, and snowboarding lessons in the Banner Elk area.

SKIING   At 5,506 feet above sea level, **Ski Beech** (⊠ *Rte. 184, Beech Mountain* ☎ *828/387–2011 or 800/438–2093*) is the highest resort in the eastern United States. One of the larger resorts in the area, **Sugar Mountain** (⊠ *Off Rte. 184, Banner Elk* ☎ *828/898–4521 or 800/784–2768*) has an equipment shop and lessons and tubing for the kids. A higher-end resort, **Hawksnest Ski Resort** (⊠ *2058 Skyland Dr., Seven Devils* ☎ *828/963–6561 or 800/822–4295*) has full snowmaking capability and challenging slopes. However, the golf course is closed. Call for **ski conditions** (☎ *800/962–2322*). ■TIP➔ The Gold Card, sold in limited numbers beginning in August of each year, allows unlimited skiing with no blackout dates at six North Carolina ski resorts (Sapphire Valley, Sugar Mountain, Appalachian Ski Mountain, Ski Beech, Cataloochee, and Wolf Ridge Ski Resort) for a fee of $775. For information, call (☎ *828/898–4521*).

SHOPPING

For hardware, firewood, a half gallon of milk, locally grown vegetables, pumpkins for Halloween, snowboard and ski rentals, gourmet bird seed, today's *Wall Street Journal,* and just about anything else you need, **Fred's General Mercantile** (⊠ *501 Beech Mountain Pkwy.* ☎ *828/387–4838*), half general store and half boutique, is the place to go in the Banner Elk and Beech Mountain areas, and has been for 30 years.

THE SOUTHERN MOUNTAINS

The Southern Mountains encompass a diverse area in 10 North Carolina counties south and west of Asheville. They include the towns of Hendersonville and Flat Rock in Henderson County, and Brevard in Transylvania County. The Southern Mountains also include Cashiers, Highlands, and Lake Toxaway, chic summer enclaves where some lakefront building lots now cost a million dollars.

HENDERSONVILLE

23 mi south of Asheville via I–26.

Hendersonville, with about 11,000 residents, has one of the most engaging and vibrant downtowns of any small city in the South. Historic Main Street, as it's called, extends 10 serpentine blocks, lined with flower boxes and about 40 shops, including many antiques stores, galleries, and restaurants. Each year from April through October Main Street has displays of public art. Within walking distance of downtown are several B&Bs.

The Hendersonville area is North Carolina's main apple-growing area, and some 200 apple orchards dot the rolling hills around town. An Apple Festival, attracting some 200,000 people, is held each year in August.

♻ The **Holmes Educational State Forest,** a 235-acre state forest, has "talking trees," a fun way for kids to learn about the forests of western North Carolina—just punch a button on a hickory or poplar, and a recording tells you about the tree. ⊠ *Crabtree Rd., 9 mi from downtown Hendersonville* ☎ *828/692–0100* ⬜ *Free* ☉ *Mid-Mar.–mid-Nov., Tues.–Fri. 9–5, weekends 11–8.*

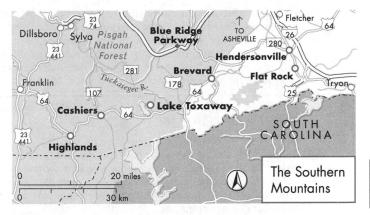

The **Historic Johnson Farm,** a 19th-century tobacco farm that is now operated by Henderson County Public Schools, has the original farmhouse, barn, outbuildings, and a museum with about 1,000 artifacts typical of farm life of the time. ✉*3346 Haywood Rd., 4 mi north of downtown Hendersonville* ☎*828/697-4733* ✆*Guided tours $3* ⊙*Tues.–Fri. 9–2:30; closed on school holidays.*

OFF THE BEATEN PATH

Thomas Wolfe's Angel. In his novel *Look Homeward, Angel,* Asheville-born Thomas Wolfe makes many references to an angel statue. The famous angel, in real life carved from Italian marble by Wolfe's father, W. O. Wolfe, stands in Hendersonville's Oakdale Cemetery, marking the graves of a family named Johnson, to whom the senior Wolfe sold the statue. The statue is protected by an iron fence. ✉*U.S. 64, just west of downtown Hendersonville.*

WHERE TO STAY & EAT

$$–$$$
AMERICAN

✕**Bistro 502.** The walls are a sedate beige, but the food here is anything but. For lunch, there's a nice selection of paninis and other sandwiches. At dinner, moderately priced entrées (mostly $15–$20, with a choice of salad or soup) include fresh fish and some comfort foods, such as seared pork loin and meat loaf. There's local art on the walls, and the tables at the front are good for people-watching on Main Street. You're invited to post your comments in a spiral-bound notebook at each table, and the musings of previous guests are fun to read. ✉*502 N. Main St.* ☎*828/697-5350* ▭*AE, MC, V* ⊙*Closed Sun.; dinner only Sat.*

$$–$$$
AMERICAN

✕**Flight Wood Grill & Wine Bar.** Located in a 1920s-era bank building, complete with the old vault, your best investments here include the many items grilled over local apple wood, including lamb chops (four for $28), chicken breast with salsa verde ($19), and the mixed grill ($22–$34 depending on which items you order). Wood-grilled pizzas ($10–$12) also are good choices. About 300 birds soar in a mobile around the ceiling. The staff is perky and pours some 40 wines by the glass. ✉*401 N. Main St.* ☎*828/694-1030* ▭*AE, MC, V* ⊙*Dinner Mon.–Sat.*

$$$–$$$$

▦**Waverly Inn.** On a warm afternoon you'll love to "sit a spell" in a rocking chair on the front porch of Hendersonville's oldest inn. All 14 rooms in the 1898 three-story Victorian, two blocks from downtown, are named after native flowers and shrubs and outfitted with antique furnishings. The Mountain Magnolia suite has a king canopy bed, and the Silverbell room, painted an airy yellow and white, has a four-poster bed and a claw-foot bathtub. **Pros:** historic small inn; walking distance of downtown; friendly and very well run. **Cons:** quite a bit of traffic in area; some rooms are on small side. ⊠*783 N. Main St.* ☎*828/698– 9193 or 800/537–8195* ⊕*www.waverlyinn.com* ➞*13 rooms, 1 suite* ⚴*In-room: DVD (some), Wi-Fi. In-hotel: Wi-Fi, no-smoking rooms* ▭*AE, D, DC, MC, V* ⊠*BP.*

NIGHTLIFE & THE ARTS

THE ARTS   The Skyland Hotel is one of the places where Jazz Age novelist F. Scott Fitzgerald stayed when he visited his wife in a mental institution in Asheville, and the building is now the **Arts Center** (⊠*538 N. Main St.* ☎*828/693–8504*), a nonprofit organization that puts on art exhibits and other cultural programs.

NIGHTLIFE   While local nightlife is limited, you can hear live music on weekend nights and enjoy one of about 125 types of beer at **Hannah Flanagan's Pub** (⊠*300 N. Main St.* ☎*828/696–1665*).

SPORTS & THE OUTDOORS

GOLF   Among the five golf courses in Hendersonville, the 6,719-yard, par-71, private **Champion Hills Golf Club** (⊠*1 Hagen Dr.* ☎*828/693–3600*) is the home course of famed golf-course designer Tom Fazio. An enjoyable public course is **Crooked Tree Golf Club** (⊠*764 Crooked Tree Rd.* ☎*828/692–2011*), where the clubhouse was once a corporate retreat owned by Warner Bros., the movie company.

SHOPPING

If you like to shop, you'll enjoy browsing the 40 shops on **Historic Main Street,** including several antiques stores, a branch of Mast General Store, and local boutiques.

FLAT ROCK

3 mi south of Hendersonville; 26 mi south of Asheville via I–26.

Flat Rock has been a summer resort since the early 19th century. It was a favorite of wealthy planters from Charleston eager to escape the Lowcountry heat. The trip from Charleston to Flat Rock by horse and carriage took as long as two weeks, so you know there must be something here that made the long trek worthwhile.

☺ The **Carl Sandburg Home National Historic Site** is the spot to which the
★ poet and Lincoln biographer Carl Sandburg moved with his wife Lillian in 1945. Guided tours of their house, Connemara, where Sandburg's papers still lie scattered on his desk, are given by the National Park Service. In summer the productions *The World of Carl Sandburg* and *Rootabaga Stories* are presented at the amphitheater. Kids enjoy a walk around the grounds of the farm, which still maintains descendants of the Sandburg family goats. ⊠*1928 Little River Rd.* ☎*828/693–4178* ⊕*www.nps.gov/carl* ⊠*$5* ☉*Daily 9–5.*

The **Flat Rock Playhouse** has a high reputation for summer stock theater. The season runs from May to mid-December. ✉*2661 Greenville Hwy.* ☎*828/693–0731* ⊕*www.flatrockplayhouse.org.*

BREVARD

40 mi southwest of Asheville on Rte. 280.

With its friendly, highly walkable downtown, Brevard is Mayberry RFD transported to the Pisgah National Forest. In fact, a popular toy store in town is called O. P. Taylor's—get it?

Brevard residents go nuts over the white squirrels, which dart around the town's parks. These aren't albinos, but a variation of the eastern gray squirrel. About one-fourth of the squirrels in town are white. The white squirrels are thought to have come originally from Hawaii by way of Florida; they possibly were released in Brevard by a visitor in the 1950s. Whatever the truth, today Brevard capitalizes on it by holding a White Squirrel Festival in late May. One of the best places to see the little devils is on the **Brevard College** (✉*400 N. Broad St.*) campus.

The oldest frame house in western North Carolina, the **Allison-Deaver House** was built in the early 1800s, and has been renovated and expanded several times. ✉*N.C. Hwy. 280, Pisgah Forest, near Forest Gate Shopping Center* ☎*828/884–5137* 🎟*Donations accepted* ⏱*Apr.–Oct., Fri. and Sat. 10–4, Sun. 1–4.*

☾ Nearby Pisgah National Forest has the **Cradle of Forestry in America**
★ **National Historic Site,** the home of the first forestry school in the United States, with a 1-mi interpretive trail, the school's original log buildings, and a visitor center with many hands-on exhibits of interest to kids. The road from Brevard to the Cradle of Foresty, a scenic byway, continues on to connect with the Blue Ridge Parkway near Mt. Pisgah. ✉*1001 Pisgah Hwy., U.S. 276* ☎*828/884–5823* ⊕*www.cradleofforestry.com* 🎟*$5* ⏱*Mid-Apr.–early Nov., daily 9–5.*

The newest addition to nature sites near Brevard is **DuPont State Forest,** which was established in 1996 and expanded in 2000. You'll find 10,400 acres with four waterfalls and 80 mi of old dirt roads to explore, with ideal conditions for biking or horseback riding. ✉*U.S. 64 and Little River Rd.* ☎*828/877–6527* ⊕*www.dupontforest.com* 🎟*Free.*

Near the road and easy to get to, **Looking Glass Falls** is a classic, with water cascading 60 feet into a clear pool. ✉*Pisgah National Forest, north of Brevard, off U.S. 276* 🎟*Free.*

☾ At the **Pisgah Center for Wildlife Education** the fish hatchery produces more than 400,000 brown, rainbow, and native brook trout each year for release in local streams. You can see the fish up close in tanks called raceways and even feed them (approved trout feed is sold for a quarter). There's also a small visitor center with information about the life cycle of trout and an educational nature trail. ✉*Rte. 475 off U.S. 276 in Pisgah National Forest* ☎*828/877–4423* ⏱*Daily 8–5* 🎟*Free.*

At **Sliding Rock** in summer you can skid 60 feet on a natural waterslide. Wear old jeans and tennis shoes and bring a towel. ⊠*Pisgah National Forest, north of Brevard, off U.S. 276* ☎*828/877–3265* ⊠*$3 per car* ☉*Late May–early Sept., daily 10–5:30.*

WHERE TO STAY & EAT

¢

AMERICAN

✗**Cardinal Drive-In.** The cheeseburgers are just fair and the onion rings are like fried cardboard, but this is an authentic piece of Americana—a real drive-in, with carhops and everything. ⊠*7328 S. Broad St.* ☎*828/884–7085* ⊟*No credit cards.*

$$$

ECLECTIC

✗**Hobnob.** You can hobnob with old and new friends at this casual spot in a colorfully painted house near downtown. The co-owners, who formerly ran a restaurant in Charleston, have brought a Lowcountry edge to dining in Brevard, with dishes like Carolina crab cake on sweet corn salad. Other dishes have a French influence. ⊠*226 Main St.* ☎*828/966–4662* ⊟*AE, MC, V.*

$–$$

▥**Red House Inn.** One of the oldest houses in Brevard, the Red House Inn was built in 1851 as a trading post and later served as a courthouse, tavern, post office, and school. Now it's an unpretentious but pleasant B&B four blocks from the center of town. There are four rooms in the main house and an efficiency cottage. **Pros:** B&B in historic house; comfortable; friendly hosts. **Cons:** not for swinging singles. ⊠*412 W. Probart St.* ☎*828/884–9349* ⊕*www.brevardbedandbreakfast.com* ⊯*4 rooms, 1 cottage* ⅁*In-room: refrigerator (some), Wi-Fi. In-hotel: no-smoking rooms* ⊟ *MC, V* ⅋*BP.*

NIGHTLIFE & THE ARTS

THE ARTS

The nationally known **Brevard Music Center** (⌂*P.O. Box 312* ☎*828/884–2011* ⊕*www.brevardmusic.org*) has a seven-week music festival each summer, with about 80 concerts from mid-June to early August. Keith Lockhart is the principal conductor.

Formerly the Jim Bob Tinsley cowboy museum, the **Transylvania Heritage Museum** (⊠ *W. Jordan St., 28712* ☎*828/884–2347*) has displays on the Brevard area and also on life and interests of Brevard native Tinsley, a musicologist and author of 10 books who played with Gene Autry.

SPORTS & THE OUTDOORS

FISHING

Catch rainbow, brown, or brook trout on the Davidson River, named one of the top 100 trout streams in the United States by Trout Unlimited. **Davidson River Outfitters** (⊠*26 Pisgah Forest Hwy.* ☎*828/877–4181*) arranges trips and also has a fly-fishing school and a fly shop.

GOLF

Etowah Valley Country Club and Golf Lodge (⊠*U.S. 64, Etowah* ☎*828/891–7141 or 800/451–8174*) has three very different (one par-72, two par-73) 18-hole courses and offers good package deals.

MOUNTAIN BIKING

The North Carolina Mountains offer some of the best mountain biking in the East. Among the favorite places for mountain biking are **Tsali**, a peninsula sticking out into Lake Fontana near Bruston City, in the Nantahala National Forest; **Dupont State Forest**, just south of Brevard; and the **Bent Creek, Davidson River,** and **Mills River** sections of the Pisgah Ranger District of the Pisgah National Forest.

⛸ Western North Carolina's largest indoor skateboard, skating, and BMX biking facility is **Zero Gravity Skatepark** (✉ *1800 Old Hendersonville Hwy.,* ☎*828/862–6700*), with fun boxes, ramps, launch boxes, ledges, roll-ins, and a pyramid and bowl.

LAKE TOXAWAY

40 mi southwest of Asheville.

A century ago a group called the Lake Toxaway Company created a 640-acre lake in the high mountains between Brevard and Cashiers. Nearby, a grand 500-room hotel built with the finest materials, providing the most modern conveniences and serving European cuisine, attracted many of the country's elite. That hotel is long gone, but the scenic area, which some still call "America's Switzerland," has a number of fine resorts and some of the priciest real estate in the North Carolina Mountains.

WHERE TO STAY

$$$$ 🏨**Earthshine Mountain Lodge.** You can have as much solitude or ★ adventure as you want at this spacious cedar log cabin with stone fireplaces. The lodge, which sits on 70 acres midway between Brevard and Cashiers on a ridge that adjoins the Pisgah National Forest, offers horseback riding, hiking, fishing, and even an opportunity to gather berries, feed the goats, pan for gems, take guided trail rides, and try the 30-foot climbing wall or zip line. In the evening families gather around an open fire to sing songs, square dance, and exchange stories. ■TIP→ Rates include all meals. On a week's stay, the seventh day is free. **Pros:** bucolic, family-oriented mountain lodge; healthful meals; beautiful setting. **Cons:** somewhat remote. ✉ *1600 Golden Rd.* ☎*828/862–4207* ⊕*www.earthshinemtnlodge.com* ⮑*10 rooms* ⚭*In-room: no TV. In-hotel: restaurant, children's programs (ages 6 and up), no-smoking rooms* ▤*D, MC, V* ⏢*FAP.*

$$$$ 🏨**Greystone Inn.** In 1915 Savannah resident Lucy Molz built a second home on Lake Toxaway. Today the six-level Swiss-style mansion is an inn listed on the National Register of Historic Places and is known for pampering its guests. Rooms have antiques or period reproductions, and suites that border the lake of this mountain resort are modern. Rates include breakfast and dinner, afternoon tea and cake, and cocktails. The inn is open weekends only January through March. **Pros:** deluxe lakeside mountain inn; pampering service; excellent food. **Cons:** very expensive. ✉*Greystone La.* ☎*828/966–4700 or 800/824–5766* ⊕*www.greystoneinn.com* ⮑*31 rooms, 2 suites* ⚭*In-hotel: restaurant, tennis courts, pool, spa, bicycles, no-smoking rooms* ▤*AE, MC, V* ⏢*MAP.*

CASHIERS

74 mi southwest of Asheville via U.S. 74 and NC 107; 14 mi west of Lake Toxaway.

Cashiers (pronounced CASH-ers) is not a quite a town. Until recently, it was just a crossroads, with a store or two, a summer getaway for wealthy South Carolinians escaping the heat. But with the building of many exclusive gated developments, the Cashiers area, at a cool 3,500-foot elevation, is seeing new restaurants, lodges, and golf courses open seemingly every month.

Whiteside Mountain is one of the highest continuous cliffs in the East. The sheer cliffs of white granite rise up to 750 feet, overlooking the Chattooga River in the Nantahala National Forest. The cliffs are popular with climbers. ⊠ *Whiteside Mountain Rd., 4.6 mi from Cashiers on U.S. 64* ☎*828/586–2155* ⊘*Closed to climbers Jan.–July.*

WHERE TO STAY & EAT

¢–$
AMERICAN
✕**Cornucopia.** In the second-oldest building in Cashiers, built in 1892, you can sit on the huge, airy, covered back porch and eat some of the best sandwiches in the region. Specialties include the "Arabian Club," with turkey, bacon, sprouts, and black olives on pita bread. The Black Angus burgers are excellent, and for a Southern treat try the Coca-Cola Ribs. ⊠*Hwy. 107 S* ☎*828/743–3750* ▤*MC, V.*

$$$
AMERICAN
✕**The Orchard.** Widely considered the best restaurant in the Cashiers area, the Orchard, in a cozy house with brown wood shakes, with an antique Jeep on display in front, puts a Southern twist on traditional American dishes. Try the mountain trout. ⊠*905 NC 107 S* ☎*828/743–7614* ⊘*Closed Mon. No lunch.*

$$$–$$$$
★
⌂**High Hampton Inn & Country Club.** On the front lawn of this old inn are some of the most ancient trees in the region, including a giant Fraser fir that is a national champion. Many of the buildings are bark-covered, and inside the main building you'll find rare wormy chestnut. With rustic rooms—30 in the main lodge and 90 in small cottages around the 1,400-acre property—the atmosphere is more down-home than country club. Meals are served buffet-style in a huge hunting lodge–style dining room. There's an 18-hold George Cobb golf course and a 35-acre private lake. On the National Register of Historic Places, and family-owned for three generations, High Hampton Inn stubbornly sticks to traditions such as requiring coats and ties for dinner and declining to install televisions or telephones in guest rooms. Many guests have been coming here for decades. A new 5,000-square-foot fitness center opened in 2006. RVs and motorcycles are not permitted on the property. **Pros:** historic mountain inn; full of tradition, like resorts used to be. **Cons:** perhaps a little old-fashioned. ⊠*1525 NC 107S, Cashiers* ☎*828/743–2411 or 800/334–2551* ⊕*www.highhamptoninn.com* ⇗*120 rooms, 18 cottages; 40 rental houses* ⌂*In-room: no a/c (some), no phone, kitchen (some), no TV, Wi-Fi. In-hotel: restaurant, golf course, tennis courts, gym, laundry service, Wi-Fi, no-smoking rooms* ▤*AE, D, DC, MC, V* ⊘*Closed mid-Nov.–mid-Apr.* ⍩*FAP.*

$$$–$$$$
⌂**Innisfree Victorian Inn.** On a hill above Lake Glenville you can indulge your literary or romantic fantasies in the Brontë Suite or one of the other garden-house rooms named after writers. And a fine fantasy it would be, with a four-poster bed and a glassed-in fireplace so you can see the fire from either the comfy bed or the two-person tub. The main inn has a wraparound veranda, an observatory, and an octagonal dining room. **Pros:** deluxe B&B; lovely mountain and lake views. **Cons:** breakfasts

so-so. ⊠*NC 107 N, Glenville* ☎*828/743–2946* ⊕*www.innisfreeinn. com* 🖙*9 rooms, 1 suite* ⅃*In-room: refrigerator (some), no TV (some), Wi-Fi. In-hotel: no-smoking rooms* ▤*AE, D, MC, V* ⦿*BP.*

SPORTS & THE OUTDOORS

GOLF   At the golf course at the **High Hampton Inn & Country Club** (⊠*1525 NC 107 S* ☎*828/743–2411*) is a par-71, 6012-yard George Cobb design, with a famous 8th hole. The newest course in the Cashiers area, a par-71, 6,699-yard semiprivate course designed by Tom Jackson, **Highlands Cove** (⊠*U.S. 64* ☎*828/526–4185*) has an elevated Highlands side and a flatter Cove side. Perched at 4,500 feet, **Trillium Links** (⊠*975 New Trillium Way* ☎*828/743–4251*), a public course built in 1998, plays to 6505 yards at par 71.

4

HIGHLANDS

85 mi southwest of Asheville; 11 mi south of Cashiers on U.S. 64.

Highlands is a tony small town of around 900 people, but the surrounding area swells to 10,000 or more in summer and fall, when those with summer homes here flock back, like wealthy swallows of Capistrano. Once Highlands billed itself as the highest town in the East, but it relinquished the title when Banner Elk and other tiny communities a little higher up in the High Country were incorporated as towns. Still, at 4,118 feet it is usually cool and pleasant when even Asheville gets hot. The town's five-block downtown is, not surprisingly given the local demographics, lined with upscale shops, antiques stores, and coffeehouses, and there's a sniff of West Palm Beach in the air.

West of Highlands via U.S. 64 toward Franklin, the **Cullasaja Gorge** (Cul-lah-SAY-jah) is an 8-mi gorge passing Lake Sequoyah and several waterfalls, including **Bridal Veil Falls** and the 200-foot **Cullasaja Falls.** During periods of extreme drought, such as the Highlands area has experienced in 2007–2008, Bridal Veil Falls almost completely dries up. ⊠*U.S. 64.*

In the center of downtown Highlands the **Highlands Botanical Garden and Biological Station,** run by Western Carolina University, is a 30-acre biological reserve of native plants. There's also a small nature center, open seasonally. ⊠*265 6th St.* ☎*828/526–2602* ⦿*Garden: daily sunrise–sunset. Nature center: June–Sept., Mon.–Sat. 10–5* ▣*Free.*

WHERE TO STAY & EAT

$$$$ ✕**Madison's.** In the Old Edwards Inn, Madison's is Highland's most
AMERICAN   upscale restaurant. The dining room is gorgeous, light and sunny with windows overlooking Highland's Main Street, and with Oriental rugs on the stone floors and Christofle silverware on the tables. Try the steamed mountain trout with fingerling potato salad and parsley-champagne vinaigrette ($26). Save room for one of the excellent desserts, such as bourbon pecan soufflé ($18) or chocolate-blackberry cheesecake ($12). Service is attentive, but sometimes not up to the restaurant's high prices. Adjacent to the restaurant, the Wine Garden is an outdoor

café serving a casual menu of sandwiches, salads, and wines by the glass. ⊠*445 Main St.* ☎*828/526–5477* ▤*AE, D, MC, V.*

$$$–$$$$ ✗**On the Verandah.** You'll enjoy views of Lake Sequoyah from the big
ECLECTIC   windows of this former speakeasy. The owner has a collection of more than 1,300 hot sauces, any of which you can sample. The menu is long and varied, and many dishes are infused with Asian or Caribbean flavors. There's live piano music nightly and an excellent wine list. ⊠*1536 Franklin Rd.* ☎*828/526–2338* ▤*D, MC, V* ⊙*Closed Dec.– mid-Mar. No lunch Mon.–Sat.*

$$$–$$$$ ✗**Ristorante Paoletti.** At this storefront restaurant on Main Street you
ITALIAN   are taken care of in a style that's more Italian-provincial than nouveau riche. The menu includes a lengthy section of fresh-made pastas, along with veal and seafood. The wine list includes more than 1,000 selections. ⊠*440 Main St.* ☎*828/526–4906* ▤*AE, MC, V* ⊙*Closed Jan. and Feb. No lunch.*

$$$–$$$$ ✗**Wolfgang's Restaurant & Wine Bistro.** Cheerful and unpretentious, Wolf-
ECLECTIC   gang's has an eclectic menu ranging from wiener schnitzel to Cajun barbecue shrimp to grilled venison. Several of the rooms have fireplaces, and in good weather there's outdoor seating. The wine list is well-chosen and extensive. ⊠*474 Main St.* ☎*828/526–3807* ▤*AE, D, MC, V* ⊙*No lunch.*

$$$$ 🏨**Old Edwards Inn and Spa.** A two-year-long, $40-million renovation
★   turned this 115-year-old inn into the smartest hotel in Highlands. Guest rooms have plasma TVs, DVDs, and a central digital-control screen for lights, music, and media. Bath amenities are by Bulgari. The hotel could be on Manhattan's Upper East Side, as could the prices, with two-night packages as much as $2,750 per couple. Just behind the main inn is The Lodge, with more rustic but still luxurious accommodations. The suites have fireplaces. Due to local liquor laws, the bar is for guests only. **Pros:** deluxe inn with plethora of amenities; central location near shops and restaurants. **Cons:** not inexpensive. ⊠*445 Main St.* ☎*828/526–8008 or 866/526–8008* ⊕*www.oldedwardsinn.com* ⇆*25 rooms, 5 suites in inn; 12 rooms, 13 suites, and 1 four-bedroom cottage in lodge* ⌂*In-room: safe, refrigerator, DVD, Internet, Wi-Fi. In-hotel: restaurant, room service, bar, gym, spa, laundry service, Wi-Fi, no-smoking rooms* ▤*AE, D, MC, V.*❍|*BP.*

THE ARTS

The well-respected **Highlands Playhouse** (⊠*Oak St.* ☎*828/526–2695*), an equity theater, puts on four or five productions each summer.

SHOPPING

The nightly antiques auctions from June through October at **Scudder's Gallery** (⊠*352 Main St.* ☎*828/526–4111*), a high-end antiques dealer and estate liquidator established in 1925, are a form of local entertainment.

Since 1963, **Elephants Foot Antiques** (⊠*U.S. 64 at Foreman Rd.* ☎*828/ 526–5451*) has sold decorative furniture, antique lamps and other antiques.

Great Smoky Mountains National Park

WORD OF MOUTH

"We like the North Carolina side [of the Smokies] near Asheville. Great scenic drives, waterfalls, Biltmore House (beautiful gardens in the spring), nice art/craft shops and dining."

—Katie7

By Lan Sluder   **GREAT SMOKY MOUNTAINS NATIONAL** Park is one of the great wild areas of the eastern United States and the most-visited national park in the U.S. From a roadside lookout or from a clearing in a trail, in every visible direction you can see the mountains march toward a vast horizon of wilderness.

Some of the tallest mountains in the East are here, including 16 peaks over 6,000 ft. The highest in the park, Clingmans Dome, was reputedly the original inspiration for the folk song "On Top of Old Smoky." It rises 6,643 ft above sea level and 4,503 ft above the valley floor. These are also some of the oldest mountains in the world, far older than those in the Rockies, the Alps, or the Andes. Geologists say the building of what are now the Great Smokies began about a billion years ago.

Today, the park hosts over 9 million visitors each year, almost twice as many as the second-most-visited national park, the Grand Canyon. Even so, with more than 814 square mi of protected land, if you get out of your car you can soon be in a remote cove where your closest neighbors are deer, bobcats, and black bears.

Due to a fortuitous combination of moderate climate and diverse geography, Great Smoky Mountains National Park is one of the most biologically rich spots on earth. Bears are the most famous animal in the park, but elk are also making the Smokies their home for the first time in 150 years. But it is not just large mammals that make it special. The Smokies has been called the "salamander capital of the world," with at least 30 different salamander species. It is also one of the few places on earth where, for a few evenings in June, you can see synchronous fireflies flashing in perfect unison.

The park offers extraordinary opportunities for other outdoor activities: it has world-class hiking, on more than 850 mi of trails, ranging from easy half-hour nature walks to week-long backpacking treks. While backcountry hiking has its wonders, some of the most interesting sights in the park are viewable from the comfort of your car or motorcycle. You can explore old farms and mountain homesteads, or watch cornmeal ground at a working gristmill.

The Great Smoky Mountains National Park headquarters is in Gatlinburg, TN, and many people think of the Smokies as being a Tennessee national park. In fact, slightly more of the park is on the eastern, or North Carolina side, than on the Tennessee side—276,000 acres to 246,000 acres to be exact. This chapter only covers the North Carolina side of the park, though there is a lot to explore on the Tennessee side as well. For a complete guide to the park, pick up a copy of *Fodor's In Focus Great Smoky Mountains National Park*.

TOP REASONS TO GO

Witness the wilderness: Great Smoky Mountains National Park is one of the last remaining big chunks of wilderness in the East. Get away from civilization in more than 800 square miles of tranquillity, with old-growth forests, clear streams, meandering trails, wildflowers, and panoramic vistas from mile-high mountains.

Get your endorphins going: Outdoor junkies can bike, boat, camp, fish, hike, ride horses, raft white water, watch birds and wildlife, and even ski cross-country.

Experience mountain culture: Visit restored mountain cabins and tour "ghost towns" in the park, with old frame and log buildings preserved much as they were 100 years ago.

Spot wildlife: You can see black bears, elk, white-tailed deer, wild turkeys, and other wildlife. Biologists estimate there are more than 1,500 bears, 6,000 deer, and nearly 100 elk now in the park, so your chances of seeing these beautiful wild creatures, while not guaranteed, is quite good.

Learn something new: Take advantage of the interpretative talks and walks and Junior Ranger programs for kids.

ORIENTATION & PLANNING

GETTING ORIENTED

The North Carolina side of the park boasts the highest mountain in the park—Clingmans Dome—as well as the historic Cataloochee Valley, many scenic overlooks and great hiking opportunities. It also connects to the famed Blue Ridge Parkway near Cherokee, NC.

What's Nearby. Sometimes called "the quiet side of the park," the North Carolina side of the Smokies is edged with a collection of small, low-key towns. The most appealing of these are Bryson City, Sylva, and Waynesville. Except for these towns, and the city of Asheville about 50 mi east, most of the area around the east side of the park consists of national forest lands and rural areas. On the southwestern boundary of the park is Lake Fontana, the largest lake in western North Carolina.

GREAT SMOKY MOUNTAINS NATIONAL PARK PLANNER

WHEN TO GO

There's not a bad time to visit the Smokies, though summer and the month of October are the busiest times. The biggest crowds in the park arrive mid-June to mid-August, and all of the month of October, which is peak fall color season. Weekends in October are especially crowded, and you should expect traffic delays on U.S. 441 and traffic jams in Cades Cove. Beat the crowds by coming on weekdays and also early in the day, before 10 AM. Late spring is a wonderful time to visit the park, as wildflowers are in bloom, and it's before the heat, humidity, and crowds of summer. Winter in the park can be beautiful, especially when there's snow on the ground or rime frost on the tree limbs. The air is usually clearer in the winter, with less haze, and with leaves off the trees the visibility is excellent.

GETTING HERE & AROUND
You can enter the park near the Oconaluftee Visitors Center in Cherokee. Coming from the north on I–40, take Exit 27 to U.S. 74 West toward Waynesville. Turn onto U.S. 19 and proceed through Maggie Valley to Cherokee. Turn onto U.S. 441 North at Cherokee and follow the road into the park. From the south, follow U.S. 441/U.S. 23 North. At Dillsboro merge on U.S. 74 West/U.S. 441 North. At Exit 74 merge onto U.S. 441. Follow U.S. 441 through Cherokee and into the park.

Another, and much more pleasant (but slower) route to the Smokies is the Blue Ridge Parkway, which has its southern terminus at Cherokee. *For more information on the Blue Ridge Parkway, see Chapter 4: The North Carolina Mountains.*

BY AIR The closest airport with national air service is Asheville Regional Airport (AVL), about 60 mi east of the Cherokee entrance. Asheville is served by Delta, US Air, Northwest, and Continental.

BY CAR The closest sizeable citiy to the park in North Carolina is Asheville. Asheville is about 50 mi east of Cherokee and the Oconaluftee Visitor Center. It takes a little over an hour to get from Asheville to the Cherokee entrance of the park.

Coming either from the east or west, I–40 is the main access route to the Great Smokies; from the north and south, I–75, I–81, and I–26 are primary arteries.

U.S. 441, also called Newfound Gap Road, is the main road through the park, and the only paved road that goes all the way through. It travels 31 mi between Cherokee and Gatlinburg, crossing Newfound Gap at nearly a mi high.

ESSENTIALS **Airport Information Asheville Regional Airport** (*AVL* ✉ *708 Airport Rd., Fletcher* ☎ *828/684–2226* ⊕ *www.flyavl.com*).

ABOUT THE RESTAURANTS
The closest thing to fine dining you can find in the park is a hot dog at the snackbar in Cades Cove or a Coke from a vending machine at a visitor center. You'll have to make your own fine dining with an alfresco picnic at one of the park's attractive picnic areas or leave the park for a meal.

Outside the park you'll find many more dining options, from fast food to fine dining, the latter especially in Asheville. *For more information on Asheville, see Chapter 4: The North Carolina Mountains.*

ABOUT THE CAMPGROUNDS & HOTELS
The only accommodations actually in the park, besides camping, are at one remote, rustic, and remarkable mountain lodge on the Tennessee side, LeConte Lodge. Camping, however, is abundant and reasonably priced. The park has 947 tent and RV camping spaces at 10 developed

campgrounds, in addition to more than 100 backcountry campsites and shelters. The cost ranges from free (backcountry sites and shelters) to $14–$23 per night for front-country sites. Developed campgrounds range from creekside sites in historic valleys to a campground among evergreens at over a mile high. All but one of the campgrounds accept RVs and trailers, though most have size limits. Immediately outside the park are many commercial campgrounds and RV parks.

Outside the park, you have a good selection of hotels of every ilk. The lodging on the North Carolina side is low-key; you can choose from old mountain inns, B&Bs, and motels in the small towns of Bryson City, Waynesville, and Robbinsville. A seemingly ever-expanding number of hotel towers are connected to the giant Harrah's casino in Cherokee, soon to have 1,000 rooms. About 50 mi away, in and around Asheville, you can choose from among one of the largest collections of B&Bs in the Southeast, along with hip urban hotels and classic mountain resorts.

5

WHAT IT COSTS					
	¢	$	$$	$$$	$$$$
Restaurant	under $10	$10–$14	$15–$19	$20–$24	over $24
Hotel	under $100	$100–$150	$151–$200	$201–$250	over $250
Camping	under $10	$10–$14	$15–$19	$20–$24	over $24

Restaurant prices are for a main course at dinner. Hotel prices are for two people in a standard double room in high season. Camping prices are for campsites that usually include a tent pad or parking area for RVs/trailer, fire pit or grate and/or raised grill, bear-proof food-storage lockers at some campgrounds, and picnic table; potable water and restrooms with flush toilets and running water will be nearby.

PLANNING YOUR TIME

If you only have a day to visit the Smokies, start early, pack a picnic lunch, and drive to the **Oconaluftee Visitor Center**, to pick up orientation maps and brochures. While you're there, spend an hour or so exploring the **Mountain Farm Museum**. Then, drive the ½ mi to **Mingus Mill** and see corn being ground into meal in an authentic working gristmill. Head up **Newfound Gap Road** and, via Clingmans Dome Road, to **Clingmans Dome**. The 25-mi drive takes you, in terms of the kinds of plants and trees you'll see at the mountain top, all the way to Canada. Stretch your legs and walk the ½-mi paved, but fairly steep, trail to the observation tower on Clingmans Dome, the highest point in the Smokies. If you've worked up an appetite, head back down the mountain and stop for a leisurely picnic at **Collins Creek Picnic Area** (MM 25.4). If you want a moderate afternoon hike, the 4-mi (roundtrip) **Kephart Prong** trail is nearby and wanders for 2 mi along a stream to the remains of a Depression-era Civilian Conservation Corps camp. Alternatively, and especially if it's a hot summer day, save your picnic and hike, and drive via the **Blue Ridge Parkway** and Heintooga Ridge Road to the **Heintooga Picnic Area** at Balsam Springs. At a mile high, this part of the Smokies is usually cool even in mid-July. If you're up for it, you can hike all (about 5 mi round-trip) or part of the **Flat Creek Trail**, which begins near the

Heintooga picnic area and is one of the hidden jewels of trails in the park. If you decide not to take a long hike, you may have time to drive the one-way, unpaved **Balsam Mountain Road** to Big Cove Road back to Cherokee. Catch the sunset at an overlook on your drive back.

FLORA & FAUNA

A profusion of vegetation defines the Great Smokies; it has one of the richest and most diverse collections of flora in the world. The park is about 95% forested, home to almost 6,000 known species of wildflowers, plants, and trees.

Many call the Smokies the "wildflower national park," as it has more flowering plants than any other U.S. national park. You can see wildflowers in bloom virtually year-round, from the ephemerals such as trillium and columbine in late winter and early spring, the bright red cardinal flowers, orange butterfly weed, and black-eyed Susans in summer, and Joe-pye weed, asters, and mountain gentian in the fall. However, the best time to see wildflowers in the park is the spring, especially April and early May. The second-best time to see the floral display is early summer. From early to mid-June to mid-July, the hillsides and heath balds blaze with the orange of flame azaleas, the white and pink of mountain laurel, and the purple and white of rhododendron. In the fall, typically in October, hundreds of thousands of visitors jam the roads of the park to view the autumn leaf color.

Living in Great Smoky Mountains National Park are some 66 species of mammals, over 200 varieties of birds, 50 native fish species, and more than 80 types of reptiles and amphibians.

The North American black bear is the symbol of the Smokies. Bear populations vary year to year, but biologists think that up to 1,600 bears are in the park, a density of about two per square mile. Many visitors to the park see bears, although sightings are never guaranteed.

The National Park Service has helped reintroduce elk, river otters, and peregrine falcons to the Smokies. Because of the high elevation of much of the park, you'll see birds here usually seen in more northern areas, including the common raven and the ruffed grouse.

For a few short weeks, usually from late May to mid-June, synchronous fireflies put on an amazing light show. In this illuminated mating dance, the male Photinus fireflies blink 4 to 8 times in the air, then wait about 6 seconds for the females on the ground to return a double-blink response. The Joyce Kilmer Memorial Forest just outside the park is a great place to see them.

SCENIC DRIVES

Newfound Gap Road (*U.S. 441*). Newfound Gap Road is the busiest road in the park by far, with more than a million vehicles making the 16-mi climb from 2,000-foot elevation near Cherokee to almost a mile high at Newfound Gap (and then down to Gatlinburg on the Tennessee side). It's the only road that goes all the way through the

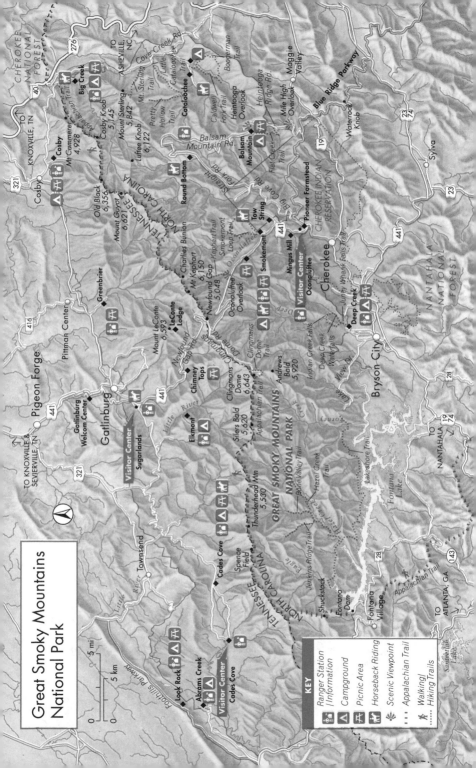

Great Smoky Mountains National Park

KEY

- Ranger Station / Information
- Campground
- Picnic Area
- Horseback Riding
- Scenic Viewpoint
- Appalachian Trail
- Walking/
- Hiking Trails

CHEROKEE NATIONAL FOREST

TO KNOXVILLE, TN

Cosby

Mt Cammerer 4,928

Big Creek

Cosby Knob 5,145

Mount Sterling 5,842

Luftee Knob 6,122

Old Black 6,356

Mount Guyot 6,621

TENNESSEE / NORTH CAROLINA

Greenbrier

Charlies Bunion

Mt Kephart 6,150

Newfound Gap 5,048

Mount LeConte 6,593

LeConte Lodge

Pittman Center

Pigeon Forge

Gatlinburg Welcome Center

Gatlinburg

Visitor Center Sugarlands

Newfound Gap Rd

Clingmans Dome Rd

Chimney Tops

Clingmans Dome 6,643

Silers Bald 5,620

Appalachian Trail

Elkmont

TO KNOXVILLE & SEVIERVILLE, TN

River Townsend

Little River

Thunderhead Mtn 5,530

Spence Field

Cades Cove

Look Rock

Abrams Creek

Visitor Center Cades Cove

Foothills Parkway

GREAT SMOKY MOUNTAINS NATIONAL PARK

TENNESSEE / NORTH CAROLINA

TO ASHEVILLE, NC

276

Cove Creek Rd

Mt. Sterling Trail

Little Cataloochee Trail

Pretty Hollow Trail

Cataloochee Trail

Cataloochee

Caldwell Fork Trail

Boogerman Trail

Heintooga Overlook

Heintooga Ridge Rd.

Mile High Overlook

Maggie Valley

Blue Ridge Parkway

Waterrock Knob

Sylva

Balsam Mountain Rd.

Balsam Mountain

Round Bottom

Straight Fork Rd

Big Cove Rd

Flat Creek Trail

Tow String

Kephart Prong Trail

Kephart Trail

Smokemont Loop Trail

Oconaluftee Trail

Smokemont

Oconaluftee Overlook

Mingus Mill

Visitor Center Oconaluftee

Pioneer Farmstead

CHEROKEE INDIAN RESERVATION

Cherokee

441

Deep Creek

Deep Creek Waterfalls

Indian Creek Falls

Juney Whank Falls Trail

NANTAHALA NATIONAL FOREST

Andrews Bald 5,920

Deep Creek Trail

Bryson City

Noland Creek

Forney Creek

Tow Valley Dr

Lakeview Dr.

Noland Divide Trail

Bote Valley Trail

Hazel Creek Trail

Eagle Creek

Forney Creek Trail

Lakeshore Trail

Jenkins Ridge Trail

Fontana Lake

Tuckasegee

Shuckstack

Fontana Dam

Fontana Village

Appalachian Trail

TO NANTAHALA

TO ATLANTA, GA

Little Tennessee

Sugarloaf Lake

0 5 mi

0 5 km

center of the park, and the only fully paved road. While it's not a route to escape from the crowds, the scenery is memorable. If you don't have time to explore the back roads or to go hiking, Newfound Gap Road will give you a flavor of the richness and variety of the Smokies. Unlike other roads in the park, Newfound Gap Road has mile markers; however, the markers run "backwards" (as far as North Carolinians are concerned), starting at 0 at the park boundary near Gatlinburg to 31.1 at the border of the park at the entrance to the Blue Ridge Parkway near Cherokee. Among the sites on the road are: Oconaluftee Visitor Center and Mountain Farm Museum (MM 30.3); Mingus Mill (MM 29.9); Smokemont Campground and Nature Trail (MM 27.2); Web Overlook (MM 17.7), from which there's a good view almost due west of Clingmans Dome; and Newfound Gap (MM 14.7), the start of the 7-mi road to Clingmans Dome.

> **AVOID THE CROWDS**
>
> If you arrive in high season, you can still avoid the crowds by avoiding Newfound Gap Road. Even if you want to stay in your car, back roads such as Balsam Mountain Road and Cove Creek Road have almost no traffic, even at peak times. In fact, you can usually drive for miles and not see another vehicle. Note that these back roads are generally unpaved, may be one-way, and some are closed in winter. Also, anytime you step out of your car and onto a hiking trail, solitude is almost guaranteed.

★ **Cove Creek Road** (*Old Highway 284*). This drive takes you to one of the most beautiful valleys in the Smokies, and to one of the most interesting destinations. The first 7 mi of Cove Creek Road is a mostly paved, winding two-lane road through a scenic rural valley. Entering the park, the road becomes gravel. ■ TIP→**Although in the park this is a two-way road, in places it is wide enough only for one vehicle, so you may have to pull over and let the oncoming vehicle pass. At points the curvy road hugs the mountainside, with steep drop-offs, making it unsuitable for large RVs or travel trailers.** As you near the Cataloochee Valley, suddenly you're on a nice, paved road again. Follow the paved road, as it is a short cut to the historic old buildings of Cataloochee. (You can also continue on the unpaved Cove Creek Road toward Crosby, TN, and in about 5 mi you can enter Cataloochee from the back side.) Follow the signs for a driving tour of the old houses, barns, churches, a school, and other buildings that are all that remain of the once-thriving Cataloochee community, which at its peak in 1910 had about 1,200 residents. You can stop and walk through most of the buildings. Keep a lookout for elk, wild turkey, deer, and other wildlife here. If you haven't had enough driving for the day, from Cataloochee you can continue on the unpaved Cove Creek Road to Big Creek campground near the North Carolina–Tennessee line, where you can reconnect with I–40 at Exit 451 on the Tennessee side.

CLOSE UP

Cataloochee, the Novel

Asheville native Wayne Caldwell's 2007 novel, *Cataloochee*, tells the story of three generations of mountain families in Cataloochee Cove. They came to this distant, beautiful valley in search of a hardscrabble version of Eden. Some may have found it, but the idyll was not to last. As the government took steps to relocate the settlers out of Cataloochee to make room for Great Smoky Mountain National Park, a tragic act of violence touched the families.

Toward the end of the novel, a preacher at the Baptist church in Little Cataloochee says:

"I heard Brother Smith over in Big Cataloochee preached about this land being Eden. I hope you see fit to forgive him, even if he is a Methodist. Because, Lord, this is pretty country right enough, but mankind tamed this forest and grubbed out these pastures, and that don't make it Paradise. You made Eden oncet and that's it."

5

WHAT TO SEE

HISTORIC SIGHTS

Fodor'sChoice ★ **Cataloochee Valley.** This is one of the most memorable and eeriest sites in all of the Smokies. At one time Cataloochee was a community of more than 1,200 people, in some 200 buildings. After the land was taken over in 1934 for the national park, the community dispersed. Although many of the original buildings are now gone, more than a dozen houses, cabins, and barns, two churches, and other structures have been kept up. You can visit the Palmer Methodist Chapel, a one-room schoolhouse, Beach Grove School, and the Woody and Messer homesteads. It's much like Cades Cove on the Tennessee side, but much less visited. On a quiet day you can almost hear the ghosts of the former Cataloochee settlers. You will almost always spot a few elk here, especially in the evening and early morning. Cataloochee is one of the most remote parts of the Smokies reachable by car, via a narrow, winding, gravel road. ⊠ *Cataloochee Community, via U.S. 276 near Maggie Valley, off Exit 20 of I–40, to Cove Creek Rd.*

★ **Mountain Farm Museum.** This museum at the Oconaluftee Visitors Center is perhaps the best re-creation anywhere of a mountain farmstead. The nine farm buildings, all dating from around 1900, were moved here from locations within the park. Besides a furnished two-story log cabin, there is a barn, apple house, corn crib, smokehouse, chicken coop, and other outbuildings. In season, corn, tomatoes, pole beans, squash, and other mountain crops are grown in the garden, and park staff sometimes put on demonstrations of pioneer activities, such as making apple butter and molasses. ⊠ *U.S. 441 at Oconaluftee Visitors Center* ☎ *828/497–1904.*

Mingus Mill. In its time, the late 19th century, this was the state-of-the-art in gristmills, the two large grist stones powered by a store-bought turbine rather than a hand-built wheel. You can watch the miller make cornmeal, and even buy a pound of it. ⊠ *U.S. 441, 2 mi north of Cherokee* ☎ *828/497–1904* ☉ *Mid-Mar.–late Nov.*

SCENIC STOPS

★ **Andrews Bald.** Getting to Andrews Bald isn't easy. You have to walk the rocky Forney Ridge trail some 1.8 mi one-way, with an elevation gain of almost 600 feet, the equivalent of a 60-story skyscraper. The payoff is several acres of grassy bald at over 5,800 feet, with stunning views of Lake Fontana and the southeastern Smokies. This is one of only two balds in the Smokies (the other is Gregory Bald on the Tennessee side) that the park service keeps clear. ⊠ *1.8 mi from the Forney Ridge trailhead parking lot, at the end of Clingmans Dome Rd.*

Big Witch Gap Overlook. The 2-mi drive on the Blue Ridge Parkway between Big Witch Gap Overlook and Noland Divide Overlook offers fine views into the eastern side of the Smokies, and in May and June the roadsides are heavily abloom with rhododendron. ⊠ *MM 461.9 on the BRP and nearby.*

★ **Cataloochee Overlook.** Coming from Cove Creek Road onto the paved section of Cataloochee Road, this is your first opportunity to stop and see the broad expanse of Cataloochee Cove. Cataloochee is taken from a Cherokee word meaning "row upon row" or "standing in rows," and indeed you'll see rows of mountain ridges here. The overlook is well-marked and has a split-rail fence. ⊠ *Cataloochee Rd.*

★ **Clingmans Dome.** At an elevation of more than 6,600 feet, this is the third-highest peak east of the Rockies, only a few feet shorter than the tallest, Mt. Mitchell. Walk up a paved, but steep, ½-mi trail to an observation tower offering 360-degree views from the "top of Old Smoky." Temperatures here are usually 10° F lower than at the entrance to the park near Cherokee. Clingmans Dome Road is closed to vehicular traffic in winter (December–March), but if there's snow on the ground you can put on your s snowshoes and hike up to the peak. ⊠ *At end of Clingmans Dome Rd., 7 mi from U.S. 441.*

★ **Heintooga Overlook.** This is one of the best spots to watch the sunset, with a sweeping view westward of the crest of the Great Smokies. ⊠ *Off Heintooga Ridge Rd., at the picnic area, 7 mi from the BRP— the entrance to Heintooga Ridge Rd. is at MM 458.2* ⊙ *Closed Mid-Oct–early May.*

Lakeview Drive Fontana Lake Overlook. This is the first scenic overlook you come to after entering the park on Lakeview Drive, better known as the Road to Nowhere. It's a little over 3 mi from the Lakeview entrance to the park. You can see parts of Fontana Lake, which marks the southwestern boundary of the park. The lake, part of the Tennessee Valley Authority system, is drawn down at times, especially in the fall, so the lake level and the shoreline change significantly depending on whether the gates on Fontana Dam, the tallest dam in the East, are open or closed. ⊠ *First scenic overlook on Lakeview Dr., 3.1 mi from Lakeview Dr. park entrance near Bryson City.*

Mile High Overlook. This overlook has a panoramic view of much of the eastern side of the Smokies. ⊠ *Heintooga Ridge Rd., 1.3 mi from the BRP—the entrance to Heintooga Ridge Rd. is at MM 458.2.*

TRIP PLANNING

The official Great Smoky Mountains National Park Web site (⊕ *www. nps.gov/grsm*) provides a wealth of information on the park. Before you go, download the **Smokies Trip Planner** at ⊕ *www.nps.gov/grsm/ planyourvisit/trip-planner.htm.*

Several commercial Web sites also are useful for trip-planning. Among the best are My Smoky Mountain Vacation (⊕ *www.mysmokymounta-invacation.com*), Romantic Asheville (⊕ *www.romanticasheville.com*), and

Bryson City & the Great Smokies (⊕ *www.greatsmokies.com*).

Once you arrive at the park, pick up the *Smokies Guide*, a free tabloid newspaper published once a season with an area map, schedule of free park programs, and information on destinations in the park, birding, wildlife, wildflowers, and hiking. The park visitor centers have shops with large collections of books on every aspect of the park.

Oconaluftee Valley Overlook. From atop the Thomas Divide, just a little below the crest of the Smokies, you can look down and see the winding Newfound Gap Road. This is also a good spot to view sunrise in the Smokies. ✉ *U.S. 441 (Newfound Gap Rd.) at MM 15.4.*

VISITOR CENTER

Oconaluftee. The park's only information center on the North Carolina side is 1½ mi from Cherokee. Inside the pleasant old stone and wood main building you'll find helpful rangers to answer your questions, bulletin boards describing upcoming park activities, information on current campsite availabilities, and a small shop selling books, maps, and souvenirs. The restrooms are downstairs, around back. A backcountry permit station is near the restrooms. A planned new visitor center, projected to open in 2010, would expand the visitor center's space sevenfold. The current plans call for a new 6,000-square-foot visitor center, a new information kiosk, and a new restroom and vending building. The existing visitor center building will remain as administrative offices. Adjoining the present visitor center, in a large, level field next to the Oconaluftee River, is the Mountain Farm Museum. If you want to take an easy hike, the 1.6-mi (3.2-mi round-trip) Oconaluftee River Trail begins nearby. ✉ *U.S. 441, 1½ mi from Cherokee* ☎ *865/436–1200* ⊙ *Nov.–Apr., daily 8–4:30; May, daily 8:30–5:30; June–Aug., daily 8–6; Sept.–Oct., daily 8:30–6.*

SPORTS & THE OUTDOORS

BICYCLING

The North Carolina side of the Smokies offers excellent cycling, and bicycles are permitted on most roads. However, you have to be selective about where you bike. ■ **TIP→Vehicular traffic on the main roads, especially Newfound Gap Road (U.S. 441), can be very heavy. Steep terrain, and curvy, narrow back roads with narrow shoulders and blind spots make biking difficult or unsafe in some areas.**

Two good places for biking on (mostly) paved roads are Lakeview Drive—the so-called Road to Nowhere near Bryson City—and Cataloochee Cove. Also, Balsam Mountain Road and Cove Creek Road offer pleasant biking with very little auto traffic. Since these roads are unpaved, with mostly gravel surfaces, you should use a mountain bike or an all-terrain hybrid. Helmets are not required by law but are strongly recommended.

MOUNTAIN BIKING

There are no mountain biking trails in the Smokies. On the North Carolina side only two hiking trails, the Oconaluftee River trail, which begins near the Oconaluftee visitor center, and the lower Deep Creek trail near Bryson City, formerly a road, allow bikes.

Near the Smokies, the **Tsali Recreation Area** in the Nantahala National Forest, about 15 mi west of Bryson City, is a popular area for biking. With about 40 mi of trails with four excellent loops, it has been rated one of the top places for mountain biking in the country. ✛ *Tsali is on a hilly peninsula reaching into Fontana Lake, at the base of the Smokies. From Bryson City, follow U.S. 19/74 to the intersection with NC 28. Follow NC 28 north about 3 mi. Look for a sign for the Tsali Recreation Area; turn right. Follow the paved road to the campground and trailhead parking lot; park in the lot with the sign* BIKERS PARK AND PAY HERE. ☉ *April to October.*

The Pisgah National Forest also offers many opportunities for cycling.

BIKE RENTALS

Nantahala Outdoor Center Bike Shop. Watch river rafters swoosh by on the Nantahala River as you get your bike tuned up or rent a bike at this friendly outfitter. Avid bikers on staff will give you tips on the best biking spots. Mountain bikes rent for $40 to $60 a day, and road bikes for $40. Off-season discounts are sometimes available. All bike rentals include a helmet and a bike rack to transport the bike on your car. ⊠ *13077 Highway 19 W, Bryson City* ☎ *828/488–2176* ⊕ *www.noc.com*

FISHING

The North Carolina side of the Smokies has one of the best wild trout fisheries in the East. Deep Creek, Little Cataloochee, and Hazel Creek are streams known to serious anglers all over the country. The North Carolina side has more than 1,000 mi of streams (not all contain trout), and all are open to fishing year-round, except Bear Creek at its junction with Forney Creek, and upstream from there.

Among the best trout streams on this side of the park are Big Creek, Cataloochee Creek, Palmer Creek, Raven Fork, Deep Creek, Hazel Creek, and Noland Creek. Often, the best fishing is in higher-elevation streams, in areas that are more difficult to reach. Streams that are easily accessible, such as the Pigeon River, have greater fishing pressure.

Another option is Lake Fontana. Its cold, deep waters provide an ideal habitat for muskie, walleye, and smallmouth bass.

FISHING RULES

To fish in the park you must possess a valid fishing license or permit from either Tennessee or North Carolina. Either state license is valid throughout the park, and no trout stamp is required. Persons under 16 don't need a license. Fishing licenses are not available in the park, but may be purchased in nearby towns or online.

Only artificial flies or lures with a single hook can be used—no live bait. Fishing is permitted from a half hour before official sunrise to a half hour after official sunset. The limit for the combined total of brook, rainbow, or brown trout, or smallmouth bass, must not exceed five fish each day. You may not have more than five fish in your possession, regardless of whether they are fresh, stored in an ice chest, or otherwise preserved. Twenty rock bass may be kept in addition to the above limit.

> **THE AT**
>
> Each spring about 1,500 hikers set out to conquer the Appalachian Trail (AT), the 2,175-mi granddaddy of all hikes. Most hike north from Springer Mountain, Georgia, toward Mt. Katahdin, Maine. By the time they get to the Great Smokies, 160 mi from the trailhead in Georgia, about one-half of the hikers will already have dropped out. Typically, only about 400 hikers per year complete the entire AT. Of course, you don't have to hike the whole thing to experience the wonders of the trail; you can get on it for a short hike from Newfound Gap Road on the North Carolina–Tennessee line.

5

The size limit is 7 inches for brook, rainbow, brown trout, and smallmouth bass. For rock bass there is no minimum size.

LICENSES **North Carolina Wildlife Resources Commission.** You can order a North Carolina inland fishing license, valid throughout the park, online. A 10-day nonresident fishing license is $10, and an annual nonresident license is $30. Licenses for North Carolina residents cost half the nonresident fee. To fish for trout outside the park, you'll also need a trout stamp, which costs an extra $10. ⊠ *1751 Varsity Drive, Raleigh, NC* ☎ *919/707–0010* ⊕ *www.ncwildlife.org*

OUTFITTERS For backcountry trips, you may want to hire a licensed guide. Full-day trips cost around $225–$300 for one angler, $300–$400 for two. Only guides approved by the National Park Service are permitted to take anglers into the backcountry.

Smoky Mountain Fly Fishing (⊠ *626 Tsali Boulevard, Cherokee, NC* ☎ *828/497–1555* ⊕ *www.smokymountainflyfishing.net*) is a park licensed guide that conducts guided flyfishing trips in the park. **Lowe Fly Shop**(⊠ *15 Woodland Drive, Waynesville, NC* ☎ *828/452–0039* ⊕ *www.loweguideservice.com*) offers guided angling trips in the Smokies for all skill levels.

HIKING

Great Smoky Mountains National Park has more than 800 mi of hiking trails, of which about half are on the North Carolina side. The trails range from short nature walks to long, strenuous hikes that gain several thousand feet in elevation. Park trails are maintained, but on many trails maintenance is seasonal. Be prepared for trail erosion and washouts, especially December through May, when staffing levels may not permit much trail work. ■**TIP→Although permits are not required for day hikes, you must have a backcountry permit for overnight or longer trips.**

Keep in mind that the park has significant elevation changes and that some summer days, especially at lower elevations, can be hot and humid. Also, high ozone levels are an issue on some days. Together, these can pose problems for people who aren't in good shape or who have heart or respiratory problems. ■**TIP→Be realistic about your physical condition and abilities. Carry plenty of water and energy-rich foods, like GORP (good old raisins and peanuts), energy bars, and fruit.**

Weather in the park is subject to rapid change. A day in March or April might start out warm and sunny, but by the time you reach a mile-high elevation the temperature may be near freezing, and it could be snowing heavily. The higher elevations of the park can get up to 80 inches of precipitation annually. ■**TIP→Dress in layers and be prepared for temperature changes, especially snow in winter. Carry rain gear and expect rain at anytime.** Be sure to allow plenty of time to complete your hike before dark. As a rule of thumb, when hiking in the Smokies you'll travel only about 1½ mi per hour, so a 10-mi hike will take almost seven hours. Remember, dogs and other pets are not allowed on park trails.

EASY **Deep Creek Waterfalls.** For the effort of a 2.4-mi hike, this trail will reward you with three pretty waterfalls, Tom Branch, Indian Creek, and Juney Whank. Deep Creek also has a picnic area and campground. Tubing on Deep Creek is fun, too. ✉ *Trailhead at end of Deep Creek Rd., near Bryson City entrance to park.*

Fodor'sChoice **Hazel Creek and Bone Valley.** This hike begins with a boat ride across Fon-
★ tana Lake, which takes some advance planning. After you've crossed the lake, your boat captain will give you directions on how to get from the Fontana docking point to the trailhead, depending on where you're dropped off, as changing lake levels make the drop-off point vary from month to month. A half-mile on the Hazel Creek Trail (known on some park maps as Lakeshore Trail) will take you to the old lumber and mining town of Proctor, which was once a booming lumber town. At about 5.1 mi, bear right onto the Jenkins Ridge Trail, which will take you to the Bone Valley Trail. Bone Valley gets its name from the herd of cattle, moved here for summer pasture in 1888, which died in a spring snowstorm. If you want to keep going, you can check out Hall Cabin at mile 7.8, or turn around and make your way back. This is an easy hike (as hikes go in the Smokies), with an elevation gain of less than 500 feet. Most of the hike is on an old road and railroad bed. However, it is a long hike, 7.8 mi one-way and nearly 16 mi round-trip, not including the boat rides. Of course, you could always do a shorter section. ■**TIP→Arrange in advance with Fontana Marina (** ☎ *800/849–2258 or 828/498–2211***) at Fontana Village on Highway 28 North to take you across the lake on a boat. The shuttle boat will drop you (and pick you up) near Proctor on Hazel Creek.** ✉ *The Hazel Creek trailhead begins near backcountry campsite 86.*

MODERATE **Clingmans Dome Trail.** If you've been driving too long and want some exercise, along with unbeatable views of the Smokies and an ecological lesson, too, take the ½-mi (1-mi round-trip) from the Clingmans Dome parking lot to the observation tower at the top of Clingmans Dome, the highest peak in the Smokies. While short and paved, the trail is fairly steep, and at well over 6,000 feet elevation you'll probably be gasping for air. Most of the fir trees here are dead, killed by the balsam wooly adelgid. ✉ *Trail begins at the Clingmans Dome parking lot* ⊙ *Clingmans Dome Rd. is closed in winter.*

> ## PETS IN THE SMOKIES
>
> Pets are allowed in campgrounds, picnic areas, and along roadways in the Great Smoky Mountains National Park; however, they must be on a leash at all times. Dogs and other pets are only allowed on two short walking paths—the Gatlinburg Trail and the Oconaluftee River Trail. They are not allowed on any other park trails or elsewhere in the backcountry. Pet excrement must be immediately collected by the owner and disposed of in a trash receptacle.

Flat Creek. This is one of the hidden gems among Smokies trails. It's little known, but it's a delightful hike, especially in the summer when this higher-elevation means respite from stifling temperatures. The pat stretches through a pretty woodland, with evergreens, birch, rhododendron, and wildflowers. The elevation gain is about 570 feet. The trail is only 2.6 mi if you use a two-car shuttle, one at the trailhead at mile 5.4 of Heintooga Ridge Road, and the other at the Heintooga picnic area; if you don't do a two-car shuttle, you'll have to walk 3.6 mi along Heintooga Ridge Rd. to your car, but even this is pleasant, with spruce and fir lining the road and little traffic. ✉ *Trail begins at Flat Creek trailhead at mile 5.4 of Heintooga Ridge Rd.; alternatively, you can begin at the trailhead at Heintooga picnic area, 3.6 mi away* ⊙ *Heintooga Ridge Rd. is closed in winter.*

Kephart Prong. A 4-mi (roundtrip) woodland trail wanders beside a stream to the remains of a Civilian Conservation Corps camp. ✉ *Trailhead is 5 mi north of Smokemont Campground on U.S. 441 (Newfound Gap Rd.).*

★ **Little Cataloochee.** No other hike in the Smokies offers a cultural and historic experience like this one. In the early 20th century Cataloochee Cove had the largest population of any place in the Smokies, around 1,200 people. Most of the original structures have been torn down or succumbed to the elements, but a few historic frame buildings remain, such as a log cabin near Davidson Gap at mi 2.6, an apple house at mi 3.3, and a church at mi 4, preserved by park staff. You'll see several of these, along with rock walls and other artifacts, on the Little Cataloochee Trail. The trail is 5.9 mi (one-way) including about 0.8 mi at the beginning on Pretty Hollow Gap Trail. It is best hiked with a two-car shuttle, with one vehicle at the Pretty Hollow Gap trailhead in Cataloochee Valley and the other at the Little Cataloochee trailhead at Old Highway 284 (Cove Creek Road). Including the time it takes to explore the historic buildings and cemeteries, you should allow at least six hours for this hike. ⊠ *The Pretty Hollow Gap trailhead is near Beech Grove School in the Cataloochee Valley.*

Smokemont Loop. A 6.1-mi (roundtrip) loop takes you by streams and, in the spring and summer, lots of wildflowers, including trailing arbutus. The trail also passes a field with old chestnut trees killed by the chestnut blight decades ago. With access off Newfound Gap Road (U.S. 441) this is an easy trail to get to. ⊠ *Bradley Fork trailhead is at D loop of Smokemont campground, follow Bradley Fork trail to Smokemont Loop trail.*

DIFFICULT **Mt. Sterling.** A 5.4-mi (round-trip) hike takes you to an old fire watchtower, which you can climb. The route is steep, with an elevation gain of almost 2,000 feet, so you should consider this a strenuous, difficult hike. ⊠ *Trailhead on Cove Creek Rd. (Old Hwy. 284), midway between Cataloochee and Deep Creek Campground.*

HORSEBACK RIDING

Get back to nature and away from the crowds with a horseback ride through the forest. Guided horseback rides are offered by one park concessionaire stable at Smokemont near Cherokee. Rides are at a walking pace, so they are suitable for even inexperienced riders.

Another option is to bring your own horse. Smoky Mountains National Park is one of the best places to ride in the Southeast. About 550 mi of the park's hiking trails are open to horses. Horses are restricted to trails specifically designated for horse use. Five drive-in horse camps, open April through October, allow you easy access to the park's horse trails and cost from $20 to $25 a night. Four of these are on the North Carolina side—Big Creek, Cataloochee, Tow String, and Roundbottom. If you bring a horse to any park horse camp or ride a horse in the park, you must have either the original or a copy of an official negative test for equine infectious anemia (called a Coggins test). Pets are permitted in the horse camps but must be on a leash.

OUTFITTERS **Smokemont Riding Stable.** The emphasis here is on a family-friendly horseback riding experience, suitable even for novice riders. Choose either the one-hour trail ride or a 2½-hour waterfall ride (departing daily at 9 and noon). Riders must be at least five years old and weigh no more than 225 pounds. Smokemont also occasionally offers wagon rides. Check with the stables for dates and times. ⊠ *135 Smokemont Riding Stable Rd. (near MM 27.2), Cherokee* ☎ *828/497–2373* ⊕ *www.smokemontridingstable.com* 🖃 *$20–$48* ⏲ *Late May–Oct., daily 9–5.*

HORSE CAMPS **Big Creek Horse Camp.** Big Creek has six tent-only horse camping sites, with flush toilets, potable water, picnic tables, grills, designated parking, refuse containers, horse stalls, and hitch racks. ⊠ *Exit 451, I-40, 16 mi southeast of Crosby, TN* ☎ *877/444–6777* ⊕ *www.recreation. gov* ⏲ *Apr.–early Nov.*

Cataloochee. Cataloochee has seven tent-only horse camping sites, pit toilets, picnic tables, grills, designated parking, refuse containers, horse stalls, and hitch racks. The horse camp has a creekside setting in the beautiful Cataloochee Valley; elk may wander into the camp. ⊠*Exit 20, I–40, 25 mi northwest of Asheville, NC; turn on Cove Creek Rd. and go 11 mi to horse camp* ☎ 877/444–6777 ⊕*www.recreation.gov* ⊗*Open Apr.–early Nov.*

Roundbottom. Roundbottom has five tent-only horse camping sites, pit toilets, picnic tables, grills, designated parking, refuse containers, horse stalls, and hitch racks. ⊠*From Cherokee: take U.S. 441 south. Just after entering the park, turn right to Big Cove Rd. Go 0.2 mi to stop sign and turn left onto Big Cove Rd. Go 8.8 mi to a tee. Turn right and go .9 mi to the end of the pavement. Take the gravel Straight Fork-Round Bottom Rd., adjacent to a trout rearing facility, 3.5 mi to the horse camp* ☎877/444–6777 ⊕*www.recreation.gov* ⊗*Open Apr.–early Nov.*

Tow String. Tow String has only two tent-only horse camping sites, pit toilets, picnic tables, grills, designated parking, refuse containers, horse stalls, and hitch racks. ⊠*4 mi north of Cherokee off Newfound Gap Road (U.S. 441). Turn right at sign for Tow String. Turn left after crossing bridge* ☎877/444–6777 ⊕*www.recreation.gov* ⊗*Open Apr.–early Nov.*

RAFTING, TUBING, AND BOATING

On a hot summer's day there's nothing like hitting the water. You can swim or go tubing on Deep Creek near Bryson City. The upper section is a little wild and woolly, with white water flowing from cold mountain springs. The put-in is at the convergence of Indian Creek and Deep Creek where the sign says NO TUBING BEYOND THIS POINT. The lower section of Deep Creek is more suitable for kids. Put-in for this section is at the swimming hole just above the first bridge on the Deep Creek trail. There are several tubing outfitters near the entrance of the park at Deep Creek. Some have changing rooms and showers. Wear a swimsuit and bring towels and dry clothes to change into which you can leave in your car. Most tubing outfitters are open April–October. Note that the National Park Service recommends against tubing and swimming in the park, due to the risk of water-related injuries and even drowning; however, many thousands of visitors to the park enjoy the experience every summer.

For a more serious water experience, go rafting on the Nantahala River or one of the other rivers near the Smokies. The Nantahala, near Bryson City, is the closest to the Smokies. It has mild but still exciting Class II and III rapids. Serious rafters and kayakers looking for a challenge on a Class IV/IV+ river should consider the Cheoah near Robbinsville, NC. The Cheoah River has reopened for rafting and kayaking, after being dammed and closed for years, but only for about 17 days a year, mostly in the summer and fall. The French Broad near Asheville is another option. However, as of this writing most rafting trips on the French Broad have been discontinued due to a regional drought that has reduced water levels to lows not seen in more than 100 years.

For lake boating near the Smokies, your best bet is Fontana Lake. This 29-mi long, 11,700-acre TVA lake offers great views of the southwestern side of the Smokies. Canoes, kayaks, and other boats are available to rent at several marinas on the lake. You can even rent a houseboat. If you're towing your own boat, there are several boat ramps, including two near Bryson City. The Old 288 ramp is west of town; turn off Everett Street and continue on Lakeview Drive, following the Tuckasegee River, to the boat ramp signs. The Lemons Branch ramp is also west of Bryson City. Follow U.S. 74, then turn north on Highway 28; look for the Tsali Recreation Area on your right and follow signs to boat launch.

OUTFITTERS &
EXPEDITIONS
You can rent an inner tube for tubing on Deep Creek for less than $5 a day at these outfitters, all located near the Deep Creek entrance to the park near Bryson City. **Deep Creek Store & Tubes** (⊠ *1840 W. Deep Creek Rd., Bryson City* ☎*828/488–9665* ⊕*www.smokymtncampground. com*) rents tubes and sells camping supplies. **Deep Creek Tube Center** (⊠ *1090 Deep Creek Rd., Bryson City* ☎*882/488–6055* ⊕*www.deepcreekcamping.com/tubing.html*) rents inner tubes and sells creek shoes and other tubing accessories in their camp store.

Nantahala Outdoor Center (*NOC* ⊠*13077 U.S. Hwy. 19 W, Bryson City* ☎*800/232–7238 or 828/488–2176* ⊕*www.noc.com*) guides more than 30,000 rafters every year on the Nantahala and eight other rivers in North Carolina, Tennessee, Georgia, and West Virginia. *For more information, see Bryson City in What's Nearby below.*

Boat rentals on Fontana Lake, including kayaks, canoes, pontoon boats, small powerboats, houseboats (around $500 a day), and Jet Skis, are available at **Fontana Village Marina** (⊠*Fontana Village, Hwy. 28 North, Fontana Dam* ☎*800/849–2258 or 828/498–2211*), open April–October. For a fast boating experience, try **Smoky Mountain Jet Boats** (⊠ *22 Needmore Rd., Bryson City* ☎*828/488–0522 or 888/900–9091*), offering half-hour rides on Fontana Lake for $28 a person. To rent a small powerboat—a 15-foot boat is $50 a day, and a 24-foot pontoon boat is $165 a day—check with **Alarka Boat Dock** (⊠ *7230 Grassy Branch Rd., Bryson City* ☎*828/488–3841*).

SKIING
It doesn't snow much at the lower elevations of the Smokies, but in winter the higher elevations of the park frequently get heavy snow. Newfound Gap, at nearly a mile high, gets almost 5 feet of snow in the average year. You can check on the amount of snow on the ground at the higher elevations by visiting the park's webcam at Purchase Knob, on the North Carolina side at about 5,000 feet (⊕*www.nature.nps.gov/ air/webcams/parks/grsmpkcam/grsmpkcam.cfm*). Some roads, including Clingmans Dome Road and Balsam Mountain Road, are closed in winter, and even the main road through the park, Newfound Gap Road, closes when there's snow and ice, cutting off access to snowy areas. If Newfound Gap Road is not closed, you can enjoy cross-country skiing and hiking in the snow along Clingmans Dome Road, which is closed to vehicles in winter. For weather information, call ☎*865/436–1200, Ext. 630* and for road closings, dial *Ext. 631.*

EDUCATIONAL OFFERINGS

Discover the flora, fauna, and mountain culture of the Smokies with scheduled ranger programs and nature walks.

⟳ **Interpretive Ranger Programs.** The National Park Service sponsors all sorts of orientation activities, such as daily guided hikes and talks. The focus of the programs vary widely, from Earthcaching (like geocaching—a high-tech treasure hunt played with GPS devices—but with an education component), using GPS units loaned by the park, to talks on mountain culture to old-time fiddle and banjo music. Most are free, though a ranger-led hayride costs $8.50. Many of the programs are suitable for older children as well as for adults. For schedules, go to the Oconaluftee Visitor Center and pick up a free copy of *Smokies Guide* newspaper, or check online. ☎*865/436–1200 ⊕www.nps.gov/grsm* ✉*Free, $8.50 hayride.*

⟳ **Junior Ranger Program for Families.** Children ages five to 12 can take part in these hands-on educational programs. Kids should pick up a Junior Ranger booklet ($3) at Oconaluftee or at other park visitor centers. After they've completed the activities in the booklet, they can stop by a visitor center to talk to a ranger and receive a Junior Ranger badge. Especially during the summer, the park offers many age-appropriate demonstrations, classes, and programs for Junior Rangers, such as Blacksmithing, Stream Splashin', Geology, Critters and Crawlies, Cherokee Pottery for Kids, and—our favorite—Whose Poop's on Our Boots? ☎*865/436–1200 ⊕www.nps.gov/grsm/forkids/index.htm* ✉*$3.*

WHERE TO EAT

There are no restaurants within the park. Picnic areas, however, provide some amenities such as restrooms and pavilions.

PICNIC AREAS

Big Creek Picnic Area. This is the smallest picnic area in the park, with only 10 picnic tables. It's accessible via Exit 451 of I–40, or the unpaved Cove Creek Road from Cataloochee. There's a small campground here, and restrooms, but no pavilion. Several good hiking trails can be reached from the picnic area. Big Creek has some Class IV rapids nearby. ✉*Off I–40 at exit 451 (Waterville). Follow the road past the Walters Power Generating Station to a 4-way intersection. Continue straight through and follow signs.*

Collins Creek Picnic Area. The largest developed picnic area in the park, Collins Creek has 182 picnic tables. Collins Creek, which runs near the picnic area, is a small stream with above-average trout fishing. The site has restrooms with flush toilets, potable water, and a 70-seat pavilion that can be reserved in advance for $20. ✉*U.S. 441 (New-found Gap Rd.) at MM 25.4, about 8 mi from Cherokee ⊙Picnic area open early Mar.–Oct.; grounds close at 8 PM May–Aug., at sunset rest of the time.*

Getting Groceries

Other than a small convenience store at Cades Cove campground, there is no place to buy picnic supplies and groceries in the park. However, you'll find good-sized supermarkets near the park entrance. In North Carolina, **Ingles** (⊠ *U.S. 19/23 at Hughes Branch Rd., Bryson City, NC* ; ⊠ *201 Barber Blvd., Waynesville, NC* ; ⊠ *251 Welch Rd., Waynesville, NC* ; ⊠ *2 Sweetwater Rd., Robbinsville, NC*) is the dominant supermarket chain, with stores in Bryson City, Waynes-ville, and Robbinsville, among other towns near the park. **Bi-Lo** (⊠ *404 Russ Ave., Waynesville, NC*), another Southeastern chain supermarket with more than 220 stores, has a location in Waynesville. In Asheville, you'll find **Greenlife** and **Earth Fare**, two regional natural foods supermarket groups, and **Fresh Market**, a regional gourmet supermarket chain. The largest farmers' market in North Carolina is in Asheville, too.

★ **Deep Creek Picnic Area.** Deep Creek offers more than picnicking. You can go tubing (rent a tube for the day for under $5 at nearby tubing centers). Hike about 2 mi to three pretty waterfalls. Go trout fishing. You can even go mountain biking here, as this is one of the few park trails where bikes are allowed. The picnic area, open year-round, has 58 picnic tables, plus a pavilion that seats up to 70. ⊠ *1912 East Deep Creek Rd., Bryson City, NC. From downtown Bryson City, follow signs for 3 mi to Deep Creek.*

Fodor'sChoice
★ **Heintooga Picnic Area.** This is our favorite developed picnic area in the park. Located at more than a mile high, and set in a stand of spruce and fir, the picnic area has 41 tables. Nearby is Mile High Overlook, which offers one of the most scenic views of the Smokies and is a great place to enjoy the sunset. For birders, this is a good spot to see golden-crowned kinglets, red-breasted nuthatches, and other species that prefer higher elevations. You're almost certain to see the common raven here. Nearby are a campground and trailheads for several good hiking trails including Flat Creek. You can return to Cherokee via an unpaved backroad, Balsam Mountain Road, which is one-way, to Big Cove Road. ⊠ *Near end of Heintooga Ridge Rd. From Cherokee, take the Blue Ridge Parkway 11 mi to the turnoff for Heintooga Ridge Rd. Follow Heintooga Ridge Rd. about 9 mi to picnic area.*

WHERE TO CAMP

There is no lodging, other than camping, inside the park on the North Carolina side. Camping is permitted only in designated campsites, whether you're in the backcountry or frontcountry. There are 10 developed campgrounds (5 in North Carolina) with almost 950 tent and RV/trailer sites, and more than 100 backcountry campsites in the Smokies. Developed campgrounds have restrooms with cold running water and flush toilets, but there are no showers or electrical or water hookups in the park. Only one campground, Big Creek, doesn't permit RVs, but most campgrounds have length limits (from 12 to 40 ft.)

on trailers and RVs. Campgrounds charge between $14–$23 a night, depending on the campground and whether you are tent camping or have an RV or trailer.

Only one developed campground, at Cades Cove, is open year-round. The rest are closed in winter, but the dates vary. ⇨ See information for each campground below for dates. Smokemont accepts reservations for the period May 15–October 31. Others are first-come, first-served. Reservations can be made by phone (☎877/444–6777) or online (⊕*www. recreation.gov*).

Outside the park, there are many commercial campgrounds at entrances to the park. Nearly all have 30 or 50 amp electrical, sewer, and water hookups, restrooms, showers, and dump stations. Many have cable TV and Internet connections. Some have swimming pools.

$

Fodor's Choice

★

Balsam Mountain Campground. If you like a high, cool campground, with a beautiful setting in evergreens, Balsam Mountain will be your favorite campground in the park. It's the highest elevation in the park, at over 5,300 feet. By evening, you may want a campfire even in summer. The 46 campsites—first-come, first served—are best for tents, but small trailers or RVs up to 30 feet can fit in some sites. Most of the 10x10-foot tent pads and the picnics tables have been recently replaced, so they're in good shape. Restrooms are clean. For the Smokies' best sunset, go to the nearby Heintooga picnic area and hike a short way to Mile High Overlook. The campground has bear boxes and requires standard food protection policies, but bears are rarely a problem in this area. Due to its somewhat remote location off the Blue Ridge Parkway, Balsam Mountain Campground is rarely full even on peak summer and fall weekends. Several good hiking trails are nearby, and you can drive or bike the unpaved Balsam Mountain Road, which is one-way from the campground, and Big Cove Road to Cherokee. **Pros:** appealing high-elevation campground, where it's cool even in summer; rarely busy; good hiking and great scenic vistas nearby. **Cons:** a little remote and a moderate drive for supplies and groceries; most campsites don't have views and are a little closer together than you'd like. ⊠ *Near end of Heintooga Ridge Rd. From Cherokee, take the Blue Ridge Parkway 11 mi to the turnoff for Heintooga Ridge Rd. Follow Heintooga Ridge Rd. about 9 mi to campground, which is just beyond the picnic area.* ☎877/444–6777 ⊕*www.recreation.gov* ⇆*46 sites for RVs/trailers up to 30 feet and tents* ⅏ *Flush toilets, drinking water, bear boxes, fire pits, grills, picnic tables* ☉ *Early May–Oct.*

$

Big Creek Campground. With just 12 campsites, Big Creek is the smallest campground in the park, and the only one that doesn't accept RVs or trailers—it's for tents only. This is a walk-in, not hike-in, campground. While you can't park your vehicle right beside your tent, you only have to tote your supplies 100 or 200 feet. Five of the 12 first-come, first-served sites (unnumbered) are beside Big Creek, which offers good swimming and fishing. Although it's not far from an I–40 exit, the campground is more remote than it looks on a map, and it's a 30-minute drive to the nearest grocery store, in Newport, Tennessee. There is a small convenience store closer by. Carefully observe bear protection rules, as there have been a number of human-bear interactions nearby. **Pros:** small escape spot by a river; tents only, no RVs. **Cons:** about a 30-minute drive to the nearest grocery. ⊠ *Cove Creek Rd. (Old Hwy. 284).* ✛ *Take I–40 to the Waterville (TN) Exit 451. Cross the Pigeon River and turn left to follow the Pigeon River upstream. Go 2.3 mi to an intersection. Go through the intersection and enter the park. Pass the Big Creek Ranger Station and go about 3.5 mi to the end of the gravel road and the campground. An alternate route is on the unpaved Cove Creek Rd. (Old Hwy. 284) from the Cataloochee Valley* ☎ *877/444–6777* ⊕ *www.recreation.gov* ⇝ *12 tent sites* ⚹ *Flush toilets, drinking water, bear boxes, fire pits, grills, picnic tables, swimming creek* ⊙ *Early Mar.–Oct.*

$$ ⚠ **Cataloochee Campground.** The appeal of this small campground is
★ its location in the beautiful and historical Cataloochee Valley. You can tour the old homesteads and churches, maintained much as they were before the coming of the park, when this valley supported some 1,200 people. You're also virtually guaranteed to see elk, along with white-tailed deer and wild turkeys. Bears are a little less common, but they do come into the campground, so follow bear-proof food storage rules and use bear boxes. Of the 27 campsites, about half a dozen set beside Cataloochee Creek fill up first. This is a first-come, first-served campground, and you can't reserve ahead. Although the campground allows RVs and trailers up to 31 feet, you may want to think twice before driving anything other than a car or truck into the valley—the unpaved Cove Creek Road is narrow, with sharp curves, and in some places you hug the mountainside, with a steep drop-off just a few feet away. There's a horse camp here, and nearby you'll find excellent hiking on several trails including Little Cataloochee and Boogerman. **Pros:** provides access to beautiful, historic Cataloochee Valley; small campground with spacious, nicely spaced sites; pleasant creekside setting. **Cons:** difficult, even scary, drive in a large RV to the campground; long drive for groceries and supplies. ⊠ Cataloochee Valley. ✛ *On I–40, take North Carolina Exit 20 and go 0.2 miles on U.S. 276. Turn right onto Cove Creek Rd. and follow the signs 11 mi to the Cataloochee Valley and Campground* ☎ *877/444–6777* ⊕ *www.recreation. gov* ⇝ *27 sites for RVs/trailers up to 31 feet and tents* ⚹ *Flush toilets, drinking water, bear boxes, fire pits, grills, picnic tables, swimming creek.* ⊙ *Early Mar.–Oct.*

$$ ⚠ **Deep Creek Campground.** Rollin', rollin', you're rollin' down the river—at least, you're floating on an inner tube down Deep Creek. This campground is near the most popular tubing spot in the Smokies. Officially, the park service doesn't recommend tubing in the streams of the Smokies, due mainly to the risk of injury from slips and slides, but thousands of kids and the young at heart do it at Deep Creek every summer. Commercial businesses near this campground rent tubes all day for $5 or less. There's also swimming in several swimming holes. (Don't confuse this park campground with a similarly named commercial campground just outside the Deep Creek entrance of the park.) Of the 92 first-come, first-served sites here, sites 1–42 are for tents only, and the other sites are for tents and small RVs/trailers up to 26 feet in length.

Nearby are several easy to moderate hiking trails, including a short loop a little over 2 mi that takes you to three waterfalls. **Pros:** lots of family tubing and swimming fun on the creek; convenient to the pleasant small town of Bryson City. **Cons:** with several private campgrounds and tube rental businesses, the entrance to the park has a commercial feel. ✉ *1912 East Deep Creek Rd., Bryson City, NC. From downtown Bryson City, follow signs for 3 mi to Deep Creek* ☎ *877/444—6777* ⊕ *www.recreation.gov* ➲ *92 sites for RVs/trailers up to 26 feet and tents* ⚓ *Flush toilets, drinking water, bear boxes, fire pits, grills, picnic tables, public telephone, swimming creek* ☉ *Early Apr.–Oct.*

\$\$–\$\$\$ ⚐**Smokemont Campground.** With 142 sites, Smokemont is the largest campground on the North Carolina side of the park. Some of the campsites are a little jammed up, but the individual sites themselves are spacious. Tent sites have a 13x13-foot tent pad, fire ring with cooking grill, and a picnic table with lantern pole. Sites in F loop, open to RVs only, are wooded and more private. Sites F2, 4, 6, 8, 34, 36, 38, 40, 42, 44, and 46 are on the river. In RV areas, generator use is restricted to 8 AM to 8 PM and prohibited altogether in loops A, B, and C from mid-May–October. The Bradley Fork River runs through the campground. There's fishing and tubing (bring your own tubes) in the river, and the campground allows access to the Bradley Fork Trail, located at the top of D loop, which leads to a number of other hiking trails. In summer and fall rangers offer interpretive talks at the campground, and there are mountain music and storytelling programs. The nearby Smokemont Stable offers horseback rides and sells firewood and ice. This campground stays open most of the year, closing only in January, February, and the first few days of March. **Pros:** pleasant, large campground; lots for families and kids to do including tubing, fishing, horseback riding, and hiking; easy access to Cherokee and to sites such as Mingus Mill and Mountain Farm Museum. **Cons:** with so many RVs, you're not exactly in the wilderness. ✉ *Off U.S. Hwy. 441 (Newfound Gap Rd.) 6 mi north of Cherokee.* ☎ *877/444–6777* ⊕ *www.recreation. gov* ➲ *142 sites for RVs up to 40 feet and trailers up to 35 feet, and tents* ⚓ *Flush toilets, drinking water, bear boxes, pit fires, grills, picnic tables, public telephone, swimming creek* ☉ *Early Mar.–Dec.*

WHAT'S NEARBY

Whether you're looking for a hot meal and a comfy bed after days of camping out or just want some "unnatural" diversion, these small towns have everything from big casinos to quaint potteries to keep you entertained.

CHEROKEE

178 mi east of Charlotte; 51 mi west of Asheville; 2 mi from entrance to Great Smoky Mountains National Park.

The 56,000-acre Cherokee reservation is known as the Qualla Boundary, and the town of Cherokee is its capital. Truth be told, there are two Cherokees. There's the Cherokee with the sometimes tacky pop culture, designed to appeal to the masses of tourists, many of whom are visiting nearby Great Smoky Mountains National Park or have come to gamble at the massive Harrah's casino (the largest private employer in the region). But there's another Cherokee that's a window onto the rich heritage of the tribe's Eastern Band. Although now relatively small in number—tribal enrollment is 12,500—these Cherokee and their ancestors have been responsible for keeping alive the Cherokee culture. They are the descendants of those who hid in the Great Smoky Mountains to avoid the Trail of Tears, the forced removal of the Cherokee Nation to Oklahoma in the 19th century. They are survivors, extremely attached to the hiking, swimming, trout fishing, and natural beauty of their ancestral homeland. The reservation is dry, with no alcohol sales anywhere, even at the casino. This also means that there are few upscale restaurants in the area (since they depend on wine and cocktail sales for much of their profits), just fast-food and mom-and-pop places.

GETTING HERE & AROUND
The Blue Ridge Parkway's southern terminus is at Cherokee, and the Parkway is by far the most beautiful route to Cherokee and to Great Smoky Mountains National Park. A faster option is U.S. 23 and U.S. 74/U.S. 441 connecting Cherokee with I–40 from Asheville or from Franklin in the south. The least pleasant route is U.S. 19 from I–40, a mostly two-lane road pocked with touristy roadside shops.

ESSENTIALS
Cherokee Visitors Center (⌖ *U.S. 441 Business* ☎ *828/497–9195 or 800/438–1601* ⊕ *www.cherokee-nc.com*).

EXPLORING
The **Museum of the Cherokee Indian,** with displays and artifacts that cover 12,000 years, is one of the best Native American museums in the United States. Computer-generated images, lasers, specialty lighting, and sound effects help re-create events in the history of the Cherokee: for example, you'll see children stop to play a butter-bean game while adults shiver along the snowy Trail of Tears. The museum has an art gallery, a gift shop, and an outdoor living exhibit of Cherokee life in the 15th century. ⌖ *U.S. 441 at Drama Rd.* ⌂ *P.O. Box 1599* ☎ *828/497–3481* ⊕ *www.cherokeemuseum.org* ⌖ *$9* ☉ *June–Aug., Mon.–Sat. 9–8, Sun. 9–5; Sept.–May, daily 9–5.*

☾ At the historically accurate, re-created **Oconaluftee Indian Village** guides in native costumes will lead you through a village of 225 years ago while others demonstrate traditional skills such as weaving, pottery, canoe construction, and hunting techniques. ⌖ *U.S. 441 at Drama Rd.* ☎ *828/497–2315* ⊕ *www.oconalufteevillage.com* ⌖ *$15* ☉ *Daily 9:30–5:30 mid-May–mid-Oct.*

☾ Every mountain county has significant deposits of gems and minerals, and at the **Smoky Mountain Gold and Ruby Mine,** on the Qualla Boundary, you can search for gems such as aquamarines. Children love panning precisely because it can be wet and messy. Here they're guaranteed a

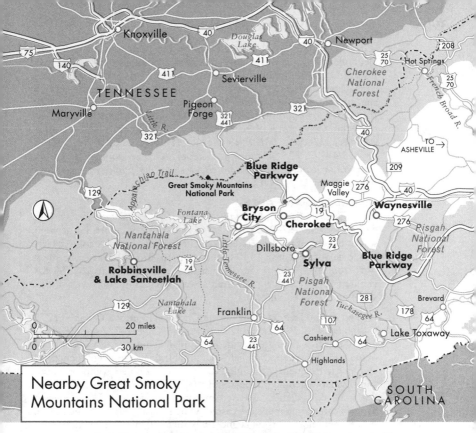

Nearby Great Smoky Mountains National Park

find. Gem ore can be purchased, too, for $4–$10 per bag: gold ore costs $5 per bag. ⊠ *U.S. 441 N* ☎ *828/497-6574* ✉ *$4–$10, depending on gems* ☉ *Mar.–Nov., daily 10–6.*

WHERE TO STAY

$–$$ 🖼 **Fairfield Inn & Suites.** This three-story chain motel is directly across from Harrah's Casino, so you can walk to the casino without worrying about parking. Rooms here are typical of the Fairfield Inn chain—comfortable and clean but not deluxe. **Pros:** convenient to casino; usual chain motel amenities. **Cons:** like all Fairfield motels. ⊠ *568 Painttown Rd.* ☎ *828/497-0400* 🖷 *828/497-4242* ⊕ *www.marriott.com* ➴ *96 rooms, 4 suites* ☼ *In-room: refrigerator, Wi-Fi. In-hotel: pool, laundry facilities, laundry service, parking (free), no-smoking rooms* ⊟ *AE, D, DC, MC, V* ⊙| *CP.*

$$$–$$$$ 🖼 **Harrah's Cherokee Casino Hotel.** The 15-story hotel, which opened in 2002 and doubled in size with an addition in 2005, towers over the mom-and-pop motels nearby and the casino next door, to which it is umbilically attached via a series of escalators and walkways. The lobby and other public areas incorporate traditional Cherokee art themes. Rooms are large, about 500 square feet, and have 32-inch TVs. For high-rollers, there are suites on the top floor. The Selu Garden Café in the hotel and the Seven Sisters restaurant in the casino are handy after

a day of playing the slots. Restaurants and the casino do not offer alcoholic drinks, as the sale of alcohol is prohibited on the Cherokee reservation. A $650 million expansion that will bring the total of hotel rooms here to over 1,000 and also add new restaurants, shops, and a spa, and increase the number of video gaming machines to over 5,000 is expected to be completed by 2012. **Pros:** supersized hotel; convenient to casino. **Cons:** hotel often fully booked due to comps and deals for gamblers; no booze. ☒*U.S. 19 at U.S. 441 Business,* ☎*800/427–7247 or 828/497–7777* ⊕*www.harrahs.com* ↩*576 rooms* ⌂*In-room: refrigerator (some), Wi-Fi. In-hotel: 5 restaurants, pool, gym, no-smoking rooms* ▤*AE, D, DC, MC, V* ⏐⏐*EP.*

NIGHTLIFE & THE ARTS

THE ARTS *Unto These Hills* (☒*Mountainside Theater on Drama Rd., off U.S. 441 N,* ☎*828/497–2111 or 866/554–4557*) is a colorful and well-staged history of the Cherokee from the time of Spanish explorer Hernando de Soto's visit in 1540 to the infamous Trail of Tears. The show runs from mid-June to late August, and tickets start at $18 ($8 for children 12 and under). The drama was updated in 2006 with a new script and new costumes.

NIGHTLIFE Owned by the Eastern Bank of the Cherokee, **Harrah's Casino** (☒*777 Casino Dr., U.S. 19 at U.S. 441 Business,* ☎*828/497–7777 or 800/427–7247*) has more than 3,600 video-gaming machines in a casino the size of more than three football fields. Digital blackjack and digital baccarat combine live dealers with digital cards. Some gamblers complain about stingy video machine payouts and the fact that alcohol is not served. Big-name stars such as Wayne Newton, Jay Leno, and Willie Nelson provide entertainment at the casino, which has a theater seating 1,500. A $650 million expansion is underway that will increase the number of gaming machines to over 5,000 and add a larger theater.

SPORTS & THE OUTDOORS

FISHING There are 30 mi of regularly stocked trout streams on the **Cherokee Indian Reservation** (☎*828/497–5201 or 800/438–1601*). To fish in tribal water you need a tribal fishing permit, available at nearly two dozen reservation businesses. The $7 permit is valid for one day and has a creel limit of 10. A five-day permit is $28. Fishing is permitted from late March to October.

HIKING A five-minute hike from the **Mingo Falls Campground** (☒*Big Cove Rd., about 4 mi north of Acquoni Rd.*) will reward you with a view of the 120-foot-high Mingo Falls. In the downtown area you can cross the Oconaluftee River on a footbridge to **Oconaluftee Islands Park & Trail** (☒*Off U.S. 441, across from Cherokee Elementary School*) and walk a trail around the perimeter of the Island Park, which also has picnic facilities.

SHOPPING

The **Qualla Arts and Crafts Mutual** (☒*U.S. 441 at Drama Rd.,* ☎*828/497–3103*), across the street from the Museum of the Cherokee Indian, is a cooperative that displays and sells items created by 300 Cherokee craftspeople. The store has a large selection of high-quality baskets, masks, and wood carvings, which can cost hundreds of dollars.

BRYSON CITY

65 mi east of Asheville; 11 mi southwest of Cherokee.

Bryson City is a little mountain town on the Nantahala River, one of the lesser-known gateways to the Great Smokies. The town's most striking feature is a city hall with a four-sided clock. Since becoming the depot and headquarters of the Great Smoky Mountains Railroad, the downtown shopping area has been rejuvenated, mostly with gift shops and ice-cream stands.

GETTING HERE AND AROUND
Bryson City is a 15-minute drive from Cherokee on U.S. 19. Near Bryson City are two entrances to the Great Smokies.

EXPLORING
The most popular river in western North Carolina for rafting and kayaking is **Nantahala River,** which races through the scenic Nantahala Gorge, a 1,600-foot-deep gorge that begins about 13 mi west of Bryson City on U.S. 19. Class III and Class IV rapids (Class V are the most dangerous) make for a thrilling ride. Several outfitters run river trips or rent equipment. Happily, the severe drought that reduced water flow on many other rivers in the region doesn't affect the Nantahala, due to daily dam releases. ■**TIP→ At several points along the river you can park your car and watch rafters run the rapids—on a summer day you'll see hundreds of rafts and kayaks going by.** ⊠*U.S. 19, beginning 13 mi west of Bryson City, .*

The popular train rides of the **Great Smoky Mountains Railroad** include excursions from Bryson City, and several special trips. Diesel-electric or steam locomotives go along the Nantahala Gorge. Open-sided cars or standard coaches are ideal for picture taking as the mountain scenery glides by. Some rides include a meal: on some Friday evenings there's a mystery theater train with dinner, and on Saturdays a gourmet dinner train. ⊠*225 Everett St., Stes. G & H, Bryson City* ☎*800/872–4681* ⊕*www.gsmr.com* ⊠*$34–$53 for standard seating; upgraded seating $12–$20 additional; rates plus $3 parking fee; most tickets include admission to the Smoky Mountain Model Reailroad Museum.*

☺ Commercial and overpriced, the **Smoky Mountain Model Railroad Museum** nevertheless appeals to kids or anyone with a fond memory of model trains. More than 2,500 model trains are displayed, around two model railroad operating layouts. This is also a retail store selling model trains of all kinds. ⊠*100 Greenlee St., near Great Smoky Mountains Railroad Depot* ☎*828/488–5200 or 866/914–5200* ⊕*www.smokymtntrains.com* ⊠*$9* ☉*Mon.–Sat. 8:30–5:30.*

5

WHERE TO STAY & EAT

$ ✕ **River's End at Nantahala Outdoor**
AMERICAN **Center.** The casual riverbank setting and high-energy atmosphere
at NOC's eatery draws lots of hungry people just returned from an
invigorating day of rafting. There
are salads, soups, and sandwiches
during the day and fancier fixins'
in the evening. The chili's a winner—there are black- and white-
bean versions ($5.25 for a bowl).
For more upscale fare at NOC, try
Relia's Garden, which specializes in
steak and trout (closed Monday–
Wednesday). ⊠*13077 Highway
19 W* ☎*828/488–2176* ▤*MC, V*
☻*Closed Nov.–Mar.*

WET OR DRY?

The mountains sometimes seem
to have a schizophrenic attitude
toward alcohol. Making moonshine
was once a major industry here,
but at the same time, many communities refuse to authorize the
legal sale of alcohol. Four counties—Clay, Graham, Mitchell, and
Yancey—are completely dry; no
alcohol can be sold, although it's
not illegal to drink. Others operate
on a spectrum. For all the details,
visit the Web site of the **North
Carolina Alcoholic Beverage
Control Commission** (⊕*www.
ncabc.com*).

$–$$ ▦ **Fryemont Inn.** An institution in
Bryson City for eight decades, the
Fryemont Inn is on the National Register of Historic Places. The lodge
exterior is bark, rooms in the main lodge are paneled in real chestnut,
and the lobby has a fireplace big enough for 8-foot logs. If you need
more luxury, choose one of the suites with fireplaces and air-conditioning. The restaurant ($$–$$$), serving Southern fare, is open to the
public for breakfast and dinner. **Pros:** historic inn; comfortably rustic;
charming restaurant with wholesome, simple food. **Cons:** rooms in
main lodge are far from posh; can be warm on a summer day; no swimming pool. ⊠*Freymont St., Box 459, Bryson City* ☎*828/488–2159
or 800/845–4879* ⊕*www.fryemontinn.com* ⊅*37 rooms, 3 suites, 1
cabin* &*In-room: no a/c (some), no phone, no TV (some). In-hotel:
restaurant, pool* ▤*D, MC, V* ☻*No lunch* ⊠*MAP.*

$–$$ ▦ **Hemlock Inn.** This folksy, friendly mountain inn on 50 acres above
Bryson City is the kind of place where you can rock, doze, and play
Scrabble. Even if you're not a guest at the inn, you can make a reservation for dinner Monday through Saturday and for lunch on Sunday.
The all-you-can-eat meals (breakfast included in the rates, dinner packages available) are prepared with regional foods and served family-style
on lazy Susans at big round tables. Fly-fishing and river rafting–kayaking and other packages are available. **Pros:** unpretentious, family-
oriented inn; delicious Southern-style food; like a visit to grandma's.
Cons: no modern conveniences like Wi-Fi, TVs, or in-room phones;
family-style meals may not suit everyone; no alcohol served; no swimming pool. ⊠*Galbraith Creek Rd.* ⊡*P.O. Box 2350* ✛*1 mi north
of U.S. 19* ☎*828/488–2885* ⊕*www.hemlockinn.com* ⊅*22 rooms,
3 cottages* &*In-room: no a/c, no phone, no TV. In-hotel: restaurant*
▤*D, MC, V* ☻ ⊠*BP.*

SPORTS & THE OUTDOORS

GOLF The par-71, 5987-yard course at semiprivate **Smoky Mountain Country Club** (✉1112 *Conley Creek Rd.,Whittier* ☎828/4497–4653 or 800/474–0070), has 400 feet of elevation change over the 18 holes, not to mention stunning views of the mountains.

HORSEBACK RIDING Privately owned **Deep Creek Stables** (✉*Deep Creek Picnic Area, near Bryson City entrance to Great Smokies National Park,* ☎828/488–8504) offers trail riding in the Smokies.

RIVER RAFTING & KAYAKING **Nantahala Outdoor Center (NOC)** (🏠 *13077 Highway 19 W* ☎800/232–7238 ⊕*www.noc.com*) guides more than 30,000 rafters every year on the Nantahala and eight other rivers: the Chattooga, Cheoah, French-Broad, Nolichucky, Ocoee, Gauley, New, and Pigeon. Due to the severe regional drought in 2007–2008, the French Broad River was at its lowest flow level in more than 100 years, and as of this writing most rafting trips on the French Broad have been discontinued. ■**TIP→ The Cheoah River has reopened for rafting and kayaking, after being dammed and closed for years, but only for about 17 days a year. Serious rafters and kayakers looking for a challenge on Class IV/IV+ river should consider the Cheoah.** NOC also rents kayaks, ducks, and other equipment. The NOC complex on the Nantahala River is virtually a tourist attraction itself, especially for young people, with three restaurants, cabin and campground rentals, an inn, a stop for the Great Smokies Railroad, and an outdoor store.

ROBBINSVILLE & LAKE SANTEETLAH

98 mi southwest of Asheville; 35 mi southwest of Bryson City.

If you truly want to get away from everything, head to the area around Robbinsville in the far southwest corner of North Carolina, a little south of the southern edge of the Great Smokies. The town of Robbinsville offers little, but the Snowbird Mountains, Lake Santeetlah, Fontana Lake, the rugged Joyce Kilmer–Slickrock Wilderness, and the Joyce Kilmer Memorial Forest, with its giant virgin poplars and sycamores, definitely are highlights of this part of North Carolina.

More than 29 mi long, **Fontana Lake & Dam** border the southern edge of the Great Smokies. Unlike most other lakes in the mountains, Fontana has a shoreline that is almost completely undeveloped, since about 90% of its 240 mi are owned by the federal government. Fishing here is excellent, especially for small-mouth bass, muskie, and walleye. On the downside, the Tennessee Valley Authority (TVA) manages the lake for power generation, and at peak visitor period in the fall the lake is drawn down, leaving large areas of mudflats. Fontana Dam, completed in 1944, at 480 feet is the highest concrete dam east of the Rockies. The Appalachian Trail crosses the top of the dam. ✉*Fontana Dam Visitor Center, off Rte. 28, 3 mi from Fontana Village* ☎865/632–2101 *TVA* 🖼*Free* ☉ *Visitor center May–Nov., daily 9–7.*

Fodor'sChoice ★ One of the few remaining sections of the original Appalachian forests, **Joyce Kilmer Memorial Forest,** a part of the 17,000-acre Joyce Kilmer–Slickrock Wilderness, has 400-year-old yellow poplars that are as much as 20 feet in circumference, along with huge hemlocks, oaks, syca-mores, and other trees. If you haven't seen a true virgin forest, you can't imagine what America must have looked like in the early days of settlement. A 2-mi trail takes you through wildflower- and moss-carpeted areas of incredible beauty. The forest is named for the early-20th-century poet, killed in World War I, who is famous for the lines "I think I shall never see / A poem lovely as a tree." ■ **TIP→ During June, the parking lot of the Joyce Kilmer Memorial Forest is an excellent spot to see the light shows of the synchronous fireflies (***Photinus caroli-nus***), which blink off and on in unison.** ⊠*15 mi west of Robbinsville, off Cherohala Skyway via Hwy. 143 and Kilmer Rd.* ☎*828/479–6431 Cheoah Ranger District* ☜*Free.*

Formed in 1928 with the construction of the Santeetlah Dam, **Lake Santeetlah,** meaning "blue waters" in the Cherokee language, has 76 mi of shoreline, with good fishing for crappie, bream, and lake trout. The lake is managed by Alcoa as a hydroelectric project, but most of the land is owned by the federal government, a part of the Nantahala National Forest. ⊠*Cheoah Point Recreation Area, Rte. 1145 off U.S. 129, about 7 mi north of Robinsville* ☎*828/479–6431 Nantahala National Forest/Cheoah Ranger District* ☜*Free.*

WHERE TO STAY

$$ ⛺**Blue Boar Inn.** On the outside, it looks like a lodge for bear and wild boar hunters, which it was—it was built in 1950 by a Cincinnati beer magnate as a hunting lodge. Today it has been totally redone inside, with upscale modern furnishings, including air-conditioning and TVs. Each spacious room has a porch. Up a hillside above the main lodge, privately owned cottages (plans are for 10 of them eventually) are available for rent for $250–$325 nightly, EP. The 1,000-square-foot cottages each have two bedrooms, two baths, kitchen, hot tubs, and fireplaces. You can kayak or canoe on nearby Lake Santeetlah, and a stocked trout pond is on the lodge grounds. A delicious full breakfast is included (lodge rooms only), and dinner is available at an extra charge. BYOB, as no wine or other alcohol is sold. **Pros:** peaceful mountain retreat; large rooms with upscale furnishings; self-catering cabins an option. **Cons:** no alcohol sold; no swimming pool; remote location. ⊠*1283 Blue Boar Rd., Robbinsville* ☎*828/479–8126 or 866/479–8126* ⊕*www.blueboarinn.com* ⇆*8 rooms, 3 two-bedroom cottages* ⅀*In-room: kitchen (some), refrigerator. In-hotel: restaurant, no-smok-ing rooms* ☰*AE, D, MC, V* ☉*Closed late Nov.–late Mar.* ⅋❘*BP.*

$$$–$$$$ ⛺**Snowbird Mountain Lodge.** The main lodge, built in 1941 and now in
Fodor'sChoice   the National Register of Historic Places, has two massive stone fire-
★   places, solid chestnut beams across the ceiling, and beautiful views across the valley. If you run out of things to do, there are 10,000 books in the library and 100 acres of grounds to explore. The restaurant serves "rustic" meals like fresh trout with grilled vegetable salsa, and the wine list is the size of a small telephone directory. For more luxury than the main lodge rooms offer, choose a room in the Chestnut Lodge or a king suite in a separate cottage. Some rooms have whirlpool baths and fireplaces. **Pros:** gorgeous mountainside setting; excellent food;

BARD OF THE MOUNTAINS

John Parris (1914–99), a native of the small town of Sylva, has been called the "Bard of the Mountains." In the course of four decades of writing a daily newspaper column "Roaming the Mountains" for the *Asheville Citizen*, Parris gathered and published more on mountain traditions and culture and language than perhaps any other writer who ever lived. Some of his daily columns were collected in five books, including *My Mountains, My People*. Sometimes sentimental, but always full of authentic detail, his daily

stories were prose poems about the mountains he loved. These lines from *Mountain Cooking* exemplify his style:

"An old farmhouse with a fire blazing on the hearth has a way of conjuring up memories.

This is particularly so when the first icy winds come prowling under the eaves and there's a smell of frost in the air.

It is then that the memories come flooding back...."

huge wine list. **Cons:** remote; no swimming pool. ⊠*4633 Santeetlah Rd., Robbinsville* ☎*828/479–3433 or 800/941–9290* ⊕*www.snow-birdlodge.com* ⇝*21 rooms, 2 suites in separate cottage* ⚘*In-room: no a/c (some), no phone, refrigerator (some), no TV. In-hotel: restaurant, tennis courts, Internet terminal, Wi-Fi, no kids under 12, no-smoking rooms* ⊟*MC, V* ⊺○*MAP.*

SYLVA

48 mi southwest of Asheville; 2 mi east of Dillsboro via U.S. 23.

Sylva, population 2,300, is the county seat of Jackson County. It has a classic small-town Main Street with stores selling furniture, hardware, watches, books, beer, and other necessities. The domed Jackson County Courthouse, built in 1914 in the Beaux Arts style, overlooks the downtown from a nearby hilltop. Noted author John Parris was a native of Sylva.

Mountain Heritage Center. In wormy chestnut-paneled quarters at Western Carolina University, this museum maintains and displays the heirlooms of hundreds of mountain families, from butter churns to baby basinets. Most exhibits rotate, but a permanent exhibit, "Migration of the Scotch-Irish People," describes the history and culture of the English and Scottish people of Northern Ireland, known as Ulster Scots, who settled the Carolina mountains in the 18th century. ⊠*150 H.F. Robinson Building, Western Carolina University, Cullowhee* ☎*828/227–7129* ⊕*www.wcu.edu/mhc* ✉*Free* ☉*Mon.–Fri. 8–5; also Sun. 2–5 in Oct. only; closed during some college holiday periods.*

WHERE TO STAY & EAT

$–$$
AMERICAN
✕**Jarrett House.** The food here may not win any awards for creative cooking, but folks love the mountain trout ($15.95), country ham with red-eye gravy ($15.95), and fried chicken ($13.95) at the Jarrett

House, in continuous operation since 1884 and now on the National Register of Historic Places. Jarrett House is best known for its dining, but you can also stay here. Rooms (¢) in this three-story country inn, with porches on all three levels, are small and unpretentious, but you can't beat the location right across from Dillsboro's shops. ⊠ *Box 219, U.S. 441, Dillsboro* ☎*828/586–0265 or 800/972–5623* ⊕*www.jarretthouse.com* ⊟*No credit cards* ⊗*Closed Jan.–Apr.*

$–$$ ⊡ **Balsam Mountain Inn.** A stay here is like going back 75 years in time, when folks rocked and chatted on the front porch, went to bed at 10 PM, and hotels didn't have amenities like air-conditioning, room TVs, swimming pool, fitness center, or, heaven forbid, Internet connections. In this rambling old wood-frame inn, the floors creak and you may overhear your neighbors through paper-thin walls. But if you can buy into the back-in-time premise, Balsam Mountain Inn is a delight, with a cozy library, friendly staff, and a wonderfully unpretentious restaurant. The rooms, most not overly large, have been redone, but old-fashioned elements such as claw-foot tubs remain. You'll enjoy the included breakfast served on the sun porch. **Pros:** friendly, down-home, old mountain inn; delicious food. **Cons:** rooms vary, and some are small, with thin walls; lights out at 10. ⊠ *68 Seven Springs Dr., Balsam* ☎*828/ or 800/224–9498* ⊕*www.balsammountaininn.com* ⚲*41 rooms, 9 suites* ⚭*In-room: no a/c, no phone, no TV. In-hotel: restaurant* ⊟*AE, D, MC, V* ⏏*BP.*

SPORTS & THE OUTDOORS

RIVER TUBING   On the Tuckaseegee River, much gentler than the Nantahala River, **Tuck-**
& KAYAKING   **aseegee Outfitters** (⊠*U.S. 74/441,* ☎*800/539–5683*) offers nonguided trips by tube, raft, and inflatable kayak.

SHOPPING

Nearby Dillsboro has a cluster of mostly tourist-oriented shops, in the several blocks adjoining the Great Smokies Railroad tracks. A co-op of more than 80 area artisans owns and runs **Dogwood Crafters** (⊠*90 Webster St.* ☎*828/586–2248*), where you can purchase pottery, rugs, baskets, and other crafts. You can see potters throwing pots at **Mountain Pottery** (⊠*152 Front St.* ☎*828/586–9183*), where pottery, including ceramics made in the Japanese raku style, by about 75 different local potters is for sale.

WAYNESVILLE

17 mi east of Cherokee on U.S. 19.

This is where the Blue Ridge Parkway meets the Great Smokies. Waynesville is the seat of Haywood County. About 40% of the county is occupied by Great Smoky Mountains National Park, Pisgah National Forest, and the Harmon Den Wildlife Refuge. The town of Waynesville is a rival of Blowing Rock and Highlands as a summer and vacation-home retreat for the well-to-do, though the atmosphere here is a bit more countrified. A Ramp Festival, celebrating the smelly local cousin of the onion, is held in Waynesville annually in early May. New B&Bs are springing up like wildflowers. Local restaurants celebrated in 2008, when the town voted to allow liquor by the drink. Ghost Town, a Wild West theme park popular with kids, is nearby, in Maggie Valley.

The **Museum of North Carolina Handicrafts,** in the Shelton House (circa 1875), has an exhibit of 19th-century heritage crafts. ✉*307 Shelton St.* ☎*828/452–1551* ✉*$5* ⊙*May–Oct., Tues.–Fri. 10–4.*

Cold Mountain, the vivid best-selling novel by Charles Frazier, has made a destination out of the real **Cold Mountain.** About 15 mi from Waynesville in the Shining Rock Wilderness Area of Pisgah National Forest, the 6,030-foot rise had long stood in relative anonymity. But with the success of Frazier's book, people want to see the region that Inman and Ada, the book's Civil War–era protagonists, called home.

For a view of the splendid mass stop at any of a number of overlooks off the Blue Ridge Parkway. Try the Cold Mountain Parking Overlook, just past mile marker 411.9; the Wagon Road Gap parking area, at mile marker 412.2; or the Waterrock Knob Interpretative Station, at mile marker 451.2. You can climb the mountain, but beware, as the hike to the summit is strenuous. No campfires are allowed in Shining Rock, so you'll need a stove if you wish to cook. Inform the **ranger station** (☎*828/877–3350*) if you plan to hike or camp.

☺   **Ghost Town in the Sky** is a Wild West theme park on top of a mountain. Originally opened in 1961, it closed in 2002 but came back to life in 2007 under new ownership. You ride up 3,300 feet in a chairlift or an inclined railway. At the top you're greeted by gunslingers who stage O.K. Corral–style gunfights. One cowhand says he's been in more than 50,000 gunfights at Ghost Town. There are 40 replica buildings meant to represent an 1880s Western town. Also at the park are thrill rides, including the new "Cliff Hanger" roller coaster. ✉*16 Fie Top Rd., Maggie Valley* ☎*828/926–1140* ⊕*www.ghosttowninthesky.com* ✉*$30 ($24 if purchased online)* ⊙*Early May, Fri.–Sun. 10–6; mid-May–early Sept., daily 10–6; and early Sept.–early Nov., Fri–Sun. 10–6.*

WHERE TO STAY & EAT

$$$–$$$$ ✕**Lomo Grill.** Waynesville's best restaurant combines Mediterranean-
ARGENTINE   style ingredients with the chef-owner's Argentine background. The grilled steaks are perfectly prepared and served with delicately cooked, fresh local vegetables. Many of the fruits and vegetables are grown in the chef's garden. In a 1920s downtown space with a high, crimson-red ceiling, Lomo Grill has superlative servers, efficient and friendly without being obsequious. Try the key lime pie—it's the best in the mountains. ✉*44 Church St.* ☎*828/452–5222* ▭*AE, D, DC, MC, V* ⊙*Closed Sun. and Mon. No lunch.*

$$$$ ▦**The Swag Country Inn.** This rustic inn sits at 5,000 feet, high atop the
★   Cataloochee Divide overlooking a deep depression in otherwise high ground. Its 250 wooded acres share a border with Great Smoky Mountains National Park. Guest rooms and cabins were assembled from six authentic log structures and transported here. All have exposed beams and wood floors and are furnished with early American crafts. New beds and other upgrades were added in 2008. Dinners here are social events, with hors d'oeuvres, conversation, and an option of family-

style or individual seating. There's a two-night minimum stay; bring your own beverages, as the inn is in a dry county. **Pros:** small inn with personality; fabulous location on a nearly mile-high mountaintop; delicious meals included. **Cons:** remote; expensive; no TV. ✉ *2300 Swag Rd.* ☎ *828/926–0430 or 800/789–7672* ⊕ *www.theswag. com* ➮ *16 rooms, 3 cabins* ⚭ *In-room: no TV, no air-conditioning. In-hotel: restaurant, no-smoking rooms* ☰ *AE, D, MC, V* ⊘ *Closed Nov.–Mar.* ⊙ *FAP.*

$$$–$$$$ ⊞ **The Yellow House on Plott Creek Road.** Just outside town, this lovely two-story Victorian sits on a low knoll, with colorful surrounding gardens. The rooms and suites are named for and decorated to evoke other destinations, from Savannah to the Caribbean island of Saba to E'staing, France. Most rooms have fireplaces, and some suites have whirlpool baths. Honeymoon and anniversary packages include fresh flowers, a picnic hamper, and a book of poetry. **Pros:** well-run B&B; lovely grounds; personal service. **Cons:** not a place for singles looking for the action. ✉ *89 Oak View Dr., at Plott Creek Rd., 1 mi west of Waynesville* ☎ *828/452–0991 or 800/563–1236* ⊟ *828/452–1140* ⊕ *www.theyellowhouse.com* ➮ *4 rooms, 6 suites* ⚭ *In-room: refrigerator (some), no TV, Wi-Fi. In-hotel: no kids under 13, no-smoking rooms* ☰ *MC, V* ⊙ *BP.*

SPORTS & THE OUTDOORS

FISHING   If you want to fly-fish for rainbow, brown, or native brook trout, try **Lowe Fly Shop and Guide Service** (✉ *15 Woodland Dr.* ☎ *828/452–0039*), which runs wading and floating trips on area streams and lakes. The owner has written two books on fly-fishing. A full-day wade trip for two with guide costs around $300.

GOLF   A public course at the Methodist conference center, **Lake Junaluska Golf Course** (✉ *19 Golf Course Rd.* ☎ *828/456–5777*) is short but surprisingly tricky, due to all the trees. At **Waynesville Country Club Inn** (✉ *176 Country Club Dr.* ☎ *828/452–4617*), you can play three 9-hole Donald Ross-designed courses in any combination.

SHOPPING

The **Downtown Waynesville** (✉ *Main St.*) shopping area stretches three blocks from the city hall to the Haywood County courthouse, with a number of small boutiques, bookstores, and antiques shops.

Myrtle Beach & the Grand Strand, SC

WORD OF MOUTH

"Who knew all this existed right near Myrtle Beach? My family certainly did not. We just wanted to look around Myrtle Beach and get away a bit—what we saw was fantastic and so is [Carolina Safari Jeep Tours.] . . . The value is excellent for a personally guided tour from qualified, fun-loving guides. We were fascinated with the beautiful birds, especially the ibis, and the alligators. My kids loved the trip to the haunted graveyard with graves going back to the 1700s."

—ElizabethAshley

Updated by
Mary Erskine

THE LIVELY, FAMILY-ORIENTED GRAND STRAND, a booming resort area along the South Carolina coast, is one of the eastern seaboard's mega–vacation centers. The main attraction, of course, is the broad, beckoning beach—60 mi of white sand, stretching from the North Carolina border south to Georgetown, with Myrtle Beach at the hub. People come to the Strand for all of the traditional beach-going pleasures: shell hunting, fishing, swimming, sunbathing, sailing, surfing, jogging, and strolling. Most of the sand is packed hard, so that at low tide you can explore for miles on a bicycle. Away from the water, golfers have more than 120 courses to choose from, designed by the likes of Arnold Palmer, Robert Trent Jones, Jack Nicklaus, and Tom and George Fazio. There are also excellent seafood restaurants; giant shopping malls and factory outlets; amusement parks, waterslides, and arcades; a dozen shipwrecks for divers to explore; campgrounds, most of them on the beach; plus antique-car and wax museums, an aquarium, the world's largest outdoor sculpture garden, an antique German band organ and merry-go-round, and a museum dedicated entirely to rice. The Strand has also emerged as a major center for country music, with an expanding number of concert halls. When it comes to diversions, you could hardly be better served.

ORIENTATION & PLANNING

GETTING ORIENTED

While most resort communities boast beaches and water activities, the Grand Strand is known for much more. Lush botanical gardens, elegant waterfronts, quirky art galleries, high-end and kitschy shopping, and tasty seafood are just some of the Strand's assets. While other coastal communities, such as Charleston or Hilton Head Island may cater to a wealthier lifestyle, the Grand Strand can accommodate both the budget conscious as well as the high-end traveler.

The Myrtle Beach Area. Myrtle Beach is sometimes unfairly nicknamed the Redneck Riviera, but though some aspects of the city live up to the moniker, there's more to enjoy. Learn a little about the shag, the South Carolina state dance, which found its birthplace in Myrtle Beach; try a local muscadine wine featuring sweet grapes grown in the region, or some candy from Canipes, a local confectioner. Add to that the miles of sandy beaches and you'll discover Myrtle Beach is a diamond in the rough.

The Southern Grand Strand. Where the tourist traps and neon of Myrtle Beach end at the border of Horry and Georgetown counties, the South Strand begins. Georgetown County, featuring the communities of seafood-centric Murrells Inlet, "arrogantly shabby" Pawleys Island, and historic Georgetown, boasts a rustic elegance in its communities. Whether by land or by sea, these smaller communities have a lot to offer, even if it's not in the nicest wrapping. You may enjoy shopping

TOP REASONS TO GO

Bike the beach: From North Myrtle Beach all the way down to Pawleys Island, Grand Strand sand is hard-packed and smooth, making it perfect for biking next to the crashing waves. If you're lucky, you'll see dolphins, who often come in close in the early morning or just before sunset.

Golf, golf, and more golf: 120 golf courses at all skill levels meander through pine forests, dunes, and marshes. The Arrowhead Course in the Briarcliffe area offers holes and vistas along the Intracoastal Waterway.

Southern culture: Explore Southern history on a plantation tour, such as the Prince George Winyah sponsored plantation tours of the Georgetown area in the Spring; taste it in the form of barbecue, boiled peanuts, and other local foods; bring it home with folk art or a hammock woven right in Pawleys Island.

Brookgreen Gardens: More than 500 works from American artists are set amid 250-year-old oaks, palm trees, and flowers in America's oldest sculpture garden. A restored plantation, nature trail, and animal sanctuary are also part of the 9,200-acre property.

Tours from the water: Paddle a kayak or ride a pontoon boat past the ruins of the rice plantations that line the shores around Georgetown. Look closely and you can often see the ancient wooden irrigation gates that were raised by hand to allow water into the paddies.

at one of the small shops surrounded by live oaks or sampling the fresh catch of the day, all without a pretense in sight.

MYRTLE BEACH & THE GRAND STRAND PLANNER

WHEN TO GO

The Grand Strand was developed as a summer resort, and with its gorgeous beaches, flowering tropical plants, and generally good—if warm—weather, it continues to shine during the height of the season. That said, the fall and spring shoulder seasons may be even more pleasant. Warm temperatures allow for beach activities, but the humidity drops and the heat of summer has passed.

Winter—November through February—isn't usually thought of as a time to visit the beach, but the region can be quite pleasant. Although there are certainly cold days here and there, for the most part golfers, tennis players, and other outdoor enthusiasts can enjoy their pursuits during these months—at rock-bottom prices.

GETTING HERE & AROUND

BY AIR The Myrtle Beach International Airport (MYR) is served by Delta, Continental, USAir, and SpiritAir.

BY BOAT & Boaters traveling the Intracoastal Waterway may dock at Barefoot
FERRY Landing, Hague Marina, Harbourgate Resort and Marina, and Marlin Quay.

BY CAR   Midway between New York and Miami, the Grand Strand isn't connected directly by any interstate highways but is within an hour's drive of Interstate 95, Interstate 20, Interstate 26, and Interstate 40. U.S. 17 Bypass and Business are the major north–south coastal routes through the Strand.

BY TAXI   Taxi services are available at several locations along the Grand Strand. Beachside Taxi Transportation serves the North Myrtle Beach area, Pawleys Yellow Cab serves the South Strand, and Ocean Boulevard Shuttle and Taxi Service serves the central Myrtle Beach area.

ESSENTIALS   **Air Contacts Myrtle Beach International Airport** (*MYR* ✉ *1100 Jetport Rd.* ☎ *843/448–1580*).

Boat & Ferry Contacts Barefoot Landing (✉ *1 Hague Dr., Myrtle Beach* ☎ *843/663–0838*). **Hague Marina** (✉ *1 Hague Dr., Myrtle Beach* ☎ *843/293–2141*). **Harbourgate** (✉ *2120 Sea Mountain Hwy., North Myrtle Beach* ☎ *843/249–8888*). **Marlin Quay** (✉ *1508 S. Waccamaw Dr., Garden City Beach* ☎ *843/651–4444*).

Taxi Contacts Ocean Boulevard Shuttle and Taxi Service (☎ *843/444–1144*). **Beachside Taxi Transportation**(☎ *843/445–9999*). **Pawleys Yellow Cab**(☎ *843/237–5599*).

ABOUT THE HOTELS & RESTAURANTS

With the sand at your feet, seafood will most likely be on your mind. Restaurants on the Grand Strand boast all types of seafood, whether you're seeking a buffet or a more intimate dining spot, there are nearly 2,000 spots to whet your whistle. The summer months see an influx of visitors, so waits at popular restaurants can reach up to an hour or more. ■**TIP➜ A good bet is to take advantage of the early-bird dinner specials offered at many restaurants or try for a reservation if they offer them.**

High-rise and kitschy beach hotels line the Grand Strand, but a variety of other accommodations is also available. Beachside camping, luxury resorts, and weekly beach-house rentals are popular choices. Most hotel accommodations offer pools, but many high-rises also offer lazy rivers or water play areas. Availability varies, but advance reservations are recommended by the majority of beach properties.

WHAT IT COSTS					
	¢	$	$$	$$$	$$$$
Restaurant	under $10	$10–$14	$15–$19	$20–$24	over $24
Hotel	under $100	$100–$150	$151–$200	$201–$250	over $250

Restaurant prices are for a main course at dinner. Hotel prices are for two people in a standard double room in high season.

PLANNING YOUR TIME

Centrally located, Myrtle Beach is the hub for family-centric activities, with amusements parks, waterslides, and beaches to choose from. Venture farther south to Murrells Inlet and Georgetown, and museums and historical tours abound. If history is your passion, spend at least a day exploring Georgetown on foot, by boat, or with a guided tour.

Myrtle Beach &
The Grand Strand

DISCOUNTS & DEALS

You can find discounts for myriad activities along the Grand Strand. Just check out any visitor's center or grocery store and grab a copy of the coupon books offered there. You'll find discounts for mini-golf, 18-hole golf courses, personal watercraft rentals, and parasailing jaunts, just to name a few.

THE MYRTLE BEACH AREA

Myrtle Beach was a late bloomer. Until 1901 it didn't have an official name; that year the first hotel went up, and oceanfront lots were selling for $25. Today, more than 13 million people a year visit the region, and no wonder: lodging, restaurants, shopping, and entertainment choices are varied and plentiful. The many golf courses in the area add to the appeal. ■TIP➔ Be sure to take note of whether an establishment is on U.S. 17 Business or U.S. 17 Bypass when getting directions—confusing the two could lead to hours of frustration. U.S. 17 Business is also referred to as Kings Highway.

Myrtle Beach has a reputation as a frenzied strip of all-you-can-eat buffets, T-shirt shops, and bars. That reputation isn't completely unwarranted, but this side of Myrtle Beach's character is generally limited to parts of Ocean Boulevard (the "strip"), Kings Highway, and Restaurant Row (sometimes called the Galleria area). Some blocks may be a bit seedy, but the pedestrian-friendly strip is generally safe and clean (though at night the sidewalks can be crowded with the young bar crowd). Attractions such as Family Kingdom Amusement Park and Myrtle Waves Water Park can add a dose of fun to your afternoon.

What may come as a surprise is that it's also not terribly difficult to spend a quiet vacation here, dining

WHAT'S IN A NAME?
When faced with the prospect of pronouncing some of the names found in town, many visitors can get a bit tongue-tied. For example, Myrtle Beach and North Myrtle Beach are located in Horry County, named for Revolutionary War icon Peter Horry. The "H" is silent—"Orr-ee"—so if you're referring to the county, please don't make it sound cheap.

in sophisticated spots after spending the day on relatively uncrowded beaches. Myrtle Beach State Park, for instance, is a bastion of peace and quiet, as are the beaches adjacent to the residential areas of Myrtle Beach at either end of the strip. ■TIP➔**Those looking for a quieter time take note: The third and fourth weeks of May find the Strand inhabited by bikers in town for the Harley Davidson Spring Rally and the Atlantic Beach Bike Fest. Traffic and noise problems are common occurrences, and hotel space is scarce.**

MYRTLE BEACH

94 mi northeast of Charleston via U.S. 17; 138 mi east of Columbia via U.S. 76 to U.S. 378 to U.S. 501.

Myrtle Beach, with its high-rises and hyperdevelopment, is the nerve center of the Grand Strand and one of the major seaside destinations on the East Coast. Visitors are drawn here for the swirl of classic vacation activity, from beaches to arcades to live music shows.

To capture the flavor of the place, take a stroll along Ocean Boulevard. Here's where you'll find an eclectic assortment of gift and novelty shops, a wax museum, and a museum of oddities. When you've had your fill, turn east and make your way back onto the beach amid the sunbathers, kite-fliers, and kids building sand castles.

GETTING HERE & AROUND
Most routes to Myrtle Beach run via interstate, I–95 and I–40, and connect to either U.S. 501 or U.S. 17. U.S. 17 Bypass and U.S. 17 Business, or Kings Highway, are the main thoroughfares through the Grand Strand. Both run parallel to the beach. Most of the city's main streets are numbered and are designated north or south, referring to the location in the city. Palmetto Tour & Travel and Gray Line offer tour packages and guide services.

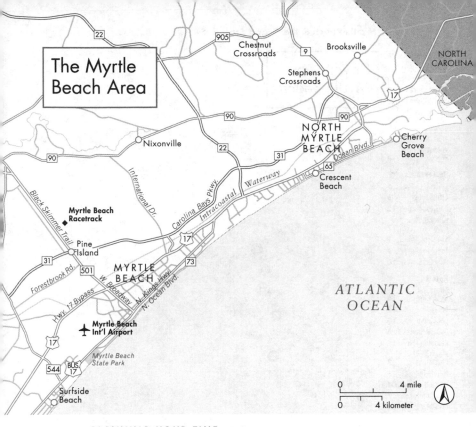

PLANNING YOUR TIME

If you have a few days in Myrtle Beach, spend a day at the beach and an evening at an amusement park. Family Kingdom is ideal for smaller children. On your second day head to Georgetown and take a tour through Winyah Bay on board a sightseeing cruise where you might see dolphins, bald eagles, and even the remains of a Civil War submarine. Brookgreen Gardens, between Pawleys Island and Murrells Inlet, is also a must. On your last day, check out the shopping and dining at Market Common, located off Farrow Parkway on the site of the old Myrtle Beach Air Force Base.

ESSENTIALS

Visitor Information **Myrtle Beach Area Chamber of Commerce and Information Center** (⊠ 1200 N. Oak St., Box 2115, Myrtle Beach ☎ 843/626–7444 or 800/356–3016 ⊕ www.myrtlebeachinfo.com ⊙ Memorial Day–Labor Day, Mon.–Fri. 8:30–5, Sat. 9–5, Sun. 10–2; Sat. 9–2, closed Sun. the rest of the year).

Tour Contacts **Gray Line Myrtle Beach** (☎ 800/261–5991). **Palmetto Tour & Travel** (☎ 843/626–2431).

EXPLORING

 On **Carolina Safari Jeep Tours** you'll visit everything from a plantation house to an alligator-laden salt marsh to an 18th-century church. The 3½-hour tour, which includes some walking, provides a surprisingly

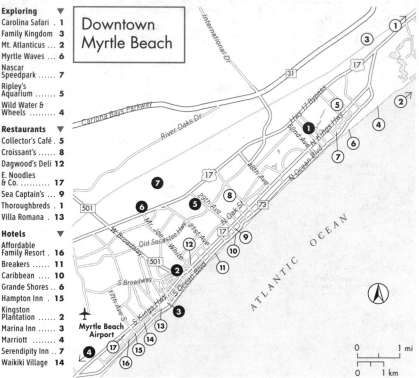

complete overview of the region and beautiful views of the Grand Strand's varied ecosystem. ☒725 Seaboard St., Unit E ☏843/497–5330 or 843/272–1177 ⊕www.carolinasafari.com ☒$40 ⊘Arrange tour times when making reservations.

❸ Dominated by a gigantic white wooden roller coaster called the Swamp
Ⓒ Fox, **Family Kingdom Amusement Park** is set right on the ocean. There are thrill and children's rides, a log flume, go-cart track, old-fashioned carousel, and the Slingshot Drop Zone, which rockets riders straight down a 110-foot tower. Operating hours can vary, so it's worthwhile to call before visiting, especially on Saturday when the park is often rented by groups. ■TIP➔Money-saving bundled tickets and multiday passes for water parks and other recreational venues are readily available, check out Web sites for more information. ☒300 S. Ocean Blvd., The Strip ☏843/626–3447 ⊕www.family-kingdom.com ☒Fees vary for individual attractions; 1-day unlimited access to most rides $22.75 ⊘June–mid-Aug., daily 4 PM–midnight, Sat. 1–midnight, Sun. 4–midnight; mid-Apr.–May and late Aug.–Sept., weekdays 6 PM–close, Sat. 1–close, Sun. 1–6.

❷ **Mt. Atlanticus Minotaur Golf.** Climb up and over several levels to experi-
Ⓒ ence the fun of this multilevel mini-golf attraction. Mount Atlanticus features two different courses, and is challenging enough to suit picky mini-golfers, while kids have plenty to look at with mythical creatures,

caves, and lagoons throughout the courses. ⊠707 N. Kings Hwy. ⊕Off 7th Ave. N, near U.S. 501, Central Myrtle Beach ☎843/444–1008 🎫$8 ☉ Daily 9 AM–midnight.

6 **Myrtle Waves** is South Carolina's largest water park. You can shoot through twisty chutes, swim in the Ocean in Motion Wave Pool, float the day away on an inner tube on the LayZee River, or ride a boogie board on the Racer River. There's beach volleyball, too, for when you've had enough water. Shaded areas with lounge chairs offer respite from the sun. Free soft drinks and sunscreen are available with the price of admission. Lockers are available to keep money and valuables safe. ■TIP➔Admission discounts are available after 2 PM daily. Wear a well-secured swimsuit if you're going on the big slides, or else you may reach the end of the slide before your suit does. ⊠U.S. 17 Bypass and 10th Ave. N, Central Myrtle Beach ☎843/913–9260 ⊕www.myrtlewaves.com 🎫$28 for full day, $18 after 2 ☉June–Aug., daily 10–6, early May and early Sept., daily 10–5.

7 At **NASCAR SpeedPark** you can drive on seven different NASCAR-replica tracks. The cars vary in their sophistication and speed; to use the most advanced track you need to be a licensed driver. The 26-acre facility also has racing memorabilia, an arcade, and miniature golf. NASCAR drivers often make scheduled appearances, so call ahead. ■TIP➔Lines at attractions are shortest on Monday. ⊠1820 21st Ave. N, corner of U.S. 17 Bypass and 21st Ave. N, Central Myrtle Beach ☎843/918–8725 ⊕www.nascarspeedpark.com 🎫$32 unlimited day pass or $3 individual tickets ☉Open daily 10 AM, closing hrs. vary, call to confirm.

5 **Ripley's Aquarium** has an underwater tunnel exhibit longer than a football field and exotic marine creatures on display, from poisonous lionfish to moray eels to an octopus. Children can examine horseshoe crabs and eels in touch tanks. Special exhibits are often included in the price of aquarium admission. ■TIP➔Admission discounts are available when combined with price of Ripley's Ocean Boulevard attractions. ⊠Broadway at the Beach, U.S. 17 Bypass between 21st Ave. N and 29th Ave. N, Central Myrtle Beach ☎843/916–0888 or 800/734–8888 ⊕www.ripleysaquarium.com 🎫$18.99☉Daily 9 AM–10 PM.

4 About 9 mi south of Myrtle Beach in Surfside Beach, **Wild Water & Wheels** has 25 water-oriented rides and activities, along with go-carts and mini-golf. If your children are old enough to navigate the park on their own, spend a few minutes at the adults-only lounge pool, where you can sit immersed in Jacuzzi-like bubbles. ⊠910 U.S. 17 S, Surfside Beach ☎843/238–3787 ⊕www.wild-water.com 🎫$24.98, $14.98 after 3 ☉Late May–early Aug., daily 10–6.

WHERE TO EAT

$$$$ ✕**Collectors Café.**A successful restaurant, art gallery, and coffeehouse
ECLECTIC rolled into one, this unpretentious arty spot has bright, funky paint-
★ ings and tile work covering its walls and tabletops. The cuisine is among the most inventive in the area. Try the grilled tuna with Indian spices, served with Cuban black-bean sauce and mango salsa—it's a far cry from standard Myrtle Beach fish-house fare. They don't serve

lunch, but you can stop in for dessert or coffee beginning at noon. ✉ *7726 N. Kings Hwy., North End* ☎ *843/449–9370* ⊕ *www.collectorscafeandgallery.com* ✉ *AE, D, MC, V* ☉ *Closed Sun. No lunch.*

¢   **✕ Croissants Bakery & Café.** The lunch
CAFÉ   crowd loves this spot, which has an on-site bakery. Black-and-white tile floors, café tables, checked tablecloths, and glass pastry cases filled

with sweets create an appetizing feel to the place. Try the chicken or broccoli salads, a Reuben or Monte Cristo sandwich, or one of the pasta specials, and save room for the peanut-butter cheesecake. Tapas are available after 4. ✉ *3751 Grissom Pkwy., Central Myrtle Beach* ☎ *843/448–2253* ⊕ *www.croissants.net* ✉ *D, MC, V* ☉ *Closed Sun.*

¢   **✕ Dagwood's Deli.** Comic-strip characters Dagwood and Blondie could
AMERICAN   split one of the masterful sandwiches at Dagwood's Deli. There are the usual suspects—ham, turkey, and the like—but you won't regret trying one of the more distinctive creations, such as blackened mahimahi with homemade pineapple salsa, or the grilled chicken breast with bacon, provolone, and ranch dressing. Salads and burgers round out the menu, and they deliver (for $1) to most of Myrtle Beach. ✉ *400 Mr. Joe White Ave.* ☎ *843/448–0100* ⊕ *www.dagwoodsdeli.com* ⚅ *Reservations not accepted* ✉ *AE, MC, V* ☉ *Closed Sun. No dinner.*

¢–$ **✕ E. Noodles & Co.** The dramatic lighting, sleek furnishings, and top-
CHINESE   notch Asian specialties transport diners out of the beach and straight to the city. The menu pulls from Chinese, Thai, and Japanese flavors. Double panfried noodles promise to foil all but the most die-hard Atkins follower. Grouper tempura is a terrific local take on the classic. ✉ *400 20th. Ave, S,* ☎ *843/916–8808* ⊕ *www.enoodlesmb.com* ⚅ *Reservations not accepted* ✉ *MC, D, V* ☉ *Closed Sun.*

$$$–$$$$ **✕ Sea Captain's House.** At this picturesque restaurant with a nautical
SEAFOOD   theme, the best seats are in the windowed porch room, which overlooks the ocean. The fireplace in the wood-panel dining room inside is warmly welcoming on cool off-season evenings. Menu highlights include Low-country crab casserole and avocado-seafood salad. The breads and desserts are baked on the premises. ✉ *3000 N. Ocean Blvd., The Strip* ☎ *843/448–8082* ⊕ *www.seacaptains.com* ✉ *AE, D, MC, V.*

$$$–$$$$ **✕ Thoroughbreds Chophouse & Seafood Grille.** For a special night out, or to
AMERICAN   fulfill a red-meat craving, Thoroughbreds, with its dark wood, leather banquettes, and top-notch meat, is a romantic escape from the whirlwind of Myrtle Beach. Fish selections are fresh and well prepared, but steaks, pork chops, and rack of lamb steal the show. There's a great wine list, too. ✉ *9706 N. Kings Hwy.* ☎ *843/497–2636* ⊕ *www.thoroughbredsrestaurant.com* ⚅ *Reservations essential* ✉ *AE, D, MC, V* ☉ *No lunch.*

$–$$ **✕ Villa Romana.** It's all about family at Villa Romana, where owners
ITALIAN   Rinaldo and Franca come in early to make the gnocchi and stick around
★   to greet customers. It's hard to resist filling up on the stracciatella soup,

bruschetta, salad, and rolls (perhaps the best on the Strand) that accompany every meal, but try. The gnocchi is a perfect foil for any of the homemade sauces, and the veal Absolut (sautéed veal in a sauce of cream, mushrooms, and vodka) is a specialty. ■TIP➔ Michael the accordion player can entertain diners with songs that range from "Mack the Knife" to "Stairway to Heaven." ✉707 S. Kings Hwy. ☎843/448-4990 ⊕www.villaromanamyrtle-beach.com ⌖Reservations essential ⊟AE, D, MC, V ✷No lunch.

FABULOUS FISH

With ocean on one side and tidal marsh and rivers on the other, the Grand Strand isn't at a loss for fresh seafood. Local shrimp, oysters, and fish, particularly grouper, are good bets, as is she-crab soup, a creamy bisquelike creation served with a cruet of sherry on the side. Don't drink the sherry—add a splash to the soup, along with a dash of hot sauce.

WHERE TO STAY

¢–$ **Affordable Family Resort.** With suites and cottages large enough to house three generations of family members, this spot is both budget conscious and family-friendly. The water play area is sure to get smiles from the kids. The resort features waterslides, pools, and even a duck pond. The Honeymoon Suite boasts a heart-shaped hot tub. Pros: pets are welcome; arcade for the kids. Cons: rooms are not rented to anyone under 25. ✉2300 S. Ocean Blvd., South End ☎888/839–4330 ⊕www.affordablefamilyresort.com ⇗13 suites, 6 cottages ⌖In hotel: pools, laundry facilities, Wi-Fi ⊟AE, D, MC, V.

$–$$ **Breakers Resort Hotel.** The rooms in this oceanfront hotel are airy and spacious, with contemporary furnishings. Most have kitchenettes and Murphy beds; the Paradise Tower has one-, two- and three-bedroom suites. There are several pools, a lazy river, and a pirate-ship facade that kids can swim in and around. The hotel is right in the middle of the Myrtle Beach Strip. ■TIP➔ There's a Starbucks coffee shop across the street. Pros: views are excellent from the tower rooms. Cons: the pool areas are on the small side for the potential number of guests. ✉2006 N. Ocean Blvd. ☎843/444–4444 or 800/952–4507 ⊕www.break-ers.com ⇗288 rooms, 384 suites ⌖In-room: refrigerator. In-hotel: 2 restaurants, room service, bar, pools, gym, children's programs (ages 4–10), laundry service ⊟AE, D, MC, V.

$$$–$$$$ **Caribbean Resort and Villas.** The Caribbean actually consists of four different properties, each offering access to the other's amenities. The Jamaican Inn is a quaint old-style motel with cheaper rates, the rustic Chelsea Condos offer a more intimate stay, while the newly constructed Cayman Tower and Dominican Oceanfront Suites offer more luxurious accommodations. Water play areas are available at all four properties, with splash areas, waterslides, and lazy rivers alongside the indoor and outdoor pools. ■TIP➔ Corner suites in the Cayman Tower feature balconies with views of the Grand Strand in all directions, plus stainless-steel appliances in the full kitchen. Pros: the views from the Cayman Tower are spectacular, floor to ceiling windows in the suites afford expansive views of the beach and the ocean. Cons: not for couples looking for a

6

quiet romantic stay; children in wet bathing suits are a regular sight in the elevators, and the pools and water activity areas are more for families than couples. ✉*30th Ave. N, The Strip* ☎*800/552–8509* ⊕*www. caribbeanresort.com* ⬦*455 rooms and suites* ♿ *In room: safe, refrigerator. In-hotel: pool, gym* ▤*AE, D, MC, V*

$$–$$$ 📷**Grande Shores.** Like many of the newer properties in Myrtle Beach—this one was built in 2001—Grande Shores is a combination of rentable condos with full kitchens and standard hotel rooms outfitted with refrigerators, coffeemakers, and, in a few cases, kitchenettes. Whichever you choose, all of the airy rooms at Grande Shores have balconies with a view of the ocean and free high-speed Internet. Pools abound: there's an indoor pool, an outdoor pool with a meandering stream that gently propels swimmers, and a rooftop garden with a pool and four hot tubs. **Pros:** there are water features for all age groups. **Cons:** only a select group of rooms actually face the ocean, most either face north or south, offering glimpses, rather than views. ✉*201 77th Ave. N,* ☎*843/692–2397 or 877/798–4074* ⊕*www.grandeshores.com* ⬦*136 rooms* ♿*In-hotel: restaurant, bar, pools, gym, parking (free)* ▤*AE, D, DC, MC, V.*

$$$–$$$$ 📷**Hampton Inn and Suites Oceanfront.** This property combines the reli-
★ ability of an established hotel chain with the joys of a beach resort. Rooms have balconies and a cheerful style; all have ocean views. There's a lazy river—a pool with a moving current—that carries swimmers along its course. **Pros:** crisp white bed linens offer a tropical, beachy feel to the rooms. **Cons:** construction projects in the area are noisy and disruptive. ✉*1803 S. Ocean Blvd., South End* ☎*843/946–6400 or 877/946–6400* ⊕*www.hamptoninnoceanfront.com* ⬦*80 rooms, 36 suites* ♿*In-room: refrigerator. In-hotel: pools, gym* ▤*AE, D, DC, MC, V* ⦿*CP.*

$$$–$$$$ 📷**Kingston Plantation.** This complex includes two hotels, as well as restaurants, shops, and one- to three-bedroom condominiums and villas, on 145 acres of ocean-side woodlands. One hotel, an Embassy Suites, has guest rooms with bleached-wood furnishings and kitchenettes. The other, a Hilton, has a more classic decor and no kitchen facilities. The villas and condos are privately owned, but you can reserve one through the central booking number and Web site. Although these options are decorated to the taste of their owners, they all have the same standard amenities such as sheets and towels, and kitchen equipment. Beachgoing is enhanced by a beach club with bathrooms, water fountains, and parking. **Pros:** lushly landscaped lawns and area. **Cons:** some condos may include a sleeper sofa in the bed count. ✉*9800 Queensway Blvd., North End* ☎*843/449–0006 or 800/876–0010* ⊕*www.kingstonplantation.com* ⬦*385 rooms, 255 suites, 414 villas, 414 condos* ♿*In-hotel: 3 restaurants, tennis courts, pools, gym.* ▤*AE, D, MC, V* ⦿*BP, Embassy Suites only.*

$$$ 📷**Marina Inn at Grande Dunes.** Geared to families, business travelers, and golf enthusiasts, this hotel oozes luxury. From the rich wood and sumptuous carpet in the lobby to the manicured lawns and amenities, the newly built Marina Inn is a little slice of paradise. Rooms and suites are large and afford views of the Intracoastal Waterway. The hotel

features a large outdoor pool with pool bar and hot tub, an indoor pool and hot tub, as well as Ping-Pong tables, fire pits, and badminton on the lawn. A Ruth's Chris Steak House is on the property, and the hotel houses the Anchor Café and WaterScapes Restaurant. **Pros:** the lobby boasts comfy couches good enough to grab a nap on. **Cons:** the proximity to U.S. 17 Bypass is a concern, and construction across the street and on the property detracts from its peaceful feel; there's no easy way to the beach. ✉ *8121 Amalfi Pl., North End* ☎ *866/437–4113* ⊕ *www.marinainnatgrandedunes.com* ⚡ *235 rooms* ♿ *In room: safe, DVD. In hotel: pools, gym, Wi-Fi* ▭ *AE, D, MC, V.*

$$$–$$$$ 🏨**Myrtle Beach Marriott Resort & Spa.** Entering this plantation-chic high-
★ rise resort, with its airy wicker furniture, giant palms, and mahogany details will take you away from the hubbub of Myrtle Beach and straight to a tropical locale. Green-and-gold guest rooms have plush carpet that makes them quiet and serene, perfect for watching the waves break on the beach. The spa, which offers a full range of treatments, is top-notch, and the health club has well-maintained, state-of-the-art machines. The golf and tennis clubs are both on-site, as is a marina with charters and personal watercraft, boat, and kayak rentals. **Pros:** striped hammocks swing near the dunes with views of the ocean; several pools and water features are available. **Cons:** the hotel is located near a construction site; some rooms have a view of either the parking lot or bare earth and bulldozers. ✉ *8400 Costa Verde Dr.* ☎ *843/449–8880* ⊕ *www.myrtlebeachmarriott.com* ⚡ *400 rooms* ♿ *In-room: refrigerator. In-hotel: restaurant, room service, tennis court, pools* ▭ *AE, D, MC, V* ⧉ *BP.*

¢–$ 🏨**Serendipity Inn.** This cozy Spanish-villa-style inn is about 300 yards
★ from the beach. Though the layout is much like a hotel, each guest room is decorated in a different way, most with four-poster beds and antique chests in pine or mahogany. Included in each room is a copy of the movie *Serendipity*, starring John Cusack, for your viewing pleasure. There's also a colorful pool area dotted with hanging flowers and a trickling fountain. A breakfast of homemade coffee cake, hardboiled eggs, yogurt, cereal, and fruit is served in the wicker-appointed garden room. **Pros:** the tranquil setting helps you forget the hustle and bustle of busy Myrtle Beach. **Cons:** some amenities are dated, but still pleasant; don't expect brand-new lounge chairs or an architecturally designed pool. ✉ *407 71st Ave. N, North End* ☎ *843/449–5268 or 800/762–3229* ⊕ *www.serendipityinn.com* ⚡ *12 rooms, 2 suites* ♿ *In-room: no phone, kitchen (some), refrigerator, DVD, Wi-Fi. In-hotel: pool, Wi-Fi* ▭ *MC, V* ⧉ *BP.*

¢ 🏨**Waikiki Village Motel.** If you're looking for something beyond high-rises and luxury rooms with steep price tags, try this mom-and-pop motel. The rooms, in aqua and white, are centered around a pool, and the beach is an easy stroll across Ocean Boulevard. The budget-friendly room rate doesn't increase during Bike Week or the summer months. **Pros:** friendly, helpful staff; affordable. **Cons:** no hot breakfast; couples and families are preferred. ✉ *1500 S. Ocean Blvd., South End* ☎ *843/448-8431* ⚡ *46 rooms* ♿ *In-hotel: pool.* ▭ *D, MC, V.*

SPORTS & THE OUTDOORS

BEACHES Regardless of whether you're staying on the beach, you shouldn't have too much trouble getting to a spot of sand. There are nearly 150 public beach-access points in the city, all marked with signs. Most are located off Ocean Boulevard and have parking and "shower towers" for cleaning up; few have restroom facilities. Parking can be scarce, but during the summer the city allows parallel parking on Ocean Boulevard.

Since much of Myrtle Beach's coastline is dominated by high-rise hotels, there are plenty of places to get lunch or a cool drink without having to get back in your car. Many of these hotels also rent beach chairs, umbrellas, and boogie boards. Some also have nets set up for games of beach volleyball. ■TIP→ **For a quieter beach experience, look for beach accesses away from the high-rise hotels. Spots between 30th and 48th avenues North are good bets.**

Dogs, kayaks, and surfboards are limited on many beaches from May through September. Be sure to read the ordinances posted at each access point for details. ■TIP→ **Summer heat can be brutal, so don't leave pets or food in the car during the hot summer months.**

For a more out-of-the-way experience, head south of Myrtle Beach to **Myrtle Beach State Park.** There you can swim in the ocean, hike on a nature trail, and fish in the surf or from a pier. You can also camp, but you need to book in advance. ⊠ *U.S. 17, 3 mi south of Myrtle Beach,* ☎ *843/238–5325* ☜ *$4.50 to fish off pier, no license required.*

FISHING The Gulf Stream makes for good fishing from early spring through December. Anglers can fish from 10 piers and jetties for amberjack, sea trout, and king mackerel. Surfcasters may snare bluefish, whiting, flounder, pompano, and channel bass. In the South Strand, salt marshes, inlets, and tidal creeks yield flounder, blues, croakers, spots, shrimp, clams, oysters, and blue crabs.

GOLF Many of the Grand Strand's more than 100 courses are championship layouts; most are public. **Tee Times Central** (☎ *843/347–4653 or 800/344–5590*) makes it easy to book tee times at nearly all the Strand's courses. ⚠ **Alligators have taken up residence in many of the Strand's golf courses. If you see one, don't investigate: they're faster than they look.**

Two of Myrtle Beach's courses are particularly notable. Built in the 1920s, **Pine Lakes** (⊠ *5603 Woodside Ave.* ☎ *843/315–7700*) is considered the granddaddy of Strand courses. In spring you can get mimosas on the 10th tee; in winter they serve clam chowder. Pine Lakes is a terrific walking course. The course is currently undergoing renovations, including upgrades to cart paths, new grass, and more. All changes will either maintain or enhance the course's Scottish style, and the course is slated to reopen in March 2009. Former home to the Senior PGA Tour, the Tom Fazio–designed **Tournament Players Club at Myrtle Beach** (⊠ *1189 TPC Blvd., Murrells Inlet* ☎ *888/742–8721 or 843/357–3399* ⊕ *www.tpcmyrtlebeach.com*) boasts narrow fairways amid water hazards and wetlands.

A bit less demanding, but still interesting, thanks to surprising changes in elevation, **The Witch** (⊠*1900 S.C. 544, East Conway* ☎*843/448–1300* ⊕*www.witchgolf.com*) is built on wetlands and contains nearly 4,000 feet of bridges. Known for its top-notch condition, regardless of the season, **Arrowhead** (⊠*1201 Burcale Rd.,* ☎*800/236–3243* ⊕*www.arrowheadcc.com*) is the only Raymond Floyd–designed course in the region. Several of the 27 holes run along the Intracoastal Waterway and you might spot dolphins cavorting in the smooth water.

There are a few bargains on the Myrtle Beach golfing scene. One is **Indigo Creek** (⊠*9480 Indigo Club Dr., Murrells Inlet* ☎*800/718–1830 or 843/650–1809* ⊕*www.indigocreekgolfclub.com*), which is cut through forests of huge oaks and pines. Built on the site of an old airbase, **Whispering Pines** (⊠*U.S. 17 Business and 22nd Ave. S,* ☎*843/918–2305* ⊕*www.wpinesgolf.com*) is recognized as an Audubon Cooperative Sanctuary.

SCUBA DIVING You don't have to go far off the coast of the Grand Strand to explore the underwater world. Man-made reefs boast an array of fish including sea fans, sponges, reef fish, anemones, urchins, and crabs. A number of shipwrecks are also worth exploring under the waves. Paddle-wheelers, freighters, and cargo ships lie in ruins off the coast, and are popular scuba spots. ■**TIP➔Always wanted to dive but never learned how? Most dive shops can have you PADI-certified in a weekend.**

Instruction and equipment rentals, as well as an indoor dive tank, are available in the Sports Corner shopping center from **Nu Horizons Dive and Travel** (⊠*515 U.S. 501, Ste. A* ☎*800/505–2080, 843/839–1932*).

TENNIS **Prestwick Country Club** (⊠*1001 Links Rd.* ☎*843/293–4100, 888/250–1767* offers court time, instruction, and tournament opportunities; clay and hard courts are lighted for nighttime play. **Grande Dunes Tennis** (⊠*U.S. 17 Bypass at Grande Dunes Blvd.* ☎*843/449–4486*) is a full fitness facility with 10 lighted Har-Tru courts; the club also offers lessons, clinics, camps, and match opportunities.

WATER SPORTS Hobie Cats, personal watercraft, ocean kayaks, and sailboats are available for rent at **Downwind Sails** (⊠*2915 South Ocean Blvd. at 29th Ave. S, South End* ☎*843/448–7245*); they also have banana-boat rides (where you're towed in a long, yellow inflatable raft) and parasailing. ■**TIP➔Don't forget to bring your own towels and sunscreen when you head out. Ocean Watersports** (⊠*3rd Ave. S and beach, between Family Kingdom amusement park and Westgate Resort, The Strip* ☎*843/445–7777*) rents water-sports equipment.

NIGHTLIFE & THE ARTS

CLUBS & LOUNGES South Carolina's only Hard Rock Cafe, daiquiri bar Fat Tuesday, and karaoke haven Broadway Louie's are just a few of the hot spots at **Broadway at the Beach** (⊠*U.S. 17 Bypass between 21st and 29th Aves. N, Central Myrtle Beach* ☎*843/444–3200*), which also has shopping. In the evening, dueling piano players compete to perform the most outlandish versions of audience requests at **Crocodile Rocks** (⊠*Broadway at the Beach, U.S. 17 Bypass between 21st and 29th Aves. N, Central*

6

Myrtle Beach ☎843/444–2096); singing along is part of the fun. The shag (South Carolina's state dance) is popular at **Studebaker's** (✉2000 *N. Kings Hwy., Central Myrtle Beach* ☎843/448–9747.

FILM **IMAX 3D Theatre** (✉*Broadway at the Beach, U.S. 17 Bypass between 21st and 29th Aves. N, Central Myrtle Beach* ☎843/448–4629) shows educational films on a six-story-high screen.

MUSIC & LIVE SHOWS **Carolina Opry** (✉8901A *U.S. 17 Business N, North End* ☎800/843–6779) is a family-oriented variety show featuring country, light rock, show tunes, and gospel. At **Dolly Parton's Dixie Stampede** (✉8901B *U.S. 17 Business N, North End* ☎843/497–9700 or 800/433–4401) dinner theater, dozens of actors on horseback re-create Civil War cavalry battles. **Legends in Concert** (✉301 *U.S. 17 Business S, Surfside Beach* ☎843/238–7827 or 800/960–7469) has high-energy shows by impersonators of Elvis, Garth Brooks, and the Blues Brothers.

The elegant **Palace Theatre** (✉*Broadway at the Beach, U.S. 17 Bypass between 21st and 29th Aves. N, Central Myrtle Beach* ☎843/448–0588 or 800/905–4228) hosts the acrobatic feats of Le Grande Cirque, as well as solo performances by acts such as Larry the Cable Guy. Watch knights on horseback battle for their kingdom, followed by a real jousting tournament, at **Medieval Times Dinner & Tournament** (✉2904 *Fantasy Way* ☎843/236–4635, 888/935–6878).

SHOPPING

For recreational shopping, Myrtle Beach's main attraction is **Broadway at the Beach** (✉*U.S. 17 Bypass between 21st Ave. N and 29th Ave. N*). More than 100 shops include everything from high-end apparel to Harley Davidson–theme gifts. A new endeavor that combines high-end shopping with upscale living and dining spaces, **The Market Common** (✉4017 *Deville Street* ⌖*Off Farrow Parkway, between U.S. 17 Business and U.S. 17 Bypass, South End* ☎843/839–3500 ⊕*www.marketcommonmb.com* ◷*Mon.–Sat.* 10 AM–9 PM, *Sun. noon–6*) features stores like Banana Republic, Anthropologie, and Tommy Bahama.

DISCOUNT OUTLETS The **Tanger Factory Outlet Center** (✉*U.S. 501, near Hard Rock Park,* ☎843/236–5100) is a large outlet center with Nike, Polo, Brooks Brothers, and J. Crew. **Tanger Factory Outlet Center** (✉10785 *Kings Rd., at U.S. 17, North End* ☎843/449–0491) has 75 factory outlet stores, including Gap, Banana Republic, and Old Navy.

NORTH MYRTLE BEACH

5 mi north of Myrtle Beach via U.S. 17.

North Myrtle Beach, best known as the site where the shag, South Carolina's state dance, originated, is made up of the beach towns Cherry Grove, Crescent Beach, Windy Hill, and Ocean Drive. Entering North Myrtle Beach from the south on U.S. 17, you'll see Barefoot Landing, a huge shopping and entertainment complex that sits on the Intracoastal Waterway. As you make your way east toward the ocean, then north on Ocean Boulevard South, high-rises give way to small motels, then to single beach houses, many of which are available for rent. This end of the strand marks the tip of a large peninsula, and there are lots of little islands, creeks, and marshes between the ocean and the Intracoastal to explore by kayak or canoe. ■ TIP→ Mosquitoes can be a problem on the marsh, especially in the early evening. Be sure to pack repellent.

GETTING HERE & AROUND

North Myrtle Beach is an easy jaunt up U.S. 17 from Myrtle Beach or just south of Little River. Once inside the city limits, the numbered cross streets connect to Ocean Drive, the beachfront road.

ESSENTIALS

Visitor Information North Myrtle Beach Chamber of Commerce Convention and Visitor's Bureau (✉ 270 U.S. 17 N., North Myrtle Beach ☎ 843/281–2662 or 877/332–2662 ⊕ www.northmyrtlebeachchamber.com ⊗ Weekdays 8:30 AM– 5 PM, weekends 10–4.

EXPLORING

Alligator Adventure has interactive reptile shows, including an alligator-feeding demonstration. Boardwalks lead through marshes and swamps on the 15-acre property, where you'll see wildlife of the wetlands, including a pair of rare white albino alligators; Utan, the largest known crocodile in captivity; giant Galápagos tortoises; river otters; and all manner of reptiles, including boas, pythons, and anacondas. Unusual plants and exotic birds also thrive here. (✉ U.S. 17, at Barefoot Landing ☎ 843/361–0789 ⊕ www.alligatoradventure.com ⌨ $16.95 ⊗ Daily 9 AM–11 PM.

Hawaiian Rumble is the crown jewel of Myrtle Beach miniature golf. The course hosts championship tournaments, and is best known for its smoking volcano, which rumbles and belches fire at timed intervals. (✉ 3210 33rd Ave. S, at U.S. 17 ☎ 843/272–7812 ⌨ $8 for one round, $12 for two rounds until 5 PM ⊗ Daily 8 AM–1 AM.

La Belle Amie Vineyard. This shady vineyard is off U.S. 17 just outside of North Myrtle Beach. The wines sold here are created from the sweet muscadine grapes grown on the property. Tastings and tours are available during operating hours. Saturdays are typically festival days and usually feature live music, food, and free tours of the grounds. The gift shop features everything from wine to savory dips and fun grape-themed items. (✉ 1120 St. Joseph Rd., on the corner of St. Joseph Rd. and S.C. 90, Little River ☎ 843/839–WINE ⊕ www.labelleamie.com ⌨ $8 on festival days. Call for group tour pricing ⊗ Mon.–Sat. 10–6.

SPORTS & THE OUTDOORS

FISHING   The **Cherry Grove Fishing Pier** (✉ 3500 N. Ocean Blvd. ☎ 843/249– 1625) has a two-story observation deck and reaches 985 feet into the ocean, making it the place to catch pompano, bluefish, and mackerel. You can rent tackle and buy bait at the pier. ■ TIP→ Early morning and late afternoon are the best time to catch fish. **Little River Fishing Fleet** (✉ 1901 U.S. 17 ☎ 843/361–3323 or 800/249–9388). offers half- and full-day excursions, including night fishing.

6

GOLF   In Cherry Grove Beach you'll find the much-touted 18-hole, par-72 **Tidewater Golf Club and Plantation** (✉*1400 Tidewater Dr.* ☎*843/913–2424* ⊕*www.tidewatergolf.com*), one of only two courses in the area with ocean views. The challenging fairways and high bluffs are reminiscent of Pebble Beach.

The four 18-hole championship courses at **Barefoot Resort and Golf** (✉*4980 Barefoot Resort Bridge Rd.* ☎*843/390–3200 or 800/320–6536*) were designed by Tom Fazio, Davis Love III, Pete Dye, and Greg Norman and have proven to be new favorites of Grand Strand golfers. Notable details include a replica of plantation ruins on the Love course and only 60 acres of mowable grass on the Norman course. ■**TIP➔ An online Web special features an offer to play three courses and get the fourth free.**

WATER   You can rent your own pontoon boats or Jet Skis at **Myrtle Beach**
SPORTS   **Water Sports, Inc.** (✉*4495 Mineola Ave., Little River on the docks* ☎*843/280–7777*), or try parasailing or a ride on *Sea Screamer,* touted as the World's Largest Speed Boat. Learn to scuba dive, take a dive trip, or just rent equipment at **Coastal Scuba** (✉*1501 U.S. 17 S* ☎*800/249–9388 or 843/361–3323* ⊕*www.coastalscuba.com*), which is PADI-certified.

WHERE TO EAT

$$$-$$$$ ✕**Greg Norman's Australian Grille.** Overlooking the Intracoastal Water-
ECLECTIC   way, this large restaurant in Barefoot Landing has leather booths, Aus-
★   tralian aboriginal art on the walls, an extensive wine list, and a classy bar area. The menu features grilled meats, and many of the selections have an Asian flair. (The Australian theme comes through more strongly in the decor, and the Greg Norman merchandise for sale, than in the food.) Highlights are the lobster dumplings, miso-marinated sea bass, and habanero-rubbed tenderloin. ✉*4930 U.S. 17 S* ☎*843/361–0000* ⟋*Reservations essential* ⊟*AE, D, MC, V.*

$$-$$$ ✕**Rockefellers Raw Bar.** Yes it's a raw bar—and a good one, with a
SEAFOOD   bounty of fresh seafood—but don't sell the cooked items short at this small, casual locals' joint. The oysters Rockefeller, with their splash of Pernod and fresh spinach, are the real deal, and the iron pot of steamed mussels, clams, scallops, and other goodies is a terrific version of a Lowcountry staple. ✉*3613 U.S. 17 S* ☎*843/361–9677* ⟋*Reservations not accepted* ⊟*AE, D, MC, V.*

WHERE TO STAY

$-$$ 🛏**Barefoot Resort.** This luxury golf resort includes more than 325 one-to- four-bedroom condominium units along fairways as well as in the 62-unit, 14-story North Tower, which overlooks the Intracoastal Waterway. Furnishings in each unit vary, but all have been tastefully decorated and have all the amenities of a hotel, including daily maid service. The waterfront pool covers an acre of land and is said to be one of the largest on the east coast. The Barefoot Landing shopping and entertainment center is just across the inlet. **Pros:** pretty views of the Intracoastal Waterway surround the resort. **Cons:** getting to the beach and the ocean requires driving across a busy highway. ✉*2200*

Lights Out for Sea Turtles!

You'll notice that many of the Strand's beachfront resorts keep the lights turned down low on the ocean side. This may add to the romance of a nighttime stroll along the sand, but the primary beneficiaries of the darkness aren't humans...they're turtles.

Loggerhead sea turtles have been nesting on the beaches of the Grand Strand for thousands of years. (Seeing one of these often-giant reptiles come ashore to lay eggs in the sand is a rare thrill.) Today loggerheads are a threatened species, so it's important

to cut down on obstacles to their breeding.

That's where the darkness comes in. After a 60-day incubation period, the baby turtles hatch and begin to crawl toward the ocean. But bright lights confuse their navigation systems, causing them to head toward the light instead of the water, and making them easy prey for sand crabs and sea birds. Keeping lights to a minimum allows the baby turtles to heed their instincts and make it to the ocean.

Premier Resorts Blvd., North Myrtle Beach ☎877/237-3767 ⊕*www. barefootgolfresort.com* ⤢*387 condos* ⌂*In-hotel: 3 restaurants, bar, golf courses, pools* ▤*AE, D, MC, V.*

$-$$ ⊡**Best Western Ocean Sands.** One of the few fairly small, family-owned
☾ properties left in North Myrtle Beach, the Ocean Sands has some nice touches that make it a good choice for families, including full kitchens in every room and large suites with true separate bedrooms. Although it's not luxurious, it's clean and breezy, and all rooms have balconies. ■**TIP→The exercise room is very small, with just a treadmill and stair climber.** Pros: friendly, available staff. Cons: annex building is down the street away from the central hotel. ⊠*1525 S. Ocean Blvd.* ☎*843/272–6101 or 800/588–3570* ⊕*www.oceansands.com* ⤢*80 rooms, 36 suites* ⌂*In-room: kitchen. In-hotel: pools, no-smoking rooms* ▤*AE, D, MC, V.*

NIGHTLIFE & THE ARTS

CLUBS & Sassy and saucy, but with live music that ranges from R&B to classic
LOUNGES rock to beach favorites, **Dick's Last Resort** (⊠*Barefoot Landing, 4700 U.S. 17 S,* ☎*843/272–7794*) is big and loud, and the beer is cold.

You can dance the shag at **Duck's** (⊠*229 Main St.* ☎*843/249–3858*), and take lessons from the pros. The club often hosts shag events throughout the year for dedicated and novice dancers.

MUSIC & LIVE Live acts, and country-and-western shows in particular, are a big draw
SHOWS on the Grand Strand. Music lovers have many family-oriented shows to choose from. The 2,250-seat **Alabama Theatre** (⊠*Barefoot Landing, 4750 U.S. 17 S* ☎*843/272–1111*) has a regular variety show with a wonderful patriotic closing; the theater also hosts different guest music and comedy artists during the year. The **House of Blues** (⊠*Barefoot Landing, 4640 U.S. 17 S* ☎*843/272–3000 for tickets*) showcases big names and up-and-coming talent in blues, rock, jazz, country, and

R&B on stages in its Southern-style restaurant and patio as well as in its 2,000-seat concert hall. The gospel brunch is a great deal.

SHOPPING

MALLS **Barefoot Landing** (⊠*4898 U.S. 17 S* ☎*843/272–8349*) has more than 100 specialty shops, along with numerous entertainment activities. During the summer, check out fireworks displays here every Monday night.

SPECIALTY Beach-music lovers have been finding their long-lost favorites at **Judy's**
STORES **House of Oldies** (⊠*300 Main St.* ☎*843/249–8649*), for years. Find classics on cassette and CD at this small but packed-to-the-gills music emporium.

THE SOUTHERN GRAND STRAND

Unlike the more developed area to the north, the southern end of the Grand Strand—Murrells Inlet, Litchfield, Pawleys Island, and George-town—has a barefoot, laid-back vibe that suits its small restaurants, shops, galleries, and outdoor outfitters. And what this part of the Strand lacks in glitz, it more than makes up for in natural beauty.

MURRELLS INLET

15 mi south of Myrtle Beach on U.S. 17.

Murrells Inlet, a fishing village with some popular seafood restaurants, is a perfect place to rent a fishing boat or join an excursion. A notable garden and state park provide other diversions from the beach.

GETTING HERE & AROUND

Driving south on U.S. 17 takes you through Murrells Inlet. If you stay on U.S. 17 Bypass, though, you'll miss some of the town's character. Try taking U.S. 17 Business to get a taste of the real Murrells Inlet. Most cross streets connect to the bypass if you get turned around.

EXPLORING

Fodor'sChoice Just beyond *The Fighting Stallions,* the Anna Hyatt Huntington sculp-
★ ture alongside U.S. 17, lies **Brookgreen Gardens,** one of the Grand Strand's most magnificent hidden treasures. Here, in the oldest and largest sculpture garden in the United States, are more than 550 examples of figurative American sculpture by such artists as Frederic Remington and Daniel Chester French. Each is carefully set within garden rooms and outdoor galleries graced by sprawling live oak trees, colorful flowers, and peaceful ponds. The gardens are lush and full in spring and summer, and in winter splashes of color from winter-blooming shrubs are set off against the stark surroundings.

The 9,000-acre property was originally a winter home for industrial-ist Archer Huntington and his wife Anna Hyatt Huntington, but they quickly decided to open it to the public as a sculpture garden and wild-life sanctuary. Today, more than 70 years later, their legacy endures as a center for not only American art but Lowcountry culture and nature

The Ghosts of the Grand Strand

Spend any time on the Grand Strand and you'll likely hear about two of the area's eeriest residents: Alice Flagg and the Gray Man.

Alice Flagg was the teenage sister of the wealthy owner of the Hermitage, a rice plantation near Murrells Inlet. She was sent by her family to boarding school in Charleston to keep her away from a boy who'd captured her heart. The young lovers managed to see each other on the sly and soon became secretly engaged. Alice wore her engagement ring around her neck, hidden next to her heart. She came down with a high fever and returned to the Hermitage, where she died with the name of her fiancé on her lips. Her brother discovered the ring and, in a rage, threw it in the marsh.

Although she was buried at the Hermitage, her body was later moved to the cemetery at All Saints Church near

Pawleys Island, where it now rests under a marble slab bearing only the name "Alice." For many years her ghost was seen wandering the marsh near the house, looking for the ring. Her spirit, it is said, can be summoned by walking around the grave backward 13 times.

The Gray Man, according to most renditions of his story, was a young man who, while rushing to see his sweetheart, was thrown from his horse and died. After his funeral, his love took to walking along the beach each night. One evening she was approached by a ghostly version of her lover. "Leave the island at once," he warned. "You are in great danger." She heeded the warning, and later that day a hurricane struck. Ever since, the Gray Man has delivered storm warnings to island residents, most famously before Hurricane Hugo hit in September 1989.

preservation. You'll find a wildlife park, an aviary, a cypress swamp, nature trails, and an education center. Several tours, including a boat tour of tidal creeks and a Jeep excursion into the preserve, leave from Brookgreen. ■ TIP→ **Outdoor concerts under the stars are a tradition, check the Web site for dates.** ☒ *West of U.S. 17, 3 mi south of Murrells Inlet* ☎ *843/235–6000 or 800/849–1931* ⊕ *www.brookgreen.org* ☜ *$12, good for 7 days* ☉ *June–Sept., Wed.–Fri. 9:30–9, Sat.–Tues. 9:30–5; Oct.–May, daily 9:30–5.*

Huntington Beach State Park, the 2,500-acre former estate of Archer and Anna Huntington, lies east of U.S. 17, across from Brookgreen Gardens. The park's focal point is **Atalaya** (circa 1933), their Moorish-style 30-room home. There are nature trails, fishing, an education center with aquariums and a loggerhead sea turtle nesting habitat, picnic areas, a playground, concessions, and a campground. ☒ *East of U.S. 17, 3 mi south of Murrells Inlet* ☎ *843/237–4440* ⊕ *www.huntingtonbeachsc.org* ☜ *$5* ☉ *6 AM–10 PM daily.*

WHERE TO EAT

$$$–$$$$
AMERICAN
★

✕**Bovine's Wood-Fired Specialties.** What started as a meat-lovers-only restaurant has quietly morphed into a local favorite not just for delicious mesquite-grilled beef, lamb, pork, and fish, but also for superb crisp-crusted pizzas, baked in an imported brick oven and topped with a creative assortment of toppings. Add to that a terrific view of Murrells Inlet and Surfside Beach in the distance and a sleek, modern decor, and Bovine's is a nice change from the usual waterfront establishment. ✉3979 U.S. 17 Business ☎843/651–2888 ⚓Reservations essential ☰AE, D, MC, V ⊘No lunch.

$$$–$$$$ ✗The Crab Cake Lady. A weathered yellow shack with a hand-lettered
SEAFOOD   sign heralds this unassuming spot in Murrells Inlet. While you can't sit down and eat, you can order the famous creations of An, known as the Crab Cake Lady, who fishes daily for crab to go into her handmade cakes. Creek Rolls, a twist on the classic egg roll, feature baby shrimp caught daily in the inlet. ✉4525 Wesley Rd., off U.S. 17 ☎843/651–0708 ☰AE, D, MC, V ⊘Closed Sun.

$$$–$$$$ ✗Lee's Inlet Kitchen. They're closed at lunchtime, on Sunday, and in
SEAFOOD   winter; they don't take reservations or have a view, but nobody fries
★   up a mess of seafood like Lee's. Even the biggest eaters will get their fill when they order the Shore Dinner: fried or broiled flounder, shrimp, oysters, scallops, deviled crab, and lobster, along with a shrimp cocktail, clam chowder, hush puppies, fries, and coleslaw. Sure, you can get your fish broiled or grilled, but why mess with deep-fried perfection? ✉4660 U.S. 17 Business ☎843/651–2881 ⚓Reservations not accepted ☰AE, MC, V ⊘Closed Sun., Dec., and Jan. No lunch.

$$–$$$ ✗Nance's Creekfront Restaurant. You can smell the brine and Old Bay
SEAFOOD seasoning the minute you leave your car and head toward the front
★   door of Nance's. There's not much atmosphere, but that's okay. Oysters, the small local ones that taste of saltwater and seaweed, are the specialty, available raw or steamed in an iron pot and served with butter. There are other selections on the menu, but it's really all about the oysters—and the 10-layer chocolate cake, made specially for Nance's by a local baker. ✉4883 U.S. 17 Business ☎843/651–2696 ⚓Reservations not accepted ☰D, MC, V ⊘No lunch.

NIGHTLIFE

You can have a drink, watch boats come back from a day of fishing, and enjoy the evening breeze on the deck at **Captain Dave's Dockside** (✉4037 U.S. 17 Business ☎843/651–5850), where there's live music most nights in summer. Strewn with party lights and offering live bands every night, the **Hot Fish Club** (✉4911 U.S. 17 Business ☎843/357–9175) is a happening spot with a great view.

SPORTS & THE OUTDOORS

BOATING   **Capt. Dick's** (✉ 4123 U.S. 17 Business, ☎843/651–3676) runs half- and full-day fishing and sightseeing trips. You can also rent boats and kayaks and go parasailing. The evening ghost-story cruise is scary fun.

PAWLEYS ISLAND

10 mi south of Murrells Inlet via U.S. 17.

About 4 mi long and ½ mi wide, this island, sometimes referred to as "arrogantly shabby," began as a resort before the Civil War, when wealthy planters and their families summered here. It's mostly made up of weathered old summer cottages nestled in groves of oleander and oak trees. You can watch the famous Pawleys Island hammocks being made and bicycle around admiring the beach houses, many dating to the early 1800s. Golf and tennis are nearby. ■TIP→ Parking is limited on Pawleys and facilities are nil, so arrive early and bring what you need.

GETTING HERE & AROUND

Pawleys Island is located south of Murrells Inlet on U.S. 17. Take North Causeway Drive off the main highway to experience the natural beauty of the island. A 2-mi long historic district is home to rustic beach cottages, historic buildings, and even a church.

WHERE TO EAT

$$$–$$$$

AMERICAN

★

✗ **Frank's.** This local favorite serves dishes that give traditional cooking methods and ingredients a new twist. In a former 1930s grocery store with wood floors, framed French posters, and cozy fireside seating, diners indulge in large portions of fish, seafood, beef, and lamb cooked over an oak-burning grill. The local grouper with mustard-bacon butter, served with a side of stone-ground grits, is a star. Behind Frank's is the casual (but still pricey) Outback, a lush candlelit garden with a huge stone fireplace. ■TIP→ Enjoy a before- or after-dinner drink at Outback's bar. Heaters will keep you warm in winter. ⊠ *10434 U.S. 17* ☎ *843/237–3030* ▤ *AE, D, MC, V* ⊗ *Closed Sun. No lunch.*

6

¢–$

BARBECUE

Fodor'sChoice

★

✗ **Hog Heaven.** Part barbecue joint, part raw bar (after 5), Hog Heaven's wonderful smoky aroma perfumes U.S. 17 for miles. Pulled-pork barbecue has the tang of vinegar and the taste of long hours in the pit. Although sandwiches are available, the buffet, which includes fried chicken, greens, and sweet-potato casserole, is the main event. In the evening try the seafood tray, an assortment of shellfish steamed to order and served piping hot. ⊠ *7147 U.S. 17* ☎ *843/237–7444* ⚠ *Reservations not accepted* ▤ *MC, V.*

¢

CAFÉ

✗ **Landolfi's.** This Italian pastry shop and restaurant, fourth-generation-owned, has excellent coffee, hearty hoagies, pizzas, homemade sorbet, and delicious and authentic pastries, including cannoli and *pasticciotti* (a rich cookielike pastry filled with jam). Both counter and table service is available. ⊠ *9305 Ocean Hwy.* ☎ *843/237–7900* ▤ *MC, V* ⊗ *Closed Sun. and Mon. Open until 5 PM Tues. and Wed., and until 9 Thurs.–Sat.*

$–$$

AMERICAN

✗ **Pawleys Island Tavern.** This little eatery has terrific crab cakes, hickory-smoked barbecue, roasted chicken, and pizza. On summer weekend nights tiki torches outside blaze and live music rocks the place. ⊠ *The Island Shops, U.S. 17* ☎ *843/237–8465* ▤ *AE, MC, V* ⊗ *Closed Mon.*

WHERE TO STAY

$$$

⌸ **Hampton Inn Pawleys Island/Litchfield.** Ongoing upgrades keep this hotel in tip-top condition. Like most Hampton Inns, the property offers a wide array of amenities and is clean and well maintained. The beach at Pawleys is a 10-minute drive away. **Pros:** cute turtles populate a pond outside and beg for treats. **Cons:** the beach isn't close by. ⊠ *150 Willbrook Blvd.* ☎ *843/235–2000* ⊕ *www.pawleysislandhamptoninn.com* ⌸ *66 rooms* �� *In-hotel: pool, gym* ▤ *AE, D, DC, MC, V* ⦾ *BP.*

$–$$　　▣ **Litchfield Beach and Golf Resort.** This beautifully landscaped 4,500-
Fodor's Choice　acre resort runs along both sides of U.S. 17. The almost 2-mi stretch
★　of oceanfront accommodations ranges from condos to the 160-room
Litchfield Inn, which has motel rooms; other options, such as high-rise
condos, duplexes, and even Charleston-style beach houses, overlook
fairways, lakes, or the marsh. All accommodations are grouped into
miniresorts, each with its own pool and tennis courts. A bike trail connects them all to the large lake, which has a small fishing dock and a
couple of resident alligators. There's a one-week minimum for oceanfront rentals during June, July, and August, except at the Inn, where
the minimum is three nights. ■ **TIP**➡ Resort guests have access to Litchfield's oceanfront cabana, where there's parking, bathrooms, and a water
fountain. Pros: geared to all kinds of travelers. Cons: some properties
are as much as a 15-minute walk to the beach. ⊠ *U.S. 17, 2 mi north of
Pawleys Island, Litchfield Beach* ☎ *843/237–3000 or 800/845–1897*
⊕ *www.litchfieldbeach.com* ⤸ *140 rooms, 216 suites, 200 condominiums, cottages, and villas* ♿ *In-hotel: 2 restaurants, golf courses, tennis
courts, pools, gym, bicycles* ⊟ *AE, D, MC, V*

$$$–$$$$　▣ **Litchfield Plantation.** Period furnishings adorn suites of this impeccably
★　restored 1750 rice-plantation manor house–turned–country inn. All
of the rooms are lovely, with rich fabrics and views of lakes, woods,
or creeks. Use of a beach-house club a short drive away is part of the
package, as is a full breakfast at the elegant Carriage House Club;
guests also have golf privileges at eight nearby courses. The resort is
approximately 2 mi south of Brookgreen Gardens on U.S. 17 (turn
right at the Litchfield Country Club entrance and follow signs). **Pros:**
shared condos are ideal for a group of friends getting together. **Cons:**
shared condos can be awkward if staying with people you don't know.
⊠ *Kings River Rd.* ☎ *843/237–9121 or 800/869–1410* ⊕ *www.litch-
fieldplantation.com* ⤸ *35 rooms, 3 suites, 9 two- and three-bedroom
cottages* ♿ *In-hotel: restaurant, tennis courts, pool* ⊟ *AE, D, DC, MC,
V* ⊺◯ *BP.*

$$$–$$$$　▣ **Sea View Inn.** A "barefoot paradise," Sea View is a no-frills beach-
side boardinghouse (there are no TVs or in-room phones) with long
porches. Rooms in the main inn, with views of the ocean or marsh,
have half baths; showers are down the hall and outside. Cottage rooms
are marshside and have air-conditioning. Three meals, served family
style—with grits, gumbo, crab salad, pecan pie, and oyster pie—make
this an unbeatable deal. There's a two-night minimum stay during May
and September and a one-week minimum from June through August.
Pros: live oak trees and a nearby nature preserve keep you insulated
from resort hustle and bustle. **Cons:** no handicapped access; only six of
the 14 rooms have air-conditioning; some showers are outside of room.
⊠ *414 Myrtle Ave.* ☎ *843/237–4253* ⊕ *www.seaviewinn.com* ⤸ *20
rooms, 1 cottage* ♿ *In-room: no a/c (some), no phone, no TV. In-hotel:
restaurant* ⊟ *No credit cards* ⊘ *Closed Dec.–Mar.* ⊺◯ *FAP.*

SPORTS & THE OUTDOORS

GOLF　The live-oak alley and wonderful greens help make the **Heritage Club**
(⊠ *478 Heritage Dr.* ☎ *800/552–2660* ⊕ *www.legendsgolf.com*) one
of the South Strand's top courses, and its fees are lower than courses

of similar difficulty and condition. **Litchfield Country Club** (✉*619 Country Club Dr. off U.S. 17 S* ☏*843/235-4653*) is a mature, old-style course with tight fairways and moss-laden oaks.

Pawleys Plantation Golf & Country Club (✉*70 Tanglewood Dr. off U.S. 17 S* ☏*843/237–6100 or 800/367–9959*) is a Jack Nicklaus-designed course; several holes play along saltwater marshes.

Willbrook (✉*379 Country Club Dr., off U.S. 17 S* ☏*843/237–4900*) is on a former rice plantation and winds past historical markers, a slave cemetery, and a tobacco shack.

TENNIS You can get court time, rental equipment, and instruction at **Litchfield Country Club** (✉*U.S. 17 S* ☏*843/235–4653*).

HANGIN' AROUND

Created nearly 100 years ago by a riverboat captain tired of sleeping on his grain-filled mattress, the original Pawleys Island rope hammock is handcrafted in Pawleys Island exactly as it was by Captain Ward. More than 1,000 feet of rope are knitted by hand, pulled between oak stretcher bars, and tied with bowline knots to the body. In the 1930s Captain Ward's brother-in-law began selling the hammocks at a general store called the Hammock Shop. Still standing at the same location on U.S. Highway 17, the shop's weaving room is open to visitors most Saturdays.

SHOPPING

The **Hammock Shops at Pawleys Island** (✉*10880 Ocean Hwy.* ☏*843/237–8448*) is a complex of two dozen boutiques, gift shops, and restaurants built with old beams, timber, and ballast brick. Outside the Original Hammock Shop, in the Hammock Weavers' Pavilion, craftspeople demonstrate the 19th-century art of weaving the famous cotton-rope Pawleys Island hammocks. Also look for jewelry, toys, antiques, and designer fashions.

GEORGETOWN

13 mi south of Pawleys Island via U.S. 17.

Founded on Winyah Bay in 1729, Georgetown became the center of America's colonial rice empire. A rich plantation culture developed on a scale comparable to Charleston's, and the historic district is among the prettiest in the state. Today oceangoing vessels still come to Georgetown's busy port, and the **Harborwalk,** the restored waterfront, hums with activity. ■**TIP→** **Many of the restaurants along the riverside of Front Street have back decks overlooking the water that come alive in the early evening for happy hour.**

GETTING HERE & AROUND

Georgetown is accessible from U.S. 17, as well as S.C. 701. The heart of the town is located near the waterfront—an easy trip off the highway down any side street is worth it. Take Cannon Street to Front Street to see the harbor.

ESSENTIALS

Visitor Information Georgetown County Chamber of Commerce (⌕531 *Front St., Box 1776, Georgetown 29442* ☎843/546–8436 ⊕ www.georgetownchamber.com)

EXPLORING

Hampton Plantation State Historic Site preserves the home of Archibald Rutledge, poet laureate of South Carolina for 39 years until his death in 1973. The 18th-century plantation house is a fine example of a Lowcountry mansion. The exterior has been restored; cutaway sections in the finely crafted interior show the changes made through the centuries. The grounds are landscaped, and there are picnic areas. ✉*Off U.S. 17, at edge of Francis Marion National Forest, 16 mi south of Georgetown* ☎843/546–9361 ✆*Mansion $4, grounds free* ⊙*Mansion Mar.–Oct., Tues.–Sun. noon–4; Nov.–Feb., Thurs.–Sun. noon–4. Grounds daily 9–6.*

⟳ **Hobcaw Barony Visitors Center** is at the entrance of Hobcaw Barony, on the vast estate of the late Wall Street financier Bernard M. Baruch; Franklin D. Roosevelt and Winston Churchill came here to confer with him. A small interpretive center has exhibits on coastal ecology and history, with special emphasis on the Baruch family. There are aquariums, touch tanks, and video presentations; there are guided three-hour tours of the 17,500-acre wildlife refuge Tuesday, Wednesday, and Friday morning and Thursday afternoon. ✉*On U.S. 17, 2 mi north of Georgetown* ☎843/546–4623 ⊕*www.hobcawbarony.org* ✆*Visitors center free, tours $15* ⊙ *Weekdays 10–5; reservations necessary for tour.*

Hopsewee Plantation, surrounded by moss-draped live oaks, magnolias, and tree-size camellias, overlooks the North Santee River. The circa-1740 mansion has a fine Georgian staircase and hand-carved lighted-candle moldings. ✉*U.S. 17, 12 mi south of Georgetown* ☎843/546–7891 ⊕*www.hopsewee.com* ✆*Mansion $15; grounds only $5 per car; parking fees apply toward tour* ⊙*Mansion and grounds Feb.–Nov., weekdays 10–4; Dec.–Jan. by appointment.*

Overlooking the Sampit River from a bluff is the **Kaminski House Museum** (circa 1769). It's especially notable for its collections of regional antiques and furnishings, its Chippendale and Duncan Phyfe furniture, Royal Doulton vases, and silver. ✉*1003 Front St.* ☎843/546–7706 ✆*$7* ⊙*Mon.–Sat. 9–5, Sun. 1–5.*

Prince George Winyah Episcopal Church (named after King George II) still serves the parish established in 1721. It was built in 1737 with bricks brought from England. ✉*Broad and Highmarket Sts., Georgetown* ☎843/546–4358 ✆*Free, donation suggested* ⊙ *Mar.–Oct., weekdays 11:30–4:30.*

⟳ The graceful market and meeting building in the heart of Georgetown, topped by an 1842 clock and tower, has been converted into the **Rice Museum,** with maps, tools, and dioramas. At the museum's Prevost Gallery next door is the Brown's Ferry river freighter, the oldest American-built water-going vessel in existence. The museum gift shop has local pine needle baskets, African dolls, and art (including baskets made from whole cloves), and carries South Carolina rice and honey. ⊠*Front and Screven Sts.* ☎*843/546–7423* ✉*$7* ⊙*Mon.–Sat. 10–4:30.*

WHERE TO EAT

¢–$
CAFÉ
Fodor'sChoice
★

✕**Kudzu Bakery.** Come here for the justifiably famous key lime pie and red velvet cake, both of which are available whole or by the slice, and can be eaten in the garden. Kudzu is also a great source for ready-to-cook specialties such as cheese biscuits, macaroni and cheese, and quiche. In addition, you'll find fresh bread, deli items, and a terrific selection of wines. ⊠*120 King St.* ☎*843/546–1847* ▤*MC, V* ⊙*Closed Sun. No dinner.*

$$$–$$$$
AMERICAN
★

✕**Rice Paddy.** At lunch, locals flock to this Lowcountry restaurant for the shrimp and bacon quesadilla and the creative salads and sandwiches. Dinner in the Victorian building, with windows overlooking Front Street, is more relaxed. Grilled local tuna with a ginger-soy glaze is a winner, as are the crab cakes, which you can get uncooked to go. ⊠*732 Front St.* ☎*843/546–2021* ⚔*Reservations essential* ▤*AE, MC, V* ⊙*Closed Sun.*

$–$$
SEAFOOD

✕**River Room.** This restaurant on the Sampit River specializes in char-grilled fish, Cajun fried oysters, seafood pastas, and steaks. For lunch you can have shrimp and grits or your choice of sandwiches and salads. The dining room has river views from most tables. It's especially romantic at night, when the oil lamps and brass fixtures cast a warm glow on the dark wood and brick interior of the early-20th-century building. ⊠*801 Front St.* ☎*843/527–4110* ⚔*Reservations not accepted* ▤*AE, MC, V* ⊙*Closed Sun.*

¢
SOUTHERN

✕**Thomas Café.** There's great fried chicken, homemade biscuits, and pie at this lunch counter, not to mention grits, eggs, country ham, and other breakfast favorites served every day but Sunday (when the café opens at 11 AM instead of 7). Join the regulars at the counter, or sit in one of the booths or café tables in the 1920s storefront building. ⊠*703 Front St.* ☎*843/546–7776* ▤*MC, D, V* ⊙*No dinner.*

WHERE TO STAY

$

🏨**Hampton Inn Georgetown Marina.** Watch boats cruise up and down the river at this riverside resort; spectacular sunsets are an easy trade for being a little farther from the beach. An upgraded Hampton Inn, the Georgetown property offers a hot breakfast, signature Cloud 9 bedding, and a choice of pillows. Suites have pull-out sofas, all rooms have a microwave, refrigerator, and coffeemaker. **Pros:** there is a marina outside the hotel if you'd like to arrive by boat. **Cons:** as a chain hotel, it lacks the unique aspects of some other hotels. ⊠*420 Marina Dr.* ☎*843/545–5000 or 800/426–7866* ⊕*www.georgetownhamptoninn. com* ⇖*98 rooms, suites and deluxe suites* ⚐*In-room: refrigerator, Wi-Fi. In-hotel: pool, Wi-Fi* ▤*AE, D, MC, V.*

$–$$

🏨**Harbor House Bed and Breakfast.** Watch the shrimp boats come into the harbor from the front porch of Georgetown's only waterfront B&B; if you're lucky, innkeeper Meg Tarbox will turn some of the catch into shrimp and grits for breakfast. All four rooms (named for ships that have docked at Georgetown) have water views, as well as decades-old heart-pine floors and family antiques. Refreshments in the afternoon

6

include more of those shrimp, this time in the family's locally famous dip. **Pros:** great views of Winyah Bay. **Cons:** guests typically socialize, so those who prefer to keep to themselves might be turned off. ✉*15 Cannon St.* ☎*843/546–6532 or 877/511–0101* ⊕*www.harborhousebb.com* ⇄*4 rooms* ⌂*In-hotel: bicycles* ▤*MC, V* ⊘*Closed mid-Dec.–mid-Feb.* �‖*BP.*

SPORTS & THE OUTDOORS

BOATING   Cruise past abandoned rice plantations and hear stories about the belles who lived there with Cap'n Rod of **Lowcountry Plantation Tours** (✉*Front St., on the harbor* ☎*843/477–0287*); other tours include a lighthouse expedition and a ghost-stories cruise. Feel the spray on your face as you explore Winyah Bay aboard a 40-foot yacht with Captain Dave of **Wallace Sailing Charters** (✉*Front St., on the harbor* ☎*843/902–6999*). Each trip is limited to six passengers, so it feels like you're touring on a private yacht.

★   **Black River Outdoor Center and Expeditions** (✉*21 Garden Ave., U.S. 701* ☎*843/546–4840* ⊕*www.blackriveroutdoors.com*) offers naturalist-guided canoe and kayak day and evening tours (including moonlight tours) of the tidelands of Georgetown. Guides are well versed not just in the wildlife, but in local lore. Tours take kayakers past settings such as Drunken Jack's (the island that supposedly holds Blackbeard's booty), and Chicora Wood plantation, where dikes and trunk gates mark canals dug by slaves to facilitate rice growing in the area. It's said that digging the canals required as much manual labor as Egypt's pyramids. Black River also rents and sells equipment. ■**TIP**➔ **Wildlife tends to be more active during the early morning or late afternoon; there's a good chance you'll hear owls hooting on the evening tours, especially during the fall.**

GOLF   The premier course in the Georgetown area, and the only one with a ghost story, is the 18-hole, par-73 **Wedgefield Plantation** (✉*129 Club House La., off U.S. 701* ☎*843/448–2124 or 843/546–8587*). People have reported sightings of the ghost of a Revolutionary War-era British soldier, who lost his head to Francis Marion while guarding valuable prisoners in the plantation house. The spirit's appearance near the plantation house is accompanied by the sound of horses' hooves.

Charleston, SC

WORD OF MOUTH

"I hope you plan to stay in the historic district. A walking map is all you need. Go to the [Old City Market] for fun flea market shopping. Slip into an old church for a rest. Be cheesy . . . take a carriage ride. Eat shrimp and grits. Read some Pat Conroy before you go."

—twigsbuddy

By Eileen
Robinson
Smith

WANDERING THROUGH THE CITY'S HISTORIC district, you would swear it was a movie set. The spires and steeples of more than 180 churches punctuate the low skyline, and the horse-drawn carriages pass centuries-old mansions and carefully tended gardens overflowing with heirloom plants. It's known for its quiet charm, and has been called the most mannerly city in the country.

Immigrants settled here in 1670. They flocked here initially for religious freedom and later for prosperity (compliments of the rice, indigo, and cotton plantations). Preserved through the poverty following the Civil War, and natural disasters like fires, earthquakes, and hurricanes, many of Charleston's earliest public and private buildings still stand. And thanks to a rigorous preservation movement and strict Board of Architectural Review, the city's new structures blend with the old ones. In many cases, recycling is the name of the game—antique handmade bricks literally lay the foundation for new homes. But although locals do live—on some literal levels—in the past, the city is very much a town of today.

Take the internationally heralded Spoleto Festival, for instance. For two weeks every summer, arts patrons from around the world come to enjoy local and international concerts, dance performances, operas, improv shows, and plays at venues citywide. Day in and out, diners can feast at upscale Southern restaurants, shoppers can look for museum-quality paintings and antiques, and outdoor adventurers can explore all Charleston's outlying beaches, parks, and marshes. But as cosmopolitan as the city has become, it's still the South, and just outside the city limits are farm stands cooking up boiled peanuts, recently named the state's official snack.

ORIENTATION & PLANNING

GETTING ORIENTED

The heart of the city is on a peninsula, sometimes just called "downtown" by the nearly 60,000 residents who populate the area. Walking Charleston's peninsula is the best way to get to know the city.

North of Broad. The main part of the historic district, where you'll find the lion's share of the historic district's homes, B&Bs, and restaurants, is the most densely packed area of the city and will be of the greatest interest to tourists. King Street, Charleston's main shopping street, is here as well.

The Battery & South of Broad. The southern part of the historic district is heavily residential, but it still has a few important sights and even some B&Bs, though many fewer restaurants and shops.

Mount Pleasant & Vicinity. East of Charleston, across the Arthur Ravenel Jr. Bridge, Mount Pleasant, a pleasant city just across the river from Charleston, will be of some interest to tourists. Further afield, the out-

TOP REASONS TO GO

Dining out: Charleston has become a culinary destination, with talented chefs who offer innovative twists on the city's traditional cuisine. Bob Waggoner at the Charleston Grill is one outstanding example.

Seeing art: The city is home to more than 100 galleries, so you'll never run out of places to see world-class art. The Charleston Museum and dozens of others add to the mix.

Spoleto Festival USA: If you're lucky enough to visit in late May and early June, you'll find a city under siege: Spoleto's flood of indoor and outdoor performances (opera, music, dance, and theater) is impossible to miss and almost as difficult not to enjoy.

The Battery: The views from the point—both natural and man-made—are the loveliest in the city. Look west to see the harbor; to the east you'll find elegant Charleston mansions.

Historic homes: Charleston's preserved 19th-century houses, including the Nathaniel Russell House, are highlights; outside the city, plantations like Boone Hall, with its extensive garden and grounds, make scenic excursions.

lying islands have the region's best beaches and resorts. There are a few good places to stay in Mount Pleasant itself.

West of the Ashley River. Beyond downtown, the area of Charleston west of the Ashley River will be of some interest to tourists, though the sights here are spread out over a much greater area than in the historic downtown.

CHARLESTON PLANNER

GETTING HERE & AROUND

You don't need a car to explore the historic sistrict, where few of the hotels and B&Bs offer free parking, but you'll need a car if you want to explore the area.

BY AIR Charleston International Airport, about 12 mi west of downtown, is served by American Eagle, Continental, Delta, United Express, Northwest, US Airways, and Air Tran. Wings Air, a commuter airline that flies to and from Atlanta, operates out of the Charleston Executive Airport.

Several cab companies serve the airport, including the Charleston Black Cab Company, which has London-style taxis ($50 for 2 to 5 passengers). Airport Ground Transportation arranges shuttles ($14 per person). Star Limousine Service offers stretch limo service.

BY BOAT & The Charleston Water Taxi is a delightful way to travel between
FERRY Charleston and Mount Pleasant ($10 round-trip). It departs from the Charleston Maritime Center. The water taxi departs every hour from 2:30 PM to 5:30 PM.

BY BUS The Charleston Area Regional Transportation Authority, the city's public bus system, takes passengers around the city and to the suburbs. Bus 11, which goes to the airport, is convenient for travelers. CARTA operates DASH, which runs buses that look like vintage trolleys along three downtown routes; a single ride is $1.25 (exact change only), and a daylong pass is $4.

BY TAXI Fares within the city average about $5 to $10 per trip. Companies include Charleston Black Cab Company, Safety Cab, and Yellow Cab; the latter two are available 24 hours a day.

Pedicabs can take you anywhere in the historic district for $4.50 per person per 10 minutes, and they can be called. Three can squeeze into the one seat.

BY TRAIN The Amtrak station is somewhat isolated, but a visible police presence means there are few reports of crime in the area. Taxis meet every train; a ride to downtown averages $25.

VISITOR INFORMATION The Charleston Area Convention & Visitors Bureau runs the Charleston Visitor Center, which has information about the city as well as Kiawah Island, Seabrook Island, Mount Pleasant, North Charleston, Edisto Island, Summerville, and the Isle of Palms. The Historic Charleston Foundation and the Preservation Society of Charleston have information on house tours.

ESSENTIALS **Airport Contacts Charleston Executive Airport** (⊠ *2700 Fort Trenholm Rd., John's Island* ☎ *877/754–7285*). **Charleston International Airport** (⊠ *5500 International Blvd., North Charleston* ☎ *843/767–1100*). **Mt. Pleasant Regional Airport** (⊠ *700 Airport Rd., Mount Pleasant* ☎ *843/884–8837*).

Airport Transfers Airport Ground Transportation (☎ *843/767–1100*). **A Star Limousine** (☎ *843/745–6279*). **Charleston Black Cab Company** (☎ *843/216–2627 or 843/216–1206*).

Boat & Ferry Contacts Charleston Water Taxi (⊠ *Charleston Maritime Center, 10 Wharfside St., Upper King* ☎ *843/330–2989*).

Bus Contacts CARTA (⊠ *3664 Leeds Ave., North Charleston* ☎ *843/747–0922* ⊕ *www.ridecarta.com*). **Charleston Bus Station** (⊠ *3610 Dorcester Rd., North Charleston* ☎ *843/744–4247*).

Taxi Contacts Charleston Bike Taxi (☎ *843/532–8663*). **Charleston Black Cab Company** (☎ *843/216–2627 or 843/216–1206*).**Charleston Ped-Cab** (☎ *843/577–7088*). **Charleston Rickshaw Company** (☎ *843/723–5685*).**Safety Cab** (☎ *843/722–4066*). **Yellow Cab** (☎ *843/577–6565*).

Train Contacts Amtrak (⊠ *4565 Gaynor Ave., North Charleston* ☎ *843/744–8264*).

Visitor Information Contacts Charleston Visitor Center (⊠ *375 Meeting St., Upper King* 🎫 *423 King St., 29403* ☎ *843/853–8000 or 800/868–8118* ⊕ *www. charlestoncvb.com*). **Historic Charleston Foundation** (☎ *843/723–1623* ⊕ *www. historiccharleston.org*). **Preservation Society of Charleston** (☎ *843/722–4630* ⊕ *www.preservationsociety.org*).

TOURS

AIR TOURS Flying High Over Charleston provides aerial tours of the city and surrounding areas. Trips begin at $60 per person.

BOAT TOURS Charleston Harbor Tours offers tours that give the history of the harbor; it's the oldest harbor tour boat company (since 1908) and gives a good narrated tour of the harbor (excluding Fort Sumter). Spiritline Cruises, which runs the ferry to Fort Sumter, also offers harbor tours and dinner cruises ($47 to $52). Sandlapper Tours has tours focused on regional history, coastal wildlife, and ghostly lore ($15 to $25); you must make reservations by phone in advance, since there is no ticket office where the harbour tours depart. On the authentic, 84-foot tall *Schooner Pride* (capacity 49 persons), you can enjoy a diesel-free sail and the natural sounds of Charleston harbor ($27 to $39).

BUS TOURS Adventure Sightseeing leads bus tours of the historic district. Associated Guides of Historic Charleston pairs local guides with visiting tour groups. Doin' the Charleston, a van tour, makes a stop at the Battery. Sites and Insights is a van tour that covers downtown and nearby islands. Gullah Tours focuses on sights significant to African-American culture. Chai Y'All shares stories and sights of Jewish interest.

CARRIAGE TOURS Carriage tours are a great way to see Charleston. Carolina Polo & Carriage Company, Old South Carriage Company, and Palmetto Carriage Tours run horse- and mule-drawn carriage tours of the historic district. Each tour lasts about one hour. Most carriages queue up at North Market and Anson streets. Charleston Carriage and Polo picks up passengers at the Doubletree Guest Suites Historic Charleston on Church Street.

ECOTOURS Barrier Island Ecotours, at the Isle of Palms Marina, runs three-hour pontoon-boat tours to a barrier island. Coastal Expeditions has half-day and full-day naturalist-led kayak tours on local rivers. Charleston Explorers leads educational boat tours that are great for kids.

WALKING TOURS Walking tours on various topics—horticulture, slavery, or women's history—are given by Charleston Strolls and the Original Charleston Walks. Bulldog Tours has walks that explore the city's supernatural side. Listen to the infamous tales of lost souls with Ghosts of Charleston, which travel to historic graveyards. Military history buffs should consider Jack Thompson's Civil War Walking Tour. The food-oriented tours by Carolina Food Pros explore culinary strongholds—gourmet grocers, butcher shops, and restaurants, sampling all along the way.

TOUR ESSENTIALS **Air Tour Contacts Flying High Over Charleston** (⊠ *Mercury Air Center, W. Aviation Ave., North Charleston* ☎ *843/569–6148* ⊕ *www.flyinghighovercharleston.com*).

Boat Tour Contacts Charleston Harbor Tours (⊠ *Charleston Maritime Center, 10 Wharfside St., Upper King* ☎ *843/722–1112, 800/979–3370; 212/209–3370* ⊕ *www.charlestonharbortours.com*). **Sandlapper Tours** (⊠ *Charleston Maritime Center, 10 Wharfside St., Upper King* ☎ *843/849–8687* ⊕ *www.sandlappertours. com*) **Schooner Pride** (⊠ *Aquarium Wharf, Upper King* ☎ *843/559–9686 or 843/722–1112* ⊕ *www.schoonerpride.com*). **Spiritline Cruises** (⊠ *360 Concord St. [Aquarium Wharf], Upper King area* ☎ *843/881–7337 or 800/789–3678* ⊕ *www. spiritlinecruises.com*).

Bus Tour Contacts **Adventure Sightseeing** (☎843/762–0088 or 800/722–5394 ⊕ www.touringcharleston.com). **Associated Guides of Historic Charleston** (☎843/724–6419 ⊕ www.historiccharleston.org). **Chai Y'All** (☎843/556–0664). **Doin' the Charleston** (☎843/763–1233 or 800/647–4487 ⊕ www.dointhecharlestontours.com). **Gullah Tours** (☎843/763–7551 ⊕ www.gullahtours.com). **Sites and Insights** (☎843/762–0051 ⊕ www.sitesandinsightstours.com).

Carriage Tour Contacts **Charleston Carriage & Polo Company** (☎843/577–6767 ⊕ www.cpcc.com). **Old South Carriage Company** (☎843/723–9712 ⊕ www. oldsouthcarriagetours.com). **Palmetto Carriage Tours** (☎843/723–8145).

Ecotour Contacts **Barrier Island Ecotours** (✉ Isle of Palms Marina, off U.S. 17, Isle of Palms ☎843/886–5000 ⊕ www.nature-tours.com). **Charleston Explorers** (✉40 Patriots Point Rd., Mount Pleasant ☎843/723–5656 ⊕ www. charlestonexplorers.org). **Coastal Expeditions** (✉514-B Mill St., Mount Pleasant ☎843/884–7684 ⊕ www.coastalexpeditions.com).

Walking Tour Contacts **Bulldog Tours** (✉40 N. Market St., Market area ☎843/568–3315 ⊕ www.cobblestonewalkingtours.com). **Carolina Food Pros** (✉701 E. Bay St., Market area ☎843/723–3366 ⊕ www.carolinafoodpros.com). **Charleston Strolls** (✉ Charleston Pl., 130 Market St., Market area ☎843/766–2080 ⊕ www.charlestonstrolls.com). **Ghosts of Charleston** (✉184 E. Bay St., French Quarter ☎843/723–1670 or 800/723–1670). **Jack Thompson's Civil War Walking Tour** (✉ Mills House Hotel, 115 Meeting St., Market area ☎843/722–7033). **Original Charleston Walks** (✉58½ Broad St., South of Broad ☎843/577–3800 or 800/729–3420).

PLANNING YOUR TIME

The best way to get acquainted with Charleston is to take a carriage ride, especially those that take you through the South of Broad neighborhood. After the ride, carriage companies drop you off near the Old City Market in the North of Broad neighborhood, where you can wander looking for souvenirs. You can get acquainted with Charleston's historic district at your leisure, especially if you can devote at least three days to the city. You'll have time to explore some of the plantations west of the Ashley River. With another day, you can explore Mount Pleasant, and if you have more time, head out to the coastal islands, where you can play golf or visit the beach; you can even stay in a condo or villa out here and enjoy the fresh sea breezes.

EXPLORING CHARLESTON

The heart of the city is on a peninsula, sometimes just called "downtown" by the nearly 60,000 residents who populate the area. Walking Charleston's peninsula is the best way to get to know the city. The main downtown historic district is roughly bounded by Lockwood Boulevard to the west, Calhoun Street to the north, the Cooper River to the east, and the Battery to the south. Nearly 2,000 historic homes and buildings occupy this fairly compact area divided into South of Broad (Street) and North of Broad. King Street, the main shopping street in town, cuts through Broad Street, and the most trafficked tourist area ends a few blocks south of the Crosstown, where U.S. 17 cuts across

Upper King. Downtown is best explored by foot. Otherwise, there are bikes, pedicabs, and trolleys. Street parking is irksome, as meter readers are among the city's most efficient public servants. Parking garages, both privately and publicly owned, charge around $2 an hour.

Beyond downtown, the Ashley River hugs the west side of the peninsula, and the region on the far shore is called West Ashley. The Cooper River runs along the east side of the peninsula, with Mount Pleasant on the opposite side and the Charleston Harbor in between. Last, there are outlying sea islands—James' Island with its Folly Beach, John's Island, Kiawah and Seabrook Islands, Isle of Palms, and Sullivan's Island—with their own appealing attractions. Everything that entails crossing the bridges is best explored by car or bus.

NORTH OF BROAD

Large tracts of available land made the area North of Broad ideal for suburban plantations during the early 1800s. A century later, the peninsula had been built out, and today the area is a vibrant mix of residential neighborhoods and commercial clusters, with verdant parks scattered throughout. This area is comprised of three primary neighborhoods: Upper King, the Market area, and the College of Charleston. Though there are a number of majestic homes and pre-Revolutionary buildings in this area, the main draw is the area's collection of stores, museums, restaurants, and historic churches. The farther north you travel (up King Street in particular), the newer and more commercial development becomes. In times past, Broad Street was considered the cutoff point for the most coveted addresses. Those living in the area Slightly North of Broad were called mere "SNOBs," and their neighbors South of Broad were nicknamed "SOBs."

TOP ATTRACTIONS

②★☾ Charleston Museum. Founded in 1773, the country's oldest museum is housed in a contemporary complex. (The original Greek Revival pillars are all that remain standing at the museum's former home on Rutledge Avenue.) The museum's decorative-arts holdings and its permanent Civil War exhibit are extraordinary. There are more than 500,000 items in the collection, including silver, toys, snuffboxes, and Indian artifacts. There are also fascinating exhibits on natural history, archaeology, and ornithology. The suspended whale skeleton (the museum's mascot to many locals) is a must-see. ■TIP→**Combination tickets that give you admission to the Joseph Manigault House and the Heyward-Washington House are a bargain at $22.** ⊠*360 Meeting St., Upper King* ☎*843/722–2996* ⊕*www.charlestonmuseum.org* ⊠*$10* ☾*Mon.–Sat. 9–5, Sun. 1–5.*

⑪★ Charleston Place. The city's most renowned hotel is flanked by upscale boutiques and specialty shops. Stop by for afternoon tea at the classy Thoroughbred Club. The city's finest public rest rooms are downstairs by the shoe-shine station. Entrances for the garage and reception area are on Hasell Street between Meeting and King streets. ⊠*130 Market St., Market area* ☎*843/722–4900.*

7

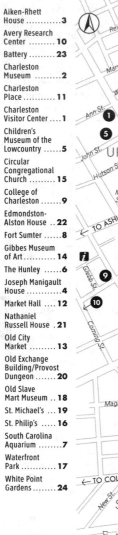

1 **Charleston Visitors Center.** The center's 20-minute film *Forever Charleston* is a fine introduction to the city. ■**TIP**➔**The first 30 minutes are free at the parking lot.** ✉*375 Meeting St., Upper King* ☎*843/853–8000 or 800/868–8118* ⊕*www.charlestoncvb.com* ✆*Free* ☉*Apr.–Oct., daily 8:30–5:30; Nov.–Mar. 31, daily 8:30–5.*

5 **Children's Museum of the Lowcountry.** Hands-on exhibits at this top-notch
★ museum keep kids up to 12 occupied for hours. They can climb on a
☼ replica of a local shrimp boat, play in exhibits that show how water evaporates, and wander the inner workings of a medieval castle. ✉*25 Ann St., Upper King* ☎*843/853–8962* ⊕*www.explorecml.org* ✆*$7* ☉*Tues.–Sat. 10–5, Sun. 1–5.*

NEED A BREAK?

Take a break with an icy treat at **Paolo's Gelato Italiano** (✉ *41 John St., Upper King* ☎*843/577-0099*). **Flavors include various fruits and florals, as well as traditional flavors like pistachio. It also serves crepes covered with delicious sauces.**

15 **Circular Congregational Church.** The first church building erected on this site in the 1680s gave bustling Meeting Street its name. The present-day Romanesque structure, dating from 1890, is configured on a Greek-cross plan and has a breathtaking vaulted ceiling. Explore the grave-yard, the oldest in the city, with records dating to 1696. ✉*150 Meeting St., Market area* ☎*843/577–6400* ⊕*www.circularchurch.org.*

9 **College of Charleston.** Randolph Hall—an 1828 building with a majes-tic Greek Revival portico designed by Philadelphia architect William Strickland—anchors the central Cistern area of the college. Draping oaks envelop the Cistern's lush green quad, where graduation ceremo-nies and concerts take place. The college was founded in 1770. Scenes from *Cold Mountain* were filmed here. ✉*St. Philip and George Sts., College of Charleston Campus* ⊕*www.cofc.edu.*

8 **Fort Sumter National Monument.** The first shot of the Civil War was fired
★ at Fort Sumter on April 12, 1861. After a 34-hour battle, Union forces
☼ surrendered the fort, which became a symbol of Southern resistance. The Confederacy held it, despite almost continual bombardment, from August 1863 to February 1865. When it was finally evacuated, the fort was a heap of rubble. Today the National Park Service oversees it.

The **Fort Sumter Liberty Square Visitor Center,** next to the South Carolina Aquarium, contains exhibits on the Civil War. This is a departure point for ferries headed to the island where you find Fort Sumter itself. ✉*340 Concord St., Upper King* ☎*843/577–0242* ✆*Free* ☉*Daily 8:30–5.*

Rangers conduct guided tours of the restored **Fort Sumter.** To reach the fort, you have to take a ferry; boats depart from Liberty Square Visi-tor Center and from Patriot's Point in Mount Pleasant. There are six crossings daily between mid-March and mid-August. The schedule is abbreviated the rest of the year, so call ahead for details. ✉*Charleston Harbor* ☎*843/577–0242* ⊕*www.nps.gov/fosu* ✆*Fort free; ferry $15, kids 9 and under $5.* ☉*Mid-Mar.–early Sept., daily 10–5:30; early Sept.–Mar., daily 10–4 (11:30–4 Jan.–Feb.).*

7

⑭ Gibbes Museum of Art. Housed in a beautiful Beaux Arts building, this museum boasts a collection of 10,000 works, principally American with a local connection. Each year there are a dozen special exhibitions, often of contemporary art. The museum shop is exceptional, with artsy, Charlestonian gifts. ⊠*135 Meeting St., Market area* ☎*843/722–2706* ⊕*www.gibbesmuseum.org* ▣*$9* ⊙*Tues.–Sat. 10–5, Sun. 1–5.*

④ Joseph Manigault House. An outstanding example of federal architecture, this home was designed by Charleston architect Gabriel Manigault in 1803. It's noted for its carved-wood mantels, grand staircase, elaborate plasterwork, and garden "folly." The pieces of rare tricolor Wedgwood are noteworthy. ⊠*350 Meeting St., Upper King* ☎*843/722–2996* ⊕*www.charlestonmuseum.org* ▣*$10* ⊙*Mon.–Sat. 10–5, Sun. 1–5.*

⑬ Old City Market. This area is often called the Slave Market because it's ℭ where house slaves once shopped for produce and fish. Today stalls are lined with restaurants and shops selling children's toys, leather goods, and regional souvenirs. Local "basket ladies" weave and sell sweetgrass, pine-straw, and palmetto-leaf baskets—a craft passed down through generations from their West African ancestors. ⊠*North and South Market Sts. between Meeting and E. Bay Sts., Market area* ⊙*Daily 9–dusk.*

⑱ Old Slave Mart Museum. This is likely the only building still in existence Fodor'sChoice that was used for slave auctioning, which ended in 1863. It is part of a ★ complex called Ryan's Mart, which contains the slave jail, the kitchen, and the morgue. The history of Charleston's role in the slave trade is recounted here. ⊠*6 Chalmers St., Market area* ☎*843/958–6467* ⊕*www.charlestoncity.info* ▣*$7* ⊙*Mon.–Sat. 9–5.*

⑯ St. Philip's (Episcopal) Church. The namesake of Church Street, this graceful late-Georgian building is the second on its site: the congregation's first building burned down in 1835 and was rebuilt in 1838. During the Civil War the steeple was a target for shelling; one Sunday a shell exploded in the churchyard. The minister bravely continued his sermon. Afterward, the congregation gathered elsewhere for the duration of the war. Notable Charlestonians like John C. Calhoun are buried in the graveyard. ⊠*146 Church St., Market area* ☎*843/722–7734* ⊕*www.stphilipschurchsc.org* ⊙*Church weekdays 9–11 and 1–4; cemetery daily 9–4.*

⑦ South Carolina Aquarium. The 380,000-gallon Great Ocean Tank has ★ the tallest aquarium window in North America. Exhibits display more ℭ than 10,000 creatures, representing more than 500 species. You travel through the five major regions of the Southeast Appalachian Watershed: the Blue Ridge Mountains, the Piedmont, the coastal plain, the coast, and the ocean. Little ones can pet stingrays at one touch tank and horseshoe crabs and conchs at another. ⊠*100 Aquarium Wharf, Upper King* ☎*843/720–1990 or 800/722–6455* ⊕*www.scaquarium. org* ▣*$16* ⊙*Mid-Apr.–mid-Aug., Mon.–Sat. 9–5, Sun. noon–5; mid-Aug.–mid-Apr., Mon.–Sat. 9–4, Sun. noon–4.*

⑰ **Waterfront Park.** Enjoy the fishing
★ pier's porch-style swings, stroll
along the waterside path, or relax
in the gardens overlooking Charleston Harbor. Home to two fountains, one known as the "Pineapple
Fountain," the other a walk-in (or
jump-in) fountain to refresh you
on hot summer days. The park is
at the foot of Vendue Range, along
the east side of Charleston Harbor and Cooper River. ⊠ *Prioleau
St., Market area* ☎ *843/724–7321*
⊠ *Free* ⊘ *Daily 6 AM–midnight.*

> ## ON THE CHEAP
>
> A $44.95 Charleston Heritage
> Passport, sold at the Charleston
> Visitors Center, gets you into
> the Charleston Museum, Gibbes
> Museum of Art, the Nathaniel Rus-
> sell House, the Edmondston-Alston
> House, the Aiken-Rhett House,
> Drayton Hall, and Middleton Place.
> It's good for two days. It can now
> be bought online, too, at ⊕ *www.
> travelocity.com.*

WORTH NOTING

③ **Aiken-Rhett House.** This stately 1818 mansion still has its original wallpaper, paint schemes, and even some of its furnishings. The kitchen,
slave quarters, and work yard are much as they were when the original
occupants lived here, making this one of the most complete examples of
urban slave life. Confederate general P. G. T. Beauregard made his headquarters here in 1864. ⊠ *48 Elizabeth St., Upper King* ☎ *843/723–
1159* ⊕ *www.historiccharleston.org* ⊠ *$10; $16 with admission to
Nathaniel Russell House* ⊘ *Mon.–Sat. 10–5, Sun. 2–5.*

⑩ **Avery Research Center for African-American History and Culture.** This center, part museum and part archive, was once a school for freed slaves.
Collections include slavery artifacts like badges, manacles, and bills
of sale. A riveting mural chronicles the Middle Passage—the journey
slaves made from Africa to Charleston's shores. The free tours include
a brief film. ⊠ *125 Bull St., College of Charleston Campus* ☎ *843/953–
7609* ⊕ *www.cofc.edu* ⊠ *Free* ⊘ *Weekdays noon–5, mornings by
appointment.*

⑥ **The Hunley.** The *Hunley* became the world's first successful submarine
when it was built for the Confederacy in 1864, and then suddenly
disappeared into the depths of the sea. Lost for over a century, it was
found in 1995 off the coast of Sullivan's Island and raised in 2000.
It is being preserved and excavated in a 90,000-gallon tank. A full
military funeral with honors was given in 2000 for those men that per-
ished aboard. Tour tickets can be ordered in advance online or on the
phone, but you have to pay a service charge. ⊠ *1250 Supply St., Old
Charleston Naval Base* ☎ *843/743–4865 Ext. 10, 877/448–6539 for
tour reservations* ⊕ *www.hunley.org, www.etix.com (for tour reservations only)* ⊠ *$12* ⊘ *Sat. 10–5, Sun. noon–5.*

⑫ **Market Hall.** Built in 1841, this imposing restored landmark was modeled after the Temple of Nike in Athens. The hall contains the **Confederate Museum,** in which the United Daughters of the Confederacy
display flags, uniforms, swords, and other Civil War memorabilia.
⊠ *188 Meeting St., Market area* ☎ *843/723–1541* ⊠ *$5* ⊘ *Tues.–Sat.
11–3:30.*

7

SOUTH OF BROAD

The heavily residential area south of Broad Street and west of the Battery brims with beautiful private homes, most of which bear plaques with a short written description of the property's history. Mind your manners, but feel free to peek through iron gates and fences at the verdant displays in elaborate gardens. Although an open gate once signified that guests were welcome to venture inside, that time

> ### IF THE SHOE FITS
>
> Wear good walking shoes, because the sidewalks, brick streets, and even Battery Promenade are very uneven. Take a bottle of water, or take a break to sip from the fountains in White Point Gardens, as there are practically no shops south of Broad Street.

has mostly passed—residents tell stories of how they came home to find tourists sitting in their front porch rockers. But you never know when an invitation to look around from a friendly owner-gardener might come your way. Several of the city's lavish house museums call this famously affluent neighborhood home.

TOP ATTRACTIONS

㉓ **Battery.** From the intersection of Water Street and East Battery you
Fodor's Choice can look east toward the city's most-photographed mansions; look
★ west for views of Charleston Harbor and Fort Sumter. Walk south along East Battery to White Point Gardens, where the street curves and becomes Murray Boulevard. ⊠*East Bay St. and Murray Blvd., South of Broad.*

㉑ **Nathaniel Russell House.** One of the nation's finest examples of Adam-
★ style architecture, the Nathaniel Russell House was built in 1808. The interior is distinguished by its ornate detailing, its lavish period furnishings, and the "free flying" staircase that spirals three stories with no visible support. The garden is well worth a stroll. ⊠ *51 Meeting St., South of Broad* ☎*843/724–8481* ⊕*www.historiccharleston.org* ☚*$10; $16 with admission to Aiken-Rhett House* ☾ *Mon.–Sat. 10–5, Sun. 2–5.*

㉙ **St. Michael's Episcopal Church.** The cornerstone of St. Michael's was set in place in 1752, making it Charleston's oldest surviving church. Through the years other elements were added: the steeple clock and bells (1764); the organ (1768); the font (1771); and the altar (1892). The pulpit—original to the church—was designed to maximize natural acoustics. ⊠ *14 St. Michael's Alley, South of Broad* ☎*843/723–0603* ⊕*www. stmichaelschurch.net* ☾ *Weekdays 9–4:30, Sat. 9–noon.*

㉔ **White Point Gardens.** Pirates once hung from gallows here; now it's a
★ serene park with Charleston benches—small wood-slat benches with
☺ cast-iron sides—and views of the harbor and Fort Sumter. Children love to climb on the replica cannon and pile of cannonballs. ⊠*Murray Blvd. and E. Battery, South of Broad* ☎*843/724–7327* ☾ *Weekdays 9–5, Sat. 9–noon.*

WORTH NOTING

㉒ Edmondston-Alston House. First built in 1825 in late-Federal style, the Edmondston-Alston House was transformed into the imposing Greek Revival structure you see today during the 1840s. Tours of the home—furnished with antiques, portraits, silver, and fine china— are informative. ✉*21 E. Battery, South of Broad* ☎*843/722–7171*

⊕*www.middletonplace.org* ✉*$10; $41 with combination ticket for Middleton Place* ⊗*Tues.–Sat. 10–4:30, Sun. and Mon. 1:30–4:30.*

㉑ Old Exchange Building & Provost Dungeon. Originally a customs house with a waterside entrance, this building was used by the British to house prisoners during the Revolutionary War. Today costumed guides bring the Revolutionary era to life. ✉*122 E. Bay St., South of Broad* ☎*843/727–2165* ⊕*www.oldexchange.com* ✉*$7* ⊗*Daily 9–5.*

MOUNT PLEASANT & VICINITY

East of Charleston, across the Arthur Ravenel, Jr. Bridge, the largest single-span bridge in North America, is the town of Mount Pleasant, named not for a mountain or a hill but for a plantation in England from which some of the area's settlers hailed. In its Old Village neighborhood are antebellum homes and a sleepy, old-time town center with a drugstore where patrons sidle up to the soda fountain and lunch counter for egg-salad sandwiches and floats. Along Shem Creek, where the local fishing fleet brings in the daily catch, several seafood restaurants serve the area's freshest (and most deftly fried) seafood. Other attractions in the area include military and maritime museums, plantations, and, farther north, the Cape Romain National Wildlife Refuge.

TOP ATTRACTIONS

★ **Boone Hall Plantation & Gardens.** A ½-mi drive through a live-oak alley draped in Spanish moss introduces you to the still-operating plantation, the oldest of its kind. Tours take you through the 1935 mansion, the butterfly pavilion, the heirloom rose garden, and nine antebellum-era brick slave cabins. Seasonal Gullah culture performances in the theater are laudable. Stroll along the winding river, tackle the fields to pick your own strawberries, pumpkins, or tomatoes. Across the highway are a farmers' market and gift shop. ✉*1235 Long Point Rd., off U.S. 17 N, Mount Pleasant* ☎*843/884–4371* ⊕*www.boonehallplantation. com* ✉*$17.50* ⊗*Apr.–early Sept., Mon.–Sat. 8:30–6:30, Sun. 1–5; early Sept.–Mar., Mon.–Sat. 9–5, Sun. 1–4.*

Fort Moultrie National Monument. Here Colonel William Moultrie's South Carolinians repelled a British assault in one of the first Patriot victories of the Revolutionary War. Completed in 1809, this is the third fort on this site at **Sullivan's Island,** reached on Route 703 off U.S. 17 N (10 mi southeast of Charleston). A 20-minute film tells the history of the fort.

7

FODOR'S FIRST PERSON

Pat Conroy
Writer

"I know of no more magical place in America than Charleston's South of Broad. I remember seeing this area near the Battery when I was a kid and I was stunned as to how beautiful it was. In meeting with my Doubleday publisher about writing this latest book, now entitled *South of Broad*, which is set there, she wanted to understand the big draw of this neighborhood. I said, "It is the most beautiful area of this gorgeous city. It is what the Upper East Side is to Manhattan, what Pacific Heights is to San Francisco, or what Beverly Hills is to L.A. S.O.B. is mysterious. It keeps drawing you back like a magnetic force. I am fortunate, that my writer friend Ann Rivers Simms lets me stay in her carriage house there when I come to town. As a cadet at The Citadel, I would walk along the Battery and watch the ships come in and out of port. They looked so close you thought you could touch them."

Conroy talks of other Charleston favorites: "When my children come to town I go to the aquarium with my grandchildren. It is small enough to take in. Aquariums always make me believe in God. Why? You see the incredible shapes of things and the myriad capacity for different forms of animals. And there is that wonderful outdoor area where you can look at the fish tanks and then look out to the river and see porpoises playing."

"Thanks to Mayor Riley, (the city's mayor for more than 30 years) who has been like Pericles for Charleston, there are so many parks and open spaces. Waterfront Park is a great example."

"And one of the true joys of Charleston in these last decades is its restaurant renaissance."

■**TIP**➔ Plan to spend the day relaxing bicycling through Sullivan's Island, which is characterized by its cluster of early-20th-century beach houses. ✉*1214 Middle St., Sullivan's Island* ☏*843/883–3123* ⊕*www.nps. gov* 🎫*$3* 🕐*Daily 9–5.*

🔄 **Patriots Point Naval & Maritime Museum.** Ships berthed here include
★ the aircraft carrier USS *Yorktown,* the World War II submarine USS *Clamagore,* the destroyer USS *Laffey,* and the Coast Guard cutter *Ingham,* responsible for sinking a U-boat during World War II. A Vietnam exhibit showcases naval air and watercraft used in the military action. ✉*Foot of Ravenel Bridge, Mount Pleasant* ☏*843/884–2727* ⊕*www. patriotspoint.org* 🎫*$15* 🕐*Daily 9–6:30.*

WORTH NOTING

Charles Pinckney National Historic Site. Across the street from Boone Hall Plantation, this is a remnant of the country estate of Charles Pinckney, drafter and signer of the Constitution. A self-guided tour focuses on African-American farm life, including the plantation owner–slave relationship. You can also tour an 1820s tidewater cottage. ✉*1254 Long Point Rd., off U.S. 17N, Mount Pleasant* ☏*843/881–5516* 🖶*843/881–7070* ⊕*www.nps.gov* 🎫*Free* 🕐*Daily 9–5.*

Old Village. This neighborhood is distinguished by white-picket-fenced colonial cottages, antebellum manses, tiny neighborhood churches, and restored (or new) waterfront homes with pricetags in the millions. It's a lovely area to stroll or bike. The Blessing of the Fleet seafood festival takes place each April. ⊠*South of Alhambra Park, Mount Pleasant.*

> **BASKET LADIES**
>
> Drive along U.S. 17 N, through and beyond Mount Pleasant, to find the basket ladies set up at rickety roadside stands, weaving sweetgrass, pine-straw, and palmetto-leaf baskets. Baskets typically cost less on this stretch than in downtown Charleston. Each purchase supports the artisans, who are becoming fewer and fewer each year. Nevertheless, be braced for high prices.

WEST OF THE ASHLEY RIVER

Ashley River Road, Route 61, begins a few miles northwest of downtown Charleston, over the Ashley River Bridge. Sights are spread out along the way and those who love history, old homes, and gardens may need several days to explore places like Drayton Hall, Middleton Place, and Magnolia Plantation and Gardens. Spring is a peak time for the flowers, although the gardens are in bloom throughout the year.

TOP ATTRACTIONS

Magnolia Plantation and Gardens. The extensive informal garden, begun in 1685, has evolved into an overflowing collection of plants that bloom year-round, including a vast array of azaleas and camellias. You can take a tram or boat to tour the grounds, travel through the 125-acre Waterfowl Refuge, or explore the 30-acre Audubon Swamp Garden walking its new network of boardwalks and bridges. You can traverse the more than 500 acres of trails. (Regrettably, you can no longer rent a canoe or a bike, though you can bring them into the grounds.) There are also a petting zoo, a miniature-horse ranch, and an antebellum cabin (a guide gives a slave talk). You can tour the 19th-century plantation house, which originally stood in Summerville. (The original burned.) The home was taken apart, floated down the Ashley River, and reassembled here. The Audubon Swamp Garden is the only individual attraction that can be visited without first paying the $15 admission fee for the grounds. ⊠*3550 Ashley River Rd., West Ashley* ☎*843/571–1266 or 800/367–3517* ⊕*www.magnoliaplantation.com* ☜*Grounds $15; tram $7; boat $7; house tour $7; Audubon Swamp Garden $7* ⊙*Daily 8–5:30.*

Fodor'sChoice
★
Middleton Place. Blooms of all seasons form floral *allées* (alleys) along terraced lawns, and around ornamental lakes shaped like butterfly wings. Much of the year, the landscaped gardens, begun in 1741, are ablaze with camellia, magnolia, azalea, and rose blossoms. A large part of the mansion was destroyed during the Civil War, but the gentlemen's wing has been restored and houses impressive collections of silver, furniture, paintings, and historic documents. In the stable yard craftspeople use authentic tools to demonstrate spinning, weaving, and other skills from the plantation era. Farm animals, peacocks, and other creatures roam

freely. The Middleton Place Restaurant serves Lowcountry specialties for lunch and dinner. It has a cozy character, a real sense of history, and is a charming, tranquil spot. (You do not have to pay admission to have dinner, and dinner guests can walk the grounds between 5 until dusk.) There is also a delightful museum gift shop that carries local arts, crafts, and souvenirs; a garden shop sells rare seedlings. You can sign up for kayak, bike, wagon, or carriage rides. Finally, you can stay overnight at the contemporary Middleton Inn, where floor-to-ceiling windows splendidly frame the Ashley River. ✉ *4300 Ashley River Rd., West Ashley* ☎ *843/556–6020 or 800/782–3608* ⊕ *www.middletonplace.org* ⌂ *Grounds $25, house tour $10, carriage tours $15; all-inclusive day-pass $45* ۞ *Grounds daily 9–5; house tours Tues.–Sun. 10–4:30, Mon. noon–4:30.*

WORTH NOTING

★ **Charles Towne Landing State Historic Site.** Commemorating the site of the
۞ original 1670 Charleston settlement, this park has a reconstructed village and fortifications, a new museum, which allows you to relive the first colonists' experiences up to modern-day life, and English park gardens with bicycle trails and walkways. A new replica of the colonists' 17th-century sailing vessel is being constructed, and at this writing was expected to be moored in the tidal creek by late 2008. In the animal park (Charleston's only zoo), more than 20 native (American) species roam freely—among them alligators, bison, pumas, bears, and wolves. Bicycle rentals are available. It has a new and inviting entrance which winds through a preserved wooded area. The paths will take you to the marshes, creek, and animal park. ✉ *1500 Old Towne Rd., Rte. 171, West Ashley* ☎ *843/852–4200* ⊕ *www.southcarolinaparks.com* ⌂ *$5* ۞ *Daily 8:30–5.*

Drayton Hall. Considered the nation's finest example of unspoiled Georgian–Palladian architecture, this mansion is the only plantation house on the Ashley River to have survived the Civil War. A National Trust historic site, built between 1738 and 1742, it's an invaluable lesson in history as well as in architecture. Drayton Hall has been left unfurnished to highlight the original plaster moldings, opulent hand-carved woodwork, and other ornamental details. Watch *Connections,* which details the conditions under which slaves were brought from Africa. You can also see copies of documents that recorded the buying and selling of local slaves. Tours depart on the hour; guides are known for their in-depth knowledge of the era. ✉ *3380 Ashley River Rd., West Ashley* ☎ *843/769–2600* ⊕ *www.draytonhall.org* ⌂ *$14* ۞ *Mar.–Oct., daily 9:30–4; Nov.–Feb., daily 9:30–3.*

WHERE TO EAT

Eating is a serious pastime in Charleston. You can dine at nationally renowned restaurants serving the best of Southern nouveau, or if you prefer, a waterfront shack with some of the best fried seafood south of the Mason-Dixon line. Local chefs have earned reputations for preparing Lowcountry cuisine with a contemporary flair, and there is plenty of

Charleston Preserved

It's easy to think Charleston is a neverland, sweetly arrested in pastel perfection. But look at Civil War–era images of the Battery mansions on East Bay Street, one of the most photographed areas in town today, and you see the surrounding homes disfigured with crippling battle scars. Because of the poverty that followed the Civil War, on the whole locals simply couldn't afford to build anew from the late 1860s through the early part of the 20th century, so they put the homes they had back together.

In the 1920s it was community activism that rescued the old homes from being destroyed. According to Jonathan Poston, author of *Buildings of Charleston,* the preservation movement began when an Esso gas station was slated to take the place of the Joseph Manigault House. Citizens formed the Society for the Preservation of Old Dwellings (the first such group in the nation) and saved what's now a popular house museum. By 1931 Charleston's City Council had created the Board of Architectural Review (BAR), and designated the historic district protected from unrestrained development—two more national firsts. The Historic Charleston Foundation was established in 1947, and preservation is now second nature (by law).

As you explore, look for Charleston single houses: just one room wide, these houses were built with the narrow end streetside and multistory south or southwestern porches (often called piazzas) to catch prevailing breezes. Cool air drifts across these shaded porches, entering houses through open windows.

You'll see numerous architectural vestiges along Charleston's preserved streets. Many houses have plaques detailing their history, and others have Carolopolis Awards given for fine restoration work. Old fire-insurance plaques are more rare; they denote the company that insured the home and that would extinguish the flames if a fire broke out. Notice the bolt heads and washers that dot house facades along the Battery; some are in the shape of circles or stars, and others are capped with lion heads. These could straighten sagging houses when tightened via a crank under the floorboards.

Note the iron spikes that line the tops of some residential gates, doors, walls, and windows. Serving the same purpose as razor wire atop prison fences, most of these *cheveux de frise* (French for frizzy hair) were added after a thwarted 1822 slave rebellion, to deter break-in—or escape.

incredible young talent in the city's kitchens. The local food revolution began in the early 1980s, with the reintroduction of original Lowcountry cuisine onto restaurant menus. As Lowcountry cuisine evolved and contemporary adaptations became commonplace, the city's remarkable pool of talented chefs grew, and Charleston began to be thought of as a destination for foodies.

Reservations are a good idea for dinner year-round, especially on weekends, as there is almost no off-season for tourism. Tables are especially hard to come by during the Southeastern Wildlife Expo (President's Day weekend in February) and the Spoleto Festival (late May to mid-

June). The overall dress code is fairly relaxed: casual khakis and an oxford or polo shirt for men, casual slacks (or a skirt), top, and sandals for women work in most places just fine, but in the fine-dining restaurants, particularly on weekends, people tend to dress up.

PRICES

Fine dining in Charleston can be expensive. One option to keep costs down might be to try several of the small plates that many establishments offer. To save money, drive over the bridges or go to the islands, including James's and John's islands.

WHAT IT COSTS					
	¢	$	$$	$$$	$$$$
Restaurant	under $10	$10–$14	$15–$19	$20–$24	over $24

Restaurant prices are for a main course at dinner, not including taxes (7.5% on food, 8.5% tax on liquor).

NORTH OF BROAD

$$
SOUTHERN
✕**Blossom.** Exposed white rafters and linenless tables make this place casual and yet upscale. The terrace with a view of St. Philip's majestic spire, the dining room, and the bar are heavily populated with young professionals. The open, exhibition kitchen adds to the high-energy atmosphere. Lowcountry seafood is a specialty, and the pastas are made on the premises. Special seasonal menus can be expected, and the new bar menu is available as late as 1 AM on Friday and Saturday nights. ✉171 E. Bay St., Market area ☎843/722–9200 ▭AE, DC, MC, V.

$$–$$$$
SEAFOOD
✕**Boathouse Restaurant.** Large portions of fresh seafood at reasonable prices make both Charleston-area branches of this restaurant wildly popular. The shrimp hush puppies with spicy mayonnaise and lightly battered fried shrimp and oysters are irresistible. Entrées come with mashed potatoes, grits, collard greens, or blue-cheese coleslaw. The original, Isle of Palms location is right on the water, so tables are hard to come by. At the Upper King branch, which is in a more central location, the architecture is strikingly contemporary, with a fisherman's boat hoisted at the bar. Brunch is popular on Sunday. ✉549 E. Bay St., Upper King ☎843/577–7171 ✉101 Palm Blvd., Isle of Palms ☎843/886–8000 ⚓Reservations essential ▭AE, DC, MC, V ⊘No lunch Mon.–Sat.

$$
SEAFOOD
✕**Bubba Gump.** If you loved Forrest, Jenny, Lieutenant Dan, and the others from the movie *Forrest Gump,* then head to this chain eatery. The food, particularly the shrimp with mango-pineapple salsa, can be surprisingly good. You won't be able to resist the chocolate-chip-cookie sundae. Children who weren't even born when the movie came out in 1994 adore the Gumpisms scrawled on the walls of the indoor dining room and that if you flip the license plate on the table, the server will come back. Young kids love to race the rubber duckies in the mock creek and to get a slushy drink in a glowing plastic cup that is available

in the cutsey gift shop. ⊠*96 S. Market St., Market area* ☎*843/723–5665* ⊟*AE, DC, MC, V.*

\$\$\$\$
SOUTHERN
Fodor'sChoice
★

✕**Charleston Grill.** Michelle Weaver's groundbreaking New South cuisine is now served in a dining room highlighted by pale wood floors, flowing drapes, and elegant Queen Anne chairs. A jazz ensemble adds a hip, yet unobtrusive, element. As it was hoped, the Grill, which has been reborn in a more relaxed form, now attracts a younger and more vibrant clientele than its original incarnation. The affable and highly talented chef raised the culinary bar in this town and continues to provide what many think of as its highest gastronomic experience. He utilizes only the best produce, such as the organic vegetables used in the golden beet salad. The menu is now in four quadrants: simple, lush (foie gras and other delicacies), cosmopolitan, and Southern. A nightly tasting menu offers a way to sample it all. The pastry chef sends out divine creations like chocolate caramel ganache. Sommelier Rick Rubel has 1,300 wines in his cellar, with many served by the glass. ⊠*Charleston Place Hotel, 224 King St., Market area* ☎*843/577–4522* ⌕*Reservations essential* ⊟*AE, D, DC, MC, V* ⊘*No lunch.*

\$\$\$\$
SOUTHERN
★

✕**Circa 1886.** If you're celebrating, come to this dining room in a carriage house behind the Wentworth Mansion, where the sound level is low enough that you needn't strain to hear your companions. There's a formality here, and the wait staff has both skill and decorum. Chef Marc Collins has created dishes that are real originals; don't resist the Vidalia onion cream soup or the foie gras with crushed almonds. Crab is the central ingredient in his signature soufflé. The coffee-rubbed strip loin with corn pudding, asparagus, and truffles is remarkable. After all that beef, you may experience a chemical need for dessert—try the chocolate tasting with wonders like chocolate-chunk-brownie gelato. ⊠*149 Wentworth St., Lower King* ☎*843/853–7828* ⌕*Reservations essential* ⊟*AE, D, DC, MC, V* ⊘*Closed Sun. No lunch.*

\$\$\$–\$\$\$\$
ECLECTIC
★

✕**Cypress Lowcountry Grille.** From the owners of Magnolias and Blossom comes a renovated 1834 brick-wall building with an urbane contemporary decor. Rust-color leather booths, a ceiling with light sculptures that change color, and a "wine wall" of 5,000 bottles keeps things interesting. The cuisine is high-end Southern-American, with fresh local ingredients accented with exotic flavors, notably from the Pacific Rim. Try fabulous salads, like the hearts of palm and baby greens with local goat cheese topped with a walnut vinaigrette. The duck is a good entrée choice, as is the fillet cooked over hickory wood and topped with a Madeira wine sauce. Executive chef Craig Deihl consistently creates simple yet elegant fare, and you can do the same with his cookbook called, of course, *Cypress.* ⊠*167 E. Bay St., Market area* ☎*843/727–0111* ⌕*Reservations essential* ⊟*AE, DC, MC, V* ⊘*No lunch.*

\$\$\$
SOUTHERN

✕**82 Queen.** In a city with a vibrant but ever-evolving restaurant scene, this is one of the landmarks. Wildly popular as a social meeting ground in the 1980s, it has settled down into its primary role, as an atmospheric fine-dining establishment. Multiple dining areas in both indoor and garden settings make this a great place to linger, perhaps under a gazebo or in an elegant, art-rich (and air-conditioned) room inside the historic residence. Also notable are the genuinely caring service and

7

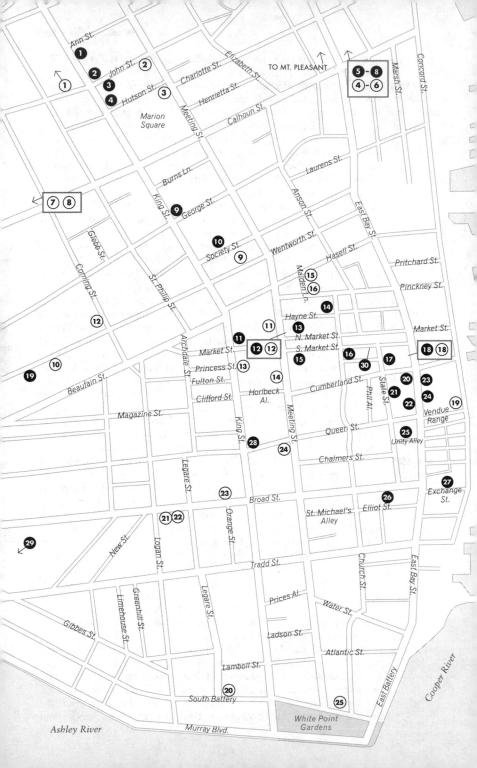

Where to Stay & Eat in Charleston

7

```
0          1/4 mile
|----------|

0          400 meters
|----------|
```

KEY

① *Hotels*

❶ *Restaurants*

extensive wine list featuring new varietal blends (no house wine here) which have earned it high and consistent praise. As always, its food has strong Southern leanings, with seafood highlights including Charleston bouillabaisse; don't miss the creamy grits (perfection) or authentic fried green tomatoes. ⊠*82 Queen St., Lower King* ☎*843/723–7591* ⚲*Reservations essential* ▤*AE, MC,V*

$$$
ECLECTIC
★

✕**Fish.** Since its European chef, Nico Romo, raised it to a high culinary level, settling into the niche of French/Asian cuisine with the freshest of seafood, the popularity of Fish has soared. The dim sum appetizer is more beautiful than a flower arrangement. The sweet-chili calamari and other petite plates give the menu a new kick. The bouillabaisse with coconut-lemongrass broth and ginger croutons is one-of-a-kind. Increasing business has triggered a major redo of the spaces, which blend antiqued mirrors and stainless steel, and a new dining room has gone into the adjacent building. The original bar has tripled in size. Some "jazzy" contemporary musicians play on "Wine Wednesdays," when bottles of wine are half-price from 6 to 8. ⊠*440–442 King St., Upper King* ☎*843/722–3474* ⚲*Reservations essential* ▤*AE, MC,V* ⊘*Closed Sun., no lunch Sat.*

$$$$
STEAK
Fodor'sChoice

✕**Grill 225.** This atmospheric establishment has been stockpiling accolades over the years and has never been better. Its popularity and status as a special-occasion restaurant makes it popular year-round as a superior dining experience, with a staggering array of excellent wines and professional, caring service. Dress up and add to the elegance created by wood floors, white linens, and red-velvet upholstery. It makes sense to opt for the USDA prime steaks; the fillet with foie gras with a fig demi-glace (hold the béarnaise) may be the best you will ever have anywhere. You will need to share a side or two, such as the mashed sweet potatoes with Boursin cheese. Presentation is at its best with the appetizers like the tuna tower tartare. Expect hefty portions, but save room for the pastry chef's shining creations, which include a contemporized version of baked Alaska, with a nutty crust, flambéed tableside. ⊠*Market Pavilion Hotel, 225 E. Bay St., Market area* ☎*843/266–4222* ▤*AE, D, DC, MC, V.*

$$$–$$$$
SEAFOOD

✕**Hank's Seafood.** A lively spot with a popular bar and a community table flanked by paper-topped private tables, Hank's is an upscale fish house with such Southern adaptions as Lowcountry bouillabaisse. Seafood platters come with sweet-potato fries and cole slaw. It has a true bistro atmosphere, with waiters in long white aprons buzzing about. It's super popular with the thirtysomething crowd and those who live inland and want the freshest seafood. With a location just off the Old Market, the sister restaurant to the fancy-pants Peninsula Grill is a noteworthy landmark on Charleston's dining scene. ⊠*Church and Hayne Sts., Market area* ☎*843/723–3474* ▤*AE, D, DC, MC, V* ⊘*No lunch.*

$$$–$$$$
SOUTHERN
★

✕**High Cotton.** Chef Anthony Gray, who has been with the restaurant since 1991, has taken over as chef, and so far the transition has gone smoothly. Lazily spinning paddle fans, palm trees, and brick walls still create a plantation ambience. As for the food, Gray combines wonderful flavors and flawless presentation for memorable meals. His Southern and Italian background translates to such specialties as homemade sausages and excellent sauces and marinades for meat. You can feast on bourbon-glazed pork and white-cheddar grits. The chocolate soufflé with blackberry sauce and the praline soufflé are both remarkable. Sunday brunch is accompanied by musicians who sweeten the scene. At night the bar is enlivened with jazz. ⊠*199 E. Bay St., Market area* ☏*843/724–3815* ⚑*Reservations essential* ▤*AE, D, DC, MC, V* ⊘*No lunch weekdays.*

$$–$$$
FRENCH
✕**La Fourchette.** French owner Perig Goulet moves agilely through the petite dining room of this unpretentious bistro. With back-to-back chairs making things cozy (and noisy), this place could be in Paris. Kevin Kelly chooses the wines—predominately French and esoteric, and they befit the authentic fare. Perig boasts of his country pâté, from a recipe handed down from his *grand-mère*. Other favorites include duck salad, scallops sautéed in cognac, and shrimp in a leek sauce. Dieters may be shocked by the golden *frites* fried in duck fat and served with aioli, but they keep putting their hungry hands in the basket. Check the blackboard for fish straight off the boats. ⊠*432 King St., Upper King* ☏*843/722–6261* ▤*AE, MC, V* ⊘*Closed Sun. No lunch Aug.–Mar.*

$$$$
AMERICAN
★
✕**McCrady's.** Young chef Sean Brock has come of age, turning McCrady's into a superb culinary venture. Passionate about his profession, he spends his nights coming up with innovative pairings that are now working, although he favors meat on the rare side for some tastes. For your appetizer, try the slow-cooked lobster tail with parsnips, leeks, almond puree, and citrus; follow with a main course such as spice-roasted rack of lamb with eggplant, pine nuts, and golden raisins. The bar area has a centuries-old tavern feel and is frequented by well-heeled downtown residents. The encyclopedia-size wine list is matched by some wonderful wines by the glass. The cold soft chocolate with a mascarpone filling is one of the impressive desserts; the sorbet is easily shared: nine tiny cones filled with vivid flavors. ⊠*2 Unity Alley, Market area* ☏*843/577–0025* ⚑*Reservations essential* ▤*AE, MC, V* ⊘*No lunch.*

$$$
ITALIAN
✕**Mercato.** Mercato is the new darling of those in Charleston who like to see and be seen. Placed throughout the two floors are 18th-century antiques and Venetian lighting fixtures juxtaposed with contemporary artworks hung on elaborately plastered walls. Reserve a banquette under the 24-foot-long oil painting inspired by an early Italian circus banner. Music four nights a week, like the incredible gypsy band, is kept low-key until after the normal dinner hour. (There's a late-night menu, too.) Thereafter, the volume goes up, adding fuel to the firey bar scene. Kudos go to the house-made pastas and raviolis (like duck and wild mushrooms with pine nuts plus). The beef marsala with wild mushrooms will make any chilly night as warm as Tuscany in the summer. Desserts like the panna cotta and the warm chocolate cake with vanilla gelato are most agreeable with a small glass of limoncello. ⊠*102 N. Market St., Market area* ☏*843/722–6393* ▤*AE, D, DC, MC, V* ⊘*No lunch.*

7

¢   ✗**Modica.** Known to most for its gelato, Modica often has a line of
ITALIAN   gelato-lovers in the evenings, especially during Spoleto, after a performance lets out of the Sotille Theater across the street. Less well known are the fat, sassy, panini and garden-crisp salads like the piquant, which gets heat from the Sopressata salami and crunch from roasted pistachios. The house soup is a broth made from portobello mushroom, and on a given day there might also be one made from carrot and sage or creamy Gorgonzola. You can order a decadent gelato cake for a celebration with 24 hours notice. And Italian patrons say that it has the only true espresso in town—Moak, from Sicily—just like owner Marcello and his cousin Vince. ⊠ *41A George St., Lower King* 🕾 *843/723–8868* ▤ *MC, V* ⊘ *No dinner Sun.*

$$$ ✗**Muse Restaurant & Wine Bar.** If you want to go to Europe without
MEDITERRANEAN   going through customs or security, spend the evening at Muse, preferably on Thursday night when there is live piano music. Just off King, on a lovely historic block, it's a draw as much for its popular Wine Bar (which serves premium liquors and cocktails, too), where a charming bartender will give you a good pour and where more than 100 wines by the glass are offered. Then you can move on to your designated table in one of four dining rooms decorated in the styles of Greece, Italy, France, and Spain. Owner Beth Anne Crane recruited Chef Jason Houser, then the sous-chef at the famed Charleston Grill, to realize her dream. Expect a contemporary take on Mediterranean cuisine like sumac-rubbed duck breast with dates and pomegranate jus, or pasta with unsweetened cocoa, lemon ricotta, and pesto. ⊠ *82 Society St., Lower King* 🕾 *843/577–1102* ⚖ *Reservations essential* ▤ *AE, MC, V* ⊘ *No lunch.*

$$$$ ✗**Oak Steakhouse.** In a 19th-century bank building, this dining room
STEAK   juxtaposes antique crystal chandeliers with contemporary art. Reserve a table on the third floor for the full effect and the best vistas. It's pricey, but the filet mignon with a foie-gras-black-truffle butter is excellent, and the side dishes, such as creamed spinach, are perfectly executed. Favorite appetizers include beef carpaccio and Gorgonzola fondue. Service is professional and cordial. This is a personality place, with chef/owner Chef Brett McKee "the man." He is nationally known and celebrities like Dennis Hopper fly him out to cook for their dinner parties. On Sunday nights a reasonably priced, family-friendly prix-fixe Italian supper is now served. An expansion, which will affect the first floor, is being planned at this writing. ⊠ *17 Broad St., Market area* 🕾 *843/722–4220* ▤ *AE, MC, V* ⊘ *No lunch.*

$$$$ ✗**Peninsula Grill.** Eighteenth century–style portraits hang on walls cov-
SOUTHERN   ered in olive-green velvet in this dining room. You sit beneath black-
★   iron chandeliers feasting on longtime executive chef Robert Carter's imaginative entrées, including rack of lamb with a sesame-seed crust and a coconut-mint pesto. If you start with the foie gras with a duck barbecue biscuit and peach jam—superb—you might want to go simple. Carter prepares fresh, thick fillets, such the black grouper, perfectly; all you have to do is to chose your sauce, say a ginger-lime butter. Palate cleanse with the homemade sorbet or the signature dessert, a three-way chocolate dessert that comes with a shot of ice-cold milk. The servers,

who work in tandem, are pros; the personable sommelier makes wine selections that truly complement your meal, anything from bubbly to clarets and dessert wines. The atmosphere is animated and convivial. ⊠*Planters Inn, 112 N. Market St., Market area* ☏*843/723–0700* ⚬*Reservations essential* ▭*AE, D, DC, MC, V* ⊘*No lunch.*

$$$$
CONTINENTAL
★

✕**Robert's of Charleston.** Owner Robert Dickson is both a classically trained chef and an effusive baritone who belts out show tunes in the intimate dining room. Accompanied by a pianist, he can sing in Italian, too, and even an Italian rendition of "Home on The Range." A Charleston mainstay since the 1970s, the restaurant tends to draw an older crowd, although honeymooners sometimes hold hands across the table while Robert croons to them. It's a popular spot for anniversaries and birthdays. The five-course prix-fixe menu changes and is now one of the most praiseworthy meals in Charleston. It might include scallop mousse with curried lobster sauce, duck with a balsamic fig sauce and creamy polenta, and chateaubriand with a Cabernet demi-glace. Manager Joseph Raya picks the wines to pair with each course. The restaurant is a family-run affair, which puts a warm spin on the experience. Joseph's wife (and Robert's daughter), Maria-Elena, now reigns in the kitchen. ⊠*182 E. Bay St., Market area* ☏*843/577–7565* ⚬*Reservations essential* ▭*D, MC, V* ⊘*Closed Sun.–Wed. No lunch.*

$$$–$$$$
SOUTHERN
★

✕**Slightly North of Broad.** This former warehouse with brick-and-stucco walls has a chef's table that looks directly into the open kitchen. It's a great place to perch if you can "take the heat," as chef Frank Lee, who wears a baseball cap instead of a toque, is one of the city's culinary characters. Known for his talent in preparing game, his venison is exceptional. Many of the items come as small plates, which make them perfect for sharing. The braised lamb shank with a ragout of white beans, arugula, and a red demi-glace is divine. Lunch can be as inexpensive as $9.95 for something as memorable as mussels with spinach, grape tomatoes, and smoked bacon. ⊠*192 E. Bay St., Market area* ☏*843/723–3424* ▭*AE, D, DC, MC, V* ⊘*No lunch weekends.*

$$$
FRENCH
★

✕**39 Rue de Jean.** In classic French-bistro style—gleaming wood, cozy booths, and white-papered tables—Charleston's trendy set wines and dines until the wee hours on such favorites as steamed mussels in a half-dozen preparations. Order them with *pomme frites,* as the French do. Each night of the week there's a special, such as the bouillabaisse on Sunday. Rabbit with a whole-grain mustard sauce was so popular it jumped to the nightly menu. The duck confit with lentils, braised endive, and blood orange velouté is the most popular new item. If you're seeking quiet, ask for a table in the dining room on the right. It's noisy—but so much fun—at the bar, especially since it has the city's best bartenders. ⊠*39 John St., Upper King* ☏*843/722–8881* ⚬*Reservations essential* ▭*AE, D, DC, MC, V.*

$$$–$$$$
SOUTHERN
Fodor'sChoice
★

✕**Tristan.** Within the French Quarter Inn, this fine dining room has a sleek, contemporary style with lots of metal, glass, contemporary art, and fresh flowers. The menu has been purposely tailored to complement the decor: it's ultrachic, innovative, and always evolving. The banquettes that line the wall are sought after, so ask for one when you reserve. The young talent who has moved up to executive chef, Aaron

7

Deal, has expanded the prix-fixe lunch, consisting of three courses from the dinner menu, for a mere $20—less than that chicken wings place down the block. Imagine sitting down to a lunch of baby beet salad, then lamb ribs with a chocolate barbecue sauce, and moving on to violet crème brûlée. After dark the prices escalate—it's a status place with a sophisticated bar scene. On Sunday there's a fab brunch with a jazz trio and residents of the Holy City reserve for after church. ⊠*French Quarter Inn, 55 S. Market St., Market area* ☎843/534–2155 ▤*AE, D, MC, V.*

$$
SOUTHERN

✕**Virginia's on King.** This Charleston newcomer is a tribute to an old Southern tradition, mom's home-cooked Southern family meals. In this case, the mother is Ms. Virginia Bennett, and she has shared her recipes for traditional fare that she still prepares for her extended family. Ms. Virginia makes sure prices here are affordable. Starters are such classics as tomato pie, fried green tomatoes, she-crab soup, okra soup, oyster stew, tomato aspic, and Waldorf salad. Supper might be a creamy chicken and dumplings or country-fried steak with red-eye gravy. And sides? Oh yes—collard greens, grits, sweet-potato fries, and more. ⊠ *412 King St., Upper King,* ☎*843/735–5800* ▤*AE, D, DC, MC, V* ⊘ *No lunch Sat. No dinner Sun.*

SOUTH OF BROAD

$$$–$$$$
SOUTHERN

✕**Carolina's.** On a quiet side street between East Bay Street and Waterfront Park, this longtime favorite occupies a former wharf building. The smartened-up decor includes romantic banquettes. The evolving menu has a strong emphasis on healthful ingredients. (Owner Richard Stoney also owns Kensington Plantation, where most of the produce is grown.) Lowcountry favorites stand next to original dishes like scallops with roasted cauliflower. Local grouper works amazingly well with a port-wine broth. Ask about the special prix-fixe dinners, including ones with beer pairings. On Sunday and Monday bottles of wine are half-price. The free valet parking is much appreciated. ⊠*10 Exchange St., South of Broad* ☎*843/724–3800* ⚠*Reservations essential* ▤*D, MC, V* ⊘*No lunch weekends*

MOUNT PLEASANT & VICINITY

$$$
SOUTHERN

✕**Old Village Post House.** If you've been on the road too long, this circa-1888 inn will provide warmth and sustenance. Many residents of this tree-lined village consider this their neighborhood tavern. The second, smaller dining room is cozy, and the outdoor space under the market umbrellas is open and airy. Expect contemporary takes on Southern favorites like lump crab cakes, shrimp and grits, and especially the fresh vegetables, like a butter beans mélange. From the open kitchen, the chefs do a perfect sautéed catch of the day. Here pork tenderloin may have a ginger-peachy glaze. In season, plump soft-shell crabs are deftly fried. Frank Sinatra serenades as you cleanse your palate with a tart, key lime pie with a crunchy crust and passion-fruit couli. ⊠*101 Pitt St., Mount Pleasant* ☎*843/388–8935* ▤*AE, MC, V* ⊘*No lunch Mon.–Sat.*

\$\$\$–\$\$\$\$ ✕**Sienna.** Ken Vedrinkski, who achieved 5-star status for The Wood-
ITALIAN lands, continues to enjoy rave reviews for this, his own laid-back eatery.
★ Sumptuous meals here have all the flavor, complexity, and flair befitting
a celebrity chef—but without the pomp. You may taste things here that
you have never heard of before, and the menu changes daily according
to the seasonal markets. Every day Ken hand-makes his gnudis (like a
gnocchi but made with cheese instead of potato) or "naked raviolis"
with such fillings as morel mushrooms in a Parmesan broth. Four- and
seven-course tasting menus are the way to dine, and they can be paired
with wine. Well worth the drive over the bridges, it's the best of downtown dining, minus the crowds and paid parking. ✉*901 Island Park
Dr., Daniel Island* ☎*843/881–9211* ▤*AE, MC, V* ⊘*Closed Sun. No
lunch summer and weekends.*

\$\$ ✕**The Wreck of the Richard and Charlene.** At first glance you think the
SEAFOOD name might refer to the waterfront restaurant—a shabby, screened-
★ in porch. In actuality, the *Richard and Charlene* was a trawler that
slammed into the building during a hurricane in 1989. Located in the
old village of Mount Pleasant, the kitchen serves up Southern tradition on a plate: boiled peanuts, fried shrimp, and stone crab claws.
The best deal is the most expensive: the mixed seafood platter with
fried flounder, shrimp, oysters, and scallops. This seafood shack is a
hoot. Know that it closes by 8:30 Tuesday through Thursday, and at
9:15 on Friday and Saturday nights. ✉*106 Haddrell St., Mount Pleasant* ☎*843/884–0052* ⚖*Reservations not accepted* ▤*No credit cards*
⊘*No lunch. Closed Sun. and Mon.*

GREATER CHARLESTON

\$\$ ✕**Charleston Crab House.** When you cross over the Wapoo Creek Bridge
SEAFOOD to James Island, you catch a glimpse of this tiered restaurant, whose
decks are splashed by the waters of the Intracoastal Waterway. Boaters
tie up and mingle with the fun crowd. Bus tours do come to the James
Island location, however. Crab is the specialty, of course, with she-crab
soup a perennial favorite. Owner John Keener gives the place its large
fun quotient and takes pride in the excellent crab cakes and baked
oysters. Servers and bartenders are young and fun, but don't expect
professional-level service. ✉*125A Wappoo Creek Dr., James Island*
☎*843/795–1963* ✉*1101 Stockade La., Mount Pleasant* ☎*843/884–
1617* ✉*41 S. Market St., Market area* ☎*843/853–2900* ▤*AE, DC,
MC, V.*

\$ ✕**J B's Smokeshack.** At the sign of the pig (not to mention other rudi-
SOUTHERN mentary signs stuck in the ground like CATFISH), this is one of the area's
best barbecue joints. A funky find, you will see evidence of the diverse
crowd, beat-up pickup trucks to new BMWs—the latter often guests
at nearby Kiawah Island. (JB's will deliver out there—for \$35.) Most
people have the buffet, which includes the barbecue pork, applewood-
smoked chicken, and all of the Southern veggies—usually including
okra gumbo, butter beans, and coleslaw—plus desserts like banana
pudding you can eat for one (very) low price. Barbecue connoisseurs
know that JB's takes the big prizes at the competitions and that the ribs

7

and the Angus beef brisket are top-shelf. To further flavor the smoky meats, sauces are served on the side. Just come early, because dinner is over by 8:30. ✉ *3406 Maybank Hwy., John's Island* ☎ *843/577–0426* ▤ *MC, V* ⊘ *Closed Sun.–Tues.*

WHERE TO STAY

Charleston is known for lovingly restored mansions that are now atmospheric bed-and-breakfasts, as well as deluxe inns, all found in the residential blocks of the historic district. Upscale, world-class hotels are in the heart of downtown as well as unique, boutique hotels that provide a one-of-a-kind experience. All are within walking distance of the shops, restaurants, and museums housed within the nearly 800 acres that makes up the historic district.

The major chains line the busy, car-trafficked Meeting Street in the historic district; you'll find others in West Ashley, Mount Pleasant, and North Charleston. Mount Pleasant is considered the most upscale suburb; North Charleston is the least, but if you need to be close to the airport or are participating in events in its Coliseum, it is probably the cheapest of alternatives.

BED & BREAKFAST AGENCIES

As prices escalate, more and more downtown residents are renting out a room or two through the reservation service, **Historic Charleston Bed & Breakfast Association** (☎ *843/722–6606* ⊕ *www.historiccharleston-bedandbreakfast.com*). They can be in up-and-coming revitalized neighborhoods or even on The Battery. Handsomely furnished, these rooms can be less expensive than commercial operations. However, since the owners or families are usually on-site, they may not offer the same level of privacy as more traditional B&Bs or small inns.

PRICES

Charleston's downtown lodgings have three seasons: high season (March to May and September to November); mid-season (June to August); and low season (late November to February). Prices drop significantly during the short low season, except during holidays and special events. High season is summer at the island resorts; rates drop for weekly stays and during off-season. Free parking is a rarity downtown; factor in that savings if your hotel offers it.

WHAT IT COSTS				
¢	$	$$	$$$	$$$$
Hotel under $100	$100–$150	$151–$200	$201–$250	over $250

Prices are for two people in a standard double room in high season, not including 12.5% tax.

DOWNTOWN CHARLESTON

$-$$ ⌂**Broad Street Guesthouse.** Hadassah Rothenberg, an accomplished cook and baker, has realized her dream of opening the city's first kosher B&B. She completely transformed this 1880s frame house, artfully decorating it with a mix of Victorian furnishings, religious art, and vintage family photos. On Friday evening guests can join in traditional prayers and partake in a multicourse Shabbat dinner. Rothenberg's kosher dishes are delicious and fresh, the baked goods delectable. The wholesome breakfast is even better when taken on the terrace. **Pros:** impeccably clean; a fascinating learning experience if you are non-Jewish; decor has a museum quality to it. **Cons:** only three rooms; you cannot bring in foods that are not kosher; innkeeper fussy about noise in the main house. ⊠ *133 Broad St., South of Broad* ☎ *843/577–5965* ⊕ *www.charlestonkosherbedandbreakfast.com* ⇆ *2 suites, 1 cottage* 丸 *In-room: no phone, no TV, kitchen. In-hotel: public Wi-Fi, parking (free), no-smoking rooms* ☰ *AE, D, MC, V* ⎮◎⎮ *BP.*

$$$$ ⌂**Charleston Place.** Even casual passersby enjoy gazing up at the
★   handblown Murano glass chandelier in the hotel's open lobby, clicking across the Italian marble floors, and admiring the antiques from Sotheby's. A gallery of upscale shops completes the ground-floor offerings. Rooms are furnished with period reproductions. The impeccable service is what you would expect from an Orient-Express property, particularly on the Club Level, where rooms carry a $100 surcharge that gets you a breakfast spread, afternoon tea, and cocktails and pastries in the evening. A truly deluxe day spa, with an adjacent fitness room, has an inviting indoor salt- and mineral-water pool with a retractable roof and illuminated skylight for night swimming. **Pros:** two great restaurants; located in the historic district on the best shopping street; pet-friendly. **Cons:** no Wi-Fi; rooms aren't as big as one would expect for the price; much of the business is conference groups in shoulder seasons. ⊠ *130 Market St., Market area* ☎ *843/722–4900 or 800/611–5545* ⊕ *www.charlestonplacehotel.com* ⇆ *400 rooms, 42 suites* 丸 *In-room: safe, refrigerator, Internet. In-hotel: 2 restaurants, bars, pool, gym, spa, Internet terminal, parking (paid), some pets allowed, no-smoking rooms* ☰ *AE, D, DC, MC, V* ⎮◎⎮ *EP.*

$$$-$$$$ ⌂**Embassy Suites Historic Charleston.** A courtyard where cadets once marched is now an atrium with skylights, palm trees, and a fountain. The restored brick walls of the breakfast room and some guest rooms in this contemporary hotel contain original gun ports, reminders that the 1822 building was the Old Citadel. Handsome teak and mahogany furniture and sisal rugs in the common areas recall the British-colonial era. Guest rooms are not nearly as chic, but are clean and serviceable. **Pros:** near Marion Square, where events take place including Saturday's farmers' market; close to newly refurbished Upper King's business and retail district; complementary manager's reception nightly that extends to the courtyard. **Cons:** the suites themselves are chain-hotel standard, not handsome and atmospheric like the lobby; no longer inexpensive. ⊠ *337 Meeting St., Upper King* ☎ *843/723–6900 or 800/362–2779* ⊕ *www.embassysuites.com* ⇆ *153 suites* 丸 *In-room:*

7

refrigerator, Wi-Fi. In-hotel: restaurant, pool, gym, laundry facilities, parking (paid), no-smoking rooms ⊟*AE, D, DC, MC, V* ⦿*BP.*

$$$$ ⊡**French Quarter Inn.** The first architectural detail you'll notice in this
★   boutique hotel known for its chic French style is a circular staircase with a wrought-iron bannister embellished with iron leaves. Guests appreciate the lavish breakfasts, the afternoon wine and cheese reception, and evening cookies and milk. The pillow menu is a luxury; you can order whatever kind you desire, including big body pillows. Some rooms have fireplaces, others balconies. Among the best are No. 220, a business suite with a corner office niche overlooking the courtyard, and No. 104, with a spacious L-shape design. You'll get champagne at check-in, too. **Pros:** located in the heart of the market area yet a quiet haven; excellent restaurant (Tristan) on premises. **Cons:** no pool or fitness area; being smack in the busy Market has its downside. ✉*166 Church St., Market area* ☎*843/722–1900 or 866/812–1900* ⊕*www. fqicharleston.com* ⇘*46 rooms, 4 suites* ♿*In-room: safe (some), refrigerator (some), Internet. In-hotel: restaurant, bar, Wi-Fi, parking (paid), no-smoking rooms* ⊟*AE, MC, V* ⦿*CP.*

$$$$ ⊡**Governors House Inn.** This quintessential Charleston lodging radiates
★   18th-century elegance. Its stately architecture typifies the grandeur, romance, and civility of the city's bountiful colonial era. A National Historic Landmark, it's filled with antiques and period reproductions in the public rooms and the high-ceilinged guest rooms, some of which have whirlpool tubs. The best room is the Rutledge Suite, a legacy to the original owner, Governor Edward Rutledge. Nice touches include a proper afternoon tea where wine and cheese are also served. **Pros:** you can take breakfast on the veranda or have it delivered; evening sherry and Godiva chocolates with turndown service. **Cons:** older children are welcome in the former kitchen-house rooms, but the main house is not the appropriate environment; no glorious views. ✉*117 Broad St., South of Broad* ☎*843/720–2070 or 800/720–9812* ⊕*www.governorshouse.com* ⇘*10 rooms, 1 jr. suite* ♿*In-room: kitchen (some), Internet, Wi-Fi. In-hotel: Internet terminal, Wi-Fi, parking (free), no-smoking rooms* ⊟*AE, D, MC, V* ⦿*BP.*

$$$ ⊡**Hampton Inn–Historic District.** Hardwood floors and a fireplace in the lobby of what was once an 1800s warehouse help elevate this chain hotel a bit above the rest. Spindle posts on the headboards give guest rooms a little personality. Rooms are not large but have little perks like coffeemakers. The location is perfect for exploring downtown. There is always something to eat and drink in the lobby. **Pros:** hot breakfast; located near the business and retail district of Upper King and near a couple of really good restaurants. **Cons:** a long walk to the Market area; rooms are smallish and not atmospheric. ✉*373 Meeting St., Upper King* ☎*843/723–4000 or 800/426–7866* ⊕*www.hamptoninn. com* ⇘*166 rooms, 5 suites* ♿*In-room: refrigerator, Wi-Fi. In-hotel: pool, laundry facilities, parking (paid), no-smoking rooms* ⊟*AE, D, DC, MC, V* ⦿*BP.*

$$$–$$$$ ⊡**HarbourView Inn.** Ask for a room facing the harbor, and you can gaze down at the landmark "Pineapple Fountain" of Waterfront Park. Calming earth tones and rattan soothe and relax; four-poster beds and sea-grass rugs complete the Lowcountry look. Some of the rooms are in a former 19th-century shipping warehouse with exposed brick walls, plantation shutters, and whirlpool tubs. Afternoon wine and cheese and evening milk and cookies are included. **Pros:** continental breakfast can be delivered to room; service notable; closest hotel to the harbor and Waterfront Park. **Cons:** rooms are off long, modern halls; rooms are not particularly spacious. ⊠*2 Vendue Range, Market area* ☎*843/853–8439 or 888/853–8439* ⊕*www.harbourviewcharleston.com* ⇨*52 rooms* ⌂*In-room: safe, refrigerator, Wi-Fi. In-hotel: Internet terminal, Wi-Fi, parking (paid), no-smoking rooms* ⊟*AE, D, DC, MC, V* ⦿*BP.*

$$–$$$ 📷**Indigo Inn.** A former indigo warehouse in Charleston's colonial times is painted an appealing smoky green. The location is convenient to King Street and to the Market, yet it is solidly quiet, with a parklike, inner courtyard. There you can take your complimentary Hunt Breakfast or the wine and hors d'oeuvres that are set out nightly. All-day beverages, from lemonade to coffee, are available in the petite lobby, which is the meeting ground for guests. The front desk and long-term management of this family-owned hotel are particularly welcoming and helpful; repeat guests are the norm. Rooms are comfy, done in period reproductions, some with four-posters; a couple have desks. The free in-room Wi-Fi is a plus, as is the adjacent parking lot, but there is a $10 fee. **Pros:** location, location; mini-bottles of liquor and good bottles of wine can be purchased from front desk; free local calls. **Cons:** rooms are not large and some are dark; opened in 1981, and rooms are a little dated. ⊠*1 Maiden La. Lower King* ☎*843/577–5900* ⊕*www.indigoinn.com* ⇨*40 rooms* ⌂*In-room: Wi-Fi. In-hotel: Internet terminal, Wi-Fi, parking (paid), some pets allowed, no-smoking rooms* ⊟*AE, D, MC, V* ⦿*BP.*

$$$–$$$$ 📷**Jasmine Inn.** Not as publicized as most downtown properties, this is as close to living in a grand Charleston home as you may ever get without a real estate closing. This 1843 mansion was decorated handsomely when it opened in the 1980s. Walking down the quiet, tree-lined street and coming upon this glorious Greek Revival mansion—yellow with white columns—you simply want in. If indeed, you do decide to stay here, it will be like staying in a friend's home. The housekeeper is there by day, but otherwise this inn shares its front desk, phone system, and parking lot with its sister property, Indigo Inn. The main house has royally large rooms; several, including the Canton Room, which opens to the second-story verandah, has an ante-room called a "card room." The separate carriage-house "dependency," which looks out to a leafy courtyard, has four cozy rooms of its own. **Pros:** complimentary beverages (hot and cold in the kitchen); evening wine and cheese spreads on the sideboard; carriage-house rooms were more recently decorated and are aesthetically more appealing. **Cons:** no on-site Internet or Wi-Fi (though guests can use Indigo Inn's next door); bedding could be more plush. ⊠*64 Hassell St., Lower King* ☎*843/577–5900* ⊕*www.jasminehouseinn.com* ⇨*10 rooms* ⌂ *In-hotel: parking (paid), no kids under 18, no-smoking rooms* ⊟*AE, MC, V* ⦿*BP.*

$$$$
★

▓ **John Rutledge House Inn.** In 1791 George Washington visited this elegant mansion, residence of one of South Carolina's most influential politicians, John Rutledge. This National Historic Landmark has spacious accommodations within the lovingly restored main house (Nos. 6, 8, and 11 are the most appealing). Solid painted walls—in forest green and buttercream yellow—complement the billowy fabrics on the four-poster beds. Parquet floors sit beneath 14-foot ceilings adorned with plaster moldings. Families gravitate to the privacy and quiet of the two carriage houses overlooking the shaded brick courtyard. A scrumptious afternoon tea is served in the former ballroom. Breakfast—continental as well as at least one hot item—can be taken in the ballroom or courtyard. **Pros:** at night, when you "go home" and pour a sherry, it's like being a blue-blood Charlestonian; the building has a New Orleans-esque exterior with its wrought-iron architectural details; nice, quiet back courtyard. **Cons:** the two carriage houses can cost more than the main and are not nearly as grand; you can hear some street and kitchen noise in the first-floor rooms. ✉*116 Broad St., South of Broad* ☎*843/723–7999 or 800/476–9741* ⊕*www.charminginns.com* ⌨*16 rooms, 3 suites* ⚅*In-room: refrigerator, Wi-Fi. In-hotel: Wi-Fi, parking (paid), no-smoking rooms* ▤*AE, D, DC, MC, V* ⦿*BP.*

$$$$
Fodor'sChoice
★

▓ **Market Pavilion Hotel.** The melee of one of the busiest corners in the city vanishes as soon as the uniformed bellman opens the lobby door to dark, wood-paneled walls, antique furniture, and chandeliers hung from high ceilings. It resembles a European grand hotel from the 19th century, and you feel like visiting royalty. Get used to being pampered—smartly attired bellmen and butlers are quick at hand. Rooms are decadent with French-style chaises and magnificent marble baths. One of Charleston's most prestigious fine-dining spots, Grill 225, is here. All guests enjoy delectable refreshments in their respective lounge, with those on the executive 4th floor getting a hot breakfast, afternoon tea, and (good) wine service. **Pros:** opulent furnishings; architecturally impressive, especially the tray ceilings; conveniently located for everything. **Cons:** the building was constructed to withstand hurricane-force winds, which thus far has prohibited Wi-Fi and can limit cell phone reception; those preferring a minimalist decor may find the opulent interior too elaborate. ■**TIP→Join sophisticated Charlestonians who come for cocktails and appetizers at the rooftop Pavilion Bar.** ✉*225 E. Bay St., Market area* ☎*843/723–0500 or 877/440–2250* ⊕*www.marketpavilion.com* ⌨*61 rooms, 9 suites* ⚅*In-room: Internet. In-hotel: restaurant, bar, pool, Internet terminal, no-smoking rooms* ▤*AE, D, DC, MC, V* ⦿*EP.*

$$$–$$$$

▓ **Meeting Street Inn.** This 1874 house with second- and third-story porches originally had a tavern on the ground floor; the nightly wine and cheese reception in the lobby, often with live music, is the reincarnation of a more genteel time. Rooms overlook a lovely courtyard with fountains and a garden; many have hardwood floors and hand-woven rugs. Four-poster or canopy beds, chair rails, and patterned wallpaper create a period feel. Despite its good downtown location, the inn has managed to keeps its prices more affordable than some places. **Pros:** all rooms have free Wi-Fi, and more expensive rooms have desks and a veranda; within the courtyard is a large heated spa tub. **Cons:** rooms have 19th-century style (reproductions) but could use some updated decor; some employees are excellent, while others are somewhat taciturn. ⊠*173 Meeting St., Market area* ☎*843/723–1882 or 800/842–8022* ⊕*www.meetingstreetinn.com* ⚓*56 rooms* ⚐*In-room: refrigerator, Wi-Fi. In-hotel: bar, Wi-Fi, parking (paid), no-smoking rooms* ⊟*AE, D, DC, MC, V* ⎮⊙⎮*BP.*

$$$–$$$$ ⊞**Mills House.** A favorite local landmark, the Mills House is reconstruction of an 1853 hotel where Robert E. Lee once waved from the wrought-iron balcony. All of the guest rooms have been completely refurbished and have nice touches like antique reproductions and a Charleston motif with Oriental accents. There are some additions to the original design, such as a fitness center and a delightful pool and deck. Lowcountry specialties are served in the Barbados Room, which opens onto the terrace courtyard. **Pros:** convenient to business district, historic district, and art galleries; a popular Sunday brunch spot. **Cons:** staffers are too inexperienced for a hotel of this quality; rooms are small, which is typical of hotels of this time period. ⊠*115 Meeting St., Market area* ☎*843/577–2400 or 800/874–9600* ⊕*www.millshouse.com* ⚓*199 rooms, 16 suites* ⚐*In-room: Wi-Fi. In-hotel: restaurant, bar, pool, gym, parking (paid), no-smoking rooms* ⊟*AE, D, DC, MC, V* ⎮⊙⎮*EP.*

$$$$ ⊞**Planters Inn.** Part of the Relais & Châteaux group, this boutique
★ property is a stately sanctuary amid the bustle of Charleston's Market. Light streams into a front parlor with its velvets and Oriental antiques. It serves as the lobby for this exclusive inn that has both an historic side and a new building wrapped around a two-story piazza and overlooking a tranquil garden courtyard. Rooms all look similar and are beautifully maintained, but the main building has more atmosphere and a more residential feel. Service is genteel and unobtrusive but not stuffy, and the hospitality feels genuine. The best rooms have fireplaces, verandas, and four-poster canopy beds; the "piazza" suites with whirlpool baths and top-tier suites are suitably over the top in terms of comfort. Packages that include either breakfast or dinner at the on-site Peninsula Grill are a good value. **Pros:** triple-pane windows render the rooms soundproof; the same front desk people take your initial reservation and know your name upon arrival; the continental and full breakfasts are exceptional. **Cons:** no pool; no fitness center; views are not outstanding. ⊠*112 N. Market St., Market area* ☎*843/722–2345 or 800/845–7082* ⊕*www.plantersinn.com* ⚓*56 rooms, 6 suites* ⚐*In-room: safe, Wi-Fi. In-hotel: restaurant, Wi-Fi, parking (paid), no-smoking rooms* ⊟*AE, D, DC, MC, V* ⎮⊙⎮*EP.*

$$$–$$$$ ⊞**Renaissance Charleston Hotel Historic District.** A sense of history prevails in this hotel, one of Charleston's newest upscale properties. Legend has it that British Admiral George Anson won this neighborhood, now dubbed Ansonborough, in a card game in 1726. (This is why his image is on the playing cards in the library lounge.) The hotel has a delightful courtyard where you can enjoy cocktails. Guest rooms are smallish but have nice touches like period-style bonnet beds. This is one of the few downtown hotels with a pool. The Wentworth Grill serves a mix of French and Lowcountry specialties and is a gem. **Pros:** Built in 2000, the rooms were renovated for the first time in 2008, as was the lobby; located in the King Street shopping district. Cons: Wi-Fi limited to the lobby; rooms have the feel of a chain hotel. ⊠68 *Wentworth St., Ansonborough* ☎843/534–0300 ⊕*www.renaissancecharlestonhotel. com* ⇆163 rooms, 3 suites ⚡In-room: Internet. *In-hotel: restaurant, bar, pool, public Wi-Fi, parking (paid), no-smoking rooms* ▤AE, D, DC, MC, V ⎮○⎮EP.

$$$–$$$$ ★ 🖫**Two Meeting Street.** As pretty as a wedding cake, this Queen Anne mansion has overhanging bays, colonnades, balustrades, and a turret. While rocking on the front porch you can look through soaring arches to White Point Gardens and the Ashley River. Tiffany windows, carved-oak paneling, and a crystal chandelier dress up the public spaces. Some guest rooms have a veranda and working fireplace. Expect to be treated to afternoon high tea as well as a delightful, creative Southern breakfast. Pros: 24-hour free on-street parking; community refrigerator on each floor; ringside seat for a Battery view and horse-drawn carriages clipping by. Cons: not wheelchair-accessible, some rooms have thick walls and make Wi-Fi spotty; small TVs only get local stations (no cable at all). ⊠2 *Meeting St., South of Broad* ☎843/723–7322 ⊕*www.twomeetingstreet.com* ⇆9 rooms ⚡In-room: no phone, safe, Wi-Fi. *In-hotel: no kids under 12, parking (free), no-smoking rooms* ▤No credit cards ⎮○⎮BP.

$$$ $$$$ 🖫**Victoria House Inn.** Victoria has the unique position of being immediately between its two sister properties, the Fulton Lane Inn and the King's Courtyard Inn. Though each is a separate entity with its own staff and personality, all are connected by stairways and similarly priced. These charming, personable siblings were originally a YMCA in the 1850s. Victoria has the Richardson Romanesque style; its ground floor still houses some King Street retail and antiques shops. The inn is a favorite with returnees, who appreciate the personal service from caring concierges. Breakfast is served in the namesake courtyard of King's Courtyard Inn (or indoors with air-conditioning), or breakfast can be brought your room. All guests can use the outdoor Jacuzzi at the King's Courtyard. Wine and cheese service makes every evening a social event. Pros: room decor is a cozy and feminine, with Victorian-style furnishings; some rooms have working fireplaces and whirlpool tubs. Cons: rooms on King Street can pick up some street noise, so chose an interior room like No. 317; bedding could be finer, but there are new cushy mattresses underneath. ⊠208 *King St., Lower King* ☎843/720–2944 or 800/933–5464 ⊕*www.thevictoriahouseinn.com* ⇆27 rooms ⚡In-room: refrigerator, Wi-Fi. *In-hotel: Internet terminal, Wi-Fi, parking (paid), no-smoking rooms* ▤AE, D, MC, V. ⎮○⎮BP.

$$$$ Fodor'sChoice ★ 🖫**Wentworth Mansion.** Charlestonian Francis Silas Rodgers made his money in cotton; in 1886 he commissioned this four-story mansion with such luxuries as Austrian crystal chandeliers and hand-carved marble mantles. Now guests admire the Second Empire antiques and reproductions, the rich fabrics, inset wood paneling, and original stained-glass windows. In the colder months, the baronial, high-ceilinged guest rooms have the velvet drapes drawn and the gas fireplaces lighted. The complimentary evening wine and delectable hors d'oeuvres

are now served in the sunny, glass-enclosed porch. Breakfast, with a new expanded hot menu, has been moved to Circa 1886, the inn's laudable restaurant, which shares the former carriage house with the spa. Pros: luxury bedding, including custom-made mattresses, down pillows, and Italian linens; new carpet and furnishings lend a fresh look. Cons: not child-friendly; Second Empire style can strike some people as foreboding; the building has some of the woes of an old building, including loudly creaking staircases. ⊠ *149 Wentworth St., College of Charleston Campus* ☎843/853–1886 or 888/466–1886 ⊕*www. wentworthmansion.com* ⌁*21 rooms* ⌂*In-room: Internet. In-hotel: restaurant, spa, no-smoking rooms* ⊟*AE, D, DC, MC, V* ⏀*BP.*

MOUNT PLEASANT

$$$–$$$$ 🖼 **Charleston Harbor Resort & Marina.** Mount Pleasant's finest hotel sits on Charleston Harbor, so you can gaze at the city's skyline, yet a water taxi from the marina will get you across the harbor in 10 minutes. A lot goes on here, from splashy boat shows at the marina to wedding celebrations on the man-made white-sand beach. Ask for one of the renovated rooms with fireplaces and plasma TVs. Children can jump into the mini-mariners' program while parents are navigating a sailboat. A number of annual sailing events are held here, and the bar scene is fun. Pros: the most accessible hotel to downtown that's not in downtown (approximately 6 mi away); a "trolley" runs to the Old Market from 10–10 daily; renovations have made a huge difference. Cons: no gym or spa (both are planned at this writing, however); the lobby and the restaurant are not memorable. ⊠*20 Patriots Point Rd., Mount Pleasant* ☎843/856–0028 or 888/856–0028 ⊕*www.charleston-harborresort.com* ⌁*160 rooms, 6 suites* ⌂*In-room: safe (some), refrigerator (some), Wi-Fi. In-hotel: restaurant, bar, pool, water sports, children's programs (ages 7–12), parking (free), no-smoking rooms.* ⊟*AE, DC, MC, V* ⏀*BP.*

$–$$ 🖼 **Old Village Post House.** This white wooden building anchoring Mount Pleasant's historic district is a cozy inn, an excellent restaurant, and a neighborly tavern. Up the high staircase, rooms have hardwood floors and reproduction furnishings that will remind you of Cape Cod. The dark-wood furnishings feel right at home in a building with roots in the 1880s. The food is wonderful, from the pastries at breakfast to the dinners downstairs in the Southern bistro. On Sundays you can order off the brunch menu. Staying in this charming, tree-lined village, you're within walking distance of Charleston Harbor and the nearby fishing community. Pros: unique lodging experience in Mount Pleasant; prices are as affordable as some chain motels on the highway; close to Sullivan's Island and Isle of Palms. Cons: some minor old-building woes including creeky wood floors; not plush and has few cushy creature comforts. ⊠*101 Pitt St., Mount Pleasant* ☎843/388–8935 ⊕*www. oldvillageposthouse.com* ⌁*6 rooms* ⌂*In-room: Wi-Fi. In-hotel: restaurant, bar, parking (free), Wi-Fi, no-smoking rooms* ⊟*AE, D, DC, MC, V* ⏀*BP.*

7

ELSEWHERE IN CHARLESTON

$-$$ ⚏ **Charleston Marriott.** This great river-view hotel was completely trans-formed less than five years ago into a top-notch property. A glamorous glass addition with a cascading waterfall houses the concierge desk. The sunset views from the balconies are better as you go higher and especially good from the classy, rooftop terrace where drinks and tapas are served. The pool area is resort-like, with plenty of palms and a gazebo. The aromas from the brick oven in Saffires are intoxicating, as are the myriad flatbreads it produces. The cuisine is laudable—contemporary dishes with refreshingly flavorful low-calorie options. The new Aqua Terrace, a rooftop lounge, has live jazz nightly. **Pros:** free shuttle downtown until 10:30 PM, concierge floor is excellent and a real added value; located near The Citadel, MUSC, and marinas. **Cons:** not in the historic district; Wi-Fi available but for a hefty charge; concierge floor does not have breakfast on weekends. ⊠ *170 Lockwood Dr., Charleston* ☎ *843/ 723–3000* ⊕ *www.marriott.com* ⬤ *337 rooms, 3 suites ⅄ In-room: safe, refrigerator, Internet, Wi-Fi. In-hotel: restaurant, room service, bar, pool, laundry service, Internet terminal, Wi-Fi, parking (free), no-smoking rooms.* ⊟ *AE, DC, MC, V* ⎮○⎮ *EP.*

$$$-$$$$ ⚏ **Kiawah Island Golf Resort.** Choose from one- to four-bedroom villas
Fodor's Choice   and three- to seven-bedroom private homes in two upscale resort vil-
★   lages on 10,000 wooded and oceanfront acres. The decades-old inn complex is no longer open, but a number of the smaller two-bedroom condo-villas are still fairly affordable. Or you can opt to stay at the Sanctuary at Kiawah Island, an amazing 255-room luxury waterfront hotel and spa. Its vast lobby is stunning, with walnut floors covered with hand-woven rugs and a wonderful collection of artworks. When a pianist plays in the lobby lounge it is dreamlike. The West Indies theme is evident in the guest rooms; bedposts are carved with impressionistic pineapple patterns, and plantation-style ceilings with exposed planks are painted white. The Ocean Room has incredible architectural details—wrought-iron gates and sculptures and a stained-glass dome. Its contemporary cuisine is of an international caliber. Along with the 10 mi of island beaches, recreational options include kayak and surfboard rental, nature tours, and arts-and-crafts classes. **Pros:** one of the most prestigious resorts in the country, it is still kid-friendly; the Ocean Room is an ideal venue for an anniversary or a proposal. **Cons:** not all hotel rooms have even an angular view of the ocean; it is pricey and a substantial drive from town. ⊠ *12 Kiawah Beach Dr., Kiawah Island* ☎ *843/768–2121 or 800/654–2924* ⊕ *www.kiawahresort.com* ⬤ *255 rooms, 600 villas and homes ⅄ In-room: safe (some), refrigerator, Internet, Wi-Fi. In-hotel: 10 restaurants, golf courses, tennis courts, pools, gym, spa, beachfront, water sports, children's programs (ages 3–12), Internet terminal, Wi-Fi, parking (free), no-smoking rooms* ⊟ *AE, D, DC, MC, V* ⎮○⎮ *EP.*

$$-$$$ ⚏ **Seabrook Island.** The most private of the area's island resorts, Seabrook is endowed with true Lowcountry beauty. Wildlife sightings are common: look for white-tailed deer and even bobcats. Going to the beach is as popular as playing golf or tennis, but erosion has whisked away a lot of the sand. About 200 fully equipped one- to six-bedroom

homes are available, but the smallest units are often priced as cheaply as a hotel room. The Beach Club and Island House are centers for dining and leisure activities, and there is a quality equestrian center that is just inside the gates and open to the public. As each villa is individually owned, the Internet capabilities will vary accordingly. **Pros:** physically beautiful, relatively unspoiled island; the pool complex has ocean views and is immediately adjacent to the clubhouse; great safe haven for kids and biking. **Cons:** beach has eroded despite the seawall in front of the club; accommodations consist only of villas, with no regular hotel rooms. ⊠*3772 Seabrook Island Rd., Seabrook Island* ☎*843/768–1000 or 800/845–2233* 🖷*843/768–2361* ⊕*www.seabrook.com* ➪*200 units* ᗷ*In-room: kitchen Internet (some), Wi-Fi (some). In-hotel: 3 restaurants, bar, golf courses, tennis courts, pools, gym, beachfront, water sports, bicycles, children's programs (ages 4–17), parking (free), no-smoking rooms* ☰*AE, D, DC, MC, V* ⊚*EP.*

$$$$ ★ 🖭 **Wild Dunes Resort.** This 1,600-acre island resort has as its focal point the plantation-style Boardwalk Inn. It sits among a cluster of villas that have been painted in pastels to resemble Charleston's Rainbow Row. The guest rooms and suites on the fourth and fifth floors have balconies that overlook the ocean. You can also choose from one- to six-bedroom villas that sit near the sea or the marshes. Guests have a long list of recreational options here, including Tom Fazio golf courses and nationally ranked tennis programs; packages including golf and tennis are available. Nearby is a yacht harbor on the Intracoastal Waterway. Chef Enzo Steffenelli reigns over the highly-rated Sea Island Grill. A new complex, the Village Condos (135 units) opened next to the inn in 2008 and has a family-friendly restaurant serving three meals daily. In the adjacent plaza there are music performances, family bingo, and (in the summer) musicians and jugglers. **Pros:** golf courses and marina are appealing; free shuttle runs from 7 AM to 11 PM to wherever you need to go within the complex. **Cons:** in peak summer season the number of kids in the pool areas and the boardwalk is high indeed; a congested, high-density feel in all the main facilities. ⊠*Palm Blvd. at 41st Ave., Isle of Palms* 🖃*Box 20575, Charleston 29413* ☎*843/886–6000 or 888/845–8926* ⊕*www.wilddunes.com* ➪*560 units, 93 rooms* ᗷ*In-room: safe, refrigerator (some), Internet, Wi-Fi. In-hotel: 3 restaurants, golf courses, tennis courts, pools, gym, water sports, bicycles, Internet terminal, Wi-Fi, children's programs (ages 3–12), parking (free) no-smoking rooms* ☰*AE, D, DC, MC, V* ⊚*EP.*

SPORTS & THE OUTDOORS

BASEBALL

The **Charleston Riverdogs** (⊠*Joseph P. Riley, Jr. Stadium, 360-Fishburne St.* ☎*843/577–3647* ⊕*www.riverdogs.com*) play at "The Joe," on the banks of the Ashley River near to the Citadel. Kids love their mascot, Charlie T. Riverdog. After games, fireworks often illuminate the summer sky in this all-American pastime. With "Fun is Good" as their motto, they have theme nights which attract various audiences. The season runs from April through September. Tickets cost a reasonable $7 to $12.

BEACHES

The Charleston area's mild climate means you can swim from March through October. Public beaches, operated by the Charleston County Parks & Recreation Commission, generally have lifeguards in season, snack bars, restrooms and dressing areas, outdoor showers, umbrella and chair rental, and large parking lots. The resorts on Kiawah Island have all the extras like beach umbrellas, etc. Some will allow you to park on-site and use their facilities for a fee.

Trees, palmettos, and other natural foliage cover the interior, and there's a river that winds through **Folly Beach County Park.** The beach, 12 mi southwest of Charleston, is more than six football fields long. ✉*1100 W. Ashley Ave., off U.S. 17, Folly Island* ☎*843/588–2426* ⊕*www. ccprc.com* ✍*$10 per car* ☉*Apr., Sept., and Oct., daily 10–6; May–Aug., daily 9–7; Nov.–Mar., daily 10–5.* Play beach volleyball or rent a raft at the 600-foot-long beach in the **Isle of Palms County Park.** ✉*1 14th Ave., Isle of Palms, Mount Pleasant* ☎*843/886–3863 or 843/768–4386* ⊕*www.ccprc.com* ✍*$10 per car* ☉*May–Aug., daily 9–7; Apr., Sept., and Oct., daily 10–6; Nov.–Mar., daily 10–5.* The public **Kiawah Beachwalker Park,** about 28 mi southwest of Charleston, has 500 feet of deep beach. ✉*Beachwalker Dr., Kiawah Island* ☎*843/768–2395* ⊕*www.ccprc.com* ✍*$10 per car* ☉*Mar., weekends 10–5; Apr. and Oct., weekends 10–6; May–Aug., daily 10–7; Sept., daily 10–6.*

BIKING

The historic district is ideal for bicycling as long as you stay off the busier roads. Many of the city's green spaces, including Colonial Lake and Palmetto Islands County Park, have biking trails. If you want to rent a bike, expect to pay about $15 for a half-day (three hours), and $25 for a full day.

BTB Bike Rentals (✉*6 Vendue Range, Market area* ☎*843/853–2453* ⊕*www.bicyclecharleston.com*) can set you up to ride the paths on the spectacular Arthur Ravenel, Jr. Bridge. You'll get a map, a self-guided tour booklet, and free water-taxi ride back. You can also rent comfort bikes, road bikes, tandems for 2, unicycles, jogging strollers, and tag-alongs. You can rent bikes at the **Bicycle Shoppe** (✉*280 Meeting St., Market area* ☎*843/722–8168* ✉*1539 Johnnie Dodds Blvd., Mount Pleasant* ☎*843/884–7433).* **Island Bike and Surf Shop** (✉*3665 Bohicket Rd., John's Island* ☎*843/768–1158*) rents island cruisers (beach bikes) for a very moderate weekly rate $34.95. The shop will even deliver to Kiawah and Seabrook Islands. If you just want a bike for a day or two ($12.90 per day), you have to pick it up and return it.

BOATING

Kayak through isolated marsh rivers and estuaries to outlying islands, or explore Cape Romain National Wildlife Refuge. Rates vary of course, depending on location and if you take a guided tour. Typically you can expect to pay $35 a person in a single or double kayak for a two-hour guided tour. Rentals can be $12 a person per hour. Weekly rentals are about $150 a week. The resort islands, especially Kiawah and Wild Dunes, tend to be higher.

If you want a sailing or motor yacht charter, perhaps a beach barbecue, or ecotour, or just to go offshore fishing, contact **AquaSafaris** (⊠ *Patriots Point Marina, Mount Pleasant* ☎ *843/886–8133* ⊕ *www.aqua-safaris. com*). Check the Web site, because prices vary depending on vessel size, be it the catamaran or an offshore fishing trip. Outings for individuals, families, and groups are provided by **Coastal Expeditions** (⊠ *514B Mill St., Mount Pleasant* ☎ *843/884–7684*). **Island Bike & Surf Shop** (⊠ *3665 Bohicket Rd., John's Island* ☎ *843/768–1158*) rents surfboards and kayaks and will deliver to the resort islands. Boards cost $15 a day. You can rent kayaks from **Middleton Place Plantation** (⊠ *4300 Ashley River Rd., West Ashley* ☎ *843/556–6020* ⊕ *www.theinnatmiddletonplace. com*) and glide along the Ashley River. Do make advance reservations. Take your family sailing, be at the helm, and learn how to command your own 26-foot sailboat on Charleston's beautiful harbor with the guidance of an instructor at **Ocean Sailing Academy** (⊠ *24 Patriots Point Rd., Mount Pleasant* ☎ *843/971–0700* ⊕ *osasailing.com*).

7

FISHING

For inshore (saltwater) fly-fishing, guides generally charge $350 (for two people) for a half-day, $450 for an hour more. Deep-sea fishing charters cost about $1,400 for 12 hours for a boatload of anglers.

Bohicket Marina (⊠ *1880 Andell Bluff Blvd., John's Island* ☎ *843/768– 1280* ⊕ *www.bohicket.com*) has half- and full-day charters on 24- to 48-foot boats. For inshore fishing, expect to pay about $395 for 3 hours minimum (4 to 6 people), including bait, tackle, and licenses. Saltwater fly-fishers looking for an Orvis-endorsed guide do best by calling **Captain Richard Stuhr** (⊠ *547 Sanders Farm La., North Charleston* ☎ *843/881–3179* ⊕ *www.captstuhr.com*), who has been fishing the waters of Charleston, Kiawah, and Isle of Palms since 1991; he'll haul his boat, a 19-foot Action Craft, to you. **Palmetto Charters** (⊠ *224 Patriots Point Rd., Mount Pleasant* ☎ *843/849–6004*) has guided trips that take you out in the ocean or stay close to shore. They also handle power yacht charters, crewed sailboat charters, and bareboats, both locally and in the Caribbean. There is a litany of prices, from the luxury category on down.

GOLF

With fewer golfers than in Hilton Head, the courses around Charleston have more choice starting times available. Nonguests can play at private island resorts, such as Kiawah Island, Seabrook Island, and Wild Dunes. There you will find breathtaking ocean views within a pristine setting. They offer enchantment and escape from the stresses of the workaday world. Don't be surprised if a white-tailed deer is grazing a green or if there is a gator drinking from the water holes. For the top courses like Kiawah's Ocean Course, nonguests can expect to pay $240 to $350 (peak season spring and early fall).Municipal golf courses are a golfing bargain, from $29 to $37 for 18 holes. Somewhere in between are the Shadowmoss Golf Club, West of the Ashley for $45 to $86, and The Links at Stono Ferry in Hollywood for $45 to $86.

The public **Charleston Municipal Golf Course** (⊠ *2110 Maybank Hwy., James Island* ☎*843/795–6517)* is a walker-friendly course. Green fees run $29 to $37. The **Dunes West Golf Club** (⊠*3535 Wando Plantation Way, Mount Pleasant* ☎*843/856–9000)* has great marshland views and lots of modulation on the greens. Green fees are $45 to $92. There are three championship courses at **Kiawah Island Resort** (⊠*12 Kiawah Beach Dr., Kiawah Island* ☎*800/576–1570)*: Gary Player–designed Marsh Point; Tom Fazio–designed Osprey Point; and Jack Nicklaus–designed Turtle Point. All three charge the same greens fees: $175 for resort guests, $219 for nonguests. **Links at Stono Ferry** (⊠*4812 Stono Links Dr., Hollywood* ☎*843/763–1817)* is a popular public course with reasonable rates. Green fees are $45 to $86. The prestigious **Ocean Course** (⊠*1000 Ocean Course Dr., Kiawah Island* ☎*843/266-4670),* designed by Pete Dye, was the site of the 1991 Ryder Cup. Unfortunately, its fame translates to green fees of $298 for resort guests, $350 for nonguests. (It is a walking-only facility until noon.) **Seabrook Island Resort** (⊠*Seabrook Island Rd., Seabrook Island* ☎*843/768–2529)* has two championship courses: Crooked Oaks, by Robert Trent Jones Sr., and Ocean Winds, by Willard Byrd. Green fees are $95 to $150. **Shadowmoss Golf Club** (⊠*20 Dunvegan Dr., West Ashley* ☎*843/556–8251)* is a well-marked, forgiving course with one of the best finishing holes in the area. **Green fees are $28** to **$52.** Tom Fazio designed the Links and the Harbor courses at **Wild Dunes Resort** (⊠*10001 Back Bay Dr., Isle of Palms* ☎*843/886–2180* ⊠*5881 Palmetto Dr., Isle of Palms* ☎*843/886–2301).* Green fees are $140 to $165.

HORSEBACK RIDING

★ Put your foot in the stirrup and get a leg up! You will love seeing the beaches, maritime forests, marshlands, and former rice fields from horseback. Several good stables in the area offer trail rides, and there are also equestrian centers, lessons, and jumping rings, which you can also enjoy. Trail rides average from $40 for wooded terrain to $85 for an advanced beach ride; they go out for about an hour.

Middleton Equestrian Center (⊠*4280 Ashley River Rd., West Ashley* ☎*843/556–8137* ⊕*www.middletonplace.org)* is a long-established stable that specializes in English riding lessons. It now offers trail rides through wooded and open terrain and former rice fields. All experience levels are welcome, and headgear is provided. The price is $40 for the trail, but only children 10 and older can ride. **Seabrook Island Equestrian Center** (✉ *Seabrook Island Rd., Seabrook Island* ☎ 843/768–7541 www.discoverseabrook.com) is open to the public. The center, 24 miles south of Charleston, has trail rides through the maritime forests, for $65 (children must be eight years old and up) and beach rides for advanced riders for $85, for 45 minutes to an hour. About 7 mi south of Charleston, **Stono River Stables & Farms** (✉ *2962 Hut Rd., John's Island* ☎ *843/559–0773* ⊕ *www.stonoriverstable.com*) is a well-established and caring school/stable that offers trail rides through 300 acres of maritime forests, with excellent instructors and guides. It employs the only farm manager in the state who is a member of Phi Beta Kappa. Rides must be arranged in advance, and it is $55 an hour; mainly English saddles are used. It is about 7 mi from Kiawah and Seabrook Islands. Non-riders can walk the nature trails for $15 a day.

SPAS

Charleston Place Spa (✉ *130 Market St., Market area* ☎ 843/722–4900 ⊕ *www.charlestonplacespa.com*), a truly deluxe day spa, has nine treatment rooms and a wet room where seaweed body wraps and other treatments are administered. Four-handed massages for couples are a popular option. Locker rooms for men and women have showers and saunas; men also have a steam room. Adjacent is a fitness room, an indoor pool with skylights, and a spacious hot tub. In a historic Charleston "single house," **Stella Nova** (✉ *78 Society St., Lower King* ☎ *843/723–0909* ⊕ *www.stella-nova.com*) is just off King Street. It's serious about all of its treatments, from waxing to salt scrubs. For couples, there are aromatherapy massages and men's services, too. You enjoy refreshments on the breezy verandas and it is open daily, even on Sunday, when street parking is easier to find.

TENNIS

Whether your interest in tennis is casual or serious, the Charleston area, especially its resort islands, offers tennis options for every level of play. Spring and fall are simply ideal for play. You can play for free at neighborhood courts, including several near Colonial Lake and at the Isle of Palms Recreation Center. If you want the privilege of playing where stars like the Williams sisters compete, at the Family Circle Tennis Center, the cost is $15 per hour for a clay court, and $10 per hour for a hard court. The resort islands are the most costly, depending on whether you are a guest or not.

The women's tennis Family Circle Cup is hosted each April at the **Family Circle Tennis Center** (✉ *161 Seven Farms Dr., Daniel Island* ☎ *843/534–2400* ⊕ *www.familycirclecup.com*). The 17 lighted courts (13 clay, four hard) are open to the public. A signature event for women's tennis, this annual tourney has brought in the sport's top names.

WATER SPORTS

Island Bike and Surf Shop (✉ *3665 Bohicket Rd., John's Island* ☎ *843/768–1158* rents surfboards, shredders, and kayaks and will deliver to the resort islands. Boards cost $15 a day. The pros at **McKevlin's Surf Shop** (✉ *8 Center St., Folly Beach* ☎ *843/588–2247*) can teach you what you need to know about surfing at Folly Beach County Park. Surfboard rentals and instruction can be arranged. **Sun & Ski** (✉ *1 Cedar St., Folly Beach* ☎ *843/588–0033*) rents Jet Skis off the beach, just to the left of the fishing pier. You can also rent a chair and umbrella here for five hours for $20.

NIGHTLIFE & THE ARTS

THE ARTS

CONCERTS
The **Charleston Symphony Orchestra** (☎ *843/723–7528* ⊕ *www.charlestonsymphony.com*) season runs from October through April, with pops series, chamber series, family-oriented series, and holiday concerts. This symphony is nationally and even internationally renown, as it is also the Spoleto Festival Orchestra.

VENUES
Bluegrass, blues, and country musicians step onto the historic stage of **Charleston Music Hall** (✉ *37 John St., Upper King* ☎ *843/853–2252* ⊕ *www.charlestonmusichall.com*)especially for Piccolo Spoleto performances. **Gaillard Municipal Auditorium** (✉ *77 Calhoun St., Upper King* ☎ *843/577–7400*) hosts symphony and ballet companies, as well as numerous festival events. The box office is open weekdays from 10 to 6. Dance, symphony, and theater productions are among those staged at the **North Charleston Performing Art Center** (✉ *5001 Coliseum Dr., North Charleston* ☎ *843/529–5050* ⊕ *www.coliseumpac.com*). Performances by the College of Charleston's theater department and music recitals are presented during the school year at the **Simons Center for the Arts** (✉ *54 St. Phillips St., College of Charleston Campus* ☎ *843/953–5604*).

NIGHTLIFE

You can find it all here, across the board, for Charleston loves a good party. The more mature crowd goes to the sophisticated spots, and there are many: piano bars, wine bars, lounges featuring jazz groups or a guitarist/vocalist, rooftop bars, and cigar lounges. Many restaurants have live entertainment on at least one weekend night or every night. But Charleston is also a college town, and the College of Charleston students line up to get into the latest in-spot, which is usually located in the Market area. ⚠ **A city ordinance mandates that bars must close by 2 AM and that patrons must be out of the establishment and doors locked by that hour.**

CLOSE UP

Celebrating Charleston

Spoleto USA is only the beginning—there are dozens of festivals held throughout the city each year. Some focus on food and wine, whereas others are concerned with gardens and architecture. Charleston is one of the few American cities that can claim a distinctive regional cuisine. The **BB&T Charleston Food + Wine Festival** (☎ 843/763–0280 or 866/369–3378 ⊕ www.charlestonfoodandwine.com) allows the city to "strut its stuff" at an annual festival in Marion Square in early March. Some of the most sought-after events sell out early, such as the Restaurant Dine-Around with celebrity chefs, and the Saturday Night Celebration with incredible food stations and live music. Cooking demonstrations under the big tent give guests an opportunity to learn from some of the country's finest chefs.The **Fall Tours of Homes and Gardens** (☎ 843/722–4630 ⊕ www. preservationsociety.org), sponsored by the Preservation Society of Charleston in September and October, provides an inside look at Charleston's private buildings and gardens. More than 100 private homes, gardens, and historic churches are open to the public for tours during the **Festival of Houses and Gardens** (☎ 843/722–3405 ⊕ www.historiccharleston.org), held during March and April each year. There are also symphony galas in stately drawing rooms, plantation oyster roasts, and candlelight tours. **Piccolo Spoleto** (☎ 843/724–7305 ⊕ www.piccolospoleto.org) is the spirited companion festival of Spoleto Festival USA, showcasing the best in local and regional talent from every artistic discipline. There are hundreds of events—from jazz performances to puppet shows and expansive art shows in Marion Square—from mid-May through early June, and many of the performances are free.

7

BARS & BREWERIES

Club Habana (✉ 177 Meeting St., Market area ☎ 843/853–5900) is a chic martini and cognac bar upstairs and a shop for cigar aficionados downstairs. Adjacent rooms of dark hardwood are dimly lit, furnished with sectional sofas in an intimate (at-home) ambience. This is the only establishment in town where you can still smoke inside the club. Atop the Market Pavilion Hotel, the outdoor **Pavilion Bar** (✉ 225 E. Bay St., Market area ☎ 843/266–4218 offers panoramic views of the city and harbor. Sit at the east overlook to appreciate the grand architecture of the Customs House. Enjoy appetizers, delicacies created with lobster and duck and such, with a signature martini. This can be your beginning before dining downstairs at the hotel's famous Grill 225. Or you can make a night of it here, and be soothed by the sounds of the cascading pool. Inevitably, you will meet new sophisticated friends. This is Charleston's best rooftop bar. **Social Restaurant & Wine Bar** (✉ 188 E. Bay St., Market area ☎ 843/577–5665) offers 60 wines by the glass, as well as bottles and flights (to better compare and contrast several wines in smaller portions). Light menu choices are available, and there are pizzas and flavorful microbrews, too. **Southend Brewery** (✉ 161 E. Bay St., Market area ☎ 843/853–4677) has a lively bar serving beer brewed on the premises; try the wood-oven pizzas and the smokehouse

Fodor's Choice

barbecue. Thursday is salsa night, Friday showcases a bluegrass band, and Saturday night a guitarist. You can dance if the music moves you. In fact, it is encouraged.

DANCE CLUBS

There's a see-and-be-seen crowd at **City Bar** (⊠*5 Faber St., Market area* ☎*843/577–7383*). This club frequently promotes theme parties, special groups, and contests in a fun and creative format. The throbbing dance beat of DJ Amos draws the crowds at **Club Light** (⊠*213C E. Bay St., Market area* ☎*843/722–1311*), a lively and lighthearted part of downtown's single scene. Only open Thursday through Saturday nights, there is a cover charge after 11 PM. You can stick around 'til last call. Thursday is Latin Night at the **Trio Club** (⊠*139 Calhoun St., Upper King* ☎*843/965–5333*), where funky 1970s and '80s sounds are perennially popular. This dance club starts late and runs hard until closing. Live music keeps this fashionable clientele moving. Although populated mainly by the young, it is one dance club frequented by all ages, but it's open only from Thursday through Saturday.

DINNER CRUISES

Dine and dance the night away aboard the wide-beamed motor yacht **Spirit of Carolina** (☎*843/881–7337* ⊕*www.spiritlinecruises.com*). *Dinner is generally aged beef tenderloin or crab cakes. The dance band appeals to an older crowd, but for all ages it is nice to be out on the water, hold your partner close, and see the lights of the harbor by night. There's also a cash bar.* ■TIP➔ Remember that reservations are essential for evening cruises.

JAZZ CLUBS

★ The elegant **Charleston Grill** (⊠*Charleston Place Hotel, 224 King St., Market area* ☎*843/577–4522*) has live jazz nightly and draws a mature, upscale clientele, hotel guests, and more recently an urbane thirtysomething crowd. Those who want to stare into each others eyes choose either a high cocktail table or a comfy chair in the lounge in front of the musicians. Make a reservation for dinner, or you can have something at the classy, sophisticated bar. At **Mistral** (⊠*99 S. Market St., Market area* ☎*843/722–5709*) live blues and jazz make patrons feel good on Monday, Tuesday, Thursday, and Saturday nights. On Wednesday two French musicians sing their renditions of pop and folk songs. On Friday a Dixieland band really animates those who grew up with this music. During Spoleto, fabulous groups like a Brazilian combo electrify the room. Mistral's French onion soup is fabulous if you want a late-night refuel.

LIVE MUSIC

Mercato (⊠*102 N. Market St., Market area* ☎*843/722–6393*) is a popular restaurant that has become almost as well known for its entertainment, which begins on Wednesday nights (from 7 to 10), when there is customarily a jazz vocalist. The music usually cranks up from Thursday to Saturday at 8 and goes until 11. At this writing, there's a gypsy swing band on Thursday, a jazz trio on Friday, and a Cuban fusion band on Saturday night. There is no cover, but come early to get a seat at the

CLOSE UP

Spoleto Festival USA

For 17 glorious days in late May and early June, Charleston gets a dose of culture from the **Spoleto Festival USA** (☎ *843/722–2764* ⊕ *www. spoletousa.org*). This internationally acclaimed performing-arts festival features a mix of distinguished artists and emerging talent from around the world. Performances take place in magical settings, such as beneath a canopy of ancient oaks or inside a centuries-old cathedral. Everywhere you turn, the city's music halls, auditoriums, theaters, and outdoor spaces (including the Cistern at the College of Charleston) are filled with the world's best in opera, music, dance, and theater.

Because events sell out quickly, insiders say you should buy your Spoleto tickets several months in advance. (Tickets to mid-week performances are a bit easier to secure.) Hotels definitely fill up quickly, so book a room at the same time and reserve your tables for our trendy downtown restaurants. You may not be able to get in if you wait until the last minute.

long, elegant bar. All ages come, though most are youngish. **The Thoroughbred Club** (⊠ Charleston Place Hotel, *130 Market St., Market area* ☎ *843/722–4900*) is both fun and classy, with a horse-racing theme and excellent appetizer menu. Go for the impressive afternoon tea (even with alcoholic libations), or sip a cocktail and enjoy the soothing piano being played Monday through Saturday after 1 PM (or Sunday after 5). Each of the pianists has a different repertoire, so depending on the song requests, they can infect the patrons with a wonderful spirit and camaraderie. Listen to authentic Irish music at **Tommy Condon's** (⊠ *15 Beaufain St., Market area* ☎ *843/577–3818*).

SHOPPING

SHOPPING DISTRICTS

The Market area is a cluster of shops and restaurants centered around the **Old City Market** (⊠ *E. Bay and Market Sts., Market area*). Sweetgrass basket weavers work here and you can buy the resulting wares, although these artisan crafts have become expensive. The shops run the gamut, from inexpensive stores selling T-shirts and souvenirs to upscale boutiques catering to the sophisticated tourist. In the covered, open-air market vendors have stalls with everything from jewelry to dresses and purses. **King Street** is the major shopping street in town. Lower King (from Broad to Market streets) is lined with high-end antiques dealers. Middle King (from Market to Calhoun streets) is a mix of national chains like Banana Republic and Pottery Barn. Upper King (from Calhoun Street to Cannon Street) is the up-and-coming area where fashionistas like the alternative shops such as Putumayo. That area has been dubbed the Design District as well, for the furniture and interior-design stores selling home fashion. Some are minimalist contemporary, others carry Euro-antiques, and they all will ship.

Fodor'sChoice

SPECIALTY STORES

ANTIQUES

Birlant & Co. (⊠*191 King St., Lower King* ☎*843/722–3842*) mostly carries 18th- and 19th-century English antiques, but keep your eye out for a Charleston Battery bench, for which they are famous. **English Rose Antiques** (⊠*436 King St., Upper King* ☎*843/722–7939*) has country-style accessories at some of the best prices on the Peninsula. **Haute Design** (⊠*489 King St., Upper King* ☎*843/577–9886*) sells antiques, chandeliers, and French and Italian furniture, as well as custom-designed pieces like tables and mirrors. Belgian linen and hand-screen-printed fabrics are a specialty, and available accessories include Vinnini blown glass and "antique" pillows. Interior design services are available. If you don't live locally, they will ship your treasures. The **King Street Antique Mall** (⊠*495 King St., Upper King* ☎*843/723–2211*) is part flea market, part antiques store.

ART GALLERIES

The downtown neighborhood known as the French Quarter, named after the founding French Huguenots, has become a destination for art lovers. The French Quarter Gallery Association consists of roughly 30 art galleries within the original walled city. Galleries here host a delightful art walk, with wine and some refreshments, from 5 to 8 PM on the first Friday in March, May, October, and December.

Serious art collectors head to **Ann Long Fine Art** (⊠*12 State St., Market area* ☎*843/577–0447*) for neoclassical and modern works. **Charles II Gallery** (⊠*2 Queen St., Market area* ☎*843/577–7101*) is a contemporary gallery featuring international and regional artists. It holds the city's exclusive outlet for the work of Belgian artist Fred Jamar, known for his "bubble-tree" Charleston cityscapes. The **Charleston Renaissance Gallery** (⊠*103 Church St., South of Broad* ☎*843/723–0025*) carries museum-quality Southern art. **Ellis-Nicholson Gallery** (⊠*1.5 Broad St., South of Broad* ☎*843/722–5353*) showcases artists and sculptors who span many levels, from emerging artists to those with international recognition. It has a premier selection of oils, acrylics, mixed media, bronze,

★ clay, glass, and handcrafted jewelry. The **Eva Carter Gallery** (⊠*132 E. Bay St., Market area* ☎*843/722–0506*) displays the most recognized abstract paintings in the area of owner Eva Carter, and abstract works by the late William Halsey. **Horton Hayes Fine Art** (⊠*30 State St., Market area* ☎*843/958–0014*) carries the sought-after Lowcountry paintings depicting coastal life by Mark Kelvin Horton, who paints architectural and figurative works as well. Shannon Rundquist is among the other Lowcountry artists shown; she has a fun, whimsical way of painting

Fodor's Choice local life and is known for her blue crab art. The **Martin Gallery** (⊠*18 Broad St., South of Broad* ☎*843/723–7378*), in a former bank building, is the city's most impressive gallery, selling art by nationally and internationally acclaimed artists, sculptors, and photographers. The gallery is known especially for its bronzes and large wooden sculptures, as well as glass sculpture and custom-designed jewelry. **Smith-Killian Fine Art** (⊠*9 Queen St., Market area* ☎*843/853–0708*) exhibits the contemporary paintings of Lowcountry-scapes by Betty Smith and her talented triplets Jennifer, Shannon, and Tripp. Her son is a nature photographer specializing in black-and-white images. **Wells Gallery** (⊠*125 Meeting St., Market area* ☎*843/853–3233*) has relocated to a new, larger location. Stop by to see the glass floor panel that reveals an underground cistern found during the renovation of the building. Wells showcases the talents of many fine artists, their Lowcountry-scapes, still-lifes, black-and-white photographs, and hand-blown glass vases.

CLOTHING

Charleston's own **Ben Silver** (⊠*149 King St., Lower King* ☎*843/577–4556*), premier purveyor of blazer buttons, has more than 800 designs, including college and British regimental motifs. He also sells British neckties, embroidered polo shirts, and blazers.Need a ball gown? **Berlins** (⊠*114 King St., Lower King* ☎*843/723–5591*) is the place for designer outfits. **Christian Michi** (⊠*220 King St., Market area* ☎*843/723–0575*) carries chichi women's clothing and accessories. Designers from Italy, such as Piazza Sempione and Bella Harari, are represented. High-end fragrances add to the luxurious air. Shop **Copper Penny** (⊠*311 King St., Market area* ☎*843/723–2999*) for trendy dresses and names like Trina Turk and Nanette Lepore. Boutique favorite **Finicky Filly** (⊠*303 King St., Lower King* ☎*843/534–0203*) carries exceptional women's apparel and accessories by such designers as Lela Rose, Molly B., and Etro. **The Trunk Show** (⊠*281 Meeting St., Market area* ☎*843/722–0442*) is an upscale consignment shop selling designer dresses, handbags and shoes, and vintage apparel. The back room is all about interior design. The shop has become known for its estate jewelry and also custom-made jewelry from semiprecious stones. It has an excellent selection of gowns and evening wear. Many items now come in new from other shops.

FOODSTUFFS

Charleston Candy Kitchen (⊠*32A N. Market St., Market area* ☎*843/723–4626*) sells freshly made fudge, Charleston chews, and sesame-seed wafers. Make time to stop at **Market Street Sweets** (⊠*100 N. Market St., Market area* ☎*843/722–1397*) for the melt-in-your-mouth pralines and fudge.

FURNITURE

Carolina Lanterns (⊠*917 Houston Northcutt Blvd., Mount Pleasant* ☎*843/881–4170* ⊕*www.carolinalanterns.com*) sells gas lanterns based on designs from downtown's historic district. **Historic Charleston Reproductions** (⊠*105 Broad St., South of Broad* ☎*843/723–8292*) has superb replicas of Charleston furniture and accessories, all authorized by the Historic Charleston Foundation. Royalties from sales contribute to restoration projects.At the **Old Charleston Joggling Board Co.** (⊠*652 King St., Upper King* ☎*843/723–4331*) these Lowcountry oddities (on which people bounce) are for sale.

GIFTS

Charleston Cooks/ Maverick Kitchen Store (⊠*194 E. Bay St., Market area* ☎*843/722–1212*) carries just about any gourmet kitchen tool or accessory you can think of. Regional food, cookbooks, and culinary gifts abound. And you can also enjoy cooking classes and demonstrations. If you want to learn to cook, the store focuses on Lowcountry cuisine by day and has a litany of other classes in the evening. You get to taste what is prepared, with wine as a complement. Gift certificates are offered, too. **ESD** (⊠*314 King St., Lower King* ☎*843/577–6272*) is a top local interior-design firm, and the company's King Street shop sells coffee-table books, jewelry, and pillows. **Indigo** (⊠*4 Vendue Range, Market area* ☎*843/723–2983*) stocks funky home and garden accessories. Artsy and hip baby gear, housewarming gifts, jewelry, books, and even office supplies make the mundane fun at **Worthwhile** (⊠*268 King St., Market area* ☎*843/723–4418*).

JEWELRY

Dixie Dunbar Jewelry (⊠*192 King St., Lower King* ☎*843/722–0006* deals in artisitic, unique jewelry. The hand-made pieces here can be delightfully unpredictable.

SHOES & ACCESSORIES

Bob Ellis (⊠*332 King St., Lower King* ☎*843/722–2515*) sells shoes from Dolce & Gabbana, Prada, and Manolo Blahnik, among other high-end designers. **Dona Hay Store** (⊠*160 E. Bay St., Market area* ☎*843/723–1400*) is a must-see store for the handbag connoisseur and the most-visited destination in the city for high-end bags. With something for any and every occasion to complement every fashion, Italian leather bags are a specialty. **Farushga** (⊠*337-A King St., Lower King* ☎*843/722–3131*) sells high-quality, cutting-edge Italian shoes for both men and women, from chic daytime looks to pulling-out-all-the-stops evening glamour. But the real beauty of Farushga is that you will not find the same fine brands sold at every other upscale Italian shoe stores. Husband and wife team Massimo and Eva specialize in those sold mainly in Europe, and thanks to their Italian connections, their prices are much lower than one would expect for hand-made Italian shoes. Be warned, this boutique carries only one pair per size for every style, so if you see something you like, you may want to buy it on the spot. **Magar Hatworks** (⊠*57 Cannon St., Upper King* ☎*843/577–7740*) sells handcrafted headgear. This young designer/millener has withstood the test of some time now and has introduced her love of hats to the young and fashionable. Her wholesale business includes sales to Barneys New York, and she has received national attention. She has relocated into a single house in a residential neighborhood, and will be hosting tea parties, too. **Mary Norton's** (⊠*316 King St., Lower King* ☎*843/534–2233*), formerly Moo Roo, has now gone big-time. This young Charleston mother has started handcrafting purses in her home. She also sells celebrity-made handbags and shoes to complement them, as well as a line of jewelry and scarves.

SIDE TRIPS FROM CHARLESTON

Gardens, parks, and the charming town of Summerville are good reasons to travel a bit farther afield for day trips. As Charleston and the surrounding suburbs—particularly Mount Pleasant—grow up, it is good to know that Southern country towns still exist close to Charleston. Sit out on that screen porch after some Southern home cooking, paddle around a haunting cypress swamp, and tell preternatural stories, the kind that Southern children are raised on. If the closest you have ever been to an abbey is watching *The Sound of Music,* you can visit Mepkin Abbey and see the purity of the simple religious life. If an overnight at the stellar Woodlands is out of your budget range, go for a memorable fine-dining experience; Sunday brunch there is both celebratory and more affordable. Drive the tars and gravel and let the towering pines shade you. Turn off the a/c and breath in the fresh air. This is a more genuine part of South Carolina.

SUMMERVILLE

25 mi northwest of Charleston via I–26 and Rte. 165.

Victorian homes, many of which are listed on the National Register of Historic Places, line the public park. Colorful gardens brimming with camellias, azaleas, and wisteria abound. Downtown and residential streets curve around tall pines, as a local ordinance prohibits cutting them down. Visit for a stroll in the park, or to go antiquing on the downtown shopping square. Summerville was originally built by wealthy planters. It has become a town that is being populated with young, professional families and well-to-do retirees transplanted from the cold climes. It has an artsy bent to it, and some trendy eateries have opened. The presence of the revered resort the Woodlands adds a lot to the genteel, aristocratic ambience.

For more information about Summerville, stop by the **Greater Summerville/Dorchester County Chamber of Commerce and Visitor Center** (✉ *402 N. Main St.* ☎ *843/873–2931* ⊕ *www.summervilletourism.com*).

WHERE TO STAY

$$$$ 🖳 **Woodlands Resort & Inn.** With the distinct feel of an English coun-
Fodor's Choice try estate, this Relais & Châteaux property has individually decorated
★ rooms with nice touches like Frette linens. This 1906 Greek Revival-style inn completed a much-needed, major refurbishment of its interior and all of its guest rooms. A new casual dining option was created, too. The service and quality of the accommodations are exceptional, and the restaurant ($$$$) is one of the finest in this part of the country. Talented young chef Tarver King continues to prove himself with every challenging, multicourse tasting menu. Diners can also choose from the à la carte menu. Sunday brunch is locally popular, too, but there is no Sunday dinner. The wine events, cooking demonstrations, and tastings are well worth doing. Wine pairings by long-standing sommelier Stéphane Peltier are perfection. **Pros:** a country retreat excellent for de-stressing; well-geared for weddings and honeymoons; luxurious bedding and electronic blinds (with drapes) make it ideal for sleeping. **Cons:** far (45 minutes) from downtown Charleston, so not a good base for exploring the city; not near any beaches; very traditional style might feel stuffy to some. ✉ *125 Parsons Rd.* ☎ *843/875–2600 or 800/774–9999* ⊕ *www.woodlandsinn.com* ⌨ *10 rooms, 9 suites* ⌂ *In-room: safe, DVD, Wi-Fi. In-hotel: restaurant, tennis courts, pool, spa, bicycles, parking (free), some pets allowed, no-smoking rooms* ⊟ *AE, D, DC, MC, V* ⏧ *EP.*

Hilton Head, SC & the Lowcountry

WORD OF MOUTH

"Fripp, especially at south end, has a wide beach. During high tide north beach disappears. Fripp can be traversed on foot in about 30 minutes, if the marsh deer get out of your way. They're everywhere. Enjoy."

—Lex1

"[A] visit to Beaufort would . . . be a really nice addition to your stay. It's smaller and really manageable but quite lovely."

—cpdl

By Eileen
Robinson
Smith

THE ACTION-PACKED ISLAND OF HILTON Head anchors the southern tip of South Carolina's coastline and attracts 2.5 million visitors each year. Although it historically has drawn an upscale clientele, and it still does, you'll find that the crowd here is much more diverse than you might think. Although it has more than its fair share of millionaires (you might run into director Ron Howard at the Starbucks, for instance), it also attracts families in search of a good beach.

This half-tame, half-wild island is home to more than 25 world-class golf courses and even more resorts, hotels, and top restaurants. Still, it's managed development thanks to building restrictions that aim to marry progress with environmental protection. North of Hilton Head, the coastal landscape is peppered with quiet small towns and flanked by rural sea islands. Beaufort is a cultural treasure, a graceful antebellum town with a compact historic district and waterfront promenade. Several of the 18th- and 19th-century mansions have been converted to bed-and-breakfasts.

Continuing north, midway between Beaufort and Charleston is Edisto Island, where you can comb the beach for shells and camp out on the mostly barren Edisto Beach State Park, or rent the modest waterfront cottages that have been in the same families for generations. Ocean Ridge, the one resort property there, formerly a Fairfield resort, is now a Wyndham.

ORIENTATION & PLANNING

GETTING ORIENTED

Hilton Head is just north of South Carolina's border with Georgia. It's so close to Savannah that they share an airport. This part of the state is best explored by car, as its points of interest spread over a flat coastal plain that is a mix of wooded areas, marshes, and sea islands, the latter of which are sometimes accessible only by boat or ferry. Take U.S. 170 and 17 to get from one key spot (Hilton Head, Beaufort, and Edisto) to another. It's a pretty drive that winds through small towns and over old bridges. Charleston, the Queen Belle of the South, is at the northern end of the region.

Hilton Head Island. One of the southeast coast's most popular tourist destinations, Hilton Head is known for its golf courses and tennis courts. It's a magnet for timeshare owners and retirees.

Beaufort & Vicinity. This charming town just inland from Hilton Head is a destination in its own right, with a lively dining scene and cute B&Bs. Nearby Fripp Island offers a family-friendly beach escape.

Daufuskie Island. A scenic ferry ride from Hilton Head, Daufuskie is now much more developed than it was during the days when Pat Conroy wrote *The Water is Wide,* but it's still a beautiful island to explore, even on a day-trip. You can also stay for a few days at a deluxe resort with good golf and tennis.

TOP REASONS TO GO

Beaufort: A small, antebellum town that has offers large doses of heritage and culture; nearly everything you might want to see is within its downtown historic district.

Beachcombing: Hilton Head has 12 mi of beaches. You can swim, soak up the sun, or walk along the sand. The differential between the tides leaves a multitude of shells, sand dollars, and starfish.

Challenging golf: Hilton Head's nickname is "Golf Island," and its many challenging courses have an international reputation.

Serving up tennis: One of the nation's top tennis destinations, with academies run by legends like Stan Smith, former Wimbleton champion.

Staying put: This semitropical island has been a resort destination for decades, and it has all of the desired amenities for visitors: a vast array of lodgings, an endless supply of restaurants, and excellent shopping.

Edisto Island. More down-home than the other coastal islands, Edisto has one time-share resort as well as several vacation homes for rent, and a lovely state park, where you can rent bare-bones cabins.

HILTON HEAD & THE LOWCOUNTRY PLANNER

GETTING HERE & AROUND

You can fly into Savannah's airport, which is about an hour from Hilton Head, but then you absolutely must have a car to get around.

BY AIR Hilton Head Island Airport is served by US Airways Express. Most travelers use the Savannah/Hilton Head International Airport, less than an hour from Hilton Head, which is served by American Eagle, Continental Express, Delta, Northwest, United Express, and US Airways.

BY BUS The Lowcountry Regional Transportation Authority has a bus that leaves Beaufort in the morning for Hilton Head that costs $2.50. Exact change is required. This same company has a van that, with 24-hour notice, will pick you up at your hotel and drop you off at your destination for $3. You can request a ride weekdays 7 AM to 10 AM or 12:30 PM to 3 PM.

BY TAXI At Your Service and Gray Line Lowcountry Adventures are good options in Hilton Head.

ESSENTIALS **Airport Contacts Hilton Head Island Airport** (✉ *120 Beach City Rd., Hilton Head, SC* ☎ *843/689-5400* ⊕ *www.hiltonheadairport.com*). **Savannah/Hilton Head International Airport** (✉ *400 Airways Ave., Savannah, GA* ☎ *912/964-0514* ⊕ *www.savannahairport.com*).

Bus Contacts The Lowcountry Regional Transportation Authority (☎ *843/757-5782* ⊕ *www.gotohhi.com/bus*).

Taxi Contacts At Your Service (☎ *843/837-3783*). **Gray Line Lowcountry Adventures** (☎ *843/681-8212*).

8

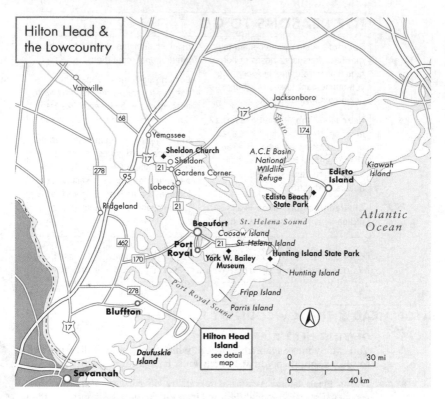

TOURS

Hilton Head's Adventure Cruises hosts dinner, sightseeing, and murder-mystery cruises. Several companies, including H20 Sports and Low-country Nature Tours in Hilton Head, run dolphin-watching, shark fishing, and delightful environmental trips. Carolina Buggy Tours show you Beaufort's historic district by horse-drawn carriage. Gullah Heritage Trail Tours give a wealth of history about slavery and the Union takeover of the island during the Civil War. Gullah 'n' Geechie Mahn Tours lead groups throughout Beaufort with a focus on African-American culture. Costumed guides sing and act out history during walking tours by the tour group, Spirit of Old Beaufort.

TOUR
ESSENTIALS

Tour Contacts Adventure Cruises (✉ *Shelter Cove Marina, 9 Shelter Cove Lane, Mid-Island, Hilton Head Island* ☎ *843/785–4558* ⊕ *www.hiltonheadisland.com*). **Carolina Buggy Tours** (✉ *901 Port Republic St., Beaufort* ☎ *843/525–1300*). **Gullah 'n' Geechie Mahn Tours** (✉ *671 Sea Island Pkwy., Beaufort* ☎ *843/838–7516* ⊕ *www.gullahngeechietours.net*). **H2O Sports** (✉ *Harbour Town Marina, 149 Lighthouse Rd., South End, Hilton Head Island* ☎ *843/363–2628* ⊕ *www.h2osportsonline. com*). **Low Country Nature Tours** (✉ *Shelter Cover Marina, Shelter Cove Lane, Mid-Island, Hilton Head Island* ☎ *843/683–0187* ⊕ *www.lowcountrynaturetours. com*). **Spirit of Old Beaufort** (✉ *103 West St., Beaufort* ☎ *843/525–0459* ⊕ *www. thespiritofoldbeaufort.com*).

ABOUT THE RESTAURANTS

Given the proximity to the Atlantic and small farms on the mainland, most locally owned restaurants are still heavily influenced by the catch of the day and seasonal field harvests. There are numerous national chain and fast-food restaurants within commercial complexes or malls. Although hard to fathom, relatively few restaurants on Hilton Head are on the water or even have a water view. Although you will find more high-end options, there are still holes-in-the-wall or that serve good-tasting fare and are frequented by locals.

Most restaurants open at 11 and don't close until 9 or 10, but some take a break between 2:30 and 6. Most of the more expensive restaurants have an early dining menu aimed at seniors, and this is a popular time to dine. During the height of the summer season reservations are essential at all times, though in the off-season you may need them only on weekends (still, more and more of the better restaurants require them).

ABOUT THE HOTELS

Hilton Head is known as one of the best vacation spots on the East Coast, and its hotels are a testimony to the reputation. The island is awash in regular hotels and resorts that are called plantations, not to mention beachfront or golf-course-view villas, cottages, and mansions. Here and on private islands you can expect the most modern conveniences and world-class service at the priciest places. Clean, updated rooms and friendly staff are everywhere—even at lower-cost hotels—this is the South, after all. Many international employees add a cosmopolitan atmosphere. Staying in cooler months, for extended periods of time, or commuting from nearby Bluffton, where there are some new limited-service properties, chains like Hampton Inn, can mean better deals.

8

WHAT IT COSTS				
¢	$	$$	$$$	$$$$
Restaurant	under $10	$10–$14	$15–$19	$20–$24	over $24
Hotel	under $100	$100–$150	$151–$200	$201–$250	over $250

Restaurant prices are for a main course at dinner. Hotel prices are for two people in a standard double room in high season. Tax of rooms is 12%; restaurant tax is 7.5% for food, and 8.5% for alcohol.

HILTON HEAD ISLAND

No matter how many golf courses pepper its landscape, Hilton Head will always be a semitropical barrier island. That means the 12 mi of beaches are lined with towering pines, palmetto trees, and wind-sculpted live oaks; the interior is a blend of oak and pine woodlands and meandering lagoons. Rental villas, lavish private houses, and luxury hotels line the coast as well.

Since the 1950s, resorts like Sea Pines, Palmetto Dunes, and Port Royal have sprung up all over. Although the gated resorts, called "plantations," are private residential communities, all have public restaurants, marinas, shopping areas, and recreational facilities. All are secured, and cannot be toured unless arrangements are made at the visitor office near the main gate of each plantation. Hilton Head prides itself on strict laws that keep light pollution to a minimum. ■ TIP➜ **The absence of streetlights makes it difficult to find your way at night, so be sure to get good directions.**

EXPLORING HILTON HEAD & VICINITY

Driving Hilton Head by car or tour bus is the only way to get around. Off Interstate 95, take Exit 8 onto U.S. 278, which leads you through Bluffton and then onto Hilton Head proper. A 5¾-mi Cross Island Parkway toll bridge ($1) is just off 278, and makes it easy to bypass traffic and reach the south end of the island, where most of the resort areas and hotels are. Know that U.S. 278 can slow to a standstill at rush hour and during holiday weekends, and the signs are so discreet that it's easy to get lost without explicit directions. ■ TIP➜ **Be careful of putting the pedal to the metal, particularly on the Cross Island Parkway. The speed limits change dramatically.**

GETTING HERE AND AROUND
Hilton Head Island is 19 mi east of I–95. Take Exit 8 off I–95 South and then Hwy. 278 directly to the bridge. If you're heading to the southern end of the island, your best bet to save time and avoid traffic is to take the Toll Expressway. The cost is $1 each way.

ESSENTIALS
Visitor Information Welcome Center of Hilton Head (⊠ *100 William Hilton Pkwy.* ☎ *843/689–6302 or 800/523–3373* ⊕ *www.hiltonheadisland.org.*

WHAT TO SEE
Audubon-Newhall Preserve, in the south, is 50 acres of pristine forest, where native plant life is tagged and identified. There are trails, a self-guided tour, and seasonal walks. ⊠ *Palmetto Bay Rd., near southern base of Cross Island Pkwy., South End,* ☎ *843/842–9246* ⊕ *www. hiltonheadaudubon.org* ☜ *Free* ⊗ *Daily dawn–dusk.*

★ **Bluffton.** Tucked away from the resorts, charming Bluffton has several old homes and churches, a growing artists' colony, several good restaurants (including Truffles Cafe), and oak-lined streets dripping with Spanish moss. You could grab Southern-style picnic food and head to the boat dock at the end of Pritchard Street for great views. There are interesting little shops and galleries and some limited-service B&Bs that provide a nearby alternative to Hilton Head's higher prices. This town and surrounding area are experiencing some rapid growth, since Hilton Head has little remaining undeveloped land. Much of the area's work force, especially its young, Latin, and international employees, live here. ⊠ *Route 46, 8 mi northwest on U.S. 278,.*

★ **Coastal Discovery Museum.** The museum has relocated to what was the Horn Plantation, and it's an all-new and wonderful Lowcountry learning experience, especially for visitors and children. Although a small

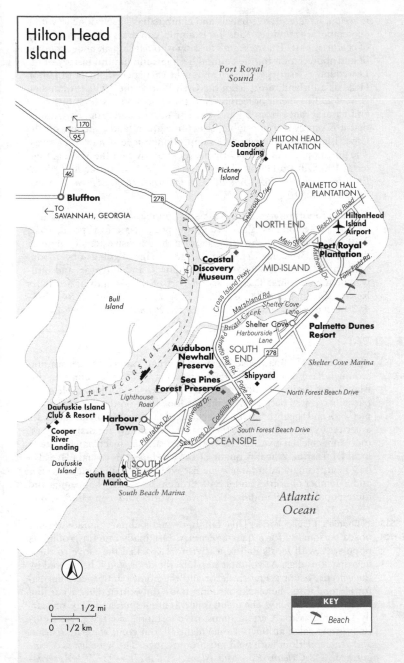

Hilton Head Island

Port Royal Sound

170
95

46

278

O **Bluffton**
← TO
SAVANNAH, GEORGIA

Waterway

HILTON HEAD
PLANTATION

**Seabrook
Landing**

*Pickney
Island*

PALMETTO HALL
PLANTATION

Seabrook Drive

NORTH END

Main Street

Beach City Road

**HiltonHead
Island
Airport**

**Port Royal
Plantation**

Matthews Dr.

Folly Field Rd.

**Coastal
Discovery
Museum**

MID-ISLAND

Cross Island Pkwy.

Marshland Rd.

*Shelter Cove
Lane*

Broad Creek

Shelter Cove O

*Harbourside
Lane*

**Palmetto Dunes
Resort**

*Bull
Island*

278

SOUTH
END

Shelter Cove Marina

Palmetto Bay Rd.

**Audubon-
Newhall
Preserve**

**Sea Pines
Forest Preserve**

Shipyard

North Forest Beach Drive

*Lighthouse
Road*

Greenwood Dr.

Pope Ave.

Cordillo Pkwy.

Intracoastal

**Daufuskie Island
Club & Resort**

**Harbour
Town** O

Plantation Dr.

Sea Pines Dr.

OCEANSIDE

South Forest Beach Drive

**Cooper
River
Landing**

*Daufuskie
Island*

**South Beach
Marina**

SOUTH
BEACH

South Beach Marina

*Atlantic
Ocean*

0 ___ 1/2 mi
0 ___ 1/2 km

8

museum, its interpretive panels and exhibits have been done in with a contemporary mind-set. Kids, for example, can dress up in the clothing of centuries past. The museum's mission is to develop an understanding of and appreciation for the cultural heritage and natural history of the Lowcountry. Visitors will learn about the early development of Hilton Head as an island resort from the Civil War to the 1930s. Admission is free, and its menu of lectures and tours on subjects both historical and natural range from $3 and up. The terrace and grounds are such that it is simply a comfortable, stress-free green landscape just off the Cross Island Parkway entrance ramp, though it feels a century away. The gift shop remains in its original location, within the Visitors Center at 100 William Hilton Pkwy. ⊠*Hwy. 278 at Gumtree Rd., North End,* ☎*843/689–6767* ⊕*www.coastaldiscovery.org* ☜*Free* ☉*Mon.– Sat. 9–5, Sun. 10–3.*

Sea Pines Forest Preserve. At this 605-acre public wilderness tract, walking trails take you past a stocked fishing pond, waterfowl pond, and a 3,400-year-old Indian shell ring. Pick up the extensive activity guide at the Sea Pines Welcome Center to take advantage of goings-on—moonlight hayrides, storytelling around campfires, and alligator- and bird-watching boat tours. The preserve is part of the grounds at Sea Pines Resort. ⊠*Off U.S. 278, Sea Pines Resort, South End,* ☎*843/363– 4530* ⊕*www.seapines.com* ☜*$5 per car* ☉*Daily dawn–dusk.*

WHERE TO EAT

$$$
SEAFOOD

✕**Boathouse 11.** Boathouse 11 is an actual waterfront restaurant; although hard to fathom, waterfront dining is difficult to find on this island. To soak in the salty atmosphere, reserve an outdoor table on its partially covered patio, where the bar looks out on the charter fishing pier. Fish and shellfish are the best choices here; for lunch you can order a perfect oyster po'boy. Yes, there are a few landlubber main courses, too. Want chicken instead? Ask for the teriyaki sandwich named after a local DJ. Distinguished by quality, fresh produce, this casual place also has a surprisingly admirable wine list with reasonably-priced glasses and a number of bottles under $40. Brunch is a Sunday happening and quite popular. ⊠*397 Squire Pope Rd., North End* ☎*843/681–3663* ☐*AE, D, MC, V*

$$$$
FRENCH

✕**Charlie's L'Etoile Verte.** This family-owned culinary landmark has oozed personality for a quarter-century. Originally one tiny room, its popularity with locals nad repeat visitors sparked the move to these new spacious digs. At you first step into the door, you'll be wowed by the eclectic, country French decor and the homey ambience. Unusual for Hilton Head, the blackboard menu is handwritten daily according to market availability. The menu is just as homespun and cozy, primarily French classics. Certain items are constants, like the perfect curried shrimp salad at lunch. Come nightfall, out come the pâté maison and veal tenderloin with wild mushroom sauce. The wine list is distinguished. ⊠*8 Orleans Rd., Mid-Island,* ☎*843/785–9277* ⚓*Reservations essential* ☐*AE, MC, V* ☉*Closed Sun. No lunch Mon.*

$$$$
ECLECTIC
Fodor's Choice
★

✗CQs. If you heard that all island restaurants are in shopping centers and lack atmosphere, then you need to experience CQs. Its rustic ambience—heart-pine floors, sepia-toned island photos, and a lovely second-story dining room—coupled with stellar cuisine, a personable staff, live piano music, and a feel-good spirit put most of the island's other restaurants to shame. Chef Eric Sayer's imaginative, original creations are divine. Imagine a lobster triumvirate as an appetizer, with an incredible lobster cheesecake the standout. Imagine a golden-brown Alaskan halibut afloat in a crab cream sauce. Manager Drew can pair your wine perfectly from an impeccable list. The gate pass for Sea Pines ($5) will be reimbursed with purchase of one main course or more. ⊠*Harbour Town, 140 Lighthouse La., South End* ☎*843/671–2779* ⌂*Reservations essential* ▤*AE, MC, V* ☽*No lunch.*

$$$–$$$$
ITALIAN
Fodor's Choice
★

✗Michael Anthony's. This throwback goes back to the days when the most exotic, ethnic restaurant in most towns was a family-owned Italian spot. This is that kind of place, but contemporized and more upscale, with fresh, top-quality ingredients, simple yet elegant sauces, and waiters who know and care about the food they serve. Owned by a talented, charismatic Philadelphia family, the restaurant has a convivial spirit, and its innovative pairings and plate presentations are au courant. Locals file in for the early-dining menu, which includes three courses and a glass of wine; this is a superior value for about $20. But you can order off the à la carte menu, and after homemade gnocchi or a succulent veal chop with wild mushroom sauce, you can finish happily with a Sambuca and panna cotta. ⊠*Orleans Plaza, 37 New Orleans Rd., Ste. L, South End* ☎*843/785–6272* ⌂*Reservations essential* ▤*AE, D, MC, V* ☽*Closed Sun. No lunch.*

$$$–$$$$
CONTINENTAL
★

✗Old Fort Pub. Overlooking the sweeping marshlands of Skull Creek, this romantic restaurant has almost panoramic views. It offers one of the island's best overall dining experiences: the building is old enough to have some personality, and the professional waiters do their duty. More important, the kitchen serves flavorful food, including a great appetizer of roasted calamari with sun-dried tomatoes and olives. Entrées like duck confit in rhubarb sauce and filet mignon with shiitake mushrooms hit the spot. The wine list is extensive, and there's outdoor seating plus a third-floor porch for toasting the sunset. Sunday brunch is celebratory and includes a mimosa. ⊠*65 Skull Creek Dr., North End* ☎*843/681–2386* ▤*AE, D, DC, MC, V* ☽*No lunch.*

¢
AMERICAN

✗Signe's Heaven Bound Bakery & Café. Every morning locals roll in for the deep-dish French toast, crispy polenta, and whole-wheat waffles. Since 1974, European-born Signe has been feeding islanders her delicious soups (the chilled cucumber has pureed watermelon, green apples, and mint), curried chicken salad, and loaded hot and cold sandwiches. The beach bag ($10 for a cold sandwich, pasta or fresh fruit, chips, a beverage, and cookie) is a great deal. The key-lime bread pudding is amazing, as are the melt-in-your mouth cakes and the rave-worthy breads, especially the Italian ciabatta. If you want to become part of the Hilton Head scene, you need to know Signe. ⊠*93 Arrow Rd., South End* ☎*843/785–9118* ▤*AE, D, MC, V* ☽*Closed Sun. No dinner.*

8

WHERE TO STAY

$$$–$$$$ ⬚ **Crowne Plaza Hilton Head Island Beach Resort.** Decorated in a classy nautical theme and set in a luxuriant garden, the Crowne Plaza is appropriately resplendent. It's the centerpiece of Shipyard Plantation, which means guests have access to all its amenities. It also has one of the more elegant lobbies and public spaces; however, this resort has the fewest oceanfront rooms of the majors and is the farthest from the water. Its latticed bridge and beach pavilion have seen many an island wedding. **Pros:** it is the closest hotel to all the restaurants and night-life in Coligny Plaza and Park Plaza; parking is free, although valet parking costs $10. **Cons:** Wi-Fi and cell service problematic due to low-rise, older concrete structures; large and sometimes impersonal. ⊠ *Shipyard Plantation, 130 Shipyard Dr., Mid-Island* ☎*843/842–2400 or 800/334–1881* ⊕*www.ichotelsgroup.com* ⇆*331 rooms, 9 suites* ⅋*In-room: refrigerator, Internet. In-hotel: 3 restaurants, golf courses, pools, gym, bicycles, Wi-Fi, children's programs (ages 3–12), parking (free), no-smoking rooms.* ⊟*AE, D, DC, MC, V* ⎟◎⎟*EP.*

$ ⬚ **Hampton Inn on Hilton Head Island.** Tree-shaded, this hotel, which is sheltered from the noise and traffic, is a good choice if you have kids. The two-bedroom family suites are surprisingly upscale; the parents' rooms are tastefully appointed, and the kids' rooms are cool enough to have foosball tables. King-size studios with sleeper sofas are another alternative for families. Breakfast is as Southern as country gravy and biscuits or as European as Belgian waffles. Major renovations throughout the buildings included the replacement of carpets, bedspreads, and other fabrics. **Pros:** good customer service; clean; eight different break-fast menus. **Cons:** not on a beach (the closest is Folly Field, 2 mi away); grounds are not memorable, and your view is often the parking lot. ⊠*1 Dillon Rd., Mid-Island* ☎*843/681–7900* ⊕*www.hampton-inn. com* ⇆*115 rooms, 7 suites* ⅋*In-room: Internet. In-hotel: pool, Wi-Fi, parking (free), no-smoking rooms* ⊟*AE, D, DC, MC, V* ⎟◎⎟*BP.*

$$$$ ⬚ **Hilton Head Marriott Resort & Spa.** Marriott's standard rooms get a
★ tropical twist at this palm-enveloped resort: sunny yellow-and-green
☾ floral fabrics and cheery furnishings are part of the peppy decor. All guest rooms have private balconies (spring for an oceanfront room), writing desks, and down comforters. The tallest granddaddy of the island's resorts, it's looking good after a major renovation in 2008 that includes revamped pool areas and restaurants, notably Conroy's. To take in the sea views, you can lounge by the pool or lunch at the fun, outdoor snack bar. On rainy days and at dusk, the indoor pool under a glass dome is a great alternative. Kids love Dive-in Theater nights and the real sand castle in the lobby. Hammocks have been added to the sandy knoll adjacent to the pool area. A new spa is also a must-do. **Pros:** the multicultural staff has a great spirit; a full-service Marriott, it is one of the best-run operations on the island. **Cons:** rooms could be larger; in summer kids are everywhere; in-room Wi-Fi costs $9.95 a day. ⊠*1 Hotel Circle, Palmetto Dunes, Mid-Island* ☎*843/686–8400 or 888/511–5086* 🖷*843/686–8450* ⊕*www.hiltonheadmarriott.com* ⇆*476 rooms, 36 suites* ⅋*In-room: safe, kitchen (some), Wi-Fi. In-hotel: restaurant, bar, golf courses, tennis courts, pools, gym, spa,*

beachfront, water sports, bicycles, Wi-Fi, children's programs (ages 3–12), no-smoking rooms ☰*AE, D, DC, MC, V* ⊙|*EP.*

$$–$$$ ⊞ **Hilton Oceanfront Resort.** There's a Caribbean sensibility to this five-story chain hotel; the grounds are beautifully landscaped with deciduous and evergreen bushes, and palms run along the beach. This resort is far more casual, laid-back, and more family- than business-friendly. The smallest accommodations are large, commodious studios with a kitchenette; they go on up to two-bedroom suites. Many rooms face the ocean, and all are decorated with elegant wood furnishings, such as hand-carved armoires. A new, urbane lounge called the XO is a happening nightspot. HH Prime is the steak house, and the excellent deli/breakfast restaurant is being expanded at this writing. The resort has three pools, one strictly for little children, another for families, and an adults-only pool overlooking the ocean. Prices span a long range; online deals can be the best, with outdoor cabana massages, breakfast, and a bottle of wine included in some packages. **Pros:** competes more with condos than hotels because of the size of its accommodations; lots of outdoor dining options. **Cons:** boisterous wedding parties can be too noisy; problems with cell reception; minimum stay is two nights during summer. ⊠*23 Ocean La., Palmetto Dunes, Mid-Island* ⌂*Box 6165, 29938* ☎*843/842–8000 or 800/845–8001* ⊕*www.hiltonheadhilton. com* ↝*303 studios, 20 suites* ⚲*In-room: kitchen, Internet. In-hotel: restaurants, golf courses, pools, gym, water sports, bicycles, Wi-Fi, children's programs (ages 5–12), no-smoking rooms* ☰*AE, D, DC, MC, V* ⊙|*EP.*

$$$–$$$$ ⊞ **Holiday Inn Oceanfront Resort.** This high-rise, on one of the island's busiest beaches, is within walking distance of major South End shops and restaurants. Standard rooms are spacious and furnished in a contemporary style, recently renovated in bright and bold color schemes. It attracts a diverse crowd, from budget-minded vacationers, mainly families, corporate travelers, and meeting groups and those liking the fun, social aspects of the beach scene. Golf and tennis packages are available, and rates with breakfast included are the better deal. A resort fee is charged, $8.95 a day that includes Wi-Fi and parking. The two-bedroom suites with ocean views usually have to be booked a month in advance, particularly in summer. The outdoor Tiki Hut lounge, a poolside bar, is hugely popular at one of the island's most populated beaches. Pets are allowed, but not during peak season. **Pros:** the price is a good value for Hilton Head, particularly for families; strong professional management and corporate standards; microwaves in rooms. **Cons:** if you are looking for posh, it is not; in summer, the number of kids raises the noise volume; small front desk can back up. ⊠*S. Forest Beach Dr., South End* ⌂*Box 5728 29938* ☎*843/785–5126 or 800/423–9897* ⊟*843/785–6678* ⊕*www.hihiltonhead.com* ↝*201 rooms* ⚲*In-room: refrigerator, Internet, Wi-Fi. In-hotel: restaurant, bar, pool, gym, bicycles, Wi-Fi, children's programs (ages 3–12), no-smoking rooms* ☰*AE, D, DC, MC, V* ⊙|*EP.*

$$$ ⊞ **The Inn at Harbour Town.** The most buzz-worthy of Hilton Head's properties is this European-style boutique hotel. A proper staff, clad in kilts, pampers you with British service and a dose of Southern charm.

8

Butlers are on hand any time of the day or night, and the kitchen delivers around the clock. The spacious guest rooms, decorated with neutral palettes, have luxurious touches like Frette bed linens, which are turned down for you each night. The back patio with its upscale furnishings, landscaping, and brickwork is enviable and runs right up to the greens of the fairways of the Harbour Town course. The lobby isn't a lobby per se; it just has a concierge desk for check-in. The Harbour Town Grill serves some of the best steaks on the island. Parking is free and easy, and valet service only costs $10. **Pros:** a service-oriented property, it is a centrally located Sea Pines address; unique, it is one of the finest hotel operations on island; complimentary parking. **Cons:** some concierges give you too much information to digest; no water views; golf-view rooms are $20 extra. ⊠*Lighthouse La., off U.S. 278, Sea Pines South End* ☎*843/363–8100 or 888/807–6873* ⊕*www.seapines.com* ⌨*60 rooms* ⅋*In-room: refrigerator, Wi-Fi. In-hotel: restaurant, golf courses, tennis courts, bicycles, laundry service, Wi-Fi, parking (free), no-smoking rooms* ⊟*AE, D, DC, MC, V* ⅋⅋*EP.*

$$$$
Fodor'sChoice
★
⬚**The Inn at Palmetto Bluff.** Fifteen minutes from Hilton Head, this is the Lowcountry's most luxurious resort. This 22,000-acre property has been transformed into a perfect replica of a small island town, complete with its own clapboard church. As a chauffeured golf cart takes you to your cottages, you'll pass the clubhouse, which resembles a mighty antebellum great house. All of the cottages are generously sized—even the one-bedrooms have more than 1,100 square feet of space. The decor is coastal chic, with sumptuous bedding, gas fireplaces, surround-sound home theaters, and marvelous bathroom suites with steam showers. Your screened-in porch puts you immediately in touch with nature. New is the Canoe Club with its restaurant, family pool, and bar. The spa puts you close to heaven with its pampering treatments. Dinner at its River House Restaurant is definitely worth an excursion from Hilton Head even if you do not stay here. **Pros:** the tennis/boccie/croquet complex has an atmospheric, impressive retail shop; the river adds both ambience and boat excursions; pillared ruins dotting the grounds are like sculpture. **Cons:** the mock Southern town is not the real thing; not that close to the amenities of Hilton Head. ⊠*476 Mount Pelia Rd., Bluffton* ☎*843/706–6500 or 866/706–6565* ⊕*www.palmettobluffresort. com* ⌨*50 cottages* ⅋*In-room: safe, refrigerator, Wi-Fi. In-hotel: 4 restaurants, bars, golf course, pools, water sports, bicycles, Internet terminal, Wi-Fi, no-smoking rooms* ⊟*AE, MC, V* ⅋⅋*EP.*

$$–$$$
Fodor'sChoice
★
⬚**Main Street Inn & Spa.** This Italianate villa has stucco facades ornamented with lions' heads, elaborate ironwork, and shuttered doors. Staying here is like being a guest at a rich friend's estate. Guest rooms have velvet and silk brocade linens, feather duvets, and porcelain and brass sinks. An ample breakfast buffet is served in a petite, sunny dining room. In the afternoon there's complimentary wine at cocktail hour; before that, you can get gourmet coffee and homemade cookies which can be taken into the formal garden. Wi-Fi is free. The spa offers treatments ranging from traditional Swedish massages to Indian Kyria massages. Four king-size junior suites overlook the pool and gardens and are the inn's largest. Some rooms have balconies and fireplaces.

Pros: when someone plays the piano while you are having your wine, it's super-atmospheric; the lion's head fountains and other Euro-architectural details. **Cons:** weddings can overwhelm the resort, especially on weekends and throughout June; regular rooms are small. ⊠*2200 Main St., North End* ☎*843/681–3001 or 800/471–3001* ⊕*www.mainstreetinn.com* ↩*29 rooms, 4 jr. suites* ♿*In-room: refrigerator, Wi-Fi. In-hotel: pool, spa, Internet terminal, Wi-Fi, no-smoking rooms* ⊟*AE, D, MC, V* ⅋*BP.*

$$$$ ⚅ Fodor's Choice ★

🖥 **Westin Hilton Head Island Resort & Spa.** A circular drive winds around a metal sculpture of long-legged marsh birds as you approach this luxury resort. The lush landscape lies on the island's quietest, least inhabited stretch of sand. Guest rooms, most with ocean views from the balconies, have homey touches, crown molding, and contemporary furnishings. If you need space to spread out, there are two- and three-bedroom villas. The service is generally efficient and caring. A new spa opened in 2007 and has become the big buzz on the island. This continues to be one of the top resorts on Hilton Head, particularly for honeymooners. **Pros:** the number and diversity of children's activities is amazing; a good destination wedding hotel, ceremonies are performed on the beach and at other atmospheric outdoor venues; the beach here is absolutely gorgeous. **Cons:** in the off-seasons, the majority of its clientele are large groups; the hotel's phone service can bog down; difficult to get cell-phone reception indoors. ⊠*2 Grass Lawn Ave., North End* ☎*843/681–4000 or 800/228–3000* ⊕*www.westin.com* ↩*412 rooms, 29 suites* ♿*In-room: Internet, Wi-Fi. In-hotel: 3 restaurants, golf courses, tennis courts, pools, gym, beachfront, bicycles, children's programs (ages 4–12), no-smoking rooms.* ⊟*AE, D, DC, MC, V* ⅋*EP.*

PRIVATE VILLA RENTALS

ResortQuest (☎*843/686–8144 or 800/448–3408* ⊕*www.resortquesthiltonhead.com*) boasts that it has the most comprehensive selection of accommodations (500-plus) on Hilton Head, from oceanfront to golf views, all in premier locations including the plantations. Guests receive a card giving them discounts on the island. Generally, guests renting from this company can play tennis for free and get preferred golf rates at the most prestigious courses. Departure cleaning is not included in the quoted rates.

Resort Rentals of Hilton Head Island (☎*843/686–6008 or 800/845–7017* ⊕*www.hhivacations.com*) represents some 300 homes and villas island-wide from the gated communities to some of the older non-gated areas that have the newest homes. Stays are generally Saturday to Saturday during the peak summer season; three- or four-night stays may be possible off-season. Most of the properties are privately owned. In addition to the rental fee, you'll pay 11% tax, a $60 reservation fee, and a 4% administration fee. Linens and departure cleaning are included in the quoted rates, but daily maid service or additional cleaning is not.

Sea Pines Resort (☎*843/842–1496* ⊕*www.seapines.com*) operates in its own little world on the far south end of the island. The vast majority of the overnight guests rent one of the 500 suites, villas, and beach houses.

8

In addition to quoted rates, expect to pay an additional 19.5% to cover the combined taxes and resort fees. Minimum rental periods are one-week in summer, three nights otherwise. All houses have landlines and most have Wi-Fi. In general, housekeeping throughout the week is additional, and price depends on the size of the villa, but departure cleaning is included.

SPORTS & THE OUTDOORS

BEACHES

Although resort beach access is reserved for guests and residents, there are four public entrances to Hilton Head's 12 mi of ocean beach. The two main parking spots are off U.S. 278 at Coligny Circle in the South End, near the Holiday Inn, and on Folly Field Road, Mid-Island. Both have changing facilities. South of Folly Field Road, Mid-Island along U.S. 278, Bradley Beach Road and Singleton Road lead to beaches where parking space is limited. ■TIP➜ **A delightful stroll on the beach can end with an unpleasant surprise if you don't put your towels, shoes, and other earthly possessions way up on the sand. Tides here can fluctuate as much as 7 feet. Check the tide chart at your hotel.**

BIKING

There are more than 40 mi of public paths that crisscross Hilton Head Island, and pedaling is popular along the firmly packed beach. The island keeps adding more to the "boardwalk" network as visitors are utilizing it and it is such a safe alternative for kids. Keep in mind when crossing streets that in South Carolina, vehicles have the right-of-way. ■TIP➜ **Bikes with wide tires are a must if you want to ride on the beach. They can save you a spill should you hit loose sand on the trails.**

Bicycles can be rented at most hotels and resorts. You can also rent bicycles from the **Hilton Head Bicycle Company** (✉112 Arrow Rd., South End ☎843/686–6888 ⊕www.hiltonheadbicycle.com). **Pedals Bicycles.** ✉71 Pope Ave., South End ☎843/842–5522. **South Beach Cycles** (✉Sea Pines Resort, off U.S. 278, South End ☎843/671–2453 ⊕www.southbeachracquetclub.com) rents bikes, helmets, tandems, and adult tricycles.

CANOEING & KAYAKING

This is one of the most delightful ways to commune with nature on this commercial but physically beautiful island. You paddle through the creeks and estuaries and try to keep up with the dolphins!

Outside Hilton Head (✉Sea Pines Resort, off U.S. 278, South End ✉Shelter Cove Lane at U.S. 278, Mid-Island ☎843/686–6996 or 800/686–6996 ⊕www.outsidehiltonhead.com) is an ecologically sensitive company that rents canoes and kayaks; it also runs nature tours and dolphin-watching excursions.

FISHING

Captain Jim of **The Stray Cat** (✉The Docks at Charlie's Crab, 3 Hudson La., North End ☎843/683–5427 ⊕www.straycatcharter.com) will help you decide whether you want to fish "in-shore" or go offshore into the deep blue. You can go for four, six, or eight hours, and the price is $120 an hour; bait and tackle are provided, but you must bring your own lunch.

GOLF

Hilton Head is nicknamed "Golf Island" for good reason: the island itself has 25 championship courses (most semiprivate), and the outlying area has 16 more. Each offers its own packages, some of which are great deals. Almost all charge the highest greens fees in the morning and lower the rates as the day goes on. Some offer lower rates in the hot summer months. It's essential to book tee times in advance, especially in the busy summer season; resort guests and club members get first choices. Most courses can be described as casual-classy, so you will have to adhere to certain rules of the greens.

GOLF SCHOOLS **The Academy at Robert Trent Jones** (⊠ *Palmetto Dunes Resort, 7 Trent Jones La., Mid-Island* ☎*843/785–1138* ⊕*www.palmettodunes.com*) offers one-hour lessons, daily clinics, one- to three-day schools, and clinics by Doug Weaver, former PGA tour pro. **The TOUR Academy of Palmetto Hall Plantation** (⊠ *Palmetto Hall Plantation, 108 Fort Hollow Dr., North End* ☎*843/681–1516* ⊕*www.palmettohallgolf.com*) is the only golf school on island affiliated with the PGA. This academy is known for its teaching technologies that include video analysis. Students can chose from a one-hour private lesson to up to five days of golf instruction to include a round of golf with an instructor.

GOLF COURSES **Arthur Hills at Palmetto Hall** (⊠ *Palmetto Hall, 108 Fort Howell Dr., North End* ☎*843/689–9205* ⊕*www.palmettohallgolf.com* ⛳*18 holes. 6918 yds. Par 72. Green Fee: $60–$104*) is a player favorite from the renowned designer Arthur Hills; this course has his trademark: undulating fairways. The course, punctuated with lakes, gently flows across the island's rolling hills, winding around moss-draped oaks and towering pines.Although it's part of a country club, the course at **Country Club of Hilton Head** (⊠*70 Skull Creek Dr. , North End* ☎*843/681–4653 or 888/465–3475* ⊕*www.golfisland.com* ⚑*Reservations essential* ⛳*18 holes. 6919 yds. Par 72. Green Fee: $50–$119*) is open for public play. A well-kept secret, it's never overcrowded. This 18-hole Rees Jones–designed course is a more casual environment than many of the others. Jack Nicklaus created **Golden Bear Golf Club at Indigo Run** ⊠*Indigo Run, 72 Golden Bear Way, North End* ☎*843/689–2200* ⊕*www. goldenbear-indigorun.com* ⛳*18 holes. 6643 yard, part 72, Green Fee $85–$109*). Located in the upscale Indigo Run community, it's in a natural woodlands setting and offers easy-going rounds. It is a course that requires more thought than muscle, yet you will have to earn every par you make. And there are the fine points—the color GPS monitor on every cart and women-friendly tees. After an honest, traditional test of golf, most golfers finish up at the plush clubhouse and with some food and drink at Just Jack's Grille.

Fodor'sChoice ★ **Harbour Town Golf Links** (⊠*Sea Pines Resort, 11 Lighthouse La., South End* ☎*843/842–8484 or 800/955–8337* ⊕*www.golfisland.com* ⛳*18 holes. 6973 yds. Par 71. Green Fee: $153–$295*) is considered by many

8

golfers to be one of those must-play courses. Designed by Pete Dye, the layout is reminiscent of Scottish courses of old. The Golf Academy is ranked among the top 10 in the country. **The May River Golf Club** (⊠*Palmetto Bluffs, 476 Mt. Pelia Rd., Blufton* ☎*843/706–6500* ⊕*www.palmettobluffresort.com/golf* ⚑.*18 holes. 7171 yds., Par 72. Green Fee: $90–$260*), an 18-hole Jack Nicklaus course, has several holes along the banks of the scenic May River and will challenge all skill levels. The greens are covered by Paspalum, the latest eco-friendly turf. Caddy service is always required, even if you chose to rent a golf cart, and then no carts are allowed earlier than 9 AM. **Old South Golf Links** (⊠*50 Buckingham Plant Dr., Blufton* ☎*843/785–5353* ⊕*www. golfisland.com* ⚑.*18 holes. 6772 yds. Par 72. Green Fee: $75–$85*) has scenic holes with marshland and views of the Intracoastal Waterway. A recent internet poll had golfers preferring it over the famous Harbour Town Golf Links and **Robert Trent Jones at Palmetto Dunes** (⊠*7 Robert Trent Jones Way, North End* ☎*843/785–1138* ⊕*www.palmettodunes. com* ⚑.*18 holes. 7005 yds. Par 72. Green Fee: $125–$165*), which is one of the island's most popular layouts. Its beauty and character are accentuated by the par-5, 10th hole, which offers a panoramic view of the ocean. It's one of only two oceanfront holes on Hilton Head.

HORSEBACK RIDING

🕑 **Lawton Stables** (⊠*Sea Pines Resort, Plantation, off U.S. 278, South End*
★ ☎*843/671–2586*) gives riding lessons and pony rides, in addition to having horseback tours through the Sea Pines Forest Preserve. The latter can be troop movements, with many participants. It is a safe ride, if not adrenaline-racing.

SPAS

The low-key **Faces** (⊠*The Village at Wexford, 1000 William Hilton Pkwy., North End* ☎*843/785–3075* ⊕*www.facesdayspa.com*) has been pampering loyal clients for 20 years, with body therapists and cosmetologists who do what they do well. It has a fine line of cosmetics and does makeovers or evening makeups. Open seven days a week,
Fodor'sChoice Monday night is for the guys. **Heavenly Spa by Westin** (⊠*Westin Resort*
★ *Hilton Head Island, Port Royal Plantation, 2 Grasslawn Ave., North End* ☎*843/681–4000, Ext. 7519*) is a new facility at the Westin resort offering the quintessential sensorial spa experience. Unique is a collection of treatments based on the energy from the color indigo, once a cash crop in the Lowcountry. The full-service salon, the relax room with its teas and healthy snacks, and the adjacent retail area with products like sweet-grass scents are heavenly, too. The **Spa at Main Street Inn** (⊠*2200 Main St., North End* ☎*843/681–3001* ⊕*www.mainstreetinn.com*) has holistic massages that will put you in another zone. A petite facility, it offers deep muscle therapy, couples massage, hydrotherapy soaks and outdoor courtyard massages. Jack Barakatis instructs both his students and his own clients in the art of de-stressing, with a significant dose of spirituality. The **Spa at Palmetto Bluffs** (⊠*476 Mount Pelia Rd., Blufton* ☎*843/706–6500* ⊕*www.palmettobluffresort.com*) has been dubbed the "celebrity spa" by locals, for this two-story facility is the ultimate pamper palace. It is as creative in its names that often have a Southern

accent, as it is in its treatments. There are Amazing Grace and High Cotton bodyworks and massages, sensual soaks and couples massage, special treatments for gentlemen/golfers and Belles and Brides packages as this is a premier wedding destination. Nonguests are welcome. **Spa Soleil** (⊠ *Marriott Hilton Head Resort & Spa, Palmetto Dunes, 1 Hotel Circle, Mid-Island* ☎ *843/686–8400* ⊕ *www.csspagroup.com*) is one of the newest spas on island; this $7-million facility has the atmosphere and professionalism, the therapies, and litany of massages found in the country's finest spas. Since the facility is all new, everything is still quite pristine. The colors, aromas, teas, and snacks make your treatment a soothing, therapeutic experience.

TENNIS

There are more than 300 courts on Hilton Head. Tennis comes in at a close second as the island's premier sport after golf. It is recognized as one of the nation's best tennis destinations. Hilton Head has a large international organization of coaches. Spring and Fall are the peak seasons for cooler play with numerous tennis packages available at the resorts and through the schools.

Palmetto Dunes Tennis Center (⊠ *6 Trent Jones La., Mid-Island* ☎ *843/ 785–1152* ⊕ *www.palmettodunes.com*) welcomes nonguests. **Port Royal** (⊠ *15 Wimbledon Ct., North End* ☎ *843/686–8803* ⊕ *www.heritagegolfgroup.com*) has 16 courts, including two grass. **Sea Pines Racquet Club** (⊠ *Sea Pines Resort, off U.S. 278, 32 Greenwood Dr., South End* ☎ *843/363–4495*) has 23 courts, instructional programs, and a pro-shop. Highly rated **Van der Meer Tennis Center/Shipyard Racquet Club** (⊠ *Shipyard Plantation, 19 de Allyon Rd., Mid-Island* ☎ *843/686– 8804* ⊕ *www.vandermeertennis.com*) is recognized for tennis instruction. Four of its 28 courts are covered.

8

NIGHTLIFE

Hilton Head has always been a party place, and that's true now more than ever. A fair number of clubs cater to younger visitors, others to an older crowd, and still others that are "ageless" and are patronized by all generations. As a general rule, local haunts tend to be on the north end of the island, closer to where the locals live.

BARS

Reggae bands play at **Big Bamboo** (⊠ *Coligny Plaza, N. Forest Beach Dr., South End* ☎ *843/686–3443*), a bar with a South Pacific theme. The **Hilton Head Brewing Co.** (⊠ *Hilton Head Plaza, Greenwood Dr., South End* ☎ *843/785–2739*) lets you shake your groove thing to 1970s-era disco on Wednesday. There's live music on Friday and karaoke on Saturday. **Jazz Corner** (⊠ *The Village at Wexford, C-1, South End* ☎ *843/842–8620*) will always be known and remembered for its live music and fun, New Orleans–style atmosphere. The restaurant has a newly updated menu, so to assure yourself of a seat on busy nights, make reservations for dinner. **Jump & Phil's Bar & Grill** (⊠ *3 Hilton Head Plaza, South End* ☎ *843/785–9070*) is a happening scene, especially for locals, and you could pass this nondescript building by if you didn't know. "Jump," whose real name is John Griffin, is an author of thriller novels under the pen name John R. Maxim, and this place is a magnet for area writers and football fans during the season. **The Metropolitan Lounge** (⊠ *Park Plaza, Greenwood Dr., South End* ☎ *843/785–8466*) is the most sophisticated of several fun places on Park Plaza. With a Euro-style that appeals to all ages, it is known for its martini menu. On weekends there is dancing in an anteroom separated by a wrought-iron gate. Here you will see all ages, from golf guys to the island's sassy, young, beautiful people. **Monkey Business** (⊠ *Park Plaza, Greenwood Dr., South End* ☎ *843/686–3545*) is a dance club popular with young professionals. On Friday there's live beach music. One of the island's latest hot spots, **Santa Fe Cafe** (⊠ *Plantation Center in Palmetto Dunes, 700 Plantation Center North End* ☎ *843/785–3838*) is where you can lounge about in front of the adobe fireplace or sip top-shelf margaritas on the rooftop. The restaurant's clientele is predominately local residents and tends to be older than those who frequent the Boathouse because of its Southwestern atmosphere, unique on the island, and its guitarist(s). **Turtle's** (⊠ *The Westin Hilton Head Resort & Spa, 2 Grass Lawn Ave.,North End* ☎ *843/681–4000*) appeals to those who still likes to hold their partner when they dance.

SHOPPING

ART GALLERIES

Linda Hartough Gallery (⊠ *Harbour Town, 140 Lighthouse Rd., South End* ☎ *843/671–6500*) is all about golf. There's everything from landscapes of courses to golden golf balls to pillows embroidered with sayings like "Queen of the Green." The **Red Piano Art Gallery** (⊠ *220 Cordillo Pkwy., Mid-Island* ☎ *843/785–2318*) showcases 19th- and 20th-century works by regional and national artists.

GIFTS

The **Audubon Nature Store** (⊠ *The Village at Wexford, U.S. 278, Mid-Island* ☎ *843/785–4311*) has gifts with a wildlife theme. **Outside Hilton Head** (⊠ *The Plaza at Shelter Cove, U.S. 278, Mid-Island* ☎ *843/686–6996 or 800/686–6996*) sells Pawleys Island hammocks (first made in the late 1800s) and other items that let you enjoy the great outdoors.

JEWELRY

The **Bird's Nest** (⊠ *Coligny Plaza, Coligny Circle and N. Forest Beach Dr., South End* ☎ *843/785–3737*) sells locally made shell and sand-dollar jewelry, as well as island-theme charms. The **Goldsmith Shop** (⊠ *3 Lagoon Rd., Mid-Island* ☎ *843/785–2538*) carries classic jewelry and island charms. **Forsythe Jewelers** (⊠ *71 Lighthouse Rd., South End* ☎ *843/342–3663*) is the island's leading jewelry store.

The World of Gullah

In the Lowcountry, Gullah refers to several things: a language, a people, and a culture. Gullah (the word itself is believed to be derived from *Angola*), an English-based dialect rooted in African languages, is the unique language of the African-Americans of the Sea Islands of South Carolina and Georgia, more than 300 years old. Most locally born African-Americans of the area can understand, if not speak, Gullah.

Descended from thousands of slaves who were imported by planters in the Carolinas during the 18th century, the Gullah people have maintained not only their dialect but also their heritage. Much of Gullah culture traces back to the African rice-coast culture and survives today in the art forms and skills, including sweetgrass basket-making, of Sea Islanders. During the colonial period, when rice was king, Africans from the West African rice kingdoms drew high premiums as slaves. Those with basket-making skills were extremely valuable because baskets were needed for agricultural and household use. Made by hand, sweetgrass baskets are intricate coils of a marsh grass with a sweet, haylike aroma.

Nowhere is Gullah culture more evident than in the foods of the region. Rice appears at nearly every meal—Africans taught planters how to grow rice and how to cook and serve it as well. Lowcountry dishes use okra, peanuts, *benne* (the African word for sesame seeds), field peas, and hot peppers. Gullah food reflects the bounty of the islands: shrimp, crabs, oysters, fish, and such vegetables as greens, tomatoes, and corn. Many dishes are prepared in one pot, a method similar to the stew-pot cooking of West Africa.

On St. Helena Island, near Beaufort, Penn Center is the unofficial Gullah headquarters, preserving the culture and developing opportunities for Gullahs. In 1852 the first school for freed slaves was established at Penn Center. You can delve into the culture further at the York W. Bailey Museum.

On St. Helena, many Gullahs still go shrimping with hand-tied nets, harvest oysters, and grow their own vegetables. Nearby on Daufuskie Island, as well as on Edisto, Wadmalaw, and Johns islands near Charleston, you can find Gullah communities as well. A famous Gullah proverb says: *If oonuh ent kno weh oonuh dah gwine, oonuh should kno weh oonuh come f'um.* Translation: If you don't know where you're going, you should know where you come from.

8

BEAUFORT

38 mi north of Hilton Head via U.S. 278 and Rte. 170; 70 mi southwest of Charleston via U.S. 17 and U.S. 21.

Charming homes and churches grace this old town on Port Royal Island. Come here on a day-trip from Hilton Head, Savannah, or Charleston, or to spend a quiet weekend at a B&B while you shop and stroll through the historic district. Tourists are drawn equally to the town's artsy scene (art walks are regularly scheduled) and the area's water-sports possibilities. Actually, more and more transplants have decided to spend the rest of their lives here, drawn to Beaufort's small-town charms, and the area is burgeoning. A truly Southern town, its picturesque backdrops have lured filmmakers here to film *The Big Chill*, *The Prince of Tides*, and *The Great Santini*, the last two being Hollywood adaptations of best-selling books by author Pat Conroy. Conroy has waxed poetic about the Lowcountry and calls the Beaufort area home. The city closest to the Marine base on Parris Island, Beaufort also has a naval hospital.

GETTING HERE & AROUND

Beaufort is 25 mi east of Interstate 95, on U.S. 21. The only way here is by private car.

ESSENTIALS

Visitor Information Beaufort Visitors Center (✉ *2001 Boundaray St.,Beaufort* ☎ *843/525–8523*). **Regional Beaufort Chamber of Commerce** (✉ *1106 Carteret St., Box 910, Beaufort* ☎ *843/986–5400* ⊕ *www.beaufortsc.org*).

EXPLORING

John Mark Verdier House Museum, built in the Federal style, has been restored and furnished as it would have been between its construction in 1805 and the visit of Lafayette in 1825. It was the headquarters for Union forces during the Civil War. A combination ticket that gets you into the Beaufort Museum & Arsenal (under renovations until Spring 2009) and the John Mark Verdier House Museum saves you $1. ✉ *801 Bay St.29901* ☎ *843/379–6335* 🔳 *$5* 🕐 *Mon.–Sat. 10–3:30.*

Henry C. Chambers Waterfront Park, off Bay Street, is a great place to survey the scene. Trendy restaurants and bars overlook these 7 landscaped acres along the Beaufort River. There's a farmers' market here on Saturday, April through August, 8 to noon.

St. Helena Island, 9 mi southeast of Beaufort via U.S. 21, is the site of the Penn Center Historic District. Established in the middle of the Civil War, Penn Center was the South's first school for freed slaves; now open to the public, the center provides community services, too. This island is both residential and commercial, with nice beaches, cooling ocean breezes, and a great deal of natural beauty.

The **York W. Bailey Museum** has displays on the Penn Center, and on the heritage of Sea Island African-Americans; it also has pleasant grounds shaded by live oaks. The Penn Center (1862) was one of the first schools for the newly emancipated slaves. These islands are where Gullah, a musical language that combines English and African languages, developed. This is a major stop for anyone interested in the Gullah history and culture of the Lowcountry. ✉ *16 Martin Luther King Jr. Blvd., St. Helena Island* ☎ *843/838–2432* ⊕ *www.penncenter. com* 🔳 *$5* 🕐 *Mon.–Sat. 11–4.*

★ Secluded **Hunting Island State Park** has nature trails and about 3 mi of public beaches—some dramatically and beautifully eroding. Founded in 1993 to preserve and promote its natural existence, it harbors 5,000 acres of rare maritime forests. Nonetheless, the light sands decorated with driftwood and the raw, subtropical vegetation is breathtaking. Stroll the 1,300-foot-long fishing pier, among the longest on the East Coast, or you can go fishing or crabbing. You will be at one with nature. The fit can climb the 181 steps of the **Hunting Island Lighthouse** (built in 1859 and abandoned in 1933) for sweeping views. The nature center has exhibits, an aquarium, and lots of turtles. The park is 18 mi southeast of Beaufort via U.S. 21; if you want to stay on the island, be sure to call for reservations. From April 1 to October 31 there is a one-week minimum stay, November 1 to March 31 the minimum is two nights. Cabins that sleep up to six or eight ($–$$) must be reserved far in advance for summer weekends (there are only 12). Expect to pay about $25 for campsites with electricity, $17 without. ⊠ *1775 Sea Island Pkwy., off St. Helena Island, Hunting Island* ☎ *843/838–2011* ⊕ *www.southcarolinaparks.com* ⊠ *$4* ⊘ *Park: Apr.–Oct., daily 6* AM–9 PM; *Nov.–Mar., daily 6–6. Lighthouse daily 11–4.*

WHERE TO EAT

$$$$ ✕ **Bateaux.** This contemporary restaurant, which was formerly on Lady's
ECLECTIC   Island, has a new home in a historic brick building in Port Royal, 6 mi
Fodor'sChoice   southwest of Beaufort. The location affords waterfront views, which
★   are best from the second story, although some downstairs tables also offer a glimpse of the blue. The move has brought major changes; lunch is no longer served, and "Chip" Ulbrich is no longer a partner. For now, owner Richard Wilson is in the kitchen. He continues creating imaginative Southern cuisine, and the menu keeps evolving. The food is fresh, elegant, and artistically presented. Foodies love that they can get foie gras in crepes and other dishes. Seafood is the obvious specialty; try the shrimp and scallops over red-pepper risotto with fried prosciutto and spinach. The staff is well-trained and knowledgeable. ⊠ *610 Paris Ave., Port Royal* ⬚ *Box 2179, Port Royal 29935* ☎ *843/379–0777* ⊟ *AE, MC, V* ⊘ *Closed Sun. No lunch.*

$$$ ✕ **Emily's Restaurant & Tapas Bar.** Long, narrow, and wood-paneled, Emi-
AMERICAN   ly's is a lively restaurant, definitely a haunt where the cool locals hang out. It has full dining service, mainly simple fare—heavy on steaks, which come with a generous salad. Crowds linger over the tapas, including spring rolls, garlic beef, and even baby lamb chops. This is a great place to come early or late, since the kitchen serves from 4 PM to 10 PM., Friday and Saturday nights at the bar can go on 'til late. At this writing, the restaurant was considering whether to start opening at lunch and the piano bar had gone quiet but was still hoping for a comeback. ⊠ *906 Port Republic St.29901* ☎ *843/522–1866* ⊟ *AE, MC, V* ⊘ *Closed Sun. No lunch.*

$–$$ ✕ **Plums.** Down the alley behind Shipman's Gallery is this homey frame
AMERICAN   house with plum-colored awnings shading the front porch. Plums still uses old family recipes for its crab-cake sandwiches and curried chicken salad, but now it also offers a blue cheese and portobello mushroom sandwich. Dinner has creative and affordable pasta and seafood dishes. The crowd is a mix of locals, particularly twenty- to thirtysomethings, and tourists, often with children. Its downtown riverfront location, fun

8

atmosphere, and reasonable prices are the draw. There's live music on weekends, starting at around 10 PM and geared to the younger crowd. ⊠904½ Bay St. 29901 ☎843/525–1946 ☐AE, MC, V.

$$$$
ECLECTIC
Fodor'sChoice
★

✕**Saltus River Grill.** Owner Lantz Price has given this 19-century loft a classy sailing motif, with portals and oversized photos of sailboats. The hippest eatery in Beaufort wins over epicureans with its cool design (subdued lighting, mod booths, dark-wood bar), waterfront patio, and nouveau Southern menu. Come early (the kitchen opens at 4 PM) and sit outdoors on the river with your cocktails. There are separate menus for sushi and oysters. A flawless dinner might start off with the skillet crab cakes with corn relish and beurre blanc sauce, then segue to the skewered, grilled quail with Oriental glaze. The wine list is admirable, and the staff is adept at pairings. Desserts change nightly; if offered, the pineapple upside-down cake can be the perfect end to your meal. ⊠802 Bay St.29001 ☎843/379–3474 ☐AE, D, MC, V.

$–$$
SEAFOOD

✕**Shrimp Shack.** On the way to Fripp and Hunting Islands, follow the cue of locals and stop at this endearing little place where Ms. Hilda, the owner, will take good care of you. All seating is outdoors, and once seated, you can't see the water. The menu includes all the typical Lowcountry fried plates, as well as South Carolina crab cakes, boiled shrimp, and gumbo, but it is best known for its shrimp burgers, sweet-potato fries, and sweet tea. Dinner is served only until 8 PM. Doors open at 11 AM. ⊠1929 Sea Island Pkwy., 18 mi southeast of Beaufort, St. Helena ☎843/838–2962 ☐No credit cards ⊘Closed Sun.

WHERE TO STAY

$$–$$$

⚏**Beaufort Inn.** This peach-painted 1890s Victorian inn charms you with its gables and wraparound porches. Pine-floor guest rooms have period reproductions, striped wallpaper, and comfy chairs. Several have fireplaces and four-poster beds. This is a homey place right in the heart of the historic district, and most rooms have views of the surrounding buildings. Room options in the main inn range from a standard queen-size room to suites, which are the most popular. Deluxe Suites have living rooms and are in separate cottages. There's also one two-bedroom, two-bathroom apartment in a separate, historic building overlooking Bay St. Garden Cottages are modern buildings and don't have the same traditional feel, but they do have garden or courtyard views; decor here is more contemporary, with heavier, darker woods and replica claw-foot tubs. Regrettably, the restaurant has closed, which is a loss to Beaufort's culinary scene. **Pros:** located in the heart of the historic district; continental breakfast has a chef-attended omelet station; the evening social hour includes snacks, refreshments, and wine. **Cons:** atmosphere may feel too dated for those seeking a more contemporary hotel; no more restaurant; deluxe suites have the worst views of all—the parking lot. ⊠809 Port Republic St. ☎843/521–9000 ⊕www.beaufortinn.com ⇆28 rooms ⟁In-room: DVD. In-hotel: bicycles, no kids under 8, parking (free), no-smoking rooms ☐AE, D, MC, V ⟊BP.

$$$-$$$$ ⊡ **Cuthbert House Inn.** Named after the original Scottish owners, who
★   made their money in cotton and indigo, this 1790 home is filled with
18th- and 19th-century heirlooms. It retains the original Federal fire-
places and crown and rope molding. When Beaufort was occupied
by the Union army during the Civil War, this home was used as the
generals' headquarters. Guest rooms and oversized suites have endear-
ing architectural details, comfortable with hand-knotted rugs on the
pine floors and commanding beds piled high with quilts. Chose one
that looks out on the bay and the glorious sunset. The Mariner's Suite
has a veranda, too. Beautifully lighted at night, this antebellum house,
with white pillars and dual verandas, typifies the Old South. Wed-
ding parties can rent out the whole inn, and many couples spend their
honeymoon nights here. But it appeals foremost to an older genera-
tion. A renovation of all rooms was in progress at this writing and
was expected to be finished by mid-2009. **Pros:** owners are accommo-
dating; other guests provide good company during the complimentary
wine service. **Cons:** some furnishings are a bit busy; some artificial
flower arrangements; stairs creak. ✉ *1203 Bay St.* ☎ *843/521–1315
or 800/327–9275* ⊕ *www.cuthberthouseinn.com* ➴ *6 rooms, 2 suites*
⚘ *In-room: refrigerator, DVD, Wi-Fi. In-hotel: bicycles, no kids under
12, no-smoking rooms* ▤ *AE, D, MC, V* ⍒ *BP.*

$$$ ⊡ **Fripp Island Resort.** This resort sits on the island made famous in
★   *Prince of Tides,* with 3½ miles of miles of broad, white beach and
⟳   unspoiled sea island scenery. It has long been known as one of the more
affordable and casual of the island resorts. It is private and gated, a
safe haven, where kids are allowed to be free, to go crabbing at low
tide, bike the trails, and swim, swim, swim. Families love the narrated
nature cruise and love Camp Fripp, the nature center, not to mention all the teen activities. Most residents are retired and happily tool
around in golf carts. Golf carts, mopeds, and bikes can be rented. This
is no swinging-singles destination, but it is a good getaway for sporty
couples who like to kayak and canoe. Of course, you can play highly-
rated golf or tennis and go fishing out of the marina as well. There are
more than 200 individual villas here insead of a hotel, though there
are a variety of small efficiencies. There's a pavilion with shops and a
choice of restaurants often with live entertainment, from the rollicking
Bonito Boathouse to the sophisticated Beach Club. ✉ *1 Tarpon Blvd.,
19 mi south of Beaufort, Fripp Island* ☎ *843/838–3535 or 877/374–
7748* ⊕ *www.frippislandresort.com* ➴ *210 units* ⚘ *In-room: kitchen,
DVD (some). In-hotel: 5 restaurants, golf courses, tennis courts, pools,
bicycles, children's programs (ages 3–12), laundry facilities, parking
(free), no-smoking rooms* ▤ *AE, D, DC, MC, V* ⍒ *EP.*

$$$-$$$$ ⊡ **Rhett House Inn.** Art and antiques abound in a circa-1820 home
Fodor's Choice   turned storybook inn. Look for the little luxuries—down pillows and
duvets, a CD player in each room, and fresh flowers. The best rooms
open out onto the veranda (No. 2) or the courtyard garden (No. 7).
The interior decor is Beaufort traditional coupled with Manhattan
panache. Breakfast, afternoon tea, evening hors d'oeuvres, and dessert
are included in the rate. Visiting celebrities have included Barbra Stre-
isand, Jeff Bridges, and Dennis Quaid. The remodeled (not so historic)

8

house across the street has eight more rooms, each of which has a gas fireplace, a whirlpool bath, a private entrance, and a porch. **Pros:** all guests come together for breakfast and other social hours; more private in annex. **Cons:** annex does not have the charisma of the main inn; in the main house you can hear footsteps on stairs and in hallways. ⊠*1009 Craven St.* ☎*843/524–9030* ⊕*www.rhetthouseinn.com* ⮑*16 rooms, 1 suite* ♿*In-hotel: restaurant, bicycles, no kids under 5, parking (free), no-smoking rooms* ⊟*AE, D, MC, V* ⦿|*BP.*

SPORTS & THE OUTDOORS

CANOE & BOAT TOURS

Beaufort is where the Ashepoo, Combahee, and Edisto rivers form the A.C.E. Basin, a vast wilderness of marshes and tidal estuaries loaded with history. For sea kayaking, tourists meet at the designated launching areas for fully-guided, two-hour tours.

Adults pay $40 at **Beaufort Kayak Tours** (⊠*600 Linton La.* ☎*843/525–0810* ⊕*www.beaufortkayaktours.com*). **A.C.E. Basin Tours** (⊠*1 Coosaw River Dr., Coosaw Island* ☎*843/521–3099* ⊕*www.acebasintours. com*) might be the best bet for the very young, or anyone with limited mobility, as it operates a 38-foot pontoon boat tour. A tour costs $35.

GOLF

Most golf courses are about a 10- to 20-minute scenic drive from Beaufort.

Fripp Island Golf & Beach Resort (⊠*201 Tarpon Blvd., Fripp Island* ☎*843/838–2131 or 843/838–1576* ⊕*www.frippislandresort.com* ⚐*Ocean Creek: 18 holes. 6643 yds. Par 71. Ocean Point: 18 holes. 6,556 yds. Par 72. Green Fee: $89–$99*) has a pair of championship courses. Ocean Creek Golf Course, designed by Davis Love, has sweeping views of saltwater marshes. Designed by George Cobb, Ocean Point Golf Links runs along the ocean the entire way. This is a wildlife refuge, so you'll see plenty of it, particularly marsh deer. That coupled with the ocean or marsh views, you have to focus to keep your eyes on the ball. Nonguests should call the golf pro to make arrangements to play.

SHOPPING

ART GALLERIES

At **Bay Street Gallery** (⊠*719 Bay St.29901* ☎*843/525–1024 or 843/522–9210*) Laura Hefner's oils of coastal wetlands magically convey the mood of the Lowcountry.At **Four Winds Gallery** (⊠*709 Bay St.29901< ☎843/838–3295*) Marianne Norton imports folk art, antiques, sculpture, photography, furniture, rugs, textiles, and weavings, connecting cultures and artists and artisans around the world. Southern art, both Gullah and New Orleans artwork, is new. The **Rhett Gallery** (⊠*901 Bay St.29901* ☎*843/524–3339*) sells Lowcountry art by four generations of the Rhett family, as well as antique maps and Audubon prints.

DAUFUSKIE ISLAND

13 mi (approx. 45 minutes) from Hilton Head via ferry.

From Hilton Head you can take a 45-minute ferry ride to nearby Daufuskie Island, the setting for Pat Conroy's novel *The Water Is Wide*, which was made into the movie *Conrack*. The boat ride may very well be one of the highlights of your vacation. The Lowcountry beauty unfolds before you, as pristine and unspoiled as you can imagine. Since the island is nestled between Hilton Head and Savannah, you can also travel from there. Many visitors come for the day, but you can also spend the night and explore your surroundings at leisure on a bike, golf cart, or on horseback. A guided tour is a good idea if time is short.

GETTING HERE & AROUND

The only way to Daufuskie is a ferry from Hilton Head or Savannah. It's possible to come on a day-trip. On arrival you can rent a golf cart or bicycle or take a tour. If you are coming to Daufuskie Island for a multiday stay with luggage and/or groceries, and perhaps a dog, be absolutely certain that you allow a full hour to park and check in for the ferry, particularly on a busy summer weekend. Whether you are staying on island or just day-tripping, the ferry costs $40 round-trip from Hilton Head ($45 from Savannah).

WHERE TO STAY

$$$$ **Daufuskie Island Resort & Breathe Spa.** Overnight visitors can stay at the Inn at Melrose, in rooms that are twice as large as those of most of the hotels on the main island. Rooms are traditional but contemporary in style and have a separate sitting area. Families might be tempted to opt for the even larger space of the cottages, the two-bedroom ones the most popular. (It is a pet-friendly resort, too, though pets are allowed only in some cottages.) Corporate groups usually take both inn rooms and cottages. Note that those run high-occupancy in the summer, especially on weekends and for holidays such as Thanksgiving. In June, especially, it is a destination resort for weddings. Sophisticated dining at Jack's Grill (named after J. Nicklaus) and its golf motif is the adult choice, whereas families enjoy the Beach Club Restaurant. ✉ *Embarkation Center, 421 Squire Pope Rd., North End* ☎ *843/341–4820 or 800/648–6778* 🌐 *www.daufuskieresort.com* *52 rooms* *In-room: kitchen (some), refrigerator, Internet. In-hotel: 4 restaurants, room service, bars, golf courses, tennis courts, pools, gym, spa, beachfront, water sports, bicycles, laundry facilities, parking (free), some pets allowed, no-smoking rooms* *AE, D, MC, V* *EP.*

SPORTS & THE OUTDOORS

Calibogue Cruises (✉ *Broad Creek Marina, 164B Palmetto Bay Rd., Mid-Island* ☎ *843/342–8687* 🌐 *www.freeport-marina.com*) has several Daufuskie tour options, including guided tours with lunch and gospel-music performances starting at $40. **Vagabond Cruises** (✉ *Harbour Town Marina, South End* ☎ *843/785–2662* 🌐 *www.vagabond-*

cruise.com) conducts daytime boat rides, from dolphin tours to runs to Savannah, sails on the *Stars & Stripes* of America's Cup fame, and dinner cruises.

EDISTO ISLAND

62 mi northeast of Beaufort via U.S. 17 and Rte 174; 44 mi southwest of Charleston via U.S. 17 and Rte. 174.

On rural Edisto (pronounced *ed*-is-toh) Island, magnificent stands of age-old oaks festooned with Spanish-moss border quiet streams, and side roads; wild turkeys may still be spotted on open grasslands and amid palmetto palms. Twisting tidal creeks populated with egrets and herons wind around golden marsh grass. Edisto is one of the less-costly, more down-home of the Carolina sea islands. Adults sing their hearts out on karaoke nights while their kids sip rocking root beer floats. And now bingo is big, and not just for seniors.

The small "downtown" beachfront is a mix of public beach-access spots, restaurants, and old, shabby-chic beach homes that are a far cry from the palatial villas rented out on the resort islands. The outlying Edisto Beach State Park is a pristine wilderness and camper's delight. The one actual resort was bought by Wyndham, and although houses time-share units, they have a number of rental accommodations.

GETTING HERE & AROUND
Edisto is connected to the mainland by a causeway. The only way here is by private car.

ESSENTIALS
Visitor Information Edisto Island Chamber of Commerce (⊠ *430 Rte. 174, Box 206, Edisto Island* ☎ *843/869–3867 or 888/333–2781* ⊕ *www.edistochamber. com).*

EXPLORING

○ **Edisto Beach State Park** covers 1,255 acres and includes marshland and
Fodor'sChoice tidal rivers, a 1½-mi-long beachfront, towering palmettos, and a lush
★ maritime forest with a 3½-mi trail running through it. The one-time CCC project park has the best shelling on public property in the Lowcountry. Overnight options include rustic furnished cabins (with basic, no-frills decor) by the marsh and campsites by the ocean (although severe erosion is limiting availability). Sites are $23 with electricity, $17 without. This park stays extremely busy, so with only seven cabins (the park system struggles to maintain their livability), you have to reserve far in advance. They are so sought-after that reservations sometimes go on the lottery system. The campsites are another story; reservations are on a first come, first served basis. Deluxe resort development has begun to encroach around the edges of the park. ⊠ *Rte. 174, off U.S. 17* ☎ *843/869–2156* ⊕ *www.southcarolinaparks.com* ⊠ *$4* ○ *Early Apr.–late Oct., daily 8 AM–10 PM; Late Oct.–early Apr., daily 8–6.*

The ruins of **Sheldon Church,** built in 1753, make an interesting stop if you're driving from Beaufort or Charleston to Edisto Island. The church burned down in 1779 and again in 1865. Only the brick walls and columns remain. With its moss-draped live oaks, it has an eerie Lowcountry beauty about it. At dusk it takes on a preternatural cast, the kind of atmosphere that gives rise to the ghost stories that Southern children are raised on. On weekends in and around June you can almost always witness a wedding. No matter, it is a good spot to get off the highway and stretch a spell. You can pick up a snack or some fixin's at the filling station nearby at Gardens Corner. It was modernized about 10 years back, but this highway landmark is still shades of decades past. ✉*18 mi northwest of Beaufort; Hwy. 17 S.*

WHERE TO EAT

¢–$ ✕**Po' Pigs Bo-B-Q.** Step inside the super-casual restaurant for pork bar-
SOUTHERN becue that has South Carolinians raving. Sample the different sauces
★ (sweet mustard, tomato, or vinegar) and wash it all down with a tall glass of sweet tea. Don't miss down-home sides like squash casserole, pork skins, lima beans and ham, and red rice. The blink-and-you-miss-it location is on the tail end of an undeveloped road. ✉*2410 Rte. 174* ☎*843/869–9003* ▭*No credit cards* ◷*Closed Sun.–Tues.*

WHERE TO STAY

¢ 🏠**Atwood Vacations.** For complete privacy, rent out a family-owned cottage on Edisto, which will be much more comfortable than the bare-bones ones that the park maintains. The list of properties includes everything from one-bedroom condos to six-bedroom homes. All kitchens are stocked with appliances and dishes, but you need to bring your own bed linens. Two-day minimum stays are required. ✉*495 Rte. 174* ☎*843/869–2151* ⊕*www.atwoodvacations.com* ♿*In-room: kitchen* ▭*AE, MC, V* ⦿*EP.*

$ 🏠**Wyndham Ocean Ridge Resort.** Looking for resort amenities in a get-
♻ away-from-it-all escape? You've found it here, at the only resort on the island. This is the former Fairfield Ocean Ridge, which was taken over by Wyndham in 2006. It is a time-share, so all of the attractive units are individually owned and decorated according to the owner's taste. Non-owners can still rent these units, but, alas, the number available is smaller than in the past, so reserve as far in advance as possible. There is a two-day minimum stay in-season (April 1–August 30), and you will pay a $25 reservation fee. Summers are solidly booked, especially weekends; in the off-season the major holidays find few available units. Although few of the accommodations (efficiencies to five-bedroom villas and houses) are on the beach, most are just a short walk away from it. **Pros:** family-oriented staff knows how to keep kids amused; shuttle transports guests to the resort's beach cabana; admirable renovation on the Plantation Golf Course. **Cons:** no daily maid-service (nor can you pay extra for it); few accomodations directly on the beach; rental options are limited. ✉*1 King*

8

Cotton Rd., Box 27 ☎*843/869–2561; 843/869–4527 or 877/296–6335 for reservations* ⊕*www.wyndhamoceanridge.com* ⇔*38 units* ♿*In-hotel: restaurant, bar, golf course, tennis courts, pool, children's programs (ages 6–14), beachfront, bicycles, no-smoking rooms* ☰*AE, D, MC, V* ⊧◎⊧*EP.*

The Midlands & Upstate, SC

WORD OF MOUTH

"I am concluding a business trip to Columbia, SC. All I can say that it impressed me in many ways. It has a cute, walkable downtown filled with restaurants, bars, and historical sites. There are several beautiful rivers flowing through town, and [it's] very clean and green. I can tell that they have revitalized the downtown section, converting old warehouses into hip restaurants and bars."

— bkluvsNola

Updated
by Christine
Anderson

SOUTH CAROLINA'S MIDLANDS, BETWEEN THE coastal Lowcountry and the mountains, is a varied region of swamps and flowing rivers, fertile farmland—perfect for horse raising—and hardwood and pine forests. Lakes have wonderful fishing, and the many state parks are popular for hiking, swimming, and camping. Small old towns with mansions turned bed-and-breakfasts are common, and the many public gardens provide islands of color during most of the year. At the center of the region is the state capital, Columbia, an engaging contemporary city enveloping cherished historic elements. Just outside of town, Congaree Swamp National Park has the largest intact tract of old-growth floodplain forest in North America. Aiken, the center of South Carolina's thoroughbred country, is where champions Sea Hero and Pleasant Colony were trained. Towns such as Abbeville and Camden preserve and interpret the past, with old house museums, history re-creations, and museum exhibits.

The Upstate of South Carolina is a land of waterfalls and wide vistas, cool pine forests and fast rapids. Camping, hiking, white-water rafting and kayaking are less than an hour from downtown Greenville and a paddle's-throw from the small hamlets that are scattered about. Greenville itself, artsy and refined, is a modern Southern city with a thriving downtown full of trendy restaurants, boutiques, and galleries.

ORIENTATION & PLANNING

GETTING ORIENTED

South Carolina's gleaming coasts and rolling mountains are linked by its lush Midlands. Swells of sandy hills mark where the state's coastline once sat, and as you drive farther inland you'll be greeted by the beauty of the Smoky Mountain foothills. What lies between is a mixture of Southern living—in cities and rural farms—that is truly remarkable.

Columbia & the Midlands. Columbia is swarming with activity, from the University of South Carolina campus to the halls of the State House. Day or night, there is always something to do. It's worth the drive, however, to slow down the pace and get outside of town. With thick forests, quaint towns, and scores of local home-cooking restaurants, the Midlands will not disappoint.

The Upstate. The Upstate is a treasure trove of natural and historic sites. Hiking trails and waterfalls abound for visitors of all fitness levels. Even the most robust will enjoy the river and falls in Reedy Falls Park, right in the heart of downtown Greenville. History buffs will love following the South Carolina National Heritage Corridor through the area. The drive stretches through lush landscapes, making stops at historic sites and homes along the way.

TOP REASONS TO GO

Small-town charm: Small towns—most complete with shady town squares, jewel-box shops, a café or two, and historic churches—dot this region. Abbeville and Aiken are a couple of the nicest.

Rafting the Chattooga: The fact that the movie *Deliverance* was filmed here doesn't scare away rafting enthusiasts, who have discovered that some of the best white-water rafting in the country comes courtesy of the Chattooga River.

Antiquing in Camden: Camden's Art & Antique District, which comprises most of the downtown area, is a trove of well-priced furniture: chests, sideboards, and dining tables from England, France, and the South-

east; ironwork, mantles, and doors from plantations and estates; and high-quality paintings.

Congaree Swamp National Park: Massive hardwoods and towering pines form a tall canopy through which hazy light filters, transforming the woods into a hauntingly beautiful scene. Wander through 20 mi of trails or follow the 2½-mi boardwalk that meanders over lazy creeks.

Waterfalls: More than 25 waterfalls tumble from the rocks and cliffs of South Carolina's Upstate; some, like 75-foot Twin Falls, are an easy walk from the road. Others, such as the over 400-foot Raven Falls, reward more serious hikers with jaw-dropping views.

THE MIDLANDS & UPSTATE PLANNER

WHEN TO GO

Central South Carolina comes alive in spring, beginning in early March, when the azaleas, dogwoods, wisteria, and jasmine turn normal landscapes into fairylands of pink, white, and purple shaded by a canopy of pines. Late May through September can be oppressive, particularly in the Midlands. Festivals celebrating everything from peaches to okra are held in summer. Fall will bring the state fair in Columbia, SEC and ACC football to the University of South Carolina and Clemson University, rich yellows and reds of the changing trees in the mountains, and a number of art and music festivals.

GETTING HERE & AROUND

BY AIR Columbia Metropolitan Airport (CAE), 10 mi west of downtown Columbia, is served by American Eagle, ASA/DeltaConnection, Continental, Delta, Northwest, United Express, and US Airways/Express. Greenville-Spartanburg Airport (GSP), off Interstate 85 between the two cities, is served by American Eagle, Continental, Delta, Independence, Northwest, United Express, and US Airways/Express.

BY CAR Interstate 77 leads into Columbia from the north, Interstate 26 runs through north–south, and Interstate 20 east–west. Interstate 85 provides access to Greenville, Spartanburg, Pendleton, and Anderson. Interstate 26 runs from Charleston through Columbia to the Upstate, connecting with Interstate 385 into Greenville. Car rental by all the national chains is available at the airports in Columbia and Greenville.

9

BY TAXI   Companies providing service in Columbia include Blue Ribbon and Checker-Yellow. American Cab provides citywide service as well as service to other cities statewide. It's about $20 to $25 from the airport to downtown Columbia. Greenville services include Budget Cab Company, Yellow Cab of Greenville, and Greenville Metro Cab. Fares from the Greenville airport to downtown Greenville will run around $25.

BY TRAIN   Amtrak makes stops at Camden, Columbia, Denmark, Florence, Greenville, Kingstree, and Spartanburg.

ESSENTIALS   **Air Contacts Columbia Metropolitan Airport** (CAE ⊠ *3000 Aviation Way, Airport* ☎ *803/822-5000* ⊕ *www.columbiaairport.com*). **Greenville-Spartanburg Airport** (GSP ⊠ *2000 G.S.P. Dr.* ☎ *864/877-7426* ⊕ *www.gspairport.com*).

Bus Contacts Greyhound (☎ *800/231-2222*).

Taxi Contacts Blue Ribbon (☎ *803/754-8163*). **Checker-Yellow** (☎ *803/799-3311*). **American Cab** (☎ *803/238-6669*). **Budget Cab Company** (☎ *864/233-4200*). **Yellow Cab of Greenville** (☎ *864/233-6666*). **Greenville Metro Cab** (☎ *864/235--8807*).

Train Contacts Amtrak (☎ *800/872-7245* ⊕ *www.amtrak.com*).

ABOUT THE HOTELS & RESTAURANTS
Most of the smaller towns have at least one dining choice that might surprise you with its take on sophisticated fare. Larger cities such as Columbia and Greenville have both upscale foodie haunts and ultracasual grits-and-greens joints. Plan ahead: many places close on Sunday.

Your best bet is to stay in an area inn or B&B. Count on just a handful of rooms, family favorites for breakfast, and, if you're lucky, a garden for wandering and a restored town square just steps away. What you gain in charm, however, you may have to give up in convenience.

WHAT IT COSTS				
¢	**$**	**$$**	**$$$**	**$$$$**
Restaurant	under $10	$10–$14	$15–$19	$20–$24	over $24
Hotel	under $100	$100–$150	$151–$200	$201–$250	over $250

Restaurant prices are for a main course at dinner. Hotel prices are for two people in a standard double room in high season.

PLANNING YOUR TIME
The Midlands and Upstate have a wonderful mix of larger cities and small towns and villages. Columbia and Greenville are destinations on their own, with plenty of sites, stores, and high-end eateries. However, the dozens of surrounding towns offer great day trips and shopping excursions, especially if you're looking to go antiquing. Aiken offers a chance to spend the day with the horses at major events like the Triple Crown each spring and Sunday polo matches every fall.

Miles of forested land and winding rivers offer plenty of reasons to stay outdoors. With options covering everything from hiking and mountain biking to motorcycle paths and bridle trails, it's easy to find an excuse

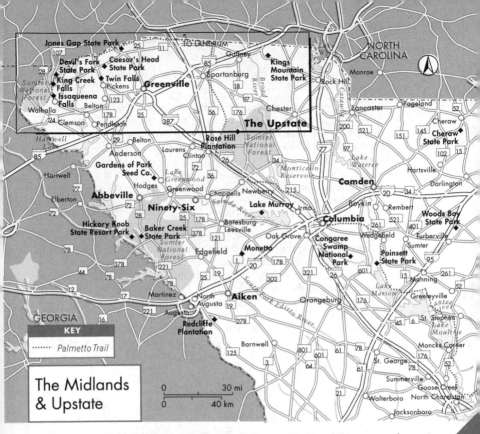

to head into the woods. The Palmetto Trail stretches across the entire state and can be walked in segments. The South Carolina National Heritage Corridor allows visitors to take a driving tour of some of South Carolina's major historic sites from the foothills of the Smokies to the coast of Charleston. The Ninety Six National Historic Site offers a mile-long loop through the woods, past Revolutionary War battlegrounds.

COLUMBIA & THE MIDLANDS

The wide swath of land that comprises the Midlands may have only one large city—the state capital, Columbia—but its profusion of small and medium-size towns makes this area a patchwork quilt of history and activity. The local museums and historic homes that line the shady streets often house surprisingly deep collections on everything from Civil or Revolutionary War battles to the lifestyle on 1850's plantations. Well-informed and friendly docents are happy to share stories, not to mention some tips on who's got the best peach pie that day.

COLUMBIA

112 mi northwest of Charleston via I–26; 101 mi southeast of Greenville via I–385 and I–26.

Old as Columbia may be, trendy and collegiate neighborhoods have given the city an edge. The symphony, two professional ballet companies, several theaters that stage live—and often locally written—productions, and a number of engaging museums keep culture alive. The city is a sprawling blend of modern office blocks, suburban neighborhoods, and the occasional antebellum home. Here, too, is the expansive main campus of the University of South Carolina. Out of town, 550-acre Lake Murray is full of pontoon boats and Jet Skis, and Congaree Swamp National Park is waiting to be explored.

In 1786 South Carolina's capital was moved from Charleston to Columbia, along the banks of the Congaree River. One of the nation's first planned cities, Columbia has streets that are among the widest in America, because it was then thought that stagnant air in narrow streets fostered the spread of malaria. The city soon grew into a center of political, commercial, and cultural activity, but in early 1865 General William Tecumseh Sherman invaded South Carolina and incinerated two-thirds of Columbia. A few homes, public buildings, and historic sights were spared. The First Baptist Church, where secession was declared, still stands because a janitor directed Sherman's troops to a Presbyterian church instead.

GETTING HERE & AROUND

Columbia lies in the heart of the state. It's two hours from the coast and just a little more than that from the mountains. Major interstates, along with airport, train, and bus terminals, make the city very accessible. Most of the action happens in the downtown neighborhoods of the Vista and Five Points. Devine Street, in the Shandon neighborhood, also offers plenty of boutique shopping and fine dining, and the university's football stadium, fair grounds, zoo, and gardens are all a short drive away. Historic Columbia runs guided tours of Columbia and rents out old properties.

ESSENTIALS

Visitor Information Columbia Metropolitan Convention and Visitors Bureau (⊠ 1101 Lincoln St., Columbia ☎ 803/545–0000 or 800/264–4884 ⊕ www.columbiaconventioncenter.com).

Tour Contacts Historic Columbia (☎ 803/252–7742 ⊕ www.historiccolumbia.org).

EXPLORING

Columbia Museum of Art contains art from the Kress Foundation collection of Renaissance and baroque treasures, sculpture, decorative arts, including art glass, and European and American paintings, including a Monet and a Botticelli; there are also changing exhibits. ⊠ *Main and Hampton Sts., Main Street area* ☎ 803/799–2810 ⊕ www.columbiamuseum.org ▨ $5; free on Sat. ⊙ Wed., Thurs., and Sat. 10–5, Fri. 10–9, Sun. 1–5.

Fodor'sChoice With more than 67,000 square feet for climbing, exploring, painting,
★ playing, building—oh, and learning, too, **EdVenture Children's Museum** is
Ↄ a full day of hands-on fun. Eddie, a 40-foot-tall statue of a boy that
can be climbed on and in by children and adults, stands as the museum
centerpiece. Each of eight galleries has a theme, such as Body Works,
World of Work, and Mission Imagination. Kids can shop in their own
grocery store, act as firemen in a full-sized fire truck, and pretend to be
newscasters. The annual Willie Wonka Halloween party is a blast too.
■TIP➔The second Tuesday of each month is family night and admission is
only $1 per person. ⊠211 Gervais St., Vista, shares campus with State
Museum ☎803/779–3100 ⊕www.edventure.org ☜$8.95 ⊙Tues.–
Sat. 9–5, Sun. noon–5.

The **Fort Jackson Museum,** on the grounds of a U.S. army–training center,
displays heavy equipment from the two world wars and has exhibits on
the training history of the fort from 1917 to the present. ■TIP➔You'll
need photo identification to enter Fort Jackson. Drivers also have to show
vehicle registration and proof of insurance. ⊠Bldg. 4442, Jackson
Blvd., East Columbia ☎803/751–7419 ☜Free ⊙Weekdays 9–4.

The **Hampton-Preston Mansion,** dating from 1818, is filled with lavish furnishings collected by three generations of two influential families. Buy
a ticket for a tour at the Historic Columbia Foundation in the Robert
Mills House. ⊠1615 Blanding St., Main Street area ☎803/252–1770
☜$6 ⊙Tues.–Sat. 10–4, Sun. 1–5.

Stop by the museum shop of the **Historic Columbia Foundation** to get
maps of walking and driving tours of historic districts. You must buy
tickets here to tour four old Columbia houses ($5 each): the Rob-
ert Mills House (on-site), the Hampton-Preston Mansion and Gardens, the Mann-Simons Cottage, and the Woodrow Wilson Family
Home. ⊠Robert Mills House, 1616 Blanding St., Main Street area
☎803/252–1770 ⊕www.historiccolumbia.org ☜Free ⊙Tues.–Sat.
10–4, Sun. 1–5.

The 41-mi-long **Lake Murray** has swimming, boating, picnicking, and
superb fishing. There are many marinas and campgrounds in the area.
The lake is off Interstate 26, 15 mi west of Columbia. ■TIP➔In summer
a massive flock of purple martins turn the sky nearly black at sunset when
they return to their roost on Bomb Island. ⊠Capital City–Lake Murray
Country Visitors Center, 2184 N. Lake Dr., Columbia ☎803/781–
5940 or 866/725–3935 ⊕www.scjewel.com.

The **Mann-Simons Cottage** was the home of Celia Mann, one of only 200
free African-Americans in Columbia in the mid-1800s. Buy a ticket
for a tour at the Historic Columbia Foundation in the Robert Mills
House. ⊠1403 Richland St., Main Street area ☎803/252–1770 ☜$6
⊙Tues.–Sat. 10–4, Sun. 1–5.

★ **Riverbanks Zoological Park and Botanical Garden** contains more than 2,000
Ↄ animals and birds, some endangered, in natural habitats. Walk along
pathways and through landscaped gardens to see sea lions, Siberian
tigers, koalas, and penguins. The South American primate collection

has won international acclaim, and the park is noted for its success in breeding endangered and fragile species. The Aquarium–Reptile Complex has South Carolina, desert, tropical, and marine specimens. At the Bird Pavilion you can view birds and wildlife under a safari-like tent. You can ride the carousel and also take a tram over the Saluda River to the 70-acre botanical gardens on the west bank. A forested section with walking trails has spectacular views of the river and passes Civil War ruins. ■TIP→Stop by the Saluda Factory Interpretive Center for more information about the site's history and its connection to the Civil War. ✉I–126 and U.S. 76, at Greystone Riverbanks exit, West Columbia ☎803/779–8717 ⊕www.riverbanks.org ☞$9.75 ◷Daily 9–5.

WORD OF MOUTH

"The State Museum is definitely worth a visit. The Vista is full of restaurants—you should not have any trouble finding someplace to eat. [Five] Points has boutique-type shops and bars. The zoo and/or Botanical Gardens are a nice several hours."

—ausc59

☸ **Riverfront Park and Historic Columbia Canal,** where the Broad and Saluda rivers form the Congaree River, was created around the city's original waterworks and hydroelectric plant. Interpretive markers describe the area's plant and animal life and tell the history of the buildings. ■TIP→A 2.5-mi paved trail weaves between the river and the canal and is filled with runners and walkers enjoying one of the region's only flat paths. ✉312 Laurel St., Vista ☎803/733–8613 ☞Free ◷Daily dawn–dusk.

The classic, columned 1823 **Robert Mills House** was named for its architect, who later designed the Washington Monument. It has opulent Regency furniture, marble mantels, and spacious grounds. ✉1616 Blanding St., Main Street area ☎803/252–1770 ☞$6 ◷Tues.–Sat. 10–4, Sun. 1–5.

☸ Exhibits in the refurbished textile mill that is the **South Carolina State Museum** explore the state's natural history, archaeology, historical development, as well as technological and artistic accomplishments. An iron gate made for the museum by Phillip Simmons, the "dean of Charleston blacksmiths," is on exhibit, as is a display on South Carolina's astronauts. In the Stringer Discovery Center children can check out microorganisms under a microscope and climb trees to observe the animals that live in the branches. Other objects include a reproduction of the Confederate submarine the *Hunley* and artifacts from the state's cotton industry and slavery. ✉301 Gervais St., Vista ☎803/898–4921 ⊕www. southcarolinastatemuseum.org ☞$5 ◷Tues.–Sat. 10–5, Sun. 1–5.

★ Six bronze stars on the western wall of the **State House** mark where direct hits were made by General Sherman's cannons. The Capitol building, started in 1851 and completed in 1907, is made of native blue granite in the Italian-Renaissance style. The interior is richly appointed with brass, marble, mahogany, and artwork. Guided tours are available throughout the day. ✉ 1100 Gervais St., Main Street area ☎803/734–2430 ☞Free ◷Weekdays 9–5, Sat. 10–5, 1st Sun. of month 1–5.

☺ Make sure it's dark out when you drive by **Tunnelvision,** a glowing optical illusion painted on the wall of the Federal Land Bank Building by local artist Blue Sky. Next to it is Sky's bigger-than-life silver "busted" Fire Hydrant, a working fountain. ⊠*Taylor and Marion Sts.,Main Street area.*

A highlight of the sprawling **University of South Carolina** is its original campus—the scenic, tree-lined **Horseshoe** (⊠*Bull St. at Pendleton St., USC Campus* ☎*800/922–9755*)—dating to 1801. Two-hour guided walking tours leave from the visitor center. Although the tours are geared to prospective students, the public is welcome. Reservations are essential. Explore the special collections on state history and genealogy at the **South Caroliniana Library** (⊠*Sumter St., USC Campus* ☎*803/777–3131* ☉*Mon., Wed., and Fri. 8:30–5, Tues. and Thurs. 8:30–8, Sat. 9–1*), established in 1840. The **McKissick Museum** (⊠*Sumter St., USC Campus* ☎*803/777–7251* ⊠*Free* ☉ *Weekdays 8–5, Sat. 11–3*) has geology, gemstone, and folklife exhibits, as well as a fine display of silver. ⊠*Sumter St., USC Campus* ☎*803/777–0169* ⊕*www.sc.edu.*

WHERE TO EAT

$$$–$$$$
SEAFOOD
Fodor'sChoice
★

✗**Garibaldi's.** Although the name is Italian, locals flock here for the creative fish dishes that might include crispy flounder, or almond crusted tilapia—the seafood menu changes slightly with the season. Creative dinner salads make interesting starters,, and the ice cream in an almond basket makes a crunchy-smooth finale to a meal. ■TIP➜**Don't miss the chocolate martini for a very grown-up dessert.** ⊠*2013 Greene St., Five Points* ☎*803/771–8888* ⚑*Reservations essential* ▤*AE, MC, V* ☉*No lunch.*

¢–$
CAFÉ

✗**The Gourmet Shop.** Sit in a black-and-white French-inspired café where mirrors and art prints decorate the walls. The Gourmet Shop has long been serving wonderful coffee and sandwiches. The chicken salad, potato salad, and the tomato, feta, and basil salad are all super. Next door, the shop sells food to go, wine, kitchen gadgets, French table linens, and fancy food items. ⊠*724 Saluda Ave., Five Points* ☎*803/799–9463* ⚑*Reservations not accepted* ▤*AE, MC, V* ☉*No dinner.*

$$$–$$$$
AMERICAN

✗**Hampton Street Vineyard.** Tucked into one of the first buildings constructed in the city after Sherman's infamous march, Hampton Street Vineyard is a cozy spot. Exposed brick walls, arched windows, and original wide-plank floors set the tone. Dinners are creative but never over the top, featuring upscale American fare such as seared breast of duck and sautéed crab cakes. The menu changes every three months. The 700-bottle wine list was the first in the state to receive *Wine Spectator*'s Best Award of Excellence. ⊠*1201 Hampton St., Downtown* ☎*803/252–0850* ⊕*www.hamptonstreetvineyard.com* ▤*AE, D, MC, V* ☉*Closed Sun. No lunch Sat.*

¢
SOUTHERN

✗**Little Pigs Barbecue.** Grab a plate, get in the buffet line and load up on barbecue, fried chicken, ribs, and fried fish, along with fixings such as collards, coleslaw, and macaroni and cheese. Since Little Pigs uses mustard-, tomato-, and vinegar-base barbecue sauces, you can sample all three and pick your favorite. ⊠*4927 Alpine Rd., Northeast Columbia* ☎*803/788–8238* ⚑*Reservations not accepted* ▤ *AE, DC, M, V* ☉*Closed Sun. and Mon. No dinner Wed.*

9

¢–$
MIDDLE
EASTERN

✕**Mediterranean Tea Room.** The name is a misnomer, since this friendly little restaurant serves Middle Eastern food. The marinated chicken breast keeps people coming back, but the *kofta* (spiced meatball), hummus, and vegetarian dishes offer patrons a break from traditional rich Southern cooking. ✉*2601 Devine St., Shandon* ☎*803/799–3118* ⚏*Reservations not accepted* ☴ *MC, V* ☻*Closed Sun.*

$$$–$$$$
SOUTHERN
★

✕**Mr. Friendly's New Southern Cafe.** Who knew that barbecue sauce could be the base for such tasty salad dressing or that lowly pimiento cheese could elevate a fillet to near perfection? Appetizers of fried pickles and country ham and spinach dip only add to the creative thinking that makes Mr. Friendly's such a treasure; the ever-changing wine-by-the-glass menu that's pulled from an eclectic list is another. ✉*2001 A Greene St., Five Points* ☎*803/254–7828* ⚏*Reservations not accepted* ☴*AE, D, MC, V* ☻*No lunch weekends.*

> ## MIDLANDS BARBECUE
>
> Barbecue in the Midlands, as elsewhere in the Carolinas and Georgia, means pork (or on rare occasion, chicken), roasted all day and basted with sauce, not just cooked on a grill. What makes Midlands barbecue distinctive is the sauce, which has a mustard base, rather than the vinegar or tomato commonly used elsewhere. The result is a flavor that's pungent but not spicy, and meat that lacks the red tint often associated with Southern barbecue. (Some places serve a variety of sauces, so you can do a taste test and see what you think of the native style.)

WHERE TO STAY

¢

🏨**Comfort Suites.** A short drive down the access road from a mall, shopping center, and cinema complex, the Comfort Suites is off Interstate 26 just west of downtown Columbia. Rooms are clean and as you'd expect from this chain. The exercise room and indoor pool are nice added benefits. **Pros:** great for avoiding heavy downtown traffic. **Cons:** too far away to go anywhere on foot. ✉*750 Saturn Pkwy., Exit 103, Harbison* ☎*803/407–4444 or 800/426–6423* ⊕*www.comfortinn.com* ⇨*82 suites* ⚒*In-room: refrigerator, Internet, Wi-Fi. In-hotel: restaurant, pool, gym, no-smoking rooms* ☴*AE, D, MC, V* ⦿*BP.*

$–$$

🏨**Embassy Suites Hotel Columbia–Greystone.** In the spacious seven-story atrium lobby—with skylights, fountains, pool, and live plants—you can enjoy your complimentary breakfast and evening cocktails. All rooms are suites that come with sleeper sofas in the living room. The staff, which caters mainly to a business clientele, works hard to please. **Pros:** right across from the zoo and botanical gardens. **Cons:** not close to many restaurants or nightlife venues. ✉*200 Stoneridge Dr., Greystone* ☎*803/252–8700 or 800/362–2779* ⊕*www.columbiagreystone. embassysuites.com* ⇨*214 suites* ⚒*In-room: refrigerator, Wi-Fi. In-hotel: restaurant, bar, pool, gym, no-smoking rooms* ☴*AE, D, DC, MC, V* ⦿*BP.*

$–$$

🏨**Hampton Inn Downtown Historic District.** This classy chain is within walking distance of restaurants and nightlife in the Vista neighborhood. The standard wood furnishings are bumped up a notch in comfort by Cloud Nine bedding. The hotel's staff provides attentive service.

Pros: the Manager's Reception offers guests free food and drinks Monday through Thursday afternoons. **Cons:** rooms along Gervais Street can be noisy from the Vista's busy nightlife. ✉*822 Gervais St., Vista* ☎*803/231–2000* ⊕*www.hamptoninncolumbia.com* ⇴*122 rooms* ⬧*In-room: refrigerator (some), Wi-Fi. In-hotel: restaurant, pool, gym, no-smoking rooms* ▤*AE, D, DC, MC, V* ⑩*BP.*

$–$$ 🏨**The Inn at Claussen's.** An old bakery warehouse in the heart of Five Points makes for a great small hotel. Traditional rooms received an update in late 2008, but kept their signature architectural features like in-suite spiral staircases. The rooms are typical hotel rooms, but service is a lot more personal. A parking lot behind the inn makes it easy for guests to explore the shopping and eateries in the area without having to fight for parking elsewhere. **Pros:** breakfast is served in-room; guests receive a complimentary glass of wine or scotch along with the daily paper. **Cons:** there is no workout room or pool. ✉*2003 Greene St., Five Points* ☎*803/765–0440 or 800/622–3382* ⊕*www.theinnatclaussens. com* ⇴*20 rooms, 8 suites* ⬧*In-room: Wi-Fi. In-hotel: no-smoking rooms* ▤*AE, D, MC, V* ⑩*BP.*

$–$$ 🏨**The Whitney Hotel.** Because they were originally built as condos, the large rooms in the Whitney have full kitchens, dining rooms, bedrooms with doors and, in the two-bedroom models, two full baths. Traditional wood and upholstered furnishings include formal desks and wingback chairs. The hotel is set among the trees in residential Shandon, so you can stroll to dinner and window-shop for trendy clothes, housewares, and shoes; there are even two grocery stores around the corner. **Pros:** much more peaceful than other hotels in the heart of town; still within walking distance of shops and restaurants; airport shuttle. **Cons:** health club access is provided, but it's off-site. ✉*700 Woodrow St., Shandon* ☎*803/252–0845* ⊕*www.whitneyhotel.com* ⇴*74 suites* ⬧*In-room: kitchen, Internet. In-hotel: restaurant, pool, no-smoking rooms* ▤*AE, D, DC, MC, V* ⑩*BP.*

NIGHTLIFE & THE ARTS

THE ARTS **Colonial Life Arena** (✉*801 Lincoln St., Vista* ☎*803/576–9200* ⊕*coloniallifearena.com*) is the largest arena in the state and hosts major entertainment events as well as University of South Carolina basketball games. The **Cultural Council of Richland and Lexington Counties** (☎*803/799–3115* ⊕*www.getcultured.org*) provides information by phone or on their Web site about local cultural events, including the ballet and symphony. **Koger Center for the Arts** (✉*1051 Greene St., at Assembly St.* ☎*803/777–7500* ⊕*www.koger.sc.edu*) presents national and international theater, ballet, and musical groups, as well as individual performers. ■**TIP→ On nights where performances are being held at several venues, parking can be difficult. Check the newspaper and plan ahead.**

The **Town Theatre** (✉*1012 Sumter St., USC Campus* ☎*803/799–2510* ⊕*www.towntheatre.com*), founded in 1919, stages seven plays a year. **Trustus** (✉*520 Lady St., Vista* ☎*803/254–9732* ⊕*www.trustus.org*) is a local professional theater group. The **Workshop Theatre of South Carolina** (✉*1136 Bull St., USC Campus* ☎*803/799–4876* ⊕*www.workshoptheatre.com*) produces a number of plays.

9

NIGHTLIFE In the hopping Vista neighborhood, the **Art Bar** (✉*1211 Park St., Vista* ☎*803/929–0198* ⊕*www.artbarsc.com*) is funky, with neon-painted walls, lighted lunch boxes, and live music for dancing. **Goatfeathers** (✉*2017 Devine St., Five Points* ☎*803/256–3325*) is a bohemian bar–café that's popular with university and law-school students, and it also appeals to late-night coffee and dessert seekers.

★ If you're more into rock, **Hunter-Gatherer Brewery & Alehouse** (✉*900 Main St., USC Campus* ☎*803/748–0540*) has it on tap most nights, along with an excellent selection of beers, some made in-house. Jazz is king at **Mac's on Main** (✉*1710 Main St., Main Street area* ☎*803/929–0037* ⊕*www.macsjazznblues.com*), where local groups often jam into the night and patrons enjoy true Southern cuisine. An ice bar and multiple water features help create the big-city feel of **Blue Tapas Bar and Cocktail Lounge** (✉*721A Lady St., Vista* ☎*803/251-4447* ⊕ *www. bluecolumbia.net*), while free valet parking and a delicious menu only add to the cool atmosphere.

SPORTS & THE OUTDOORS

CANOEING & The Saluda River near Columbia has challenging Class III and IV rap-
KAYAKING ids. Saluda access is out of town in Gardendale and Saluda Shoals Park as well as at the Riverbanks Zoo. The Broad and the Saluda rivers meet in the center of town to become the calmer Congaree River. There's public access for the Congaree behind EdVenture on Senate Street at the Senate Street Landing.

Guided Saluda and Congaree river (Saluda has rapids, Congaree is calm) trips and swamp canoeing excursions can be arranged, as can canoe rentals, at **Adventure Carolina** (✉*1107 State St., 1 mi southwest of Columbia, Cayce* ☎*803/796–4505*). You can rent canoes and kayaks or sign up for guided river or swamp expeditions at the **River Runner Outdoor Center** (✉*905 Gervais St., Vista* ☎*803/771–0353* ⊕*riverrunner.us*). Canoe and kayak rentals are available at **Saluda Shoals Park** (✉*5605 Bush River Rd., 12 mi northwest of downtown Columbia, Columbia* ☎*803/772–1228* ⊕*www.icrc.net*).

Self-guided canoe trails traverse **Congaree Swamp National Park** (✉*100 National Park Rd., Hopkins* ☎*803/776–4396*), 20 mi southeast of Columbia. Guided trips are held every Saturday and Sunday from 9–11 AM. Trips fill up quickly though, so call for reservations exactly two weeks in advance.

HIKING The 1,419 acre **Sesquicentennial State Park** -(✉*9564 Two Notch Road, Northeast* ☎*803/788–2706* ⊕*www.southcarolinaparks.com* ✉*$2* ☉*Daily 8–6*) is not far from downtown, but feels like you're in the country. A 30-acre lake sits at the heart of the park, allowing for fishing and nonmotorized boating. Visitors can enjoy picnicking areas, playgrounds, and a dog park. There are also miles of nature, hiking, and mountain-biking trails.

Fodor'sChoice **Congaree Swamp National Park** (✉*100 National Park Rd., 20 mi south-*
★ *east of Columbia, Hopkins* ☎*803/776–4396* ⊕*www.nps.gov/cong* ✉*Free* ☉*Visitor center: weekdays 8:30–5, weekends 9 AM–1 PM*) has

22 mi of trails and a ¾-mi boardwalk for people with disabilities. The alluvial floodplain, bordered by high bluffs, in the 22,200-acre park contains many old-growth bottomland hardwoods (the oldest and largest trees east of the Mississippi River). The water and trees are beautifully eerie. Hiking and canoe trails line the park, which is full of wildlife, including otters, deer, and woodpeckers, as well as the occasional wild boar. Programs, such as guided nature and history walks, are held daily. When darkness falls, join park naturalists for a hike deep into the forest to search for owls and other nighttime wildlife Friday at 8:30 PM. Call for nighttime walk reservations.

SHOPPING

Many of Columbia's antiques outlets, boutique shops, and restaurants are in the ever-growing Vista neighborhood around Huger and Gervais streets, between the State House and the river. A number of intriguing shops and cafés are in Five Points, around Blossom at Harden streets, as well as along Devine Street in the Shandon neighborhood to the east. There are also antiques shops across the river on Meeting and State streets in West Columbia.

Old Mill Antique Mall (⊠ *310 State St., West Columbia* ☎ *803/796–4229*) has items from many dealers, including furniture, glassware, jewelry, and books. The **State Farmers' Market** (⊠ *1001 Bluff Rd., USC Campus* ☎ *803/737–4664*) is one of the 10 largest in the country. Fresh vegetables, along with flowers, plants, seafood, and more, are sold Monday–Saturday 6 AM to 9 PM and Sunday 1 to 6.

CAMDEN

35 mi northeast of Columbia via I–20.

A town with a horsey history and grand colonial homes, charming Camden has never paved some of its roads for the sake of the hooves that regularly trot over them. The Carolina Cup and Colonial Cup are run here.

Camden is South Carolina's oldest inland town, dating from 1732. British General Lord Cornwallis established a garrison here during the Revolutionary War and burned most of Camden before evacuating it. A center of textile trade from the late 19th century through the 1940s, Camden blossomed when it became a refuge for Northerners escaping the cold winters. Because General Sherman spared the town during the Civil War, most of its antebellum homes still stand.

GETTING HERE & AROUND

A roughly 40-minute drive northeast of Columbia will take you to Camden. A great day trip, this town is a prime location for antiquing. Once you're in the antiques and art district, you'll have easy access to stores carrying antiques, collectibles, and one-of-a-kind art. Outside of the downtown area you will find historical homes, museums, and horse race courses. Camden Carriage Company takes you on a tour on a horse-drawn carriage through Camden's loveliest neighborhood and down unpaved roads.

ESSENTIALS

Tour Information Camden Carriage Company (☎ *803/425–5737* ⊕ *www. camdencarriage.com*).

EXPLORING

When you stop in the **Kershaw County Chamber of Commerce** for brochures and information, take note of the Chamber's building: it was designed by Robert Mills, the architect of the Washington Monument. ⊠ *607 S. Broad St.* ☎ *803/432–2525 or 800/968–4037* ⊕ *www.camden-sc.org* ⊗ *Weekdays 9–5, Sat. 11–4, and Sun. 1:30–5.*

Bonds Conway House was built by the first black man in Camden to buy his freedom. The circa-1812 home has the fine details of a skilled craftsman, including wonderful woodwork and heart-pine floors. ⊠ *811 Fair St.* ☎ *803/425–1123* ⊠ *Free* ⊗ *Thurs. 1–5 or by appointment.*

National Steeplechase Museum contains the largest collection of racing memorabilia in the United States. (A steeplechase is a horse race over open land that has been set up with obstacles.) The Equisizer, a training machine used by jockeys for practice, let's you experience the race from the jockey's perspective; don't stay on too long, unless you want to feel the race all day. ⊠ *200 Knights Hill Rd.* ☎ *800/780–8117* ⊕ *www. carolina-cup.org* ⊠ *Free* ⊗ *Sept.–May, Mon.–Sat. 10–5, Sun. and other months by appointment.*

↻ The **Historic Camden Revolutionary War Site** puts emphasis on the period surrounding the British occupation of 1780. Several structures dot the site, including the 1789 **Craven House** and the **Blacksmith Shed.** The **Kershaw House,** a reconstruction of the circa-1770 home of Camden's founder, Joseph Kershaw, also served as Cornwallis's headquarters; it's furnished with period pieces. A nature trail, fortifications, powder magazine, picnic area, and crafts shop are also here. Guided tours are available by prearrangement. ⊠ *U.S. 521, 1½ mi north of I-20* ☎ *803/432–9841* ⊠ *$5 guided tours; self guided tours are free* ⊗ *Tues.–Sat. 10–5, Sun. 2–5.*

WHERE TO STAY & EAT

$$$–$$$$
CONTINENTAL
★

✕ **Mill Pond Steak House.** It's all about steak here, and what steaks they are: aged for at least 35 days before they're cut, the fillets, rib eyes, and strips are juicy, tender, and packed with flavor. You can dine alfresco overlooking the sprawling millpond or inside a trio of old buildings. The wood paneling was reclaimed from the Boykin Tractor Shed after it was destroyed by Hurricane Hugo. The more casual side of the restaurant has a vintage saloon-style bar, which, in its first life, was the soda fountain at Zemps, a drug store in Camden. Area farmers provide most of the produce; grits for the shrimp and grits are ground at the mill next door. There is a limousine service available as well to and from Camden. ■TIP→ **Save room for homemade fruit cobbler with ice cream.** ⊠ *84 Boykin Mill Rd., 10 mi south of Camden, Boykin* ☎ *803/425–8825* ▭ *AE, MC, V, D* ⊗ *Closed Sun. and Mon. No lunch.*

$–$$

▤ **Bloomsbury Inn.** Noted Civil War diarist Mary Boykin Chestnut wrote much of her famous account in this home that was built in 1849 by her husband's family. Bedrooms are richly decorated with carved-wood or wrought-iron beds and fireplaces with antique mantels. The bathrooms are decorated with original Italian tiles from the 1930s. Breakfast is a divine extravagance that begins with a fruit course, includes homemade bread, and ends with an entrée such as freshly baked quiche with ham and asparagus. ■TIP➔ **Innkeeper Bruce Brown's history tour of the home is fascinating.** Pros: breakfast is a full gourmet event, with two to three courses each morning. Cons: no elevator and no private phone in room. ✉*1707 Lyttleton St.* ☎*803/432–5858* ⊕*www.bloomsburyinn.com* ⟿*3 rooms* ♿*In-room: no phone, Wi-Fi.* ▤*AE, D, MC, V* ¶❶*BP.*

$ ☆ ⊞**Greenleaf Inn of Camden.** The 1890 McLean house serves as the main inn, with four rooms on the second floor above the dining room; the nearby Joshua Reynolds (circa 1805) house has six more rooms. Furnishings are classic Victorian, with some four-poster beds, and all bathrooms are modern. Rooms in the main inn are more spacious, those in the separate house more private. In the dining room, high ceilings and elaborate tiled fireplaces make for an elegant breakfast. There's patio dining outside. ■TIP➔ **Cheese eggs—scrambled eggs with melted cheddar—are the comfort food you've always dreamed about.** Pros: located right in town. Cons: no elevator; the property is divided into two houses. ✉*1308 Broad St.* ☎*803/425–1806 or 800/437–5874* ⊕*www.greenleafinnofcamden.com* ⟿*10 rooms* ♿*In-hotel: restaurant, no-smoking rooms* ▤*AE, D, MC, V* ¶❶*BP.*

SPORTS & THE OUTDOORS

EQUESTRIAN EVENTS You're likely to see Thoroughbreds working out most mornings October through April at the **Springdale Race Course** (✉*200 Knights Hill Rd.* ☎*803/432–6513* ⊕*www.carolina-cup.org*). Camden puts on two steeplechase events here: the Carolina Cup, in late March or early April; and the Colonial Cup, in November.

SHOPPING

Camden is known for its antiques shopping, with the heart of the antiques and arts district along Broad Street, as well as on neighboring Rutledge, DeKalb, and Market streets.

Shop for Dutch impressionist paintings at **Andries Van Dam Investment Arts and Antiques** (✉*914 Market St.* ☎*803/432–0850*)—it's as much a gallery as an antiques shop. The **Granary** (✉*830A S. Broad St.* ☎*803/432–8811* ⊕*www.thegranaryantiques.com*), which specializes in English, French, and American antiques, also has whimsical garden furniture. **Camden Antiques Market** (✉*830 S. Broad St.* ☎*803/432–0818* ⊗*Mon.–Sat. 10–6, Sun. 1–6*) has well-priced furniture and decorative art from the 18th, 19th, and 20th centuries.

If modern pieces are more your style, stroll over to **Rutledge Street Gallery** (✉*508 Rutledge St.* ☎*803/425–0071* ⊕*www.rutledgestreetgallery.com*) for sophisticated paintings, textiles, and sculpture. Browse through the antiques mall, bookstore, and other shops that comprise the **TenEleven Galleria** (✉*1011 Broad St.* ☎*803/424–1011* ⊕*www.teneleven galleria.com*), housed in a restored warehouse. Sample almond Danish pastries, lemon bars, and macaroons at the delightful **Mulberry**

9

Market Bake Shop (⊠ *536 E. DeKalb St.* ☎ *803/424–8401*). European-style butter is key to the divine cheese sticks.

AIKEN

89 mi southwest of Camden via I-20; 56 mi southwest of Columbia via I-20 and U.S. 1.

This is Thoroughbred Country, and Aiken first earned its fame in the 1890s, when wealthy Northerners wintering here built stately mansions and entertained one another with horse shows, hunts, and lavish parties. Many up-to-60-room homes stand as a testament to this era of opulence. The town is still a center for all kinds of outdoor activity, including the equestrian events of the Triple Crown, as well as tennis and golf.

GETTING HERE & AROUND
An hour's drive southwest of Columbia will take you to the rolling green horse country of Aiken. Though not a concise town square, Laurens St. and the surrounding streets offer plenty in the way of shopping, dining, and entertainment. If you're headed to the polo matches or races, the horse district is only a five-minute drive outside the downtown area.

The City of Aiken runs a nearly two-hour tour of the historic district ($12) and will customize tours to suit individual interests.

ESSENTIALS
Visitor Information City of Aiken (☎ *888/245–3672* ⊕ *www.aikenprt.net*). **Greater Aiken Chamber of Commerce** (⊠ *121 Richland Ave. E, Box 892, Aiken* ☎ *803/641–1111* ⊕ *www.aikenchamber.net*).

EXPLORING
The area's horse farms have produced many national champions, which are commemorated at the **Aiken Thoroughbred Racing Hall of Fame and Museum.** Exhibits include horse-related decorations, paintings, and sculptures, plus racing silks and trophies. The Hall of Fame is on the grounds of the 14-acre **Hopelands Gardens,** where you can wind along paths past quiet terraces and reflecting pools. There's a Touch and Scent Trail with Braille plaques. Open-air free concerts and plays are presented on Monday evening May through August. ⊠ *135 Dupree Pl., at Whiskey Rd.* ☎ *803/642–7630* ⊡ *Free* ⊙ *Museum: Sept.–May Tues.– Fri. and Sun. 2–5, Sat. 10–5; June–Aug. Sat. 10–5, Sun. 2-5; grounds: daily dawn–dusk.*

The **Aiken County Historical Museum,** in one wing of an 1860 estate, is devoted to early regional culture. It has Native American artifacts, firearms, an authentically furnished 1808 log cabin, a schoolhouse, and a miniature circus display. ⊠ *433 Newberry St. SW* ☎ *803/642–2015* ⊡ *Donations suggested* ⊙ *Tues.–Fri. 9:30–4:30, weekends 2–5.*

Aiken surrounds **Hitchcock Woods,** 2,000 acres of Southern forest with hiking trails and bridle paths. Three times the size of New York's Central Park, it's the largest urban forest in the country and is listed on the National Register of Historic Places. ■TIP→Make use of the maps available at the entrances. The park's size makes it easy to get lost. ⊠*Enter from junction of Clark Rd. and Whitney Dr., Berrie Rd., and Dibble Rd.*

Home to James Hammond, who is credited with being first to declare that "Cotton is King," **Redcliffe Plantation** remained in the family until 1975 when it was willed to the state. The 10,000-square-foot mansion (which sits on 400 acres) remains just as it was, down to the 19th-century books on the carved shelves. Slave quarters still contain bedding pallets and other coarse furnishings. Once you've toured the house (starting at 1, 2, or 3 PM), be sure to explore the grounds on the 2-mi-long trail. ■TIP→Be warned: the house has no central heat or air-conditioning. ⊠*181 Redcliffe Rd., 15 mi southwest of Aiken, Beech Island* ☎*803/827–1473* ⊕*www. southcarolinaparks.com* 🎫*$4* ☉*Grounds: Thurs.–Mon. 9–5, House: tours run Thurs.–Mon. 1, 2, and 3* PM.

> ## CELEBRATING FOOD
>
> Summer kicks off the festival season in the Midlands, and there's plenty to celebrate. Every Fourth of July, indulge in fresh peach ice cream, or just bite into a sun-warmed peach at the **Lexington County Peach Festival** (☎*803/892–5207* ⊕*www. midnet.sc.edu/peach*) in Gilbert. In August the peanut is king at Pelion's annual **South Carolina Peanut Party** (⊕*www.scpeanutparty.com*). September's **Okra Strut** (☎*803/781–6122* ⊕*www. irmookrastrut.com*) in Irmo is slimy fun. Check out ⊕*www. scbarbeque.com* for information on South Carolina barbecue festivals.

Stephen Ferrell has an extensive collection of Edgefield pottery on display at his shop, **Old Edgefield Pottery.** Ferrell, like his father, is an accomplished potter in his own right. ■TIP→Ask to see original pieces crafted by Dave, a literate slave who created some of the first "face vessels" that have made Edgefield stoneware so collectible. ⊠*230 Simpkins St., 20 mi northwest of Aiken, Edgefield* ☎*803/637–2060* ⊕*www. edgefieldpottery.com* ☉*Tues.–Sat. 10–5.*

WHERE TO EAT

$$$–$$$$
CONTINENTAL
✕**Linda's Bistro.** Chef Linda Rooney elevates traditional European favorites, turning out excellent mushroom-Gruyère tarts, risotto with roasted mushrooms and Asiago cheese, and steak frites. Main courses come with a salad, a vegetable, and potatoes. Rum-coconut-cream bread pudding is a favorite for dessert. It's all served in an open, café-like environment. ⊠*135 York St. SE* ☎*803/648–4853* ▤*AE, MC, V* ☉*Closed Sun. No lunch.*

$$–$$$
ECLECTIC
✕**Malia's.** Locals love this busy contemporary restaurant, with dim lighting and dark fabrics that convey a cool class. The menu changes monthly and serves up a wide variety of international cuisine that includes American, Caribbean, French, and Italian entrées and even some curry dishes. Dinner reservations are recommended. ⊠*120 Laurens St. SW* ☎*803/643–3086* ⊕*www.maliasrestaurant.com* ▤*AE, D, MC, V* ☉*No lunch Mon. or weekends. No dinner Sun.–Wed.*

9

¢ ✗**New Moon Cafe.** The coffee beans are roasted right next door. Here you
AMERICAN can pair Aiken's best coffee with freshly baked muffins and sweet rolls,
panini sandwiches and salads, and homemade soups. ■ **TIP→ The black-
bean and crab bisque is particularly good.** ✉*116 Laurens St.* ☎*803/643–
7088* ⚐*Reservations not accepted* ▤*V, MC* ☾*No dinner.*

WHERE TO STAY

¢ ☷**Briar Patch.** You can learn plenty about both the Old and New South
from the knowledgeable innkeepers of this terrific B&B, which was
formerly tack rooms in Aiken's stable district. You get two choices—
either the frilly room with French-provincial furniture or the less dramatic one with pine antiques and a weather vane. **Pros:** close to the
polo fields; continental breakfast; rooms have cable TV, coffeemakers,
and private baths. **Cons:** though the house is well maintained, the clay
tennis courts and surrounding yards are overgrown and weathered.
✉*544 Magnolia La. SE,* ☎*803/649–2010* ⊕*www.bbonline.com/sc/
briar* ⮢*2 rooms* ⚭*In-room: no phone, refrigerator. In-hotel: tennis
court, no-smoking rooms* ▤*No credit cards* ☉*BP.*

$$–$$$ ☷**The Willcox.** Winston Churchill, Franklin D. Roosevelt, and the
Fodor'sChoice Astors have slept at this grand, 19th-century inn. Massive stone fire-
★ places, rosewood trim, heart-pine floors, and antiques grace the lobby.
Guest rooms and suites contain upscale furniture with classic lines, like
the sleek, dark-stain, four-poster beds dressed with down pillows and
comforters. Choose to soak in the extra-deep tub or relax beside your
fireplace. Here you can pretend, at least for one night, that you're a
Vanderbilt. Staff goes above and beyond to accommodate their guests.
Pros: the complimentary breakfast is a huge step above normal continental fare; it's a hot full Southern meal. **Cons:** though rooms have
mini-fridges stocked with water and drinks, there's no room service.
✉*100 Colleton Ave.* ☎*803/648–1898 or 877/648–2200* ⊕*www.
thewillcox.com* ⮢*15 rooms, 7 suites* ⚭*In-Room: refrigerator, Internet, Wi-Fi. In-hotel: restaurant, bar, pool, spa, some pets allowed, no-
smoking rooms* ▤*AE, D, DC, MC, V* ☉*BP.*

SPORTS & THE OUTDOORS

EQUESTRIAN In Aiken, polo matches are played at **Whitney Field** (✉*200 Mead Dr., off
EVENTS Whiskey Rd., U.S. 19* ☎ *803/643–3611* ⊕*www.aikenpoloclub.org*)
Sunday at 3, September through November and March through July.

Three weekends in late March and early April are set aside for the famed
Triple Crown (✉*Horse district, off Whiskey Rd., U.S. 19* ☎*803/641–
1111*), which includes Thoroughbred trials of promising yearlings, a
steeplechase, and harness races by young horses making their debut.

NINETY SIX

*53 mi northwest of Aiken via Rte. 19, U.S. 25, and Rte. 24; 73 mi west
of Columbia via U.S. 378, U.S. 178, and Rte. 248.*

The town of Ninety Six, on an old Native American trade route, is so
named for being 96 mi from the Cherokee village of Keowee in the Blue
Ridge Mountains—the distance a young Cherokee maiden, Cateechee,

is supposed to have ridden to warn her English lover of a threatened Native American massacre.

Ninety Six National Historic Site commemorates two Revolutionary War battles. The visitor center's museum has descriptive displays, along with a ten-minute historical film. Along the mile-long paved path through the woods and surrounding fields there are remnants of the old village, a reconstructed French and Indian War stockade, and Revolutionary-era fortifications. ✉*1103 Highway 248, 2 mi south of Ninety Six* ☎*864/543–4068* ⊕*www.nps.gov/nisi* ✉*Free* ☉*Daily 8–5.*

ABBEVILLE

★ *25 mi west of Ninety Six via Rte. 34 and Rte. 72; 102 mi west of Columbia.*

Abbeville may well be one of inland South Carolina's most satisfying lesser-known towns. An appealing historic district includes the old business areas, early churches, and residential areas. What was called the "Southern cause" by supporters of the Confederacy was born and died here: it's where the first organized secession meeting was held and where, on May 2, 1865, Confederate president Jefferson Davis officially disbanded the defeated armies of the South in the last meeting of his war council.

GETTING HERE & AROUND
Abbeville is a little more than an hour west of Columbia. Most of the sites, including the opera house, are around its quaint town square, with shopping and eateries all within walking distance. A short drive—or a long walk—past the square is the historic Burt-Stark Mansion.

ESSENTIALS
Visitor Information Greater Abbeville Chamber of Commerce (✉*107 Court Sq., Abbeville* ☎*864/366–4600* ⊕*www.abbevillescchamber.com*).

EXPLORING
The **Abbeville Welcome Center** (✉*107 Court Sq.*) has on display a series of paintings by Wilbur Kurtz, a respected authority on pre–Civil War life in the early to mid-20th century. Kurtz, a consultant on the movies *Gone With the Wind* and *Song of the South*, also painted the *Battle of Atlanta* murals on the Atlanta Cyclorama. The oversize Abbeville paintings depict Civil War scenes including the first secession meeting and Jefferson Davis's final Council of War meeting. They have been completely restored and are quite mesmerizing because of their size and detail.

In 1865 the Confederate council met at the **Burt-Stark Mansion** (1820) and Jefferson Davis disbanded the Confederate armies, effectively ending the Civil War. The house was a private residence until 1971, when Mary Stark Davis died. She willed the house to the city, with a provision that nothing be added or removed from the house. It's filled with lovely antiques, carved-wood surfaces, and old family photos. Her clothing is still in the dresser drawers. ✉*306 N. Main St.* ☎*864/366–0166*

⊕ *www.burt-stark.com* ⊠ *$3* ⊗ *Fri. and Sat. 1–5 and Mon.–Thurs. by appointment.*

The **Abbeville Opera House** faces the old town square. Built in 1908, it has been renovated to reflect the grandeur of the days when lavish road shows and stellar entertainers took center stage. Current productions range from contemporary light comedies to local renderings of Broadway musicals. Call for tours. ⊠ *Town Sq.* ☎ *864/366–2157.*

Built in 1860, **Trinity Episcopal Church** is the town's oldest church. Complete with a 125-foot spire, an original chancery window imported from England, and a rare working 1860 John Baker tracker organ, Trinity is an example of Gothic Revival architecture. ⊠ *105 Church St.* ☎ *864/366–4600* ⊠ *Free* ⊗ *Daily 10–5.*

WHERE TO STAY & EAT

$–$$
AMERICAN
★

✗**Village Grille.** The menu spans a wide variety, from hamburgers to fillets, but many locals frequent the Village Grille because of the herb rotisserie chicken. As much of the food preparation as possible is done in house, meaning burgers are ground on the spot and salads consist of locally grown organic veggies. Antique mirrors hang on pomegranate-color walls below high ceilings. The feeling here is trendy yet easygoing; the staff bends over backward to please. ⊠ *110 Trinity St.* ☎ *864/366–2500* ⊟ *AE, D, MC, V* ⊗ *Closed Sun., Mon., and Tues. nights*

¢
AMERICAN

✗**Yoder's Dutch Kitchen.** Try some authentic Pennsylvania-Dutch home cooking in this unassuming South Carolina redbrick building. There's a lunch buffet and evening smorgasbord with fried chicken, stuffed cabbage, Dutch meat loaf, breaded veal Parmesan, and plenty of vegetables. ■ TIP➔ **Shoofly pie can be purchased to go.** ⊠ *809 E. Greenwood St., east of downtown* ☎ *864/366–5556* ⊟ *AE, MC, V* ⊗ *Closed Sun.–Tues. No dinner Wed. and Thurs.*

¢

▣**Belmont Inn.** Because of the theater-dining-and-lodging packages, the Belmont Inn is a popular overnight stop for opera-house-goers. The Spanish-style redbrick building with colonnade, built in the 1900s, underwent a major update in 2008. Guest rooms are spacious, with high ceilings, pine floors, and period furniture. **Pros:** ideal location; it's mere steps away from the opera house and town square; lunch and dinner on the veranda offer great views of the town. **Cons:** breakfast is not served, so guests have to head to local restaurants. ⊠ *104 E. Pickens St.* ☎ *864/459–9625 or 877/459–8118* ⇆ *26 rooms* � &*In-room: Internet, Wi-Fi. In-hotel: restaurant, no-smoking rooms* ⊟ *AE, D, DC, MC, V* ❑*BP.*

THE UPSTATE

The Upstate, also known as the Upcountry, in the northwest corner of the state, has long been a favorite for family vacations because of its temperate climate and natural beauty. The abundant lakes and waterfalls and several state parks (including Caesar's Head, Keowee-Toxaway, Oconee, Table Rock, and the Chattooga National Wild and Scenic River) provide all manner of recreational activities. Beautiful anytime, the 130-mi Cherokee Foothills Scenic Highway (Route 11),

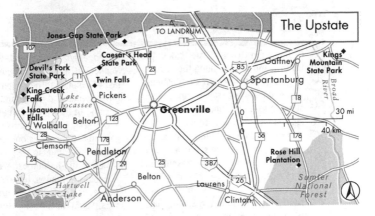

which goes through the Blue Ridge Mountains, is especially delightful in spring (when the peach trees are in bloom) and autumn.

GREENVILLE

100 mi northwest of Columbia via I–26 and I–385.

Once known for its textile and other manufacturing plants, Greenville has reinvented itself as a trendy and sophisticated city able to support a surprising number of restaurants, galleries, and boutiques along a tree-lined Main Street that passes a stunning natural waterfall. Anchored by two performance centers, the city's business district is alive well into most evenings with couples and families enjoying the energy of this revitalized Southern city. Downtown development has been so successful that many young professionals are moving here and creating interesting living spaces from old warehouses and retail establishments.

GETTING HERE & AROUND

Greenville is a little over two hours northwest of Columbia. While Columbia sits in a valley of sorts, the Greenville area is more mountainous. There is plenty of hiking and numerous waterfalls just outside of town. The revitalized Main Street area is a great base camp for your stay. The street is a long tree-lined stretch of shops, restaurants, and hotels. To the south, the road runs through Falls Park and passes the Greenville Drive Stadium. The northern end runs close to the Heritage Green neighborhood, which is a block of museums, theaters, and a library. Be prepared when driving around the outskirts of Greenville—the I–185, a connector loop of I–85 and I–385, is a toll road, so have your dollars ready.

ESSENTIALS

Visitor Information **Greater Greenville Convention and Visitors Bureau** (⊠ *206 S. Main St.* ☎ *864/233-0461 or 800/717-0023* ⊕ *www.greenvillecvb. com).* **Discover Upcountry Carolina Association** (⌂ *Box 3116, Greenville 29602* ☎ *864/233-2690 or 800/849-4766* ⊕ *www.theupcountry.com).*

CLOSE UP

The Palmetto Trail

Beginning in Oconee State Park in the Upstate and ending along the coast just north of Charleston, the Palmetto Trail is the perfect way to travel the state on foot or by mountain bike. Marked for travel in both directions by way of standard trail blazes and occasional signs, the route spans 425-miles of South Carolina's natural resources. That mileage is broken into over 20 passages that vary in length from a short 7-mi section to a multiday hike that's roughly 50 miles. The trail winds through state parks and national forests and past Revolutionary War battlefields—all with glorious views.

The best place to begin your Palmetto Trail journey is the **High Hills Outdoors Center** (✉ 2070 Hwy. 261 S, Wedgefield ☎ 803/494–5954) in Wedgefield, about 45 minutes southeast of Columbia. The center is open on weekends and hosts guided hikes on some of the Midlands' passages on a weekly basis. They also have an ongoing history series on Sundays and occasional outings to trail passages farther away. The outpost is also full of maps, information, books, and knowledgeable staff. A second outpost of the Palmetto Trail, the **Hell Hole Outdoor Center** (✉ 1174 N. Main, St. Stephen ☎ 843/567–4480) can be found in a corner of the St. Stephen Community Visitor Center near Charleston. Check out the Palmetto Trail Web site: ⊕ www.palmetto-conservation.org for more information.

EXPLORING

★ The renowned international collection of religious art at **Bob Jones University Museum & Gallery** includes works by Botticelli, Rembrandt, Rubens, and van Dyck. Note that children younger than six are not permitted. ✉ Bob Jones University, 1700 Wade Hampton Blvd. ☎ 864/242–5100 ⊕ www.bjumg.org ☞ $5; free Sun. ☉ Tues.–Sun. 2–5.

M&G is the new Bob Jones University satellite gallery. With two stories of rotating exhibits, the smaller gallery carries a tenth of the larger's collection. Upstairs you'll find hands on exhibits. Kids of all ages are allowed in this gallery. ■ TIP➜ The first Saturday of each month staff has a story time for the kids. ✉ Corner of Buncombe and Atwood Sts., Heritage Green ☎ 864/242–5100 ⊕ www.bjumg.org ☞ $5 ☉ Tues.–Sat. 10–5 and Sun. 2–5.

Exhibits at the **Upcountry History Museum** focus on the history of the 15 counties of the South Carolina Upstate. There are two floors of interactive displays and a small theater where special programs are regularly presented. The museum is self-guided, but guided trips can be arranged with reservations. ✉ 540 Buncombe St., Heritage Green ☎ 864/467–3100 ⊕ www.upcountryhistory.org ☞ $5 ☉ Tues–Sat 10–5 and Sun. 1–5. The **Greenville County Museum of Art** displays American works dating from the colonial era. Works by Andy Warhol, Georgia O'Keeffe, Andrew Wyeth, Jasper Johns, and noted Southern artists are on exhibit. ✉ 420 College St. ☎ 864/271–7570 ⊕ www.greenvillemuseum.org ☞ Free ☉ Tues., Wed., Fri., and Sat. 11–5, Thurs. 11–8, Sun. 1–5.

The **Shoeless Joe Jackson Museum and Baseball Library** is in the former home of baseball great Joseph Jackson. He, along with seven other White Sox players, were accused of throwing the 1919 World Series. Though he was found not guilty in the 1921 Black Sox Trial, Jackson was banned from playing baseball. The museum has records, artifacts, photographs, and a film, along with a library of baseball books donated from fans around the country. ✉ *356 Field St., across from Fluor Field, Historic West End* ☎ *864/235–6280* ⊕ *www.shoelessjoejackson.org* ✉ *Free* ☉ *Sat. 10–2, home game nights 5:30–7.*

OFF THE BEATEN PATH

Twin Falls. The white water swooshes over wide gray boulders on the right; the falls on the left are higher. Don't give in to the temptation to climb the rocks leading to the top of the falls; not only is the view not much better but the stones are very slippery. The trail is on public property, a ¼-mi hike one-way. ✉ *Cleo Chapman Rd., off Rte. 178, north of Pickens, 24 mi east of Greenville.*

Fodor's Choice
★
🐌

There are more than 50 mi of hiking trails within **Mountain Bridge Wilderness Area,** 30 mi north of Greenville, which encompasses two state parks. The trail leading to 420-foot-tall Raven Cliff Falls can be accessed 1 mi north of the main entrance to **Caesar's Head State Park** (✉ *8155 Geer Highway, U.S. 276, Cleveland* ☎ *864/836–6115* ⊕ *www.southcarolinaparks.com* ✉ *Overlook is free, $2 for use of hiking trails* ☉ *Office: daily 9–5, overlook daily until dark*); along the way there are spectacular views of river gorges and pine-covered mountains. Cross Matthews Creek on a suspension bridge; the view of the falls is worth the terror of knowing you're held in the air by nothing but wire. Register at Park Headquarters before you head out on the trail. Near the headquarters are Table Rock and Devil's Kitchen, a geological phenomenon that stays cool even in the heat of summer. Famous for the Rim of the Gap trail, which has views of Rainbow Falls, **Jones Gap State Park** (✉ *303 Jones Gap Rd., 6 mi east off U.S. 276, Marionetta* ☎ *864/836–3647*) is 6 mi east of U.S. 276. Access several trails from the Park Headquarters, or pick up a map and drive to one of the well-marked trailheads. ■ **TIP→ Be sure to pick up your trail map and register before venturing into the wilderness; some of the trails are long and strenuous.** ⊕ *www.southcarolinaparks.com* ✉ *$2* ☉ *Daily 7 AM–9 PM during daylight saving time, must be off trails by 8 PM; daily 9–6 rest of yr.*

Devils Fork State Park, on Lake Jocassee, has luxurious villas and camping facilities, hiking, boating, and fishing. Lower Whitewater Falls plunges more than 200 feet over huge boulders to splash into the lake waters. The falls can be viewed from an overlook or from a boat on the lake. ✉ *161 Holcombe Cr., off Rte. 11, north of Salem, 45 mi northwest of Greenville* ☎ *864/944–2639* ⊕ *www.discoversouthcarolina.com* ✉ *$2* ☉ *Daily 7–9 during daylight saving time; daily 7–7 rest of yr.; main boat ramp open 24 hrs.*

WHERE TO EAT

$$$–$$$$
AMERICAN

✕ **Augusta Grill.** Depending on what's in season, and on the whims of the chef, menu selections change daily. Seafood such as triggerfish with creamy crabmeat beurre blanc and beef with one of chef Bob Hackell's made-from-scratch sauces are typical. You can also order dinner as a series of small plates. The crab-cake special on Wednesday night packs the house. ■TIP➔ To be sure the kitchen hasn't run out of their signature blackberry cobbler by the time you have dessert, be sure to order yours at the beginning of the meal. ⊠*1818 Augusta St.* ☎*864/242–0316* ⊕*www.augustagrill.com* ▤*AE, D, MC, V* ⊘*Tues.–Sat. No lunch.*

$$$–$$$$ ✕ **Devereaux's.** The exposed brick walls and dark wood beams are
SOUTHERN   tell-tale signs of the building's former life as a 1902 cigar factory. Completely refurbished, it's now home to award winning chef Steven Devereaux Greene's restaurant. The contemporary menu has a Southern flair, and you can expect such main dishes as barbecue glazed pork loin and pine nut crusted rack of lamb, or try a little of everything with the chef's tasting menus. There are also unique desserts like the goat cheese cheesecake with lavender ice cream. The kitchen is open so patrons can watch their food being prepared. ⊠*25 E. Court St., Main Street* ☎*864/241–3030* ▤*AE, D, MC, V* ⊘*Closed Mon. No lunch.*

$$$–$$$$ ✕ **Soby's New South Cuisine.** The decorator palette of plums and golds is
SOUTHERN   a stunning contrast to the original brick and wood that was uncovered during the renovation of this 19th-century cotton exchange building. Although the menu changes seasonally, perennial favorites—a layered appetizer of fried green tomatoes and jalapeño pimiento cheese, shrimp, and locally ground grits, and the famous mind-numbing white-chocolate banana-cream pie—are always available. ⊠*207 S. Main St.* ☎*864/232–7007* ⊕*www.sobys.com* ▤*AE, MC, V* ⊘*No dinner Sun. No lunch.*

$ ✕ **Stax's Omega Diner.** This contemporary diner has both booths and
ECLECTIC   a half-circle counter with stools. The menu lists a little of everything: bacon and eggs, burgers, souvlaki, Greek-style chicken, shrimp, and grits. When you're done with your meal, check out the dessert menu from the Stax bakery next door. ⊠*72 Orchard Park Dr.* ☎*864/297–6639* ▤*AE, DC, MC, V.*

¢   ✕ **Two Chefs Delicatessen.** Mix and match from the deli's selection of deli-
AMERICAN   cious homemade sandwiches and salads. Try the roasted-potato salad, dried-cranberry-and-grilled-chicken salad, or pepper-crusted turkey on rosemary sourdough. There are a lot of tempting desserts, too, including apple-brandy cake, flourless chocolate cake, and fruit tarts. There's a second, to-go location on the east side. ⊠*104 S. Main St., Ste. 105* ☎*864/370–9336* ⊘*Closed weekends. Two Chefs To Go,* ⊠*8590 Pelham Rd.* ☎*864/284–9970* ▤*MC, V* ⊘*Closed Sun. No dinner Sat.*

WHERE TO STAY

$–$$ ▦ **Hyatt Regency Hotel.** This upscale chain offering's best asset is its location in the midst of the revitalized downtown of shops and restaurants. Rooms come with one king or queen bed or two doubles. Make sure you ask for a room overlooking the palm-filled atrium; these are far better than those without views. **Pros:** when you don't feel like fighting the busy restaurants, the Hyatt offers in-room dining. **Cons:** no airport shuttle. ⊠*220 N. Main St.* ☎*864/235–1234 or 800/233–1234* ⊕*greenville.hyatt.com* ⇪*328 rooms* ⌂*In-hotel: restaurant, room service, bar, pool, gym, no-smoking rooms* ▤*AE, D, DC, MC, V* ⎛❘*EP.*

$$$$ ⊡ **La Bastide.** About 19 mi northwest (30 minutes) of Greenville in the
★ sloping Piedmont hills, this country inn is a wonderful experience.
Rooms have European linens, French antiques and reproductions,
elaborate wrought-iron chandeliers, and gas fireplaces. The inn is surrounded by the Crescent Mountain Vineyards, and guests have quite
a view of the vineyards and outlying mountains. **Pros:** offers driving
tours of the Blue Ridge Parkway. **Cons:** no workout or spa facilities,
and in-room massages are by appointment only. ⊠ *10 Road of Vines,
Travelers Rest* ☎*864/836–8463 or 877/836–8463* ⊕*www.labastide.
com* ⬐*13 rooms* ⸛*In-hotel: restaurant, no-smoking rooms* ⊟*AE,
D, DC, MC, V* ⎟⎥*BP.*

¢ ⊡ **Phoenix–Greenville's Inn.** Ask for a room overlooking the courtyard
gardens and pool at this accommodating Southern inn. The graceful
spindles of the four-poster beds are painted or stained according to the
room's decor (white, mahogany, cherry). Although there's no health
club on-site, guests have free access to the Greenville Sports Club, a
full-service facility that's a five-minute drive away. **Pros:** the in-house
Palms restaurant is award-winning; there's a free shuttle to the airport by appointment. **Cons:** quite a drive from the downtown area;
no elevator. ⊠*246 N. Pleasantburg Dr.* ☎*800/257–3529* ⊕*www.
phoenixgreenvillesinn.com* ⬐*181 rooms, 3 suites* ⸛*In-room: Wi-Fi.
In-hotel: restaurant, bar, pool, no-smoking rooms* ⊟*AE, D, DC, MC,
V* ⎟⎥*BP.*

¢–$ ⊡ **Westin Poinsett Hotel.** A 1925, 12-story hotel has been brought back to
life by Westin. In the public spaces intricate moldings adorn the many
columns, ironwork rails and chandeliers are apparent throughout, and
decorative plasterwork has been restored. The large guest rooms have
down comforters, marble baths, and high ceilings. **Pros:** located in the
middle of Main Street, so there's little reason to drive anywhere; two
rooms have exercise machines en suite. **Cons:** some guests have com-
plained that rooms are boring and beds are uncomfortable. ⊠*120 S.
Main St.* ☎*864/421–9700* ⊕*www.westin.com* ⬐*180 rooms, 9 suites*
⸛*In-room: safe, Wi-Fi. In-hotel: restaurant, room service, bar, gym,
no-smoking rooms* ⊟*AE, D, DC, MC, V* ⎟⎥*EP.*

NIGHTLIFE & THE ARTS

The **Handlebar** (⊠*304 E. Stone Ave.* ☎*864/233–6173*) has been bring-
ing small-stage live music to Greenville since 1994. Monday is known
for no cover and lots of jazz, Tuesday brings a bluegrass jam to the
bar and a swing dance to the concert hall. The 16,000-seat **Bi-Lo Center** (⊠*650 N. Academy St.* ☎*864/233–2525* ⊕*www.bilocenter.com*)
hosts major concerts and sporting events. The **Peace Center for the Arts**
(⊠*101 W. Broad St.* ☎*864/467–3030* ⊕*www.peacecenter.org*), which
sits along the Reedy River, presents star performers, touring Broadway
shows, dance companies, chamber music, and local groups.

SPORTS & THE OUTDOORS

South Carolinians sometimes prefer Upstate golf courses to those on
the coast, as they're less crowded and enjoy a slightly cooler climate.
The area's rolling hills provide an added challenge.

9

Links O'Tryon (⊠*11250 New Cut Rd., Campobello* ☎*864/472–6723*) is an 18-hole course with stunning views of the Blue Ridge Mountains and fieldstone bridges and walls in the Tom Jackson–design layout. **Rock at Jocassee** (⊠*171 Sliding Rock Rd., Pickens* ☎*864/878–2030* ⊕*www.golftherock.com*) is a mountain course with many water hazards; its signature hole has a waterfall view.

SHOPPING

The shopping area along Greenville's Main Street and adjoining West End may be just a mile or so long, but it's chockablock full of interesting shops.

O. P. Taylors (⊠*117 N. Main St.* ☎*864/467–1984*) is a super-cool toy emporium that even adults can love. Filling two floors with French linens, furniture, and home accessories, **Postcard from Paris** (⊠*631 S. Main St.* ☎*864/233–6622*) is a slice of the Left Bank in the deep South. The shop is hip, but the service is so friendly at **Augustatwenty** (⊠*20 Augusta St., at S. Main St.* ☎*864/233–2600*) that you won't feel uncomfortable browsing the racks of designer duds. Open from mid-June until the first of November, **Perdue's Mountain Fruit Farm** (⊠*Highway 11 and Tigerville Rd.* ☎*864/895–0608*) sells an always-changing selection of locally grown fruits such as peaches, blackberries, pears, apples, and raspberries. Owner Dick Perdue also makes the jams, jellies, applesauce, and ciders that fill the shelves along with local honey.

KINGS MOUNTAIN NATIONAL MILITARY PARK

70 mi northeast of Greenville via I–85.

A Revolutionary War battle considered an important turning point was fought here on October 7, 1780. Colonial Tories commanded by British major Patrick Ferguson were soundly defeated by ragtag patriot forces from the southern Appalachians. Visitor center exhibits, dioramas, and an orientation film describe the action. A paved self-guided trail leads through the battlefield. ⊠*Off Exit 2, I–85, Blacksburg* ☎*864/936–7921* ⊕*www.nps.gov/kimo* ☞*Free* ☉*Daily 9–5.*

The 6,000-acre **Kings Mountain State Park,** adjacent to the national military park, has camping, swimming, fishing, boating, and nature and hiking trails. ⊠*Off Exit 2, I–85, Blacksburg* ☎*864/222–3209* ⊕ *www.southcarolinaparks.com* ☞*$2* ☉*Daily 7 AM–9 PM during daylight savings time; daily 8–6 rest of yr.*

Savannah, GA

10

By Eileen
Robinson
Smith

GENERAL JAMES OGLETHORPE, SAVANNAH'S FOUNDER, set sail for England in 1743, never to return. His last instructions, it's said, were, "Don't change a thing until I get back." That local joke holds more than a bit of truth. Savannah's elegant mansions, dripping Spanish moss, and sticky summer heat can make the city seem sleepy and stubbornly resistant to change. Which is exactly why many folks like the place.

Savannah, Georgia's oldest city, began its modern history on February 12, 1733, when Oglethorpe and 120 colonists arrived at Yamacraw Bluff on the Savannah River to found the 13th and last of the British colonies. As the port city grew, more settlers from England and Ireland arrived, joined by Scottish Highlanders, French Huguenots, Germans, Austrian Salzburgers, Sephardic and Ashkenazic Jews, Moravians, Italians, Swiss, Welsh, and Greeks.

In 1793 Eli Whitney of Connecticut, who was tutoring on a plantation near Savannah, invented a mechanized means of "ginning" seeds from cotton bolls. Cotton soon became king, and Savannah, already a busy seaport, flourished under its reign. Waterfront warehouses were filled with "white gold," and brokers trading in the Savannah Cotton Exchange set world prices. The white gold brought in hard currency; the city prospered.

General William Tecumseh Sherman's army rampaged across Georgia in 1864, setting fire to railroads, munitions factories, bridges, and just about anything else between them and the sea. Rather than see the city torched, Savannahians surrendered to the approaching Yankees.

As the cotton market declined in the early 20th century, the city's economy collapsed. For decades Savannah's historic buildings languished; many were razed or allowed to decay. Cobwebs replaced cotton in the dilapidated riverfront warehouses. The tide turned in the 1950s, when residents began a concerted effort—which continues to this day—to restore and preserve the city's architectural heritage.

ORIENTATION & PLANNING

GETTING ORIENTED

The Historic District. A link to the past is Savannah's main draw for travelers: the 2½-square-mi Landmark Historic District is the nation's largest. It is where the city's 22 squares and most of its accommodations, restaurants, and shops are located. The borders of the District are River Street, the Savannah River, Gwinnett Street, East Broad Street, and Martin Luther King Jr. Boulevard.

Tybee Island. This island 18 mi east of Savannah, which has always been a kitschy throwback to the 1950s, but its honky-tonk atmosphere is beginning to fade. You'll find accommodations and some good restaurants here, as well as the closest good beaches to Savannah and a raft of water-sports options.

TOP REASONS TO GO

Intriguing Architecture: Close to half of the 2,500 buildings in Savannah have architectural or historic significance. The many building styles—Georgian, Gothic Revival, Victorian, Italianate, Federal, and Romanesque—make strolling the tree-lined neighborhoods a delight. The 19th-century Telfairs's Owens-Thomas house is a particular highlight.

Midnight in the Garden of Good and Evil: John Berendt's famous 1994 book about a local murder and the city's eccentric characters still draws many travelers eager to visit the places mentioned, including the Mercer-Williams House, where Jim Williams once had his lucrative antiques business.

Famous Southern Restaurants: Savannah's elegant, fine-dining restaurants, notably Elizabeth's on 37th and Olde Pink House, have well-deserved reputations. Garabaldi's has a beautiful interior and exquisite, contemporary Italian cuisine. And, of course, who hasn't heard of Paula Deen's restaurant The Lady & Sons from watching her show on the Food Network.

Historic Inns and Bed & Breakfasts: When most people dream of a trip to Savannah, they envision staying in a romantic old mansion fronting a prominent square, where they further picture themselves sipping wine on the veranda. It is an authentic and unique experience, and everyone should have it, at least once.

Savannah by Night: Savannah is known in the Southeast as a party town. If you can't have fun in the Big Savanne, then you simply may not have the capability to have fun anywhere. "To Go" cups make barhopping in this red-hot city a favorite evening activity. Nocturnal ghost tours are another popular nocturnal must-do.

SAVANNAH PLANNER

GETTING HERE & AROUND

You can fly into Savannah; you need a car only if you want to explore beyond the historic district.

BY AIR Savannah is served by Continental Express, Northwest Airlink, Delta, United Express, and US Airways/Express for domestic flights. Savannah/Hilton Head International Airport is 18 mi west of downtown.

BY BOAT & FERRY Belles Ferry provides a regular service from the City Hall dock in the Historic District to the Westin Savannah Harbor Golf Resort & Spa at the International Convention Center, on Hutchinson Island. Ferries are part of the transit system and run daily 7 AM to 11 PM, with departures every 15 minutes. The complimentary crossing takes two minutes.

BY BUS The free CAT (Chatham Area Transit) Shuttle operates throughout the Historic District, running on a north–south route once an hour. For other Savannah buses, the fare is $1. The Dot is Savannah's other free downtown transportation system. In addition to the Savannah Belles Ferry, the Dot operates an Express Shuttle around downtown and historic 1930s River Street Streetcars, which began service in late 2008.

10

BY TAXI AAA Adam Cab Co., MC Transportation, and Yellow Cab Company are the three major taxi companies in Savannah; all can be hailed on the street or called, and all operate 24 hours a day. The standard taxi fare is $1.82 or $1.92 per mile; some companies offer flat rates to and from the airport and Tybee Island.

Savannah Pedicab is a bicycle rickshaw that costs $45 per hour or $25 per half-hour (you can also rent a pedicab for the day for $150). They operate from 11 AM to midnight (2 AM on weekends). They also rent cruiser-style bikes for $20 per day, and will deliver to your inn.

BY TRAIN Amtrak runs its Silver Service/Palmetto route down the East Coast from New York to Miami, stopping in Savannah. The station is about 6 mi from downtown.

VISITOR
INFORMATION The Savannah Area Convention & Visitors Bureau's welcome center is open daily weekdays 8:30 to 5 and weekends 9 to 5. The center has a useful audiovisual overview of the city and is the starting point for a number of guided tours. Tybee Island's visitor center, just off Highway 80, is open daily 10 to 6.

ESSENTIALS **Airport Contacts Savannah/Hilton Head International Airport** (⊠ *400 Airways Ave., West Chatham* ☎ *912/964-0514* ⊕ *www.savannahairport.com*).

Boat & Ferry Contacts Savannah Belles Ferry (⊠ *900 E. Gwinnett St.* ☎ *912/233-5767* ⊕ *www.catchacat.org*).

Bus Contacts Chatham Area Transit (CAT) (☎ *912/233-5767* ⊕ *www.catchacat. org*). **The Dot** (☎ *912/447-4026* ⊕ *connectonthedot.com*).

Taxi Contacts AAA Adam Cab Incorporated (☎ *912/927-7466*). **MC Transportation** ☎ *912/786-9191*). **Savannah Pedicab** (☎ *912/232-7900* ⊕ *www. savannahpedicab.com*). **Yellow Cab** (☎ *912/236-1133*).

Train Contacts Amtrak (☎ *800/872-7245* ⊕ *www.amtrak.com*).

Visitor Information Contacts Savannah Area Convention & Visitors Bureau (⊠ *101 E. Bay St., Historic District* ☎ *912/644-6401 or 877/728-2662* ⊕ *www. savannahvisit.com*). **Savannah Area Welcome Center** (⊠ *301 Martin Luther King Jr. Blvd.* ☎ *912/944-0455* ⊕ *www.savannahvisit.com*). **Tybee Island Visitor Information Center** (⊠ *Campbell Ave. and Hwy. 80, Tybee Island* ☎ *912/786-5444 or 800/868-2322* ⊕ *www.tybeevisit.com*).

TOURS

BOAT TOURS Riverboat cruises go up the river from Factors Walk and cost about $20. The causeway is mainly commercial, with many deserted warehouses, so it's not a terribly scenic ride, but it is narrated, has a bar, plays Jimmy Buffet, and is most relaxing. The gospel dinner cruise ($35) has a Southern buffet and gospel singers to entertain.

HISTORIC
DISTRICT
TOURS Carriage Tours of Savannah, whose tours depart from the City Market or the Visitor Center (seasonally), takes you through the Historic District by day or by night at a 19th-century clip-clop pace for a modest $20 per person.The Freedom Trail Tour is a black history tour conducted twice-daily, leaving from the Savannah Welcome Center for $20 per person. ld Savannah Tours has years of experience and offers

the widest variety of tours, including a hop-on/hop-off trolley tour ($23). Old Town Trolley Tours has narrated 90-minute tours traversing the Historic District. Trolleys stop at 13 designated stops every half hour daily 9 to 4:30; you can hop on and off as you please. The cost is $23. The Hearse Ghost Tours may be like nothing you have ever done before. These black hulks can carry eight live bodies for ghost tours, cruising the cemetery and haunted inns and pub, for just $15 a head.

SPECIAL-INTEREST TOURS   Historic Savannah Foundation, a preservation organization, leads tours of the Historic District and the Lowcountry. Fees for the specialty tours start at $75 per hour, with a two-hour minimum for a private group of up to five people. Personalized Tours of Savannah is a small company offering upscale and intimate tours of the city. The owner is a longtime Savannah resident, and tours are peppered with history, anecdotes, and insider knowledge. Each has a two-hour minimum, is highly individualized, and starts at $65 per hour.

WALKING TOURS   A Ghost Talk Ghost Walk tour should send chills down your spine during an easy 1-mi jaunt that lasts 1½ hours, leaving from the middle of Reynolds Square, at the John Wesley Memorial at 7:30 and 9:30 PM, weather permitting. The cost is $10. On Savannah-by-Foot's Creepy Crawl Haunted Pub Tour, charismatic guide and storyteller Greg Proffit regales you with tales of ghosts that haunt local pubs. Tours traditionally depart from the Six Pence Pub at 8 PM. The adults-only tours cost $15 and last for 2½ hours. Sixth Sense Savannah offers the city's most sophisticated ghost tours; prices range from $18 to $56. Savannah Fun Tours is a self-guided scavenger hunt put together by a lifelong Savannahian. Solve the puzzle and collect a prize at the end. The tour book with clues for the hunt costs $25, and was designed to be used by two to four people.

TOUR ESSENTIALS   **Boat Tour Contacts Riverboat Cruises** (☎ 912/232–6404 ⊕ www.savannah-riverboat.com).

Historic District Contacts Carriage Tours of Savannah (☎ 912/236–6756 ⊕ www.carriagetoursofsavannah.com). **Freedom Trail Tours** (☎ 912/398–2785 ✎ freedomtrailtours@bellsouth.net). **Hearse Tours** (☎ 912/695–1578 ⊕ www.hearseghosttours.com). **Old Savannah Tours** (☎ 912/234–8128 or 800/517–9007 ⊕ www.oldsavannahtours.com). **Old Town Trolley Tours** (☎ 912/233–0083).

Special-Interest Tour Contacts Historic Savannah Foundation (☎ 912/234–4088 or 800/627–5030). **Personalized Tours of Savannah** (☎ 912/234–0014 or 800/627–5030 ⊕ www.savannahsites.com).

Walking-Tour Contacts A Ghost Talk Ghost Walk Tour (✉ Reynolds Sq., Congress and Abercorn Sts., Historic District ☎ 912/233–3896). **Savannah-By-Foot's Creepy Crawl Haunted Pub Tour** (☎ 912/238–3843). **Savannah Fun Tours** (☎ 912/667–9760 ⊕ www.savannahfuntours.com). **Sixth Sense Savannah** (☎ 912/501–9788 or 866/666–3323 ⊕ www.sixthsensesavannah.com).

10

PLANNING YOUR TIME

Savannah is not large, but it's atmospheric, and you want to make sure you allow sufficient time to soak in all that atmosphere. You'll need a minimum of two or three days to fully appreciate the historic district and its many sights, not to mention the food, which is an integral part of the Savannah experience. You'll need another day or two to see the sights in the surrounding area, including a jaunt out to Tybee Island to do a fishing trip or kayaking tour. Then you may wish to head north to Hilton Head or Charleston to get the full Lowcountry experience.

EXPLORING SAVANNAH

Savannah's real draw are the people who you will meet as you visit the city. They give southern charm their own special twist. As John Berendt's wildly popular book *Midnight in the Garden of Good and Evil* amply demonstrates, eccentricities can flourish in this hothouse environment.

THE HISTORIC DISTRICT

Georgia's sage founder, General James Oglethorpe, laid out the city on a perfect grid. It is as logical as a geometry solution. The Historic District is neatly hemmed in by the Savannah River, Gaston Street, East Street, and Martin Luther King Jr. Boulevard. Streets are arrow-straight, public squares of varying sizes are tucked into the grid at precise intervals, and each block is sliced in half by narrow, sometimes unpaved streets. Bull Street, anchored on the north by City Hall and the south by Forsyth Park, charges down the center of the grid and maneuvers around the five public squares that stand in its way. All the squares have some historical significance; many have elaborate fountains, monuments to heroes, and shady resting areas with park benches; all are bordered by beautiful homes and mansions that lovingly evoke another era.

TOP ATTRACTIONS

⑪ Andrew Low House. This residence was built in 1848 for Andrew Low, a native of Scotland and one of Savannah's merchant princes. The home later belonged to his son William, who inherited his wealth and married his long time sweetheart Juliette Gordon. They lived in a baronial estate in the U.K. for decades before divorcing. It was after her former husband's death, that Juliette Gorden Low returned to this house and founded the Girl Scouts here on March 12, 1912. The house has 19th-century antiques, stunning silver, and some of the finest ornamental ironwork in Savannah. But it is the story and history of the family— even a bedroom named after the family friend and visitor General Robert E. Lee—that is fascinating and well-told by the tour guides. ⊠*329 Abercorn St., Historic District* ☎*912/233–6854* ⊠*$8* ⊘ *Mon.–Wed., Fri., and Sat. 10–4:30, Sun. noon–4.*

❶ City Market. Although the 1870s City Market was razed years ago, city fathers are enacting a three-year plan to capture the authentic atmosphere and character of its bustling origins. Already a lively destination for art studios, open-air cafés, theme shops, and jazz clubs, this popular pedestrian-only area will become the ever more vibrant, youthful heart of Savannah's Historic District. You can rent a bike here or take a ride in a horse-drawn carriage. ⊠*Between Franklin Sq. and Johnson Sq. on W. St. Julian St., Historic District* ☎*912/525–2489 for current events.*

Savannah Historic District

Savannah River

Riverfront Plaza 4

River St.

Factors Walk 2

Factors Walk

3

W. Bay St.

E. Bay St.

City Market 1

Ellis Sq.

W. Bryan St.

W. Julian

Johnson Sq.

E. Julian

Reynolds Sq.

E. Bryan St.

Warren Sq.

W. Congress St.

E. Congress St.

W. Broughton St.

E. Broughton St.

Whitaker St.

Lincoln St.

Prince St.

W. State St.

Telfair Sq. 5

W. President

Wright Sq.

E. President

E. State St.

8

Oglethorpe Sq.

9

Columbia Sq.

6

W. York St.

7

E. York St.

W. Oglethorpe Ave.

E. Oglethorpe St.

Montgomery St.

Jefferson St.

Barnard St.

Drayton St.

Abercorn St.

Habersham St.

W. Hull

E. Hull

Colonial Park Cemetery

Orleans Sq.

Chippewa Sq.

W. Perry

E. Perry

W. Liberty St.

Whitaker St.

Bull St.

E. Liberty St.

13

E. Harris St.

14

Pulaski Sq.

W. Harris St.

Madison Sq. 10

W. Charlton

St. John's Episcopal Church

Lafayette Sq.

11

E. Macon St.

Troup Sq.

E. Charlton

12

Jefferson St.

Tattnall St.

W. Jones St.

E. Jones St.

Drayton St.

Lincoln St.

W. Taylor St.

Chatham Sq.

W. Wayne St.

Monterey Sq.

E. Taylor St.

Calhoun Sq.

E. Wayne St.

Whitefield Sq.

W. Gordon St.

E. Gordon St.

Prince St.

15

W. Gaston St.

E. Gaston St.

W. Huntingdon St.

Whitaker St.

Forsyth Park

Drayton St.

E. Huntingdon St.

King-Tisdell Cottage

16

W. Hall St.

E. Hall St.

W. Gwinett St.

E. Gwinett St.

W. Park Ave.

E. Park Ave.

W. Park Avenue Ln.

E. Park Avenue Ln.

0

0

1/4 mile

400 meters

Did You Know?

In Savannah many of the houses are named, but sometimes the name is the person who built the property rather than the person for whom it was built. For example, the Stephen Williams House, now restored as an elegant B&B, was named for its builder, Stephen Williams, rather than the owner, William Thorn Williams, six-time mayor of Savannah. Some houses are named for the first owner and then a subsequent owner, like the Green-Meldrim House. The good news is that they didn't add the name Sherman—General William T. Sherman, that is, who occupied the house during "The War" from 1864–1865—to the Green-Meldrim House's name. This extraordinary edifice, open for tours on certain days, is now the parish house for St. John's Episcopal Church.

② Factors Walk. A network of iron crosswalks connects Bay Street with the multistory buildings that rise up from the river level, and iron stairways descend from Bay Street to Factors Walk. The area was originally the center of commerce for cotton brokers, who walked between and above the lower cotton warehouses. Cobblestone ramps lead pedestrians down to River Street. ■TIP➔ **These are serious cobblestones, so wear comfortable shoes. Also be aware that pedicabs cannot ride over these cobblestones.** ⊠ *Bay St. to Factors Walk, Historic District,.*

■ NEED A
BREAK?
The best place for an ice-cream soda is **Leopold's** (⊠ *212 E. Broughton St., Historic District* ☎ *912/234-4442*), a Savannah institution since 1919. It's currently owned by Stratton Leopold, grandson of the original owner and a Hollywood producer. Famed lyricist Johnny Mercer grew up a block away from Leopold's and was a faithful customer.

⑯ Forsyth Park. The park forms the southern border of Bull Street. On its 30 acres are a glorious white fountain dating to 1858, Confederate and Spanish-American War memorials, and the Fragrant Garden for the Blind, a project of Savannah garden clubs. There are tennis courts and a tree-shaded jogging path. Outdoor plays and concerts often take place here. At the northwest corner of the park, in **Hodgson Hall,** a 19th-century Italianate Greek Revival building, you can find the **Georgia Historical Society,** which shows selections from its collection of artifacts and manuscripts. ⊠ *501 Whitaker St., Historic District* ☎ *912/651–2128* ⊕ *www.georgiahistory.com* ⊗ *Tues.–Sat. 10–5.*

⑩ Green-Meldrim House. Designed by New York architect John Norris and
★ built in 1850 for cotton merchant Charles Green, this Gothic Revival mansion cost $93,000 to build—a princely sum back then. The house was bought in 1892 by Judge Peter Meldrim, whose heirs sold it to St. John's Episcopal Church in the 1940s to use as a parish house. General Sherman lived here after taking the city in 1864. Sitting on Madison Square, the house has Gothic features such as a crenellated roof, oriels, and an external gallery with filigree ironwork. Inside are mantels of

Carrara marble, carved black-walnut woodwork, and doorknobs and hinges of either silver plate or porcelain. ■ TIP➔ On Sunday, admission is free after the 10:30 church service at St. John's and includes complimentary refreshments. ✉ *1 W. Macon St., Historic District* ☎*912/233–3845* ◨*$8* ⊙*Tues., Thurs., and Fri. 10–4, Sat. 10–1. Closed last 2 wks of Jan. and 2 wks before Easter.*

9 **Isaiah Davenport House.** The proposed demolition of this historic Savannah structure galvanized the city's residents into action to save their treasured buildings. By 1955 this home had a history of dilapidation that had lingered since the 1920s, when it had been divided into tenements. Semicircular stairs with some wrought iron lead to the recessed doorway of the redbrick Federal home that master builder Isaiah Davenport built for his family between 1815 and 1820. Three dormered windows poke through the sloping roof of the stately house, and the interior has polished hardwood floors and fine woodwork and plasterwork. Alas, neither the Davenports' furniture nor the pieces brought in to replicate theirs bespeak wealth. ✉ *324 E. State St., at Columbia Sq., Historic District* ☎*912/236–8097* ⊕*www.davenporthousemuseum.org* ◨*$8* ⊙*Mon.–Sat. 10–4, Sun. 1–4.*

6 **Jepson Center for the Arts.** On Telfair Square is the Telfair Museum's newest gallery (2006), an unexpectedly contemporary building amid so many 18th- and 19th-century structures that are the city's hallmark. Within the steel-and-glass edifice you can find permanent hangings of Southern art, African-American art, and photography. There's a sculpture gallery and an outdoor sculpture terrace in addition to interactive, kid-friendly exhibits. ✉ *207 W. York St., Historic District* ☎*912/232–1177 or 912/790–8800* ⊕*www.telfair.org* ◨*$10* ⊙*Mon. noon–5, Tues.–Sat. 10–5, Sun. 1–5.*

FodorsChoice
★

7 **Juliette Gordon Low Birthplace/Girl Scout National Center.** This majestic Regency town house, attributed to William Jay (built 1818–21), was designated in 1965 as Savannah's first National Historic Landmark. "Daisy" Low, founder of the Girl Scouts, was born here in 1860, and the house is now owned and operated by the Girl Scouts of America. Mrs. Low's paintings and other artwork are on display in the house, restored to the style of 1886, the year of Mrs. Low's marriage. ✉ *142 Bull St., Historic District* ☎*912/233–4501* ⊕*www.girlscouts.org/birthplace* ◨*$8* ⊙*Mon.–Sat. 10–4, Sun. 11–4.*

8 **Owens-Thomas House & Museum.** English architect William Jay's first Regency mansion in Savannah is widely considered the country's finest example of that architectural style. Built in 1816–19, the English house was constructed mostly with local materials. Of particular note are the curving walls of the house, Greek-inspired ornamental molding, half-moon arches, stained-glass panels, and Duncan Phyfe furniture and the hardwood "bridge" on the second floor. The carriage house includes a gift shop and rare urban slave quarters, which have retained the original furnishings and "haint-blue" paint made by the slave occupants. This house had indoor toilets before the White House and the Palace of Versailles. If you have to choose just one or two house-muse-

FodorsChoice
★

10

ums, let this be one. The house is owned by the Telfair Museum of Art. ⊠*124 Abercorn St., Historic District* ☎*912/233–9743* ⊕*www.telfair.org* ⬜*$10* ⊙*Mon. noon–5, Tues.–Sat. 10–5, Sun. 1–5; last tour at 4:30.*

❹ **Riverfront Plaza.** Amid this nine-block brick concourse, you can watch a parade of freighters and pug-nosed tugs. Youngsters can play in the tugboat-shaped sandboxes. There is a steady stream of outlets for shopping and eating along the Savannah River. Savannah's Riverwalk is being extended 2,000 feet eastward from the Marriott hotel, with construction slated for completion in 2009. ⊠*River St., between Abercorn and Barnard Sts., Historic District.*

> ### THE WAVING GIRL
>
> This charming statue at River Street and East Board Ramp is a symbol of Savannah's Southern hospitality and commemorates Florence Martus, the lighthouse keeper's sister who waved to ships in Savannah's port for more than 44 years. She would wave a white towel and, when young, always had her dog by her side. When she was in her last years, locals threw her a huge birthday party at Fort Pulaski with more than 5,000 guests. Despite all of her waving to so many sailors, she died without ever having been wed.

❺ **Telfair Museum of Art.** The oldest public art museum in the Southeast was
★ designed by William Jay in 1819 for Alexander Telfair and sits across the street from Telfair Square. Within its marble rooms are American, French, and Dutch impressionist paintings; German tonalist paintings; a large collection of works by Kahlil Gibran; plaster casts of the Elgin Marbles, the Venus de Milo, and the Laocoön, among other classical sculptures; and some of the Telfair family furnishings, including a Duncan Phyfe sideboard and Savannah-made silver. During the Savannah Music Festival there are intimate, classical music performances here that are memorable. ⊠*121 Barnard St., Historic District* ☎*912/232–1177* ⊕*www.telfair.org* ⬜*$10* ⊙*Mon., Wed., Fri., and Sat. 10–5; Thurs. 10–8; Sun. 12–5.*

WORTH NOTING

⑭ **Beach Institute African-American Cultural Center.** Works by African-American artists from the Savannah area and around the country are on display in this building, which once housed the first school for African-American children in Savannah, established in 1867. On permanent exhibit are more than 230 wood carvings by folk artist Ulysses Davis. ⊠*502 E. Harris St., Historic District* ☎*912/234–8000* ⊕*www.kingtisdell.org* ⬜*$4* ⊙*Tues.–Sat. noon–5.*

NEED A BREAK?

Near Congress Street, the rustic, brick-walled **Lulu's Chocolate Bar** (⊠*42 Martin Luther King Jr. Blvd., Historic District* ☎*912/238–2012*) offers opportunities for a wonderful sugar rush by day or night. It's now open for Sunday Brunch, too (11:30 AM to 4 PM). It's open until midnight from Sunday through Wednesday, until 1 AM Thursday through Saturday, and now has a Happy Hour from 5 to 7 with free cookie bites.

⓭ **Cathedral of St. John the Baptist.** Soaring over the city, this French Gothic–style cathedral, with pointed arches and free-flowing traceries, is the seat of the Catholic diocese of Savannah. It was founded in 1799 by the first French colonists to arrive in Savannah. Fire destroyed the early structures; the present cathedral dates from 1876. Its architecture, gold-leaf adornments, and the entire edifice give testimony to the importance of the Catholic parishioners of the day, which included some dispossessed French planters from Haiti as well as a strong Irish contingent. ⊠*222 E. Harris St., at Lafayette Square, Historic District,* ☎*912/233–4709* ⊕*www.savannahcathedral.org* ⊗ *Weekdays 9–5.*

❸ **City Hall.** Built in 1906 on the site of the Old City Exchange (1799–1904), this imposing structure anchors Bay Street. Its landmark tower clock and bells once played a significant role in the day-to-day business of Savannah, since the pocket watch was not mass-produced until 1897. In 2006, in honor of its centennial, this monumental municipal building underwent interior and exterior renovation. The public is welcome to come in and admire its dramatic four-story rotunda crowned with a stained-glass inner dome, mosaic tiles, marble wainscoting, mahogany and live oak pediments and banisters, and European sculptures. ⊠*1 Bay St., Historic District* ☎*912/651–6410* ⊗ *Weekdays 8:30–5.*

⓬ **Flannery O'Connor Childhood Home.** The childhood home of the celebrated Southern author is open for regularly scheduled visits on weekends only; however, you may be able to make special arrangements for other viewing times by calling the museum in advance. O'Connor lived in this house from her birth in 1925 until 1938. The home reopened in October 2008 after a substantial renovation. ⊠*207 E. Charlton St., at Lafayette Sq., Historic District* ☎*912/233–6014* ⊕*www.flanneryoconnorhome.org* ⊠*$5* ⊗ *Sat.–Sun. 1–4).*

⓯ **Ralph Mark Gilbert Civil Rights Museum.** In Savannah's Historic District, this history museum has a series of 15 exhibits on segregation, from emancipation through the civil rights movement. The role of black and white Savannahians in ending segregation in their city is detailed in these exhibits, largely derived from archival photographs. The museum also has touring exhibits. ⊠*460 Martin Luther King Jr. Blvd., Historic District* ☎*912/231–8900* ☎*912/234–2577* ⊠*$4* ⊗*Mon.–Sat. 9–5.*

10

THE SAVANNAH AREA

☾ **Fort Pulaski National Monument.** Named for Casimir Pulaski, a Polish
★ count and Revolutionary War hero, this must-see sight for Civil War buffs was designed by Napoléon's military engineer and built on Cockspur Island between 1829 and 1847. Robert E. Lee's first assignment after graduating from West Point was as an engineer here. During the Civil War the fort fell, on April 11, 1862, after a mere 30 hours of bombardment by newfangled rifled cannons. The restored fortification, operated by the National Park Service, has moats, drawbridges, massive ramparts, and towering walls. The park has trails and picnic areas. It's 14 mi east of downtown Savannah; you can see the entrance

on your left just before U.S. 80 reaches Tybee Island. ⊠*U.S. 80, Fort Pulaski* ☎*912/786–5787* ⊕*www.nps.gov/fopu* ≊*$3* ⊙*Daily 9–7.*

Mighty Eighth Air Force Heritage Museum. The famous World War II squadron the Mighty Eighth Air Force was formed in Savannah in January 1942 and shipped out to the United Kingdom. Flying Royal Air Force aircraft, the Mighty Eighth became the largest air force of the period. Exhibits at this museum begin with the prelude to World War II and the rise of Adolf Hitler and continue through Desert Storm. You can see vintage aircraft, fly a simulated bombing mission with a B-17 crew, test your skills as a waist gunner, and view interviews with courageous World War II vets. The museum also has three theaters, an art gallery, a 1940s-era English pub, a 7,000-volume library, archives, memorial garden, chapel, and museum store. ⊠*175 Bourne Ave., I–95, Exit 102, to U.S. 80, 14 mi west of Savannah, Pooler* ☎*912/748–8888* ⊕*www. mightyeighth.org* ≊*$10* ⊙*Daily 9–5.*

Tybee Island. *Tybee* is an Indian word meaning "salt." The Yamacraw Indians came to this island in the Atlantic Ocean to hunt and fish, and legend has it that pirates buried their treasure here. The island is about 5 mi long and 2 mi wide, with seafood restaurants, chain motels, condos, and shops—most of which sprang up during the 1950s and haven't changed much since. Tybee Island's entire expanse of taupe sand is divided into a number of public beaches, where you go shelling and crabbing, charter fishing boats, parasail, bike, jet ski, kayak, and swim. Nearby, the misnamed Little Tybee Island, actually larger than Tybee Island, is entirely undeveloped. **Tybee Island Lighthouse & Museum** (⊠*30 Meddin Dr.* ☎*912/786–5801* ⊕ *www.tybeelighthouse.org*) has been well restored; the Head Keeper's Cottage is the oldest building on the island, and should be on your list of must-sees on the island. The lighthouse opens daily at 9 AM, with the last tour at 4:30 PM; admission is $6. Kids will enjoy the **Marine Science Center** (⊠*1510 Strand Ave.* ☎*912/786–5917* ⊕ *www.tybeemsc.org*), which houses local marine life such as the Ogeechee corn snake, turtles, and the American alligator. It is open daily from 9 to 5 during the summer, from 10 to 5 otherwise; admission is $4. ✛*Tybee Island is 18 mi east of Savannah; take Victory Drive (U.S. 80)* ☎*800/868–2322 for Tybee Island Convention & Visitors Bureau* ⊕*www.tybeevisit.com.*

WHERE TO EAT

Savannah has excellent seafood restaurants, though locals also have a passion for spicy barbecued meats. Most of the River Street restaurants are high-volume and touristy. The Historic District yields a culinary cache, but mainstay restaurants can no longer live off their laurels. Several of the city's restaurants have drawn members of the culinary upper crust to the region for decades; others, such as the restaurant owned by Paula Deen, the Southern Queen of the Food Network, are more recent. Savoring the local flavors should not be limited just to the Historic District. You'll soon discover that good, even fine dining, can be found on nearby Tybee Island.

HOURS, PRICES & DRESS

Most popular restaurants serve both lunch and dinner, usually until 9 or 10 PM, later on Friday and Saturday nights. Sunday brunch is a beloved institution, but many restaurants close on Sunday night. Jeans are fine at most River Street tourist restaurants or casual eateries; however, if you are going to an upscale restaurant, dress a bit better.

WHAT IT COSTS					
	¢	$	$$	$$$	$$$$
Restaurant	under $10	$10–$14	$15–$19	$20–$24	over $24

Restaurant prices are for a main course at dinner and do not include tax.

HISTORIC DISTRICT

$$$–$$$$
AMERICAN
★

✕**700 Drayton Restaurant.** This is a one-of-a-kind Savannah experience that begins as you walk up the stairs of the former Keyton Mansion into a lounge that dazzles with eclectic furnishings like a Versace leopard-skin print chair, a suitable spot for a long power lunch or a romantic dinner. You will have a delectable meal made from regionally-inspired cuisine utilizing fresh local produce. As an appetizer, the scallops with asparagus and mushrooms with a vanilla sauce are sublime. The Moroccan-spiced rack of lamb is one of the best entrées, but the lime-and-whiskey-marinated snapper, pan-seared with herb grits and tomatillo/lime sauce, is also divine. Leopold's has made the restaurant its own luscious ice cream flavor, "Old Savannah." Breakfast is also served daily, and the Sunday brunch is a local favorite for special occasions. ✉*700 Drayton St., Historic District* ☎*912/721–5002 or 912/238–5158* ✍*Reservations essential* ➡*AE, D, DC, MC, V.*

$$
SOUTHERN
Fodor's Choice
★

✕**B. Matthews Eatery.** A change of ownership has not changed the homey, neighborhood feel of this unpretentious restaurant, which continues to be an in spot for locals. Three meals a day are served, with Sunday brunch (reservations essential) and its bottomless mimosas renowned all over Savannah. Lunch (until 3) and dinner share the same menu, which is still star-worthy. Certain faves like the black-eyed-pea cake with Cajun remoulade and fried green tomato sandwiches (with oregano aioli) have been retained. Dinner entrées are an excellent value, and the lamb shanks with white-truffle risotto may make you moan. A good way to begin is with an exemplary wild-mushroom strudel. On Tuesdays there are half-price bottles of select wines; the wines by the glass are exceptional every day. Smoking is allowed after 10 PM and anytime at the patio tables. ✉*325 E. Bay St., Historic District* ☎*912/233–1319* ➡*AE, D, MC, V.*

$$$
ECLECTIC
★

✕**Bistro Savannah.** High ceilings, burnished heart-pine floors, and gray-brick walls lined with local art—even undressed mannequins—contribute to the bistro qualities of this spot by City Market. The menu has specialties such as roasted Vidalia onion soup, which has a natural sweetness and is finished with cream and served with an herbed Parmesan crisp. Going international, Thai-spiced mussels with lemongrass, coconut, and red curry will heat you up after a nocturnal pedicab ride. The hanger steak is lean and flavorful, and the seared jumbo scallops

10

Where to Stay & Eat in Savannah

Savannah River

River St.   Riverfront Plaza   River St.

Factors Walk   Factors Walk

W. Bay St.   E. Bay St.

Ellis Sq.   W. Bryan St.   Johnson   E. Julian   Reynolds   E. Bryan St.   Warren Sq.
            W. Julian   Sq.   Sq.   E. Congress St.

W. Congress St.

W. Broughton St.   E. Broughton St.

W. State St.   E. State St.

Telfair Sq.   W. President   Wright Sq.   E. President   Oglethorpe Sq.   Columbia Sq.

W. York St.   E. York St.

W. Oglethorpe Ave.   E. Oglethorpe St.

Orleans Sq.   W. Hull   Chippewa Sq.   E. Hull   Colonial Park Cemetery

W. Perry   E. Perry

W. Liberty St.   E. Liberty St.

Pulaski Sq.   W. Harris St.   Madison Sq.   Lafayette Sq.   E. Macon St.   Troup Sq.
              W. Charlton   E. Charlton

W. Jones St.   E. Jones St.

Chatham Sq.   W. Taylor St.   Monterey Sq.   Calhoun Sq.   E. Taylor St.   Whitefield Sq.
              W. Wayne St.   E. Wayne St.
              W. Gordon St.   E. Gordon St.

W. Gaston St.   E. Gaston St.

W. Huntingdon St.   Forsyth Park   E. Huntingdon St.

W. Hall St.   E. Hall St.

W. Gwinett St.   E. Gwinett St.

KEY

W. Park Ave.   E. Park Ave.

1 Hotels

1 Restaurants

W. Park Avenue Ln.   E. Park Avenue Ln.

0   1/4 mile

0   400 meters

are served over fresh crab succotash. The chef tries to use mostly local, organic veggies, chemical-free meats, and fresh, certified wild shrimp. Like most everything, ice creams, sorbets, and other desserts are made from scratch. Try Chef Scott Ostrander's twist on strawberry shortcake. ⊠*309 W. Congress St., Historic District* ☎*912/233–6266* ⊟*AE, MC, V* ⊗*No lunch.*

$ ✕**Blowin' Smoke BBQ.** The restaurant's name refers to the serious smok-
SOUTHERN   ing of the meats and chicken over Georgia pecan wood, before the
Ⓒ   housemade barbecue sauce is slathered on. This is a hip, contemporary barbecue shop but based on the same Southern premise as the down-home barbecue joints that are candidly shown in the artsy black-and-white photos hung on the deep-purple and yellow walls. Fellow diners are usually 70% locals, students, and families with kids. The specialties here are pork ribs and hand-pulled pork. Of the fried appetizers, the mushrooms with smoky ranch dressing are the ticket. A must is one of the local craft beers. ⊠*514 Martin Luther King Jr. Blvd., Historic District* ☎*912/231–2385* ⊟*AE, D, MC, V.*

$$$–$$$$ ✕**Cha Bella.** "Organic is the only way," say chef/owner Matthew Roher
AMERICAN   and his partner Steve Howard, who do everything possible to conform
Fodor's Choice   their restaurant to this maxim as staunch supporters of the new Mar-
★   ket at Trustee Gardens at The Morris Center. Surrounding the outdoor seating, sheltered by a tin roof, you'll find an aromatic herb garden; the restaurant also has two plots of land nearby where they grow much of their produce. The menu includes some excellent, unusual salads including grilled eggplant with warm plum tomatoes flavored with sweet basil and topped with a goat cheese cake. Among the pastas, the wild porcini pappardelle has a distinctive flavor and mix of textures. A local, all-star black grouper takes center stage, seared, over fresh succotash with lump crab meat. ⊠*10 E. Broad St., Historic District* ☎*912/790–7888* ⊟*AE, D, MC, V* ⊗ *Closed Mon. No lunch.*

$$$$ ✕**Elizabeth on 37th.** Regional specialties are the hallmark at this
SOUTHERN   acclaimed restaurant that goes so far as to credit local produce suppliers
★   on its menu. Although original chef and owner Elizabeth Terry retired in 1996, Kelly Yambor has helmed the kitchen ever since, and she replicates the blue crab cakes that sit comfortably beside Southern-fried grits and honey-roasted pork tenderloin and roasted shiitake and oyster mushrooms over dried tomatoes, black-eyed peas, and carrot ragout The extravagant Savannah cream cake is the way to finish your meal. Nightly or seasonal specialties are often the most creative. Tourists sometimes complain that more attention is paid to Old Guard locals, but many of them have been regulars here for decades. Regardless, service is always professional. ⊠*105 E. 37th St., Historic District* ☎*912/236–5547* ⚋*Reservations essential* ⊟*AE, D, DC, MC, V* ⊗*No lunch.*

$$$$ ✕**45 Bistro.** No one should mistake this for a nondescript hotel restau-
ECLECTIC   rant, just because it is located within the Marshall House. The contem-
★   porary artwork and stellar bar with its ornate glass ceiling give you the first clues that this is a separate entity; the menu posted outside will beckon you to come in. Chef Patrick Best, whose middle name should be "perfection," is an artist as well. Watch him as he cooks; he is as intense as if he were finishing a painting. His masterpieces include

10

grilled hearts of romaine with homemade croutons and dressing that can go up against the world's best Caesar salads; duck with roasted parsnips, apples, cured bacon, and blackberry glaze that is a perfect cool-weather main course; and figgy bread pudding with coconut ice cream and marsala caramel, which is hard to top. ⊠*123 E. Broughton St., Historic District* ☎*912/655–3529* ▤*AE, D, MC, V* ⊙*Closed Sun. No lunch.*

$$$–$$$$ ×**Garibaldi.** With the same owners as the Olde Pink House, Garabaldi
ECLECTIC   might appear to be just another tourist trap near the city market. Look
FodorśChoice   closer. This is a restaurant revered by the city's titans and Savannah's
★   crème de le crème. Many remember Garibaldi for it's well-priced Italian classics, but the kitchen also sends out some much more ambitious offerings, albeit at higher prices. There are such unforgettable appetizers as lamb ribs, slow-cooked with a sweet ginger sauce and a fuchsia pear-cabbage relish, and a salad with a poached pear, arugula, walnuts, and goat cheese fritters with a port-wine vinaigrette. Plump soft-shell crabs come with surprising glazes, and grouper and snapper with original treatments may be paired with house-made chutney and crab risotto. Have your knowledgeable and professional server suggest wine pairings. ⊠*315 W. Congress, Historic District* ☎*912/232–7118* ⚑*Reservations essential* ▤*AE, D, MC, V* ⊙*No lunch.*

¢   ×**Harris Baking Company.** Owner Sam Harris is the chief baker, and
CAFÉS   his raspberry-custard tarts and perfect éclairs will make your eyes roll
★   back. Facing Drayton, look for the outdoor market umbrellas and tables; inside, the café is a minimalist study in gray, taupe, and chrome, with symbolic stalks of wheat in bud vases. Order from the counter. All the baked goods are incredible, including the croissants and Euro-style artesian breads. But Sam also makes uncompromisingly good sandwiches, including a golden cibatta panini with roast beef, aioli, sautéed onions, mushrooms, and with provolone cheese. All salad dressings, the aioli, other condiments, and even the pickles are house-made. The lobster crab bisque, with homemade croutons, is particularly flavorful. And imagine banana bread pudding made with cinnamon buns and caramel sauce. ⊠*102 E. Liberty St., Historic District* ☎*912/233–6400* ▤*AE, D, MC, V* ⊙*No dinner.*

$$$ ×**The Lady & Sons.** Expect to take your place in line simply to make
SOUTHERN   reservations for lunch or dinner. Everyone patiently waits to attack the buffet, which is stocked for both lunch and dinner with moist, crispy fried chicken, mashed potatoes, collard greens, lima beans, and the like. Peach cobbler and banana pudding round off the offerings. These days the quality can sometimes suffer because of the volume. Locals will tell you that in the early days, when Paula was doing her own cooking, it was decidedly better. The atmosphere is retro and will take you back to a small Southern town of decades past. You can also order off the menu, and a crab cake burger at lunch or chicken potpie or barbecue grouper at dinner can be a good choice. ⊠*102 W. Congress St., Historic District* ☎*912/233–2600* ▤*AE, D, MC, V* ⊙*No dinner Sun.*

$$$$ ×**Local 11ten.** New Wave, American cuisine is served in what looks
AMERICAN   like an extension of the white-brick, American Legion post next door.
★   A peek inside shows that it is light years away. Upbeat and contem-

porary, this is where several of the top young chefs in Savannah come on their nights off. The menu is seasonally driven and is continually changing depending on the availability of produce and the new chef's vision on any given day. Chef Bradley Daniels came here from the prestigious Blackberry Farm in Tennessee, and his cuisine is as Southern as the area's local favorites, including plump, soft-shell crabs, but his menu also has definite Italian and French influences. At this writing, a new rooftop bar is in the works that should be open by spring 2009. ⊠ *1110 Bull Street, Historic District* ☎ *912/790–9000* ⚁ *Reservations essential* ⊟ *AE, D, MC, V* ⊘ *Closed Sun., Mon. No lunch.*

$$$–$$$$
ECLECTIC
Fodor's Choice
★

✕ **Noble Fare.** This is one superior fine-dining experience, all the way from the amuse-bouche to dessert. Most of the clientele are well-heeled, older residents out for a special occasion. The bread service includes honey butter, pistachio pesto, olive oil, and balsamic vinegar for your biscuits, flat breads, rolls, and foccacia, all of which are artistically presented on contemporary white dishes. A choice appetizer is tuna tartare with avocado, American caviar, and mango, drizzled with curry oil. The scallops are laudable, and fish is so fresh it practically moves on your plate, but if you are a venison lover go for the tenderloin with carrot puree, potatoes, greens, and Pinotage syrup. The molten love cake with raspberry sauce and custard ice cream is almost a requirement for dessert. The owners are Chef Patrick McNamara and his lovely bride Jenny, who runs the front of the house. A prix-fixe tasting menu is available. ⊠ *321 Jefferson St., Historic District* ☎ *912/443–3210* ⚁ *Reservations essential* ⊟ *AE, D, MC, V* ⊘ *No Lunch. Closed Sun. and Mon.*

$$–$$$$
SOUTHERN
★

✕ **Olde Pink House.** This pink-brick Georgian mansion was built in 1771 for James Habersham, one of the wealthiest Americans of his time. A stunning new bar, The Arches, is adjacent with curvaceous doors that can open on balmy nights for outdoor seating. Lunch includes number of creative sandwiches and both cold and hot entrées like a shrimp 'n' grits and chilled shellfish sampler. New chef Timothy O'Neil, who has both classical training and contemporary style, has been brought in to upgrade the menu. Though the offerings were still evolving at this writing, you can expect Lowcountry classics and innovative specials with as much local seafood and quality ingredients. How about a classic chicken potpie with roasted veggies, porcini cream sauce, and a sweet-potato biscuit? ⊠ *23 Abercorn St., Historic District* ☎ *912/232–4286* ⚁ *Reservations essential* ⊟ *AE, MC, V* ⊘ *Closed Sun. and Mon.*

$$$$
AMERICAN
★

✕ **Sapphire Grill.** Savannah's young and restless pack this trendy haunt with its loft-like style. Chef Chris Nason focuses his seasonal menus on local ingredients, such as Georgia white shrimp, crab, and fish. The Grill features succulent choices of steak, poultry, and fish, with a myriad interesting à la carte accompaniments such as jalapeño tartar sauce, sweet soy-wasabi sauce, and lemongrass butter. Vegetarians will delight in the elegant vegetable presentations—perhaps including roasted sweet onions, spicy peppers, rice wine-marinated watercress, or fried green tomatoes with grilled ginger; a three-course vegetarian tasting menu is available. You may find your bliss in the miniature cocoa gâteau with lavender almond ice cream. Downstairs, the decor

10

is hip and hopping; upstairs is quieter and more romantic. The six-course chef's tasting menu is $100. ✉ *110 W. Congress St., Historic District* ☎ *912/443–9962* ⅍ *Reservations essential* ▤ *AE, D, DC, MC, V* ⊘ *No lunch.*

¢–$ ✕ **Soho South Cafe.** Chef/owner Bonnie Retsas lived 25 years in New
ECLECTIC York prior to "retiring" here and opening up this small restaurant. This
★ long brick building had been an art gallery (local art, both good and amateurish, still hangs), though it still looks like the mechanic's garage that it once was. There is often a line for lunch and for Sunday brunch, though reservations are accepted now. The tables and chairs are a mismatch of Formica, wood, and enamel from the 1940s to '60s. The strength of Bonnie's food is that it is *consistent* and it tastes so homemade. Try the meat-loaf sandwich with Russian dressing or flavorful quiches. Soups like the signature tomato-basil bisque are the perfect accompaniment for the grilled cheese on sourdough with pimento aioli. Some more contemporary choices are offered now like the sandwiches of grilled portobello mushrooms or vegetables with roasted peppers and pesto mayo; a special might be organic chicken potpie. Only wine and beer are sold (only after noon on Sundays). ✉ *12 W. Liberty St., Historic District* ☎ *912/233–1633* ▤ *AE, MC, V* ⊘ *No dinner.*

$$$–$$$$ ✕ **Vic's on The River.** This upscale Southern charmer is one of the hippest
SOUTHERN fine-dining rooms in town, where local residents congregate and tour-
★ ists join in conversation at the bar as they listen to the talented pianists. Reserve a window table for the best views of the Savannah River. The young chef, Jay Cantrell, is becoming a local celebrity and is among those aggressively changing the dining scene for the better. Much of the menu is given over to classics like steaks and oysters Rockefeller. Pan-seared scallops are freshened up with crab and Andouille sausage risotto, wilted arugula, and lemon herb truffle butter. Lunch is popular with local business people and upscale tourists, and seafood po'boys and Angus burgers are sought after, as are the daily hot specials. Praline cheesecake is still very much in demand. ✉ *16 E. River St., Historic District* ☎ *912/721–1000* ⅍ *Reservations essential* ▤ *AE, D, MC, V.*

TYBEE ISLAND

$$ ✕ **Charly's.** This upscale restaurant in a colorfully restored beach cottage
CONTINENTAL (some rooms with pine floors) is a welcome alternative on an otherwise kitschy island. You will enjoy caring service, sometimes from the owner himself, Chuck Vonashek. Chef Ed Hornsby spends the quiet winter months honing a great new menu. The grilled lamb lollipops with a rosemary demi-glace are a study in well-executed simplicity. Such appetizers as potato-wrapped shrimp are surprisingly good and a great way to start your meal. The nightly specials are the most creative, and his lobster crab bisque is decadently rich. In shoulder seasons there's an early dining menu with cheaper main courses, providing even more value for the dollar, as does everything offered. ✉ *106 S. Campbell Ave., Tybee Island* ☎ *912/786–0221, 912/398–4709 for limo reservations* ▤ *AE, D, MC, V* ⊘ *Closed Mon. No lunch.*

$$$ ✕ **Hunter House.** Built in 1910 as a family beach house, this renovated
SOUTHERN brick home with its wraparound veranda offers an intimate dining experience with a dose of Victorian ambience. Owner John Hunter operates

one of the island's most consistently good restaurants, and that consistency has continued since the 1980s. Seafood dominates the menu and includes deliciously creative dishes such as a cognac-laced seafood bisque and ahi tuna with a bourbon soy glaze, nori, and a wasabi drizzle. Meat eaters need not despair: chicken and steak options are available, and the restaurant offers a delicious pot roast as the perennial house special, served with mashed potatoes and gravy, red cabbage, carrots, and green beans, which remains the cheapest main course. The key lime tart is the perfect finish. ⊠ *1701 Butler Ave., Tybee Island* ☎ *912/786-7515* ⊟ *AE, D, MC, V* ⊘ *Closed mid-Dec.–mid-Jan. Closed Sun. Labor Day–mid-Dec. and mid-Jan.–Memorial Day.*

WHERE TO STAY

Although Savannah has its share of chain hotels and motels, the city's most distinctive lodgings are in more than two dozen historic inns, guesthouses, and B&Bs gracing the Historic District. If the term *historic inn* brings to mind images of roughing it in shabby-genteel mansions with antiquated plumbing, you'll find that to be the case in a few isolated instances. Such are the woes of older buildings: the creaking staircase, the faucet that comes off in your hand, even the rumors of ghosts.

A continental or full Southern breakfast is often included in the rate, as are afternoon refreshments (usually wine and cheese, sometimes elaborate hors d'oeuvres); these extras definitely help to justify some of the escalated prices. Some B&Bs offer a pass that will give you free on-street parking; others have a few private parking spaces of their own. Nearly all the hotels and inns in the real downtown sector have paid parking, which can range from $8 at the riverfront inns to $18 a night for valet parking.

HOTEL PRICES

Savannah is not inexpensive, because demand is high almost year-round now; October is especially busy. Holiday periods push prices up; St. Patrick's Day weekend is a particularly busy period in Savannah. There are sometimes last-minute deals to be had, particularly in late summer.

10

WHAT IT COSTS					
	¢	$	$$	$$$	$$$$
Hotel	under $100	$100–$150	$151–$200	$201–$250	over $250

Hotel prices are for two people in a standard double room in high season and do not include 13% tax; most B&Bs (but not all) include breakfast in their rates.

HISTORIC DISTRICT

$$-$$$ ⊡ **Azalea Inn & Gardens.** This personable inn is owned and operated by Teresa Jacobson and her husband Jake, who can be thanked for the subtropical gardens that surround the pool. They have an easygoing, live-and-let-live attitude and a connection with the Savannah College of Art & Design, and artwork by students lines some hallways. The slightly

irreverent murals in the breakfast room depict the history of Savannah. The Forsyth Park neighborhood, near Gaston Street, offers the quiet surroundings adored by the residents—and guests. This 1889 mansion built for a Cotton Exchange powerhouse has multiple fireplaces, private verandas with overhead fans and wicker furnishings, and handsome artisan craftsmanship. Expect a generous, hospitable ambience, a reinvented Southern breakfast, and house-baked desserts, not to mention afternoon wine service with attitude—a good one. Pros: the Gentlemen's Parlor and Magnolia Place, the two best rooms; baked goods are put out during the day. Cons: typically Victorian, the decor is sometimes just too busy; the less expensive rooms are small; the carriage house is not as distinctive. ⊠ *217 Huntingdon St., Historic District* ☎ *912/236–2707 or 800/582–3823* ⊕ *www.azaleainn.com* ➫ *9 rooms, 2 suites* ⚘ *In-room: no phone, DVD, Wi-Fi. In-hotel: pool, Wi-Fi, parking (free), no kids under 12, no-smoking rooms* ▤ *AE, D, MC, V* ⍾ *BP.*

$$$–$$$$
★
🔲 **Ballastone Inn.** On the National Register of Historic Places, this sumptuous inn occupies an 1838 mansion that once served as a bordello. Rooms are handsomely furnished with antiques and fine reproductions; luxurious, scented linens and French down blankets on canopied beds; and a collection of original framed prints from *Harper's* scattered throughout. Garden (ground-floor) rooms are smaller but cozy, with exposed brick walls, beamed ceilings, and, in some cases, windows at eye level with the lush courtyard. Most rooms have working gas fireplaces, and three have whirlpool tubs. The aroma of fresh flowers permeates the air. Afternoon tea is served from a silver set and on fine china; the evening social hour features hors d'oeuvres; and a full bar stocks boutique wines. Pros: excellent location; romantic atmosphere; free passes to a downtown health club are included. Cons: limited off-street parking; this busy downtown area can be noisy. ⊠ *14 E. Oglethorpe Ave., Historic District* ☎ *912/236–1484 or 800/822–4553* ⊕ *www.ballastone.com* ➫ *16 rooms, 3 suites* ⚘ *In-room: Wi-Fi (some). In-hotel: bar, parking (free), no kids under 16, no-smoking rooms* ▤ *AE, MC, V* ⍾ *BP.*

$$–$$$
★
🔲 **Catherine Ward House.** Built by a former sea captain for his young wife in1886, this Italianate home is within a block of Forsythe Park. When Leslie Larson, co-owner and innkeeper in residence, took over the existing B&B, she updated and totally redecorated it, adding her contemporary style while keeping it an exquisite period piece—not the dark and dowdy Victorian she bought. Her class shows through with the well-chosen gilt mirrors, antique pieces, fresh roses, and the communal dining table, set beautifully for a breakfast that gets raves. Most rooms have balconies that overlook the garden oasis with its koi pond and soothing fountain. Pros: all rooms are immaculate, with antique mantles and fireplaces, some of which work; a couple of rooms have two-person whirlpool tubs, one a double-headed shower. Cons: the less expensive rooms are small, and some are on the garden level; the carriage house rooms are not as atmospheric as the main house; this is a transitional neighborhood, and you don't want to wander farther south. ⊠ *118 E. Waldburg St., Historic District* ☎ *912/234–8564 or 800/327–4270* ⊕ *www.catherinewardhouseinn.com* ➫ *9 rooms* ⚘ *In-room: no phone,*

refrigerator, DVD (some), Wi-Fi. In-hotel: Internet terminal, Wi-Fi, parking (free), no children under 18, no-smoking rooms ⊟AE, D, MC, V ⧦❘BP.

$$
Fodor's Choice
★

⌄ **East Bay Inn.** The charm of this tall, redbrick building with its hunter-green shutters and awnings, its first-floor facade fashioned from cast iron, and the half-dozen American flags, is not lost on passersby. Built in 1852, this inn was once a series of early cotton warehouses and factory offices. The cast-iron, interior pillars were left and the brick walls exposed; the effect is

LODGING TIP

When you are trying to decide on what kind of accommodation to reserve in Savannah, consider that B&Bs usually include breakfast (sometimes a lavish one), complimentary wine and cheese nightly, and even free bottled water; parking is sometimes free. Hotels, particularly the major ones, usually do not even give you a small bottle, and almost all charge substantially for parking.

handsome. The interior design is tasteful and professionally done with details that put it a step above what you will see in other similarly priced properties. Although the furnishings are reproductions, comfort has been emphasized, and all guest rooms look great. Each has one or two queen beds, a couch, and two comfy chairs, not to mention 18-foot ceilings. Breakfast is a good offering of cereals, meats, scrambled eggs, fresh fruit, and Danish. **Pros:** hospitality and service get very high marks; the evening reception goes farther than the requisite wine and cheese; great restaurant. **Cons:** not enough parking spaces (15) for the number of rooms; hallways, some art, and bathrooms are not as wonderful as the rooms; staff and clientele not as sophisticated as in more pricey inns. ✉*225 E. Bay St., Historic District* ☎*912/238–1225 or 800/500–1225* ⊕*www.eastbayinn.com* ↪*28 rooms* ⌂*In-room: safe, Internet (some), Wi-Fi. In-hotel: restaurant, laundry service, Internet terminal, Wi-Fi, parking (free), some pets allowed, no-smoking rooms* ⊟*AE, D, MC, V* ⧦❘*BP.*

$$$–$$$$
★

⌄ **Eliza Thompson House.** Eliza Thompson's loving husband Joseph built this fine town house for her and their seven children in 1847, only to leave her a widow, albeit a socially prominent one. This gracious Victorian is one of the oldest B&Bs in Savannah, first transformed by the first "new" owners in 1995, with furnishings and portraits in gold leaf frames brought over from England. The rooms are handsomely appointed, some with antiques and vintage beds, fine linens, and other designer accents. The J. Stephen's Room with its aubergine walls, plaid chairs, and Victorian couch look out to the mossy branches of a live oak. Some of the back rooms are small. A full breakfast is taken in the tranquil brick courtyard with its soothing fountains. Adjacent is the New Orleansesque carriage house, built in the 1980s; its 13 moderately-priced rooms have just been completely upgraded, furnishings and all. Afternoon wine, cheese, and appetizers and, later, luscious evening desserts and sherry are served in the atmospheric main parlor. **Pros:** on one of Savannah's most beautiful brick-lined streets in a lively, picturesque residential neighborhood; free parking passes are issued for street parking; flat-screen TV with cable in every room. **Cons:** no

10

private parking lot; breakfast can be hit or miss; unattractive carpet in halls of main house. ⊠5 W. Jones St., Historic District ☎ 912/236–3620 or 800/348–9378 ⊕www.elizathompsonhouse.com ⟿25 rooms ♿In-room: DVD, Wi-Fi. In-hotel: Internet terminal, parking (free), no kids under 12, no-smoking rooms ▤ AE, D, MC, V ⎟⚬⎟BP.

$$$–$$$$ ⊞**Gastonian.** Many of the rooms in this atmospheric inn, built in 1868, ★ underwent an extensive remodeling in 2008. Fresh flowers throughout and the outdoor covered arbor are unexpected pleasures. Guest rooms are decorated with a mix of funky finds and antiques from the Georgian and Regency periods; all have fireplaces, and most have whirlpool tubs. In a second building, identical to the main house, where the dining and socializing take place, the Lafayette Room has the most noteworthy fireplace; the Caracalla Suite is named for the oversize whirlpool tub built in front of its fireplace; the Low Room has a private wrought-iron balcony looking out on the treetops. At breakfast you can have such hot entrées as omelets with creamed spinach and goat cheese. Afternoon tea, complimentary wine with cheese and hors d'oeuvres, and evening cordials are among the treats.**Pros:** many rooms and suites are exceptionally spacious; the handsome and quiet Eli Whitney Room is one of the least expensive; cordial and caring staff. **Cons:** accommodations on the third floor are a hike; some of the furnishings are less than regal. ⊠220 E. Gaston St., Historic District ☎912/232–2869 or 800/322–6603 ⊕www.gastonian.com ⟿14 rooms, 3 suites ♿In-room: DVD, Wi-Fi. In-hotel: Wi-Fi, parking (free), no kids under 12, no-smoking rooms ▤AE, D, MC, V ⎟⚬⎟BP.

$$$–$$$$ ⊞**Hamilton-Turner Inn.** This French Empire mansion is celebrated, if not ★ in song, certainly in story. It was built ostentatiously in 1873 by Samuel Hamilton, Savannah's mayor (who made a *little* money as a blockade runner during the Civil War). By the 1990s it was the crash pad for Joe Odom in *Midnight in the Garden of Good and Evil*. It was rescued from further ignominy in 1997 by a wealthy Savannah couple, who did the initial restoration. In 2006 new owners Gay and Jim Dunlop sank their money into a massive, two-year restoration. It certainly has a "wow" effect, especially the rooms that front Lafayette Square. The original arched doors are some 15 feet tall; the bathrooms are the size of a New York City apartment. The Dunlops strive for perfection, and the Southern-mansion breakfast has baked items such as scones and hot entrées like perfect eggs Benedict. The afternoon reception features quality wine and both hot and cold hors d'oeuvres. **Pros:** CD players with CDs in rooms and free DVD library; the carriage house is the most private room, though not as atmospheric; pets are allowed in brick-walled, ground-level rooms ($50 deposit). **Cons:** sedate and not for young kids or party types; no guest elevator (except for accessible Room 201) and some rooms are on the fourth floor; no private parking (two-day street pass costs $8). ⊠330 Abercorn St., Historic District ☎912/233–1833 or 888/448–8849 ⊕www.hamilton-turnerinn.com ⟿11 rooms, 6 suites ♿In-room: refrigerator (some), DVD, Internet, Wi-Fi. In-hotel: Wi-Fi, some pets allowed, no kids under 12, no-smoking rooms ▤AE, D, MC, V ⎟⚬⎟BP.

$$$$
★ ▦**Kehoe House.** Originally the family manse of William Kehoe, this house dating from the 1890s is now a handsomely appointed B&B, one of the better choices in Savannah. The Victorian charmer has brass-and-marble chandeliers, a courtyard garden, and a music room with a baby grand piano. Guest rooms have a decidedly Victorian feel, with a mix of antiques and gilt mirrors. The beds are dressed in contemporary, fine linens. On the main floor, a double parlor houses two fireplaces and sweeps the eye upward with its 14-foot ceilings, creating an elegant setting for a beautifully served, full gourmet breakfast. Guests enjoy afternoon tea and desserts, as well as a wine and hors d'oeuvres reception. Rates include access to the Downtown Athletic Club.Pros: popular wedding and anniversary venue; the Mercer Room (the best accommodation) has private verandas; B&B is wheelchair accessible, with two elevators. **Cons:** only one king or queen bed per room; some details, including headboards and Victorian art, are not appealing; a few rooms have the sink and shower in the room, separated by drapes. ⊠*123 Habersham St., Historic District* ☎*912/232–1020 or 800/820–1020* ⊕*www.kehoehouse.com* ⇖*13 rooms* ⚷*In-room: DVD, Wi-Fi. In-hotel: Internet terminal, Wi-Fi, parking (free), no kids under 12, no-smoking rooms* ☰*AE, D, MC, V* ⦿|*BP.*

$$$$
Fodor'sChoice
★ ▦**Mansion on Forsyth Park.** Sophisticated, chic, and artsy only begin to describe this Kessler property. The newer wings blend perfectly with its historic surroundings and the original, 18,000 square-foot Victorian-Romanesque, redbrick and terra-cotta mansion. Sitting on the edge of Forsyth Park, its dramatic design, opulent interiors with a contemporary edge, and magnificently diverse collection of some 400 pieces of American and European art create a one-of-a-kind experience. Every turn delivers something unexpected—the antique hat collection; the pool with its creative water wall, and a canopied patio that looks like it's out of the *Arabian Nights*; a Nordic-looking full-service spa; back-lighted onyx panels and 100-year-old Italian Corona–marble pillars. The 700 Drayton Restaurant offers contemporary fine dining and professional, attentive service. Upstairs, Casimir's Lounge, with live piano and jazz, is one of the city's hot spots.Pros: no real breakfast, but Starbuck's coffee, pastries, and bagels are gratis in the Bösendorfer Lounge every morning; an exciting, stimulating environment that transports you from the workaday world; complimentary Lincoln Town Car and driver (limited). **Cons:** very pricey, particularly for room service and phone calls; some of the art from the early 1970s is not appealing. ⊠*700 Drayton St., Historic District* ☎*912/238–5158 or 888/711–5114* ⊕*www.mansiononforsythpark.com* ⇖*126 rooms* ⚷*In-room: safe, Internet, Wi-Fi. In-hotel: restaurant, room service, bars, spa, Internet terminal, Wi-Fi, parking (paid), no-smoking rooms* ☰*AE, D, DC, MC, V* ⦿|*EP.*

10

$$$
▦**Marshall House.** This restored hotel, with original pine floors, woodwork, and exposed brick, caters to business travelers, as well as families, yet it provides the intimacy of a B&B. A second major renovation finished in winter 2008 has made a marked difference in the guest rooms, which are now nearly swank. Rooms with their own wrought-iron balconies, which overlook the street, are decidedly the best. Some

bathrooms have a bear-claw tub and traditional shower, as well as a separate modern shower. The lobby segues into the bar and then into 45 Bistro, both are under separate management but an integral part of the inn's experience. Different spaces reflect different parts of Savannah's history, from its founding to the Civil War. Artwork is mostly by local artists. A full breakfast is offered in the lovely atrium. Pros: great location near stores and restaurants; exceptional restaurant on-site; guests get free passes to a downtown health club. Cons: no free parking; no room service; facade has somewhat of an urban motel appearance. ✉123 E. Broughton St., Historic District ☎912/644–7896 or 800/589–6304 ⊕www.marshallhouse.com ♥65 rooms, 3 suites ⚘In-room: safe, refrigerator, Internet. In-hotel: restaurant, bar, Wi-Fi, parking (paid), no-smoking rooms ☐ AE, D, DC, MC, V ⦿BP.

$$
Fodor'sChoice
★

The Stephen Williams House. Although named for its builder, this house was constructed for the honorable Mayor (six terms) William Thorn Williams in 1834. This wonderful Federal-style mansion is now owned by an equally exceptional retired physician, Dr. Albert Wall. Savannah-born, an inveterate storyteller, lover of history, antique collector, and survivor of seven historic preservation projects, he was determined to save this house, which had become one sad derelict. The sumptuous suite has an entirely separate parlor and a draped bed. The less expensive garden rooms, which share a bath, are characterized by beamed ceilings and exposed brick walls, and open out to the restored garden and walled courtyard with its lion's head fountain. Dr. Wall has a deep affection for his city, and as he pours morning coffee for his guests, he suggests his favorite things in Savannah for them to do and can arrange for bicycles to be delivered. The hotel is a superb wedding venue. Pros: elegant furnishings (a 45-year collection of period antiques, some museum-quality, some for sale); full Southern breakfast made from old Savannah recipes; beds triple-sheeted with Frette linens and choice of down pillows. Cons: occasional plumbing problems as befits an aged manse; no wine and hors d'oeuvres reception in the evening; rooms facing Liberty Street catch the bus and traffic noise. ✉4 Barnard St., Historic District ☎912/495–0032 ⊕www.thestephenwilliamshouse. com ♥4 rooms, 1 suite ⚘In-room: Wi-Fi. In-hotel:, laundry service, Wi-Fi, parking (free), no kids under 12, no-smoking rooms ☐AE, D, MC, V ⦿BP.

$$$-$$$$
★

The Zeigler House Inn. This urban mansion on one of the city's most desirable brick-paved streets will have you fantasizing about living in such a place, just like the city's upper crust. Owner Jackie Heinz came from Atlanta for a weekend and put in an offer to buy the house before she left. It is her home now, and her taste is admirable, from the hanging baskets of rare flowers to the chocolate-brown ceilings in the main parlors that make the white ceiling medallions look like art. You can tap into Savannah's good life and have a romantic stay in a beautifully appointed room or, better yet, a suite with contemporary style juxtaposed with antiques, a custom-made king bed, and fine bedding. Jackie has a unique way of handling breakfast. Each room has a kitchenette or full kitchen with a coffeemaker; she stocks the fridge with juice and milk and bakes delectable pastries daily that she leaves for breakfast.

A professional chef, she can prepare a gourmet, multicourse dinner for guests upon request. **Pros:** the privilege of being in such a lovable home; a stocked kitchen makes you feel like you really live here; lovely slate fireplaces and heart-pine floors and staircase. **Cons:** garden-level rooms have a subterranean feel; not a full-service hotel; no full, hot breakfast. ✉*121 W. Jones St., Historic District* ☎*912/233–5307 or 866/233–5307* ⊕*www.zieglerhouseinn.com* ↪*4 rooms, 2 suites* &*In-room: kitchen (some), refrigerator, DVD, Wi-Fi. In-hotel: Wi-Fi, parking (free), no kids under 12, no-smoking rooms* ▤*AE, MC, V* �†⊙†*CP.*

ELSEWHERE IN SAVANNAH

$$$$ ⊡ **Westin Savannah Harbor Golf Resort & Spa.** Within its own fiefdom, this major high-rise property lords it over small Hutchinson Island, five minutes by water taxi from Factors Walk. It has more resort amenities than any other property in the area, including tennis courts, and most importantly, a golf course. Its professional, full-service spa is affiliated with the Greenbrier's in West Virginia. The island's adjacent Savannah International Convention Center is what keeps the hotel at high occupancy levels almost year-round, since many meeting attendees stay here; leisure guests predominate on the weekends. The lobby is swanky and upscale. The Savannah Harbor Golf Course is open to the public and is best bet for golfers staying in the Historic District. The island's ferries or water taxis dock at the Savannah Belles Ferry Dock in front of the Hyatt Regency. The first one departs from the hotel at 7 AM; scheduled runs are every 20 minutes, with the last one leaving downtown at midnight. If you miss the last ferry, you can still take a taxi for about $7. **Pros:** dreamy bedding; outdoor pool is heated; rooms can come with Pilates and fitness equipment for an extra charge. **Cons:** you are close, but still removed, from downtown; this is a major chain hotel, not an atmospheric, historic inn; hotel charges an expensive and annoying resort fee. ✉*1 Resort Dr., Hutchinson Island* ☎*912/201–2000* ⊕*www.westinsavannah.com* ↪*390 rooms, 13 suites* &*In-room: safe (some), kitchen (some), refrigerator, Wi-Fi. In-hotel: 2 restaurants, room service, bars, golf course, tennis courts, pool, gym, spa, children's programs (ages 4–12), laundry service, Internet terminal, Wi-Fi, parking (free), some pets allowed, no-smoking rooms* ▤*AE, D, MC, V* ⊙*EP.*

TYBEE ISLAND

If renting a 5-star beach house, a pastel island cottage, or a waterfront condo in a complex with a pool and tennis courts is more your Tybee dream, check out **Tybee Vacation Rentals** (✉*1010 Hwy. 80 E, Tybee Island* ☎*912/786–5853 or 866/359–0297* ⊕*www.tybeevacationrentals.com*). This family-owned business has grown because these managers are so friendly and accommodating, and they now represent some 130 rentals. At the main rental office you can use their computers or Wi-Fi to get online, and there's a machine that rents DVDs 24 hours a day. Expect to pay $600 for a three-night stay (minimum) for a one-bedroom condo.

10

NIGHTLIFE & THE ARTS

Savannah's nightlife reflects the city's laid-back personality. Some clubs have live reggae, hard rock, and other contemporary music, but most stick to traditional blues, jazz, and piano-bar vocalists. After-dark merrymakers usually head for watering holes on Riverfront Plaza or the Southside.

FESTIVALS & SPECIAL EVENTS

For three days in mid-October (usually the second weekend) the free **Savannah Folk Music Festival** (⊕*www.savannahfolk.org*) becomes the city's main musical attraction. The **Savannah Jazz Festival** (⊕*www.savannahjazzfestival.org*) is a free event held each September in Forsyth Park, featuring artists from around the region. The September weather is ideal, as is the ambience of the park setting.Georgia's largest and most acclaimed music festival, the **Savannah Music Festival** (⊕*www.savannahmusicfestival.org*) begins on infamous St. Patrick's Day weekend and runs for 18 days, with four to six performances daily at some 20 downtown venues. The music ranges from foot-stomping gospel to mournful blues to frenetic Cajun zydeco.

BARS & NIGHTCLUBS

A relatively new and certainly stellar nightspot, **Casimir Lounge** (⊠*700 Drayton St., Historic District* ☎*912/721–5061 or 912/238–5158*) is not as formal as the downstairs lounge at 700 Drayton, but its decor is gorgeous, too. The real draw is the live music that plays on Friday and Saturday nights (and sometimes Thursday or Sunday), beginning about 8:30. Jazz and blues are the norm. A gay bar, **Club One Jefferson** (⊠*1 Jefferson St., Historic District* ☎*912/232–0200* ⊕*www.clubone-online.com*) has been dubbed one of the city's best dance clubs by the locals, and the notorious Lady Chablis still does cameo appearances here. Drag shows are a feature, but mostly it's a DJ keeping the dancers in motion. There's no cover. **Kevin Barry's Irish Pub** (⊠*114 W. River St., Historic District* ☎*912/233–9626* ⊕*www.kevinbarrys.com*) has a friendly vibe, a full menu until 1 AM, and traditional Irish music seven days a week (the music generally begins at 8:30). It's *the* place to be on St. Patrick's Day, but the challenge is trying to get in. The rest of the year there's a mix of tourists and locals of all ages and the Guinness flows freely.

> ### WATCH YOUR BACK
>
> Regrettably, street crime and muggings are on the rise in Savannah. While you can still enjoy yourself at night, it's important to exercise a certain amount of caution, as you would in any big city. When out and about at night, there is safety in numbers—make new friends and go around as a group. If you are a party of one, call a pedicab for transportation after 10 PM. Don't carry excess cash, and put your money in several different places. Stay out of the alleys and even the squares. Homeless people and druggies frequent these lovely parks by night.

FodorsChoice **Planters Tavern** (✉ *23 Abercorn St., Historic District* ☎*912/232–4286*), in
★ the basement of the Olde Pink House, is one of Savannah's most romantic
late-night spots for a nightcap. There's some kind of live entertainment
every night. The decor never changes, and that is part of what makes the
scene, especially the stone fireplace and the fox-hunt memorabilia.

COFFEEHOUSES

Gallery Espresso (✉ *234 Bull St., Historic District* ☎*912/233–5348*) is
a combined coffee haunt and art enclave, with gallery shows and free
Internet access for customers. Plus, it stays open until 10 PM. The staff
can be curt, but it is a real neighborhood scene and a popular destination for students at SCAD.

For traditional afternoon high tea, you can't beat the lavishly outfitted
Gryphon Tea Room (✉ *337 Bull St., Historic District* ☎*912/525–5880*).
A former old-time pharmacy, with stained glass and apothecary motifs
in tiles, this atmospheric tearoom also serves specialty coffees alongside
a full menu of scones, baklava, biscotti, and healthier salads and sandwiches. And it offers a full afternoon tea service, complete with finger
sandwiches, scones, and sweets.

LIVE MUSIC CLUBS

★ **Jazz'd Tapas Bar** (✉ *52 Barnard St., Historic District* ☎*912/236–7777*)
is a chic, basement venue featuring a range of local artists are featured
from Tuesday through Saturday. The tapas menu has healthy, contemporary small plates, and is one of the city's best values; the place usually
opens at 4. No one under 21 can enter once the kitchen closes (10 PM
weekdays, midnight on weekends); there's never a cover.
Vic's On the River (✉ *26 E. Bay St and 15 East Bay St., Historic District*
☎*912/721–1000*) is one of Savannah's best restaurants, which also
happens to have an excellent bar. The piano is manned every night.

SPORTS & THE OUTDOORS

10

BIKING

Island Bike (✉ *14 W. State St., Historic District* ✉*205 Johnny Mercer Blvd., Wilmington Island* ☎*912/236–8808 or 912/897–7474*)
rents single-speed adult bikes for $20 per day, kid's bikes for $15 per
day, and multi-speed bikes for $25 per day at both locations. Hel-
mets and locks are available only at the downtown location (for an
extra charge).On Tybee Island you can enjoy a bike-friendly environment with ocean-view trails, at half the cost of biking downtown. **Tim's
Beach Gear** (✉ *Tybee Island* ☎*912/786–8467* ⊕*www.timsbeachgear.
com*) rents bikes for adults and kids as well as in-tow carriers. This is
strictly a drop-off service, offering free delivery and pickup on Tybee
Island—for just $10 a day ($8 per day for multiday rentals), and that
includes helmets.

BOATING & FISHING

Explore the natural beauty and wildlife on a narrated boat tour with **Dolphin Magic Tours** (✉*101 River St., Historic District* ☎*800/721–1240* ⊕*www.dolphin-magic.com*). From River Street you go out to the marshlands and tidal creeks near Tybee Island. The search for dolphin encounters lasts two hours and sightings are guaranteed. Departure times vary according to the tides and the weather; the cruise costs $30. Bring sunscreen and beverages. **Lowcountry River Excursions** (✉*Bull River Marina, 8005 Old Tybee Rd. [Hwy. 80 E], Tybee Island* ☎*912/898–9222*), which operates out of Bull River Marina, allows you to experience an encounter with friendly bottlenose dolphins and enjoy the scenery and wildlife during a 90-minute cruise down the Bull River aboard a 40-foot pontoon boat. Restrooms are on board, and beverages, too. Call to confirm times and seasonal hours. Reservations are strongly advised. Capt. Judy Helmley, a long-time and legendary guide of the region, heads up **Miss Judy Charters** (✉*124 Palmetto Dr., Wilmington Island* ☎*912/897–4921 or 912/897–2478* ⊕*www.missjudycharters.com*) and provides packages ranging from two-hour sightseeing tours to 16-hour deep-sea fishing expeditions. Rates run about $500 for four hours and (up to) six people, and $650 for eight hours, and a 16-hour adventure will cost you $1,800. Most major credit cards accepted. Please don't forget to tip the mate 15% to 20%. **North Island Surf & Kayak** (✉*1C Old Tybee Rd., Tybee Island* ☎*912/786–4000* ⊕*www.northislandkayak.com*) is a young and versatile operation, but they will open up a whole new world of kayaking with their sit-on-top kayaks that are virtually unsinkable. You can put in at the company's floating dock, or launch wherever you want. All rentals include paddles, life jackets, and seat backs. Prices are $40 per day for a single, $55 for a double; there are no hourly rentals. The company also offers ecotours; although these tours require a minimum of six adults ($50), you can often join a scheduled group if you are a couple or a single. You can also rent paddleboards here for $50 a day, or a surfboard for $30. Lessons are an extra $10 an hour.

GOLF

The Club at Savannah Harbor (✉*2 Resort Dr., Hutchinson Island* ☎*912/201–2007* ⊕*www.theclubatsavannahharbor.com*) is an 18-hole course with a pro shop, spa, locker rooms, putting green, and driving range. This is the resort complex of the Westin Hotel, which is a free ferry ride from Savannah's riverfront. This championship course has unparalleled views the river and of historic downtown Savannah as it winds through wetlands. Green fees, including cart, run $60–$120.

SPAS

Spas are catching on in the city of Spanish moss, and the spa options in Savannah have now matured and expanded.

Magnolia Spa (⊠*Marriott Savannah Riverfront, 100 Gen. McIntosh Blvd., Historic District* ☎*912/373–2039* ⊕*www.marriott.com*) is a secret mother lode of pampering services that the occasional tourist may not stumble upon in their wanderings since it is at the far end of the River Walk and within the Marriott and has not been open long. The very chic **Poseidon Spa** (⊠ *The Mansion on Forsyth Park, 700 Drayton St., Historic District* ☎*912/721–5004* ⊕*www.mansiononforsythpark.com*) is a first-class European-style spa, with a number of rejuvenating treatments and refinement services. It offers manicures, pedicures, skin and body treatments, massages, and access to a 24-hour fitness center. This truly is the town's glamour spa, though in truth prices run just a little more than the rest. **Savannah Day Spa** (⊠*18 E. Oglethorpe St., Downtown* ☎*912/234–9100* ⊕*www.savannahdayspa.com*) is a former urban mansion and is a delightful place to take your treatments, be it one of the creative massages or a therapeutic facial for your particular skin issues.

SHOPPING

Find your own Lowcountry treasures among a bevy of handcrafted wares—handmade quilts and baskets; wreaths made from Chinese tallow trees and Spanish moss; preserves, jams, and jellies. The favorite Savannah snack, and a popular gift item, is the benne wafer (from the African word for sesame seeds). These thin cookies are about the size of a quarter and come in different flavors. Handmade candies, specifically Southern pralines made with brown sugar and pecans, are a big draw with the little ones, or the "sweet tooth" teased by a free sample.

Savannah has a wide collection of colorful businesses—revitalization is no longer a goal but an accomplishment. Antiques malls and junk emporiums beckon you with their colorful storefronts and eclectic offerings, as do the many specialty shops and bookstores clustered along the streets.

10

SHOPPING DISTRICTS

For generations, **Broughton Street** (⊠*Between Congress and State Sts., Historic District*) was the main shopping street of the city. After a decades-long downturn, the area is thriving once again, not only with shops but with restaurants and coffeehouses, too. West of Bull Street are more shops; East of Bull, there are fewer stores, but you'll still find some high-end boutiques on both ends, as well as chain stores. **City Market** (⊠ *W. St. Julian St. between Ellis and Franklin Sqs., Historic District*) takes its origins from a farmers' market back in 1755. Today it's a four-block emporium that has been involved in a renaissance program, and constitutes an eclectic mix of artists' studios, sidewalk cafés, jazz haunts, shops, and art galleries. **Riverfront Plaza/River Street** (⊠*Historic District*) is nine blocks of renovated waterfront warehouses (once the city's cotton exchange) containing more than 75 boutiques, galleries, restaurants, and pubs; you can find everything from popcorn to pottery here, and even voodoo spells! Leave your stilettos at home, or you'll find the street's cobblestones hard and dangerous work.

SPECIALTY SHOPS

ANTIQUES

FodorśChoice **37th @ Abercorn Antique & Design** (⊠*37th St., at Abercorn St., Historic*
★ *District* ☎*912/233–0064*) is a one-stop shop that encompasses a city block of antiques and collectibles spanning 200 years. Stroll with a cup of java from the property's European café, and peruse through the area's largest collection of quilts, antique clocks, vintage costume jewelry, and museum-quality vintage children's clothes. Visit a primitive country kitchen displaying gadgets, enamelware, and 1950s-era linens. Original Persian rugs and antique sterling silver jewelry are among other unique items available.

ART GALLERIES

Compass Prints, Inc./Ray Ellis Gallery (⊠*205 W. Congress St., Historic District* ☎*912/234–3537*) sells original artwork, prints, and books by internationally acclaimed artist Ray Ellis.

FodorśChoice **Grand Bohemian Gallery**(⊠*The Mansion at Forsyth Park, 700 Drayton*
★ *St., Historic District* ☎*912/238–5158, ext. 5007*)is within the city's most luxurious hotel, and although it is a separate shop, the entire hotel showcases the Kessler Collection, which was acquired by the gallery's owner, Richard Kessler, a native Georgian. Much of his artwork can be purchased. Within the actual gallery you'll find the work of acclaimed artists, especially contemporary paintings, blown glass art, ceramics, whimsical sculpture, and some incredibly innovative jewelry pieces. Check on the schedule of imaginative workshops and lectures conducted
FodorśChoice by some of the most respected artists worldwide. **ShopSCAD** (⊠*340 Bull*
★ *St., Historic District* ☎*912/525–5180* ⊕*www.shopscadonline.com*) sells amazing works by faculty, alumni, and students of SCAD, including handcrafted jewelry, clothing, furniture, glass work, and original postcards. Just remember that these originals do not come cheap.

BOOKS

"The Book" Gift Shop and Midnight Museum (⊠*127 E. Gordon St., Historic District* ☎*912/233–3867*) sells all things related to *Midnight in the Garden of Good and Evil,* including souvenirs and author-autographed copies. It may not have a long life, in that the keen interest in the subject is on the wane. In the meantime, if you have never read this Savannah classic, you can pick it up here. Seeing the decline, the shop is now wisely capitalizing on the various ghost tours and has a lot of haunt-y items. **E. Shaver Booksellers** (⊠*326 Bull St., Historic District* ☎*912/234–7257*) is the source for 17th- and 18th-century maps and new books on regional subjects. It carries travel guides for Savannah and books on just about whatever you would want to know about the city, from its colonial beginnings to what there is for children to do. This shop occupies 12 rooms of an historic building, and it alone is something to see. The booksellers are knowledgeable about their wares.

CLOTHING FOR WOMEN

Fodor'sChoice
★ **Copper Penny** (✉22 W. *Broughton St., Historic District* ☎912/629–6800) was conceptualized by owner Penny Vaigneur in Charleston (there's a store there and in Myrtle Beach). Carrying Trina Turk, Nanette Lapore, and Hudson Jeans, to name a few of the designers popular with young fashionistas, the more mature shopper comes to get some edgy pieces to contemporize her wardrobe. "Attached" is Copper Penny Shooz, where you'll find shoe fashion statements by BCB Girls, Kate Spade, Michael Kors, and the like. Great-looking purses complement the shoes; you'll find names like Francesco Biasia, Hype Handbags, and Tano. Love those Lucchese boots.

> **PARK AND SAVE**
>
> Drivers be warned: Savannah patrollers are quick to dole out parking tickets. Tourists may purchase two-day parking passes ($8) at the Savannah Visitors Center and at some hotels and inns. Passes are valid in metered spots as well as in the city's lots and garages; they allow parkers to exceed the time in time-limit zones.

FOOD STUFFS

The Lady and her sons have another hit to their credit. They have transformed what was the grungiest of bars into the fabulous **Paula Deen Store** (✉108 W. *Congress St., Historic District* ☎912/232–1607), which is filled with cookbooks by the Southern Queen of the Food Network. Two full floors of cooking goodies and gadgets are cleverly displayed against a backdrop of brick walls. The shop is adjacent to Deen's famous Southern-style restaurant, so you may get lucky, for her
Fodor'sChoice son Jamie may be signing cookbooks on your day. **River Street Sweets**
★ (✉13 E. *River St., Historic District* ☎912/233–6220) opened in 1973, and it is Savannah's self-described "oldest and original" candy store. The aroma of creamy homemade fudge will draw you in, along with hot and fresh pralines, which are made all day long. The store is also known for milk-chocolate bear claws. It's a great place to find a unique, edible gift. You'll always receive excellent customer service here.

HOME DECOR

Fodor'sChoice
★ **The Paris Market & Brocante** (✉36 W. *Broughton St., Historic District* ☎912/232–1500) is a Francophile's dream, from the time you open the antique front door and take in the intoxicating aroma of lavender. This two-story emporium with chandeliers and other lighting fixtures is a classy version of the Paris flea market, selling furniture, vintage art, garden planters and accessories, and Euro-home fashions like boudoir accessories and bedding. And although the store will ship, there are numerous treasures that can be easily carried away, like the soaps, candles, vintage jewelry, kitchen and barware, and dried lavender.

10

The Coastal Isles & the Okefenokee, GA

WORD OF MOUTH

"Well, my favorite is Jekyll Island, but it is decidedly NOT upscale. St. Simons is more so. Cumberland is deserted sans some campers and the Greyfield Inn. It's wonderful because it IS so deserted."

—starrs

"St. Simon's has that same wooded feel as Hilton Head Island and [is] much less developed. I'm not a fan of the beach [on St. Simon's] though; it's not as nice as Hilton Head Island's [beach]."

—Brian_in_Charlotte

Updated by
Christine Van
Dusen

GEORGIA'S COASTAL ISLES ARE A string of lush barrier islands meandering down the Atlantic coast from Savannah to the Florida border. Notable for their subtropical beauty and abundant wildlife, the isles also strike a unique balance between some of the wealthiest communities in the country and some of the most jealously protected preserves found anywhere. Until recently large segments of the coast were in private hands, and as a result much of the region remains as it was when the first Europeans set eyes on it 450 years ago. The marshes, wetlands, and waterways teem with birds and other wildlife, and they're ideal for exploring by kayak or canoe. Though the islands have long been a favorite getaway of the rich and famous, they no longer cater only to the well-heeled. There's mounting pressure to develop these wilderness shores and make them even more accessible.

The Golden Isles—St. Simons Island, Little St. Simons Island, Sea Island, and Jekyll Island—are the more developed of the coastal isles, although by Georgia law Jekyll is only able to develop 35% of its land. (Jekyll's future, at this writing, was in dispute as developers pushed for revitalization and residents and activists resisted.) Although Little St. Simons Island and Sea Island cater primarily to the wealthy looking to get away from it all, St. Simons Island and Jekyll Island are diverse havens with something for everyone from beach bums to family vacationers to the suit-and-tie crowd. Though it has only a few hundred full-time residents, Sea Island is one of the wealthiest zip codes in America.

Generally unmarred by development, the more remote Sapelo Island and Cumberland Island National Seashore, with their near-pristine ecology, are alluring for anyone seeking an authentic getaway. Both are excellent for camping, with sites ranging from primitive to (relatively) sophisticated. Noncamping accommodations are limited and require booking well in advance. Miles of untouched beaches, forests of gnarly live oak draped with Spanish moss, and swamps and marshlands teeming with birds and wildlife combine to make these islands unique. The best way to visit them is on either public or private guided tours.

The Okefenokee National Wildlife Refuge, 60 mi inland from St. Marys near Folkston, is one of the largest wetlands in the United States. Spread over 700 square mi of southeastern Georgia and northeastern Florida, the swamp is a trove of flora and fauna that naturalist William Bartram called a "terrestrial paradise" when he visited in the 1770s. From towering cypress swamps to alligator- and snake-infested waters to prairielike grasslands, the Okefenokee is a mosaic of ecosystems, much of which has never been visited by humans.

ORIENTATION & PLANNING

GETTING ORIENTED

Coastal Georgia is a complex jigsaw wending its way from the ocean and tidal marshes inland along the intricate network of rivers. U.S. 17, the old coastal highway, gives you a taste of the slower, more rural

TOP REASONS TO GO

Saltwater marshes: Fringing the coastline, waist-high grasses transform both sunlight and shadow with their lyrical textures and shapes. This landscape inspired Georgia poet Sidney Lanier to describe the marshes as "a silver-wrought garment that clings to and follows the firm sweet limbs of a girl."

Sapelo Island: When land was set aside as an independent state of freed slaves, it became known as Georgia's Black Republic. Vestiges of that community remain at Sapelo, and have made it an island of contrasts—rich in history and ecowilderness, and home to Hog Hammock, a one-of-a-kind community that echoes the culture and practices of its African slave heritage.

Horses of Cumberland: Cumberland Island is about as far removed from civilization as you can get, and seeing the majesty of these horses run wild across the shore is worth every effort of planning ahead. There are some 200 feral horses, descendants of those that were abandoned by the Spanish in the 1500s.

Jekyll Island Club: Originally the winter retreat of the exceptionally rich, this millionaire's village of mansion-size "cottages" is an elegant exposé of how the royalty of corporate America once played. Once an exclusive club, today you can wander around the community at your leisure.

Go for a ride: The level terrain on all the islands makes for great biking, though the most scenic is Jekyll Island. It offers 20 mi of paved bike paths that traverse salt marshes, maritime forest, and beach, as well as the island's National Historic Landmark District.

South. But because of the subtropical climate, the lush forests tend to be dense along the mainland and there are few opportunities to glimpse the broad vistas of salt marsh and islands. To truly appreciate the mystique of Georgia's coastal salt marshes and islands, make the 40-minute ferry crossing from Meridian to Sapelo Island.

Sapelo Island. Reachable only by ferry from Meridien, less-developed Sapelo is the home of the Geechee, who are descended directly from former African slaves. Note that you must have a reservation for a day tour or a reservation to camp or stay at one of the island's small hotels in order to take the ferry over.

Little St. Simons Island. Little St. Simons, a private island with accommodations for a limited number of overnight guests and day-trippers, is accessible by private launch from the northern end of St. Simons.

Sea Island. One of the wealthiest private communities in the U.S., Sea Island is accessible only to residents and guests at The Cloister, the island's swanky resort hotel.

St. Simons Island. The most developed of the Golden Isles is a well-rounded vacation destination with a variety of hotels and restaurants in varying price ranges.

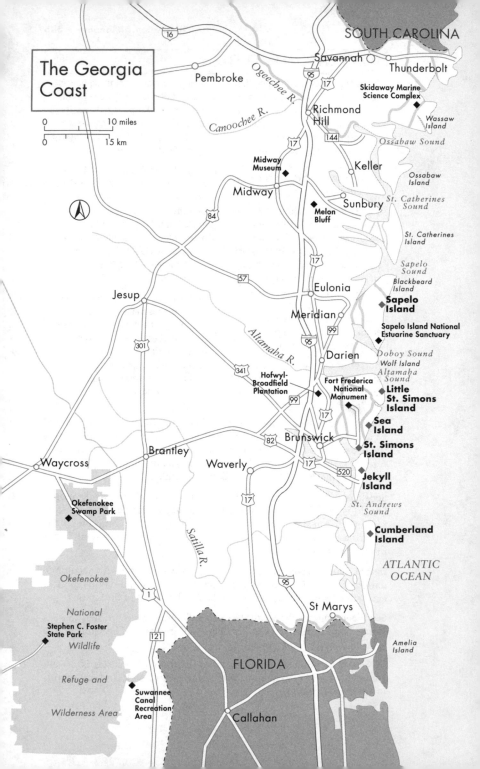

Jekyll Island. Once the playground for the rich and famous, Jekyll is now more egalitarian. It's pristine beaches are uncommercialized and open to all, and the range of resorts and restaurants appeals to a wide range of travelers.

Cumberland Island. Reachable only by ferry, this virtually pristine island is a national seashore and has only one accommodation (a former Carnegie family mansion) and a few campgrounds.

Okefenokee National Wildlife Range. The Okefenokee is a mysterious world where, as a glance at a map will indicate, all roads suddenly disappear. This large, interior wetland is navigable only by boat, and it can be confusing and intimidating to the uninitiated. None of the individual parks within the area give a sense of the total Okefenokee experience—each has its own distinct natural features. Choose the park that best aligns with your interests and begin there.

THE COASTAL ISLANDS & OKEFENOKEE PLANNER

GETTING HERE & AROUND

Visiting the region is easiest by car, particularly Sapelo Island, because many of the outer reaches of Georgia are remote places with little in the way of transportation options. Touring by bicycle is an option for most of the region, but note that the ferries at Sapelo and Cumberland do not allow bicycles on board. Except for Little St. Simons, the Golden Isles are connected to the mainland by bridges around Brunswick and are the only coastal isles accessible by car. Sapelo Island and the Cumberland Island National Seashore can only be reached by ferry from Meridian and St. Marys, respectively.

BY AIR   The coastal isles are served by the Brunswick Golden Isles Airport, 6 mi north of Brunswick, and the McKinnon St. Simons Airport on St. Simons Island. McKinnon accommodates light aircraft and private planes. The closest major airports are in Savannah and Jacksonville, FL.

BY BOAT &   Cumberland Island, Sapelo Island, and Little St. Simons are accessible
FERRY   only by ferry or private launch. The *Cumberland Queen* serves Cumberland Island and the *Anne Marie* serves Sapelo Island. The Lodge on Little St. Simons Island operates a private launch that is available only to overnight or day-trip guests by prior arrangement.

BY CAR   From Brunswick take the Jekyll Island Causeway ($3 per car) to Jekyll Island and the Torras Causeway to St. Simons and Sea Island. You can get by without a car on Jekyll Island and Sea Island, but you'll need one on St. Simons. You cannot bring a car to Cumberland Island, Little St. Simons, or Sapelo.

BY TAXI   Courtesy Cab provides taxi service from Brunswick to and from the islands for a set rate that ranges from $15 to $25 to St. Simons and from $25 to Jekyll Island with a $2 per person surcharge to a maximum of seven persons. Island Cab Service can shuttle you around St. Simons for fares that range between $7 and $15 depending on your destination.

ESSENTIALS Air Contacts **Atlantic Southeast Airlines** (☎ *800/282–3424, 800/221–1212, or 912/267–1325*). **The Brunswick Golden Isles Airport** (✉ *500 Connole St.* ☎ *912/265–2070* ⊕ *www.glynncountyairports.com*). **McKinnon St. Simons Island Airport** (✉ *Off Demere Rd.* ☎ *912/628–8617*).

Boat & Ferry Contacts **Anne Marie** (✉ *Sapelo Island Visitors Center, Rte. 1, Box 1500, Darien* ☎ *912/437–3224* ⊕ *www.sapelonerr.org*). **Cumberland Queen** (☞ *Cumberland Island National Seashore* ⌂ *Box 806, 101 Wheeler St., St. Marys 31558* ☎ *912/882–4336 or 877/860–6787* 🖷 *912/673–7747* ⊕ *www.nps.gov/ cuis*). **The Lodge on Little St. Simons Island** (⌂ *Box 21078, Little St. Simons Island 31522* ☎ *912/638–7472 or 888/733–5774* 🖷 *912/634–1811* ⊕ *www. littlestsimonsisland.com*).

Taxi Contacts **Courtesy Cab** (✉ *4262B Norwich Exit, Brunswick* ☎ *912/264–3760*). **Island Cab Service** (✉ *708 E. Island Square Dr., St. Simons* ☎ *912/634–0113*).

TOURS

St. Simons Transit Company offers year-round bus, boat, and trolley tours from St. Simons Island and Jekyll Island that explore the surrounding marshes and rivers and get you up close and personal with dolphins, manatees, and other marine life. Kayaks and canoes are also a great way to explore the creeks. Tour operators include Southeast Adventure Outfitters, St. Simons Island, and Brunswick.

TOUR ESSENTIALS Tour Contacts **St. Simons Transit Company** (✉ *105 Marina Dr., St. Simons* ☎ *912/638–5678*. **Southeast Adventure Outfitters** (✉ *313 Mallory St., St. Simons* ☎ *912/638–6732* ⊕ *www.southeastadventure.com*).

ABOUT THE RESTAURANTS

Restaurants range from fish camps—normally rustic dockside affairs— to the more upscale eateries that tend to spawn around the larger towns. And though there's still room for growth, the area now has several menus gaining not only local but nationwide attention. The rising tide of quality has begun to lift all boats. Some restaurants still serve food family style.

ABOUT THE HOTELS

Hotels run the gamut from Victorian mansions to Spanish-style bed-and-breakfasts to some of the most luxurious hotel–spa accommodations found anywhere. Since options are somewhat limited, make your reservations as far in advance as possible. Most hotels offer the full range of guest services, but as a matter of philosophy many B&Bs do not provide televisions or telephones in the rooms. Lodging prices quoted here may be much lower during non-peak seasons, and specials are often available on weekdays even in high season.

WHAT IT COSTS					
	¢	$	$$	$$$	$$$$
Restaurant	under $10	$10–$14	$15–$19	$20–$24	over $24

Restaurant prices are for a main course at dinner. Hotel prices are for two people in a standard double room in high season.

WHAT IT COSTS					
	¢	$	$$	$$$	$$$$
Hotel	under $100	$100–$150	$151–$200	$101–$250	over $250

Restaurant prices are for a main course at dinner. Hotel prices are for two people in a standard double room in high season.

PLANNING YOUR TIME

Although Georgia's coastal islands are along a strip of coastline that is less than 60 mi long, each has a different feel, and a visit requires at least a day. The complications of ferries to Sapelo or Cumberland make it difficult to visit either of those in less than a day, and these visits must generally be planned far in advance. It's possible to base yourself on busy St. Simons Island (or any of the Golden Isles for that matter) and visit much of the region on a series of day trips. The Okefenokee is a bit farther out of the way, but can be visited on a day trip from almost any of the islands, or if you have more time it can be an overnight trip.

SAPELO ISLAND

8 mi northeast of Darien.

The fourth-largest of Georgia's coastal isles—and bigger than Bermuda—Sapelo Island is a unique community in North America. It still bears evidence of the early-Paleo-Indians who lived here some 4,500 years ago, and is home to the Geechee, direct descendants of African slaves who speak a creole of English and various African languages. This rapidly dwindling community maintains many traditional African practices, including the making of sweetgrass baskets and the use of herbal medicines made from recipes passed down for generations. It's also a nearly pristine barrier island with miles of undeveloped beaches and abundant wildlife. To take the 40-minute ferry ride from Meridian on the mainland through the expanse of salt marshes to Sapelo Island is to enter a world seemingly forgotten by time.

GETTING HERE & AROUND

You can explore many historical periods and natural environments here, but facilities on the island are limited. Note that you can't simply walk up to the dock and catch the ferry—you need to have a reservation for a tour, a campsite, or one of the island's lodgings (or have prearranged plans to stay with island residents). Bring insect repellent, especially in summer, and leave your pets at home. You can rent a bicycle on the island, but you cannot bring a bicycle on the ferry.

EXPLORING SAPELO ISLAND

Start your visit at the **Sapelo Island Visitor Center** in Meridian on the mainland near the Sapelo Island ferry docks. Here you can see exhibits on the island's history, culture, and ecology, and you can purchase tickets for a round-trip ferry ride and bus tour of the island. The sights that make up the bus tour vary depending on the day of the week, but always included are the marsh, the sand-dune ecosystem, and the wildlife management area. On Friday and Saturday the tour includes the 80-foot **Sapelo Lighthouse**, built in 1820, a symbol of the cotton and lumber industry once based out of Darien, a prominent shipping center of the time. To see the island's **Reynolds Mansion**, schedule your tour for Wednesday or Saturday. To get to the visitor center and Meridian Ferry Dock from downtown Darien, go north on Route 99 for 8 mi, following signs for the Sapelo Island National Estuarine Research Reserve. Turn right onto Landing Road at the Elm Grove Baptist Church in Meridian. The visitor center is about ½ mi down the road. ⊠ *Rte. 1, Box 1500, Darien* ☎ *912/437–3224, 912/485–2300 for group tours* ⊕ *www.sapelonerr.org.*

Hog Hammock Community is one of the few remaining sites on the south Atlantic coast where ethnic African-American culture from the slave era has been preserved. The "Salt Water Geechee," Georgia's sea-island equivalent to the Gullah, are descendants of slaves who worked the island's plantations during the 19th century. Hog Hammock's 40 residents are the last members of a disappearing culture with its own distinct language and customs. **The Spirit of Sapelo Tours** (✉ *Box 7, Sapelo Island 31327* ☎ *912/485–2170*) provides private guided bus tours led by an island native who discusses island life, culture, and history. **Sapelo Culture Day** (☎ *912/485–2197* ⊕ *www.sapeloislandgeorgia.org*), a celebration of Geechee folklore, music, food, handcrafts, and art, takes place in Hog Hammock every year on the third weekend in October. Reservations are required.

OFF THE
BEATEN
PATH

Colonial Coast Birding Trail. Georgia's vast network of rivers, marshes, and barrier islands provides ideal habitat for hundreds of species of birds, from nesting wood storks to red painted buntings. This "trail" is a string of 18 sites along the coast from the border of South Carolina to Florida, straddling U.S. 17 and Interstate 95. Four of the sites (Harris Neck National Wildlife Refuge, Jekyll Island, Cumberland Island, and the Okefenokee National Wildlife Refuge) have been designated Important Birding Areas (IBAs) by the Georgia Audubon Society. With more than 330 species of birds to watch for, the staffs of visitor centers along the way have maps and plenty of bird-watching suggestions for both skilled and novice birders. ☎ *912/262–3128* ⊕ *georgiawildlife.dnr.state.ga.us.*

WHERE TO EAT

$$
SEAFOOD
★

✕ **Mudcat Charlie's.** This tabby-and-wood restaurant on the Altamaha River sits right in the middle of the Two Way Fish Camp and is a favorite haunt of locals from nearby Darien. The restaurant overlooks the boats moored in the marina, and the seafood is local. Crab stew, fried oysters, and shrimp are the specialties, and the peach and apple pies are made in-house. It's 1 mi south of Darien on U.S. 17, just after the third bridge. Look for the Two Way Fish Camp sign. ⊠ *250 Ricefield Way* ☎ *912/261–0055* ⊟ *AE, D, MC, V.*

$$
SEAFOOD
★

✕ **Skipper's Fish Camp.** You can find this upscale take on the fish camp theme at the foot of Skipper's dock on the Darien River, where the working shrimp boats moor. It has a beautiful courtyard pond that uses water from the river and an open-air oyster bar. Popular menu items include Georgia white shrimp, ribs, and fried flounder. There's usually a wait on weekends, so get there early. At the southern end of Darien, turn right at Broad just before the river bridge, then take the first left down to the docks. ⊠ *85 Scriven St.* ☎ *912/437–3474* ⚓ *Reservations not accepted* ▤ *AE, D, MC, V.*

WHERE TO STAY

$–$$ ▦ **The Blue Heron Inn.** Bill and Jane Chamberlain's airy, Spanish-style home sits on the edge of the marsh and is only minutes from the ferry at the Sapelo Island Visitors Center. The downstairs dining and living areas have an open, Mediterranean feel, with a large, rustic fireplace and a sweeping view of the marsh. Guest rooms are simply decorated with colorful quilts; most have four-poster beds, and all have a view of the marsh. The proprietor, an Athens native, provides drinks and hors d'oeuvres on the third-floor terrace overlooking the Doboy Sound every evening, and his breakfast specialties include lime French toast and sweet Georgia shrimp omelets. **Pros:** deliciously inventive breakfasts; decks provide great views. **Cons:** the small number of rooms means the place can book up fast. ⊠ *1 Blue Heron La., Meridian* ☎🖷 *912/437–4304* ⊕ *www.blueheroninngacoast.com* ↪ *4 rooms* ♿ *In room: no phone, no TV. In-hotel: Wi-Fi* ▤ *MC, V* �101 *BP.*

$ ▦ **Open Gates.** Built by a timber baron in 1876, this two-story, white-★ frame house on Darien's Vernon Square is filled with antiques and Victorian atmosphere. Each room is beautifully decorated. Innkeepers Kelly and Jeff Spratt hold masters degrees in biology and arrange guided tours of the Altamaha River and surrounding area. A full Southern breakfast and evening cocktails are included in your stay. **Pros:** the library has an excellent collection of books of local historical interest. **Cons:** limited restaurant choices in the area; not a hot spot for singles. ⊠ *301 Franklin St., Box 662, Darien* ☎ *912/437–6985* 🖷 *912/882–9427* ⊕ *www.opengatesbnb.com* ↪ *5 rooms, 4 with bath* ♿ *In room: no TV. In-hotel: pool* ▤ *MC, V* 101 *BP.*

¢ ▦ **The Wallow Lodge.** Cornelia Walker Bailey's memoir of life growing up Geechee on Sapelo, *God, Dr. Buzzard, and the Bolito Man,* has made her a folk hero and focused awareness on the disappearing communities of descendants of African slaves. A stay at Bailey's Wallow Lodge offers a chance to experience the island's distinct culture. Cotton chenille, a tradition on Sapelo, and quilted spreads cover the beds. **Pros:** each room is decorated with furniture and memorabilia from residents of the island. **Cons:** the lodge has a communal kitchen, so unless you make prior arrangements for meals, you must bring your own supplies from the mainland. ⊠ *1 Main Rd., Box 34, Sapelo Island* ☎ *912/485–2206* 🖷 *912/485–2174* ⊕ *www.gacoast.com/geecheetours* ↪ *6 rooms, 5 with bath* ♿ *In room: no phone, no TV* ▤ *No credit cards* 101 *EP.*

CLOSE UP

The Nile of the East Coast

The Altamaha River is a national treasure. Formed by the confluence of the Ocmulgee and Oconee rivers near Hazelhurst, it's the longest undammed river and the second largest watershed in the eastern United States, covering almost 15,000 square mi. After running its 137-mi course, it spills into the Altamaha Sound, between Sapelo Island and Little St. Simons, at a rate of 100,000 gallons every second, or more than 3 trillion gallons a year—a flow comparable to Egypt's Nile.

The Altamaha's greatest value lies in the 170,000 acres of river swamps that shoulder the length of its course, serving as refuge to at least 130 endangered plant and animal species, including several freshwater mussels found nowhere else in the world. The swamps are also incubators for life-giving organic matter such as leaves, twigs, and other detritus. Spring floods flush this matter downstream, where it's trapped by the salt marshes that stretch between the mouth of the river and Georgia's barrier islands. This natural fertilizer feeds marsh grasses, which in turn feed fungi and phytoplankton, and so on up the food chain.

WHERE TO CAMP

⚠ **Comyam's Campground.** The name of Hog Hammock's only campground comes from the Geechee word meaning "come here." And the marsh-side view is just for backpackers coming for a more rustic taste of the island life. ☐ *Box 7, Sapelo Island, Tom's Hole 31327* ☐ *Flush toilets, showers* ☐ *30 sites* ☎ *912/485–2170* 🖷 *912/485–2174* ⊕ *www. gacoast.com/geecheetours* ☐ *Reservations essential* ☐ *$10 per person per day, not including ferry.*

SPORTS & THE OUTDOORS

CANOEING & KAYAKING

The Altamaha River, the largest undammed river on the East Coast, runs inland from near Darien. You can take expeditions along it with **Altamaha Coastal Tours** (☒ *229 Fort King George Dr., Darien* ☎ *912/437–6010*), which rents equipment and conducts guided trips from the waterfront in Darien. With them you can explore tidal swamps, marshlands, and Queen and Sapelo islands.

NIGHTLIFE

It seems appropriate that the only watering hole in Hog Hammock is named the **Trough** (☒ *1 Main Rd.* ☎ *912/485–2206*). It's a small, bare-bones, belly-up-to-the-bar establishment, but owner Julius Bailey serves his beer ice-cold, and there's usually a good conversation going on. It's next to the Wallow Lodge (operated by Julius's wife, Cornelia), right "downtown."

**EN
ROUTE**

Rice, not cotton, dominated Georgia's coast in the antebellum years, and the **Hofwyl-Broadfield Plantation** is the last remaining example of a way of life that fueled an agricultural empire. The main farmhouse, in use since the 1850s when the original house burned, is now a museum with family heirlooms accrued over five generations, including extensive collections of silver and Canton china. A guide gives an insightful talk on rural plantation life. Though grown over, some of the original dikeworks and rice fields remain, as do some of the slave quarters. A brief film at the visitor center complements exhibits on rice technology and cultivation, and links to Sierra Leone, from where many slaves were taken because of their expertise in growing rice. ⊠ *5556 U.S. 17 N, 4 mi south of Darien* ☎ *912/264–7333* ⊕ *www.gastateparks.org/ info/hofwyl* ⊠ *$5* ⊙ *Tues.–Sat. 9–5, Sun. 2–5:30.*

ST. SIMONS ISLAND

22 mi south of Darien, 4 mi east of Brunswick.

St. Simons may be the Golden Isles' most developed vacation destination: here you can swim and sun, golf, hike, fish, ride horseback, tour historic sites, and feast on local seafood at more than 50 restaurants. (It's also a great place to bike and jog, particularly on the southern end, where there's an extensive network of trails.) Despite the development, the island has managed to maintain some of the slow-paced Southern atmosphere that made it such a draw in the first place. Upscale resorts and restaurants are here for the asking, but this island the size of Manhattan has only 20,000 year-round residents, so you can still get away from it all without a struggle. Even down in the village, the center of much of St. Simons's activity, there are unpaved roads and quiet back alleys of chalky white sand that seem like something out of the past.

GETTING HERE & AROUND
Reach the island by car via the causeway from Brunswick. In the village area, at the more developed south end of the island, you can find shops, several restaurants, pubs, and a popular public pier. For $20 a quaint **"trolley"** (☎ *912/638–8954*) takes you on a 1½-hour guided tour of the island, leaving from near the pier at 11 AM and 1 PM in high season and at 11 AM in winter.

ESSENTIALS
Visitor Information Brunswick and the Golden Isles Visitors Center (⊠ *4 Glynn Ave., Brunswick* ☎ *912/265–0620* ⊠ *530 Beachview Dr., St. Simons* ☎ *912/638– 9014* ☎ *800/809–1790* ⊕ *www.bgicvb.com).* **St. Simons Visitors Center** (⊠ *St. Simons, F.J. Torras, Causeway at U.S. 17, St. Simons Island* ☎ *912/265–6620* ⊕ *www.bgicvb.com).*

EXPLORING ST. SIMONS ISLAND

ᘓ Named after St. Simons slave Neptune Small, **Neptune Park** (⊠ *550 Beachview Dr.* ☎ *912/279–2836*), on the island's south end in the village, has picnic tables, a children's play park, miniature golf, and beach access. The casino swimming pool ($4 per person) is open each summer near the St. Simons Lighthouse. Bathrooms are in the library beside the visitor center.

★ **St. Simons Lighthouse,** one of only five surviving lighthouses in Georgia, has become a symbol of the island. It's been in use since 1872; a predecessor was blown up to prevent its capture by Union troops in the Civil War. The **Museum of Coastal History,** occupying two stories of the lightkeeper's cottage, has period furniture and a gallery with photo displays illustrating the significance of shipbuilding on St. Simons, the history of the lighthouse, and the life of James Gould, the first lighthouse keeper. The keeper's second-floor quarters contain a parlor, kitchen, and two bedrooms furnished with period pieces, including beds with rope mattress suspension. ⌧*101 12th St.* ☎*912/638–4666* ⊕*www. saintsimonslighthouse.org* ⌧*$5* ⊙*Mon.–Sat. 10–5, Sun. 1:30–5.*

At the north end of the island is the **Fort Frederica National Monument,** the ruins of a fort built by English troops in the mid-1730s to protect the southern flank of the new Georgia colony against a Spanish invasion from Florida. At its peak in the 1740s, it was the most elaborate British fortification in North America. Around the fort are the foundations of homes and shops and the partial ruins of the tabby barracks and magazine. Start your visit at the National Park Service Visitors Center, which has a film and displays. ⌧*Off Frederica Rd. near Christ Episcopal Church* ☎*912/638–3639* ⊕*www.nps.gov/fofr* ⌧*$3* ⊙*Daily 9–5.*

The white-frame, Gothic-style **Christ Episcopal Church** was built by shipwrights and consecrated in 1886 following an earlier structure's desecration by Union troops. It's surrounded by live oaks, dogwoods, and azaleas. The interior has beautiful stained-glass windows, and several of the pews were handmade by slaves. ⌧*6329 Frederica Rd.* ☎*912/638–8683* ⌧*Donations suggested* ⊙*Weekdays 2–5.*

☾ **Maritime History Museum.** At the restored 1936 Historic Coast Guard Station, this new center is geared as much to kids as adults. It features the life of a "Coastie" in the early 1940s through personal accounts of the military history of St. Simons Island and has illustrative displays on the ecology of the islands off the coast of Georgia. ⌧*East Beach Causeway* ☎*912/638–4666* ⌧*$6* ⊙*Mon.–Sat. 10–5, Sun. 1:30–5.*

WHERE TO EAT

$
BARBECUE ✗**The Beachcomber BBQ and Grill.** No shoes, no shirt, no problem in this small, rustic eatery where the walls are covered with reed mats and the barbecue smokes away on a cooker right beside the front door. Despite the name, it doesn't boast a beachfront location. However, it's one of the best barbecue joints on the island, offering everything from sandwiches to pulled pork, ribs, and brisket by the pound. ■TIP➔ **The freshly squeezed lemonade is to die for.** ⌧*319 Arnold Rd.* ☎*912/634–5699* ⊕*beachcomberbbq.com* ▤*AE, MC, V.*

$$
AMERICAN ✗**Bennie's Red Barn.** The steaks are cut fresh daily and cooked over an oak fire in this barn of a restaurant that has been serving St. Simons for

Where Legends Landed

In May 1803 an "Igbo" chief and his West African tribesmen became Geechee folk legends when they "walked back to Africa," drowning en masse rather than submitting to a life of slavery. Captured in what is modern-day Nigeria, the tribesmen disembarked their slave ship at **Ebo Landing** and headed straight into Dunbar Creek, chanting a hymn. Though the site is now private property, it can be seen from the road. *From the F. J. Torras Causeway, turn left on Sea Island Rd. After Hawkins Island Dr., look left (north) just before crossing small bridge at Dunbar Creek. The landing is at bend in creek.*

50 years. Though there's room for 200 people, it feels just like family with the checkered tablecloths and the big open fireplace. There's also fresh local seafood. The pies are homemade. And there's music next door at Ziggy's on weekends. ✉*5514 Frederica Rd.* ☎*912/638–2844* ⊕*benniesredbarn.com* ▤*AE, D, MC, V* ⊘*No lunch.*

$$$
SOUTHERN
★
✗**CARGO Portside Grill.** This superb bistro beside the port in Brunswick has a menu that reads like a foodie's wish list, with succulent coastal fare from many ports. Chef Kate Buchanan puts a creative spin on Southern fare, whether it's sesame catfish, or pasta with grilled chicken in a chipotle cream sauce, or pork chops in a sauce flavored with Jack Daniels. Save room for the Georgia peach pound cake. ✉*1423 Newcastle St., Brunswick* ☎*912/267–7330* ⊕*cargoportsidegrill.com* ▤*AE, MC, V* ⊘*Closed Sun. and Mon. No lunch.*

$$$–$$$$
CONTINENTAL
✗**Christie's.** A young husband and wife have poured their hearts into this trendy restaurant. Chef Jayson Riddinger is intent on whimsical innovation, be it in his original dishes or contemporary takes on classics like oysters Rockefeller, which he finishes off on the grill. The Grand Marnier–glazed salmon works beautifully (some of his other creations don't). The house-made green tea ice cream and apple cider panna cotta are superlative. Pricing is fair, particularly for the exceptional lunch menu. ✉*1618 Newcastle St., Brunswick* ☎*912/262–0699* ⊕*christiesrestaurant.net* ▤*AE, MC, V* ⊘*Closed Sun. No lunch Sat.*

$
AMERICAN
✗**Gnat's Landing.** There's more than a little bit of Margaritaville in this Key West–style bungalow catering to the flip-flop crowd. Seafood is their specialty, with a gumbo that's outta sight. Besides being the strangest item on the menu, the fried dill pickle is also the most popular. Sandwiches and salads are also offered. And, of course, there's the "$8,000 margarita," which is about how much owner Robert Bostock spent in travel and ingredients coming up with the recipe. There's live music most Sunday nights, and once a year there's "Gnatfest," a party blowout with live bands for all those pesky regulars. ✉*310 Redfern Village* ☎*912/638–7378* ⊕*gnatslanding.com* ▤*AE, D, MC, V.*

$$$$
AMERICAN
★
✗**Halyards.** This elegant restaurant with a laid-back attitude makes everything except the ketchup right on the premises. Chef-owner Dave

Snyder's devotion to quality has earned a faithful following of discerning locals. Slide into a cozy, tufted booth or sit at the sophisticated bar lined with photos of yachts. Headliners include the seared, sushi-grade tuna with a plum wine reduction and the Asian-style diver scallops. A tasting menu with five courses is paired with wines selected from the restaurant's impressive cellar. The signature coffee hits the mark with the coconut/lime panna cotta with a dark rum gelée layer. ✉*55 Cinema La.* ☎*912/638–9100* ⊕*halyardsrestaurant.com* ⚑*Reservations essential* ▤*AE, D, MC, V* ⊙*Closed Sun. No lunch.*

$$
AMERICAN

✕**Mullet Bay.** After 9 PM the older beach-bar crowd has this place hopping, and on weekends the bar and wraparound porches can be standing-room only until the wee hours. By day, however, this spacious and casual restaurant is great for families, serving a good selection of burgers, pastas, and salads. The kids' menu starts at $1.95. ∎**TIP➜The platters of fried popcorn shrimp are delicious and perfect for sharing.** ✉*512 Ocean Blvd.* ☎*912/634–9977* ⊕*mulletbayrestaurant.com* ▤*AE, D, MC, V.*

¢
SEAFOOD
★

✕**Rafters.** If you're looking for cheap, delicious food and a raucous good time, this is the place. Revelers sit together at long tables and partake of the offerings from the prodigious bar and the equally generous kitchen. The restaurant serves ocean fare such as "u-shuck-'em" oysters, baked mussels, and a shrimp quesadilla with caramelized papaya, lime, and molasses. Rafters is open late and presents live entertainment Wednesday through Saturday. ✉*315½ Mallery St.* ☎*912/634–9755* ▤*AE, D, MC, V* ⊙*Closed Sun.*

$$$
ITALIAN

✕**Tramici.** This is the new baby of David Snyder, owner of the more refined Halyards. Tramici is billed as a neighborhood restaurant, although it's in a shopping center. It certainly is kid-friendly, with spaghetti and meatballs and pizzas piled with favorite toppings. There's a remarkable antipasto with prosciutto and asparagus and a superb take on veal marsala over pasta, with sun-dried tomatoes as the mystery ingredient. ✉*75 Cinema La.* ☎*912/634–2202* ⊕*tramicirestaurant. com* ▤*AE, D, MC, V.*

WHERE TO STAY

$

⌂**Holiday Inn Express.** With brightly decorated rooms at great prices, this no-smoking facility is an attractive option in this price category. The executive rooms have sofas and desks. **Pros:** good value. **Cons:** some guests complain that the walls are too thin. ✉*Plantation Village, 299 Main St.* ☎*912/634–2175 or 888/465–4329* ⊕*www.hiexpress. com/stsimonsga* ⇆*60 rooms* ⌂*In-hotel: pool, bicycles, laundry service, Wi-Fi, no-smoking rooms* ▤*AE, D, MC, V* ⦿*BP.*

$$–$$$

⌂**King and Prince Beach & Golf Resort.** This resort is a cushy retreat with spacious guest rooms and luxurious two- and three-bedroom villas. Guests get golf privileges at the Hampton Club at the Hampton Plantation on St. Simons, as well as access to many outdoor activities such as sailing and tennis. The villas are all privately owned, so the total number available for rent varies from time to time. **Pros:** sprawling suites; access to Hampton Club; speedy room service. **Cons:** amenities here are fairly basic. ■TIP➔The historic main building has been refurbished to include a Starbucks. ✉*201 Arnold Rd.* ☎*912/638–3631 or 800/342–0212* 🖷*912/634–1720* ⊕*www.kingandprince.com* ⇆*145 rooms, 2 suites, 41 villas* ♿*In-hotel: restaurants, room service, bar, tennis courts, pools, bicycles, Wi-Fi* ▭*AE, D, MC, V* ⦺*EP.*

$$$$

Fodor'sChoice

★

▣**The Lodge at Sea Island Golf Club.** Simply put, this small resort overlooking the sea is one of the top golf and spa destinations in the country. It has the feel of an English-country manor, with exposed ceiling beams, walls covered with tapestries, hardwood floors softened by oriental rugs, and your own private butler, on call 24 hours a day. Dashingly decorated rooms and suites have water or golf-course views. The lodge serves as the clubhouse for the Sea Island Golf Club (though the name is misleading—all of the facilities are on St. Simons Island). Seaside, the first of three courses built here, was inspired by St. Andrews in Scotland and has breathtaking panoramas of coastal Georgia. **Pros:** fantastic golfing; elegant interiors. **Cons:** only guests can visit the restaurants or bars. ✉*St. Simons Island* ☎ *888/732–4752* ⊕*www. seaisland.com* ⇆*40 rooms, 2 suites* ♿*In-room: refrigerator, DVD, Internet. In-hotel: restaurant, bar, golf courses, tennis court, pool, spa, children's programs (ages 3–19)* ▭*AE, D, DC, MC, V* ⦺*EP.*

$–$$

▣**Sea Palms Golf and Tennis Resort.** If you're looking for an active getaway, this contemporary complex could be the place for you—it has golf, tennis, a fitness center loaded with state-of-the-art equipment, a beach club, sand-pit volleyball, horseshoes, and bicycling. The guest rooms, touted to be the largest standard rooms in the Golden Isles, have balconies with views of the Marshes of Glynn and the golf course. **Pros:** guests have beach club privileges. **Cons:** the furnishings are somewhat unimaginative. ✉*5445 Frederica Rd.* ☎*912/638–3351 or 800/841–6268* ⊕*www.seapalms.com* ⇆*112 rooms, 23 suites, 11 villas* ♿*In-hotel: 2 restaurants, golf course, tennis courts, pools, gym, bicycles* ▭*AE, DC, MC, V* ⦺*EP.*

$–$$

▣**St. Simons Inn.** This Spanish-style inn sits in a prime spot by the lighthouse, only minutes on foot from the village and the beaches. Rooms are nothing fancy, but they're clean and comfortable. Suites have whirlpools, and apartments are fully equipped. There's a two-night minimum during high season. Discounts are available for longer stays. **Pros:** excellent location. **Cons:** basic rooms. ✉*609 Beachview Dr.* ☎*912/638–1101* ⊕*www.stsimonsinn.com* ⇆*35 rooms* ♿*In-room: refrigerator. In-hotel: pool, Wi-Fi* ▭*AE, D, DC, MC, V* ⦺*BP.*

$$

▣**The Village Inn & Pub.** The black-and-white photographs hanging of the wall are the only clue that this inn was once a cinder-block beach house. In the heart of the village, this lodging has won awards for design. The best guest rooms have king-size beds and double half-moon balconies. All are named after Georgia celebrities like author Eugenia Price, whose books line one shelf. Breakfast may include make-your-own Belgian waffles. **Pros:** owners have taken care to preserve the mossy live oaks. **Cons:** rooms are standard-issue motel quality. ✉*500 Mallery St.* ☎*912/634–6056 or 888/635–6111* ⊕*www.villageinnand-pub.com* ⇆*28 rooms* ♿*In-hotel: restaurant, bar, pool, Wi-Fi* ▭*AE, D, DC, MC, V* ⦺*BP.*

SPORTS & THE OUTDOORS

BIKING

St. Simons has an extensive network of bicycle trails, and you can ride on the beach as well. **Ocean Motion** (⊠*1300 Ocean Blvd.* ☎*912/638–5225 or 800/669–5215*) rents bikes for the entire family, from trail bikes to beach bikes to seats for infants. At **Wheel Fun** (⊠*532 Ocean Blvd., just off intersection with Mallory St.* ☎*912/634–0606*) you can rent anything from multispeed bikes to double surreys with bimini tops that look like antique cars and carry four people.

CRABBING & FISHING

☺ There's no simpler fun for the kids than to grab a crab basket or fishing pole and head to St. Simons Island Pier next to Neptune Park. **St. Simons Island Bait and Tackle** (⊠*121 Mallory St.* ☎*912/634–1888*) is near the foot of the pier and is open 364½ days a year. Owners Mike and Trish Wooten have everything from crabbing and fishing gear to snacks and cold drinks. They also sell one-day, weekly, and yearly licenses.

GOLF

The top-flight golf facilities at the Lodge at Sea Island are available only to members and guests, but St. Simons has two other high-quality courses open to the general public. **The Hampton Club** (⊠*100 Tabbystone St.* ☎*912/634–0255* ⊕*www.hamptonclub.com*), at the north end of St. Simons on the site of an 18th-century cotton, rice, and indigo plantation, is a *Golf Digest* "Places to Play" 4-star winner. The par-72 course designed by Joe Lee lies amid towering oaks, salt marshes, and lagoons. **Sea Palms Golf and Tennis Resort** (⊠*5445 Frederica Rd.* ☎*912/638–3351 or 800/841–6268* ⊕*www.seapalms.com*) on a former cotton plantation, offers 27 holes of golf and a driving range.

KAYAKING & SAILING

After an instructional clinic, head off to explore the marsh creeks, coastal waters, and beaches with **Ocean Motion** (⊠*1300 Ocean Blvd.* ☎*912/638–5225 or 800/669–5215*), which has been giving kayaking tours of St. Simons for more than 20 years. If sailing is your thing, try **Barry's Beach Service** (⊠*On the beach, near the Beach Club North Breaker Condominiums* ☎*912/638–8053 or 800/669–5215*) for Hobie Cat rentals and lessons in front of the King and Prince Beach and Golf Resort on Arnold Road. Barry's also rents kayaks, boogie boards, and beach funcycles (low, reclining bikes), and conducts guided ecotours.

SCUBA DIVING

Gray's Reef, off Sapelo island, is one of only 12 National Marine Sanctuaries, home to Loggerhead turtles, and part of the northern right whale breeding grounds, all of which makes it an attractive place for diving. **Island Dive Center** (⊠*101 Marina Dr., in Morningstar Marina on F.J. Torras Causeway* ☎*912/638–6590 or 800/940–3483*) is the place to go for scuba and snorkeling instruction, equipment rental, and charter trips. They also have Jet Skis for rent. ■**TIP→ If underwater photography is your thing, this is the place for underwater classes.**

LITTLE ST. SIMONS ISLAND

10–15 min by ferry from Hampton River Club Marina on St. Simons Island.

Little St. Simons is 15 minutes by boat from St. Simons, but in character it's a world apart. The entire island is a privately owned resort; there are no telephones and no televisions in the only habitations, which are a rustic, former hunting lodge on the riverfront, two upscale cottages, and three river houses. This compound is so at one with its surroundings that the deer graze in the open. "Luxury" on Little St. Simons means having the time and space to get in tune with the rhythms of nature.

The island's forests and marshes are inhabited by deer, armadillos, raccoons, gators, otters, and more than 200 species of birds. As a guest at the resort, you can take part in guided activities, including tours, horseback rides, canoe trips, and fly-fishing lessons, all for no additional charge. You're also free to walk the 7 mi of undisturbed beaches, swim in the mild surf, fish from the dock, and seine for shrimp and crab in the marshes.

GETTING HERE & AROUND

From June through September up to 10 nonguests per day may visit the island for a fee of $100, which includes the ferry to the island, a tour by truck, lunch at the lodge, and a beach walk. Contact the Lodge on Little St. Simons Island for more information.

WHERE TO STAY

$$$$ 🏨 **Lodge on Little St. Simons Island.** Privacy and simplicity are the star
★   attractions on this 10,000 acre island with its rustic island 1917 lodge and four cottages, with a capacity of only 30 guests. The newer Cedar House and Helen's Cottage are the better accommodations. A stay here is all-inclusive: you get three meals a day, use of all equipment and facilities, and drinks at cocktail hour. On staff are three full-time naturalists who lead nature talks and tours. Meals, taken family style, feature platters heaped with fresh fish and homemade breads and pies. Transportation from St. Simons Island is also part of the package. **Pros:** friendly, attentive staff. **Cons:** close quarters and family-style meals might not suit those looking for more alone time. ⌖ *Box 21078 31522* ☎ *888/733–5774* 🖷 *912/634–1811* ⊕ *www.littlestsimonsisland.com* 🛏 *14 rooms, 1 suite* ♿ *In-room: no phone, no TV. In-hotel: restaurant, pool, beachfront, water sports, bicycles* ▤ *AE, D, MC, V* ⊚ *FAP.*

SEA ISLAND

5 mi northeast of St. Simons Island.

Tiny Sea Island—with a full-time population of less than 200—is one of the nation's wealthiest communities. Established by Howard Coffin, the wealthy Detroit auto pioneer who also owned Sapelo Island,

Sea Island has been the domain of the well-heeled since 1928. The hub of activity is the very swanky Cloister, whose recent renovations made it even more exclusive (and expensive). Now a gated community, Sea Island is accessible only to registered guests and Sea Island Club members.

GETTING HERE & AROUND

Though accessible by causeway, the island is restricted to owners and guests of the single hotel.

WHERE TO STAY

Do-it-yourselfers and families on a budget have many options beyond hotels and campsites. For vacation cottage rentals throughout the islands, contact **By the Sea Vacations** (☎*912/638–6610 or 866/639-6610 ⊕www.bytheseavacations.com*). In addition to real-estate sales, **Parker-Kaufman Realty** (☎*912/638–3368 or 888/227–8573 ⊕www. parker-kaufman.com*) manages a range of rental homes.

$$$$
Fodor's Choice
★

☷ The Cloister. It's easy to see why this grande dame was chosen as the site of the G-8 Summit in 2004: the Mediterranean-style, waterside resort—tucked behind a secure gate and impeccably appointed with tropical landscaping, rich rococo fabrics, stained glass. and dark woods—is fit for dignitaries. In 1928 Calvin Coolidge kicked off the Cloister's presidential tradition of planting a commemorative oak tree and was followed by Presidents Eisenhower, Ford, Carter, and George W. Bush. There are all the luxuries you would expect, such as a sprawling two-story spa, as well as those that are a wonderful surprise, like the bi-level water garden. Try the ceviche at Big George's, or grab a cone at the ice-cream parlor. Families are welcome, and on-site programs abound for kids. **Pros:** elegant getaway; golfing galore; horseback riding; pristine beach; sprawling guest rooms. **Cons:** the winding paths and property layout may be a bit confusing for first-time visitors. ⊠*Sea Island ☎912/638–3611 or 866/465–3563 ⊕www.seaisland. com ⇆153 rooms, 3 suites ⚿In-room: safe, Internet, Wi-Fi. In hotel: 4 restaurants, bars, golf courses, tennis courts, pools, beachfront, water sports, children's programs (ages 3–19) ⊟AE, D, DC, MC, V ⊧EP.*

JEKYLL ISLAND

18 mi south of St. Simons Island, 90 mi south of Savannah.

For 56 winters, between 1886 and 1942, America's rich and famous faithfully came south to Jekyll Island. Through the Gilded Age, World War I, the Roaring '20s, and the Great Depression, Vanderbilts and Rockefellers, Morgans and Astors, Macys, Pulitzers, and Goodyears shuttered their 5th Avenue castles and retreated to elegant "cottages" on their wild coastal island. It's been said that when the island's distinguished winter residents were all "in," a sixth of the world's wealth was represented. Early in World War II the millionaires departed for the last time. In 1947 the state of Georgia purchased the entire island for the bargain price of $675,000.

Jekyll Island is still a 7½-mi playground, but it's no longer restricted to the rich and famous. A water park, picnic grounds, and facilities for golf, tennis, fishing, biking, and jogging are all open to the public. One side of the island is lined by nearly 10 mi of hard-packed Atlantic beaches; the other by the Intracoastal Waterway and picturesque salt marshes. Deer and wild turkeys inhabit interior forests of pine, magnolia, and moss-veiled live oaks. Egrets, pelicans, herons, and sandpipers skim the gentle surf. Jekyll Island's clean, mostly uncommercialized public beaches are free and open year-round. Bathhouses with restrooms, changing areas, and showers are open at regular intervals along the beach. Beachwear, suntan lotion, rafts, snacks, and drinks are available at the Jekyll Shopping Center, facing the beach at Beachview Drive. Visitors must pay a fee of $3, which is used to support conservation of the island's natural and cultural resources.

GETTING HERE & AROUND

Jekyll Island is connected to the mainland by the Sidney Lanier Bridge. Once on the island, you'll need a car or a bicycle to get around.

ESSENTIALS

Visitor Information Jekyll Island Welcome Center (⊠ *1 Downing Musgrove Causeway, Jekyll Island* ☎ *912/635–3636* ⊕ *www.jekyllisland.com*).

EXPLORING JEKYLL ISLAND

The**Georgia Sea Turtle Center,** a new must-see on Jekyll Island, aims to increase awareness of habitat and wildlife conservation challenges for the endangered loggerhead turtles through turtle rehabilitation, research, and education programs. The center includes educational exhibits and a "hospital," where visitors can view rescued turtles, which lay their eggs along Jekyll Island beaches from May through August, and read their stories. ⊠ *214 Stable Rd.* ☎ *912/635–4444* ⊕ *www.georgiaseaturtlecenter.org* ⊠ *$6* ⊙ *Daily 10–6.*

The **Jekyll Island History Center** gives tram tours of the Jekyll Island National Historic Landmark District. Tours originate at the museum's visitor center on Stable Road four times a day. Tours at 11 and 2 include two millionaires' residences in the 240-acre historic district. Faith Chapel, illuminated by stained-glass windows, including one Tiffany original, is open daily 2–4. ⊠ *100 Stable Rd., I–95, Exit 29* ☎ *912/635–4036* ⊠ *912/635–4004* ⊕ *www.jekyllisland.com* ⊠ *$10– $17.50* ⊙ *Daily 9–5; tours daily, 10, 11, 2, and 4.*

☼ **Summer Waves** is an 11-acre park using more than a million gallons of water in its 18,000-square-foot wave pool, water slides, children's activity pool with two slides, and circular river for tubing and rafting. Inner tubes and life vests are provided at no extra charge. ⊠ *210 S. Riverview Dr.* ☎ *912/635–2074* ⊕ *www.summerwaves.com* ⊠ *$19.95*

⊙*Late May–early Sept., Sun.–Thurs. 10–6, Sat. 10–8; hrs vary at beginning and end of season.*

┌──
| OFF THE
| BEATEN
| PATH

Driftwood Beach. If you've ever wondered about the effects of erosion on barrier islands, head at low tide to this oceanfront boneyard on North Beach, where live oaks and pines are being consumed by the sea at an alarming rate. The snarl of trunks and limbs and the dramatic, massive root systems of upturned trees are an eerie and intriguing tableau of nature's slow and steady power. It's been estimated that nearly 1,000 feet of Jekyll's beach have been lost since the early 1900s. ■**TIP→ Bring your camera; the photo opportunities are terrific and this is the best place to shoot St. Simons Lighthouse.** ✛*Head to far north of Jekyll on Beachview Dr. to large curve where road turns inland. When ocean is visible through forest to your right, pull over and take one of the many trails through trees to beach.*

WHERE TO EAT

$$$$
MEDITERRANEAN

✕**Courtyard at Crane.** When it was built in 1917, Crane Cottage—actually an elegant Italianate villa—was the most expensive winter home on Jekyll Island. Now, as part of the Jekyll Island Club Hotel, the Courtyard at Crane offers casual alfresco dining in quirky little dining areas. The menu has a Mediterranean flair with salads at lunch and more substantial dishes in the evening, like marinated grilled rib eye and cioppino. The bread served at dinner, a warm loaf specked with vegetables, is especially tasty. ⊠*375 Riverview Dr., Jekyll Island Club Hotel* ☎*912/635–2600* ▤*AE, D, DC, MC, V* ⊙*No dinner Fri. and Sat.*

$$$$
SOUTHERN
★

✕**Grand Dining Room.** The colonnaded Grand Dining Room of the Jekyll Island Club maintains a tradition of fine dining first established in the 19th century. The huge fireplace, views of the pool, and sparkling silver and crystal all contribute to the sense of old-style elegance. Signature dishes are the pistachio-crusted rack of lamb, grouper flamed with hazelnut liqueur, and the filet mignon. The menu also includes local seafood and regional dishes such as Southern fried quail salad. The wine cellar has its own label cabernet, merlot, white zinfandel, and chardonnay, made by Round Hill Vineyards. ⊠*Jekyll Island Club, 371 Riverview Dr.* ☎*912/635–2400* ⚖*Reservations essential* ⑩*Jacket required* ▤*AE, D, DC, MC, V.*

$$$
SEAFOOD

✕**Latitude 31.** Right on the Jekyll Island Club Wharf, in the middle of the historic district, Latitude 31 wins the prize for best location. The menu has everything from oysters Rockefeller to seafood crepes to bourbon peach- and pecan-glazed pork tenderloin. There's also a kids' menu. ⊠*Jekyll Island Club Wharf* ☎*912/635–3800* ▤*D, MC, V* ⊙*Closed Mon.*

$$
SEAFOOD
★

✕**The Rah Bar.** A tiny swamp shack right on the end of the Jekyll Island Club Wharf (connected to Latitude 31), the Rah Bar is the place for a hands-on experience. It's elbow-to-elbow dining (unless you eat at the tables outside on the wharf) with "rah" oysters, "crawdaddies," and "u peel 'em" shrimp. As you eat, you look out on the shrimp boats and the beautiful salt-marsh sunsets. ⊠*Jekyll Island Club Wharf* ☎*912/635–3800* ▤*D, MC, V* ⊙*Closed Mon.*

$$
SEAFOOD ✕ **SeaJay's Waterfront Café & Pub.** A casual tavern overlooking the Jekyll Harbor Marina, SeaJay's serves delicious, inexpensive seafood, including a crab chowder that locals love. This is also the home of the wildly popular Lowcountry boil buffet: an all-you-can-eat feast of local shrimp, corn on the cob, smoked sausage, and new potatoes. There's live music Thursday through Saturday night. ■ **TIP➡ Bring the kids, their special menus run from $3.95.** ✉*1 Harbor Point Rd., Jekyll Harbor Marina* ☎*912/635–3200* ▭*AE, D, MC, V.*

WHERE TO STAY

The Buccaneer Beach Resort closed in 2007 after 48 years; plans are underway to replace it with Canopy Bluff Resort, an upscale 300-room facility with 120 condo rentals.

$$-$$$ ▦ **Beachview Club.** Grand old oak trees shade the grounds of this luxury, all-suites lodging. Rooms are either on the oceanfront or have a partial ocean view; some rooms are equipped with hot tubs and gas fireplaces. Efficiencies have one king-size or two double beds, a desk, and a kitchenette. The interior design reflects an understated island theme, and the unique meeting room in the Bell Tower accommodates up to 35 people for business events. Higher-end suites have full kitchens. **Pros:** friendly and eager staff; property near the beach. **Cons:** room decor is somewhat out of date; not much for kids to do here. ✉*721 N. Beachview Dr.* ☎*912/635–2256 or 800/299–2228* 🖷*912/635–3770* ⊕*www.beachviewclub.com* ⟋*38 rooms, 6 suites* &*In-room: kitchen (some). In-hotel: bar, pool, bicycles, Wi-Fi, parking (free)* ▭*AE, D, DC, MC, V* ¶◎*EP.*

$$$-$$$$
★ ▦ **Jekyll Island Club Hotel.** This sprawling 1886 resort was once described as "the richest, the most exclusive, the most inaccessible club in the world." Not so today. The comfortable resort's focal point is a four-story clubhouse, with its wraparound verandas and Queen Anne–style towers and turrets. Rooms, suites, apartments, and cottages are decorated with mahogany beds, armoires, and plush sofas and chairs. Two beautifully restored former "millionaires' cottages"—the Crane and the Cherokee—add 23 elegant guest rooms to this gracefully groomed compound. The B&B packages are a great deal. **Pros:** on the water; old-world charm, with traditional room keys; close proximity to restaurants, shopping, and sea-turtle center. **Cons:** room decor and some appliances could use an update. ✉*371 Riverview Dr.* ☎*912/635–2600 or 800/535–9547* 🖷*912/635–2818* ⊕*www.jekyllclub.com* ⟋*138 rooms, 19 suites* &*In-room: Internet, Wi-Fi. In-hotel: restaurant, bar, pool, beachfront, bicycles, Wi-Fi, parking (free)* ▭*AE, D, DC, MC, V* ¶◎*EP.*

$-$$ ▦ **Jekyll Oceanfront Resort & Spa.** At the largest oceanfront resort hotel on the island, the buildings are spread across 15 verdant acres. Popular with families, the inn accommodates children under 17 free when they stay with parents or grandparents. Packages include summer family-focused arrangements and romantic getaways. The restaurant offers basic, hearty fare, including an all-you-can-eat Saturday night seafood buffet. As of this writing, a major renovation was underway.

Pros: beachfront location is a plus; staff is responsive. Cons: pre-renovation, some rooms are reportedly dingy. ✉975 N. Beachview Dr. ☎912/635–2531 or 800/736–1046 🖷912/635–2332 ⊕www.jekyllinn.com ↩260 rooms and villas ⌂In-room: refrigerator. In-hotel: restaurant, bars, pool, spa, beachfront, children's programs (ages 5–12), parking (free) ▤AE, D, DC, MC, V ⏐◎⏐EP.

$–$$ ▣**Oceanside Inn and Suites.** After more than $1.5 million in renovations, Oceanside Inn and Suites, the former Buccaneer's sister resort, has been completely refurbished and now has a new restaurant called the SandBar and Grill. It's a two-story, motel-style property directly on the ocean. **Pros:** lovely views; laundry facilities. **Cons:** some rooms still need improvements, particularly to the bathrooms. ✉711 N. Beachview Dr. ☎912/635–2211 ⊕www.oceansideinnandsuites.com ↩152 rooms, 26 suites ⌂In-hotel: restaurant, bar, tennis court, pool, bicycles, parking (free) ▤AE, D, DC, MC, V ⏐◎⏐EP.

WHERE TO CAMP

⚠**Jekyll Island Campground.** At the northern end of Jekyll across from the entrance to the fishing pier, this campground lies on 18 wooded acres with more than 200 sites that can accommodate everything from backpackers looking for primitive sites to RVs needing full hookups. Pets are welcome, but there's a $2 fee. ✉1197 Riverview Dr. ☎912/635–3021 ▤AE, MC, V ◈$30–$42. ⌂Flush toilets, dump station, guest laundry, showers, electricity, public telephone

SPORTS & THE OUTDOORS

CYCLING

The best way to see Jekyll is by bicycle: a long, paved trail runs right along the beach, and there's an extensive network of paths throughout the island. **Jekyll Island Mini Golf and Bike Rentals** (✉N. Beachview Dr. at Shell Rd. ☎912/635–2648) has a wide selection, from the surrey pedal cars, which can hold four people, to lay-down cycles, to the more traditional bikes. **Wheel Fun** (✉60 S. Oceanview Dr. ☎912/635–9801) sits right in front of the Days Inn and is easy to get to Jekyll's southern beachfront.

FISHING

With 40 years of experience in local waters, Captain Vernon Reynolds of **Coastal Expeditions** (✉Jekyll Harbor Marina ☎912/265–0392 ⊕www.coastalcharterfishing.com) provides half-day and full-day trips in-shore and offshore for fishing, dolphin-watching, and sightseeing. Aside from his ample angling skills, Larry Crews of **Offshore Charters** (✉Jekyll Harbor Marina ☎ 912/265–7529 ⊕www.offshore-charters.com) also offers his services as captain to tie the knot for anyone who's already landed the big one.

GOLF

The **Jekyll Island Golf Club** (⊠*322 Capt. Wylly Rd.* ☎*912/635–2368*) has 63 holes, including three 18-hole, par-72 courses, and a clubhouse. Green fees are $40, good all day, and carts are $17 per person per course. The nine-hole, par-36 **Oceanside Nine** (⊠*N. Beachview Dr.* ☎*912/635–2170*) is where Jekyll Island millionaires used to play. Green fee is $22, and carts are $7.25 for every nine holes.

HORSEBACK RIDING

Take a sunset ride through the maritime forest along the North Beach with **Victoria's Carriages and Trail Rides** (⊠*100 Stable Rd., in stables at Jekyll Island History Center* ☎*912/635–9500*). Morning and afternoon rides include visits to the salt marsh and Driftwood Beach, a boneyard of live oaks and pine trees being reclaimed by the sea. Rides leave from the Clam Creek picnic area across from the Jekyll Island Campground.

SUMMER PROGRAMS

☾ The **Tidelands Nature Center,** a 4H program sponsored by the University of Georgia, has summer classes for kids and adults on everything from loggerhead sea turtles to live oaks to beach ecology. You can learn how the maritime forest evolves or get a lesson in seining and netting. There are guided nature walks, kayak tours, and canoe and paddleboat rentals. The center also has touch tanks and exhibits on coastal ecology. ⊠*100 Riverview Dr.* ☎*912/635–5032* ⊕*www.tidelands4h.org* ☜*$1 for exhibit* ⊙*Mar.–Oct., Mon.–Sat. 9–4, Sun 10–2; Nov.–Feb., weekdays 9–4, Sat. 10–2.*

TENNIS

The **Jekyll Island Tennis Center** (⊠*400 Capt. Wylly Rd.* ☎*912/635–3154* ⊕*www.gate.net/~jitc*) has 13 clay courts, with seven lighted for nighttime play. The facility hosts six USTA-sanctioned tournaments throughout the year and provides lessons and summer camps for juniors. Courts cost $18 per hour daily 9 AM to 10 PM. Reservations for lighted courts are required and must be made prior to 6 PM the day of play.

CUMBERLAND ISLAND

Fodor's Choice *47 mi south of Jekyll Island; 115 mi south of Savannah to St. Marys*
★ *via I–95; 45 min by ferry from St. Marys.*

Cumberland, the largest of Georgia's coastal isles, is a national treasure. The 18-mi spit of land off the coast of St. Marys is a nearly unspoiled sanctuary of marshes, dunes, beaches, forests, lakes, and ponds. And although it has a long history of human habitation, it remains much as nature created it: a dense, lacework canopy of live oak shades sand roads and foot trails through thick undergrowths of palmetto. Wild horses roam freely on pristine beaches. Waterways are homes for gators, sea turtles, otters, snowy egrets, great blue herons, ibises, wood storks, and more than 300 other species of birds. In the forests are armadillos, wild horses, deer, raccoons, and an assortment of reptiles.

In the 16th century the Spanish established a mission and a garrison, San Pedro de Mocama, on the southern end of the island. But development didn't begin in earnest until the wake of the American Revolution, with timbering operations for shipbuilding, particularly construction of warships for the early U.S. naval fleet. Cotton, rice, and indigo plantations were also established. In 1818 Revolutionary War hero Gen. "Lighthorse" Harry Lee, father of Robert E. Lee, died and was buried near the Dungeness estate of General Nathaniel Greene. Though his body was later moved to Virginia to be interred beside his son, the gravestone remains. During the 1880s the family of Thomas Carnegie (brother of industrialist Andrew) built several lavish homes here. In the 1950s the National Park Service named Cumberland Island and Cape Cod as the most significant natural areas on the Atlantic and Gulf coasts. And in 1972, in response to attempts to develop the island by Hilton Head–developer Charles Fraser, Congress passed a bill establishing the island as a national seashore. Today most of the island is part of the national park system.

GETTING HERE & AROUND

The only access to the island is on a National Park Service ferry, the *Cumberland Queen*. Ferry bookings are heavy in summer. Cancellations and no-shows often make last-minute space available, but don't rely on it. You can make reservations up to six months in advance. ■ TIP→ Note that the ferry does not transport pets, bicycles, kayaks, or cars.

EXPLORING CUMBERLAND ISLAND

Though the **Cumberland Island National Seashore** is open to the public, the only public access to the island is via the *Cumberland Queen*, a reservations-only, 146-passenger ferry based near the National Park Service Information Center at St. Marys. From the Park Service docks at the island's south end, you can follow wooded nature trails, swim and sun on 18 mi of undeveloped beaches, go fishing and bird-watching, and view the ruins of Thomas Carnegie's great estate, **Dungeness**. You can also join history and nature walks led by Park Service rangers. Bear in mind that summers are hot and humid and that you must bring everything you need, including your own food, soft drinks, sunscreen, and insect repellent. There's no public transportation on the island. ⌂*Cumberland Island National Seashore, Box 806, St. Marys 31558* ☎*912/882–4335 Ext. 254* ⊕*www.nps.gov/cuis* ✉*Round-trip ferry $17, day pass $4* ⊙*Mar.–Sept., ferry departure from St. Marys daily 9 AM and 11:45 AM; from Cumberland, Sun.–Tues. 10:15 AM and 4:45 PM, Wed.–Sat. 10:15 AM, 2:45 PM, 4:45 PM. Oct. and Nov., ferry departure from St. Marys daily 9 AM and 11:45 AM; from Cumberland 10:15 AM and 4:45 PM. Dec.–Feb., Thurs.–Sun., ferry departure from St. Marys 9 AM and 11:45 AM, from Cumberland 10:15 AM and 4:45 PM.*

Ⓒ If the heat has you, and the kids are itching to get wet, head to the **St. Marys Aquatic Center** (✉*301 Herb Bauer Dr., St. Marys* ☎*912/673–8118* ⊕*www.funatsmac.com*), a full-service water park where you can get an inner tube and relax floating down the Continuous River, hurtle

11

CLOSE UP

Georgia's Black Republic

After capturing Savannah in December 1864, General William Tecumseh Sherman read the Emancipation Proclamation at the Second African Baptist Church and issued his now famous Field Order No. 15, giving freed slaves 40 acres and a mule. The field order set aside a swath of land reaching 30 mi inland from Charleston to northern Florida (roughly the area east of Interstate 95), including the coastal islands, for an independent state of freed slaves.

Under the administration of General Rufus Saxton and his assistant, Tunis G. Campbell, a black New Jersey native who represented McIntosh County as a state senator, a black republic was established with St. Catherines Island as its capital. Hundreds of former slaves were relocated to St. Catherines and Sapelo islands, where they set about cultivating the

land. In 1865 Campbell established himself as virtual king, controlling a legislature, a court, and a 275-man army. Whites called Campbell "the most feared man in Georgia."

Congress repealed Sherman's directive and replaced General Saxton with General Davis Tillison, who was sympathetic to the interests of former plantation owners, and in 1867 federal troops drove Campbell off St. Catherines and into McIntosh County, where he continued to exert his power. In 1876 he was convicted of falsely imprisoning a white citizen and sentenced, at the age of 63, to work on a chain gang. After being freed, he left Georgia for good and settled in Boston, where he died in 1891. Every year on the fourth Saturday in June, the town of Darien holds a festival in Campbell's honor.

down Splash Mountain, or corkscrew yourself silly sliding down the Orange Crush.

OFF THE BEATEN PATH

The First African Baptist Church. This small, one-room church on the north end of Cumberland Island is where John F. Kennedy Jr. and Carolyn Bessette were married on September 21, 1996. Constructed of whitewashed logs, it's simply adorned with a cross made of sticks tied together with string and 11 handmade pews seating 40 people. It was built in 1937 to replace a cruder 1893 structure used by former slaves from the High Point–Half Moon Bluff community. The Kennedy–Bessette wedding party stayed at the Greyfield Inn, built on the south end of the island in 1900 by the Carnegie family. ⊠ *North end of Cumberland near Half Moon Bluff.*

WHERE TO EAT

$$
SEAFOOD

✕ **Lang's Marina Restaurant.** Everything's made from scratch at this popular waterside restaurant, including the desserts. And the seafood comes fresh from the owner's boats. You can order shrimp, scallops, and oysters, or opt for the Captain's Platter and get some of everything. Fish is available fried, grilled, or blackened. ⊠ *307 W. St. Marys St., near waterfront park, St. Marys* ☎ *912/882–4432* ⊟ *MC, V* ⊙ *Closed Sun. and Mon. No dinner Tues. No lunch Sat.*

$ ✗The Williams' Saint Marys Seafood and Steak House. Don't let the tabby-
SEAFOOD   and-porthole decor fool you. In a region rife with seafood restaurants,
this one's full of locals for a reason. The food is fresh, well prepared,
and plentiful, and the price rarely gets so right. The menu includes
frogs' legs and alligator tail for more adventurous eaters. ⊠*1837
Osborne Rd., St. Marys* ☎*912/882–6875* ▤*MC, V.*

WHERE TO STAY

ON THE ISLAND

$$$$ **Greyfield Inn.** Once described as a "Tara by the sea," this turn-of-the-last-
★   century Carnegie family home is Cumberland Island's only accommodation. Built in 1900 for Lucy Ricketson, Thomas and Lucy Carnegie's
daughter, the inn is filled with period antiques, family portraits, and
original furniture that evoke the country elegance of a bygone era. And
with a 1,000-acre private compound, it offers a solitude that also seems
a thing of the past. Prices include all meals, transportation, tours led
by a naturalist, and bikes. Nonguests can dine at the restaurant ($$$$)
on delicious dishes that change daily. **Pros:** air-conditioned during summer; lack of telephone service means complete solitude. **Cons:** no stores
on Cumberland; communications to the mainland are limited. ⊠ *Cumberland Island* ☎*904/261–6408 or 866/401–8581* ⊕*www.greyfield-
inn.com* ⇖*16 rooms, 4 suites* ♿*In-room: no phone, no TV. In-hotel:
restaurant, bar, bicycles* ▤*D, MC, V* ⸙*FAP.*

⚠**Hickory Hill, Yankee Paradise, Stafford Beach, Brickhill Bluff, and Sea
Camp.** The island has five camping sites in a National Wilderness
Area, all of which require reservations usually at least two months in
advance. Sea Camp is the ideal spot for first-time campers. It's a half-
mile from the dock and has restrooms and showers nearby. None of the
sites allow pets or fires, and stays are limited to seven days. The other
locations are primitive sites and are a 4- to 10-mi hike. ■TIP➔Because
ferry reservations are mandatory to camp, book the boat at the same time.
⌖*Cumberland Island National Seashore, Box 806, St. Marys 31558*
☎*912/882–4335 or 877/860–6787* 🖷*912/673–7747* ⊕*www.nps.
gov/cuis* ⸙*Park access, $4 per person; backcountry sites, $2 per person per day; Sea Camp, $4 per person per day.*

ON THE MAINLAND

$ ▦**Cumberland Island Inn & Suites.** Children under 18 stay free at this
modern, moderately priced hotel on Osborne Road, 3 mi from the
St. Marys waterfront. The spacious suites have complete kitchens,
large refrigerators, sleeper sofas, executive work desks with ergonomic
chairs, and free high-speed Internet access. Some suites feature Jacuzzis.
Pros: clean, large rooms. **Cons:** not in historic area. ⊠*2710 Osborne
Rd., St. Marys* ☎*912/882–6250 or 800/768–6250* 🖷*912/882–4471*
⊕*www.cumberlandislandinn.com* ⇖*79 rooms* ♿*In-room: refrigerator, Internet. In-hotel: restaurants, bar, pool, laundry facilities* ▤*AE,
D, MC, V* ⸙*BP.*

¢   ▦**Riverview Hotel.** A giant step back in time, this 1916 hotel looks
straight out of the Old West. The lobby resembles a museum, with

old cameras in a glass case and high-backed typewriters on display. A Tiffany lamp—the real thing—hangs over the reception desk. Guest rooms with river views have ornate iron beds and antique furniture from the owner's family. The popular Seagles's Waterfront Café features steaks and seafood, including delicious rock shrimp. Picnic lunches can be packed for your Cumberland Island excursion. **Pros:** old-time touches; excellent location. **Cons:** some rooms seem a little bit shabby; no air-conditioning in common areas. ⊠*105 Osborne St., St. Marys* ☎*912/882–3242* ⊕*www.riverviewhotelstmarys.com* ⮐*18 rooms* ⚹*In-room: no phone. In-hotel: restaurant, bar* ☐*AE, D, DC, MC, V* ⧆*BP.*

$-$$ ⚏ **Spencer House Inn.** At this pink Victorian inn, built in 1872, some rooms have expansive balconies which overlook the neatly tended grounds, and some have antique claw-foot bathtubs. Innkeepers Mike and Mary Neff will prepare picnic lunches if you ask. The inn is listed in the National Register of Historic Places, and is a perfect base for touring the St. Marys and Cumberland Island area. **Pros:** short walk to the ferry; rocking chairs on its balcony. **Cons:** not recommended for young singles in search of a party; pets not welcome. ⊠*200 Osborne St., St. Marys* ☎*912/882–1872 or 888/840–1872* 🖷*912/882–9427* ⊕*www.spencerhouseinn.com* ⮐*13 rooms, 1 suite* ⚹*In-hotel: Wi-Fi* ☐*AE, D, MC, V* ⧆*BP.*

SPORTS & THE OUTDOORS

KAYAKING

Whether you're a novice or skilled paddler, **Up The Creek Xpeditions** (⊠*111 Osborne St., St. Marys* ☎*912/882–0911*) can guide you on kayak tours through some of Georgia and Florida's most scenic waters. Classes include navigation, tides and currents, and kayak surfing and racing. Trips include Yulee, the St. Marys River, and the Cumberland Sound. The sunset dinner paddle includes a meal at Borrell Creek Restaurant overlooking the marsh.

NIGHTLIFE

The closer you get to borders, the more pronounced allegiances become. A case in point is **Seagle's Saloon and Patio Bar** (⊠*105 Osborne St., St. Marys* ☎*912/882–1807*), a smoky watering hole not far from the Florida state line that's festooned with University of Georgia memorabilia. Bawdy bartender Cindy Deen is a local legend, so expect some Southern sass.

EN ROUTE On your way back from Cumberland Island, stop in at the **St. Marys Submarine Museum** (⊠*102 W. St. Marys St., across from Cumberland Island Ferry office* ☎*912/882–2782* ⊕*stmaryssubmuseum.com*). This small, fascinating museum is a natural in a town that owes much of its existence to the nearby Kings Bay Naval Base, home of the Atlantic Trident fleet. The museum has an extensive collection of photos and artifacts, including uniforms, flags, scale models, designs, sonar consoles, hatches, working steering positions, and a working periscope.

OKEFENOKEE NATIONAL WILDLIFE REFUGE

Larger than all of Georgia's barrier islands combined, the Okefenokee National Wildlife Refuge covers 730 square mi of southeastern Georgia and spills over into northeastern Florida. From the air, all roads and almost all traces of human development seem to disappear into this vast, seemingly impenetrable landscape, the largest intact freshwater wetlands in the contiguous United States. The rivers, lakes, forests, prairies, and swamps all teem with seen and unseen life: alligators, otters, bobcats, raccoons, opossums, white-tailed deer, turtles, bald eagles, red-tailed hawks, egrets, muskrats, herons, cranes, red-cockaded woodpeckers, and black bears all make their home here. The term *swamp* hardly does the Okefenokee justice. It's the largest peat-producing bog in the United States, with numerous and varied landscapes, including aquatic prairies, towering virgin cypress, sandy pine islands, and lush subtropical hammocks.

During the last Ice Age, 10,000 years ago, this area was part of the ocean flow. As the ocean receded, a dune line formed, which acted as a dam, forming today's refuge. The Seminole Indians named the area "Land of the Quivering Earth." And if you have the good fortune to walk one of the many bogs, you can find the earth does indeed quiver like Jell-O in a bowl.

GETTING HERE & AROUND

There are three gateways to the refuge: an eastern entrance at the U.S. Fish and Wildlife Service headquarters in the Suwannee Canal Recreation Area, near Folkston; a northern entrance at the Okefenokee Swamp Park near Waycross; and a western entrance at Stephen C. Foster State Park, outside the town of Fargo. Visiting here can feel frustrating, because none of the parks encompass everything the refuge has to offer; you need to determine what your highest priorities are and pick your gateway on that basis. The best way to see the Okefenokee up close is to take a day trip from whichever gateway you choose. You can take an overnight canoeing-camping trip into the interior, but be aware that access is restricted by permit. Plan your visit between September and April to avoid the biting insects that emerge in May, especially in the dense interior.

SUWANNEE CANAL RECREATION AREA

8 mi southwest of Folkston via Rte. 121.

The east entrance of the Okefenokee near Folkston offers access into the core of the refuge by way of the man-made Suwannee Canal. The most extensive open areas in the park—Chesser, Grand, and Mizell Prairies—branch off the canal and contain small natural lakes and gator holes. The prairies are excellent spots for sport fishing and birding, and it's possible to take one- and two-hour guided boat tours of the area leaving from the Okefenokee Adventures concession, near the visitor center. The concession also has equipment rentals and food at the Camp Cornelia Cafe. The visitor center has a film, exhibits, and a mechanized mannequin that tells stories about life in the Okefenokee (it sounds hokey but it's surprisingly informative). A boardwalk takes you over the water to a 50-foot observation tower. Hikers, bicyclists, and private motor vehicles are welcome on the Swamp Island Drive; several interpretive walking trails may be taken along the way. Picnicking is permitted. *Refuge headquarters* ⊠ *Rte. 2, Box 3330, Folkston* ☎ *912/496–7836* ⊕ *www.fws.gov/okefenokee* ⊠ *$5 per car* ☺ *Refuge: Mar.–Oct., daily ½ hr before sunrise–7:30 PM; Nov.–Feb., daily ½ hr before sunrise–5:30 PM.*

WHERE TO STAY & EAT

¢ ✕ **Okefenokee Restaurant.** Everything's home-cooked at this half-cen-
SOUTHERN tury-old, local institution, and from the fried shrimp to the black-eyed peas, it's all good. They open early for breakfast and have a daily lunch buffet from 11 to 2, which includes a drink, for less than $8. ⊠ *103 S. 2nd St., Folkston* ☎ *912/496–3263* ▤ *D, MC, V* ☺ *Closed Sun.*

¢–$ ▦ **The Folkston House.** This white, two-story B&B built in 1900 is filled with antiques and period furniture in rooms with names like Victorian Lace, Suite Destiny and Jardin de Lune. Each evening homemade refreshments are served in the parlor, and in the morning there's a full Southern breakfast in the Victorian dining room or outside on the dining porch. **Pros:** elegantly furnished; excellent breakfast. **Cons:** no children under eight permitted. ⊠ *802 Kingsland Dr., Folkston* ☎ *904/219–4240* ⊕ *www.folkstonhouse.com* ⊅ *7 rooms* ◷ *In-room: no phone (some). In-hotel: no kids under 8, no-smoking rooms.* ▤ *AE, D, MC, V* ¶◎¶*BP.*

$–$$ ▦ **The Inn at Folkston.** Eight miles from the Suwannee Canal Recreation Area entrance to the Okefenokee, the Inn at Folkston is a minirefuge with a huge front veranda, hot tub, porch swings, and rocking chairs. This Craftsman-style inn is filled with antiques, and each room is uniquely decorated. The romantic Lighthouse Room has a king-size bed, a fireplace, and a screened-in porch; the International Family Room is decorated in vibrant reds and includes books on Persian wisdom. And get set for a terrific breakfast: the four-cheese soufflé with artichokes and the classic eggs Benedict with hollandaise sauce are particularly good. **Pros:** inn is beautifully restored; owners make you feel like welcome relatives; great place for train enthusiasts. **Cons:** the many trains that pass by can be noisy. ■ **TIP➜ Ask about midweek business rates for a good deal.** ⊠ *509 W. Main St., Folkston* ☎ *912/496–6256 or 888/509–6246* ⊕ *www.innatfolkston.com* ⊅ *4 rooms* ◷ *In-room: no TV, Wi-Fi. In-hotel: no-smoking rooms* ▤ *AE, D, MC, V* ¶◎¶*BP.*

SPORTS & THE OUTDOORS

CANOEING & Wilderness canoeing and camping in the Okefenokee's interior are
CAMPING allowed by reserved permit only (for which there's a $10 fee per person per day). Permits are difficult to come by, especially in the cooler seasons. Reservations can be made only by phone. You need to call **refuge headquarters** (☎ *912/496–3331* ☺ *Weekdays 7 AM–10 AM*) within two months of your desired starting date to make a reservation. Guided overnight canoe trips can be arranged by **Okefenokee Adventures** (⊠ *Rte. 2, Box 3325, Folkston* ☎ *912/496–7156* ⊕ *www.okefenokeeadventures.*

com). They also do one- and two-hour boat tours ($12.50, $20.50) and have boat and canoe rentals. As of this writing, the company was not renting motorboats, due to the drop in water levels.

OKEFENOKEE SWAMP PARK

⟳ *8 mi south of Waycross via U.S. 1.*

This park serves as the northern entrance to the Okefenokee National Wildlife Refuge, offering easy access as well as exhibits and orientation programs good for the entire family. The park has a 1-mi nature trail, observation areas, wilderness walkways, an outdoor museum of pioneer life, and boat tours into the swamp that reveal its unique ecology. A boardwalk and 90-foot tower are excellent places to glimpse cruising gators and birds. A 1½-mi train tour (included in the admission price) passes by a Seminole village and stops at Pioneer Island, a re-created pioneer homestead, for a 30-minute walking tour. ⊠*5700 Okefenokee Swamp Park Rd., Waycross* ☎*912/283-0583* 🖷*912/283-0023* ⊕*www.okeswamp.com* 🖅*$12, plus $4–$16 for boat tours* ☉*Daily 9–5:30.*

WHERE TO STAY

🖸 **Holiday Inn Waycross.** What makes this chain hotel stand out is its bargain package deal: for $90 you get a double room and two adult admissions to the Okefenokee Swamp Park, including the boat ride, train ride, and attractions. **Pros:** affordable rooms in convenient location. **Cons:** older hotel; beverages not included with complimentary breakfast. ⊠*1725 Memorial Dr.* ☎*912/283-4490 or 800/465-4329* 🖷*912/283-4490* ⊕*www.ichotelsgroup.com* 🖅*142 rooms, 9 suites* △*In-hotel: bar, pool, laundry facilities, some pets allowed (fee)* ☐*AE, D, DC, MC, V* ◐*BP.*

🖸 **Pond View Inn.** Though the pond is long gone, everything else is just as it should be in one of the more elegant dining options ($$$–$$$$; closed Sunday and Monday, no lunch) in Waycross. This restaurant in the historic district has 18-foot ceilings, hardwood floors, and white tablecloths, and the food makes some interesting variations on a Southern theme. The crab cakes are excellent. For dessert, try the bread pudding with rum-butterscotch sauce. Sara and David Rollison's small B&B is just upstairs and has a similar elegance. There's a sense of refinement in these double rooms with views of the downtown historic district. Rooms feature queen beds, private baths, and Jacuzzis. ⊠*311 Pendleton St., Waycross* ☎*912/283-9300 or 866/582-5149* ⊕*www. pondviewinn.com* 🖅*4 rooms* △*In-room: Wi-Fi. In-hotel: restaurant, no-smoking rooms* ☐*AE, MC, V* ◐*BP.*

△ **Laura S. Walker State Park.** One of the few state parks named for a woman, this 600-acre park honors a Waycross teacher who championed conservation. The park, 9 mi northeast of the Okefenokee Swamp Park, has campsites with electrical and water hookups. Be sure to pick up food and supplies on the way. Boating and skiing are permitted on the 120-acre lake, and there's an 18-hole golf course. Rustic cabins cost $20 per night, plus $2 parking. ⊠*5653 Laura Walker Rd.,*

Waycross ☎*912/287–4900, 800/864–7275, 912/285–6154 for golf course* ⊕*gastateparks.org/info/lwalker* ⇒*44 tent, trailer, RV campsites; group campsite sleeps 142* ⚲ *Pool.*

STEPHEN C. FOSTER STATE PARK

18 mi northeast of Fargo via Rte. 177.

Named for the songwriter who penned "Swanee River," this 80-acre island park is the southwestern entrance to the Okefenokee National Wildlife Refuge and offers trips to the headwaters of the Suwannee River, Billy's Island—site of an ancient Indian village—and a turn-of-the-20th-century town built to support logging efforts in the swamp. The park is home to hundreds of species of birds and a large cypress-and-black-gum forest, a majestic backdrop for one of the thickest growths of vegetation in the southeastern United States. Park naturalists lead boat tours and recount a wealth of Okefenokee lore while you observe alligators, birds, and native trees and plants. You may also take a self-guided excursion in a rental canoe or a motorized flat-bottom boat. Campsites and cabins are available. ⊠*Rte. 1, Box 131, Fargo* ☎*912/637–5274* ⊕*gastateparks.org/info/scfoster* ⊠*$5 per vehicle for National Wildlife Refuge* ⊙ *Mar.–mid-Sept., daily 6:30* AM–8:30 PM; *mid-Sept.–Feb., daily 7* AM–7 PM.

OFF THE BEATEN PATH

Suwannee River Visitors Center. A high-definition film and exhibits on swamp, river, and timbering history are part of the fare at this visitor center in Fargo. There are also animal exhibits featuring black bears, bobcats, otters, snakes, fish, and birds. The 7,000-square-foot facility is eco-friendly, employing solar-powered fans, composting toilets that use no water, decking made from recycled plastic, insulation from recycled newspapers, and a retaining wall made from recycled dashboards and electrical cables. Guided boat tours are available, as are canoe and boat rentals. ⊠*125 Suwannee River Dr., at U.S. 441 bridge over Suwannee River, near Fargo* ☎*912/637–5274* ⊕*gastateparks.org/info/scfoster* ⊠*Free* ⊙ *Wed.–Sun. 9–5.*

WHERE TO STAY

Stephen C. Foster State Park. The park has sites for all types of camping as well as basically equipped, two-bedroom cottages that can sleep up to eight. Be aware that the gates of the park are closed between sunset and sunrise—there's no traffic in and out for campers, so you need to stock up on supplies before the sun goes down. You can book sites and cabins up to 11 months in advance. ⌂*Rte. 1, Box 131, Fargo 31631* ☎*912/637–5274 or 800/864–7275* ⊕*gastateparks.org/info/scfoster* ⇒*66 tent, trailer and RV sites, pioneer camping, 9 cottages.*

Southwest Georgia

WORD OF MOUTH

"Thomasville . . . has a number of fine old homes, etc., on display. It is also well known for its rose gardens and Rose Festival."

—aileen679

"Callaway Gardens is a nice day trip destination from Atlanta—under two hours, I think. There's a neat butterfly house, and a lake with sandy beach. We have rented bicycles there."

—noe847

Updated by
Christine Van
Dusen

THE ROLLING AGRICULTURAL LANDSCAPES OF a slower, older South, where things remain much the same as they were for generations, can be found within a couple of hours' drive of Atlanta's high-rise bustle. Here small towns evoke a time when the world was a simpler place, where people lived close to the land and life was measured on a personal scale. In southwest Georgia, peanuts, corn, tobacco, and cotton are the lifeblood of the local economies, and you're as likely to see a tractor on a country road as a car.

People here live far from the hassles of Atlanta's modernity—the daily grind of traffic jams and suburban sprawl. The accents are slow and seductive. Small towns and petite country hamlets beckon with their charming town squares and elegant bed-and-breakfasts. In southwest Georgia the inclination simply to relax is contagious—it can saturate you slowly but completely, like syrup on a stack of pancakes. And the Southern pride is palpable: sometimes seen in yellow ribbons scattered throughout entire communities or heard in conversations that still refer to "the War between the States" rather than the Civil War.

Despite the quiet pace of life here, this is the land of such greats as President Jimmy Carter, writers Erskine Caldwell and Carson McCullers, singers "Ma" Rainey and Otis Redding, and baseball-legend Jackie Robinson. For a time even Franklin Delano Roosevelt was drawn here; he returned again and again for the healing mineral waters of Warm Springs.

ORIENTATION & PLANNING

GETTING ORIENTED

Scattered along a vast coastal plain that covers much of the southern part of the state, the small towns of southwest Georgia are best explored by car or by the SAM Shortline. The touring train chugs through the countryside between Cordele and Archery.

Western Foothills & Farmland. Take a walk through the past with a visit to Franklin Roosevelt's Little White House retreat or tiptoe through the tulips at the 14,000-acre Callaway Gardens. This area also is home to Georgia's largest state park and the massive Fort Benning.

The Southwest Corner. Antiques shopping, peach picking, golf courses, and country inns are abundant in this part of the state, particularly in Thomasville, which is celebrated most for its Victorian homes, plantations, and historic churches.

SOUTHWEST GEORGIA PLANNER

WHEN TO GO

Because many of the towns in the region are off the beaten path, crowds are rarely a problem, though spring (which comes early) and fall (which comes late) are the most popular seasons. If you're not fond of the heat,

TOP REASONS TO GO

Callaway Gardens Resort and Preserve: 14,000 acres of gardens and parkland make this the raison d'être for visiting Pine Mountain. In spring the rhododendrons and wild azaleas take your breath away. If flowers really aren't your thing, then there's golf, fishing, tennis, a spa, and arts and crafts programs at Callaway Gardens Resort.

Thomasville Plantations: Nowhere is the lore of the deep South better understood than in and around the plantations of Thomasville. Because many have been restored as country inns, or are open to the public, they are almost like living museums. The entire region could be renamed "Tarasville."

FDR's Little White House: The cottage where President Franklin Delano Roosevelt stayed while taking in the healing waters of Warm Springs looks much as it did in his day. You can even see the pools where he was treated for polio.

Jimmy Carter's home town: President Jimmy Carter and First Lady Rosalynn Carter still live in Plains, Georgia, and still worship at the Maranathan Baptist Church. There are a number of museums and historic sites in Plains dedicated to Carter's legacy, including his boyhood farm and his high school–turned–museum.

12

March to May and September to December are the best times to visit. During this time, book well in advance for the more popular hotels and B&Bs in Pine Mountain, Warm Springs, and Thomasville.

GETTING HERE & AROUND

BY AIR Delta Airlines has daily flights into Columbus Metro Airport (CSG) from Atlanta.

BY CAR A car is the best way to tour this part of Georgia. Interstate 75 runs north–south through the eastern edge of the region and connects to several U.S. and state highways that traverse the area. Interstate 85 runs southwest through LaGrange and Columbus. Do explore backcountry roads—they offer the landscapes and ambience of the real South. Just be sure to travel with a good road map or GPS, and expect detours for photo opportunities.

BY TRAIN A great means of seeing the countryside, the SAM Shortline Southwest Georgia Excursion Train originates in Cordele and runs west through Georgia Veteran's State Park, Leslie, Americus, Plains, and Archery. You can get on or off at any of the stations, stop over for the night, and take the train again the next morning (check the schedule to be sure there's a train running the next day).

ESSENTIALS **Air Contacts Columbus Metro Airport** (CSG ⊠ *3250 W. Britt David Rd., Columbus* ☎ *706/324–2449* ⊕ *www.flycolumbusga.com).*

Train Contacts SAM Shortline Southwest Georgia Excursion Train (⊠ *105 E. 9th Ave., Box 845, Cordele* ☎ *229/276–0755 or 877/427–2457* ⊕ *www.sam-shortline.com).*

ABOUT THE HOTELS & RESTAURANTS

This region of Georgia does lovely things by slow-cooking pork over green oak. Pit barbecue joints in the area are homey, hands-on, and relatively inexpensive.

Lodging in the area runs the gamut from elegant, luxurious properties to low-profile but unique B&Bs to reliable and inexpensive chain hotels. RV parks and campgrounds are also available.

WHAT IT COSTS				
	¢	$	$$	$$$	$$$$
Restaurants	under $10	$10–$14	$15–$19	$20–$24	over $24
Hotels	under $100	$100–$150	$151–$200	$201–$250	over $250

Restaurant prices are for a main course at dinner. Hotel prices are for two people in a standard double room in high season.

PLANNING YOUR TIME

A traveler could easily get lost on the backroads of southwest Georgia, so perhaps the best way to take in the sites of this region is to park your car and board the SAM Shortline Excursion Train in Cordele. The ride will take you to Georgia Veterans State Park, The Rural Telephone Museum, Habitat for Humanity's Global Village, the Rylander Theatre, Windsor Hotel, and Plains. This way you'll get a sense of what spots deserve more time and which are suited for a drive-by.

If you'd prefer to spend the majority of your visit outdoors, southwest Georgia has its share of parks, with fishing, hunting, boating, and hiking opportunities.

WESTERN FOOTHILLS & FARMLAND

You won't be able to visit this slice of Georgia without feeling the influence of two generations of American presidents, Franklin Roosevelt and Jimmy Carter. About 100 mi south of Atlanta, near the Alabama border, Pine Mountain and Warm Springs are the rural retreats they have always been since FDR used to visit, and have retained much of their ambience from yesteryear. The Little White House is among its historical highlights. Plains (Jimmy Carter country) seems cut from the pages of the past.

WARM SPRINGS

97 mi southwest of Atlanta via I–85 and U.S. 27.

Renowned for centuries for the supposed healing properties of its thermal waters, Warm Springs is where the Creek Indians brought their wounded warriors when all other treatments had failed. In the early 1920s news spread that a young Columbus native and polio victim, Louis Joseph, had made a dramatic recovery after extensive therapy in the springs. Word reached Franklin Delano Roosevelt (1882–1945),

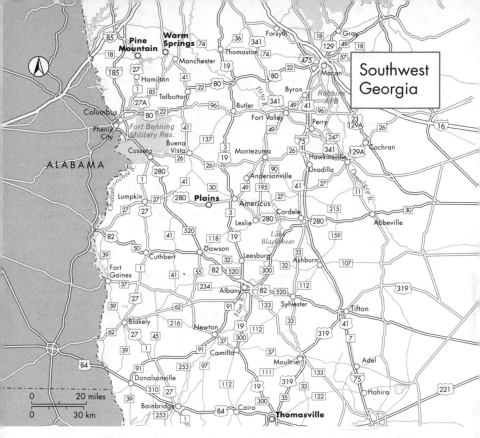

who had contracted polio, and a 20-year relationship began between him and this remote mountain village, where he built a cottage for his visits that came to be known as the Little White House. Roosevelt's experiences here led to the effort to eradicate polio around the world through the founding of the March of Dimes, and his encounters with his poor rural neighbors fueled ideas for his Depression-era New Deal recovery programs. After Roosevelt's death, the town fell on hard times, but an influx of crafts and antiques shops in the 1980s has revitalized Warm Springs.

GETTING HERE & AROUND

The best way to visit Warm Springs is to travel from Atlanta on I–85 South to Exit 41. Take a left turn onto Highway 27A/41, then continue for 35 miles to Warm Springs. Columbus is another good point to embark from; Warm Springs is about 40 miles south on Georgia 85 North. Much of Warm Springs is walkable, but a car is necessary if you want to hit all the high points.

Visitor Information Warm Springs Welcome Center (⌧ *1 Broad St., Warm Springs* ☎ *706/655–3322 or 800/337–1927* ⊕ *www.warmspringsga.com*).

EXPLORING

Fodor's Choice The **Little White House Historic Site/FDR Memorial Museum,** at the south end
★ of town, contains the modest three-bedroom cottage in which Roosevelt
stayed during his visits here. The cottage, built in 1932, remains much
as it did the day he died here (while having his portrait painted) and
includes the wheelchair Roosevelt designed from a kitchen chair. The
unfinished portrait is on display along with the 48-star American flag
that flew over the grounds when Roosevelt died. The FDR Memorial
Museum includes an interesting short film narrated by Walter Cronkite,
exhibits detailing Roosevelt's life and New Deal programs, and some
of Roosevelt's personal effects, such as his 1938 Ford, complete with
the full hand controls he designed. ■ TIP→ **Admission here allows you
to also visit the nearby pools where Roosevelt took his therapy.** ⊠*401
Little White House Rd.* ☎*706/655–5870* ⊕*www.fdr-littlewhitehouse.
org* ⊠*$7* ⊗*Daily 9–4:45.*

WHERE TO STAY

$–$$ ⊡ **Hotel Warm Springs Bed & Breakfast Inn.** Right in downtown Warm
Springs, this old hotel has plenty of character and is a great bargain.
The guest rooms have oak furniture and 12-foot ceilings with crown
molding. Prices are even cheaper if you opt not to have breakfast,
though this means you'll miss out on a Southern breakfast with cheese
grits. ■ TIP→ **Whether you stay or not, the Tuscawilla Soda Fountain off the
lobby is a treat to visit—it was the town's original drug store and soda fountain, often frequented by FDR himself. Pros:** convenient to Warm Springs'
sights; storied history. **Cons:** no elevator; sometimes harried staff; not
large enough for group travel. ⊠*47 Broad St.* ☎*706/655–2114 or
800/366–7616* ⊕*www.hotelwarmspringsbb.org* ⇆*10 rooms, 3 suites*
⊟*AE, D, MC, V* ⊠*BP.*

PINE MOUNTAIN

14 mi west of Warm Springs via Rte. 18 and Rte. 194.

Pine Mountain Ridge is the last foothill of the Appalachian chain, and
the town of Pine Mountain rests at the same elevation as Atlanta, making it generally cooler than the surrounding communities. The flora
and fauna here reflect the town's Appalachian connections. Most visitors are lured by the surrounding area's large-scale attractions—such
as Callaway Gardens Resort and Preserve—and are then pleasantly
surprised that the small-town berg has a folksy, inviting downtown
square. Antiques figure prominently in the area economy, and shops
abound in the town center.

GETTING HERE & AROUND

Pine Mountain can be reached by car from Atlanta via I–85 South and
sits 14 mi west of Warm Springs, via Rtes. 18 and 194.

ESSENTIALS

Visitor Information Pine Mountain Welcome Center (⊠*101 E. Broad St., Pine
Mountain* ☎*706/663–4000 or 800/441–3502* ⊕*www.pinemountain.org).*

EXPLORING

Just south of the village lies the area's main draw: **Callaway Gardens Resort and Preserve**, a 14,000-acre, nonprofit, family-style golf and tennis resort with a combination of elaborate, cultivated gardens and natural woodlands. This botanical wonderland was developed in the 1930s by textile magnate Cason J. Callaway and his wife Virginia, who were determined to breathe new life into the area's dormant cotton fields. With more than 1,000 varieties, the **Day Butterfly Center** is one of the largest free-flight conservatories in North America. **Mountain Creek Lake** is well stocked with largemouth bass and bream. **Ida Cason Callaway Memorial Chapel**—a favorite wedding venue—is a lovely stone chapel nestled in the woods alongside a lake and babbling stream. ⊠ *17800 U.S. 27* ☎ *706/225–5292 or 800/225–5292* ⊕ *www. callawaygardens.com* ⊠ *$13; free to overnight guests* ⊙ *Daily 9–5.*

At the **Wild Animal Safari,** a few miles northwest of town, you can either drive yourself or ride a bus through a 500-acre animal preserve. You may not believe you're still in Georgia: camels, llamas, antelopes, and hundreds of other exotic animals traipse around freely, often coming close to vehicles. An added plus is the **Old McDonald's Farm,** a petting zoo with jovial monkeys and writhing-reptile pits. ■**TIP**→ **The park sells special food for you to offer the animals, and some will scamper over your car to get it. Leave your new car at home.** ⊠ *1300 Oak Grove Rd.* ☎ *706/663–8744 or 800/367–2751* ⊕ *www.animalsafari. com* ⊠ *$16.95* ⊙ *Mar. and Apr., daily 10–6:30; May–Labor Day, daily 10–7:30; Labor Day–Feb., daily 10–5:30; call to confirm hrs and tour-bus schedule.*

WHERE TO EAT

$$$
ECLECTIC
✕**Carriage & Horses.** International cuisine is served in this Victorian house just north of town and overlooking the horse pastures of Grey Eagle Farm. The eclectic menu includes escargots, alligator with mushroom and lemon sauce, grilled trout (a house specialty), and filet mignon served with garlic mashed potatoes. The restaurant's oversize windows and patio make it a local favorite for sunset dining, and often local artists play assorted easy-listening '40s and '50s music. ⊠ *607 Butts Mill Rd.* ☎ *706/663–4777* ⚑ *Reservations essential* ⊟ *AE, D, MC, V* ⊙ *Closed Mon.*

WHERE TO STAY

$–$$
🏨 **Callaway Gardens Resort and Preserve.** Stay at this sprawling resort and your room key gains you access to its famous gardens from dawn until dusk. Accommodations range from fairly basic motel-style guest rooms to fully furnished one- to four-bedroom cottages and villas, all of them with lovely panoramic vistas and verdant garden settings. There's also the new Spa Prunifolia, with 13 treatment rooms. A 10-mi paved bike trail meanders through the property. There's great fishing in 13 stocked ponds, and the golf courses are famously impressive. Various meal and recreation packages are available. **Pros:** access to the gardens; several types of accommodations available. **Cons:** some guests say the look is outdated and housekeeping is slow to respond. ⊠ *17800 U.S. 27* ☎ *706/663–2281 or 800/225–5292* ⊕ *www.callawaygardens.com*

🛏453 rooms, 20 suites, 155 –cottages, 50 villas ⅏In-room: kitchen. In-hotel: 4 restaurants, bars, golf courses, tennis courts, gym, spa, beachfront, bicycles ☰AE, D, MC, V.

$ ⊞Chipley Murrah House B&B. One mile from the Callaway Gardens entrance and near downtown Pine Mountain, this lavish inn occupies a high-style Queen Anne Victorian dating to 1895. A favorite perch in this period-decorated house is the wraparound porch, decked out with rockers, swings, and wicker chairs. Hardwood floors, 12-foot ceilings, and decorative molding are among the beautifully preserved original details. In addition to the guest rooms there are three cottages, one with two bedrooms and two with three bedrooms. ■TIP➔ Cottage rentals are a great bet for families at $150 to $260 a night. Pros: welcoming owners; clean accommodations; spectacular stained glass. Cons:breakfast is not included with the cottages; no pets allowed; kids under 12 only allowed in the cottages. ✉207 W. Harris St., Box 1154, ☎706/663–9801 or 888/782–0797 ⊕www.chipleymurrah.com 🛏4 rooms, 3 cottages ☰AE, MC, V ⊘Closed Jan. ❦BP.

¢ ⊞Days Inn. There are no surprises at this old standby, but it's clean and close to downtown Pine Mountain and area attractions. Check the Web site for significantly cheaper specials. **Pros:** good breakfast; inexpensive lodging close to Callaway Gardens. **Cons:** small rooms and sometimes iffy customer service. ✉368 S. Main Ave., Box 1570 ☎706/663–2121 or 800/325–2525 ⊕www.daysinn.com 🛏60 rooms ⅏In-room: refrigerator, Wi-Fi. In-hotel: pool, some pets allowed ☰AE, D, MC, V ❦BP.

CAMPING

¢–$ ⚠Pine Mountain Campground. This large, well-kept campground just north of town has everything from tent sites to full RV hookups to cabins. "Megasites" are paved sites with patios, grills, and fences for privacy. You can swim in the pool and play miniature golf, volleyball, and horseshoes. Pets on a leash are welcome. The property recently added 30 acres and now has about 220 sites with full hookups, along with two cabins. **Pros:** convenient to Callaway Gardens; helpful staff. **Cons:**may be too sprawling and modern for some campers' tastes. ✉8804 Hamilton Rd., U.S. 27 ☎706/663–4329 ⊕www.camppine-mountain.com 🛏 220 full hookups ⅏Flush toilets, full hookups, partial hookups (electric and water), dump station, drinking water, guest laundry, showers, public telephone, general store, play area, swimming (pool) ☰MC, V.

SPORTS & THE OUTDOORS

CANOEING & About 45 minutes from Pine Mountain between Thomaston and
KAYAKING Columbus is the **Flint River Outdoor Center** (✉4429 Woodland Rd., Rte. 36 at Flint River, Thomaston ☎706/647–2633), with 5 mi of river courses where you can test your skills in everything from a float tube to kayaks running Class II rapids. The more daring can try Yellow Jacket Shoals, the Flint's only Class III/IV run—rumored to have destroyed more canoes than any other rapids in the Southeast.

HORSEBACK The mountain terrain makes the Pine Mountain area an interesting
RIDING place for horseback riding. **Roosevelt Stables** (✉1063 Group Camp

Rd. ☎706/628–7463 or 877/696–4613), in Franklin D. Roosevelt State Park, has 28 mi of trails and offers everything from one-hour rides to overnight trips complete with cowboy breakfasts.

EN ROUTE **LaGrange,** which lies 70 mi southwest of Atlanta via Interstate 85 and 27 mi northwest of Pine Mountain, makes for a pleasant diversion. A major cotton-growing region before the Civil War, the town's relative isolation from the battlefronts made it an ideal location for hospitals and convalescent centers. This was also home to the "Nancy Harts," the only all-female militia unit to serve in the war. Today the inviting town center is set around lovely LaFayette Square. Named for the Marquis de Lafayette, a major-general under General George Washington in the Revolutionary War, here's where to find the small but impressive **LaGrange Art Museum** (✉112 *LaFayette Pkwy., 1 block off Sq.* ☎706/882–3267) and its exhibits by regional contemporary artists. A little farther afield is **Bellevue** (✉204 *Ben Hill St.* ☎706/884–1832), a stately, colonnaded 1850s house, listed on the National Register of Historic Places, and considered one of the finest examples of Greek Revival architecture in Georgia.

> **STRETCH YOUR LEGS**
>
> **Pine Mountain Trail** is a favorite of the nearly 40 mi of trails in Franklin D. Roosevelt State Park that are designated for hikers only. Although each part of the trail is interesting in its own right, Dowdell's Knob Loop, near the center, makes a great day hike at 4.7 mi. The 6.5 mi Wolfden Loop is another beautiful part of the trail, traveling past beaver dams, over Hogback Mountain, and along the Mountain Creek Nature Trail, which features all manner of plant life. Trail maps are available at the State Park office and at Callaway Gardens Country Store.

PLAINS

85 mi southeast of Pine Mountain via U.S. 27.

This rural farming town—originally named the Plains of Dura after the biblical story of Shadrach, Meshach, and Abednego—is the birthplace and current home of former president Jimmy Carter and his wife Rosalynn. The Carters still live in a ranch-style brick house on the edge of town—the only home they have ever owned, and they still worship at the **Maranatha Baptist Church** (*148 GA 45 N* ☎ *229/824-7896* ⊕ *mbc-plains.com*). ■TIP→President Carter teaches Sunday school here once a month at 10 AM; doors open at 8:30 AM and the class fills up fast so arrive early. Call or check the Web site for the schedule. Although it's the hub of a thriving farming community, the one-street downtown paralleling the railroad tracks resembles a 1930s movie set.

GETTING HERE & AROUND

From I–85 or I–75, look for the exit to Rt. 280, then exit for Plains.

ESSENTIALS

Visitor Information Plains Welcome Center (✉1763 *U.S. 280, Plains* ☎229/824-7477 ⊕www.plainsgeorgia.com).

EXPLORING

Each September the town comes alive with the **Plains Peanut Festival,** which includes a parade, live entertainment, arts and crafts, food vendors, and races. The annual softball game pitting President Carter and Secret Service agents against alumni from Plains High School is always a festival highlight.

★ At the **Jimmy Carter National Historic Site** you can still see the late-1880s **railroad depot** that housed his 1976 presidential-campaign headquarters; in January 1977 the "Peanut Special," an 18-car train filled with supporters, departed from here for Carter's inauguration in Washington. The vintage phones here play recordings of Carter discussing his grassroots run for the White House. A couple of miles outside of town on the Old Plains Highway is the 360-acre **Jimmy Carter Boyhood Farm,** where the Carter family grew cotton, peanuts, and corn; it has been restored to its original appearance before electricity was introduced. Period furniture fills the house, and the battery-powered radio plays Carter's reminiscences of growing up on a Depression-era farm. **Plains High School,** in which the Carters were educated, is now a museum and the headquarters of the historic site. You can visit these places and tour the town by picking up a self-guided tour book at the visitor center or the high school. ⊠*Plains High School, 300 N. Bond St.* ☎*229/824–4104* ⊕*www.nps.gov/jica* ⊠*Free* ☉*Daily 9–5.*

WORD OF MOUTH

"I joined folks in the sanctuary of Maranatha Baptist Church to hear Jimmy Carter teach Sunday School. He teaches Sunday School quite often and the calendar is listed on the church's Web site. The lesson was wonderful. We stayed for church [afterwards], of course.... I was a bit surprised when Jimmy and Rosalynn sat a couple of pews behind me.... But, then, during the last hymm, I HEARD him—and leaned over to my father and whispered "That's Jimmy Carter singing!" That's one memory that I don't think will ever fall away."

—starrs

NEED A BREAK? For a local spot to refuel in Plains, try **Mom's Kitchen in Plains** (⊠*203 E. Church St.* ☎*229/824-5458*) which serves up buffet-style Southern food. **Old Bank Café** (⊠*118 Main St.* ☎*229/824-4520*)has soup, salads, and sandwiches.

WHERE TO STAY

¢–$ **Plains Historic Inn.** Each spacious room of this inn, set in a turn-of-the-20th-century furniture store directly above the Antiques Mall on Main Street, is decorated to reflect the aesthetics of a particular decade between the 1920s and the 1980s. The street-side rooms have a view across Main Street, where Billy Carter's old gas station still sits along with the railroad depot from which President Carter ran his bid for the White House. ■TIP→ The inn books up fast during the Peanut Festival; reserve six months in advance. Pros: very close to tourist attractions; cozy and comfortable; claw-foot tubs in some bathrooms. Cons: breakfast is self-serve; not many eating options nearby. ⊠*106 Main*

St. ☎229/824–4517 ⊕ *www.plainsinn.net* ⊅7 *suites* ♿*In-hotel: no-smoking rooms* ▤*AE, D, MC, V* ⦿❙*BP.*

EN ROUTE Warp back in time to the mid-19th century at **Westville Village** (⌂*Box 1850, Lumpkin 31815* ☎*229/838–6310 or 888/733–1850* ⊕ *www. westville.org* ⛁*$10* ⊙*Tues.–Sat. 10–5*). In Lumpkin, at the junction of I–85 and Hwy. 27, 7 mi east of Plains, this replica of an 1850s town has more than 30 pre–Civil War buildings, relocated and authentically restored. The village comes alive with hearth-cooked food, mules and wagons, and period-dressed townspeople and tradesmen demonstrating skills such as candle making, quilting, and cotton baling.

Founded in 1832, Americus is the only city in the United States named for explorer Amerigo Vespucci (1454–1512). Today this small town 11 miles east of Plains via U.S. 280 is best known as the site of the international headquarters of **Habitat for Humanity** (✉*121 Habitat St.* ☎*229/924–6935 or 800/422–4828* ⊕*www.habitat.org* ⛁*Headquarters: free. Global Village: $6 suggested donation* ⊙*Headquarters: Tues.–Sat. 8–5. Global Village weekdays 9–5, Sat. 10–2.*), an organization dedicated to building decent, affordable housing for low-income families around the world. You can tour the headquarters and watch videos discussing the group's work. A few blocks farther west on West Church Street is **Habitat's Global Village & Discovery Center,** which examines different housing conditions around the world. You can climb into the Papua New Guinea house on stilts, make compressed-earth blocks, or try your hand at roof tiles, just like Habitat builders in Africa and Asia.

THE SOUTHWEST CORNER

Thomasville is the highlight of Georgia's southwest corner. It's among the nation's most appealing small towns, thanks to an inviting town square, shaded glens, and an easygoing air; you can also find some fine country inns here.

THOMASVILLE

236 mi south of Atlanta via I–75 and U.S. 319.

The early fortunes of this appealing small town in the Tallahassee Red Hills paralleled the rise and fall of the antebellum cotton plantations that lined the region's famed "Plantation Trace." Following the Civil War, thousands of Union prisoners who had been evacuated from the nearby Andersonville prison to Thomasville brought home stories of the curative effects of the balsam breezes of the pine-scented air. These stories fueled the second boom in the region's fortunes, during which Northerners fleeing the cold wintered here. The wealthier among them built elegant estates in and around the town.

Although Thomasville's golden era has long since ended and there's little left of the old-growth forests that brought winter vacationers south, the distinct pine-scented air remains, as does the Victorian elegance of

CLOSE UP

King Cotton

Such was Georgia's preeminence in world cotton production at the turn of the 20th century that the international market price was set at the Cotton Exchange in Savannah. And the huge plantations of southwest Georgia were major players in the engine driving the state's economic prosperity. For more than 100 years, from the first time it was planted in Georgia in 1733 until the beginning of the Civil War, cotton was the most commercially successful crop in the state. But because the seeds had to be separated from the lint by hand, production was laborious and output was limited. In 1793 a young Yale graduate named Eli Whitney (1765–1825) came to Savannah's Mulberry Grove Plantation as a tutor to the children of Revolutionary War hero Nathaniel Greene. After watching the difficulty workers were having separating the seeds from the cotton, he invented a simple machine of two cylinders with combs rotating in opposite directions. The "gin," as he called it (short for engine), could do the work of 50 people and revolutionized the cotton industry. So significant was its immediate impact on the U.S. economy that President George Washington personally signed the patent issued to Whitney.

In 1900 the boll weevil came to the U.S. via Mexico and quickly undermined cotton production. The weevil was a major cause of the onset of the economic depression that spread throughout the South. Cotton production was at an all-time low in Georgia by 1978; in 1987 the state began a boll weevil eradication program that has all but wiped out the threat. And the result is that today Georgia is once again one of the top producers in the nation.

the town's heyday. Thomasville retains the stately vestiges of a once-posh resort, but without the crowds. Known as the "City of Roses," it draws thousands of visitors each spring to its annual Rose Festival (the fourth weekend in April). And during the Victorian Christmas, locals turn out in period costumes to enjoy horse-drawn carriage rides, caroling, and street theater.

GETTING HERE & AROUND
Thomasville, with its rich atmosphere of a bygone era, sits 55 miles south of Tifton and can be reached from Atlanta via I–75 and U.S. 319.

ESSENTIALS
Visitor Information Thomasville Welcome Center (⊠ *144 E. Jackson St., Thomasville* ☎ *229/228–7977 or 866/577–3600* ⊕ *www.thomasvillega.com).*

EXPLORING
One of Thomasville's more interesting sights is the **Lapham–Patterson House,** built by Chicago shoe manufacturer Charles W. Lapham. At the time of its construction in 1884, the three-story Victorian house was state-of-the-art, with gas lighting and indoor plumbing with hot and cold running water. Each room was built with at least five or six walls. But the most curious feature of this unusual house is that Lapham, who had witnessed the Great Chicago Fire of 1871, had 45

exit doors installed because of his fear of being trapped in a burning house. The house is now a National Historic Landmark because of its unique architectural features. ✉*626 N. Dawson St.* ☎*229/ 225–4004* ⊕*www.gastateparks. org/info/lapham* ✑*$5* ☉*Tues.– Sat. 9–5, Sun. 2–5:30.*

☺ The **Birdsong Nature Center** encompasses 565 acres of lush fields, forests, swamps, and butterfly gardens, plus miles of walking trails. It's a wondrous haven for birds and scores of other native wildlife. Nature programs are offered year-round. ✉*2106 Meridian Rd.* ☎*229/377–4408 or 800/953–2473* ⊕*www. birdsongnaturecenter.org*✑*$5* ☉*Wed., Fri., and Sat. 9–5, Sun. 1–5.*

★ For a glimpse of the grandeur of Southern life Tara-style, visit **Pebble Hill Plantation,** listed on the National Register of Historic Places and the only plantation in the area open to the public. Pebble Hill dates to 1825, although most of the original house was destroyed in a fire in the 1930s. Highlights of the current two-story main house include a dramatic horseshoe-shape entryway, a wraparound terrace on the upper floor, and an elegant sunroom decorated with a wildlife motif. Surrounding the house are 34 acres of immaculately maintained grounds that include gardens, a walking path festooned with jasmine, a log-cabin school, a fire station, a carriage house, kennels, and a hospital for the plantation's more than 100 dogs (prized dogs were buried with full funerals, including a minister). The sprawling dairy-and-horse-stable complex resembles an English village. Grab a cup of lemonade from the large thermos under the oak tree opposite the Plantation Store—it's compliments of the house. ✉*5 mi south of Thomasville on U.S. 319* ☎*229/226–2344* ⊕*www.pebblehill.com* ✑*Grounds $5, house tour $10* ☉*Oct.–Aug., Tues.–Sat. 10–5, Sun. 1–5; last tour at 4.*

WHERE TO EAT

¢–$
SEAFOOD
✗**George & Louie's.** The fresh gulf seafood served at this airy Key West–style restaurant is as good as you can find anywhere. Try the broiled shrimp, cooked in olive oil with a smattering of fresh garlic; fresh mullet dinner; or combination platter with homemade deviled crab, shrimp, oysters, scallops, and flounder for one, two, or three people. The fried green tomatoes sprinkled with feta are cooked to perfection, and the burgers are a local favorite. Vintage music from the '40s plays on the sound system, and there's outdoor dining under umbrellas. ✉*217 Remington Ave.* ☎*229/226–1218* ▭*No credit cards* ☉*Closed Sun.*

$$$$
ECLECTIC
✗**Liam's Restaurant.** With a flair for the unexpected, this bistro turns out a rotating seasonal menu with such updated Southern dishes as Jamaican pork loin with sweet red-onion marmalade, and duck with cottage cheese, pecans, and corn cake with a blueberry sauce. Liam's also serves a full cheese cart of various artisan cheese from Europe, as well as local selections. It's especially proud of its humongous Euro-

ANTIQUE ANTICS

Toscoga Marketplace (✉*209 S. Broad St., Thomasville,* ☎*229/ 227–6777*) is home to some 90 antiques dealers and, as south Georgia's largest antiques mall, is the local sponsor of the greatly heralded *Antiques Roadshow* TV show.

12

pean breakfast served every Saturday. Wine is not on the menu, but you're free to bring your own bottle. An open kitchen, garden dining, and paintings by local artists create a cozy dining room. ✉*113 E. Jackson St.* ☎*229/226–9944* 🌐*www.liamsofthomasville.com* 💳*MC, V* ⏲*Closed Sun. and Mon. No dinner Tues. and Wed.*

$$–$$$ ITALIAN ✕**Mom and Dad's Italian Restaurant.** That's definitely oregano you smell when entering Mom and Dad's—but also expect to hear a Southern drawl. These go together perfectly at this restaurant, a great place for Italian food made with rich cheeses and thick red tomato sauce. The garlic bread is served warm and strong enough to turn your breath into a blowtorch. ✉*1800 Smith Ave. 31792* ☎*229/226–6265* 💳*AE, MC, V* ⏲*Closed Sun. and Mon. No lunch.*

WHERE TO STAY

$$–$$$ ★ **1884 Paxton House Inn.** Each room is unique in this immaculate property, a stately blue Victorian mansion with a wraparound veranda. Antiques and period reproductions decorate the public spaces and guest rooms. Thoughtful details include designer fabrics, Egyptian-cotton bath towels, goose-down pillows, evening turndown service, and homemade cranberry, orange, or blueberry bread for breakfast. Accommodations are spread among the main inn, a pool house, a garden cottage, and a carriage house. Afternoon tea and lemonade socials are part of the fun of this inn in the downtown historic district. **Pros:** no kids under 12, lap pool and Jacuzzi at pool house, old-time charm with modern amenities. **Cons:** no kids; modern amenities may be a turn-off. ✉*445 Remington Ave.* ☎*229/226–5197* 🌐*www.1884paxtonhouseinn.com* *10 rooms* *In-room: DVD, Internet, Wi-Fi. In-hotel: pool, no kids under 12* 💳*AE, MC, V* *BP.*

Atlanta, GA

WORD OF MOUTH

"Reading Tom Wolfe's *A Man in Full* [before your visit] is an excellent idea if you are of the mind. Then a visit to the High Museum, a drive down West Paces Ferry and into the heart of Buckhead would take on a different feel."

—cpdl

"The CityPass allowed us to bypass the ticket line [at the Georgia Aquarium] which saved us standing in the Georgia heat. One tip: If there is not an event go up to the ballroom above the food court. It is not part of the traffic flow (and indeed signs say 'no live exhibits,' but the ballroom has a huge window to the beluga whale tank."

—palmettoprincess

Updated by
Christine Van
Dusen

A WARM EMBRACE GREETS VISITORS to Atlanta. Top-notch shopping, world-class dining, and major attractions are among the greatest rewards these days. In the past, many of the big draws—Stone Mountain Park, for example—were outside the city limits. Today there's plenty in town to keep you occupied. The Georgia Aquarium, the largest in the world, draws visitors who want to get up close and personal with whale sharks. The Woodruff Arts Center is a cultural hub where you can catch a performance by the Atlanta Symphony Orchestra or gaze on treasures from the Louvre on loan at the High Museum of Art. And the fizzy World of Coke is dedicated to the hometown beverage.

Atlanta continues to experience explosive growth. The latest estimates place the city's population at 486,411. But the 20-county Atlanta Metropolitan Statistical Area counts more than 5 million residents. A good measure of the city's expansion is the ever-changing skyline; condominium developments appear to spring up overnight, while rundown properties seem to disappear in a flash. In Buckhead—once home to a noisy, raucous bar district—most of the taverns have been razed and work is underway on what developers are hoping will become the Rodeo Drive of the South. Office and residential towers have risen throughout the Midtown, Downtown, and outer perimeter (fringing Interstate 285, especially to the north) business districts. Residents, however, are less likely to measure the city's growth by skyscrapers than by the increase in traffic jams and crowds, higher prices, and the ever-burgeoning subdivisions that continue to push urban sprawl farther and farther into surrounding rural areas.

Originally built as the terminus of the Western & Atlantic Railroad, Atlanta is still a transportation hub. The city now serves the world through Hartsfield-Jackson Atlanta International Airport—now ranked as the busiest in the world. It serves nearly 89 million passengers annually. Direct flights to Europe, South America, Africa, and Asia have made Atlanta easily accessible to the more than 50 countries that have representation in the city through consulates, trade offices, and chambers of commerce. Atlanta is the world headquarters for such Fortune 500 companies as Home Depot, Coca-Cola, United Parcel Service, and SunTrust Banks.

"The city too busy to hate," Atlanta has become the best example of the New South, a fast-paced modern city proud of its heritage. Transplanted Northerners and those from elsewhere account for more than half the population and have undeniably affected the mood of the city, as well as the mix of accents of its people. Irish immigrants played a major role in the city's early history, along with Germans and Austrians. Since the 1980s, Atlanta has seen spirited growth in its Asian and Latin-American communities. Related restaurants, shops, and institutions have become part of the city's texture.

TOP REASONS TO GO

The Georgia Aquarium: Wildly successful after its opening in late 2005, the world's largest aquarium draws visitors from all over the globe.

A stroll through the park: April in Paris has nothing on Atlanta, especially when the abundant azaleas and dogwoods are blooming in Atlanta Botanical Garden, Centennial Park, and Piedmont Park.

Following in King's footsteps: Home of Martin Luther King Jr., Atlanta was a hub of the civil rights movement. Not to be missed is a visit to the King Center and a tour through his childhood home on Auburn Avenue.

Civil War history: Atlanta may have been burned during General William Sherman's march to the sea, but artifacts in the city's museums—as well as at historic sites in nearby Kennesaw, Marietta, and Roswell—give history buffs the chance to revisit those difficult times.

Southern cooking, and then some: Good Southern food has always been easy to find in Atlanta; visit JCT Kitchen on Howell Mill Road for a high-class take on chicken and dumplings or try red velvet cake at Thelma's Kitchen in Sweet Auburn. Southern cooking isn't your only option in this town, though—the richness of Atlanta's ethnic diversity makes it a great place to sample a wide range of cuisines.

13

ORIENTATION & PLANNING

GETTING ORIENTED

Atlanta, the state's capital and seat of Fulton County, was founded in 1837 and sits on the Piedmont Plateau in northern Georgia. Though the metro area spans 8,000 square miles, don't let the sprawling size— or all the transplanted "Yankees"—fool you into thinking Southern hospitality is dead. It's alive and well in Atlanta's pith-helmeted downtown ambassadors, drawling coffee mug-fillers, waving neighbors, and good ol' boy politicians.

Downtown Atlanta. Downtown has begun to shake its reputation for being desolate and a bit dangerous, now that tourists are flocking to sites like the Georgia Aquarium and more residents are looking at living in the city center. Daytime is when the area is most active with workers, conventioneers and, yes, panhandlers. But these days there is some activity after twilight at the district's restaurants and lounges.

Sweet Auburn. This mile and a half along Auburn Avenue, considered the epicenter of African-American history and achievement in Atlanta, has undergone restoration since landing on a 1992 list for endangered historic places. Here you can visit Dr. Martin Luther King Jr.'s birth home, church, and grave.

Midtown. You'll see Atlanta's most beautiful and chic people in Midtown, living in luxurious high-rise condos and frequenting the district's trendy restaurants, clubs, and shops. Regular folks fit in here too, enjoying sunny days at the Atlanta Botanical Garden and in the grassy oasis that is Piedmont Park.

Buckhead. Buckhead was known for its glamorous condos, majestic homes, and moneyed residents like Elton John, along with a notorious entertainment district that looked like college Spring Break every night. The latter is now largely gone, soon to be replaced by Buckhead Avenue's luxury retailers and ritzy boutiques.

Virginia Highland & the Emory Area. Stroll through the leafy neighborhood at the intersection of Virginia and North Highland avenues and you'll find a concentration of trendy stores, patio bars, cozy music venues, and tasty eateries. The area has a sunny disposition, and sits not far from the venerable Emory University and a collection of shops, pizza joints, and bars.

Little Five Points & Inman Park. There's a lively mix here, with the majestic old mansions and adorable bungalows of Inman Park situated just down Euclid Avenue from the quirky assortment of bars, restaurants, tattoo parlors, vintage-clothing shops, and street characters of Little Five Points. The area remains fiercely off-beat and independent.

ATLANTA PLANNER

WHEN TO GO

Atlanta isn't called "Hotlanta" for nothing—in the late spring and summer months the mosquitoes feast and the temperatures can reach a sticky and humid 99°F (thankfully, almost every place in the city is air-conditioned). July 4th weekend can be particularly hectic, due to the influx of runners for the annual 10K Peachtree Road Race. The best time to visit is in the fall and early winter, when many other cities are beginning to get cold and gray but Atlanta typically maintains a steady level of sunshine and cool breezes. Airfares are fairly reasonable at most times of the year, given that the city is a transportation hub and most Atlanta attractions aren't seasonal.

GETTING HERE & AROUND

BY AIR   Hartsfield-Jackson Atlanta International (ATL), the busiest passenger airport in the world, is served by more than 26 airlines, including Air-Tran, Continental and Delta. Although an underground train and moving walkways help you reach your gate more quickly, budget a little extra time for negotiating the massive facility. Because of the airport's size, security lines can be long, especially during peak travel periods. The airport typically suggests arriving two hours before your flight.

The airport is 13 mi south of Downtown. There are large parking facilities, which tend to fill up quickly. Check their current capacity, which is available on the airport's Web site. Locals know that MARTA, the regional subway system, is the fastest and cheapest way to and from the airport, but taxis are available. The fare to Downtown is about $35 for one person. From the airport to Buckhead, the fare is $38 for one person (though some politicians are trying to raise it). Buckhead Safety Cab and Checker Cab offer 24-hour service.

AIRPORT SHUTTLES Atlanta Airport Superior Shuttle vans run daily every 15 minutes between 6 AM and 11:30 PM to Perimeter Center offices, hotels, and residences. The trip can take 30 to 45 minutes, depending on the traffic. The cost typically ranges from $27 to $32 one-way. Atlanta Link operates vans every 15 minutes between 6 AM and midnight to Downtown, Midtown, and the Buckhead–Lenox area. Vans heading Downtown cost a minimum of $17 for the 20-minute trip. Vans to Midtown cost a minimum of $19 for the 40-minute trip, and vans to the Buckhead–Lenox area cost about $21 for the 45-minute trip.

Airport Metro Shuttle operates shuttles around-the-clock to destinations around the region. Reservation must be made at least 12 hours in advance. Typical fee is $48 for one passenger to Marietta.

BY BUS MARTA operates more than 100 routes covering more than 1,000 mi, but the bus system isn't popular among visitors. The fare is $1.75, and exact change or a Breeze card is required. Service is limited outside the perimeter of Interstate 285, except for a few areas in Clayton, DeKalb, and north Fulton counties.

BY CAR The city is encircled by Interstate 285. Three interstates also crisscross Atlanta: Interstate 85, running northeast–southwest from Virginia to Alabama; Interstate 75, running north–south from Michigan to Florida; and Interstate 20, running east–west from South Carolina to Texas.

Some refer to Atlanta as the "Los Angeles of the South," because driving is virtually the only way to get around. Atlantans have grown accustomed to frequent delays at rush hour—the morning and late-afternoon commuting periods seem to get longer every year. **The South as a whole may be laid-back, but Atlanta drivers are not; they tend to drive faster and more aggressively than drivers in other Southern cities. Rarely do Atlantans slow down at a yellow light.**

If you plan to venture beyond the neighborhoods served by MARTA, you will want to rent a car. Many national agencies have branch offices all over the city, as well as at Hartsfield-Jackson Atlanta International Airport.

BY SUBWAY MARTA has clean and safe subway trains with somewhat limited routes that link downtown with many major landmarks, like the CNN Center and the Martin Luther King Jr. Memorial. The system's two main lines cross at the Five Points station. MARTA uses a smart-card fare system called Breeze. The cards are available at RideStores and from vending machines at each station by using cash or credit cards. The one-way fare is $1.75, but the cards offer several options, including weekend, weekly, and monthly passes.

Trains generally run weekdays 5 AM to 1 AM and weekends and holidays 6 AM to 12:30 AM. Most trains operate every 15 to 20 minutes; during weekday rush hours, trains run every 10 minutes.

■TIP➔ Locals take MARTA to and from Hartsfield-Jackson International Airport, which has the traffic snarls common with larger airports. The $1.75 fare (plus a $0.50 charge for a Breeze Ticket or $5 for a reloadable Breeze

Card) is a fraction of the amount charged by shuttles or taxis. Airport travelers should be careful about catching the right train. One line ends up at North Springs station to the north. The other at Doraville station, to the northeast. Daily parking is free at MARTA parking facilities. Long-term parking rates range from $4 to $7 daily. All stations do not have lots, however.

BY TAXI   Taxi service in Atlanta can be uneven. Drivers often lack correct change, so bring along plenty of small bills. You can also charge your fare, as many accept credit cards. Drivers may be as befuddled as you may be by the city's notoriously winding streets, so if your destination is somewhere other than a major hotel or popular sight, bring along printed directions.

In Atlanta taxi fares begin at $2.50, then add 25¢ for each additional 1/8 mi. Additional passengers are $2. If you remain within the Downtown Convention Zone, the Midtown Zone, or the Buckhead Zone, a flat rate of $8 for one person and $2 for each additional passenger is charged to any destination.

You generally need to call for a cab, as Atlanta is not a place where you can hail one on the street. Buckhead Safety Cab and Checker Cab offer 24-hour service.

BY TRAIN   Amtrak operates daily service from Atlanta's Brookwood Station to New York; Philadelphia; Washington, DC; Baltimore; Charlotte, North Carolina; Greenville, South Carolina; and New Orleans.

VISITOR   The Atlanta Convention & Visitors Bureau, which provides informa-
INFORMATION   tion on Atlanta and the outlying area, has several information centers in Atlanta: Hartsfield-Jackson Atlanta International Airport, in the Atrium; Underground Atlanta; and the Georgia World Congress Center.

ESSENTIALS   **Airport Contacts Hartsfield-Jackson Atlanta International Airport** (*ATL* ✉ *6000 N. Terminal Pkwy., Atlanta* ☎ *404/530–7300* ⊕ *www.atlanta-airport. com*).

Bus & Train Contacts Amtrak (✉ *Brookwood Station, 1688 Peachtree St., Buckhead* ☎ *404/881–3060 or 800/872–7245* ⊕ *www.amtrak.com*).

Subway Contact MARTA (☎ *404/848–5000* ⊕ *www.itsmarta.com*).

Taxi & Shuttle Contacts Atlanta Airport Superior Shuttle (☎ *404/766–5312* ⊕ *atlsuperiorshuttle.com*). **Atlanta Link** (☎ *404/524–3400* ⊕ *www.theatlantalink. com*). **Airport Metro Shuttle** (☎ *404/766–6666* ⊕ *airportmetro.com*). **Buckhead Safety Cab** (☎ *404/233–1152*). **Checker Cab** (☎ *404/351–1111*).

Visitor Information Atlanta Convention & Visitors Bureau (✉ *233 Peachtree St., Suite 100, Downtown* ☎ *404/521–6600* ✉ *Underground Atlanta, 65 Upper Alabama St., Downtown* ☎ *404/523–2311* ✉ *Georgia World Congress Center, 285 International Blvd., Downtown* ☎ *404/223–4000* ⊕ *www.atlanta.net*).

PLANNING YOUR TIME

Because it would take too long to explore the city end-to-end in one fell swoop, consider discovering Atlanta one pocket at a time. In Downtown you can stroll through the Georgia Aquarium, tour the CNN Center and meander through the World of Coca-Cola, then finish off the day with dinner and draughts at Marietta Street sports bar Stats or with a classy glass of wine down the street at Thrive. Another good pocket includes three very walkable neighborhoods, all known for their canopies of trees, cute shops, and fun bistros: Virginia-Highland, Little Five Points, and Inman Park. From there you can drive to East Atlanta, one of the slower-transitioning in-town neighborhoods, and check out its casual bars, tattoo shops, vegetarian restaurants, and live music. Your third pocket should be Buckhead, and depending on when you go you will either see a neighborhood in metamorphosis or, if all goes according to plan, a shopper's mecca. Two constants there are Lenox Mall and Phipps Plaza, great shopping spots in their own right.

13

DISCOUNTS & DEALS

Visitors can take advantage of the deal offered with **Atlanta CityPass**, "the ticket to a New and Old South vacation." As of this writing, an adult pass—which is valid for a nine-day period—cost $69 and provided access to six attractions: Georgia Aquarium, World of Coca-Cola, Zoo Atlanta, and a choice between Inside CNN Atlanta Studio Tour or Atlanta Botanical Garden, and a choice of either High Museum of Art or Atlanta History Center. Visit ⊕*www.citypass.com/city/atlanta.html* or call ☎*888/330–5008* for details.

EXPLORING ATLANTA

The greater Atlanta area embraces several different counties. The city of Atlanta is primarily in Fulton and DeKalb counties, although its southern end and the airport are in Clayton County. Outside Interstate 285, which encircles the city, Cobb, Gwinnett, and northern Fulton counties are experiencing much of Atlanta's population increase.

Atlanta's lack of a grid system confuses many drivers, even locals. Some streets change their names along the same stretch of road, including the city's most famous thoroughfare, Peachtree Street, which follows a mountain ridge from downtown to suburban Norcross, outside Interstate 285: it becomes Peachtree Road after crossing Interstate 85 and then splits into Peachtree Industrial Boulevard beyond the Buckhead neighborhood and the original Peachtree Road, which heads into Chamblee. Adding to the confusion, dozens of other streets in the metropolitan area use "Peachtree" in their names. ■TIP➜ **Before setting out anywhere, get the complete street address of your destination, including landmarks, cross streets, or other guideposts, as street numbers and even street signs are often difficult to find.**

Atlanta proper has three major areas—Downtown, Midtown, and Buckhead—as well as many smaller commercial districts and intown neighborhoods. Atlanta's Downtown is filled with government staffers and office workers by day, but at night the visiting conventioneers—and, as city improvements take hold, residents—come out to play. Midtown, Virginia-Highland, Buckhead, and Little Five Points are the best places to go for dinner, nightclubs, and shows. Other neighborhoods like East Atlanta, Grant Park, and Kirkwood have unique characteristics that merit exploration.

The city's public transportation system, the Metropolitan Atlanta Rapid Transit Authority (MARTA), operates bus and rail networks in Atlanta and Fulton and DeKalb counties. The two major rail lines, which run east–west and north–south (there's a northern spur, so consult a map before you jump on board), extend roughly to the edges of Interstate 285. ■TIP➔ MARTA is best for traveling to and from the airport and within Downtown, Midtown, and Buckhead; if you plan to venture beyond those regions, you should call a taxi or rent a car.

DOWNTOWN ATLANTA

Downtown Atlanta clusters around the hub known as Five Points. Here you'll find the MARTA station that intersects the north–south and east–west transit lines, both of which run underground here. On the surface, Five Points is formed by the intersection of Peachtree Street with Marietta, Broad, and Forsyth streets. It's a crowded area, and traffic can be snarled in the early morning and late afternoon. With the opening of the Georgia Aquarium and the new World of Coca-Cola, which join the Imagine it! Children's Museum and the CNN Center, Downtown has taken on greater interest for travelers. Lush Centennial Olympic Park—built for the 1996 Olympic Games—is a great place to let your children play in the Fountain of Rings or to enjoy a take-out lunch.

TOP ATTRACTIONS

❶ ★ Atlanta Cyclorama & Civil War Museum. A building in Grant Park (named for a New England–born Confederate colonel, not the U.S. president) houses a huge circular painting depicting the 1864 Battle of Atlanta, during which 90% of the city was destroyed. A team of expert European panorama artists completed the painting in Milwaukee, Wisconsin, in 1887; it was donated to the city of Atlanta in 1897. On the second level, a display called "Life in Camp" displays rifles, uniforms, and games soldiers played to pass the time. An outstanding bookstore has dozens of volumes about the Civil War. Guided tours are available every hour on the half hour. To get here by car, take Interstate 20 east to Exit 59A, turn right onto Boulevard, and then follow signs to the Cyclorama. The museum shares a parking lot and entrance walkway with Zoo Atlanta. ⊠ *800C Cherokee Ave., Grant Park* ☎ *404/658-7625* ⊕ *www.atlantacyclorama.org* ✉ *$8* ⊙ *Tues.–Sun. 9:30–4:30.*

❶ FodorsChoice ★ ☾ Centennial Olympic Park. This 21-acre swath of green was the central venue for the 1996 Summer Olympics. The benches at the Fountain of Rings allow you to enjoy the water and music spectacle—eight tunes are timed to coincide with water displays that shoot sprays 15 feet to 30 feet high. The All Children's Playground is designed to be accessible

Downtown Atlanta & Sweet Auburn

to kids with disabilities. Nearby is the world's largest aquarium and Imagine It! Children's Museum. The park also has a café, restrooms, and a playground, and typically offers ice-skating in winter. ■TIP➔ **Don't miss seeing Centennial Olympic Park at night, when eight 65-foot-tall lighting towers set off the beauty of the park. These stylized reproductions represent the kind of markers that led ancient Greeks to significant public events.** ✉*Marietta St. and Centennial Olympic Park Dr., Downtown* ☎*404/223-4412* ⊕*www.centennialpark.com* ⊗*Daily 7 AM–11 PM.*

❶❺ **CNN Center.** The home of Cable News Network occupies all 14 floors
★ of this dramatic structure on the edge of Downtown. The 55-minute CNN studio tour—difficult for some people because it descends eight flights of stairs—is a behind-the-scenes glimpse of the control room, news rooms, and broadcast studios. Tours depart approximately every 10 minutes. You can make reservations by telephone or online. ✉*1 CNN Center, Downtown* ☎*404/827-2300* ⊕*www.cnn.com/studiotour* ▢*Tour $12* ⊗*Daily 9–5.*

❶❹ **Georgia Aquarium.** With 8 million gallons of water, this wildly popular
Fodor'sChoice attraction is the world's largest aquarium. The 550,000-square-foot
★ building, an architectural marvel resembling the bow of a ship, has
♻ tanks of various sizes filled with more than 80,000 animals, representing 500 species. The aquarium's 6.3-million-gallon Ocean Voyager Gallery is the world's largest indoor marine exhibit, with 4,574 square feet of viewing windows. In the gigantic tanks you'll see dramatic white beluga whales, a favorite with many visitors, and massive whale sharks. Not everything has gills, however: there are also penguins, sea lions, sea otters, river otters, sea turtles, and giant octopi. As of this writing, the aquarium had announced plans to add a $110 million dolphin exhibit by 2010. Hordes of kids—and many adults—can always be found around the touch tanks. A cartoon show featuring Deepo, the aquarium mascot, is an extra $5.50 for adults and $4 for children. One-hour behind-the-scenes tours are $50. Cafe Aquaria serves sandwiches, salads, and other light fare. There are often huge crowds, so arrive early or late for the best chance of getting a close-up view of the exhibits. ■TIP➔ **Purchase tickets at least a week ahead. Online ticketing is best, as you are e-mailed tickets you can print out at home.** ✉*225 Baker St., Downtown* ☎*404/581-4000 or 877/434-7442* ⊕*www. georgiaaquarium.org* ▢*$23* ⊗*Sun. to Fri. 10–5, Sat. 9–6.*

❽ **Imagine It! The Children's Museum of Atlanta.** In this colorful and joyfully
★ noisy museum geared to children ages eight and younger, kids can build
♻ sand castles, watch themselves perform on closed-circuit TV, operate a giant ball-moving machine, and get inside an imaginary waterfall (after donning raincoats, of course). Other exhibits rotate every few

months. ✉ *275 Centennial Olympic Park Dr. NW, Downtown* ☎ *404/659–5437* ⊕ *www.imagineit-cma.org* ✉ *$11 for ages 2 and above* ⊙ *Weekdays 10–4, weekends 10–5.*

16 **World of Coca-Cola.** Read all about ⟳ it: New Coke replaces original Coke! No, no—we're not referring to the 1980s marketing flop. The Atlanta-based beverage company closed down its original museum and in May 2007 emerged anew near the Georgia Aquarium. This World of Coca-Cola—a shrine to the brown soda's image, products, and marketing—is, at 62,000 square feet, twice the size of the previous building and features more than 1,200 artifacts never before displayed to the public. You can sip samples of Coca-Cola Company products from around the world and peruse more than a century's worth of memorabilia from the corporate archives. The gift shop sells everything from refrigerator magnets to evening bags. ■**TIP➜Visits begin with the screening of a promotional movie. Some visitors love it; others see it as an annoyingly long commercial.** ✉ *121 Baker St. NW, Downtown* ☎ *404/676–5151* ⊕ *www.woccatlanta.com* ✉ *$9* ⊙ *June–Aug., Mon.–Sat. 9–6, Sun. 11–5; Sept.–May, Mon.–Sat. 9–5, Sun. 11–5.*

> ## WORD OF MOUTH
>
> "Just returned from visiting our three-year-old grandson in Atlanta. The Children's Museum (Imagine It!) is wonderful. It is basically a very large room with different play areas (including one for babies and young toddlers). Lots of interactive play, plus places to sit and read. There is limited food available inside. Parking in one of the garages nearby ($12). It was a great way to spend a rainy day."
>
> —TrvlMaven

13

2 **Zoo Atlanta.** This zoo has nearly 1,000 animals and 250 species living in ⟳ naturalistic habitats. The gorillas and tigers are always a hit, as are two giant pandas named Yang Yang and Lun Lun. Children can ride the Nabisco Endangered Species Carousel and meet new friends at the petting zoo; the whole family can take a ride on the Norfolk Southern Zoo Express Train. To reach the zoo by car, take Interstate 20 east to Exit 59A and turn right on Boulevard. Follow the signs to the zoo, which is right near the Atlanta Cyclorama & Civil War Museum. ✉ *800 Cherokee Ave. SE, Grant Park* ☎ *404/624–5600* ⊕ *www.zooatlanta.org* ✉ *$17.99* ⊙ *Daily 9:30–5:30.*

WORTH NOTING

3 **Flatiron Building.** The English-American Building, as it was originally known, was designed by Bradford Gilbert. Similar to the famous New York City Flatiron Building, built in the early 1900s, this 11-story building dates from 1897 and is the city's oldest steel-framed skyscraper. ✉ *84 Peachtree St. NW, Downtown* ⊙ *Weekdays 9–5:30.*

12 **Georgia Dome.** This arena, opened in 1992, accommodates 71,250 spectators, with good visibility from every seat; it's the site of Atlanta Falcons football games and other sporting events, conventions, and trade shows. The white, plum, and turquoise 1.6 million-square-foot, seven-level facility is crowned with the world's largest cable-supported oval, giving the roof a circus-tent top. As of this writing, the tour was closed. ✉*1 Georgia Dome Dr., Downtown* ☎*404/223–4636* ⊕*www.gadome.com.*

⑱ Georgia State Capitol. The capitol, a Renaissance-style edifice, was dedi-
★ cated on July 4, 1889. The gold leaf on its dome was mined in nearby
Dahlonega. Inside, the **Georgia Capitol Museum** houses exhibits on
its history. On the grounds, state historical markers commemorate the
1864 Battle of Atlanta, which destroyed nearly the entire city. Stat-
ues memorialize a 19th-century Georgia governor and his wife (Joseph
and Elizabeth Brown), a Confederate general (John B. Gordon), and
a former senator (Richard B. Russell). Former governor and president
Jimmy Carter is depicted with his sleeves rolled up, a man at work.
■**TIP➔Those who wish to honor Martin Luther King Jr. should visit the
governor's wall, where a portrait of the civil rights leader was unveiled
in 2006.** ✉*206 Washington St., Downtown* ☎*404/656–2844* ⊕*sos.
georgia.gov/archives/state_capitol* ⊘*Museum weekdays 8–5; guided
tours weekdays at 10, 11, 1, and 2.*

❾ Hurt Building. Named for Atlanta developer Joel Hurt, this restored
1913 Chicago-style, 18-story high-rise is known for its intricate grill-
work. Enter at street level and take the sweeping marble staircase up to
the excellent City Grill restaurant. ✉*50 Hurt Plaza, Downtown.*

⑪ J. Mack Robinson College of Business. Atlanta architect Phillip Trammel
Shutze designed this 14-story edifice, originally known as the Empire
Building, in 1901. In 1929 Shutze refashioned the first three floors,
bestowing on them a decidedly Renaissance look. This was one of
the city's first steel-frame structures, but during the renovation Shutze resheathed the base with masonry. The edifice is also known as
the Bank of America Building, the NationsBank Building, the Citizens
& Southern National Bank Building, and the Atlanta Trust Company
Building. ✉*35 Broad St., Downtown* ☎*404/413-7000.*

❺ Margaret Mitchell Square. A cascading waterfall and columned sculpture
are highlights of this park named for one of Atlanta's most famous
authors, whose masterpiece is *Gone With the Wind.* ✉*Peachtree St.
at Forsyth St. NW and Carnegie Way, Downtown.*

❼ Museum of Design Atlanta. In the Peachtree Center in the Marquis Two
★ Tower, MODA is the only museum in the Southeast devoted exclu-
sively to design. It features exhibitions on fashion, graphics, archi-
tecture, furniture, and product design. ✉*285 Peachtree Center Ave.,
Downtown* ☎*404/979–6455* ⊕*www.museumofdesign.org* ▢*Free*
⊘*Tues.–Sat. 11–5.*

❻ Peachtree Center. John Portman designed this skyscraper complex,
built between 1960 and 1992. Across the street from this collection of
shops and restaurants, connected by skywalks, is the massive **Ameri-
casMart-Atlanta** wholesale market. Two additional Portman creations,
the **Atlanta Marriott Marquis** and the **Hyatt Regency Atlanta** hotels,
are also connected by skywalks. A MARTA station is convenient to
Peachtree Center. ✉*225 Peachtree St. NE, Downtown* ☎*404/524-
3787* ⊕*www.peachtreecenter.com.*

⑲ Shrine of the Immaculate Conception. During the Battle of Atlanta, pastor Thomas O'Reilly persuaded Union forces to spare his church and several others around the city. That 1848 structure was then torn down to make room for this much grander building, whose cornerstone was laid in 1869. The church was nearly lost to fire in 1982 but has been exquisitely restored. ■TIP→ To view the church, contact the rectory for an appointment. ✉️*48 Martin Luther King Jr. Dr. SW, Downtown* ☎️*404/521–1866* ⊙*By appointment only.*

⑩ Statue of Henry Grady. Alexander Doyle's bronze sculpture honors Henry Grady, editor of the old *Atlanta Constitution* and early advocate of the so-called New South. The memorial was raised in 1891, after Grady's untimely death at age 39. ✉️*Marietta and Forsyth Sts., Downtown.*

13

⑰ Underground Atlanta. Underground has seen more than its share of ups and downs. It was created from the web of subterranean brick streets, ornamental facades, and tunnels that fell into disuse in 1929, when the city built viaducts over the train tracks. The six-block district opened in 1969 as a retail and entertainment center and remained fairly popular until it was closed in 1980 for the MARTA train project. After a $142 million renovation, it reopened with eateries, retail, and specialty shops. In the following years, the spot's popularity waned. In 2005 the developers tried to revive interest in the district as a nighttime hot spot, opening six nightclubs on New Year's Eve, and saw mixed success. These days Underground remains relatively quiet during the daytime but hops at night for a largely African-American clientele, drawn to clubs like Sugar Hill and The House. As of this writing, the property was looking to charge $2 for entry to the district as a whole. ■TIP→ AtlanTIX, a half-price ticket outlet theater and cultural attractions, is in Underground Atlanta. It's open 11 to 6 Tuesday to Saturday, noon to 4 Sunday. ✉️*50 Upper Alabama St., Downtown* ☎️*404/523–2311* ⊕*www.underground-atlanta.com.*

OFF THE BEATEN PATH

Wren's Nest House Museum. Joel Chandler Harris, author of the Uncle Remus tales, lived in this rambling cottage in Atlanta's West End from 1881 until his death in 1908. Forty years later Walt Disney filmed *Song of the South,* based on Harris's stories, on the property. ✉️*1050 Ralph David Abernathy Blvd., West End* ☎️*404/753–7735* ⊕*www. wrensnestonline.com* 💲*$8* ⊙*Tues.–Sat. 10–2:30.*

④ Woodruff Park. This triangular park named for the city's great philanthropist, Robert W. Woodruff, the late Coca-Cola magnate, fills during lunchtime on weekdays with business executives, street preachers, university students, and homeless people. Chess games abound, and nearby sits a row of restaurants on Broad Street. ✉️*Bordered by Edgewood and Peachtree Sts., Downtown* ⊕*www.woodruffpark.com.*

SWEET AUBURN

Between 1890 and 1930, the historic Sweet Auburn district was Atlanta's most active and prosperous center of black business, entertainment, and political life. Following the Depression, the area went into an economic decline that lasted until the 1980s, when the residential area where civil rights leader Reverend Martin Luther King Jr. (1929–68) was born, raised, and later returned to live was declared a National Historic District.

TOP ATTRACTIONS

㉑ **African American Panoramic Experience (APEX).** The museum's quarterly exhibits chronicle the history of black people in America. Videos illustrate the history of Sweet Auburn, the name bestowed on Auburn Avenue by businessman John Wesley Dobbs, who fostered business development for African-Americans on this street. ✉*135 Auburn Ave., Sweet Auburn* ☎*404/521–2739* ⊕*www.apexmuseum.org* ✉*$4* ⊙*Tues.–Sat. 10–5, Sun. 1–5.*

> **HELP AT HAND**
>
> Need a helping hand—or simply directions—while exploring Downtown? Watch for a member of the **Atlanta Ambassador Force** (⊕*www.atlantadowntown.com/ambassador.asp*). The members, easily recognized by their pith helmets, are a traveler's best friend.

㉘ **Ebenezer Baptist Church.** A Gothic Revival–style building completed in 1922, the church came to be known as the spiritual center of the civil rights movement. Members of the King family, including the slain civil rights leader, preached at the church for three generations. The congregation itself now occupies the building across the street. ■TIP➔ A federally funded restoration project is underway at the original church. Call before visiting. ✉*407 Auburn Ave. NE, Sweet Auburn* ☎*404/688–7300* ✉*Free* ⊕*www.historicebenezer.org.*

Fodor's Choice
★

㉖ **Martin Luther King Jr. National Historic Site and Birth Home.** The modest Queen Anne–style residence is where Martin Luther King Jr. was born and raised. Besides items that belonged to the family, the house contains an outstanding multimedia exhibit focused on the civil rights movement. To sign up for guided tours, go to the **National Park Service Visitor Center** (✉*450 Auburn Ave., Sweet Auburn*), across the street from the Martin Luther King Jr. Center for Nonviolent Social Change. Parking is on the corner of John Wesley Dobbs Street and Boulevard, behind the visitor center. ■TIP➔ A limited number of visitors are allowed to tour the house each day. Advance reservations are not possible, so sign up early in the day. ✉*501 Auburn Ave., Sweet Auburn* ☎*404/331-6922* ⊕*www.nps.gov/malu* ✉*Free* ⊙*Tours: daily 10–5.*

Fodor's Choice
★

㉗ **Martin Luther King Jr. Center for Nonviolent Social Change.** The Martin Luther King Jr. National Historic District occupies several blocks on Auburn Avenue, a few blocks east of Peachtree Street in the black business and residential community of Sweet Auburn. Martin Luther King Jr. was born here in 1929; after his assassination in 1968, his widow, Coretta Scott King, established this center, which exhibits such personal items as King's Nobel Peace Prize, bible, and tape recorder, along with memorabilia and photos chronicling the civil rights movement. In the courtyard in front of Freedom Hall, on a circular brick pad in the middle of the rectangular Meditation Pool, is Dr. King's white-marble tomb; the inscription reads; FREE AT LAST, FREE AT LAST, THANK GOD

ALMIGHTY I'M FREE AT LAST. Nearby, an eternal flame burns. A chapel of all faiths sits at one end of the reflecting pool. Mrs. King, who passed away in 2006, is also entombed at the center. ⊠ *449 Auburn Ave., Sweet Auburn* ☎*404/526–8900* ⊕*www.thekingcenter.org* ⊒*Free* ⊙*Daily 9–5.*

WORTH NOTING

㉓ Atlanta Daily World Building. This simple two-story brick building, banded with a white frieze of lion heads, was constructed in the early 1900s. Since 1945 it has housed one of the nation's oldest black newspapers. Publisher M. Alexis Scott is the granddaughter of William A. Scott II, who founded the paper in 1928. ⊠*145 Auburn Ave., Sweet Auburn* ☎*404/659–1110* ⊕*www.atlantadailyworld.com.*

OFF THE BEATEN PATH

Herndon Home. Alonzo Herndon (1858–1927) emerged from slavery and founded both a chain of successful barbershops and the Atlanta Life Insurance Company. He traveled extensively and influenced the cultural life around Atlanta's traditionally black colleges. Alonzo's son, Norris, created a foundation to preserve the handsome Beaux-Arts home as a museum. ⊠*587 University Pl. NW, near Morris Brown College, Vine City* ☎*404/581–9813* ⊒*$5* ⊙*Tours Tues. and Thurs. 10–4, or by appointment on Sat.*

㉕ Auburn Avenue Research Library on African-American Culture and History. An extension of the Atlanta-Fulton Public Library, this unit houses a noncirculating collection of about 60,000 volumes dealing with topics of African-American interest. The archives contain art and artifacts, transcribed oral histories, and rare books, pamphlets, and periodicals. There are frequent special events, all free to the public. ⊠*101 Auburn Ave., Sweet Auburn* ☎*404/730–4001* ⊕*www.afplweb.com/aarl* ⊙*Mon.–Thurs. 10–8, Fri. and Sat. noon–6, Sun. 2–6.*

㉒ Baptist Student Union. This restored Victorian building adjacent to the Georgia State University campus once contained the Coca-Cola Company's first bottling plant. ⊠*125 Edgewood Ave., Sweet Auburn* ☎*404/659–8726.*

OFF THE BEATEN PATH

Oakland Cemetery. Established in 1850 in the Victorian style, Atlanta's oldest cemetery was designed to serve as a public park as well as a burial ground. Some of the 70,000 permanent residents include six governors, five Confederate generals, and 6,900 Confederate soldiers. Also here are novelist Margaret Mitchell and golfing great Bobby Jones. You can bring a picnic lunch or take a tour conducted by the Historic Oakland Foundation. The King Memorial MARTA station on the east–west line also serves the cemetery. ⊠*248 Oakland Ave., Grant Park* ☎*404/688–2107* ⊕*www.oaklandcemetery.com* ⊙*Tours: Mar.–Nov., Sat. at 10, 2, 6:30, Sun. at 2, 6:30. Weekday group tours by appointment.*

㉕ Odd Fellows Buildings. The Georgia Chapter of the Grand United Order of Odd Fellows was a trade and social organization for African-Americans. In 1912 the membership erected this handsome Romanesque Revival–style building. Terra-cotta figures adorn the splendid entrance.

Now handsomely restored, the building houses offices. ✉ *236 and 250 Auburn Ave., Sweet Auburn* ☎ *404/525–5027* ⏲ *Weekdays 9–5.*

24 **Sweet Auburn Curb Market.** The market, an institution on Edgewood Avenue since 1923, sells flowers, fruits, and vegetables, and a variety of meat—everything from fresh catfish to foot-long oxtails. Vendors also include an Italian deli, an organic coffee shop, and a smoothie shop. Individual stalls are run by their owners, making this a true public market. Don't miss the splendid totemic sculptures by Atlanta artist Carl Joe Williams. ✉ *209 Edgewood Ave., Sweet Auburn* ☎ *404/659–1665* 🌐 *www.sweetauburncurbmarket.com* ⏲ *Mon.–Sat. 8–6.*

MIDTOWN

Midtown Atlanta—north of Downtown and south of Buckhead—has earned its own place in the Atlanta landscape. Four-miles square, its skyline of gleaming office towers rivals that of Downtown. The renovated mansions and bungalows in its residential section have made it a city showcase. The newly expanded Woodruff Arts Center, the nation's largest performing- and visual-arts center, is here, as are 25 other arts and cultural venues. Piedmont Park and the Atlanta Botanical Garden are also here. The neighborhood is the hub for the city's sizeable gay community.

TOP ATTRACTIONS

34 **Atlanta Botanical Garden.** Occupying 30 acres inside Piedmont Park, the grounds contain acres of display gardens, including a 2-acre interactive children's garden; a hardwood forest with walking trails; the Fuqua Conservatory, which has unusual flora from tropical and desert climates; and the award-winning Fuqua Orchid Center, with a spectacular collection of tropical and high-elevation orchids. A variety of special exhibits take place throughout the year. ✉ *1345 Piedmont Ave., Midtown* ☎ *404/876–5859* 🌐 *www.atlantabotanicalgarden.org* 🎟 *$12* ⏲ *Apr.–Oct., Tues.–Sun. 9–7, Thurs. 9–10; Nov.–Mar., Tues.–Sun. 9–5.*

Fodor's Choice ★

29 **Bank of America Plaza Tower.** At 1,023 feet, this is the South's tallest building. The 1992 skyscraper's graceful birdcage roof is easily visible from the highway. The elegant marble central lobby is worth a glimpse. ✉ *600 Peachtree St. NE, Midtown* ☎ *404/607–4850* ⏲ *Mon.–Thurs. 8:30–4, Fri. 8:30–6.*

37 **Center for Puppetry Arts.** The largest puppetry organization in the country houses a museum where you can see more than 350 puppets from around the world. Make sure to check out the furry and funny creatures from Jim Henson's productions. Elaborate performances, which include original works and classics adapted for stage, are presented by professional puppeteers. In particular, the popular Christmas performance of *The Velveteen Rabbit* is a truly magical experience. Kids also love the create-a-puppet workshops. ✉ *1404 Spring St., at 18th St., Midtown* ☎ *404/873–3391* 🌐 *www.puppet.org* 🎟 *$16* ⏲ *Wed.–Sat. 9–5, Sun. 11–5.*

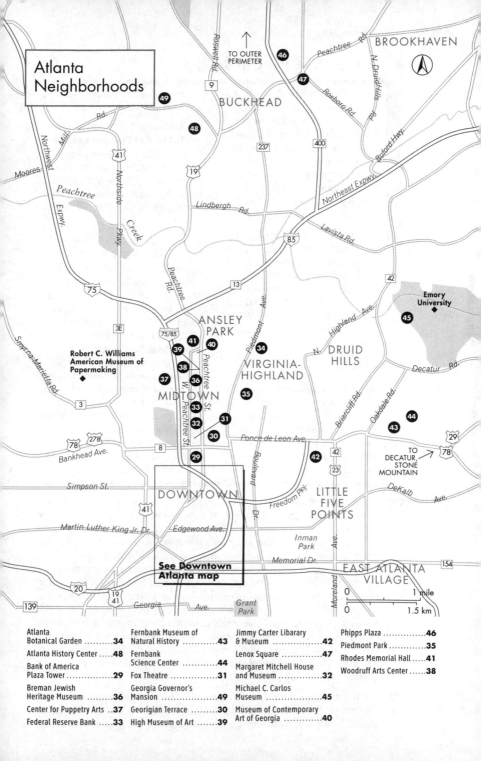

Atlanta Neighborhoods

BROOKHAVEN

TO OUTER PERIMETER

BUCKHEAD

Peachtree Rd.

N. Druid Hills Rd.

Roxboro Rd.

Northwest

Moores

Mill Rd.

Peachtree Expwy.

Northside Pkwy.

Creek

Lindbergh Rd.

Northeast Expwy.

Buford Hwy.

Lavista Rd.

Smyrna-Marietta Rd.

Robert C. Williams
American Museum of
Papermaking ◆

ANSLEY PARK

MIDTOWN

W. Peachtree St.

Peachtree St.

VIRGINIA-HIGHLAND

N. DRUID HILLS

N. Highland Ave.

Emory University ◆

Decatur Rd.

Briarcliff Rd.

Oakdale Rd.

Ponce de Leon Ave.

Boulevard

Bankhead Ave.

Simpson St.

DOWNTOWN

Martin Luther King Jr. Dr.

Edgewood Ave.

Freedom Pkwy.

TO DECATUR, STONE MOUNTAIN

LITTLE FIVE POINTS

DeKalb Ave.

Inman Park

Memorial Dr.

See Downtown
Atlanta map

EAST ATLANTA VILLAGE

Georgia Ave.

Grant Park

0   1 mile
0   1.5 km

In Search of the Old South

Gone With the Wind enthusiasts coming to Atlanta for the first time are often disappointed to discover that Scarlett O'Hara's beloved plantation, Tara, was no more real than Scarlett herself. But history buffs can find antebellum treasures in towns like Marietta and Kennesaw (about 20 mi northwest of Atlanta) and Roswell (about 23 mi north of Atlanta).

The **Marietta Museum of History** (⊠ *1 Depot St., Marietta* ☎ *770/794-5710* ⊕ *www.mariettahistory.org*), on the 2nd floor of the historic 1845 Kennesaw House, traces the history of Cobb County. The **Marietta Gone With the Wind Museum** (⊠ *18 Whitlock Ave.* ☎ *770/794-5576* ⊕ *www.mariettaga.gov/gwtw/default.aspx*) pays homage to the movie with props and costumes.

The 2,884-acre **Kennesaw Mountain National Battlefield** (⊠ *Old U.S. 41 and Stilesboro Rd., Kennesaw* ☎ *770/427-4686* ⊕ *www.nps.gov/kemo*) was the site for crucial battles in 1864. The National Park Service maintains 16 mi of well-used hiking trails. A small museum has uniforms, weapons, and other items from the era.

The fascinating **Southern Museum of Civil War and Locomotive History** (⊠ *2829 Cherokee St., Kennesaw* ☎ *770/427-2117* ⊕ *www.southernmuseum.org*) is the home of the General, a locomotive stolen by Union forces from the Confederates during the Civil War.

Barrington Hall (⊠ *535 Barrington Dr., Roswell* ☎ *770/640-3253* ⊕ *www.cvb.roswell.ga.us/barrington-hall.html*) is widely recognized as one of the nation's best examples of Greek Revival architecture. **Bulloch Hall** (⊠ *180 Bulloch Ave., Roswell* ☎ *770/640-3253* ⊕ *www.cvb. roswell.ga.us/bulloch-hall.html*) was the childhood home of Mittie Roosevelt, mother of President Teddy Roosevelt and grandmother of Eleanor Roosevelt. It has a nice museum shop. The original furniture of the Archibald Smith family fills **Smith Plantation** (⊠ *935 Alpharetta St., Roswell* ☎ *770/640-3253* ⊕ *www.cvb.roswell. ga.us/smith-plantation-home.html*).

OFF THE BEATEN PATH

East Atlanta Village. This earthy outpost of edgy-cool shops and restaurants evolved, beginning in 1996, thanks to a group of proprietors with dreams much bigger than their bank accounts: spurning the high rents of fancier parts of town, they set up businesses in this then-blighted but beautiful ruin of a neighborhood 4 mi southeast of downtown. Soon artists and hipsters came to soak up the ensuing creative atmosphere. East Atlanta, which is centered at Flat Shoals and Glenwood avenues, just southeast of Moreland Avenue at Interstate 20, has had its ups and downs, but after new streetscapes were installed in 2005, it's seeing a resurgence. The majestic homes have almost all been renovated, and what remains unrestored seems simply to romanticize the area's hint of "fashionable" danger. Check out the delightfully funky gift shop **Traders Neighborhood Store** (⊠ *485-B Flat Shoals Ave., East Atlanta* ☎ *404/522-3006*).

31 **Fodor's**Choice ★

Fox Theatre. One of a dwindling number of vintage movie palaces in the nation, the Fox was built in 1929 in a fabulous Moorish-Egyptian style. The interior's crowning glory is its ceiling, complete with moving clouds and twinkling stars above Alhambra-like minarets. Threatened by demolition in the 1970s, the Fox was saved from the wrecking ball by community activists. Today it's still a prime venue for musicals, rock concerts, dance performances, and film festivals. ■ TIP→ **Tours, conducted by Atlanta Preservation Center, should be scheduled in advance.** ⊠ *660 Peachtree St. NE, Midtown* ☎ *404/881–2100 for box office, 404/688–3353 for tours* ⊕ *www.foxtheatre.org* 🎫 *Tour: $10* 🕙 *Tour: Mon., Wed., and Thurs. at 10, Sat. at 10 and 11.*

13

39 ★ **High Museum of Art.** This museum's permanent collection includes 19th- and 20-century American works, including many by African-American artists. It also displays contemporary art. The building itself is a work of art; the American Institute of Architects listed the sleek structure, designed by Richard Meier, among the 10 best works of American architecture of the 1980s. An expansion designed by Renzo Piano, which opened in 2005, doubled the museum's size to 312,000 square feet with three new aluminum-paneled buildings. The roof features a system of 1,000 "light scoops" that filter light into the skyway galleries. A recent partnership with the Louvre Museum in Paris has brought hundreds of works from the Parisian museum's collection. ■ TIP→ **On the third Friday of every month, the museum is open for Friday Jazz until 10** PM. ⊠ *Woodruff Arts Center, 1280 Peachtree St., Midtown* ☎ *404/733– 4400, 404/733–4444 recorded information* ⊕ *www.high.org* 🎫 *$15* 🕙 *Tues., Wed., Fri., and Sat. 10–5, Thurs. 10–8, Sun. noon–5.*

32 **Margaret Mitchell House & Museum.** While she wrote her masterpiece, the author of *Gone With the Wind* lived in a turn-of-the-20th-century apartment house she called "the Dump." Volunteers gathered the funds necessary to restore the building in the early 1990s. To many Atlantans, the Margaret Mitchell House symbolizes the conflict between promoting the city's heritage and respecting its roots. The house has been struck by fire twice, in 1994 and 1996. Arson was strongly suspected but no on was ever caught. Some say the city's most famous writer should not be lauded, as her book includes stereotypes of African-Americans during the Civil War. However, her fans point out that she helped to fund medical-school scholarships to Morehouse College for scores of African-American students. The visitor center exhibits photographs, archival material, and personal possessions. ⊠ *990 Peachtree St., at Peachtree Pl., Midtown* ☎ *404/249–7015* ⊕ *www.gwtw.org* 🎫 *$12* 🕙 *Daily 9:30–5, Sun. 12–5.*

WORTH NOTING

36 **The William Breman Jewish Heritage Museum.** The history of the Jewish community in Atlanta is told through a permanent exhibit called "Creating Community." Other exhibits document the Holocaust and the immigrant experience in America. The facility—the largest archive of Georgia Jewish history—also contains a research library and an education center. ⊠ *1440 Spring St., Midtown* ☎ *678/222–3700* ⊕ *www. thebreman.org* 🎫 *$10* 🕙 *Mon.–Thurs. 10–5, Fri. 10–3, Sun. 1–5.*

33 **Federal Reserve Bank.** The exhibits within this grand monetary museum explain the story of money as a medium of exchange and the history of the U.S. banking system. Items displayed include rare coins, uncut sheets of money, and a gold bar. The self-guided tour includes a video called *The Fed Today*. ✉*1000 Peachtree St. NE, Midtown* ☎*404/498–8777* ⊕*www. frbatlanta.org* 🎫*Free* ⊗*Tours: Mon.–Fri., 9:30, 11, and 1.*

⓿ **Georgian Terrace.** The oldest hotel in the city of Atlanta, Georgian Terrace is known as the Grande Dame of the South. Built in 1911, the Beaux-Arts style hotel housed the stars of the film *Gone With the Wind* when it premiered in 1939 at the nearby Loew's Theater (now demolished). Stars of the Metropolitan Opera stayed at the hotel when the Met used to make its annual trek to Atlanta, and according to locals, Enrico Caruso routinely serenaded passersby from its balconies. President Calvin Coolidge is among the other dignitaries who slept here. Renovated in 1991, the building is now a luxury hotel. ✉*659 Peachtree St. NE, Midtown* ☎*404/897–1991* ⊕*www.thegeorgianterrace.com.*

> ## GARDEN SPOTS
>
> Atlantans love their gardens—and the chance to show them off. **Garden tours** are plentiful in spring, so check the *Atlanta Journal-Constitution* (⊕ www. ajc.com) for listings. December brings tours of the inside of many similar houses, all done up for the holidays.

⓿ **Museum of Contemporary Art of Georgia (MOCA GA Midtown).** Georgia's visual artists are showcased in small gallery, housed in an office-building lobby. More than 500 paintings, sculptures, and other works are part of the permanent collection. ✉*75 Bennett St., Midtown* ☎*404/881–1109* ⊕*www.mocaga.org* 🎫*Free* ⊗*Tues.–Sat. 10–5.*

⓿ ★ ☺ **Piedmont Park.** The city's outdoor recreation center, this park has been a popular destination since the late 19th century. Tennis courts, a swimming pool, a popular dog park and paths for walking, jogging, and rollerblading are part of the attraction, but many retreat to the park's great lawn for picnics with a smashing view of the Midtown skyline. ✉*Piedmont Ave. between 10th St. and Monroe Dr., Midtown* ⊕*www. piedmontpark.org.*

⓿ **Rhodes Memorial Hall.** This former residence, now headquarters of the **Georgia Trust for Historic Preservation,** is one of the finest works of Atlanta architect Willis F. Denny II. It was built at the northern edge of the city in 1904 for Amos Giles Rhodes, the wealthy founder of a Southern furniture chain. The stained-glass windows in the hall depict the rise and fall of the Confederacy. ✉*1516 Peachtree St., Midtown* ☎*404/881–9980* ⊕*www.georgiatrust.org* 🎫*$5; $8 for Sun. behind-the-scenes tour* ⊗*Tues.–Fri. 11–4, Sat. 10–2, Sun. noon–3.*

Robert C. Williams Paper Museum. More than 10,000 tools, machines, papers, and watermarks, plus more than 2,000 manuscripts and books, trace the history of papermaking from its origins. The museum is housed at the Georgia Institute of Technology's Institute of Paper Science and Technology. ✉*500 10th St. NW, Midtown* ☎*404/894–7840* ⊕*www.ipst.gatech.edu/amp* 🎫*Free* ⊗*Weekdays 9–5.*

③⑧ Woodruff Arts Center. The center includes the world-renowned **Atlanta Symphony Orchestra**, the **High Museum of Art**, and the **Alliance Theatre**, plus the nearby **14th Street Playhouse**, which has several repertory companies. Both theaters present contemporary dramas, classics, and frequent world premieres. ✉*1280 Peachtree St. NE, Midtown* ☎*404/733–4200* ⊕*www.woodruffcenter.org.*

BUCKHEAD

13

Atlanta's sprawl doesn't lend itself to walking between major neighborhoods, so take a car or MARTA to reach this neighborhood's fine dining and shopping. Finding a parking spot on the weekends and at night can be a real headache, and long waits are common in the hottest restaurants.

TOP ATTRACTIONS

④⑧ Atlanta History Center. Life in Atlanta, the South, and the Civil War are

FodorsChoice the focus of this fascinating museum. Displays are provocative, juxta-
★ posing *Gone With the Wind* romanticism with the grim reality of Ku Klux Klan racism. Located on 33 acres in the heart of Buckhead, this is one of the Southeast's largest history museums with a research library and archives that annually serve more than 10,000 patrons. Visit the elegant 1928 **Swan House** mansion and the plantation house that is part of **Tullie Smith Farm**. The Kenan Research Center houses traveling exhibitions and an extensive archival collection. Lunch is served at the Swan Coach House, which also has a gallery and a gift shop. ✉*130 W. Paces Ferry Rd. NW, Buckhead* ☎*404/814–4000* ⊕*www.atlantahistorycenter.com* 🎟*$15* ⊙*Mon.–Sat. 10–5:30, Sun. noon–5:30.*

WORTH NOTING

④⑨ Georgia Governor's Mansion. This 24,000-square-foot 1967 Greek Revival mansion contains 30 rooms with Federal-period antiques. It sits on 18 acres that originally belonged to the Robert Maddox family (no relation to Georgia governor Lester Maddox, who was its first occupant). ■TIP➔ **Reservations are necessary for parties of 10 or more.** ✉*391 W. Paces Ferry Rd. NW, Buckhead* ☎*404/261–1776* 🎟*Free* ⊙*Tours: Tues.–Thurs. 10–11:30.*

④⑦ Lenox Square. Anchored by Bloomingdale's, Neiman Marcus, and Macy's, this mall is a popular shopping destination. It offers more than 250 chain and specialty stores and several upscale restaurants, as well as an extensive food court. A MARTA station sits nearby. ✉*3393 Peachtree Rd., Buckhead* ☎*404/233–6767* ⊕*www.lenoxsquare.com.*

④⑥ Phipps Plaza. The luxury marble-floor mall is one of Atlanta's premier

THE BUC STOPS HERE

The Buc (☎*404/812-7433* ⊕*www.bucride.com*) is a free bus shuttle service linking two MARTA stations, the Buckhead station and the Lenox station during peak commute and lunchtime hours on weekdays. It also stops at major hotels in central Buckhead, making it an easy way to get to the subway. Route maps are available at all stops.

shopping areas, with nearly 100 upscale chain stores, including Nordstrom and Saks Fifth Avenue. It also includes a 14-screen movie theater. ✉ *3500 Peachtree Rd., Buckhead* ☎ *404/262–0992 or 800/810–7700* ⊕ *www.phippsplaza.com.*

VIRGINIA-HIGHLAND & THE EMORY AREA

Restaurants, art galleries, and boutiques are sprinkled throughout Virginia-Highland/Morningside, northeast of Midtown. Like Midtown, this residential area was down-at-the-heels in the 1970s. Reclaimed by writers, artists, and a few visionary developers, Virginia-Highland (as well as bordering Morningside) is a great place to explore. To the east, the Emory University area is studded with enviable mansions. Near the Emory University campus is Druid Hills, the location for the film *Driving Miss Daisy,* by local playwright Alfred Uhry. The neighborhood was designed by the firm of Frederick Law Olmsted, which also designed New York's Central Park.

MAIN ATTRACTIONS

㊾ Fernbank Museum of Natural History. One of the largest natural-history
★ museums south of the Smithsonian Institution in Washington, D.C., this
☾ museum offers 17 galleries and an on-site IMAX theater. The "Giants of the Mesozoic" exhibit includes an exact replica of the world's largest dinosaur. The café, with an exquisite view of the forest, serves great food. ✉ *767 Clifton Rd., Emory* ☎ *404/929–6300* ⊕ *www.fernbankmuseum.org* ▣ *$15* ⊘ *Museum Mon.–Sat. 10–5, Sun. noon–5; IMAX Mon.–Thurs. 10–5, Fri. 10–10, Sat. 10–5, Sun. noon–5.*

㊷ Jimmy Carter Presidential Library & Museum. This complex occupies the
★ site where Union General William T. Sherman orchestrated the Battle of Atlanta (1864). The museum and archives detail the political career of former president Jimmy Carter. The adjacent Carter Center, which is not open to the public, focuses on conflict resolution and human rights issues. Outside, the Japanese-style garden is a serene spot to unwind. Both Carter and former First Lady Rosalynn Carter maintain offices here. ✉ *441 Freedom Pkwy., Virginia-Highland* ☎ *404/865–7100* ⊕ *www.jimmycarterlibrary.org* ▣ *$8* ⊘ *Mon.–Sat. 9–4:45, Sun. noon–4:45.*

㊺ Michael C. Carlos Museum. Housing a permanent collection of more than
☾ 16,000 objects, this excellent museum designed by renowned American architect Michael Graves exhibits artifacts from Egypt, Greece, Rome, the Near East, the Americas, and Africa. European and American prints and drawings cover the Middle Ages through the 20th century. The gift shop sells rare art books, jewelry, and art-focused items for children. The museum's Caffé Antico is a good lunch spot. ✉ *Emory University, 571 S. Kilgo Circle, Emory* ☎ *404/727–4282* ▣ *$7* ⊕ *www.carlos.emory.edu* ⊘ *Tues.–Sat. 10–5, Sun. noon–5.*

ALSO WORTH SEEING

44 **Fernbank Science Center.** The museum, in the 65-acre Fernbank Forest, focuses on ecology, geology, and space exploration. In addition to the exhibit hall, there's an observatory open Thursday and Friday from 8 PM to 10:30 PM. ✉ *156 Heaton Park Dr., Emory* ☎ *678/874–7102* ⊕ *fsc.fernbank. edu* 🖼 *$4* ☉ *Mon.–Wed. 8:30–5, Thurs. and Fri. 8:30 AM–10 PM, Sat. 10–5, Sun. 1–5.*

13

OFF THE BEATEN PATH

Inman Park and Little Five Points. Since this neighborhood about 4 mi east of downtown was laid out by famous developer Joel Hurt in 1889, the area has faded and flourished a number of times, which explains the vast gaps in opulence evident in much of the architecture here. Huge, ornate Victorian mansions sit next to humble bungalows. But no matter the exact address or style of home—be it modest or massive—Inman Park now commands considerable cachet among all types, from young families to empty-nesters to gays and lesbians. Here you'll also find the delightfully countercultural Little Five Points section, with funky boutiques, neighborhood bars, and gritty music venues that draw urban hipsters and suburban gawkers alike. Check out the kooky wigs, rubber corsets, and water pipes at **Junkman's Daughter** (✉ *464 Moreland Ave. NE, Little Five Points* ☎ *404/577–3188*), a funky-junky department store. The **Clothing Warehouse** (✉ *420 Moreland Ave., Little Five Points* ☎ *404/524–5070*) is one of the many colorful vintage-clothing stores here. Hot fashion can be found at **Cherry Bomb** (✉ *1129 Euclid Ave., Little Five Points* ☎ *404/522–2662*). If all that shopping makes you hungry, grab a bite—try the salt and vinegar popcorn or the hush puppies with smoked bacon and applesauce—at **The Porter Beer Bar** (✉ *1156 Euclid Ave., Little Five Points* ☎ *404/223–0393*). **A Cappella Books** (✉ *484 Moreland Ave., Inman Park* ☎ *404/681–5128*) stocks new and out-of-print titles. And don't miss **Charis Books** (✉ *1189 Euclid Ave., Little Five Points* ☎ *404/524-0304*), the South's oldest and largest feminist bookstore.

OTHER AREA ATTRACTIONS

It's essential to drive to most of these venues, so plan your visits with Atlanta's notorious rush hours in mind.

Chattahoochee Nature Center. Birds and animals in their natural habitats may be seen from nature trails and a boardwalk winding through 124 acres of woodlands and wetlands. A gift shop, exhibits, birds-of-prey aviaries, and a picnic area are on the property. ✉ *9135 Willeo Rd., Roswell* ☎ *770/992–2055* ⊕ *www.chattnaturecenter.com* 🖼 *$5* ☉ *Mon.–Sat. 9–5, Sun. noon–5.*

Decatur Historical Courthouse. Known as the Old Courthouse on the Square, this charming building was constructed in 1898 and now houses the DeKalb History Center. It's in the midst of the shops and coffeehouses of Decatur's quaint main square. Free concerts are sometimes held in the gazebo behind the Old Courthouse. ■TIP➡ **Getting here is easy, as Decatur has its own stop on MARTA's east-west rail line.** ✉ *101 E. Court Sq., Ponce de Leon Ave., east 8 mi to Decatur Sq. at Clairmont Ave., Decatur* ☎ *404/373-1088* ⊕ *www.dekalbhistory.org* ✉ *Free* ⊙ *Weekdays 9–4.*

> ### THE NAME GAME
>
> Founded in 1837 by the Western & Atlantic Railroad, Atlanta has changed names several times. It was nicknamed Terminus, for its location at the end of the tracks. Marthasville was its first official name, in honor of the then-governor's daughter. It switched soon afterward to Atlanta, the feminine of Atlantic—another nod to the railroad.

ᶜ **Six Flags Over Georgia.** Georgia's major theme park with heart-stopping roller coasters, family rides, and water attractions (best saved for last so you won't be damp all day), is a child's ideal playground. The new Goliath is a giant among roller coasters—at 200 feet, it's the largest in the Southeast. The heart-clenching ride hits speeds of 70 mph. The park also has well-staged musical revues, concerts by top-name artists, and costumed characters such as the Justice League. ■TIP➡ **To get here, take MARTA's west line to the Hamilton Homes station and then hop aboard the Six Flags bus.** ✉ *I–20W at 275 Riverside Pkwy., Austell* ☎ *770/948–9290* ⊕ *www.sixflags.com* ✉ *$29.99* ⊙ *June–mid-Aug., open daily; mid-Aug.–Oct. and Mar.–May, open weekends; hrs vary.*

★ **Stone Mountain Park.** At this 3,200-acre state park you'll find the larg-
ᶜ est exposed granite outcropping on earth. The Confederate Memorial on the north face of the 825-foot-high mountain is the world's largest sculpture, measuring 90 feet by 190 feet. There are several ways to see the sculpture, including a cable car that lifts you to the mountaintop and a steam locomotive that chugs around the mountain's base. Summer nights are capped with the **Lasershow Spectacular,** an outdoor light display set to music and projected onto the side of Stone Mountain—attendance is a rite of passage for new Atlantans. There's also a wildlife preserve, an antebellum plantation, a swimming beach, two golf courses, a campground, a hotel, a resort, several restaurants, and two Civil War museums. Crossroads, an entertainment complex with an 1870s-Southern-town theme, offers costumed interpreters and a movie theater. The newest addition is Sky Hike, a family-friendly ropes course at 12 feet, 24 feet, or 40 feet high. ✉ *U.S. 78E, Stone Mountain Pkwy., exit 8, Stone Mountain* ☎ *770/498–5600* ⊕ *www. stonemountainpark.com* ✉ *$8 per car, $25 per adult for an Adventure Pass* ⊙ *Daily 6 AM–midnight.*

★ **Your DeKalb Farmers Market.** This sprawling warehouse store 9 mi east of Atlanta may not be a true farmers' market, but it's truly a market experience to remember. Rows of bins of produce from around the world are perhaps the biggest attraction: root vegetables from Africa, greens from Asia, wines from South America, cheeses from Europe. The store also has one of the largest seafood departments in the country (a few species still swimming) and sizable meat, deli, and wine sections. The reasonably priced cafeteria serves dishes ranging from lasagna to goat stew. ■TIP→ The market is accessible by MARTA bus from the Avondale rail station. ⊠*3000 E. Ponce de Leon Ave., Decatur* ☎*404/377–6400* ⊕*www.dekalbfarmersmarket.com* ⊘*Daily 9–9.*

WHERE TO EAT

13

This is a city known for its food; many a trip to Atlanta is planned around meals in its barbecue shacks, upscale diners, and chic urban eateries. Traditional Southern fare—including Cajun and creole, country-style and plantation cuisine, coastal and mountain dishes—thrives, as do Asian fusion, Peruvian tapas, creative vegan, and mouth-scorching Indian food. Catch the flavor of the South at breakfast and lunch in modest establishments that serve only these meals. Reserve evenings for culinary exploration, including some of the new restaurants that present traditional ingredients and dishes in fresh ways.

Many restaurants will accept you just as you are; dress codes are extremely rare in this casual city, except in the chicest of spots. While many restaurants accept reservations, some popular spots operate on a first-come, first-served basis on weekends. Waits at some hot dining locales can exceed an hour, especially if you arrive after 7 PM.

PRICES
Eating in Atlanta is surprisingly affordable, at least when compared to cities like New York and Chicago. Some of the pricier restaurants offer early-bird weeknight specials and prix-fixe menus. Ask when you call to make reservations.

A dining option that has become very popular in recent years is counter-service restaurants. These usually casual eateries require guests to place their order at a counter, which cuts staffing expenses. In general, the food quality remains quite high. Many local restaurant names operate under this system, including Fellini's Pizza, Figo, Little Azio, Tacqueria Del Sol, Willy's, and Moe's Southwest Grill.

WHAT IT COSTS					
	¢	$	$$	$$$	$$$$
Restaurant	under $10	$10-$14	$15–$19	$20–$24	over $24

Restaurant prices are for a main course at dinner, excluding sales tax of 6%–8%.

BEST BETS IN ATLANTA DINING

With hundreds of restaurants to choose from, how will you decide where to eat? Fodor's writers and editors have selected their favorite restaurants by price, cuisine, and experience in the Best Bets lists below. In the first column, Fodor's Choice properties represent the "best of the best" in every price category. You can also search by neighborhood for excellent eats—just peruse our reviews on the following pages.

FODOR'S CHOICE

Bacchanalia $$$$
The Dining Room $$$$
Joël $$$$
Madras Chettinaad $
MF Sushibar $$-$$$
Swallow at the Hollow $

Best by Price

BEST ¢

Fellini's Pizza
Flying Biscuit
Taqueria del Sol

BEST $

Madras Chettinaad
Swallow at the Hollow

BEST $$

MF Sushibar
Tamarind Seed

BEST $$$

Food 101
Hi Life Kitchen & Cocktails

BEST $$$$

Bacchanalia
The Dining Room
Joël

Best by Cuisine

AMERICAN

Food 101 $$$
Ted's Montana Grill $-$$

MEXICAN

Taqueria del Sol ¢-$
Zocalo $

SOUTHERN

Mary Mac's Tea Room $
Thelma's Kitchen ¢
Watershed $$-$$$

THAI

Spicy Basil $
Tamarind Seed $$

Best by Experience

BRUNCH

Babette's Cafe $$-$$$
Canoe $$$-$$$$
Flying Biscuit ¢-$
Gato Bizco ¢

HOT SPOTS

MF Sushibar $$-$$$
Shaun's $$$
Straits $$$

MOST ROMANTIC

Bacchanalia $$$$
Joël $$$$

BUSINESS DINING

City Grill $$$$
Ted's Montana Grill $-$$

Thrive $$$

OUTDOOR SEATING

Fellini's Pizza ¢
Fox Bros. Bar-B-Q $
JCT Kitchen & Bar $$-$$$

FREE WI-FI

The Earl ¢
Flying Biscuit ¢-$

PEOPLE WATCHING

Eclipse di Luna $$$
MF Sushibar $$-$$$
Straits $$-$$$

GRAND INTERIORS

Bacchanalia $$$$
City Grill $$$$
Joël $$$$
Park 75 $$$-$$$$

SPECIAL OCCASION

Bacchanalia $$$$
The Dining Room $$$$
Joël $$$$
Nam $-$$

DOWNTOWN

$$$$
SOUTHERN

✕**City Grill.** A posh power-lunch spot in Atlanta, City Grill has made the most of its grand location—at the top of a sweeping double marble staircase—in the elegantly renovated historic Hurt Building. Get a load of the hand-painted murals depicting a magical forest. An extensive wine list accompanies the menu, which includes a variety of hickory-grilled meats. Desserts range from peach cobbler to key lime parfait to Coca-Cola cake. ⊠*50 Hurt Plaza, Downtown* ☎*404/524–2489* ▱*AE, D, DC, MC, V* ⊘*Closed Sun. No lunch Sat.*

$–$$
AMERICAN
★

✕**Ted's Montana Grill.** The Ted in question is CNN founder Ted Turner, who has left a significant mark on this city. That's why Atlantans feel a sense of ownership for this chain specializing in bison meat. Chicken, beef, and salmon also play a role on the menu. Tin ceilings, a cheerful waitstaff, and mahogany paneling add to the comfortable feel. Ted himself is known to stop by this location a lot; he lives in the building's penthouse. ⊠*133 Luckie St., Downtown* ☎*404/521-9796* ⚄*Reservations not accepted* ▱*AE, D, DC, MC, V.*

$$$
ASIAN

✕**Thrive.** Locals know that Downtown typically isn't the best place to go for a high-class meal; this neighborhood is more the domain of lunchtime sandwich shops and other eateries that close when workers go home. But Thrive bucks the trend, bringing to Downtown a modern, Asian-inspired restaurant with sake by the bottle and specialty cocktails with flavors like lychee and pomegranate. Some of the sushi rolls flavor flash over substance, so try the salmon sashimi instead— it's fresh-tasting and simple—and the fried oysters on a bed of sea salt, which strikes the perfect balance between spicy, salty, and meaty. Finish off your meal with the truly sinful chocolate cake. ⊠*101 Marietta St., Downtown* ☎*404/389–1000* ▱*AE, D, DC, MC, V.*

$
SOUTHERN

✕**Thelma's Kitchen.** After losing her original location to make way for Centennial Olympic Park, Thelma Grundy moved her operation to Auburn Avenue. The new location—more cheerful than the earlier spot—serves favorites like okra pancakes, fried catfish, slaw, and macaroni and cheese, all of which are among the best in town. Thelma's desserts, including lemon cheese pound cake, sweet-potato pie, red velvet cake, and pecan pie, are worth the trip. ⊠*302 Auburn Ave., Sweet Auburn* ☎*404/688–5855* ⚄*Reservations not accepted* ▱*No credit cards* ⊘*Closed Sun. No dinner.*

MIDTOWN

$$$$
AMERICAN
Fodor'sChoice
★

✕**Bacchanalia.** Often called the city's best restaurant, Bacchanalia has been a special-occasion destination since it opened in Buckhead in 1993. Chef-owners Anne Quatrano and Clifford Harrison helped transform an industrial zone west of Midtown when they moved to their current location in 2000. The renovated warehouse, known for its 20-foot ceilings, is decorated in deep, inviting tones. The kitchen focuses on locally grown organic produce and seasonal ingredients. Items on the prix-fixe menu change frequently, but could include crab fritters, wood-grilled beef tenderloin, and warm chocolate cake. ⊠*1198 Howell Mill Rd.,*

13

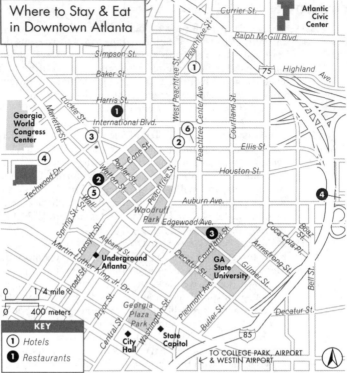

Where to Stay & Eat in Downtown Atlanta

KEY

① Hotels

❶ Restaurants

West Midtown 📞404/365–0410 ⏰*Reservations essential* ▭*AE, DC, MC, V* 🚫*Closed Sun.*

$ ✕**Doc Chey's Noodle House.** Claim
ASIAN your share of bench space at the crowded rows of tables, smile at the folks crammed in next to you, and then dig in to the big bowls of flavorful soups and rice dishes. Entrées such as noodles and eggplant with tomato-ginger sauce and Thai-style curry over rice come with your choice of chicken, tofu, shrimp, or salmon. ✉*1424 N. Highland Ave., Virginia-Highland* 📞*404/888–0777* ⏰*Reservations not accepted* ▭*AE, D, MC, V* ✉*1556 N. Decatur Rd., Emory* 📞*404/378–8188* 🚫*No lunch Sun.*

$$–$$$ ✕**JCT Kitchen & Bar.** This comfortable, airy restaurant—with pale wood,
SOUTHERN white, and silver accents—is a welcome addition to the now-bustling
★ Westside Urban Market, home to the city's famed Bacchanalia restaurant and counter-service favorites Tacqueria del Sol and Figo. JCT, a

---

WORD OF MOUTH

"We once spent a whole week in Atlanta and enjoyed the time up to the last minute. And we came back last year.... In the Quinones room at Bacchanalia, we were served the best meal we ever had in the USA. Spectacular! (But pricey, around $200 per person including wines.)"

—traveller1959

"farmstead bistro" with Southern flair, is a great place for a business-casual lunch or a dinner date. The deviled eggs are to die for, as are the perfectly crisp truffle-parmesan fries. Service is hit or miss. ⊠*1198 Howell Mill Rd., Suite 18, West Midtown* ☎*404/355–2252* ⚒*Reservations essential* ▤*AE, DC, MC, V* ✪*No lunch Sun.*

$ | ✗**Mary Mac's Tea Room.** Local celebrities and ordinary folks line up for
SOUTHERN | the country-fried steak, fried chicken, and fresh vegetables. Here, in the Southern tradition, waitresses will call you "honey" and pat your arm to assure you that everything's all right. It's a great way to experience Southern food and hospitality all at once. ⊠*224 Ponce de Leon Ave., Midtown* ☎*404/876–1800* ▤*AE, MC, V.*

$$–$$$ | ✗**MF Sushibar.** The "MF" stands for Magic Fingers, and once you try
JAPANESE | the spicy tuna tartar or the top-notch sushi rolls, you'll understand
Fodor's Choice | why. Whether you take a seat at the bar or at one of the tables, you're
★ | going to enjoy some of the best fish in town. Particularly popular is the Godzilla roll—shrimp tempura topped with smoked salmon, eel, and avocado. The ginger salad is a refreshing treat. ⊠*265 Ponce de Leon Ave., Midtown* ☎*404/815–8844* ▤*AE, D, DC, MC, V.*

$–$$ | ✗**Nam.** Brothers Alex and Chris Kinjo paid tribute to their mother's
VIETNAMESE | homeland with this stylish eatery. Gauzy curtains separate the tables,
★ | and sleek servers whisk by dressed in black and red. The crab-and-asparagus soup is packed with plenty of meat. Rich caramelized onions add mouthwatering depth to spicy clay-pot catfish. And the lemongrass tofu is just the right mix of crispy, spicy, and soft. ⊠*931 Monroe Dr., Suite A-101, Midtown* ☎*404/541–9997* ▤*AE, D, MC, V* ✪*No lunch Mon. or weekends.*

$$–$$$ | ✗**One Midtown Kitchen.** An unassuming warehouse entrance down a
AMERICAN | side street near Piedmont Park leads to a seductively lighted, industrial-chic restaurant. The dining room is energetic but can be loud; the back porch, on the other hand, is quieter and offers a serene view of the park and the city skyline. Small plates like the wood-roasted pizza are outstanding, as is the price-tiered wine list. Order a glass or bottle, choose several plates for the table, and share the red snapper crudo, the chicken satays, and the pancetta gnocchi with lady peas, preserved lemon butter, and quail egg. This eatery is owned by the Concentrics group, which also runs hot spots Two Urban Licks and Trois. ⊠*559 Dutch Valley Rd., Midtown* ☎*404/892–4111* ▤*AE, MC, V* ✪*No lunch.*

¢–$ | ✗**Osteria del Figo.** High-quality counter-service restaurants like this one
ITALIAN | have changed the face of Atlanta dining. In exchange for standing in a short line and paying up front, you get excellent food at a reasonable price. That's the concept behind this Italian eatery, which keeps it simple with pasta dishes, salads, and a few desserts. Try the bruschetta, which has a generous amount of fresh, juicy tomato chunks. Be sure to bring an appetite, as the portions are hefty. ⊠*1210 Howell Mill Rd., West Midtown* ☎*404/351–3700* ⚒*Reservations not accepted* ▤*MC, V.*

$$$–$$$$ | ✗**Park 75.** This swanky establishment inside the Four Seasons Hotel
AMERICAN | features a seasonal menu that includes standouts like Kobe short ribs and filet of Angus beef, served with fingerling potatoes. The six-course Sunday brunch—featuring dishes like egg-white frittata, chocolate

13

waffle, Indian-style samosas, passion-fruit sorbet, and truffled Brie de Meaux—is also popular. ⊠*Four Seasons Hotel, 75 14th St., Midtown* ☎*404/253–3840* ☱*AE, D, DC, MC, V* ⊗*No dinner Sun.*

$$–$$$
SOUTHERN
★

✕**South City Kitchen.** The culinary traditions of South Carolina inspire the dishes served at this cheerful restaurant. This is the place to get fried green tomatoes with goat cheese, she-crab soup, or buttermilk fried chicken. The chef prepares catfish in many intriguing ways. Crab hash, served with poached eggs and chive hollandaise, is a classic. Don't miss the chocolate pecan tart. Within walking distance of the Woodruff Arts Center, the spare, art-filled restaurant attracts a hip crowd. ⊠*1144 Crescent Ave., Midtown* ☎*404/873–7358* ☱*AE, DC, MC, V.*

$$–$$$
ASIAN

✕**Straits.** Ludacris, a former hometown radio personality turned acclaimed rapper and actor, adds restaurateur to his résumé with his co-ownership of this sleek Singaporean restaurant, in the spot formerly occupied by trendy Spice. The interior hasn't changed much—it's still dark, sexy and chic—but the menu is more inspired. Think lobster pad thai, crisp flatbread with curry dipping sauce, and house specialty chicken Kung Pao lollipops. The space also features the intimate Opium Lounge. ⊠*793 Juniper St., NE, Midtown* ☎*404-877-1283* ⌕*Reservations essential* ☱*AE, DC, MC, V.*

$$
THAI

✕**Tamarind Seed.** All that is good about Thai flavors—refreshing lime, spicy basil, hot peppers, cooling coconut, and smoky fish sauces—is even better at this standout known for excellent service. Favorite dishes include chicken with green curry and sea bass with three-flavor sauce. Meals are served in a simple, subdued, but elegant setting. ⊠*1197 Peachtree St. Midtown* ☎*404/873–4888* ☱*AE, MC, V* ⊗*No lunch Fri. and Sat.*

¢–$
MEXICAN
★

✕**Taqueria del Sol.** Don't let the long lines outside at this counter-service eatery discourage you. They move quickly, and you'll soon be rewarded with a full bar, a wide selection of tacos and enchiladas, unusual sides like spicy collard greens and jalapeño coleslaw, and a fabulous trio of salsas. Don't pass up the chunky guacamole. ⊠*1200-B Howell Mill Rd., West Midtown* ☎*404/352–5811* ⌕*Reservations not accepted* ☱*AE, MC, V* ⊗*Closed Sun. No dinner Mon.*

$$$–$$$$
ITALIAN

✕**Veni Vidi Vici.** Gleaming wood and sleek furnishings create the perfect environment for an indulgent Italian meal. Start with *piatti piccoli* (savory appetizers) before moving on to the mushroom risotto, linguine with white clam sauce, or osso buco. Gnocchi with Gorgonzola is another favorite, as are the fragrant rotisserie meats. ⊠*41 14th St., Midtown* ☎*404/875–8424* ☱*AE, D, DC, MC, V* ⊗*No lunch weekends.*

$
MEXICAN

✕**Zocalo.** People come to this restaurant's inviting open-air patio—warmed in the winter by giant heaters—for the city's best Mexican food. Order the guacamole, prepared tableside, as a starter before moving on to dishes like chicken breast simmered in a thick mole sauce or shrimp sautéed in chipotle salsa. The bar has an excellent selection of top-shelf tequilas. ■TIP➔There is also a location near the Decatur Courthouse on the square, and a new location will be opening near Grant Park. ⊠*187 10th St., Midtown* ☎*404/249-7576* ⌕*Reservations not accepted* ☱*AE, D, DC, MC, V.* ⌕*123 East Court Sq., Deca-*

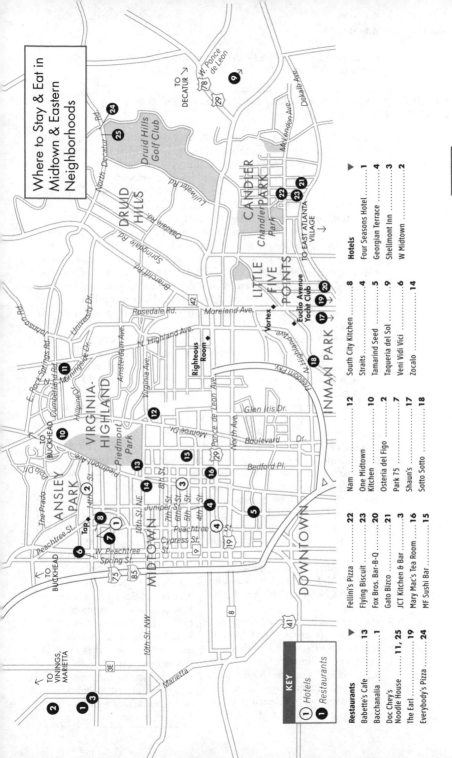

Where to Stay & Eat in Midtown & Eastern Neighborhoods

13

tur ☎404/270–9450 ᇂ*Reservations not accepted* ▤*AE, D, MC, V*
🕑*No lunch Sun.*

EMORY AREA, INMAN PARK, CANDLER PARK & EAST ATLANTA VILLAGE

$$–$$$
CONTINENTAL

✗**Babette's Cafe.** Sunny yellow walls and back-porch seating add to the homey charm of this renovated bungalow. The restaurant, which describes its cuisine as European country, offers such seasonal dishes as halibut with potato-leek gratin and beef tenderloin with Gorgonzola sauce. Loyal locals love the Sunday brunch. ✉*573 N. Highland Ave., Inman Park* ☎*404/523–9121* ▤*AE, D, DC, MC, V* 🕑*Closed Mon.*

¢
AMERICAN

✗**The Earl.** A scrappy yet delightful first stop on the East Atlanta bar scene, the Earl has a hearty menu of classic pub food, as well as a few entrées that are more innovative, such as jerk tuna. A favorite here is the "Greenie Meanie Chicken," a char-grilled chicken breast topped with roasted poblano peppers and salsa verde. Pass through to the stage and bar in the back, and you'll get a chance to see the country's best up-and-coming indie acts. ✉*488 Flat Shoals Ave., East Atlanta Village, East Atlanta* ☎*404/522–3950* ᇂ *Reservations not accepted* ▤*AE, D, MC, V.*

¢–$
PIZZA

✗**Everybody's Pizza.** With two locations in Atlanta, this restaurant and bar feels like a comfortable neighborhood joint. Traditional slices and pies are available, but what Everybody's is most known for is its pizza-crisps, with very thin crusts and inventive topping combos, like shrimp and artichoke or Thai chicken. The salads are a standout too—build your own with goat cheese, roasted peanuts, and the creamy Italian dressing. ✉*1593 N. Decatur Rd., Emory* ☎*404/377-7766* ᇂ*Reservations not accepted* ▤*AE, D, DC, MC, V.*

¢
PIZZA

✗**Fellini's Pizza.** This local chain, with seven parlors in the Atlanta area, puts together a mean 'za with a no-frills, order-at-the-counter approach. This particular location features a wide-open patio that looks out on the small and quirky commercial district in Candler Park. The slices are big and fresh. Some detractors say the stuff lacks flavor, but locals love the garlicky-good white pizza and the ham and pineapple combo. ✉*1634 McLendon Ave., Candler Park* ☎*404/687-9190* ▤*AE, D, DC, MC, V.*

¢–$
SOUTHERN
★

✗**Flying Biscuit.** There's a long wait on weekends at this spot famous for its biscuits served with cranberry-apple butter. Other huge hits include sausage made with free-range chicken and sage, and bean cakes with tomatillo salsa. Fancier dinners include roasted

CORN CRAZY

One defining ingredient in Southern cooking is corn—a Native American legacy. Parch the corn with lye, which swells the grains, and you get hominy. Grind the corn, white or yellow, and you have grits. Sift the grits, and you have cornmeal for making corn bread, fluffy spoon bread, corn pone, hoecakes, hush puppies, and johnnycake (or Native American "journey" cake). Ferment the grain, and you get corn whiskey, also known as white lightning or moonshine (and arguably like Southern grappa).

chicken and turkey meat loaf with pudge (mashed potatoes). There are also plenty of vegetarian options. Next door is a bakery serving biscuits to go, as well as freshly baked muffins and cookies. Though this restaurant and its sister location in Midtown were purchased by a local chain, the service and food haven't suffered. ✉*1655 McLendon Ave., Candler Park* ☎*404/687–8888* ⚏*Reservations not accepted* ☰*AE, MC, DC, V.*

$ ✗**Fox Bros. Bar-B-Q.** In a spot that has
BARBECUE seen its share of failed restaurants— anybody remember Gringo's?—this local barbecue business is making a go of it with specialties like brisket, pulled pork, fried pickles, fried mac-and-cheese, and an artery cloggin take on tater tots, served smothered in Brunswick stew and melted cheese. Try to get a seat on the patio, a great place to soak up sun and sip a cold beer. ✉*1238 Dekalb Ave., Candler Park* ☎*404/577–4030* ⚏*Reservations not accepted* ☰*AE, D, MC, V.*

¢ ✗**Gato Bizco.** Brunch is big business in Atlanta, and sometimes the waits
AMERICAN at the best spots can span an hour. But this little eatery, across the street from the always-packed Flying Biscuit, somehow always seems to have room on a stool or in one of the six booths. Sitting at the counter is like sitting in your friend's kitchen while she cooks; the work is done right there in front of you by the easygoing, tattooed staff. The food may take longer to arrive, but it's worth the wait for fluffy omelets and great pancakes—locals rave about the sweet-potato pancakes. Hours are limited—9 AM to 2:30 PM—so plan accordingly. ✉*1660 McLendon Ave., Candler Park* ☎*404/371–0889* ⚏*Reservations not accepted* ☰*MC, V* ☻*Closed Tues.*

$$$ ✗**Shaun's.** Local superstar chef Shaun Doty—formerly with MidCity
AMERICAN Cuisine, Mumbo Jumbo, and Table 1280—brings to this corner spot in residential Inman Park a small bistro that offers inventive seasonal cuisine. Standouts include melt-in-your-mouth Chinese pork buns and a Maryland-style crab cake that is all crab, no filler. The place is comfy-chic, with an inviting bar and butcher paper on the tables. Park on the street, or take MARTA to the Inman Park stop—it's right across the street. ✉*1029 Edgewood Ave., Inman Park* ☎*404/577–4358* ⚏*Reservations essential* ☰*AE, DC, MC, V* ☻*Closed Mon. and Tues.*

$$$$ ✗**Sotto Sotto.** This hot spot close to downtown has an adventurous take
ITALIAN on Italian cuisine. The former commercial space hops with young, hip patrons dining on wood-roasted duck breast with couscous, spaghetti with sun-dried mullet roe, and utterly perfect *panna cotta* (custard). ✉*313 N. Highland Ave., Inman Park* ☎*404/523–6678* ☰*AE, DC, MC, V* ☻*No lunch.*

> ## WORD OF MOUTH
>
> "I'm going to be in Atlanta for a couple of days. Where can I find great biscuits for breakfast? We are staying in Virginia Highland and we'll have a car." —sunny16
>
> "The Flying Biscuit, obviously! Either the original Candler Park or the Midtown location, but both are hugely popular, so expect a long wait. If you're too impatient to wait an hour or two, try the Silver Skillet on 14th Street or Java Jive on Ponce de Leon Avenue."
>
> —cherylj

BUCKHEAD

$$$–$$$$
CONTINENTAL
✕**Aria.** The rustic heartiness of the entrées here also appeals to the epicurean palate. Chef Gerry Klaskala's talent is best captured by his love of "slow foods"—braises, stews, roasts, and chops cooked over a rolltop French grill. This makes for very weighty plates, but Klaskala lovingly flavors every ounce. Pork shoulder is presented with a delicious balsamic reduction and Gorgonzola polenta. Don't miss renowned pastry chef Kathryn King's mouthwatering dessert menu, including Valrhona-chocolate-cream pie with Drambuie sauce. ✉*490 E. Paces Ferry Rd., Buckhead* ☎*404/233–7673* ⌖*Reservations essential* ▤*AE, D, DC, MC, V* ☉*Closed Sun. No lunch.*

$$$–$$$$
AMERICAN
✕**Canoe.** This popular spot on the bank of the Chattahoochee River overflows with appreciative patrons nearly all day. In nice weather the outdoor dining spaces allow the best view of the river. The restaurant has built a reputation based on such dishes as crispy pheasant croquettes with brown-butter sweet potatoes and huckleberry sauce; seared mountain trout with smoked salmon ravioli; and slow-roasted rabbit with wild mushroom ravioli and Swiss chard. Sunday brunch—with smoked-salmon eggs Benedict, housemade English muffins with citrus hollandaise, and other offerings—is superb. The restaurant's tagline, "tucked away, not far away," is no joke—call for directions. ✉*4199 Paces Ferry Rd. NW, Buckhead* ☎*770/432–2663* ▤*AE, D, DC, MC, V.*

$$
SOUTHERN
✕**Colonnade Restaurant.** For traditional Southern food—fried chicken, ham steak, and turkey with dressing—insiders head to Colonnade, a local institution since 1927 and a magnet for hip gay men and the elderly. The interior, with patterned carpeting and red banquettes, is a classic version of a 1950s restaurant. ✉*1879 Cheshire Bridge Rd., Buckhead* ☎*404/874–5642* ⌖*Reservations not accepted* ▤*No credit cards* ☉*No lunch Mon. and Tues.*

$$$$
CONTINENTAL
Fodor'sChoice
★
✕**The Dining Room.** Chef Arnaud Berthelier's prix-fixe menu includes dishes such as Four Story Hill Farm lamb, fried spinach and ricotta raviolis with apricot chutney, and crispy Wild John Dory "pavé," morel duxelle, wild asparagus, and chanterelle jus. The menu is served in an elegant dining room within the Ritz-Carlton featuring apple-green silk walls and floral upholstery with a slight Asian influence. The bronze sculpture that dominates the center of the room is a work by 18th-century French sculptor Paul Comolera, who helped create the Arc de Triomphe in Paris. ✉*Ritz-Carlton, Buckhead, 3434 Peachtree Rd. NE, Buckhead* ☎*404/237–2700* ⌖*Reservations essential. Jacket required* ▤*AE, D, DC, MC, V* ☉*Closed Sun. and Mon. No lunch.*

$$$
MEDITERRANEAN
✕**Eclipse di Luna.** This hot spot has captured the fancy of twentysomethings, who flock here on weekends. The lunch menu includes sandwiches and salads; evening fare consists of tapas such as *patatas bravas* (potatoes with olive oil and spicy sauce). The only real entrée is traditional paella: saffron-flavored rice overflowing with fresh seafood, chicken, and chorizo. A vegetarian version is available. The restaurant is tucked at the very end of the Miami Circle design center. ✉*764 Miami Circle, Buckhead* ☎*404/846–0449* ▤*AE, MC, V* ☉*No lunch Sun. or Mon.*

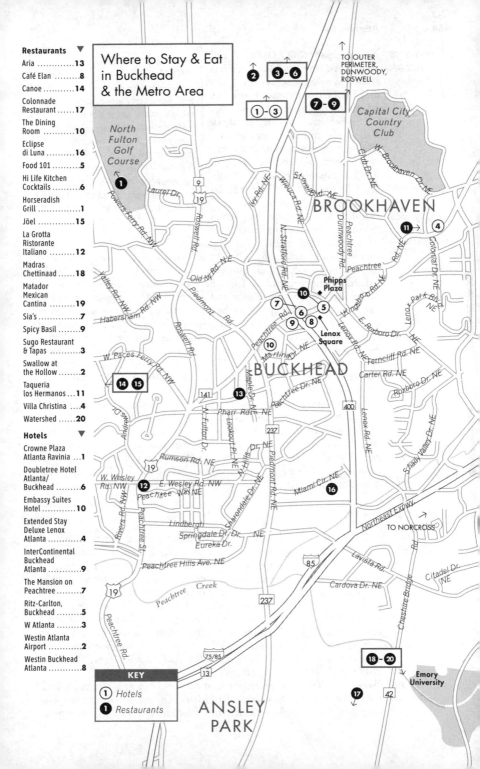

Restaurants ▼

Hotels ▼

Where to Stay & Eat in Buckhead & the Metro Area

North Fulton Golf Course

Capital City Country Club

BROOKHAVEN

Phipps Plaza

Lenox Square

BUCKHEAD

TO OUTER PERIMETER, DUNWOODY, ROSWELL

TO NORCROSS

TO Emory University

ANSLEY PARK

KEY

① Hotels

❶ Restaurants

$$$–$$$$
MODERN
SOUTHERN

✕**Horseradish Grill.** Once a red horse barn, this establishment has arched windows across the front that brighten the space. It may be a little noisy, but it's a good spot for authentic, if upscale, Southern dishes. The menu changes seasonally, with entrées ranging from venison stew to skillet-fried chicken. ✉*4320 Powers Ferry Rd., Buckhead* ☎*404/255–7277* ▭*AE, D, DC, MC, V* ⊘*No lunch Sat.*

> ### TEA: SWEET OR UNSWEET?
>
> Iced tea usually arrives at your table with the sugar already added. Needless to say, it's often very sweet. If you're unaccustomed to sweet tea, order a half-and-half—a blend of sweet and unsweet tea—before you move on to the real stuff. If you want a cup of hot tea, be specific.

$$$$
FRENCH
Fodor's Choice
★

✕**Joël.** When founder and James Beard Award–winning chef Joël Antunes decided to leave this elegant brasserie to work at New York City's Plaza Hotel, many a foodie worried that the French-inflected menu would go downhill. But non. Antunes remains a partner in the Atlanta enterprise, and chef Cyrille Holota now occupies the famed dream kitchen, an immaculate and roomy 5,000-square-foot space so vast its creation almost halved the restaurant's seating capacity. Holata does Joël proud. The tomato tart is the perfect mix of fresh vegetables and basil on a crispy cracker, and the truffle grits are so creamy they feel like custard. The atmosphere is romantic, making a visit feel even more special. ✉*3290 Northside Pkwy, Buckhead* ☎ *404/233–3500* ⌨*Reservations essential* ▭*AE, D, DC, MC, V* ⊘*No lunch Sat. Closed Sun.*

$$$–$$$$
ITALIAN

✕**La Grotta Ristorante Italiano.** Overlook the location in the ground level of a posh condominium—this place is a class act. The burgundy-and-cream interior is elegant, and the staff is excellent. Old northern Italian favorites such as prosciutto with grilled pears and mascarpone cheese and potato-and-herb gnocchi with a wild mushroom sauce are the core of the menu. ✉*2637 Peachtree Rd., Buckhead* ☎*404/231–1368* ⌨*Reservations essential* ▭*AE, D, DC, MC, V* ⊘*Closed Sun. No lunch.*

METRO ATLANTA

$$$$
AMERICAN
★

✕**Café Elan.** Located within the sprawling grounds of the Chateau Elan Winery and Resort, this cozy eatery offers more than just a great glass of wine from grapes grown on-site. The pasta frutti de mare is divine, chock-full of seafood and topped with a cream tomato sauce. Their salad of smoked grapes and fava beans with halloumi cheese and lemon thyme vinaigrette strikes the right balance between sweet and savory. After dinner, visit the wine market for a take-home bottle and vino-inspired gifts. The French country resort is also a great place to stay, with four championship golf courses, a teaching kitchen, ropes course, nature trails, and a spa. ✉*100 Rue Charlemagne, Braselton* ☎*800/233–9463* ▭*AE, MC, V.*

$$$
AMERICAN

✕**Food 101.** This restaurant north of Atlanta is a hit, given its contemporary twist on comfort food—Kobe beef brisket burrito with jalapeño lime slaw, for example, or buttermilk fried chicken with whipped potatoes, green beans, and slaw. Wine lovers come to sample from their 50 selections available by the glass. ⊠*4969 Roswell Rd., Sandy Springs* ☎*404/497–9700* ▭*AE, D, MC, V* ⊘*No lunch Sat.*

$$$–$$$$ ✕**Hi Life Kitchen & Cocktails.** This upscale-casual restaurant 20 mi north-
AMERICAN east of downtown Atlanta presents an eclectic menu of American favorites, with Asian-inspired appetizers like crab with sesame rick cakes, sweet soy and wasabi caviar, and American entrées like truffle honey-glazed lamb rack. It's a good alternative to Buckhead for those in the 'burbs ⊠*3380 Holcomb Bridge Rd., Norcross* ☎*770/409–0101* ▭*AE, DC, MC, V* ⊘*No lunch weekends, closed Sun.*

$ ✕**Madras Chettinaad.** The chef from beloved Madras Saravana Bhavan
INDIAN moved here after it closed, taking with him a loyal following. Favorites
Fodor's Choice include cheese *masala dosai* (lentil flour crepe with spiced potatoes),
★ mango *lassi (yogurt smoothie),* and *chat samosas* (vegetable turnovers topped with onions, chickpeas, crispy noodles, sweet and sour sauces, and cilantro). The service is fast and the restaurant is spacious, with big-screen televisions playing Bollywood music videos. There are meat dishes as well as many vegetarian options, and it's easy to get a table. ⊠*2201 Lawrenceville Hwy., Decatur* ☎*404/636–6614* ▭*AE, D, DC, MC, V.*

¢ ✕**Matador Mexican Cantina.** Recognized by *Atlanta Magazine* for its
MEXICAN inventive tacos like lobster, barbecue pulled pork, and tofu, the Mata-dor offers authentic Mexican fare. Enchiladas, *chiles poblanos* (chiles topped with cheese, egg, and beans), *camarones del inferno* (spicy shrimp), and fish tacos are good bets. The service isn't always stellar, but the low prices, good quality, and regular beer specials help make up for that. ⊠*350 Mead Rd., Decatur* ☎*404/377–0808* ▭*AE, MC, V.*

$$$–$$$$ ✕**Sia's.** "Creative American" is how this sleek suburban restaurant
AMERICAN describes its contemporary cuisine, which includes such entrées as pan-seared wild salmon and cranberry-grilled lamb chops. A cozy bar tucked away from the open circular dining room is a nice place to stop for drinks, too. ⊠*10305 Medlock Bridge Rd., Duluth* ☎*770/497–9727* ▭*AE, D, DC, MC, V* ⊘*Closed Sun. No lunch weekends.*

$ ✕**Spicy Basil.** The unappealing food photos on the restaurant's Web site
THAI and the long drive to a strip mall in the burbs might turn you off from
★ this casual eatery. But then you'd be missing out on some of the best Thai food in the Atlanta area. Start with the "bubble ball," a Thai-style taro and sweet corn fritter, and move on to a perfectly sweet, sour, and salty pad Thai. Though the food is great, it's not a date place—the booths and flat-screen televisions give it a sports-bar feel. ⊠*3675 Sat-ellite Blvd. , Duluth* ☎*770/232–2803* ▭*AE, MC, V.*

$–$$ ✕**Sugo Restaurant and Tapas.** This very romantic restaurant, part of a
ITALIAN small chain, has Spanish-red walls, flowing tapestries, and stone urns filled with fresh tomatoes and pasta. Try the pork tenderloin served caprese style with fresh mozzarella, basil, carmelized onions, mild Ital-ian sausage and crispy, long-stem artichokes. The dishes are derived from the Greek-Italian background of owner Federico Castellucci, the fourth generation to run this family-owned restaurant. ⊠*Clock Tower Place, 408 S. Atlanta St., Roswell* ☎*770/641–9131* ▭*AE, D, DC, MC, V.*

13

$ ✕**Swallow at the Hollow.** Bring your biggest appetite when visiting this
BARBECUE legendary barbecue restaurant and country music venue where every-
Fodor'sChoice thing is homemade, from the sausages to the pickles. Belly up to the
★ long picnic tables for some of the region's best ribs, smoked meats, and
cabin bread. There's even a delicious vegetarian option: the pit-cooked
portabello mushroom sandwich with smoked gouda and fried green
tomatoes. The place gets packed, so be prepared to wait on the homey
front porch. If you want to catch the music, call ahead for a reservation. ✉1072 Green St., Roswell ☎678/352–1975 ⟐Reservations
essential ▭AE, D, DC, MC, V ⊘Closed Mon. and Tues.

¢–$ ✕**Taqueria los Hermanos.** At this tiny storefront restaurant in a shopping
MEXICAN center, the Ballasteros brothers serve marinated pork tacos, delicate
chiles rellenos, and, occasionally, their mother's handmade tamales.
Don't leave without tasting the tres leches cake (cake soaked in three
milks—evaporated, sweetened, condensed—and cream). ✉Killian
Hills Crossing shopping center, 4760 Lawrenceville Hwy., Lilburn
☎678/380–3727 ▭AE, D, MC, V ✉4418 Hugh Howell Rd., Tucker
☎678/937–0660 ▭AE, D, MC, V.

$$$$ ✕**Villa Christina.** Look no farther for elegant Italian food with a twist.
ITALIAN You enter down a lighted path resplendent with gardens, a waterfall,
and a stone bridge. The dining room doubles as an art gallery, with two
murals depicting a glorious Tuscan landscape. Entrées include seared
wild striped sea bass on a bed of spinach, and grilled Tuscan veal chops
with a sweet-onion brûlée of Parma ham. The house specialty, seafood
cioppino, is a medley of succulent shellfish swimming in a saffron-
tomato stew. ✉4000 Summit Blvd., Dunwoody ☎404/303–0133
▭AE, D, DC, MC, V ⊘Closed Sun. No lunch Sat.

$$–$$$ ✕**Watershed.** Indigo Girl Emily Saliers and three of her friends launched
SOUTHERN this casual restaurant in a converted gas station. Chef Scott Peacock,
★ coauthor of The Gift of Southern Cooking, specializes in elegant takes
on classic Southern fare: the planet's best shrimp salad, homemade
pimento cheese with sharp cheddar, roasted or fried chicken, an outstanding chocolate cake, and Georgia pecan tart with a scrumptious
shortbread crust. Also a wine bar, Watershed sells wine both retail in
bottles and by the glass at the comfy bar. When she's not in the record-
ing studio, Saliers makes a fine sommelier and loves to talk about wine.
✉406 W. Ponce de Leon Ave., Decatur ☎404/378–4900 ▭AE, MC,
V ⊘No dinner Sun.

WHERE TO STAY

One of America's most popular convention destinations, Atlanta offers
plenty of variety in terms of lodgings. More than 76,000 rooms are
in metro Atlanta, with about 12,000 downtown, close to the Georgia
World Congress Center, Atlanta Civic Center, and Philips Arena. Other
clusters are in Buckhead, in the north Interstate 285 perimeter, and
around Hartsfield-Jackson Atlanta International Airport.

PRICES

Atlanta lodging facilities basically have two seasons: summer and convention (conventions are generally held year-round, though there are fewer in summer).

WHAT IT COSTS					
	¢	$	$$	$$$	$$$$
Hotel	under $100	$100–$150	$151–$200	$201–$250	over $250

Hotel prices are for two people in a standard double room in high season, excluding service charges and 6%–8% sales tax, plus a 7% bed tax.

13

DOWNTOWN

$$–$$$ Atlanta Marriott Marquis. Immense and coolly contemporary, the building seems to go up forever as you stand under the lobby's huge fabric sculpture that hangs from the skylighted roof 47 stories above. Guest rooms, which open onto this atrium, are decorated in dark greens and tans. Fresh flowers fill the major suites, two of which have grand pianos and ornamental fireplaces. You don't even have to walk outside to reach the Peachtree Center MARTA station; it's connected via an indoor walkway. **Pros:** great views; convenient access to MARTA. **Cons:** lobby noise can carry to the lower floors. ☒265 *Peachtree Center Ave., Downtown* ☎404/521–0000 *or* 888/855–5701 ⊕*www.marriott.com* ⇌*1,569 rooms, 94 suites* ♿*In-room: Internet, Wi-Fi. In-hotel: 4 restaurants, bars, pool, gym, Internet terminal, parking (paid), no-smoking rooms* ⊟*AE, D, DC, MC, V.*

> ### WORD OF MOUTH
>
> "Keep this in mind about staying at the Marriott Marquis downtown. You will not have to go outside your hotel to hop on the metro because it is connected to Peachtree Plaza. It is a big deal because July in Atlanta is hot and you can stay in the AC."
>
> —GoTravel

$$–$$$ Ellis Hotel. This renovated boutique hotel provides Southern hospitality in a restored 1913 historic landmark. Each of the rooms has pillow-top mattresses, LCD televisions, and Wi-Fi. The hotel has a number of unique features, like neckties on hand free of charge and a women's-only floor, which provides secure entry to its stylish rooms, which have in-room amenities such as curling and straightening irons and Spanx hosiery. The MARTA is across the street and top attractions are just 10 minutes away. **Pros:** 24-hour fitness and business centers; free in-room Wi-Fi. **Cons:** small rooms with considerable street noise; on-site restaurant closes at 10 PM; breakfast-only room service. ☒176 *Peachtree St. NW, Downtown* ☎404/523–5155 ⊕*www.ellishotel.com* ⇌*127 rooms, 13 suites* ♿*In-room: Internet, Wi-Fi. In-hotel: restaurant, room service, bar, gym, laundry service, public Wi-Fi, parking (paid), no-smoking rooms* ⊟*AE, D, DC, MC, V.*

$$–$$$ Glenn Hotel. This boutique hotel is a mix of New York sophistication and Miami sex appeal. The rooms are small, but a thoughtful renovation makes the best of the space. Glass walls between the oversize showers and the sleeping areas mean you won't miss a minute of the program on your plasma TV. The contemporary decor is sleek and sophisticated. **Pros:** new business center; complimentary Wi-Fi. **Cons:** dim lighting might be a bit dark for some guests. ✉*110 Marietta St. NW, Downtown* ☎*404/521–2250 or 866/404–5366* ⊕*www.glennhotel.com* ⥂*93 rooms, 16 suites* ♿*In-room: Internet, Wi-Fi. In-hotel: restaurant, bar, gym, parking (paid)* ▤*AE, D, DC, MC, V.*

$$$　　▢**Omni Hotel at CNN Center.** Adjacent to the home of the Cable News Network is this sleek two-towered hotel with an ultramodern marble lobby overlooking Centennial Olympic Park through floor-to-ceiling windows. Creams, browns, and rich red accents decorate the rooms and complement the mahogany furniture. The hotel is at MARTA's CNN Center station. **Pros:** convenient location for downtown tourists; easy access to MARTA. **Cons:** panhandlers likely outside. ✉*100 CNN Center, Downtown* ☎*404/659–0000 or 800/444–6664* ⊕*www. omnihotels.com* ⥂*1,036 rooms, 31 suites* ♿*In-room: Internet, Wi-Fi. In-hotel: 2 restaurants, bar, pool, gym, spa, public Internet, parking (paid), no-smoking rooms* ▤*AE, D, DC, MC, V.*

¢–$　　▢**Quality Hotel Downtown.** This quiet, older downtown hotel two blocks off Peachtree Street is priced reasonably for its location; this, along with the hotel's proximity to the Georgia World Congress Center and the AmericasMart complex, makes the hotel popular during conventions. Note that prices go up when conventions are in town. Sofas and a grand piano fill the marble lobby. **Pros:** good breakfast; convenient to downtown attractions; check-in starts at 10 AM. **Cons:** one elevator, so it can take a while to get to your floor; little in the way of amenities. ✉*89 Luckie St., Downtown* ☎*404/524–7991 or 888/729–7705* ⊕*www.qualityinn.com* ⥂*75 rooms* ♿*In-room: Internet, Wi-Fi. In-hotel: Internet terminal, parking (paid), no-smoking rooms* ▤*AE, D, DC, MC, V* ❢◉▮*BP.*

$$$–$$$$　　▢**Ritz-Carlton, Atlanta.** Traditional afternoon tea—served in the inti-
★ mate, sunken lounge beneath an 18th-century chandelier—sets the mood. Notice the 17th-century Flemish tapestry when you enter from Peachtree Street. All suites have flat-screen TVs. All rooms have bay-window views of the downtown skyline. The Atlanta Grill is one of downtown's few outdoor dining spots. It's opposite MARTA's Peachtree Center station. **Pros:** top-notch restaurant; ideal for doing business downtown. **Cons:** this part of the city shuts down after dusk. ✉*181 Peachtree St., Downtown* ☎*404/659–0400* ⊕*www.ritzcarlton.com* ⥂*422 rooms, 22 suites* ♿*In-room: Internet, Wi-Fi. In-hotel: restaurant, bar, gym, laundry service, Internet terminal, no-smoking rooms* ▤*AE, D, DC, MC, V.*

MIDTOWN

$$$$　　▢**Four Seasons Hotel.** From the lobby a sweeping staircase leads up to
★ Park 75, the hotel's chic dining establishment. Rose-hue marble creates a warm feeling in the public spaces and lounges. Amenities abound throughout: marble bathrooms with extra-large soaking tubs, lemon

or celadon color schemes, comfy mattresses, and brass chandeliers. The hotel prides itself on its immensely courteous staff—it's considered scandalous if a call to reception rings more than twice before it's answered. Stewards and other staff members are on hand the moment you need their help. **Pros:** staff is professional; dining options inside the hotel are quite good. **Cons:** fairly close to the action in Midtown, but you'll probably need to drive or take a cab to get to most of the bars, restaurants and clubs. ☒*75 14th St., Midtown* ☎*404/881–9898* ⊕*www.fourseasons.com* ⬫*226 rooms, 18 suites* ⌂*In-room: DVD, Internet, Wi-Fi. In-hotel: restaurant, bar, pool, gym, spa, Internet terminal, parking (paid), some pets allowed, no-smoking rooms* ▤*AE, D, DC, MC, V.*

$$-$$$ ⌹**Georgian Terrace.** Enrico Caruso and other stars of the Metropolitan Opera once lodged in this 1911 hotel across the street from the Fox Theatre. The fine hotel, which has always housed the rich and famous, is now on the National Register of Historic Places. The columned lobby is striking, and breathtaking terraces traverse the exterior, making it a popular venue for wedding receptions. All the suites are pastel and plush, providing adequate if not luxurious comfort. **Pros:** the front terrace is a great place for people-watching, and having a glass of wine before a show at the Fox. **Cons:** some rooms are a little bit old-fashioned and cramped. ☒*659 Peachtree St., Midtown* ☎*404/897–1991* ⊕*www.thegeorgianterrace.com* ⬫*308 rooms* ⌂*In-room: kitchen (some), Internet, Wi-Fi. In-hotel: restaurant, pool, gym, Internet terminal, parking (paid)* ▤*AE, D, MC, V.*

$$$-$$$$ ⌹**Shellmont Inn.** Designed in 1891 by architect Walter T. Downing, this distinctive lodging is on the National Register of Historic Places. The mansion, which is named for its recurring shell motif, has antique stained, leaded, and beveled glass, enhanced by artfully carved woodwork and charming stencils. Victorian-style antiques fill the guest rooms. **Pros:** homey touches like hand-painted stenciling in rooms; verandas overlook gardens and a Victorian fishpond. **Cons:** low-powered hair dryers in rooms; not ideal for people with disabilities. ☒*821 Piedmont Ave. NE, Midtown* ☎*404/872–9290* ⊕*www.shellmont. com* ⬫*5 rooms, 2 suites, 1 carriage house* ⌂*In-room: DVD, Internet, Wi-Fi* ▤*AE, D, DC, MC, V* ❢*BP.*

$$$$ ⌹**W Midtown.** A trip to this new, ultrachic hotel in Midtown feels less like Atlanta and more like New York City, with slick details and more black-suited security guards and velvet ropes than seems necessary. Still, it's a special experience to stay here—the rooms, in grays and purples, feature exquisitely comfortable beds, and the staff operates under a "whatever whenever" service philosophy. There's also an in-house Bliss Spa and Southeast Asian specialties at The Spice Market. If you want to feel like a VIP, skip Whiskey Park bar and look instead for the lounge hidden under the stairs. **Pros:** beautiful people, beautiful views; Manhattan-style chic. **Cons:** a bit self-consciously hip and elitist. ☒*188 14th St., Midtown* ☎*404/892–6000* ⊕*www.starwood-hotels.com* ⬫*433 rooms, 30 suites* ⌂*In-room: Internet, Wi-Fi. In-hotel: restaurant, bars, pool, Internet terminal, parking (paid), some pets allowed, no-smoking rooms* ▤*AE, D, DC, MC, V.*

BUCKHEAD & OUTER PERIMETER

$$ 🏨**Crowne Plaza Atlanta Ravinia.** If you're visiting one of the many businesses in Atlanta's Perimeter Center, about a 10-minute drive north of Buckhead, you can't beat the convenience of this hotel and conference center. A lushly landscaped atrium lobby echoes the surrounding woodlands. All rooms were refurbished in early 2006. **Pros:** walking paths behind the hotel; courteous check-in staff. **Cons:** not the place to stay if you want easy access to Atlanta and its attractions. ⊠*4355 Ashford-Dunwoody Rd., Dunwoody* ☎*770/395–7700* ⊕*www.crowneplaza. com* ⇌*473 rooms, 30 suites* &*In-room: Internet, Wi-Fi. In-hotel: 3 restaurants, bar, tennis court, pool, gym, laundry service, Internet terminal, parking (paid), no-smoking rooms* ⊟*AE, D, DC, MC, V.*

$–$$ 🏨**Doubletree Hotel Atlanta/Buckhead.** If the complimentary fresh-baked chocolate-chip cookies that welcome you don't convince you to stay here, maybe the excellent location, spacious rooms, and reasonable rates will. The hotel, which offers complimentary transportation within 3 mi, is adjacent to the Buckhead MARTA station. **Pros:** a warm welcome; comfortable beds. **Cons:** small bar; pay to park. ⊠*3342 Peachtree Rd., Buckhead* ☎*404/231–1234 or 800/222–8733* ⊕*www.doubletree.com* ⇌*230 rooms* &*In-room: Internet, Wi-Fi. In-hotel: restaurant, Internet terminal, parking (paid), no-smoking rooms* ⊟*AE, D, DC, MC, V.*

$–$$ 🏨**Embassy Suites Hotel.** Just blocks from the shopping meccas of Lenox Square and Phipps Plaza is this modern high-rise. There are several different kinds of suites—from deluxe units with amenities like wet bars to more basic sleeping-and-sitting-room combinations. All of the rooms open onto a sunny atrium that towers 16 stories above the lobby. Rates include afternoon cocktails. **Pros:** location convenient to major shopping destinations. **Cons:** no flat-screen television, and Internet is not free. ⊠*3285 Peachtree Rd., Buckhead* ☎*404/261–7733* ⊕*www. embassysuites.com* ⇌*316 suites* &*In-room: Internet, Wi-Fi. In-hotel: restaurant, pool, gym, parking (paid), no-smoking rooms* ⊟*AE, D, DC, MC, V* �BP.

$ 🏨**Extended Stay Deluxe Atlanta-Lenox.** The next-door grocery store is handy at this comfortable hotel with kitchenettes in the studio suites. Earthy tones contribute to the homey feel. The property is 1 mi north of Lenox Square and across the street from the Brookhaven MARTA station. **Pros:** convenient for travelers without cars. **Cons:** small rooms; not much ambience; noise from the nearby train. ⊠*3967 Peachtree Rd., Brookhaven* ☎*404/237–9100* ⊕*www.extendedstayhotels.com* ⇌*91 suites* &*In-room: kitchen, DVD, Wi-Fi. In-hotel: pool, gym, laundry service, some pets allowed, no-smoking rooms* ⊟*AE, D, DC, MC, V* ⊚modBP.

$$$–$$$$ 🏨**InterContinental Buckhead Atlanta.** Marble bathrooms with separate
★ soaking tubs and glass showers, 300-thread-count Egyptian-cotton linens, plush bathrobes and slippers, and twice-daily housekeeping are some of the highlights of the traditional-style rooms in this hotel, the flagship for the Atlanta-based InterContinental Hotels Group. Bar XO has outdoor terrace seating overlooking Peachtree Street. **Pros:** 24-hour fitness center; excellent French food at restaurant Pied du Cochon.

Cons: small spa. ✉ *3315 Peachtree Rd. NE, Buckhead* ☎ *404/946–9000* ⊕ *www.ichotelsgroup.com* ⬦ *400 rooms, 22 suites* ♿ *In-room: Internet, Wi-Fi. In-hotel: restaurant, bar, pool, gym, spa, Internet terminal, parking (paid), no-smoking rooms* ▤ *AE, D, DC, MC, V.*

$$$$
Fodor's Choice
★
▦ **The Mansion on Peachtree.** It's almost possible to forget you're in the middle of bustling Buckhead when you sit down with a book or a cocktail in the English garden at this new hotel and residences. The floral oasis, with benches and a shallow reflecting pool, is just one of the many luxuries available here. Set back from the busy street, the 42-story tower features a sophisticated spa, a full-sized fitness center and cozy seating areas decked out in soothing cream and brown tones. The expansive rooms feature several flat-screen televisions (including one that hides behind a painting, and another in the bathroom), a large soaking tub, and personal butler service. In-house eatery NEO is quiet and boasts impeccable service, but foodies are more excited about the soon-to-open Craft Atlanta, the latest venture from *Top Chef* judge and famed restaurateur Tom Colicchio. **Pros:** apartment-style living; delicious, fresh juices for breakfast at NEO; personalized service; relaxing spa. **Cons:** as of this writing, the indoor pool was not yet complete. ✉ *3376 Peachtree Rd., Buckhead* ☎ *404/995–7500* ⊕ *www.rwmansiononpeachtree.com* ⬦ *96 rooms, 31 suites, 45 residences* ♿ *In-room: Internet, Wi-Fi. In-hotel: restaurant, bar, gym, parking (fee)* ▤ *AE, D, DC, MC, V.*

$$$$
Fodor's Choice
★
▦ **Ritz-Carlton, Buckhead.** Decorated with 18th- and 19th-century antiques, this elegant hotel is a regular stopover for visiting celebrities. The richly paneled Lobby Lounge is a respite for shoppers from nearby Lenox Square and Phipps Plaza; afternoon tea and cocktails are popular. The Dining Room is one of the city's finest restaurants, and many of the area's top chefs have passed through its kitchen doors. The spacious guest rooms are furnished with traditional reproductions. The Club Level, with a separate lounge and concierge, showers you with everything from a bountiful continental breakfast in the morning to chocolates and cordials at night. The large gift shop, called the Boutique, sells everything from linens to luggage. As of this writing, a renovation was wrapping up, adding numerous guest rooms and six luxury suites. **Pros:** elegant; convenient to shopping; occasional celeb sightings. **Cons:** drab exterior doesn't seem very ritzy. ✉ *3434 Peachtree Rd. NE, Buckhead* ☎ *404/237–2700* ⊕ *www.ritzcarlton.com* ⬦ *453 rooms, incl. 58 suites, 6 luxury suites* ♿ *In-room: Internet, Wi-Fi. In-hotel: 3 restaurants, bar, pool, gym, spa, Internet terminal, parking (paid), no-smoking rooms* ▤ *AE, D, DC, MC, V.*

$$$–$$$$
★
▦ **W Atlanta.** This ultrachic property makes good on its promise to pamper business travelers. Its sage, blue, and cream "living room" is highlighted by candlestick chandeliers covered with glass domes. Guest rooms are sweepingly large and have all the comforts of home—assuming your home is a dazzling showcase furnished with impeccable taste. In your room you'll find a plush robe and a coffeemaker complete with the hotel's own brand of specialty coffee. **Pros:** chic lobby; bottled water offered upon arrival; car service to local shopping mall. **Cons:** parking fees; sometimes snooty staff. ✉ *111 Perimeter Center*

13

W, Dunwoody ☎770/396–6800 ⊕*www.whotels.com* ⇔*121 rooms,
154 suites* ♿*In-room: DVD, Internet, Wi-Fi. In-hotel: restaurant, bar,
pool, gym, Internet terminal, parking (paid), no-smoking rooms* ⊟*AE,
D, DC, MC, V.*

$$ 🏨**Westin Atlanta Airport.** Currently undergoing an $18 million renova-
tion, the first since 1996, this former airport pit stop it is being trans-
formed into a high-class accommodation, with some rooms that rival
any W Hotel. The 500 guest rooms, many of which are already com-
pleted, now feature Westin's signature "heavenly bed" along with a
flat-screen TV, Starbuck's Coffee, and beige, brown, and sage interiors.
The hotel's bar, lighting, and carpeting are also being updated, bright-
ened, and replaced. All work is expected to be complete by the end
of 2008. ■TIP➔**Several airlines are participating in the hotel's "bags"
program that, for $10, allows you to check your bags and receive a board-
ing pass from the hotel lobby. Pros:** incredibly convenient to the airport;
"bags" program saves time. **Cons:** not near any restaurants, cool neigh-
borhoods, or cultural attractions in Atlanta. ✉*4736 Best Rd., Airport*
☎*404/762-7676* ⊕*www.westin.com* ⇔*495 rooms* ♿*In-hotel: res-
taurant, pool, gym, Internet terminal* ⊟*AE, D, DC, MC, V*

$$$ 🏨**Westin Buckhead Atlanta.** Behind the chic glass-and-white-tile exte-
rior of this hotel overlooking Lenox Square is a chic interior. From the
sweeping two-level lobby to the rooms, the hotel offers a contemporary
but comfortable look. The decor focuses on natural colors—greens,
beiges, browns—accented by exotic foliage. The Palm restaurant is
noted for its steaks. **Pros:** the wonderful "heavenly bed"; plenty of restaurants nearby. **Cons:** small pool. ✉*3391 Peachtree Rd., Buckhead*
☎*404/365–0065* ⊕*www.westin.com/buckhead* ⇔*355 rooms, 10
suites* ♿*In-room: DVD (some), Internet, Wi-Fi. In-hotel: restaurant,
bar, pool, gym, Internet terminal, parking (paid), some pets allowed,
no-smoking rooms* ⊟*AE, D, DC, MC, V.*

NIGHTLIFE & THE ARTS

THE ARTS

For the most complete schedule of cultural events, check the weekly
"Access Atlanta" section of the *Atlanta Journal-Constitution or the*
city's lively and free alternative weekly, *Creative Loafing.* The *Atlanta
Daily World,* serving the African-American community, is also published weekly.

AtlanTIX Ticket Services (☎*404/588–9890* ⊕*www.atlantaperforms.com/
discount-tickets/atlantix-half-price.html*), at Underground Atlanta and
Lenox Square, sells half-price same-day tickets for performances as
well as half-price same-day and next-day tickets for cultural events.
Tickets are available Monday to Saturday 11 to 6, Sunday noon to 4.
Ticketmaster (☎*404/249–6400 or 800/326–4000* ⊕*www.ticketmaster.
com*) handles tickets for Fox Theatre, Atlanta Civic Center, Philips
Arena, and other venues.

CONCERTS

The **Atlanta Symphony Orchestra (ASO)** (☎404/733–5000 ⊕*www.atlantasymphony.org*), under the musical direction of Robert Spano, has 23 Grammy awards to its credit. It performs the fall–spring subscription series in the 1,800-seat Symphony Hall at Woodruff Arts Center. In summer the orchestra regularly plays with big-name popular and country artists in the outdoor Chastain Park Amphitheatre.

Emory University (✉*201 Dowman Dr., Emory* ☎404/727–6123 ⊕*www.emory.edu*), an idyllic campus surrounded by picturesque homes, has five major venues where internationally renowned artists perform.

Georgia State University (✉*Florence Kopleff Recital Hall, Peachtree Center Ave. and Gilmer St., Downtown* ☎404/651–4636 or 404/651–3676 ⊕*www.music.gsu.edu*) hosts concerts that are free and open to the public. The entrance is on Gilmer Street, and there's parking in the lot at the corner of Edgewood and Peachtree Center avenues.

DANCE

The **Atlanta Ballet** (✉*1400 W. Peachtree St., Midtown* ☎404/892–3303 or 404/873–5811 ⊕*www.atlantaballet.com*), founded in 1929, is the country's oldest continuously operating ballet company. It has been internationally recognized for its productions of classical and contemporary works. Artistic director John McFall has choreographed such dance greats as Mikhail Baryshnikov and Cynthia Gregory; only the third director in the company's history, McFall brings a constant stream of innovative ideas and vision to the group. Most performances, except for the annual *Nutcracker*, are held at the Cobb Energy Performing Arts Centre.

FESTIVALS

The **Atlanta Jazz Festival** (☎404/817–6815 ⊕*www.atlantafestivals.com*), held Memorial Day weekend, gathers the best local, national, and international musicians for free concerts at Atlanta's Piedmont Park.

The **National Black Arts Festival** (✉*659 Auburn Ave., Sweet Auburn* ☎404/730–7315 ⊕*www.nbaf.org*), celebrating literature, dance, visual arts, theater, film, and music in venues throughout the city, is held the third week in July. Maya Angelou, Cicely Tyson, Harry Belafonte, Spike Lee, Tito Puente, and Wynton Marsalis have appeared at past events. Admission to events varies.

OPERA

The **Atlanta Opera** (✉*1575 Northside Dr., Midtown* ☎404/881-8801 ⊕*www.atlantaopera.org*) now mounts its productions at the Cobb Energy Centre. Major roles are performed by national and international guest artists; the chorus and orchestra come from the local community.

13

PERFORMANCE VENUES

Boisfeuillet Jones Atlanta Civic Center (⊠*395 Piedmont Ave., Midtown* ☎*404/523–6275* ⊕*www.atlantaciviccenter.com*), christened after the improbably named Atlanta philanthropist, presents touring Broadway musicals, pop concerts, dance performances, and opera.

Chastain Park Amphitheatre (⊠*4469 Stella Dr. NW, Buckhead* ☎*404/ 233–2227 or 404/733–5000* ⊕*www.classicchastain.com*), home to Atlanta Symphony Orchestra's summer series and other pop concerts, feels more like an outdoor nightclub than a typical performance venue. Pack a picnic, bring a blanket if you've snagged some seats on the lawn, and prepare to listen to your favorite performers over the clink of dishes and the chatter of dinner conversation.

The **Coca-Cola Roxy** (⊠*3110 Roswell Rd., Buckhead* ☎*404/233–7699* ⊕*www.atlantamusicguide.com/the_roxy.htm*) was once a theater, so its sloped floors make for an ideal concert hall. Shows range from comedy to rock, jazz and hip-hop.

Ferst Center for the Performing Arts (⊠*349 Ferst Dr., Georgia Tech* ☎*404/894–9600* ⊕*www.ferstcenter.org*), at Georgia Institute of Technology, hosts performances that run the gamut from classical and jazz to dance and theater. There's ample free parking on weekends.

Fox Theatre (⊠*660 Peachtree St., Midtown* ☎*404/881–2100* ⊕*www. foxtheatre.org*), a dramatic faux-Moorish theater, is the principal venue for touring Broadway shows and national productions, as well as the home of the Atlanta Ballet.

Gwinnett Center and Arena (⊠*6400 Sugarloaf Pkwy., Duluth* ☎*770/813– 7500 or 800/224–6422* ⊕*www.gwinnettcenter.com*), 30 mi north of downtown Atlanta, houses the 702-seat performing-arts center and the 13,000-seat arena. The arena hosts national touring acts as well as conventions, outlet sales, and jewelry shows.

Lakewood Amphitheatre (⊠*2002 Lakewood Ave., Downtown* ☎*404/443–5000* ⊕*www.hob.com*), 4 mi south of downtown Atlanta, draws national popular music acts all summer. There's seating for up to 19,000 in reserved areas and on its sloped lawn.

Mable House Barnes Amphitheatre (⊠*5239 Floyd Rd., Mableton* ☎*770/819–7765* ⊕*mablehouseamphitheater.com*), a 2,200-seat venue 6 mi west of downtown Atlanta, stages classical, jazz, and country music.

With a seating capacity of 21,000, **Philips Arena** (⊠*1 Philips Dr., Downtown* ☎*404/878–3000* ⊕*www.philipsarena.com*) is the major venue downtown. In addition to hosting the biggest musical acts, it's also the home of the Atlanta Hawks and the Atlanta Thrashers. The Philips Arena MARTA station makes getting here a snap.

Rialto Center for the Performing Arts (⊠*80 Forsyth St. NW, Downtown* ☎*404/413–9849* ⊕*www.rialtocenter.org*), developed by Georgia State University in a beautifully renovated and restructured former movie theater, shows film, theater, and dance, as well as musical performances by local and international performers.

★ **Spivey Hall** (✉*2000 Clayton State Blvd., Morrow* ☎*678/466–4200* ⊕*www.spiveyhall.org*) is a gleaming, modern, acoustically magnificent performance center at Clayton State University, 15 mi south of Atlanta. The hall is considered one of the country's finest concert venues. Internationally renowned musicians perform everything from chamber music to jazz.

Tabernacle (✉*152 Luckie St., Downtown* ☎*404/659–9022* ⊕*www. tabernacleatl.com*) began its postchurch life as a House of Blues venue during the 1996 Olympics. Now it hosts top acts of all genres in an intimate setting. Seating is limited; the main floor of the former sanctuary is standing-room only. A tornado in 2008 caused some damage, but the resilient venue goes on.

Variety Playhouse (✉*1099 Euclid Ave., Little Five Points* ☎*404/524-7354* ⊕*www.variety-playhouse.com*), a former movie theater, is one of the cultural anchors of the hip Little Five Points neighborhood. Its denizens don't don fancy frocks to listen to rock, bluegrass and country, blues, reggae, folk, jazz, and pop.

Woodruff Arts Center (✉*1280 Peachtree St. NE, Midtown* ☎*404/733-4200* ⊕*www.woodruffcenter.org*) houses the Alliance Theatre and the Atlanta Symphony Orchestra.

THEATER

14th Street Playhouse (✉*173 14th St., Midtown* ☎*404/733–4750* ⊕*www.14thstplayhouse.org*) is part of the Woodruff Arts Center. Resident companies include Art Within, Atlanta Classical Theatre, and Theatre Gael. Musicals, plays, and sometimes opera are presented.

Actor's Express (✉*887 W. Marietta St. NW, Downtown* ☎*404/607-7469* ⊕*www.actors-express.com*), an acclaimed theater group, presents an eclectic selection of classic and cutting-edge productions in the 150-seat theater of the King Plow Arts Center, a stylish artists' complex hailed by local critics as a showplace of industrial chic.

Alliance Theatre (✉*1280 Peachtree St. NE, Midtown* ☎*404/733–5000* ⊕*www.alliancetheatre.org*), Atlanta's premier professional theater, presents everything from Shakespeare to the latest Broadway and off-Broadway hits. It's in the Woodruff Arts Center.

The **Atlanta Shakespeare Company** (✉*499 Peachtree St., Midtown* ☎*404/874–5299* ⊕*www.shakespearetavern.com*) stages plays by the Bard and his peers, as well as by contemporary dramatists, at the New American Shakespeare Tavern. Performances vary in quality but are always fun. The Elizabethan-style playhouse is a real tavern, so alcohol and pub-style food are available.

★ **Georgia Shakespeare** (✉*4484 Peachtree Rd. NE, Buckhead* ☎*404/264-0020* ⊕*www.gashakespeare.org*), a tradition since 1986, brings plays by the Bard and other enduring authors to the 509-seat Conant Performing Arts Center, on the campus of Oglethorpe University, from June to November.

Horizon Theatre Co (✉*1083 Austin Ave., Little Five Points* ☎*404/584–7450* ⊕*www.horizontheatre.com*), a professional troupe established in 1983, produces premieres of provocative and entertaining contemporary plays in its 175-seat theater.

NIGHTLIFE

Atlanta has long been known for having more bars than churches, and in the South that's an oddity. The pursuit of entertainment—from Midtown to Buckhead—is known as the "Peachtree shuffle." Atlanta's vibrant nightlife includes everything from coffeehouses to sports bars, from country line dancing to high-energy dance clubs.

BARS

You can't get a Budweiser or Coors at the **Brick Store Pub** (✉*125 E. Court Sq., Decatur* ☎*404/687–0990*), but you can choose from hundreds of other bottled and draft brews—including high-altitude beers—along with some very good burgers, salads, and sandwiches. The interior, particularly upstairs, is cavelike but comfortable.

East Andrews Cafe (✉*56 E. Andrews Dr., Suite 10., Buckhead* ☎*404/869–1090*) offers upscale food, signature martinis and live indie, '80s, and party music at the bar and at the upstairs music venue.

If you're looking for a spot to become a "regular," **Euclid Avenue Yacht Club** (✉*1136 Euclid Ave. NE, Little Five Points* ☎*404/688–2582*) is the kind of place where everybody knows your name. The cans of PBR and friendly staff make everyone from hipsters to motorcycle riders feel welcome.

The food's far from fantastic at **Manuel's Tavern** (✉*602 N. Highland Ave., Virginia-Highland* ☎*404/525–3447*), but it's still a local landmark and a favorite of left-leaning politicos and media gadflies. The crowd gathers around the wide-screen TVs when the Atlanta Braves play.

Righteous Room (✉*1051 Ponce De Leon Ave., Virginia-Highland* ☎*404/874–0939*) is tiny and nestled in between a movie theater and an Urban Outfitters store, but good things come in small packages: good grub (try the fried onion straws) and a jukebox with a moody playlist await.

TAP (✉*1180 Peachtree St., Midtown* ☎*404/347–2221*) is one of Atlanta's few great gastropubs, serving upscale food like their mahi sandwich and watercress and cornichon salad alongside a variety of specialty brews and wine. One of the best features here is the patio—typically populated with after-work execs and trendy Midtowners—which sits out on busy Peachtree Street and provides ample opportunity for people-watching.

Vortex (✉*438 Moreland Ave., Little Five Points* ☎*404/688–1828*) prides itself on being impolite—a look at the "rules" will show you they take no guff—but really it's a friendly bar with great burgers and fried zucchini. Just look for the huge skull, a landmark of Little Five Points, and you've found the front door.

COMEDY

In the Startime Entertainment complex in Roswell, 20 mi north of downtown Atlanta, is **Funny Farm** (✉*608 Holcomb Bridge Rd., Roswell* ☎*770/817–4242*). Admission usually ranges from $10 to $14.

Punchline (✉*280 Hilderbrand Dr., Balconies Shopping Center, Sandy Springs* ☎*404/252–5233*), the city's oldest comedy club, books major national acts. The small club is popular, so you need a reservation. Cover charges can be $20 for some acts, but it's usually worth it.

COUNTRY

The 44,000-square-foot **Cowboys Concert Hall** (✉*1750 N. Roberts Rd., Kennesaw* ☎*770/426–5006*) attracts national talent twice a month. On Thursday to Sunday, line-dancing and couple-dancing lessons bring out the crowds. The cover is $7—more if an unusually high-profile act is slated.

Billing itself as the nation's largest country-music dance club and concert hall, **Wild Bill's** (✉*2075 Market St., Duluth* ☎*678/473–1000*) has room for 5,000 dancin', drinkin', partyin' cowpokes. The cover is $8 to $10 most nights.

DANCE

El Bar (✉*939 Ponce de Leon Ave., Midtown* ☎*404/869–8484*) is called one of Atlanta's best-kept secrets. Located behind the El Myr restaurant on Ponce de Leon Avenue, this tightly packed dance room features live DJs, cold drinks and a refreshingly unpretentious clientele. It's open from 10 PM to 3 AM and closed Sunday, Monday, and Wednesday.

You may have heard of the infamous **Clermont Lounge** (✉*789 Ponce de Leon Ave., Midtown* ☎*404/874–4783*), which truly is a strip club but unlike any other—the women who rule the roost at this local landmark are older, sassier, and less concerned about personal appearance than your average exotic dancer. And really, they're just a sideshow on Saturday nights when the dance floor opens up and the DJ plays old-school disco, funk, pop and R&B. The well drinks are strong, the bathrooms are dirty, and the clientele is cool—all making for a textured and entertaining night out in Atlanta.

In the hopping Crescent Street entertainment district you'll find **Opera** (✉*1150B Peachtree St., Midtown* ☎*404/874–0428*), a sleek dance club with a theater-like main lounge, balcony VIP boxes, and banquettes with personal cocktail service. The outdoor area looks like it's straight out of South Beach, with private cabanas and bottle service. Parking in this area can be tricky—street parking often leads to break-ins—so be prepared to pay garage fees.

13

GAY & LESBIAN

Most of the city's many lesbian and gay clubs are in Midtown, but a few can be found in Buckhead and the suburbs. For up-to-the-minute information on the scene, pick up a free copy of *Southern Voice* (⊕*www.sovo.com*) throughout the city.

Blake's on the Park (✉*227 10th St., Midtown* ☎*404/892–5786*) is a favorite spot with weekly drag shows, a diverse crowd, and plenty of people-watching.

A fixture on the gay scene since 1978, **Bulldogs** (✉*893 Peachtree St., Midtown* ☎*404/872–3025*) is the place to hang out with friends or dance to hip-hop, house, or R&B. The cover is $3 to $5.

Burkhart's (✉*1492 Piedmont Rd., Suite F, Ansley Square Shopping Center, Midtown* ☎*404/872–4403*) caters to a mostly male clientele with pool, karaoke, and drag shows. It's more of a neighborhood hangout than a dance club.

LeBuzz (✉*585 Franklin Rd., Marietta* ☎*770/424–1337*) got new owners this year, and they're reinvigorating the place with contests and events like "Drag Idol" and the "Men of Playgirl" revue from Las Vegas. Cover charges vary.

My Sister's Room (✉*1271 Glenwood Ave., East Atlanta* ☎*770/424–1337*), a lesbian club formerly located in Decatur, is now located in East Atlanta and bills itself as the city's "most diverse ladies' bar," with hip-hop music, DJs and karaoke.

New Order (✉*1544 Piedmont Rd., Ansley Mall, Midtown* ☎*404/874–8247*) has been around since the 1970s and attracts a slightly older male demographic for open mike nights, free pool on Tuesdays, and an overall relaxed atmosphere.

★ **Mary's** (✉*1287 Glenwood Ave., East Atlanta* ☎*404/624–4411*) is often mentioned as one of the best gay bars in Atlanta, known for hosting "Project Runway" viewing parties and a karaoke night they call "Mary-oke."

Woofs (✉*2425 Piedmont Rd., Midtown* ☎*404/869-0112*) is Atlanta's first and only gay sports bar, with sports on 25 televisions, pool, darts, and Internet access.

JAZZ & BLUES

Blind Willie's (✉*828 N. Highland Ave., Virginia-Highland* ☎*404/873–2583*) showcases New Orleans and Chicago blues groups. Cajun and zydeco are also on the agenda from time to time. The name honors Blind Willie McTell, a native of Thomson, Georgia; his original compositions include "Statesboro Blues," made popular by the Georgia–based Allman Brothers. Cover charges run $3 to $10.

Churchill Grounds (✉*660 Peachtree St., Midtown* ☎*404/876–3030*) celebrates jazz with weekly jam sessions and great local and national acts. Cover charges typically range from $5 to $15.

Resembling a ship, **Dante's Down the Hatch** (✉ *3380 Peachtree Rd., Buckhead* ☎*404/266–1600*) is as popular for its music as it is for its sultry sensibility. Most nights music is provided by a jazz trio, which conjures silky-smooth tunes.

Sambuca (✉ *3102 Piedmont Rd., Buckhead* ☎*404/237–5299*), a lively bar with good blues and jazz music, attracts a young crowd.

ROCK

10 High Club (✉ *816 N. Highland Ave., Virginia-Highland* ☎*404/873–3607*), a brick-walled space in the basement of the Dark Horse Tavern, hosts local and regional bands that are guaranteed to be loud. ■ **TIP→** You can rock out to heavy-metal karaoke with the live band Metalsome backing you up a few nights a week. Covers rarely exceed $10.

Eddie's Attic (✉ *515B N. McDonough St., Decatur* ☎*404/377–4976*) is a good spot for catching local and some national rock, folk, and country-music acts. It has a full bar and restaurant and is near the Decatur MARTA station. Cover charges range from $5 to $20.

Lenny's Bar and Grill (✉ *486 Decatur St., Cabbagetown* ☎*404/577–7721*) is a dingy, no-frills hipster haven sometimes referred to as the CBGBs of Atlanta (if CBGBs even existed in New York City anymore, which it doesn't). You'll often see members of the women's roller-derby team and local rockers at the bar while well-known indie bands thrash on stage. Lenny's also hosts the annual Corndogorama, a summertime music festival that, yes, features corn dogs. Cover charges vary.

Smith's Olde Bar (✉ *1578 Piedmont Ave., Midtown* ☎*404/875–1522*) schedules different kinds of talent, both local and regional, in its acoustically fine performance space. Food is available in the downstairs restaurant. Covers vary depending on the act, but are usually $5 to $15.

★ **Star Community Bar** (✉ *437 Moreland Ave., Little Five Points* ☎*404/681–9018*) is highly recommended for those who enjoy grunge and rockabilly. Bands play almost nightly, with covers of $5 to $8, depending on the act. The bar used to be a bank—the Elvis shrine in the vault must be seen to be believed.

SPORTS & THE OUTDOORS

At almost any time of the year, in parks, private clubs, and neighborhoods throughout the city, you'll find Atlantans pursuing everything from tennis to soccer to rollerblading. The magazine *Atlanta Sports & Fitness* (☎*404/843–2257* ⊕*www.atlantasportsmag.com*), available free at many health clubs and sports and outdoors stores, is a good link to Atlanta's athletic community.

BASEBALL

Atlanta's most beloved team, Major League Baseball's **Atlanta Braves** (✉ *755 Hank Aaron Dr., Downtown* ☎*404/522–7630* ⊕*braves.mlb. com*), play in Turner Field, formerly the Olympic Stadium.

BASKETBALL

The **Atlanta Hawks** (⌗*1 Philips Dr., Downtown* ☏*404/878–3800* ⊕*www.nba.com/hawks*) play downtown in Philips Arena.

BIKING

Closed to traffic, **Piedmont Park** (⌗*Piedmont Ave. between 10th St. and Monroe Ave., Midtown* ⊕*www.piedmontpark.org*) is popular for biking, running, dog-walking, and other recreational activities.

Connecting Atlanta with the Alabama state line, the **Silver Comet Trail** (☏*404/875–7284* ⊕*www.pathfoundation.org*) is very popular with bikers. The trail is asphalt and concrete.

Skate Escape (⌗*1086 Piedmont Ave., across from Piedmont Park, Midtown* ☏*404/892–1292*) rents and sells bikes and in-line skates.

Part of the Atlanta–DeKalb trail system, the **Stone Mountain/Atlanta Greenway Trail** (☏*404/875–7284* ⊕*www.pathfoundation.org*) is a mostly off-road paved path that follows Ponce de Leon Avenue east of the city into Stone Mountain Park. The best place to start the 17-mi trek is the Jimmy Carter Presidential Library & Museum.

FOOTBALL

The **Atlanta Falcons** (⌗*1 Georgia Dome Dr., Downtown* ☏*404/223–8000* ⊕*www.atlantafalcons.com*) play at the Georgia Dome. In July and August, training camp is held in Flowery Branch, about 40 mi north of Atlanta. There's no charge to watch a practice session.

Georgia Force (⌗*Philips Arena, 1 Philips Dr., Downtown* ☏*404/223–8000* ⊕*www.georgiaforce.com*) is part of the Arena Football League, whose season runs February to May.

GOLF

Golf is enormously popular here, as the numerous courses attest.

Bobby Jones Golf Course. Named after the famed golfer and Atlanta native and occupying a portion of the site of the Civil War's Battle of Peachtree Creek, this is the only public course within sight of downtown Atlanta. Despite having some of the city's worst fairways and greens, the immensely popular course is always crowded. ⌗*384 Woodward Way, Buckhead* ☏*404/355–1009* ⚑*18 holes. 6455 yds. Par 71. Green Fee: $36/$39.* ⌔*Facilities: Driving range, putting green, pitching area, golf carts, pull carts, rental clubs, pro-shop, golf academy/lessons, restaurant, bar.*

North Fulton Golf Course. This course has one of the best layouts in the area. It's at Chastain Park, within the Interstate 285 perimeter. ⌗*216 W. Wieuca Rd., Buckhead* ☏*404/255–0723* ⚑*18 holes. 6570 yds. Par 71. Green Fee: $36/$40.* ⌔*Facilities: golf carts, rental clubs, golf academy/lessons.*

Stone Mountain Golf Club. Stone Mountian has two courses: Stonemont and Lakemont. Stonemont, with several challenging and scenic holes, is the better of the two. ⌗*1145 Stonewall Jackson Dr., Stone Mountain* ☏*770/465–3272* ⊕*www.stonemountaingolf.com* ⚑*18 holes. 6837* *yds. Par 70. Green Fee: $49/$64. ☞Facilities: Driving range, putting green, golf carts, pull carts, rental clubs, pro-shop, golf academy/lessons, restaurant, bar.*

HOCKEY

Their name sounds tough, but the National Hockey League's **Atlanta Thrashers** (✉*1 Philips Dr., Downtown* ☎*404/878–3300* ⊕*atlantathrashers.com*) are named for the state bird, the brown thrasher. They play downtown in Philips Arena.

13

The **Gwinnett Gladiators** (✉*Arena at Gwinnett Center, 6400 Sugarloaf Pkwy., Duluth* ☎*770/497–5100* ⊕*gwinnettgladiators.com*), a farm team for the Atlanta Thrashers, play in the East Coast Hockey League. Games are played October to April.

RUNNING

Check the **Atlanta Track Club's** Web site (⊕*www.atlantatrackclub.org*) for weekly Atlanta area group runs.

Chattahoochee National Recreation Area (✉*1978 Island Ford Pkwy.* ☎*678/538–1200*) contains different parcels of land that lie in 16 separate units spread along the banks of the Chattahoochee River, much of which has been protected from development. The area is crisscrossed by 70 mi of trails.

The longest running path in **Piedmont Park** (✉*Piedmont Ave. between 10th St. and Monroe Ave., Midtown* ⊕*www.piedmontpark.org*) is the Park Loop, which circles the park in 1.68 miles.

TENNIS

Bitsy Grant Tennis Center (✉*2125 Northside Dr., Buckhead* ☎*404/609–7193*), named for one of Atlanta's best-known players, is the area's best public facility. There are 13 clay courts (six of which are lighted) and 10 lighted hard courts. Before 6 PM it costs $3 per hour for the hard courts and $6 for the clay courts. After 6 PM the prices bump up to $5 and $6.25.

Piedmont Park (✉*400 Park Dr., Midtown* ☎*404/853–3461*) has 12 lighted hard courts. Access the tennis center from Park Drive off Monroe Drive; even though the sign says DO NOT ENTER, the security guard will show you the parking lot. Hours are weekdays 10 to 9, Saturday 9 to 6, and Sunday 10 to 6. The cost for out-of-towners is $3 per hour before 6 and $3.50 after 6.

SHOPPING

Atlanta's department stores, specialty shops, indoor malls, and antiques markets draw shoppers from across the Southeast. Most stores are open Monday through Saturday 10 to 9, Sunday noon to 6. The sales tax is 7% in the city of Atlanta and Fulton County and 6%–7% in the suburbs.

SHOPPING NEIGHBORHOODS

Nostalgic and cutting-edge at the same time, **Atlantic Station** was built to look like it's been around for a while. Actually, this combo of living, working, and recreational spaces opened in 2005. It covers about 10 square blocks, clustered around a green space known as Central Park. Retailers range from IKEA and Dillard's to Banana Republic and Z Gallerie. It's easy to reach by car, but is also accessible by free shuttle buses from the Arts Center MARTA station. An on-site concierge is happy to help you find your way around or make dinner reservations at the more than a dozen restaurants. ⊠*1380 Atlantic Dr.* ☎*404/685–1841* ⊕*www.atlanticstation.com.*

Buckhead, a commercial district with many specialty shops and strip malls, is no minor shopping destination. Boutiques, gift shops, and some fine restaurants line East and West Paces Ferry roads, Pharr Road, East Shadowlawn Avenue, and East Andrews Drive. Cates Center has similar stores. Others are on Irby Avenue and Paces Ferry Place. And soon what once was the thriving entertainment district will become, according to its developers, the "Rodeo Drive of the South."

Decatur Square, a quaint town quad with a sophisticated, artistic vibe, is teeming with interesting specialty shops and delectable coffeehouses and cafés. Lively downtown Decatur, 8 mi east of Midtown Atlanta, is one of the metro area's favorite spots for sidewalk strolling and window-shopping.

Little Five Points attracts "junking" addicts who find happiness in Atlanta's version of Greenwich Village. There are vintage-clothing emporiums, used record and bookshops, and some stores that defy description.

The town of **Marietta,** about 20 mi northwest of downtown Atlanta, is home to a charming town square. The surrounding streets offer dozens of antiques shops and other shopping opportunities.

Quaint **Roswell,** about 23 mi north of Atlanta, is a great place to shop for antiques, visit art galleries, and enjoy outstanding restaurants.

Virginia-Highland is a wonderful urban neighborhood for window-shopping, thanks to its boutiques, antiques shops, and art galleries. Parking can be tricky in the evening, so be prepared to park down a side street and walk a few blocks.

MALLS

Lenox Square (⊠*3393 Peachtree Rd., Buckhead* ☎*404/233–6767*), one of Atlanta's oldest and most popular shopping centers, has branches of Neiman Marcus, Bloomingdale's, and Macy's looming next to specialty shops such as Cartier and Mori. Valet parking is available at the front of the mall, but free parking is nearby. You'll do better at one of the several good restaurants in the mall—even for a quick meal—than at the food court.

The Mall at Peachtree Center (⊠*231 Peachtree St., Downtown* ☎*404/654–1296*) has specialty shops, such as International Records, Touch of Georgia, and the Atlanta International Museum gift shop.

Perimeter Mall (✉ *4400 Ashford-Dunwoody Rd., Dunwoody* ☎ *770/394–4270*), known for upscale family shopping, has Nordstrom, Macy's, Dillard's, and Bloomingdale's and a plentiful food court. Its restaurants include the Cheesecake Factory, Goldfish, and Maggiano's Little Italy.

Phipps Plaza (✉ *3500 Peachtree Rd., Buckhead* ☎ *404/262–0992*) has branches of Tiffany & Co., Saks Fifth Avenue, and Gucci, as well as such shops as Niketown and Teavana.

13

OUTLETS

The interstate highways leading to Atlanta have discount malls similar to those found throughout the country. About 60 mi north of the city on Interstate 85 at Exit 149 is a huge cluster of outlets in the town of Commerce.

Discover Mills Mall (✉ *5900 Sugarloaf Pkwy., Lawrenceville* ☎ *678/847–5000*), 25 mi northeast of downtown Atlanta, has bargain stores like Off 5th Saks Fifth Avenue and Last Call Neiman Marcus.

North Georgia Premium Outlets (✉ *800 Hwy. 400 S, at Dawson Forest Rd., Dawsonville* ☎ *706/216–3609*) is worth the 45 minutes it takes to get here from Atlanta's northern perimeter. This shopping center has more than 140 stores, including Williams-Sonoma, OshKosh B'Gosh, Bose, and numerous designer outlet shops: Coach, Ann Taylor, and Ralph Lauren.

SPECIALTY SHOPS

ANTIQUES &
DECORATIVE
ARTS

Bennett Street in Buckhead has antiques shops, home-decor stores such as John Overton Oriental Rugs-Antiques, and art galleries, including the Bennett Street Gallery. The Stalls on Bennett Street is a good antiques market.

Chamblee Antique Row (☎ *404/606–3367* ⊕ *www.antiquerow.com*) is a browser's delight. At Peachtree Industrial Boulevard and Broad Street in the suburban town of Chamblee, it's just north of Buckhead and about 10 mi north of downtown.

Buckhead's **Miami Circle,** is an upscale enclave with shops for antiques and decorative-arts lovers.

ART GALLERIES

The city is overflowing with art galleries—some new, some well established. For more information on the Atlanta art-gallery scene, including openings and location maps, consult *Museums & Galleries* (☎ *770/992–7808* ⊕ *www.nwpublications.com/publications/museums.php*), a magazine distributed free around the city.

Fay Gold Gallery (✉ *764 Miami Circle, Buckhead* ☎ *404/233–3843*) displays works by regional and national contemporary artists, featuring paintings, sculpture, and photography.

Jackson Fine Art Gallery (✉ *3115 E. Shadowlawn Ave., Buckhead* ☎ *404/233–3739*) exhibits fine-art photography.

Marcia Wood Gallery (✉ *263 Walker St., Castleberry Hill* ☎ *404/827–0030*) shows contemporary paintings, sculpture, and photography.

Mason Murer Fine Art (✉ *199 Armour Dr., Midtown* ☎*404/879–1500*) has a 24,000-square-foot gallery offering the finest in contemporary and regional art.

Vespermann Glass Gallery (✉ *309 E. Paces Ferry Rd., Buckhead* ☎*404/266–0102*) carries lovely handblown glass objects and jewelry.

The **Young Blood Gallery and Boutique** (✉ *636 N. Highland Ave., Virginia-Highland* ☎*404/254–4127*) is an edgy hipster hangout featuring artwork, crafts, and gifts created by indie artists.

FOOD **Star Provisions** (✉ *1198 Howell Mill Rd., West Midtown* ☎*404/365–0410*) is a chef's dream, with fine cookware, gadgets, and tableware for sale, plus top-of-the-line cheeses, meats, and baked goods.

Trader Joe's (✉ *931 Monroe Dr. NE, Midtown* ☎*404/815-9210*) is the bargain gourmand's obsession, with high-quality, low-priced, store-brand goodies and groceries.

The health-wise can take comfort at **Whole Foods Market** (✉ *77 W. Paces Ferry Rd. NW, Buckhead* ☎*404/324–4100* ✉*2111 Briarcliff Rd., Druid Hills* ☎*404/634–7800* ✉*650 Ponce de Leon Ave. NE, Midtown* ☎*404/853–1681*), with a dizzying amount of pesticide-free produce, hormone-free meats, and fresh seafood.

Your DeKalb Farmers Market (✉ *3000 E. Ponce de Leon Ave., Decatur* ☎*404/377–6400*) has 175,000 square feet of exotic fruits, cheeses, seafood, sausages, breads, and delicacies from around the world. The cafeteria-style buffet, with a selection of earthy and delicious hot foods and salads, is alone worth the trip.

Central Georgia

WORD OF MOUTH

"Athens is worth a visit if you want to see a college town. It has some nice shopping, a good local music scene, and definitely good food. But depending on when you go, it could be packed full of rowdy students."

—nycgirl1

"You really should go to Madison, Georgia. The drive from Milledgeville to Madison is a lovely rural drive and Madison is one of the prettiest antebellum towns in the U.S."

—starrs

Updated by
Christine Van
Dusen

TOOL DOWN U.S. 441—THE ANTEBELLUM Trail—to Macon, and you'll quickly see that the elegance of the Old South is all very new again, with many historic buildings returned to their original splendor.

If possible, make it to Macon in March, when the city's cherry trees are in full, spectacular flower. The annual festival celebrating the trees is a blast. And you can rock year-round at Macon's Georgia Music Hall of Fame, paying tribute to the state's musicians who have contributed so much to America's musical culture. Ray Charles, James Brown, the Allman Brothers Band, Chet Atkins, and Otis Redding are but a few of the legends honored in the hall.

In Athens, you can find remnants of antebellum Georgia. As home of the University of Georgia, it also pulses with college life—especially when the Bulldogs are playing. The birthplace of REM and the B-52s, Athens still has a thriving entertainment scene.

Augusta is home of the Masters Tournament. Even if you're not drawn to the tees, this city—like so many communities in Georgia—is undergoing a renaissance of its waterfront and historic districts to create a visitor destination outside of the annual Masters bash.

ORIENTATION & PLANNING

GETTING ORIENTED

Central Georgia roughly forms a triangle defined by Athens, Macon, and Augusta, which together give you a real flavor of Georgia's elegant past and vibrant future. Madison epitomizes small-town America with its charming antebellum and Victorian architecture. Eatonton, 20 mi down the highway, also has its share of stately historic houses, although your attention will be drawn to the statue of the giant rabbit on the courthouse lawn. It's part of the town's tribute to favorite son Joel Chandler Harris, creator of Br'er Rabbit and Uncle Remus.

Macon & the Antebellum Trail. The Antebellum Trail begins in Athens and travels 100 miles through seven communities that survived General Sherman's march through Georgia. Stop in Macon for its musical heritage and the National Landmark Hay House, which some say held Confederate gold in a secret room.

Augusta. Though the Masters Tournament of Golf put this 200,000-person city on the map, Augusta also charms with its antebellum mansions and tree-lined streets dotted with shops.

CENTRAL GEORGIA PLANNER

WHEN TO GO

Summertime in the South can be unpleasant; temperatures of 90° or higher (plus humidity) cause even the most Southern of Southerners to wilt. The best time to visit this region is the fall, when temperatures often hover in the pleasant 60s and there are plenty of recreational

TOP REASONS TO GO

Small town, big heart: Madison has been called America's Number One Small Town as much for its history as for its charm, much of w hich you can experience first hand around the town square—there's a restaurant in a converted 1800s bank and a couple of stores that are a hybrid of antiques, funky collectibles, and estate pieces.

The Antebellum Trail: Whether you're a fan of *Gone With the Wind* or not, traveling this picturesque trail between Macon and Athens will cast you back in time and give you a warming perspective as to the elegance of the Old South. Historic homes, plantation lands, and heritage townships are as authentic as you'll find anywhere.

Lovely lakes: Lake Okone, between Madison and Eatonton, has terrific golf courses and excellent fishing if you're tempted to drop a line. Lake Sinclair, on your way to Milledgeville is another honey-hole for fish.

Sunset cruise on the Augusta Canal: Paddle under your own steam or chug along aboard an oversize St. Petersburg barge to absorb Augusta's canal history. You pass by historic mills, homes, and gardens, as well as riverbanks teeming with wildlife such as blue herons and egrets.

Marvels of Macon: Boasting no fewer than 5,500 individual structures in the National Register of Historic Places, Macon is a city worth a stroll. Stay a while and explore everything from splendid Hay House to the quaint charm of Sidney Lanier's childhood home.

14

activities to enjoy. Springtime is lovely as well, but hotels book up for the Masters Tournament.

GETTING HERE & AROUND

Depending on where along the Antebellum Trail you begin your journey, you may want to fly into the regional airport in Macon or Augusta. Tickets can be pricey, though, so consider flying to Atlanta and renting a car. You'll need it anyway, if you want to get around the towns in this part of the state. At the time of this writing, Athens Ben Epps Airport was planning an Atlanta-to-Athens shuttle.

BY AIR Athens Ben Epps Airport (AHN) is served by U.S. Airways with connecting flights via Charlotte, NC. Augusta Regional Airport (AGS) is served by Delta Airlines and US Airways. Middle Georgia Regional Airport (MCN) is served by Delta Airlines.

BY CAR U.S. 441, known as the Antebellum Trail, runs north–south, merging with U.S. 129 for a stretch and connecting Athens, Madison, Eatonton, and Milledgeville. Macon is on Route 49, which splits from U.S. 441 at Milledgeville. Washington lies at the intersection of U.S. 78, running east from Athens to Thomson, and Route 44, running south to Eatonton. Interstate 20 runs east from Atlanta to Augusta, which is about 93 mi east of U.S. 441.

ESSENTIALS **Air Contacts Athens Ben Epps Airport** (*AHN* ✉ *1010 Ben Epps Dr.* ☎ *706/613–3420* ⊕ *www.athensairport.net).* **Augusta Regional Airport** (*AGS* ✉ *1501 Aviation*

Way ☏ *706/798-3236).* **Middle Georgia Regional Airport** *(MCN ✉1000 Terminal Dr., Rte. 247 at I-75* ☏*478/788-3760).*

Visitor Information Georgia Welcome Center (✉ *Box 211090, Martinez 30917* ☏ *706/737-1446* ⊕ *www.georgia.org).*

ABOUT THE HOTELS & RESTAURANTS

Central Georgia isn't the first place to look for haute cuisine—even haute Southern cuisine—but there are plenty of opportunities to eat simply and well at reasonable prices. Things get spiced up a bit in Athens, which presents the greatest variety of choices.

The most attractive lodging options here tend to have been around for a long time; the structures, at least, often date from the 19th century. At such places—most commonly B&Bs, but sometimes larger inns—you're likely to find big porches with rocking chairs and bedrooms decorated with antiques. If that's more Southern charm than you're after, you can choose from a smattering of chain hotels.

WHAT IT COSTS					
	¢	$	$$	$$$	$$$$
Restaurant	under $10	$10–$14	$15–$19	$20–$24	over $24
Hotel	under $100	$100–$150	$151–$200	$201–$250	over $250

Restaurant prices are for a main course at dinner. Hotel prices are for two people in a standard double room in high season.

PLANNING YOUR TIME

The best way to catch everything this region has to offer is to head from Athens down U.S. 441 toward Macon. Be prepared to take your time as you pass through smaller towns such as Milledgeville and Eatonton, each of which provides pockets of history.

MACON & THE ANTEBELLUM TRAIL

The antebellum South, filtered through the romanticized gauze of *Gone With the Wind,* evokes graciousness, gentility, and a code of honor that saw many a duel between dashing gentlemen. Certainly, the historic architecture along the Antebellum Trail would endorse this picture, and even though many of the white-column mansions were built with the sweat of slaves, there is much to appreciate. Anchored between Macon and Athens, the trail was designated a state trail in 1985, and links the historical communities of Watkinsville, Madison, Eatonton, Milledgeville, and Old Clinton, all of which escaped the rampages of General Sherman's army on his march in 1864 from Atlanta to Savannah.

MACON

85 mi southeast of Atlanta via I-75.

At the state's geographic center, Macon, founded in 1823, has more than 100,000 flowering cherry trees, which it celebrates each March

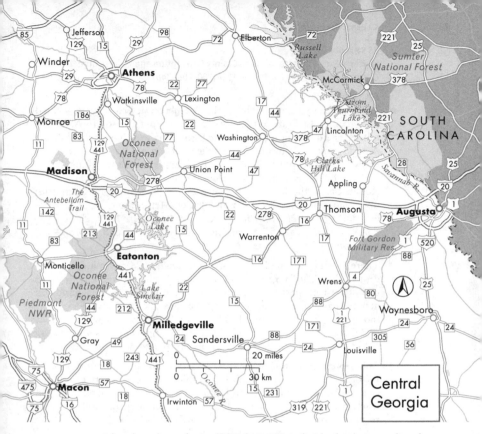

with a knockout festival. With 5,500 individual structures listed on the National Register of Historic Places, its antebellum and Victorian homes are among the state's best-preserved, and an ongoing program of restoration is revitalizing the downtown core. Following a $1.2 million restoration, the Capitol Theatre (originally founded as a bank in 1897) is open for movies and concerts; after a three year renovation, St. Joseph's Catholic Church is more impressive than ever; and the old Armory, complete with its first-floor dance hall, is finding new life as an office and retail complex.

Daily news is reported in the *Telegraph;* the *Georgia Informer* and the upscale *Macon Magazine* are good sources of information on local arts and cultural events.

GETTING HERE & AROUND

Poet Raymond Farr, in his piece "Back Roads to Macon," writes of a cozy roadside diner, the sprawling farmland, and a folksy bit of wisdom scrawled on a mailbox in the nearby town of Cordele: "Whatever your destination, thank God you arrive." These kinds of small touches add charm to the back roads to Macon. Or, for a speedier and somewhat less scenic route, jump on U.S. 441.

ESSENTIALS

Visitor Information Macon-Bibb County Convention and Visitors Bureau (⊠ *200 Cherry St., Macon* ☎ *478/743–3401 or 800/768–3401* ⊕ *www.maconga.org*).

EXPLORING

★ Among the city's many sights is the **Georgia Music Hall of Fame,** located in Macon as a tribute to the city's extensive contribution to American music. The museum recognizes the Georgians who have helped define America's musical culture. Among the honorees are Ray Charles, James Brown, Little Richard, the Allman Brothers Band, Chet Atkins, REM, and the B-52s. Exhibits also celebrate classical musicians, including Robert Shaw, the late director of the Atlanta Symphony Orchestra; opera singers Jessye Norman and James Melton; and violinist Robert McDuffie. ⊠ *200 Martin Luther King Jr. Blvd., 31201* ☎ *478/750–8555 or 888/427–6257* ⊕ *www.gamusichall.com* ◪ *$8* ⊙ *Mon.–Sat. 9–5, Sun. 1–5.*

☾ There's family fun to be had at the **Georgia Children's Museum,** adjacent to the Georgia Sports Hall of Fame. Adults can relax with a cup of hot java in the Lost Parents Café while kids engage in hands-on activities and theater performances. Be sure to check out the evolving model-train diorama about the history and industry of Georgia. ⊠ *370, 382 Cherry St.* ☎ *478/755–9539* ⊕ *www.georgiachildrensmuseum.org* ◪ *$3* ⊙ *Tues.–Sat. 10:30–5:30. Closed Sun. and Mon.*

☾ The **Georgia Sports Hall of Fame,** with its old-style ticket booths, has the look and feel of an old ballpark. Exhibits include a variety of interactive, touch-screen kiosks, and honor sports—including baseball, golf, track and field, and football—at all levels, from prep and college teams to professional. ⊠ *301 Cherry St.* ☎ *478/752–1585* ⊕ *www.gshf.org* ◪ *$8* ⊙ *Mon.–Sat. 9–5, Sun. 1–5.*

★ The unique **Hay House,** designed by the New York firm T. Thomas & Son in the mid-1800s, is a study in fine Italianate architecture prior to the Civil War. The marvelous stained-glass windows and many technological advances, including indoor plumbing, make a tour worthwhile. ■**TIP**→ Hay House was featured on America's Castles on the A&E Channel. ⊠ *934 Georgia Ave.* ☎ *478/742–8155* ⊕ *www.georgiatrust.org* ◪ *$8* ⊙ *Tues.–Sat. 10–4, Sun. 1–4*

African-American entrepreneur Charles H. Douglass built the **Douglass Theatre** in 1921. Great American musicians have performed here, among them Bessie Smith, "Ma" Rainey, Cab Calloway, Duke Ellington, and locals Little Richard and Otis Redding. It's currently a venue for movies, plays, and other performances. You can take a guided tour of the building. ⊠ *355 Martin Luther King Jr. Blvd.* ☎ *478/742–2000* ⊕ *www.douglasstheatre.org* ⊙ *Weekdays 10–5.*

☾ The **Macon Museum of Arts and Sciences and Mark Smith Planetarium** displays everything from a whale skeleton to fine art. Discovery House, an interactive exhibit for children, is modeled after an artist's garret. ⊠ *4182 Forsyth Rd.* ☎ *478/477–3232* ⊕ *www.masmacon.com* ◪ *$7* ⊙ *Mon.–Sat. 10–5, Sun. 1–5.*

Just 3 mi east of downtown Macon is the **Ocmulgee National Monument,** a significant archaeological site. It was occupied for more than 10,000 years; at its peak, between AD 900 and AD 1100, it was populated by the Mississippian peoples. There's a reconstructed earth lodge and displays of pottery, effigies, and jewelry of copper and shells discovered in the burial mound. ✉*1207 Emery Hwy., take U.S. 80 east* ☎*478/752–8257* ⊕*www.nps.gov/ocmu* ⊑*Free* ☉*Daily 9–5.*

> **ON THE TRAIL**
>
> A meander along the new **Ocmulgee Heritage Trail** is a delightful diversion. The trailhead is at Gateway Park, at the corner of MLK Boulevard and Riverside Drive. Although at this writing the entire path was not yet complete, by 2009 the trail will connect the Ocmulgee National Monument along the river to a park and recreation area underway at the old Macon Waterworks.

14

America has more tributes to Sidney Lanier, famous poet and musician of the Old South, than the years he lived. And it all starts at his birthplace, **Sidney Lanier Cottage,** a charming 1840 structure that features much of Lanier's writings among the period furnishings. Even his bride's tiny wedding gown is on show. Lanier died of consumption at 39 years of age after he was captured in 1864 for running the blockade. ✉*935 High St.* ☎*478/743–3851* ⊕*www.historicmacon.org* ⊑*$5* ☉*Mon-Sat 10–4.*

★ The **Tubman African American Museum** honors the former slave who led more than 300 people to freedom as one of the conductors of the Underground Railroad. A mural depicts several centuries of black culture. The museum also has an African artifacts gallery. ✉*340 Walnut St. 31201* ☎*478/743–8544* ⊕*www.tubmanmuseum.com* ⊑*$5* ☉*Mon.–Sat. 9–5.*

OFF THE BEATEN PATH

Museum of Aviation. This museum at Robins Air Force Base has an extraordinary collection of 90 vintage aircraft and missiles, including a MiG, an SR-71 (Blackbird), a U-2, and assorted other flying machines from past campaigns. From Macon take Interstate 75 south to Exit 146 (Centerville/Warner Robins), and turn left onto Watson Boulevard, 7 mi to Route 247/U.S. 129, then right for 2 mi. ✉*Rte. 247/U.S. 129 at Russell Pkwy., 20 mi south of Macon, Warner Robins* ☎*478/926–6870* ⊕*www.museumofaviation.org* ⊑*Free; film $2* ☉*Daily 9–5.*

WHERE TO EAT

$$$

AMERICAN

✕**Downtown Grill.** In the heart of a city block of renovated warehouses, this popular restaurant can be hard to find. But it's well worth the search. The old Georgian brick gives a romantic flair to the decor, and the menu has many classic favorites such as pork tenderloin, filet mignon, and a tasty mixed grill with options for fish lovers and vegetarians. ■TIP→ Be prepared to walk a block; the approach alleys aren't always accessible by car. ✉*562 Mulberry St. La.* ☎*478/742–5999* ⊑*AE, MC, V* ☉*Closed Sun.*

WHERE TO STAY

$$$ ⬚ **1842 Inn.** With its grand white-pillar front porch and period antiques, it's easy to see why this place is considered to be one of America's top inns. The rooms have an aristocratic flair, with plush coverlets and embroidered pillows. There are also love seats, ornate window stoops, and tile fireplaces, as well as period antiques and heirloom-quality accessories. In the morning you can eat breakfast in your room, in one of the parlors, or in the gorgeous courtyard. It's an easy walk to downtown and the historic district. **Pros:** offers a true taste of antebellum grandeur. **Cons:** the parlor may be a bit too quiet for more social guests. ⊠*353 College St.* ☎*478/741–1842 or 800/336–1842* ⊕*www.the1842inn.com* ⌁*19 rooms, 1 guesthouse* ⌂*In-room: Internet, Wi-Fi. In-hotel: laundry service* ⊟*AE, DC, MC, V* ⦿*BP.*

> A REAL FIND
>
> Bag a deal at **Ginger Michelle** (⊠*466 1st St., 31201* ☎*478/746–3025*), a sleek shop featuring contemporary and eclectic clothing, accessories, and shoes. Owners Steve and Ginger Hess are also multi-award-winning furniture designers. Much of their work, Ginger's handbags in particular, is carried in upscale stores across the nation and in Europe at considerably higher prices than you'll find here.

$$–$$$ ⬚ **Henderson Village.** At this resort, 38 mi south of Macon, you can find stunning 19th- and early-20th-century Southern homes and refurbished tenant cottages clustered around a green. Guest rooms have a rustic elegance, with fine antiques and access to inviting wraparound porches; suites are even nicer, with fireplaces and whirlpool tubs. **Pros:** the 1838 Langston House restaurant has three dining rooms and a lovely glassed-in veranda. **Cons:** no fitness center currently on-site. ⊠*125 S. Langston Circle, Perry* ☎*478/988–8696 or 888/615–9722* ⊕*www.hendersonvillage.com* ⌁*19 rooms, 5 suites* ⌂*In-hotel: restaurant, bar, pool* ⊟*AE, MC, V* ⦿*BP.*

$$ ⬚ **Ramada Plaza Macon.** Its central location is what makes this 16-story,
★ modern and comfortable chain hotel a winner. You can park the car and walk to many historic sites. **Pros:** newly refurbished Executive Level Rooms; sizeable conference center. **Cons:** may have lost some luster when it switched from a Crowne Plaza to a Ramada in 2006. ⊠*108 1st St., Macon* ☎*478/746–1461 or 877/227–6963* ⊕*www.crowneplaza.com* ⌁*293 rooms, 4 suites* ⌂*In-room: Internet, Wi-Fi. In-hotel: restaurant, bar, pool, gym* ⊟*AE, MC, V.*

MILLEDGEVILLE

32 mi northeast of Macon on GA 49.

Locals believe ghosts haunt what remains of the antebellum homes in Milledgeville. Laid out as the state capital of Georgia in 1803 (a title it held until Atlanta assumed the role in 1868), the town was not as fortunate as Madison in escaping being torched during the Civil War. Sherman's troops stormed through here with a vengeance after the general heard hardship stories from Union soldiers who had escaped from a prisoner-of-war camp in nearby Andersonville.

GETTING HERE & AROUND

Travel by car to Milledgeville, then park and hop aboard the Milledgeville Trolley Tour. This red coach will take you through the city's landmark historic district, with stops at such spots as the Old Governor's Mansion and the Stetson-Sanford House. The tour leaves from the Convention and Visitors Bureau and is available weekdays from 10–2 and Saturday at 2 for $10.

ESSENTIALS

Visitor Information Milledgeville Convention & Visitors Bureau (✉ *200 W. Hancock St.* ☎ *478/452–4687* ⊕ *www.milledgevillecvb.com*).

EXPLORING

The 1838 Greek Revival **Old Governor's Mansion** became Sherman's headquarters during the war. His soldiers are said to have tossed government documents out of the windows and fueled their fires with Confederate money. The mansion has been home to 10 Georgian governors and has undergone a $10-million restoration. Guided tours of the building, now a museum, are given daily, on the hour. ✉ *120 S. Clark St.* ☎ *478/445–4545* ⊡ *$5* ⊙ *Tues.–Sat. 10–4, Sun. 2–4.*

14

One of the most famous alumni of Georgia College and State University was novelist and short-story writer Flannery O'Connor, author of such acclaimed novels as *Wise Blood* and *The Violent Bear It Away*. O'Connor did most of her writing at the family farm, Andalusia, just north of Milledgeville on U.S. 441. The newly expanded **Flannery O'Connor Room,** inside the GCSU Museum, has many of the author's handwritten manuscripts on display. It also contains O'Connor's typewriter and some of her furniture. ✉ *221 North Clark St.* ☎ *478/445–4391* ⊕ *www2.gcsu.edu/library/museum* ⊡ *Free* ⊙ *Weekdays 10–4.*

WHERE TO STAY & EAT

¢–$ ✕ **The Brick.** This bar-restaurant has a comfortable, worn-at-the-elbows
AMERICAN appeal—which is all-important when you're about to consume massive pizzas with tasty toppings like feta cheese and spinach. Vegetarians will appreciate the "environmentally correct" pizza platter with its all-vegetable-topping. The menu's pasta selection boasts 9,000 combinations, and also offers salads and calzones. ✉ *136 W. Hancock St.* ☎ *478/452–0089* ⊟ *AE, D, MC, V.*

¢–$ ⊞ **Antebellum Inn.** Each room in this pre–Civil War mansion has beautiful period antiques. The Southern breakfasts are fabulous—think gourmet eggs Benedict or orange-essence croissant–French toast with lemon butter curd. The inn is owned and operated by a mother–daughter team, Jane Lorenz and Jo Ann Hicks, and both are bird lovers. In spring many of the hanging planters have nesting birds. In the morning birds and woodland creatures flock to the gardens, attracted to the many decorative feeders. **Pros:** excellent home-cooked breakfasts; Southern hospitality at its best. **Cons:** its popularity causes it to book up quickly. ✉ *200 N. Columbia St.* ☎ *478/453–3993* ⊕ *www.antebelluminn.com* ↩ *5 rooms* ⚐ *In-room: Wi-Fi. In-hotel: restaurant, pool* ⊟ *AE, D, MC, V* ⊙⏐*BP.*

EATONTON

20 mi north of Milledgeville on U.S. 129/441.

Right in the middle of the Antebellum Trail, Eatonton is a historic trove of houses that still retains the rare Southern antebellum architecture that survived Sherman's torches. But this isn't the only source of pride for this idyllic town. Take a look at the courthouse lawn; it's not your imagination—that really is a giant statue of a rabbit.

GETTING HERE & AROUND
As with most cities along the Antebellum Trail, Eatonton is best reached by car. As you travel there via U.S. Highway 441, check out the scenic views of pastures, mountain valleys, and rivers.

ESSENTIALS
Visitor Information Eatonton-Putnam Chamber of Commerce (⊠ *305 N. Madison Ave., Eatonton 31024* ☎ *706/485-7701* ⊕ *www.eatonton.com*).

EXPLORING
★ Eatonton is the birthplace of celebrated novelist Joel Chandler Har-
☾ ris, of Br'er Rabbit and Uncle Remus fame. The **Uncle Remus Museum,** built from authentic slave cabins, houses countless carvings, paintings, first-edition books, and other artwork depicting the characters made famous by the imaginative author. It's on the grounds of a park. ⊠ *Turner Park, U.S. 441* ☎ *706/485-6856* ⊕ *www.uncleremus.com/ museum.html* ⌧ *$1* ☉ *Mon.–Sat. 10–5, Sun. 2–5.*

The **Eatonton-Putnam Chamber of Commerce** provides printed maps detailing landmarks from the upbringing of Eatonton native Alice Walker, who won the Pulitzer Prize for her novel *The Color Purple*. It also has information on the many fine examples of antebellum architecture in Eatonton, including descriptions and photographs of the town's prize antebellum mansions, and a walking tour of Victorian homes. ⊠ *305 N. Madison Ave., 31024* ☎ *706/485-7701.*

MADISON

22 mi north of Eatonton on U.S. 129/144.

In 1809 Madison was described as "the most cultured and aristocratic town on the stagecoach route from Charleston to New Orleans," and today, that charm still prevails, in large part because General Sherman's Union Army deliberately bypassed the town, thus saving it for posterity. From the picturesque town square, with its specialty shops and businesses, you can walk to any number of antebellum and other residences that make up one of the largest designated historic areas in Georgia.

ESSENTIALS
Visitor Information Madison/Morgan County Chamber of Commerce (⊠ *115 E. Jefferson St., Madison* ☎ *706/342-4454* ⊕ *www.madisonga.org*).

EXPLORING

★ Madison is the historic heart of Georgia, and although many of the lovely homes are privately owned, **Heritage Hall** is one Greek Revival mansion, circa 1811, that is open to the public. Rooms are furnished to the 19th century and are an elegant insight as to the lifestyle of an average well-to-do family. ⊠277 S. Main St. ☎706/342–9627 ✉$5 ☉Mon.–Sat. 11–4, Sun. 1:30–4:30.

WHERE TO STAY & EAT

¢   ✕**Ye Olde Colonial Restaurant.** Housed in an old bank, this casual, all-day
SOUTHERN   restaurant is a Madison institution. Food is no-nonsense comfort for the soul—macaroni and cheese, fried chicken, barbecue pork, and squash casserole. For fun, try to grab a seat in the original bank vault; its walls are plastered with money that was used back in 1867 to fund railroad construction after the war. ⊠108 E. Washington St. ☎706/342–2211 ⚐Reservations not accepted ⊟AE, MC, V ☉Closed Sun.

$$ ⌻**The Farmhouse Inn.** On a sprawling plot, this inn offers 5 mi of wooded trails to explore, well-stocked ponds to fish, goats and miniature horses to pet, and a grassy picnic area to enjoy beside the Apalachee River. Owner Melinda Hartney even has a scavenger hunt to encourage you to get out and about. Rooms are country-fresh—one has a fly-fishing decor, another has decorative quilts, and most adjoin sunny decks. **Pros:** a great family destination. **Cons:** the rooms in the cottages are less romantic than those in the main farmhouse. ⊠1051 Meadow La. ☎706/342–7933 or 866/253–0023 ⊕www.thefarmhouseinn.com ☜5 rooms, 2 cottages ⚐In-room: kitchen (some), refrigerator (some) DVD (some) ⊟AE, MC, V ☉⃝BP.

ATHENS

30 mi northeast of Madison via U.S. 129/441; 70 mi east of Atlanta via I–85 north to Rte. 316.

Athens, an artistic jewel of the American South, is known as a breeding ground for famed rock groups such as the B-52s and REM. Because of this distinction, creative types from all over the country flock to its trendy streets in hopes of becoming, or catching a glimpse of, the next big act to take the world by storm. At the center of this artistic melee is the University of Georgia (UGA). With more than 30,000 students, UGA is an influential ingredient in the Athens mix, giving the quaint but compact city a distinct flavor that falls somewhere between a misty Southern enclave, a rollicking college town, and a smoky, jazz club–studded alleyway. Of course, this all goes "to the Dawgs" if the home team is playing on home turf; although, even then, Athens remains a truly fascinating blend of Mayberry R.F.D. and MTV. The effect is as irresistible as it is authentic.

To find out what's on in Athens, check out the Athens Banner Herald (daily) and the Flagpole.

GETTING HERE & AROUND

Parking can be scarce on the city streets. Leave yourself extra time to find a spot, then take in the city and its shopping, nightlife, campus, and culture on foot.

The Athens Welcome Center runs historic tours of downtown and surrounding neighborhoods daily at 2 PM. Tours are 90-minutes long and $15 per person.

ESSENTIALS

Visitor Information Athens Welcome Center (✉280 E. Dougherty St., ☎706/353-1820 or 800/455-1820 ⊕www.visitathensga.com).

EXPLORING

> **ROOTED IN HISTORY**
>
> In Athens the large white oak at the corner of Dearing and Finely streets, surrounded by an enclosure of granite posts and an iron chain, is the **Tree That Owns Itself.** The original tree, which fell in 1942, was granted emancipation by Colonel W.H. Jackson, who wrote: "For and in consideration of the great love I bear this tree and the great desire I have for its protection for all time, I convey entire possession of itself and the land within eight feet of it on all sides." The current tree was grown from an acorn of the original.

Although the streets bustle at night with students taking in the coffeehouse and concert life, Athens's quieter side also flourishes. The streets are lined with many gorgeous old homes, some of which are open to the public. Most prominent among them is the **Athens Welcome Center** (✉280 E. Dougherty St.), in the town's oldest surviving residence, the 1820 Church-Waddel-Brumby House.

Athens has several splendid **Greek Revival buildings** (✉570 Prince Ave.), including two on campus: the **university chapel** built in 1832, just off N. Herty Drive, and the **university president's house** that was built in the late 1850s. Easiest access to the campus in downtown Athens is off Broad Street onto either Jackson or Thomas streets, both of which run through the heart of the university. Maps are available at the Visitor Center. Another example that gives a fine sense of history is the **Taylor-Grady House** (✉634 Prince Ave.), which was constructed in 1844 and has just reopened for private events after an extensive face-lift. The 1844 **Franklin House** (✉480 E. Broad St.) has been restored and reopened as an office building. **T.R.R. Cobb House** (✉175 Hill St.) is yet another heritage building that has undergone transformation, this time turning into a museum for Civil War exhibits.

Fodor'sChoice ★ Just outside the Athens city limits is the **State Botanical Gardens of Georgia**, a tranquil, 313-acre wonderland of aromatic gardens and woodland paths. It has a massive conservatory overlooking the **International Garden** that functions as a welcome foyer and houses an art gallery, gift shop, and café. ✉2450 S. Milledge Ave., off U.S. 129/441 ☎706/542–1244 ⊕www.uga.edu/botgarden ✉Free ⊗Grounds: Apr.–Sept., weekdays 8–8; Oct.–Mar., weekdays 8–6. Visitor center: Tues.–Sat. 9–4:30, Sun. 11:30–4:30.

WHERE TO EAT

$–$$
ECLECTIC

✗**East–West Bistro.** This popular bistro—one of the busiest spots downtown—has a bar, formal dining upstairs, and casual dining downstairs. The most interesting selections downstairs are the small plates that allow you to sample cuisines from around the world—from wasabi-crusted tilapia to salmon in rice paper to roasted-garlic pork chop. And if you're not a designated driver, the chocolate martini, a blend of Godiva liqueur, ice cream, and vodka, is a must. ■TIP➔ The room upstairs is much quieter, and the booths are very romantic. ✉351 E. Broad St. ☎706/546–9378 ⚓Reservations not accepted ☐AE, D, MC, V.

14

¢
VEGETARIAN
★

✗**The Grit.** This vegetarian paradise has been a favorite in Athens for more than two decades, serving freshly-made non-meat food even carnivores adore in the casual comfort of a historic building. A popular dish of browned tofu cubes and brown rice may sound bland but it's far from it—even the tofu-fearful say it's yummy. The black-bean chili is another popular choice, with bulgur, veggies, and zesty spices. Pick up their cookbook for 130 of The Grit's best dishes. ✉199 Prince Ave. ☎706/543-6592 ⚓Reservations not accepted ☐V, MC, D.

$$–$$$
CAJUN

✗**Harry Bissett's.** Get primed to taste the offerings at one of the best restaurants in Athens, where you can expect sumptuous Cajun recipes straight from the streets of New Orleans. Nosh on oysters on the half shell at the raw bar while waiting for a table (if it's the weekend, expect to wait a while). Popular main dishes include fresh-catch Thibodaux (broiled fresh fillet smothered in crawfish étouffée) and chicken Rochambeau (a terrine of chicken breast, béarnaise sauce, shaved ham, and wine sauce). ■TIP➔ Save room for the bread pudding with whiskey sauce. ✉279 E. Broad St. ☎706/353–7065 ⊕www.harrybissetts.net ☐AE, D, MC, V.

WHERE TO STAY

¢

🏨**Best Western Colonial Inn.** A half-mile from the UGA campus, it's a favorite among relatives who come to attend graduation. Don't expect to be blown away by the architectural design, as the hotel building itself, like the rooms it offers, is basic. Rooms, however, are quite comfortable, with thick flowery bedspreads, and each room comes equipped with a coffeemaker. Excellent freshly baked cookies are offered every afternoon. ■TIP➔ Directly across the street is the famed hot dog joint, the Varsity Diner. Pros: friendly staff; good value. Cons: the walk to downtown may be a bit too steep for the elderly or physically challenged. ✉170 N. Milledge Ave. ☎706/546–7311 or 800/528–1234 ⊕www.bestwestern.com ➷70 rooms ♿In-room: Internet, Wi-Fi. In-hotel: pool ☐AE, D, DC, MC, V.

$ ⊡ **The Foundry Park Inn.** More than a hotel, this boutique village includes luxury rooms, a full-service spa, a lively pub and the Melting Point, an intimate night club that hosts musicians such as Little Feat and Ralph Stanley. The entire inn is built to be a replica of an 1820 row house; the original barn has been converted into stylish meeting rooms. There's really little need to leave, and if you do, you'll find the Classic Center Theater, the university campus, and historic downtown within easy walking distance. **Pros:** quaint setup; Melting Point's bar is comfortable and the music venue draws interesting indie acts. **Cons:** the once-heralded Hoyt House Restaurant is no longer open for dinner. ⊠295 *E. Dougherty St.* ☎706/549–7020 *or* 866/928–4367 ⊕*www.foundryparkinn.com* ⇆*119 rooms* ♿*In-room: Wi-Fi. In-hotel: restaurant, bar, spa* ⊟*AE, MC, V.*

EN ROUTE Along U.S. 78 you'll find **Washington**, a picturesque community that exudes a bustling turn-of-the-last-century charm and is a great stopover en route to Augusta. The first city chartered in honor of the country's first president, Washington is a living museum of Southern culture. Brick buildings, some of which date to the American Revolution, line the lively downtown area, which bustles with people visiting cafés and antiques shops. The Confederate treasury was moved here from Richmond in 1865, and soon afterward the half-million dollars in gold vanished. This mysterious event has been the inspiration for numerous treasure hunts, as many like to believe the gold is still buried somewhere in Wilkes County.

AUGUSTA

97 mi southeast of Athens via GA 10 and I–20; 150 mi east of Atlanta via I–20.

Although Augusta escaped the ravages of Union troops during the Civil War, nature itself was not so kind. On a crossing of the Savannah River, the town was flooded many times before modern-day city planning redirected the water into a collection of small lakes and creeks. Now the current is so mild that citizens gather to send bathtub toys downstream every year in the annual Rubber Duck Race.

Check out the *Augusta Daily Chronicle* and the *Metro Spirit* for up to the minute information of what's going on in town.

GETTING HERE & AROUND

Explore this part of the classic South via car, then park to wander the streets full of shops and restaurants. You can also canoe on the river or along the 1845 tree-lined Augusta Canal, a natural habitat for herons and other birds.

The Augusta Cotton Exchange (also known as the Augusta Visitors Bureau) conducts free tours of its historic brick building, with exhibits from its past as an arbiter of cotton prices. It also has Saturday van tours throughout the historic district of Augusta ($10). ■**TIP➔Pick up** the Augusta Gallery Pass, which gives you entrance to nine of the city's tourist attractions for half the price.

ESSENTIALS

Visitor Information Augusta Convention & Visitors Bureau (⊠ *560 Reynolds St. 30903* ☎ *706/724–4067 or 800/726–0243* ⊕ *www.augustaga.org).*

AN ONION A DAY

Vidalia onions are grown throughout Central Georgia. Because of unique soil conditions, the onions are so sweet you can eat them like apples. Watch for them on menus and at roadside stands.

EXPLORING

14

The well-maintained multilevel paths of **Riverwalk** (between 5th and 10th streets) curve along the Savannah River and are the perfect place for a leisurely stroll.

Olde Town, lying along Telfair and Greene streets, is a restored neighborhood of Victorian homes, although many are still very much works in progress.

A converted mill serves as the **Augusta Canal Interpretive Center,** a historical center where imaginative exhibits, including authentic mill equipment and looms, trace Augusta's important role in developing Georgia's textile industry. The Center is still powered by the building's original turbines (which you can see in action), and also uses the power to juice up its Petersburg canal boats. Tours of the **canal,** usually one-hour long, start here and are a fascinating trip through history. Guides are well versed in the passing sights that include assorted wildlife, a working 19th-century textile mill, and two of Georgia's only remaining 18th-century houses. ⊠ *1450 Greene St.* ☎ *706/823–0440* ⊕ *www. augustacanal.com* ⊠ *$6* ⊗ *Tues.–Sat. 9:30–5:30.*

Meadow Garden was the home of George Walton, one of Georgia's three signers of the Declaration of Independence and, at age 26, its youngest signer. It has been documented as Augusta's oldest extant residence. ⊠ *1320 Independence Dr.* ☎ *706/724–4174* ⊠ *$4* ⊗ *Weekdays 10–4, weekends by appointment.*

The **Morris Museum of Southern Art** has a splendid collection of Southern art, from early landscapes, antebellum portraits, and Civil War art through neo-impressionism and modern contemporary art. ⊠ *Riverfront Center, 1 10th St., 2nd fl.* ☎ *706/724–7501* ⊕ *www.themorris. org* ⊠ *$5, free on Sun.* ⊗ *Tues.–Sat. 10–5, Sun. noon–5.*

· ℭ Children love the National Science Center's **Fort Discovery,** an interactive high-tech playground with a moon-walk simulator, a bike on square wheels, a hot-air balloon, and a little car propelled by magnets. ⊠ *1 7th St.* ☎ *706/821–0200 or 800/325–5445* ⊕ *www.nationalsciencecenter. org* ⊠ *$8* ⊗ *Tues.–Sat. 10–5, Sun. 12–5.*

WHERE TO STAY & EAT

$$$$ **✕La Maison on Telfair.** Augusta's
CONTINENTAL finest restaurant, operated by chef-owner Heinz Sowinski, presents a classic menu of game, sweetbreads, and, with a nod to the chef's heritage, Wiener schnitzel. The experience is enhanced by the quiet and elegant room. **■TIP→ The wine and tapas bar is more casual.** ✉404 Telfair St. ☎706/722–4805 ⚖Reservations essential ☱AE, D, DC, MC, V ⊗Closed Sun. No lunch.

$$–$$$ **⊞Partridge Inn.** A National Trust Historic Hotel, this restored inn sits at the gateway to Summerville, a hilltop neighborhood of summer homes dating to 1800. There's a splendid view of downtown Augusta from the roof. Rooms are elegant, and have double-line cordless phones and high-speed Internet. The hotel's exterior has 12 common balconies and a breathtaking upper veranda accented with shaded architectural porticos over wood-plank flooring, creating a truly lustrous reprieve for a quick coffee and newspaper read. There's also videoconferencing for those who can't bear to be out of sight of their business partners. **Pros:** excellent breakfast buffet; lovely atmosphere. **Cons:** lots of stairs and occasionally uneven floors may be tricky for the elderly and physically impaired. ✉2110 Walton Way ☎706/737–8888 or 800/476–6888 ⊕www.partridgeinn.com ⇱118 rooms, 30 suites ⚐In-room: kitchen (some), Internet, Wi-Fi. In-hotel: restaurant, bar, pool, gym ☱AE, D, DC, MC, V ⊚⊩BP.

SPORTS & THE OUTDOORS

In early April Augusta hosts the much-celebrated annual **Masters Tournament** (⊕www.masters.org), one of pro golf's most distinguished events. It's broadcast in 180 countries. Tickets for actual tournament play are not available to the general public, but you can try to get tickets for one of the practice rounds earlier in the week—which, for golf addicts, is still hugely entertaining. Masters Tournament practice round tickets are awarded on a lottery basis; write to the **Masters Tournament Practice Rounds office,** (✉Box 2047, Augusta, GA 30903) by July 15 of the year preceding the tournament.

North Georgia

WORD OF MOUTH

"We drove up to Tallulah Gorge State Park. You need a permit to hike to the gorge floor—they only give out 100 a day on a first-come, first-served basis. The hike was AWESOME. The weather was perfect, and the scenery was absolutely gorgeous. . . . We had a delicious lunch at Isabelle's right there in Tallulah Falls, and then spent the afternoon driving across North Georgia."

—Meredith

Updated by
Michele Foust

NORTH GEORGIA'S ABUNDANT NATURAL WONDERS, forest trails and waterways, and its cooler Appalachian mountain air sweep visitors into relaxation. Drive a few hours—or less—from Atlanta, and you'll find clusters of old Southern settlements extending a Georgia welcome with varied attractions, outstanding food, and comfortable lodgings. It all makes for a great vacation or a weekend jaunt that's guaranteed to send travelers home rested and refreshed.

The region is home to one of the largest national forest areas in the East, the 750,000-acre Chattahoochee National Forest. About 15% of the Chattahoochee is designated as wilderness, and of this, the 35,000-acre Cohutta Wilderness is the largest national forest wilderness area in the Southeast. Several bold rivers, including the Chattahoochee, Oconee, Toccoa and Chattooga, have their headwaters in this forest. Rabun, Burton, Nottley, and Chatuge lakes offer boating and fishing. North Georgia is full of small state parks, and most have cabins for rent and inexpensive camp sites.

In Dahlonega, Blue Ridge, Clayton, Clarkesville, Ellijay, and north of metro Atlanta, visitors find shops selling fine art, as well as handmade quilts, folk art, and contemporary pottery and antiques. Farm stands offer goodies from fresh produce to famous Georgia boiled peanuts to jams and jellies. These areas also provide travelers with mountains of music and unique experiences—such as kangaroo-spying, gold panning, and local wine making. To the northwest are two important Georgia historic sites: New Echota State Historic Site and the Chickamauga & Chattanooga National Military Park.

ORIENTATION & PLANNING

GETTING ORIENTED

North Georgia's tree-lined mountain roads are a relief from the traffic jams of metro Atlanta. You can spot critters from wild turkeys to deer, and stop off for refreshing visits to waterfalls or savor shopping, lodging, and meals in quaint—and quiet—towns. The area's proximity to metro Atlanta makes it ideal for day trips and overnight stays.

The North Georgia Mountains. North Georgia has become a fascinating meld of the past and the present. Its residents wholeheartedly cherish their Appalachian roots at attractions such as the Foxfire Museum and Heritage Center and the Folk Pottery Museum of Northeast Georgia. They take pride in introducing visitors to their music, as well as their natural surroundings: mountains, hiking trails (including the Appalachian Trail), and waterfalls. But residents are embracing the mountains' potential for new ventures, as well. Award-winning wineries are springing up across the region, and a passion for fine dining is a natural accompaniment.

The Northwest. A trip to northwest Georgia reveals its fascinating history, from its Native American heritage to the state's critical role in the

TOP REASONS TO GO

Wonder at waterfalls: Climb to the top of Amicalola Falls, the tallest cascading waterfall east of the Mississippi, at 729 feet.

Surround yourself in Civil War history: The second-bloodiest battle of the Civil War was fought for two days at Chickamauga & Chattanooga National Military Park. An on-site museum documents the battle.

Take a hike: The starting point of the more than 2,100-mi Appalachian Trail is at Springer Mountain, nine miles north of Amicalola Falls State Park. Even amateurs can walk on the trail at half a dozen Georgia spots such as Dicks Creek Gap, right off the side of the road at Highway 76, 18 mi west of Clayton. A huge rock marker there offers a perfect photo-op.

Step back into Georgia's Cherokee past: Visit New Echota, the former capital of the Cherokee Nation, which offers tribute to the proud tribe. Nearby is the historic Vann House, a beautiful three-story residence of Cherokee Chief James Vann and, later, his son Joseph.

Sample local wine: Several wineries, such as Tiger Mountain Vineyards, have worked to preserve the essence of family farms; others, such as Wolf Mountain Vineyards & Winery, offer dramatic modern architecture amidst the vineyards.

15

Civil War (which is often called "the war between the states" or the "war of northern aggression" here). The Cherokee Nation once had its capital in New Echota, before the federal government forced members of the tribe on a long, tragic resettlement march to Oklahoma, marking the infamous "Trail of Tears." The first gold strike in U.S. history was discovered in the region. A few years later, the Civil War's second bloodiest battle was fought at Chickamauga & Chattanooga National Military Park, which is now commemorated by hundreds of monuments and markers in the country's first Civil War battlefield park.

NORTH GEORGIA PLANNER

WHEN TO GO

Spring, summer, and fall are prime times for travel in North Georgia. Weekends are far busier than weekdays, since many of the region's visitors drive up from nearby Atlanta for a short getaway. For the mountains, the ideal time is October and early November, when fall color is at its peak. Don't arrive in the fall without reservations, and expect traffic, even on secondary roads. The same can be true during spring and early fall festival weekends, when visitors head north to enjoy the spring wildflowers, fall apple and pumpkin harvests, and absolutely blissful weather.

GETTING HERE & AROUND

BY AIR The gateway airports for this region are Hartsfield-Jackson International Airport in Atlanta and Chattanooga Metropolitan Airport in Chattanooga, Tennessee.

BY CAR   Plan on using your car—or renting one—to get around the region. U.S. 19 runs north–south, passing through Dahlonega and up into the North Georgia mountains. U.S. 129 travels northwest from Athens eventually merging with U.S. 19. GA 75 stems off of U.S. 129 and goes through Helen and up into the mountains. U.S. 23/441 will take you north through Clayton; U.S. 76 runs west from Clayton to Dalton, merging for a stretch with GA 5/515. GA 52 runs along the edge of the Blue Ridge Mountains, passing through Ellijay. Interstate 75 is the major artery in the northwesternmost part of the state and passes near the New Echota State Historic Site and the Chickamauga and Chattanooga National Military Park.

BY TAXI   Very few North Georgia communities have taxi services. People in the area are almost completely reliant on private cars.

ESSENTIALS   **Air Contacts Chattanooga Metropolitan Airport** (CHA ✉ *1001 Airport Rd., Chattanooga, TN* ☎ *423/855–2202* ⊕ *www.chattairport.com*). **Hartsfield-Jackson Atlanta International Airport** (ATL ✉ *6000 N. Terminal Pkwy., Atlanta* ☎ *404/530–7300* ⊕ *www.atlanta-airport.com*).

Taxi Contacts Holloway Cab (✉ *5035 Broad St., Toccoa* ☎ *706/886–2839*). **Paddy's Taxi** (✉ *420 WalMart Way PMB 155, Dahlonega* ☎ *706/300–7143*).

ABOUT THE RESTAURANTS & HOTELS
The residents of small towns in lower Appalachia extend hearty hospitality to visitors. Satisfying meals range from traditional Southern fare to trendy gourmet dishes, and comfy, often scenic lodgings provide everything from bed-and-breakfasts to motels and camping to fine inns and lodges. Also, check with visitor bureaus for lists of private owners who rent cabins and cottages.

WHAT IT COSTS				
¢	$	$$	$$$	$$$$
Restaurant	under $10	$10–$14	$15–$19	$20–$24	over $24
Hotel	under $100	$100–$150	$151–$200	$201–$250	over $250

Restaurant prices are for a main course at dinner. Hotel prices are for two people in a standard double room in high season.

PLANNING YOUR TIME
These towns make good day or overnight trips from Atlanta, as they're only one to two hours away.

DISCOUNTS & DEALS
It's hard not to bring back antiques and crafts from North Georgia. But those in the know also make time for a stop at the popular **North Georgia Premium Outlets** (✉ *800 GA 400 South, Dawsonville* ☎ *706/216-3609* ⊕ *www.premiumoutlets.com*), which offers 140 name-brand stores.

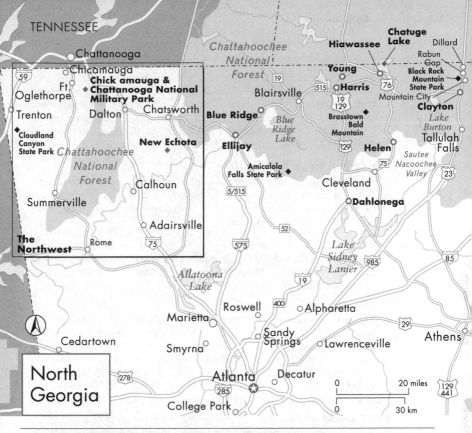

THE NORTH GEORGIA MOUNTAINS

To most Georgians, "North Georgia" means the northeast and north central mountains and foothills—from Clayton and Dillard in the east to Hiawassee and Lake Chatuge in the north, and Blue Ridge and Ellijay and the Cohutta Wilderness to the west. Dahlonega, Helen, and several state parks—Black Rock Mountain, Moccasin Creek, Unicoi, Vogel, and Amicalola Falls—are contained within the broad arc of this scenic mountain region.

DAHLONEGA

Fodor'sChoice *65 mi northeast of Atlanta via GA 400 and GA 60.*

★

Hoards of fortune-seekers stormed the town of Dahlonega (pronounced Dah-LON-eh-gah), in the 1820s after the discovery of gold in the nearby hills. The town's name comes from the Cherokee word for "precious yellow metal." But the boom didn't last long, by 1849 miners were starting to seek riches elsewhere. In fact, the famous call "There's gold in them thar hills!" originated as an enticement to miners in the Georgia mountains to keep their minds away from the lure of the Western gold rush. It worked for a while, but government price fixing eventually made gold mining unprofitable, and by the early 1920s Dahlonega's mining operations had halted completely.

Many former mining settlements became ghost towns, but not Dahlonega. Today it thrives with an irresistible town square filled with country stores, art galleries, coffeehouses, gem shops, old small-town businesses, and several sophisticated restaurants. Gold Rush Days, a festival held the third weekend in October celebrating the first gold rush in 1828, attracts about 200,000 weekend visitors.

GETTING HERE & AROUND

It's easy to spend your entire visit in Dahlonega's quaint town square. But a short drive out of town will take you to the Kangaroo Conservation Center for a tour, allow you to climb down into a gold mine, or to taste wine at the local vintners.

ESSENTIALS

Visitor Information Dahlonega-Lumpkin Chamber of Commerce and Visitors Center (⊠ *13 Park St. S, Dahlonega* ☎ *706/864–3711 or 800/231–5543* ⊕ *www.dahlonega.org*).

EXPLORING

The **Gold Museum,** on the main square, has coins, tools, and several large nuggets on display. Built in 1836, it is the oldest public building in the state, and if you look closely at the bricks that form the building's foundation, you'll notice a sprinkling of gold dust in their formation. Along with the exhibits, the museum has a new high-definition film called *America's First Gold Rush.* ⊠ *1 Public Sq.* ☎ *706/864–2257* ⊕ *www.dahlonega.org* ⊠ *$4* ☉ *Mon.–Sat. 9–5, Sun. 10–5.*

★
⟳ At **Consolidated Gold Mine** tourists can take guided tours of a real mine, which ceased operations in 1904. With 5 mi of underground tunnels, Consolidated is said to be the largest gold mine east of the Mississippi. Enter the mine (which has been reconstructed for safety), pass through a breathtaking stone passage, and then begin a descent of 120 feet into the mine's geological wonders. Guides, a few of them former miners, expound on historical mining techniques and give demonstrations of tools, such as the "widowmaker," a drill that kicks up mining dust and caused lung disease in many miners. After the tour, guests are invited to pan for gold, prospector-style, from a long wooden sluice. Visitors can also pan for minerals and semiprecious to precious gems, such as quartz and sapphire. ⊠ *185 Consolidated Gold Mine Rd.* ☎ *706/864–8473* ⊕ *www.consolidatedgoldmine.com* ⊠ *$13* ☉ *Daily 10–5.*

Fodor'sChoice
★
⟳ The largest collection of kangaroos outside Australia is at the **Kangaroo Conservation Center,** an 87-acre wildlife park. The center has more than 300 'roos, along with blue-winged kookaburras, and a massive blue-crowned pigeon that is as large as a goose. The center has nine species of kangaroos, ranging from a less than two-pound brush-tailed Bettong kangaroo to large varieties that may reach nearly 200 pounds each. Visitors can see a boomerang demonstration, as well as relax and picnic in a lush butterfly garden. Guides are knowledgeable about kangaroos and the other Australian animals and plants that live at the center, and

The Wine Highway

Grapevines and wineries are popping up all over North Georgia, and burgundy-color signs lead the way to vineyards along the **Georgia Wine Highway.** A listing of current wineries is available at ⊕ *www.georgiawine. com.*

CLAYTON

The boutique, family-owned **Persimmon Creek Vineyards** (⊠ *81 Vineyard La., Clayton* ☎ *706/212-7380* ⊕ *persimmoncreekwine.com*) is open by appointment only, but the winery's shop, **Persimmon on the Square** (⊠ *28 E. Savannah St., Clayton* ☎ *706/212-7972*), is open Monday–Tuesday and Thursday–Saturday from 1–6.

Tiger Mountain Vineyards (⊠ *2592 Old Hwy. 44 8 minutes south of Clayton, Tiger* ☎ *706/782-4777* ⊕ *www. tigerwine.com*), started on a five-generation-old family farm in 1995 by Dr. John and Martha Ezzard, is known for unusual varietals of French and Portuguese grapes such as Touriga Nacional and Malbec, as well as the native Norton grape—grown on the slopes of Tiger Mountain. Tastings are complimentary.

HELEN

Habersham Vineyards & Winery (⊠ *7025 S. Main St., on GA 75, Helen* ☎ *706/878-9463* ⊕ *www.habershamwinery.com*) started producing in 1983 and is one of the oldest wineries in the state. Its tasting room also includes an eclectic shop full of wine-related accessories. Habersham tastings are also available at the **Dahlonega Tasting Room** (⊠ *16 N. Park St., Dahlonega* ☎ *706/864-8275* ◷ *Mon.–Sat. 10–6, Sun. 12:30–6*).

YOUNG HARRIS

Crane Creek Vineyards (⊠ *916 Crane Creek Rd., off GA 515, Young Harris* ☎ *706/379-1236* ⊕ *www. cranecreekvineyards.com*) produces 12 regional artisanal wines based on the 10 grape varieties it grows. The most popular choices are Vidal Blanc, Seyval, and Cabernet Franc.

JASPER

Sharp Mountain Vineyards (⊠ *110 Rathgeb Trail, Jasper 30143* ☎ *770/735-1210* ⊕ *www. sharpmountainvineyards.com*) produces 14 wines from 12 varietals. Visitors get great mountain vistas from the property.

15

they emphasize conservation efforts on-site and recycling and conservation at home. Plan on spending at least three hours here. Admission for the guided tour is by advance ticket purchase only, and children must be six years old and in first grade or older. Times for guided and walking tours are subject to change, so call or check the Web site before visiting. ⊠ *222 Bailey-Waters Rd., 15 mi from Dahlonega via GA 52, Dawsonville* ☎ *706/265-6100* ⊕ *www.kangaroocenter.com* ⌨ *$18–$30* ◷ *Mid-Mar.–Nov., Tues.–Sat. 9–5.*

In the Dahlonega area, visitors can find the largest concentration of wineries in Georgia. **Wolf Mountain Vineyards & Winery,** is a 25-acre vineyard on a ridgetop with hillside plantings of Cabernet Sauvignon, Syrah, Mourvedre, and Touriga Nacional. The dramatic Craftsman-style lodge housing the winery and café offers tastings for a fee and serves lunch Thursday through Saturday from noon to 3, and a popular Sunday brunch between

12:30 and 2:30. Reservations are required. Wolf Mountain also offers quarterly gourmet dinners and guided tours of the grounds on weekends at 2. Some of the winery's acclaimed labels include Plenitude, a 70% Chardonnay and 30% Viognier blend; Claret, an estate reserve Cabernet and Mourvedre; and Instinct, a Rhone-style red blend. Call for special winery tour or tasting information. ✉*180 Wolf Mountain Trail, off U.S. 19/60, north of Dahlonega* ☎*706/867–9862* ⊕*www.wolfmountainvineyards.com* ♥*Mar.–mid-Dec., Thurs.–Sun. 12–5.*

Three Sisters Vineyards, Dahlonega's first family farm winery, has 15 acres of plantings including Cabernet Franc, Merlot, Cabernet Sauvignon, Pinot Blanc, Vidal Blanc, and Chardonnay, along with American varietals such as Cynthiana-Norton. The relaxed winery is named for nearby Three Sisters Mountain, which is visible from the farm's gazebo. Deli meats and cheeses, as well as artisan breads, are available, and a patio provides a comfortable picnic spot. The down-to-earth tasting room is decorated with folk art from the North Georgia area, including a poster that proclaims "Thar's Wine in Them Thar Hills." A favorite from the winery is the robust "Fat Boy Red." Special events, including the Georgia Wine Country Festival the first weekend in June, occur monthly. ✉*439 Vineyard Way, northeast of Dahlonega* ☎*706/865–9463* ⊕*www.threesistersvineyards.com* ♥*Thurs.–Sat. 11–5, Sun. 1–5.*

Frogtown Cellars is a 50-acre vineyard and winery offering picturesque mountain views from its deck and a dramatic dining room. The winery features an underground, gravity-flow wine-making facility on three floors, which utilizes gravity in place of pumps, with wine crush on the first level, fermentation on the second, and storage in wine barrels on the third and lowest level. The winery has won dozens of awards nationwide. Lunch is available on days the winery is open; a three-course Sunday brunch and wine-tasting dinners are available by reservation. ✉*700 Ridge Point Dr., northeast of Dahlonega* ☎*706/865–0687* ⊕*www.frogtownwine.com* ♥*Feb.–Mar., Sat. noon–6, Sun. noon–5; Apr.–Aug., Fri. and Sun. noon–5, Sat. noon–6; Sept. and Oct., daily noon–5; Nov. and Dec., Sat. noon–6, Fri. and Sun. noon–5.*

BlackStock Vineyards and Winery, on 90 acres, offers more than a dozen traditional European premium-quality wines. The large outdoor deck overlooks both the vineyards and the mountains. The lodge, built with old barn wood, pulls in elements from the setting, with a stacked stone three-sided fireplace and hand-crafted wrought-iron work replicating the look of the grapevines. A cascading waterfall is a highlight of the wine cellar. Signature wines are the Viognier and Merlot. The winery's ACE—a family reserve blend of Touriga, Mourvedre, and the winery's best Merlot—is named for owners David and Trish Harris' three children: Austin, Chandler, and Eliza. Check the Web site for information on regular wine dinners, fresh fare on the grill, and live music. ✉*5400 Town Creek Rd., Dahlonega* ☎*706/219–2789* ⊕*www.bsvw.com* ♥*Mon.–Sat. 10–6, Sun. 12:30–6.*

**OFF THE
BEATEN
PATH**

Amicalola Falls. This is claimed to be the highest cascading waterfall east of the Mississippi, with waters plunging an eye-popping 729 feet through a cluster of seven cascades. The surrounding 1,021-acre state park is dotted with scenic campsites and cottages strategically situated near a network of nature trails, picnic sites, and fishing streams. The southern starting point of the more than 2,100-mi Appalachian Trail begins near Amicalola Falls. ⊠ *Off GA 52, 18 mi west of Dahlonega, Dawsonville* ☎ *706/265–8888* 🎫 *Parking $3* ☉ *Daily 7 AM–10 PM.*

WHERE TO EAT

$$–$$$
AMERICAN
★

✕ **Corkscrew Café.** This cozy and intimate restaurant has terra-cotta colored walls covered with photography from a local artist and a large covered patio. Specialties include hand-carved steaks with a portobello mushroom demi-glaze, seared sashimi-grade tuna, and rack of lamb with a curry-orange glaze. Locals love the curry squash bisque and French onion soup as well as a macadamia-crusted mahi with a grilled pineapple and mango salsa and eggplant mascarpone. Inexpensive lunch entrées, also available for dinner, include sandwiches, salads, and soup. ⊠ *51 W. Main St.* ☎ *706/867–8551* ⊕ *www.thecorkscrewcafe. com* ▭ *AE, D, MC, V* ☉ *Closed Mon.*

$–$$
AMERICAN
★

✕ **The Crimson Moon Café.** Set in the historic Parker-Nix Storehouse, a general store built in the 1850s, this funky spot offers everything from a cheesesteak wrap with roasted red peppers, mushrooms, and onions to fettuccine alfredo. Pizzas are fresh, and the less expensive lunch menu is available into the evening. Breakfast is served Friday through Sunday. The intimate venue features live acoustic music, from blues and bluegrass to Celtic, folk rock, and country, five nights a week. Tickets can be purchased in advance by phone and online. ⊠ *24 North Park St., Suite A, Dahlonega* ☎ *706/864–3982* ⊕ *www.thecrimsonmoon. com* ▭ *D, MC, V* ☉ *Closed Tues.*

WHERE TO STAY

$–$$
Fodor's Choice
★

🖼 **Amicalola Falls Lodge.** One of the most appealing mountain lodges in Georgia is part of the state park system. As you sit beside a large stone fireplace in the massive glass-windowed lobby, you'll have panoramic views over the mountains. All rooms, in fact, have mountain views except for three that overlook the woods. The rooms aren't fancy, but you can pay far less here than at a private country inn. The park also has 14 cottages for rent and a restaurant serving buffet meals year around. Weekend nature programs are presented in the lobby. **Pros:** the top of Amicalola Falls is less than a five-minute walk away, and a handicap trail is also available; stunning views of the mountains. **Cons:** no conference center; no swimming pool. ⊠ *418 Amicalola Falls Lodge Rd., 20 mi west of Dahlonega via GA 52, Dawsonville* ☎ *706/265–8888 or 800/573–9656* ⊕ *www.amicalolafalls.com* 🛏 *53 rooms, 4 suites, 14 cottages* ♿ *In-room: Wi-Fi. In-hotel: restaurant, Wi-Fi* ▭ *MC, V.*

$

🖼 **Historic Worley Bed & Breakfast.** This B&B occupies an 1845 antebellum home with two garden courtyards, and is within walking distance of the Dahlonega town square. The basic breakfast includes French toast, breakfast casserole, bacon, biscuits, and grits. **Pros:** it's the only historic B&B in the area; each room has a television and private bath.

15

Cons: the building offers some wireless hot spots, but not throughout the facility; it has no elevator and offers limited handicap access; rooms are decorated in traditional style but can feel small. ✉ *168 Main St. W* ☎ *706/864–7002 or 800/348–8094* ⊕ *www.bbonline.com/ga/worley* ⇩ *7 rooms* ⊟ *MC, V* ⦿ *BP.*

$ ⚎ **Len Foote Hike Inn.** A love of the environment is clearly evident at the
★   Len Foote Hike Inn. The inn composts all waste—even relying on self-composting toilets—uses solar panels for heating and electricity, and has four worm colonies that recycle all organic waste, from office paper to kitchen scraps and even old blue jeans. No cell phones, Blackberries, or radios are allowed. A 5-mi hike of moderate difficulty (three hours each way), leads visitors to this backcountry pack-it-in-and-pack-it-out inn at Amicalola State Park. Although the inn has electric lights, there are no electrical outlets, and the showers and bathrooms are in a separate bathhouse. Rustic wood-panel rooms each have two bunk beds and meals are served family-style in the dining hall. Dinner and breakfast are included in the stay, and sack lunches are also available. Hikers *must* check-in no later than 2 PM at the Amicalola Falls State Park visitor center. ■TIP➜ The inn is a 4½-mi hike from Springer Mountain, the southern terminus of the Appalachian Trail. Pros: lots of puzzles, board games, and books are available; guests need only backpack in with their toothbrushes, toothpaste, overnight clothes, and water bottles. Cons: reservations required by phone or online; rooms book quickly, especially on weekends and in October. ✉ *240 Amicalola Falls State Park Rd., 20 mi west of Dahlonega via GA 52, Dawsonville* ☎ *800/581–8032* ⊕ *www.hike-inn.com* ⇩ *20 rooms* ⌙ *In-room: no a/c, no phone* ⊟ *MC, V* ⦿ *MAP.*

$$ ⚎ **Lily Creek Lodge.** This eclectic-looking B&B appears slightly Bavarian on the outside, and some of the rooms echo Venice, Africa, Morocco, and Argentina with their decor. The lodge sits on 9 acres boasting native flower beds, a waterfall and an outdoor hot tub. Wireless access is available throughout. Satellite TV is available. Pros: lovely grounds; close proximity to Dahlonega, Montaluce, and Wolf Mountain Vineyards & Winery. Cons: the stairs to the uppermost room, on the front on the building, are very narrow; no elevator. ✉ *2608 Auraria Rd.* ☎ *706/864–6848 or 888/844–2694* ⊕ *www.lilycreeklodge.com* ⇩ *10 rooms, 3 suites* ⌙ *In-room: kitchen, Wi-Fi (some). In-hotel: pool, Wi-Fi* ⊟ *AE, MC, V* ⦿ *BP.*

$$–$$$ ⚎ **The Smith House.** Just a block from the town square, the Smith House
Fodor's Choice   has been serving guests for generations. Its two nearby villas have bal-
★   conies that look out on the square. The hotel offers family-style dining for lunch and dinner. During remodeling several years ago a gold mine was found 30 feet under the property. Access to the mine is free to the public. Pros: luxury linens, flat-screen TVs, and upscale bathrooms; handicap access is available on the main floor. Cons: the North Georgia College and State University parking lot and recreation facility is located right next door. ✉ *84 S. Chestatee St.* ☎ *800/852–9577 or 706/867–7000* ⊕ *www.smithhouse.com* ⇩ *9 rooms in main house, 4 in carriage house, two villas nearby.* ⌙ *In hotel: pool.* ⊟ *AE, MC, V* ⦿ *BP.*

NIGHTLIFE & THE ARTS

The **Historic Holly Theater** (✉ *69 W. Main St., Dahlonega* ☎ *706/864–3759* ⊕ *www.hollytheater.com*), a well-restored classic small-town movie theater built in 1946, stages live theater, movies, children's performances, and special events. "The Mountain Music and Medicine Show," a live production featuring bluegrass and gospel music and humorous tales from Dahlonega's past, is presented regularly.

SPORTS & THE OUTDOORS

Appalachian Outfitters (✉ *2084 S. Chestatee, Hwy. 60 S, Dahlonega* ☎ *706/864–7117 or 800/426–7117* ⊕ *www.canoegeorgia.com* ⊙ *Memorial Day–Labor Day, daily 10–3; Apr.–mid-May and early-Sept.–Oct., Thurs.–Sun. 10–3*) provides equipment and maps for self-guided canoeing and kayaking trips on the Chestatee and Etowah Rivers. Tube rentals and shuttle service are also available for tubing trips on the Chestatee.

HELEN & SAUTEE-NACOOCHEE VALLEY

15

32 mi northeast of Dahlonega, 88 mi northeast of Atlanta.

Helen was founded at the turn of the 20th century as a simple lumber outpost. In the 1960s, when logging declined, business leaders came up with a plan to transform the tiny village of 300 into a theme town, and "Alpine Helen" was born. Today many businesses along Helen's central streets sport a distinctive German facade, giving an initial impression that you've stumbled on a Bavarian vista in the middle of Appalachia. ■**TIP→Don't expect small-town prices for anything from parking to ATM charges.** This is clearly not Bavaria, but the effect can be briefly contagious, making you feel as if you've stepped into a fairy tale. If it's too touristy, move on to nearby areas for delightful crafts, shopping, and dining. Sautee and Nacoochee are the home of the Habersham Winery, the Folk Pottery Museum of North Georgia, several other small museums, and a number of other pottery and craft shops.

GETTING HERE & AROUND

While the quirky town of Helen may merit a quick stop, other nearby attractions a short drive away are also well worth visiting. Try the Folk Pottery Museum of Northeast Georgia to check out the area's centuries-old pottery tradition and Georgia's famous "face jugs." The Sautee and Nacoochee areas are accessible just south of Helen off GA 75.

ESSENTIALS

Visitor Information Helen Welcome Center (✉ *726 Bruckenstrasse 30545* ☎ *706/878–2181 or 800/858–8027* ⊕ *www.helenga.org*).

EXPLORING

Chattahoochee National Forest covers about 1-million acres of land in North Georgia. It's named after the Chattahoochee River, whose headwaters are in the North Georgia mountains. The forest was created piecemeal, beginning in 1911, from bits and pieces of often environmentally degraded and abused land, and was officially established in 1936. About 15% of the Chattahoochee is wilderness. The national forest supports an estimated 500 species of fish and wildlife, including black bears, white-tailed deer, and wild turkeys. In 1959, 96,000 acres of land in middle Georgia were added, and the combined forests are called the Chattahoochee-Oconee National Forests and total more than 865,000 acres. The forest offers a wide range of recreational opportunities such as camping, hiking, and fishing (from native trout to largemouth bass and bream). ⊠*1755 Cleveland Hwy., Gainesville* ☎*770/297–3000* ⊕*www.fs.fed.us/conf.*

☼ A child-friendly museum, **Charlemagne's Kingdom** in Helen recreates sections of Germany, from the North Sea to the Alps, all in HO model-train scale (1/87th of the actual size). The Autobahn is depicted, as is the entire walled town of Rothenburg (there are 350 building replicas) and moving hot-air balloons. There are six running trains, thousands of hand-painted figurines, and sound effects including the ocean, a carnival, and German music. The shop sells Lionel trains, Thomas the Tank Engines, and John Deere toys. Willi Lindhorst, a native of Oldenburg, Germany, created the train layout and its trappings and owns the shop with his wife Judi. ⊠*8808 N. Main St., Helen* ☎*706/878–2200* ⊕*www.georgiamodelrailroad.com* ☒*$5* ☉*Mar.–Dec., daily 10–6; Jan. and Feb., call for hrs.*

FodorśChoice
★
☼ **The Folk Pottery Museum of Northeast Georgia,** 4 mi southeast of Helen, showcases a 200-year unbroken tradition of folk pottery in northeast Georgia (especially in nearby Mossy Creek and the Gillsville-Lula area). Part of the 5,000-square-foot facility, which opened in late 2006 in a building that represents the shelters that potters built for their kilns, outlines how pottery is made and how it was used for essential household purposes. It also shows how pottery later evolved into a folk art form. Exhibits showcase a 200-piece collection donated to the museum, including the whimsical face jugs that have become an emblem of Southern folk art. Demonstrations of pottery-making are offered one Saturday a month. Call ahead for dates and times. ⊠*GA 255 N, four miles southeast of Alpine Helen, Sautee Nacoochee* ☎*706/878–3300* ⊕*www.folkpotterymuseum.com* ☒*$4* ☉*Weekdays 10–5, weekends noon–5.*

WHERE TO STAY & EAT

$$–$$$
ECLECTIC ✗**Nacoochee Grill.** Beef, chicken, and fish grilled on a wood-fired grill are the focus at this casual restaurant set in a cheerful old house in Nacoochee Village, just outside town. The roasted corn, trout, and salmon chowder is a specialty. White chili is another favorite, along with crab cakes. Pies made from local apples are available seasonally. Be aware of extra charges to share the grill's generous lunches and dinners. ⊠*7277 S. Main St., Helen* ☎*706/878–8020* ☐*AE, D, MC, V.*

$$$$
★ ▦**The Lodge at Smithgall Woods.** As part of a 5,600-acre heritage preserve park run by the state of Georgia, the lodge, set in old-growth hardwoods, consists of five separate cottages. The centerpiece is a two-story, four-bedroom cabin constructed of Montana lodge-pole pine. Dinner and breakfast, featuring locally grown fruit and vegetables and local specialties like mountain trout, are included in the rates for Friday and Saturday stays. The state park has one of the best trout

streams in Georgia, and the lodge is often used as an executive retreat by Atlanta businesspeople. Guests can book an individual room, a cottage (three to five rooms), or the entire lodge. **Pros:** a luxurious and secluded retreat; on-site chef; nearby and on-site hiking trails are available. **Cons:** no pets allowed; bring your own fishing equipment; no elevator. ✉ *61 Tsalaki Trail, Helen* ☎ *706/878–3087 or 800/318–5248* ⊕ *www.smithgallwoods.com* ⇆ *14 rooms in 5 cottages* ⚬ *In-hotel: Wi-Fi.* ⊟ *AE, D, MC, V* ❍*FAP.*

$ ▦ **The Lodge at Unicoi.** Choose either the comfortable mountain lodge, with 100 attractive lodge rooms, or a one-, two-, or three-bedroom cottage (some with a fireplace), at this state-run accommodation. You can fish, canoe, or swim in the 53-acre lake, play tennis, hike on 12 mi of trails, bike on a 7.5-mi-loop trail, or take part in educational and nature events led by park rangers. In summer and fall reservations are required and can be made up to 11 months in advance. A separate restaurant is available. **Pros:** live bluegrass and gospel music on Saturday nights from May through November; less than 3 mi from Helen. **Cons:** breakfast isn't included in the rate; 22 of the 30 cottage don't have televisions or telephones. ✉ *1788 GA 356, 3 mi north of Helen,Helen* ☎ *706/878–2201 or 800/573–9659* ⊕ *gastateparks.org* ⇆ *100 rooms, 30 cottages, 84 campsites* ⚬ *In-room: kitchen (some). In-hotel: restaurant, tennis courts, Wi-Fi* ⊟ *AE, D, MC, V.*

SPORTS & THE OUTDOORS

TUBING "Tube the Hootch" with **Cool River Tubing** (✉ *590 Edelweiss Strasse, Helen* ☎ *706/878–2665 or 800/896–4595* ❍ *Late May–early Sept.*), which shuttles you on a bus upriver to begin the float back to town. Choose the short (1″ hours) or long (2″ hours) float trip. Prices are $5 for a single trip of either length or $9 all day. Cool River also operates a waterslide. A combination all-day ticket for tubing and waterslide is $10.

SHOPPING

Fodor'sChoice In an old gristmill with beautiful views of the Soque River, **Mark of the**
★ **Potter** (✉ *9982 GA 197 N, Clarkesville* ☎ *706/947–3440*) offers an outstanding selection of pottery from more than 30 artisans. The emphasis is on functional pieces, with a great variety of clay and firing techniques and glazes in every imaginable color. Items range from coffee scoops to lamps, mugs to elaborate vases and casserole dishes. ■**TIP**➔ **The shop is legendary among Georgia pottery-lovers.** Children and adults alike will enjoy sitting on the porch and feeding the huge pet trout. A potter works on the wheel at the shop on Saturday and Sunday.

Old Sautee Store (✉ *2315 GA 17, 5 mi south of Helen, Sautee* ☎ *706/ 878–2281* ❍ *Mon.–Sat. 10–5:30, Sun. noon–5:30*) has been operating continuously for more than 130 years. The museum portion displays everything from old-time Lydia Pinkham Tonic for "women's problems" to Octagon, a lye soap often used many decades ago to wash laundry. The retail store, heavily influenced by an earlier owner's Scandinavian heritage, sells amber jewelry, Norwegian flatbread, and Swedish farmer's cheese. Shoppers can also pick up old-time candy and gums, a variety of clothing perfect for mountain hiking and visiting, and toys.

15

   The Gourd Place (✉ *2319 Duncan Bridge Rd., Sautee* ☎ *706/865–4048* ⊙ *Apr.–Dec. 23, Mon.–Sat. 10–5, Sun. 1–5; Jan.–Mar., by appointment*) is a unique museum and gourd and pottery store filled with colorful gourd collections from around the world. Owners Priscilla Wilson and Janice Lymburner sell gourds and supplies to preserve dried gourds (a Southern specialty). They also produce attractive natural-glazed stoneware and porcelain dinnerware, vases, bowls, and luminaries using liquid clay poured into gourd molds.

   Hickory Flat Pottery (✉ *13664 U.S. 197 N, 4 mi north of Mark of the Potter, Clarkesville* ☎ *706/947–0030* ⊕ *hickoryflatpottery.com* ⊙ *Jan.– Mar.: Mon., Fri., and Sat. noon–5, Sun. noon–6; Apr.–Dec., Mon.–Sat. 10–6, Sun. noon–6, closed Tues.*). This working pottery studio in a large 116-year-old roadside farmhouse is filled with lots more than "just" beautiful pottery. Vibrant stained glass, a variety of jewelry, fiber art, and copper art are featured, along with the vivid, decorative and functional stoneware of shop owner Cindy Angliss, who enjoys sharing her craft by sending little bags of clay home with children. See the Web site for kiln openings and tours.

EN ROUTE

Beginning and ending in Helen, the **Russell-Brasstown Scenic Byway** is a 41-mi loop through some of the most dramatic mountain scenery in northeastern Georgia. Start the counterclockwise drive from GA17/74 north of Helen, turn left on GA 180, left again at GA 348, and another left at GA 75 Alternate back to Helen. The loop passes the Raven Cliff Wilderness, wildlife management areas, the headwaters of the Chattahoochee River, a section of the Appalachian Trail, and goes near the state parks of Vogel, Unicoi, Smithgall Woods, and Brasstown Bald mountain.

CLAYTON

35 mi northeast of Helen via GA 356, GA 197, and U.S. 76.

The town of Clayton, with a downtown filled with shops, is a gateway to North Georgia's mountains. The beautiful lakeshore and the grandeur of Black Rock Mountain State Park and Tallulah Gorge make a day tour of this area a memorable experience. Plenty of shopping and dining is available in Clayton and Clarkesville.

GETTING HERE & AROUND

Clayton makes a good base to explore Tallulah Gorge State Park and its falls, and Black Rock Mountain State Park. A short drive northwest on U.S. 76 will take you to several of the region's most appealing lakes, including Rabun and Chatuge.

ESSENTIALS

Visitor Information Rabun County Welcome Center (✉ *232 U.S. 441N, Clayton* ☎ *706/782–4812* ⊕ *www.gamountains.com*).

EXPLORING

Fodor's Choice **Tallulah Gorge State Park** is home to a 2-mi-long, 1,000-foot-deep canyon, one of the deepest in the country. In the late 1800s this area was ★ one of the most-visited destinations in the Southeast, with 17 hotels to house tourists who came to see the roaring falls on the Tallulah River. Then, in 1912, to provide electric power, the "Niagara of the South" was dammed, and the falls and tourism dried up. Today the state of Georgia has designated more than 20 mi of the state park as walking and mountain-biking trails. There's also a 16,000-square-foot interpretive center, a 63-acre lake with a beach, a picnic shelter, and 50 tent and RV sites. Water is released for experienced canoers and kayakers a few times a year and aesthetic flows replicate the original river. See the Web site for details. ⊠ *U.S. 441, Tallulah Falls* ☎ *706/754–7970, 706/754–7979 for camping reservations* ⊕ *www. gastateparks.org/info/tallulah* ⊠ *$4 parking fee* ☉ *Daily 8 AM–dusk. Interpretive center 8–5.*

> ### HIKING TIPS
>
> Each day, 100 hiking permits are issued at the interpretive center for spectacular **Tallulah Gorge**, considered one of the most stunning gorges in the eastern United States. The hike to the floor of the 1,000-foot gorge with its lush vegetation, scenic waterfalls, and rocky bottom takes three to four hours. Tennis shoes, hiking boots, or river sandals are required for the strenuous hike. Damp walkways and riverbeds can be slick, so use extreme caution. Rim trails to overlooks are also open to visitors.

15

Fodor's Choice ★ ☙ The **Foxfire Museum and Heritage Center** is a collection of 20 log cabins, about half of which are authentic and date back as far as 1820, while others were assembled to re-create Appalachian life before the days of electricity and running water. The impetus behind the effort? Students who wrote articles for a magazine at the Rabin Gap-Nacoochee School based on generations-old family stories. Their excitement in chronicling early life in the Appalachians has led to more than a dozen Foxfire books, which have sold nearly 9 million copies. The nonprofit foundation behind Foxfire opened the center to students and teachers worldwide, inviting them to the Foxfire Course for Teachers. The site is open to the public. Homes, a grist mill, a blacksmith's shop and a church are among those represented on the paths, accessible by a rough gravel road. The educational philosophy of students passing along oral history through their writing continues today at the Rabun County High School. ⊠ *200 Foxfire La., off U.S. 441 at Black Rock Mountain Pkwy., Mountain City* ☎ *706/746–5828* ⊠ *$6* ☉ *Mon.–Sat. 8:30–4:30.*

★ The **Chattooga River** was the first river in the Southeast to be designated a Wild and Scenic River by Congress. It begins at Whiteside Mountain in North Carolina and forms the border between Georgia and South Carolina. With Class II to Class V rapids, the Chattooga is popular for white-water rafting, especially in spring and summer when water levels are highest. Movie buffs should note that this was one of the locations for the movie *Deliverance*. ⊠ *From Clayton drive east 7 mi on U.S. 76 to Hwy. 76 Bridge at Georgia–South Carolina state line.*

Lake Rabun was built in 1915, the first of six lakes in the state built by Georgia Railway and Power Co. It covers only 834 acres, but its small size is misleading as its narrow fingers dart through mountain valleys.

Lightly visited by tourists and populated with weekend homes and old boat houses, it has a low-key charm. The lake offers boating and fishing, and there's a small beach at Rabun Beach Recreation Area at the east end of the lake. ⊠ *West of U.S. 23/441 via Old Hwy. 441S and Burton Lake Rd., 2˝ mi southwest of Clayton* ☎ *888/472–5253* ⊕ *www.lakerabun.com.*

ℭ Another of the six lakes built by Georgia Railway and Power Co., the 2,700-acre **Lake Burton** is in the Chattahoochee National Forest. On the lake, at GA 197, is the **Lake Burton Fish Hatchery,** alongside Moccasin Creek State Park. It has trout raceways (used to raise trout from fingerlings), and a kids-only trout-fishing area for ages 11 and younger, as well as honorary Georgia fishing license holders (issued to disabled fishermen and those 65 and older). A catfish pond for the public is also available on the grounds without charge. ⊠ *3655 Hwy. 197, off U.S. 76, west of Clayton, Clarkesville* ☎ *706/947–3194* ☞ *$3 parking fee for park; no parking fee for hatchery.*

★ At more than 3,600 feet, **Black Rock Mountain State Park** is the highest state park in Georgia. Named for the black gneiss rock visible on cliffs in the area, the 1,738-acre park has 10 mi of trails, a 17-acre lake, 64 camp and RV sites, and 10 cottages. The park offers majestic overlooks and a trail that leads visitors along the Eastern Continental Divide, from which water flows south and east to eventually reach the Atlantic Ocean, and on the other side, north and west to the mighty Mississippi River. Stop by the ranger station for extensive information on trails. ⊠ *Black Rock Mountain Pkwy., off U.S. 441, 3 mi northwest of Clayton, Mountain City* ☎ *706/746–2141, 800/864–7275 for camping and cottage reservations* ⊕ *www.gastateparks.org/info/blackrock* ☞ *$3 daily use fee* ◷ *Daily 7 AM–10 PM.*

WHERE TO EAT

$$$–$$$$
AMERICAN
Fodor'sChoice
★

✕ **Glen-Ella Springs Inn & Meeting Place.** This gourmet restaurant serves meals in two cozy dining rooms in this more than 100-year-old lodge. Dishes are prepared with fresh herbs grown on the premises and local microgreens and produce. Entrées range from boneless filet of rainbow trout and herb-crusted rack of New Zealand lamb to macadamia-crusted chicken breast. Portions are large, but there's a charge to share. For lighter fare, try crab cakes, portobello mushrooms, and sea scallops or a variety of creative salads. Strong service and entrée presentation are a staple. ⊠ *1789 Bear Gap Rd., Clarkesville* ☎ *706/754–7295 or 877/456–7527* ⊕ *www.glenella.com* ⚭ *Reservations essential* ◷ *Daily 6 PM–9:30 PM, No lunch* ▤ *AE, D, MC, V* ⦿ *BP.*

WHERE TO STAY

¢–$ ▦**Dillard House.** An inviting cluster of cottages and motel-style rooms,
★ this establishment sits on a plateau near the state border. Some rooms
have vistas of the Blue Ridge Mountains, stone fireplaces, or interior
French doors, and many open onto a large front porch with rocking-
chairs. All rooms look out onto the beautifully landscaped grounds.
Pros: located less than a half hour from Smoky Mountain Railway;
fly-fishing and horseback riding are available for a fee; all rooms look
out onto the beautifully landscaped grounds. **Cons:** the on-site restaurant relies too much on its past reputation. ⊠*768 Franklin St., Dillard*
☎*706/746–5348 or 800/541–0671* ⊕*www.dillardhouse.com* ⟿*90
rooms, 25 chalets, 4 cottages, 6 suites* ⟁*In-room: kitchen (some),
refrigerator (some), Wi-Fi. In-hotel: restaurant, tennis courts* ▤*AE,
D, DC, MC, V.*

$$ ▦**Glen-Ella Springs Inn & Meeting Place.** This restored country inn, con-
Fodor'sChoice structed in 1875 and listed on the National Register of Historic Places,
★ has a rustic but polished charm. Nestled in a quiet out-of-the-way
location on a beautifully landscaped 17 acres, the inn's well-appointed
rooms feature antiques and comfortable, attractive furnishings. There
are no TVs in the rooms, but they are available in the large garden room,
complete with snacks and comfortable seating, as well as in the newly
redecorated lobby. You can play volleyball, badminton, horseshoes,
or croquet, or practice your swing on the mini-putting green on the
grounds, or sip wine at Glen-Ella's tasting room. **Pros:** the staff is eager
to make the stay special; picturesque perennial and herb gardens; golf,
hiking, boating, fishing, wineries, and horseback riding are all nearby;
family movie nights. **Cons:** the spring-fed swimming pool can be quite
chilly; inn on a gravel road; restaurants require a drive to Clarkesville
or Clayton. ⊠*1789 Bear Gap Rd., Clarkesville* ☎*706/754–7295 or
877/456–7527* ⊕*www.glenella.com* ⟿*12 rooms, 4 suites* ⟁*In-room:
no TV, Wi-Fi. In-hotel: restaurant, pool* ▤*AE, D, MC, V* ⊺❘*BP.*

$ ▦**Lake Rabun Hotel.** Set in shady hemlocks across the road from Lake
Rabun, this rustic hotel has rough-hewn wood paneling and a field-
stone fireplace. The inn was built in 1922. **Pros:** furniture is hand-
made; visitors can take a sunset cruise, rent a pontoon boat, fish, or
swim in the lake. **Cons:** no television in the rooms. ⊠*35 Andrea La.,
Lakemont* ☎*706/782–4946* ⊕*www.lakerabunhotel.com* ⟿*9 private
suites* ⟁*In-room: No TV. In-hotel: restaurant, bar* ▤*AE, D, MC, V.*

SPORTS & THE OUTDOORS

WHITE-WATER The North Carolina–based **Nantahala Outdoor Center** (⊠*851A Chat-
RAFTING *tooga Ridge Rd., 13 mi from Clayton off U.S. 76, Mountain Rest,
SC* ☎*800/232–7238* ⊕*www.noc.com*), the largest rafting company in
the region, runs part-day, daylong, and overnight white-water rafting
trips on the Chattooga River, from $84 per person. **Southeastern Expedi-
tions LLC** (⊠*7350 U.S. 76 E, Clayton* ☎*800/868–7238*) has full-day
trips starting at $79 per person.

15

SHOPPING

★ **Main Street Gallery** (⌧*51 N. Main St. 30525* ☎*706/782–2440* ◐*Closed Wed. and Sun.*), one of the state's best sources for folk art, carries works by more than 75 regional artists, including Sarah Rakes, O.L. Samuels, Jay Schuette, and Jimmie Lee Sudduth. The store also carries jewelry, pottery, paintings, and sculptures. A wide variety of quality local arts and crafts items, such as jewelry, paintings, pottery, stained glass, and wood carvings, are offered at **Georgia Heritage Center for the Arts** (⌧*U.S. 441,* ☎*706/754–5989*).

HIAWASSEE, YOUNG HARRIS & LAKE CHATUGE

26 mi northwest of Clayton, via U.S. 76; 21 mi north of Helen via GA 75/17.

The little town of Hiawassee, population 750, and nearby Young Harris, population 600, are near the largest lake in North Georgia, Lake Chatuge, and the tallest mountain in the state, Brasstown Bald. The lake has excellent boating and other water-themed recreation. Appealing mountain resorts are nearby as well. A half-hour drive leads to Brasstown Bald, where temperatures even on the hottest summer day rarely rise above 80° F. The Georgia Mountain Fair, held annually, has a permanent location on the shores of Lake Chatuge. A number of festivals are held at the fairgrounds every year, including the Rhododendron and Bluegrass festivals in May and the Fall Festival and State Fiddler's Convention in October. The Georgia Mountain Fair claims to be the "Country Music Capital of Georgia."

ESSENTIALS

Visitor Information Towns County Tourism Association (⌧*1411 Jack Dayton Circle, Young Harris* ☎ *706/896–4966* ⊕*www.mountaintopga.com*).

EXPLORING

Fodor'sChoice **Brasstown Bald**, in the Chattahoochee National Forest, reaches 4,784
★ feet, the highest point in Georgia. Below the Bald is Georgia's only
ⓒ cloud forest, an area of lichen-covered trees often kept wet by clouds and fog. From the observation platform at the top of the Bald on a clear day you can see Georgia, North Carolina, South Carolina, and Tennessee. A paved but steep ˝-mi foot trail leads from the parking lot (where there are restrooms and a picnic area) to the visitor center, which has exhibits and interpretative programs. You also can ride a bus ($2) to the visitor center. ⌧*GA 180 Spur, 18 mi southwest of Hiawassee via U.S. 76, GA 75, GA 180, and GA 180 Spur* ☎*706/745–6928* ⊕*www.fs.fed.us/conf* ⌧*$3 day use fee, $2 shuttle* ◐*Mid-Apr.–late May, weekends 10–5; late May–Oct., daily 10–5.*

WHERE TO STAY

$$–$$$ ▣**Brasstown Valley Resort.** For upscale, lodge-style accommodations, this
★ resort is a great option. The rooms are comfortable and spacious, in an elegant but rustic style. Some have fireplaces and balconies overlooking the valley. The stone fireplace in the lobby is an impressive 70 feet high. The resort also features a variety of sports activities. **Pros:** elegant rooms,

some with fireplaces and balconies. **Cons:** far-flung location. ✉6321 *U.S. 76, Young Harris* ☎706/379–9900 or 800/201–3205 ⊕*www. brasstownvalley.com* 🛏*102 rooms, 32 cottages, 5 suites* ☐*In-room: Wi-Fi. In-hotel: restaurant, bar, golf course, tennis courts, pool, gym* ☐*AE, D, DC, MC, V* ⦿*BP.*

<table>
<tr><td colspan="2">CLOSED ON SUNDAY?</td></tr>
<tr><td>Planning on shopping and eating out? Call ahead. Many smaller town shops—such as those in Clayton, Ellijay, Blue Ridge, and Blairsville—are closed on Sunday. But Dahlonega and Helen shops are open daily.</td></tr>
</table>

$$ 🏨 **The Ridges Resort and Club.** Many of the beautifully appointed rooms in this lodge are decorated with leather furnishings, stone steps, and rustic wood and have gorgeous views of Lake Chatuge. A nearby marina has boat rentals, including pontoons, paddleboats, sailboats, and kayaks. **Pros:** the lobby has a towering fieldstone fireplace and a floor-to-ceiling window that faces the lake; boat rentals nearby. **Cons:** two-hour drive from Atlanta; light continental breakfast. ✉*3499 U.S. 76, Hiawassee* ☎706/896–2262 or 888/834–4409 ⊕*www.theridges-resort.com* 🛏*62 rooms, 4 suites* ☐*In-room: Wi-Fi. In-hotel: 2 restaurants, tennis court, pool* ☐*AE, D, DC, MC, V* ⦿*BP.*

15

BLUE RIDGE

39 mi southwest of Hiawassee via U.S. 76/GA 515; 53 mi northwest of Dahlonega via GA 52 and U.S. 76/GA 515.

Blue Ridge is one of the most pleasant small mountain towns in North Georgia. After you've eaten breakfast or lunch and shopped for antiques, gifts, or crafts at Blue Ridge's many small shops, you can ride the revived Blue Ridge Scenic Railway to McCaysville, a town at the Tennessee line, and then back through the mountains.

ESSENTIALS

Visitor Information Fannin County Chamber of Commerce and Welcome Center (✉*3990 Appalachian Hwy., Blue Ridge* ☎*706/632–5680 or 800/899–6867* ⊕ *www.blueridgemountains.com).*

EXPLORING

☾ The **Blue Ridge Scenic Railway** makes a 4-hour, 26-mi round-trip along the Toccoa River. The trip includes a halfway stop in **McCaysville, Georgia,** smack on the Georgia–Tennessee state line. Several restaurants, shops, and artisans there make it a point to be open during the 2-hour layover. On Sundays, the trip is 3.5 hours with a 1.5 hour layover. The train, which has open and Pullman cars and is pulled by diesel engines, is staffed with friendly volunteer hosts. The ticket office, now on the National Register of Historic Places, dates from 1905 and was originally the depot of the L&N Railroad. Children of all ages enjoy the ride. ■**TIP→** In summer you may want to consider the closed, air-conditioned coaches, although many passengers prefer the thrill of open-air cars. Raft and rail ($72) and raft and tubing ($42) packages are available. ✉*241 Depot St.* ☎*706/632–9833 or 800/934–1898* ⊕*www.*

brscenic.com ⚏$26–39, *depending on season* ⊘ *Mid-Mar.–late Dec. Check Web site or call for schedules and reservations.*

ⓒ The **Swan Drive-In Theater** originally opened in 1955, and is one of only four drive-in movie theaters operating in Georgia. You can take in a movie under the stars and fill up on corn dogs, pickled eggs, funnel cakes, and popcorn from the concession stand. Window speakers have been replaced by the movie sounds broadcast to your car radio. ✉651 *Summit St.* ☎706/632–5235.

WHERE TO STAY & EAT

$–$$ ✕**Serenity Garden Café.** A relaxing spot for breakfast, lunch, and dinner, AMERICAN   this café is a charming hideaway in Blue Ridge's shopping district. Diners can choose between umbrellaed tables on a landscaped deck or a bright and cheerful, but narrow, indoor dining room. The large variety of breakfast offerings includes grits and biscuits with sausage gravy. Homemade soups are popular for lunch and dinner, as are the more than two dozen sandwiches. Dinner favorites are homemade baked meat lasagna and a handcut rib-eye steak. Takeout is also available. ✉657 *E. Main St., Blue Ridge* ☎706/258–4949 ☰*AE, D, MC, V* ⊘*Sun. and Mon. 9–4; Tues.–Sat. 9–7:45.*

¢   ▦**Copperhead Lodge.** With the popularity of two-wheel cruising in North Georgia, a motorcycle resort seems natural. The community here gets involved through concerts and events at the site's open-air amphitheatre and in the lodge, year-round. Concerts feature everything from country to classic rock to blues. There's also an on-site restaurant that's open Thursday night through Sunday. **Pros:** a gathering spot for tourists traveling on two wheels; motorcycle detailing and covered parking. **Cons:** guests must bring their own alcoholic beverages; located about 12 mi from Blue Ridge and 7 mi from Blairsville. ✉171 *Copperhead Pkwy., Blairsville* ☎706/745–8000 ⊕*www.copperheadlodge.com* ⬙*11 lodge rooms; 10 log cabins* ⅃*In room: kitchen. In hotel: pool.* ☰*D, MC, V.*

ELLIJAY

84 mi west of Clayton via U.S. 76; 37 mi northwest of Dahlonega via GA 52; 80 mi north of Atlanta via I–75, I–575, and GA 5/515.

Billed as "Georgia's apple capital," Ellijay is also popular among antiques aficionados. The town, on the site of what had been a Cherokee village called Elatseyi (meaning "place of green things"), has a colorful cluster of crafts shops and antiques markets.

The most popular time to visit Ellijay is in fall, when roadside stands brimming with delicious ripe apples dot the landscape. The annual Georgia Apple Festival takes place the second and third weekends of October. In addition to showcasing the many manifestations of the crisp fruit—apple butter, apple pie, apple cider, and so on—the very popular festival offers a host of arts and crafts exhibitions.

ESSENTIALS

Visitor Information Gilmer County Chamber of Commerce and Welcome Center (✉ *368 Craig St., E. Ellijay* ☎*706/635–7400* ⊕*www.gilmerchamber.com*).

EXPLORING

☺ Buy freshly picked apples (usually August to early December) at 80-acre **Hillcrest Orchards.** Feast on homemade jellies, jams, breads, and doughnuts at the farm's market and bakery. Also on the orchard's premises are a petting zoo, a small museum, and a picnic area. On the last three September weekends, the Apple Pickin' Jubilee features live music, wagon rides, apple-picking, and other activities. ⊠*9696 GA 52E 30536* ☎*706/273–3838* ⊕*www.hillcrestorchards.net* ⊠*$5 for special events including Apple Pickin' Jubilee; $3 for petting zoo* ⊘*Mid-Aug.–early Dec., daily 9–6.*

☺ The 3,712-acre **Fort Mountain State Park** has a 17-acre lake with sandy beach, horseback riding (for a fee), 14 mi of hiking trails, and 30 mi of mountain biking trails ($2 trail fee for biking). The gem of the park is a mysterious wall of rock, 855 feet long, thought to have been built by Native Americans around AD 500. Tent and RV sites ($23–$25) and rental cottages ($110–$130) are also on-site. ⊠*181 Fort Mountain Park Rd., Chatsworth* ☎*706/422–1932* ⊕*www.gastateparks.org* ⊠*Free; park pass fee of $3 vehicle* ⊘*Daily 7 AM–10 PM.*

WHERE TO STAY

$ ▦**Best Western Mountain View Inn.** This two-story motel sits on a hilltop above East Ellijay. Half of the rooms, indeed, have mountain views. Suites are oversize rooms with a sitting area, not true suites, but they do have two TVs. **Pros:** located close to eating and shopping areas. **Cons:** the entrance is hard to find. ⊠*43 Coosawattee Dr., East Ellijay* ☎*706/515–1500 or 866/515–4515* ⊕*www.bwmountainviewinn.com* ⥹*52 rooms* ⅄*In-room: Wi-Fi. In-hotel: pool* ▤*AE, D, DC, MC, V* ⎮◎⎮*BP.*

¢ ▦**Cohutta Lodge.** This lodge is located on 108 acres atop Fort Mountain near the Cohutta Wilderness. Outdoor activities, such as hiking and biking, can be arranged through the hotel. **Pros:** outstanding views of the Appalachian foothills; restaurant serves breakfast, lunch, and dinner. **Cons:** pets not allowed; restaurant diners say the portions are too large; no elevator. ⊠*500 Cochise Trail, off GA 52, Chatsworth* ☎*706/695–9601* ⊕*www.cohuttalodge.com* ⥹*47 rooms, 5 suites, 2 cabins* ⅄*In-room: Wi-Fi. In-hotel: restaurant, pool, Wi-Fi* ▤*AE, MC, V.*

$–$$ ▦**Whitepath Lodge.** From nearly every room you get panoramic vistas of the tranquil North Georgia mountains. The main lodge has eight suites, each with two bedrooms, three baths, a fully equipped kitchen, and washers and dryers. The neighboring Shenandoah Lodge has six two-floor suites with fireplaces and multilevel decks overlooking the woods. Sports enthusiasts will be happy with all the recreational activities nearby—18-hole golf courses, mountain biking, horseback riding, tubing, seasonal white-water rafting, boating, canoeing, kayaking, and fishing. **Pros:** roomy, well-appointed accommodations; lovely landscaped grounds with a fountain. **Cons:** off the beaten track on a gravel road; it's an 8-mi drive to any restaurants; no elevator. ⊠*987 Shenandoah Dr., Ellijay* ☎*706/276–7199* ⊕*www.whitepathlodge.com* ⥹*14 suites* ⅄*In-room: kitchen. In-hotel: tennis court, pool* ▤*MC, V.*

15

SPORTS & THE OUTDOORS

There are plenty of options for fishing, canoeing, and kayaking on the Cartecay River, which runs through town. **Mountaintown Outdoor Expeditions** (⊠122 Adventure Trail, 5 mi east of Ellijay off GA 52 on Lower Cartecay Rd. ☎706/635–2524 ⊕www.mountaintownoutdoorexpeditions.com) arranges outdoor adventures for people of all skill levels.

SHOPPING

Corks & Crumbs (⊠5 Southside Sq. ☎706/276–7622) has a Frogtown Cellars winery tasting room; a bakery serving scones, cinnamon rolls, cookies, and a handful of different breads; wine accessories; and a few antiques and collectibles.

THE NORTHWEST

Northwest Georgia is rich in history. Chickamauga & Chattanooga National Military Park reminds visitors of the devastation of the Civil War and the determination of both Southern and Northern soldiers participating in its bloodiest two-day battle. The area also pays homage to Georgia's former Cherokee residents, driven by the federal government from their verdant homeland in New Echota—once the capital of the Cherokee nation—to dusty Oklahoma on the Trail of Tears. Northwest Georgia lies along the Cumberland Plateau, with its flat-top sandstone mountains.

NEW ECHOTA

71 mi northwest of Atlanta via I–75 north to GA 225; 41 mi southwest of Ellijay via U.S. 76 to GA 382W/GA 136.

From 1825 to 1838 New Echota was the capital of the Cherokee Nation, whose constitution was patterned after that of the United States. The town was named in honor of Chota, a Cherokee town in present-day Tennessee. The public buildings and houses in town were generally log structures, among them a council house, a printing office, a Supreme Court building, and the *Cherokee Phoenix* newspaper. The first newspaper established (in 1828) by Native Americans, it utilized the 86-character alphabet developed by Sequoyah, who spent 12 years developing the written Cherokee language despite having no formal education. He is the only known person in history to have single-handedly created a written language.

The Treaty of 1835, signed in New Echota by a small group of Cherokee leaders, relinquished Cherokee claims to lands east of the Mississippi. Most Cherokees considered the treaty fraudulent. A few years later 7,000 federal and state troops began removing Cherokee from their homes in Georgia, North Carolina, and Tennessee and put them in stockades, including one in New Echota. About 15,000 Cherokee were then forced to travel west to Oklahoma on foot, horseback, and in wagons, along what is known as the "Trail of Tears." Thousands died along the way. After reaching Oklahoma in 1839, the three prin-

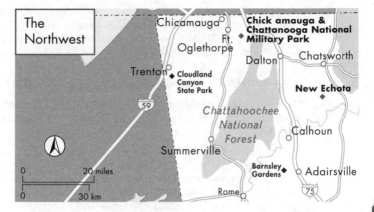

cipal signers of the Treaty of 1835 were assassinated by Cherokee who considered them traitors.

Following the removal of the Cherokee, New Echota reverted to farmland. Today one original building remains, some buildings have been reconstructed and furnished, and other structures have been moved to the site. The visitor center has a movie and a variety of books about Cherokee history. When visiting New Echota, you can stay in Calhoun, the nearest town, or in Dalton, Rome, Chickamauga, or even in Chattanooga.

GETTING HERE & AROUND

This is a good day trip from Atlanta. Take I–75 to exit 317, GA 225, for a tour of New Echota, near Calhoun, then travel 17 miles north on GA 225 to the Chief Vann House.

EXPLORING

★ A small museum and a collection of buildings at **New Echota State Historic**
☾ **Site** detail the site's history. Worcester House, a home and Presbyterian mission station, is an original building, restored in the late 1950s. The Cherokee Council House is a reconstruction of the 1819 building where the legislature met. The Supreme Court building is also a reconstruction, as is the print house, where thousands of books translated in Cherokee and the weekly *Cherokee Phoenix* were published. Other buildings—including the 1805 Vann Tavern—and outbuildings were relocated to the site. ✉*1211 Chatsworth Hwy., GA 225, 1 mi east of I–75 near Calhoun* ☏*706/624–1321* ⊕*www.georgiastateparks.org* ✑*$4* ☾*Tues.–Sat. 9–5, Sun. 2–5:30.*

The beautifully restored, three-story brick **Chief Vann House** was commissioned in 1804 by a leader of the Cherokee Nation. Moravian artisans helped construct the intricately carved interior mantles and other woodwork. The well-decorated home is furnished as it would have been when Chief Vann lived there. Of mixed Scottish and Cherokee parentage, Chief James Vann owned numerous slaves who also worked on the construction of the house. His son, Cherokee statesman Joseph Vann, lived in the house until he was evicted by the Georgia Militia in 1835 and forced to move to Cherokee Territory, in what is now Oklahoma. ⊠*82 GA 225 at GA 52A, Chatsworth* ✢*17 mi north of New Echota* ☎*706/695–2598* ⊕*gastateparks.org/info/chiefvann* ⊑*$4* ⊙*Tues.–Sat. 9–5, Sun. 2–5:30.*

CHICKAMAUGA & CHATTANOOGA NATIONAL MILITARY PARK

Fodor's Choice *110 mi northwest of Atlanta via I–75 and GA 2; 42 mi north of New*
★   *Echota State Historic Site via I–75; 12 mi south of Chattanooga, TN, via U.S. 27.*

This site, established in 1890 as the nation's first military park, was the scene of some of the Civil War's bloodiest battles. In Chickamauga alone, 34,624 were killed, missing, and wounded in September 1863. Though the Confederates won the battle at Chickamauga, the Union army retained control of Chattanooga. The normally thick cedar groves and foliage covering Chickamauga were trampled and, according to eyewitness accounts, trees were so shot up that a sweet cedar smell mingled with the blood of fallen soldiers.

Some areas around the park now suffer from suburban sprawl, but the 9,000-acre park itself is made up of serene fields and islands of trees. Monuments, battlements, and weapons adorn the roads that traverse the park, with markers explaining the action.

GETTING HERE & AROUND
Take I–75 north from Atlanta to the exit for Fort Oglethorpe and follow signs through a small but congested area to the National Military Park and to Cloudland Canyon.

EXPLORING
The **Chickamauga Battlefield Visitor Center** has an excellent small museum offering a timeline of the battle, a film on the military strategy that involved 124,000 soldiers, a collection of 346 antique military rifles, and a well-stocked bookstore. There's a 7-mi self-guided auto tour through the park, with numerous spots to stop and view the more than 700 monuments and historical markers in Chickamauga, and mid-June to September you can join a free, 90-minute auto caravan through the park, led by a park ranger. The first Civil War military park and the largest in the nation, it opened in 1890. ⊠*1 mi south of intersection of GA 2 and U.S. 27, Fort Oglethorpe* ☎*706/866–9241* ⊕*www.nps. gov/chch* ⊑*Free* ⊙*Daily 8:30–5.*

Cloudland Canyon State Park. At this 3,845-acre park you can see firsthand the unusual geology of this remote part of northwestern Georgia. Hike down the canyon, which drops 1,100 feet from the rim, and you're literally walking backward though millions of years of geologic time. If you make it all the way to the bottom—the trail totals 4″ mi—you'll be rewarded with sights of two waterfalls. ⊠*122 Cloudland Canyon Park Rd., Rising Fawn* ☎*706/657–4050* ⊕*www.georgia-stateparks.org* ⊑*$3 parking* ⊙*Daily 7* AM–*10* PM.

■ OFF THE
BEATEN
PATH

Travel Smart
The Carolinas &
Georgia

WORD OF MOUTH

"Anyplace where there are leaves changing color (in the fall) . . . there will be hordes of people (although more in October). The North Carolina beaches are awesome in September and October, and the water is plenty warm into November, typically. . . . You'll need a car."

—WannabeinaMontserrat

GETTING HERE & AROUND

∎ BY AIR

Flying time to Atlanta is 4½ hours from Los Angeles, 2½ hours from New York, 2 hours from Chicago, 2 hours from Dallas, and 9 hours from London. By plane, Charlotte is an hour northeast of Atlanta, Raleigh 75 minutes northeast, Wilmington 1½ hours east, Asheville 1 hour north, and Charleston, Hilton Head, and Savannah an hour east–southeast.

Travelers flying into the Carolinas or Georgia are likely to pass through Hartsfield-Jackson Atlanta International Airport. It's by far the most popular airport in the region, and is the busiest in the world, at least in terms of number of passengers—more than 89 million annually.

Airlines & Airports Airline and Airport Links.com (⊕ www.airlineandairportlinks.com).

Airline Security Issues Transportation Security Administration (⊕ www.tsa.gov).

AIRPORTS

The sheer number of flights at Hartsfield-Jackson Atlanta International Airport (ATL)—more than 2,700 arriving and departing flights daily—make it an obvious, if sometimes hectic, choice. With some 240 concessionaires at the airport, it's easy to find a bite to eat or something to read, and Wi-Fi is available throughout, as are laptop plug-in stations. Two interfaith chapels are open from 6 AM to midnight and a U.S. postal store is available. A customer service office and staffed customer service desks answer questions. Waiting passengers can also check out a display of Martin Luther King Jr. memorabilia on Concourse E, International Terminal. Smoking areas are located on Concourse A, B, C, D, E, and T. Overnight visitors can choose from 70 hotels and motels near the airport, most with free shuttle service. Give yourself extra time, as you'll have to tackle crowds whether waiting to buy a burger, get through secu-

rity, or board the underground train to other concourses. The airport's Web site regularly updates estimates of waits at security areas. Arrive two hours before a flight in the U.S. and allow three hours for international flights. Allow enough time to be at the gate 30 minutes before boarding and plan for extra time if returning rental cars. Keep track of laptops and be ready to collect suitcases as soon as they arrive at the carousels for security's sake.

North Carolina's Charlotte Douglas International Airport (CLT), near the border of North Carolina and South Carolina, is a US Airways hub. Although not as vast as Hartsfield-Jackson, Charlotte Douglas is quite large, and its people-moving systems work well. Tired travelers can plop down in one of the trademark, hand-crafted white rocking chairs in the Atrium, a tree-lined indoor crossroads between airport concourses that also offers a food court with mostly fast-food outlets. Within a few miles are more than a dozen hotels, most with free airport shuttles. In the center of the state, right off Interstate 40, is Raleigh-Durham International Airport (RDU), a prime gateway into central and eastern North Carolina. It sometimes feels like the airport is constantly under construction. Until the new Terminal 2 is fully complete in 2011, some carriers are using Terminal 1.

Those who live in the western reaches of the Triangle are just as likely to use the Piedmont Triad International Airport (GSO), at the convergence of four interstates in North Carolina. It primarily serves the Triad area—Greensboro, Winston-Salem, and High Point—as well as some cities in southwestern Virginia.

The portal to western North Carolina is Asheville Regional Airport (AVL), which recently expanded to include new amenities including boarding ramps, a gallery featuring regional art, and a guest services center. It provides nonstop flights to Atlanta, Charlotte, Cincinnati, Detroit, Houston, Newark, and Minneapolis-St. Paul.

For visits to the North Carolina coast, fly into Wilmington International Airport (ILM), a small facility with service by three carriers. Upstate South Carolina has the small but user-friendly Greenville–Spartanburg International Airport (GSP), which sometimes has lower fares than either the Charlotte or Asheville airports.

Airport Information Asheville Regional Airport (✉61 Terminal Dr., Fletcher, NC ☎828/684–2226 ⊕www.flyavl.com). **Charlotte Douglas International Airport** (✉5501 Josh Birmingham Pkwy., Charlotte, NC ☎704/359–4000 ⊕www.charlotteairport. com). **Hartsfield-Jackson Atlanta International Airport** (✉6000 N. Terminal Pkwy., Hapeville, GA ☎404/530–7300 ⊕www. atlanta-airport.com). **Piedmont Triad International Airport** (✉6415 Bryan Blvd., Greensboro, NC ☎336/665–5600 ⊕www.flyfrompti.com). **Raleigh-Durham International Airport** (✉2400 Terminal Blvd., Morrisville, NC ☎919/840–7700 ⊕www.rdu.com). **Wilmington International Airport** (✉1740 Airport Blvd., Wilmington, NC ☎910/341–4125 ⊕www.flyilm.com).

GROUND TRANSPORTATION

Of all the airports in the region, only Hartsfield-Jackson Atlanta International is well served by public transportation. The Metropolitan Atlanta Rapid Transit Authority, better known as MARTA, has frequent service to and from the airport. It's the quickest, cheapest, and most hassle-free way into the city. MARTA's North–South line will get you downtown in 15–20 minutes for just $1.75. MARTA riders can also travel to Midtown, Buckhead, Sandy Springs, and Doraville—reaching into north suburban Atlanta. MARTA's Airport Station is located inside the terminal and can be accessed from the north and south sides of the terminal near the baggage claim area.

Trains run weekdays 5 AM to 1 AM and weekends and holidays 5 AM to 12:30 AM. Most trains operate every 15 to 20 minutes; during weekday rush hours, trains run every 10 minutes. You can print out a copy of the rail map before your trip from the MARTA Web site or pick one up at any station.

Limited bus service—hourly from 5:25 AM to 7:25 PM—is available between the Charlotte Transportation Center in Uptown Charlotte and CharlotteDouglas International Airport. The Triangle Transit Authority (TTA) has an airport bus-shuttle service that connects to Raleigh-Durham International Airport, but the shuttle does not operate on Sunday. The airport shuttle meets TTA regional buses at the TTA Bus Center in Research Triangle Park.

Most of the airports in the region are served by taxi, limo, and shuttle services. Private limousine or van services also serve the major airports. In Atlanta, use only approved vehicles with the airport decal on the bumper, to ensure the drivers are charging legal fares and have knowledge of local destinations.

TRANSFERS BETWEEN AIRPORTS
Contacts Charlotte Area Transit System (☎704/336–7433 ⊕www.charmeck.org). **Metropolitan Atlanta Rapid Transit Authority** (☎404/848–5000 ⊕www.itsmarta.com). **Triangle Transit Authority** (☎919/549–9999 ⊕www.triangletransit.org).

FLIGHTS
Hartsfield-Jackson Atlanta International Airport is the primary hub of Delta Airlines and AirTran Airways. Altogether, more than 30 domestic and international airlines fly into Atlanta. US Airways has a hub at North Carolina's Charlotte Douglas International Airport, which is also served by more than a dozen other airlines. Raleigh-Durham International is not a hub for any carrier, but is serviced by more than a dozen airlines. Commuter airlines, including US Airways Express,

Continental Express, Delta Connection, and United Express have service between many smaller North Carolina airports as well as those in South Carolina. United Express also serves Georgia, New York, Washington, D.C., Chicago, and major Florida airports.

Airline Contacts **AirTran** (☎770/994–8258 or 800/247–8726 ⊕www.airtran.com). **American Airlines** (☎800/433–7300 ⊕www.aa.com). **Continental Airlines** (☎800/523–3273 for U.S. and Mexico reservations, 800/231–0856 for international reservations ⊕www.continental.com). **Delta Airlines** (☎800/221–1212 for U.S. reservations, 800/241–4141 for international reservations ⊕www.delta.com). **USAirways** (☎800/428–4322 for U.S. and Canada reservations, 800/622–1015 for international reservations ⊕www.usairways.com).

BY BIKE

Throughout coastal Georgia and the Carolinas, hills are few and the scenery remarkable. Many bike routes are marked on North Carolina's Outer Banks, around Savannah and Georgia's coastal islands, and greater Charleston and coastal South Carolina's Lowcountry. Mountain bikers take to North Carolina's Great Smoky Mountains and the north Georgia mountains. Larger cities in the region, especially Atlanta, can prove difficult for getting around by bicycle. While bike paths are available, riding on streets is often necessary and can prove daunting.

DeLorme's *Atlas & Gazeteer* state maps, available in bike shops and drugstores, contain useful topographic detail. Many tourist boards and local bike clubs also distribute bike maps.

Web sites can also be helpful. Southeastern Cycling (⊕*www.sadlebred.com*) has information on road and trail riding throughout the Southeast and has free ride maps. Mountain Biking in Western North Carolina (⊕*www.mtbikewnc.com*) has information on mountain trails. Trails.com (⊕*www.trails.com*) offers

information on more than 30,000 bike trails, including many in Georgia and the Carolinas. A year's subscription costs $49.95; a trial subscription is free.

Bike Maps **DeLorme** (⊠2 DeLorme Dr., Yarmouth, ME ☎800/561–5105 ⊕www.delorme.com). **Georgia Bikes** (⊕Box 49755, Atlanta, GA 30359 ☎404/441–9355 or 404/634–6745 ⊕www.georgiabikes.org). **North Carolina Division of Bicycle and Pedestrian Transportation** (⊠1552 Mail Service Center, Raleigh, NC 27699 ☎919/807–0777 ⊕www.ncdot.org/transit/bicycle/maps/maps_highways.html). **South Carolina Trails Program** (⊠1205 Pendleton St., Columbia, SC 29201 ☎803/734–0173 ⊕www.sctrails.net/trails).

BY BOAT

Ferries are a common, and necessary, way to get around coastal areas, and especially to visit North Carolina's Outer Banks and Georgia's Sea Islands.

The Ferry Division of the North Carolina Department of Transportation operates seven ferry routes over five separate bodies of water: the Currituck and Pamlico sounds and the Cape Fear, Neuse, and Pamlico rivers. Travelers use the three routes between Ocracoke and Hatteras Island, Swan Quarter, and Cedar Island; between Southport and Fort Fisher; and between Cherry Branch and Minnesott Beach. Ferries can accommodate any car, trailer, or recreational vehicle. Pets are permitted if they stay in the vehicle or are on a leash. Reservations, which can only be made by telephone, are available for the Cedar Island–Ocracoke and Swan Quarter–Ocracoke routes; on other routes, space is on a first-come, first-served basis. Schedules generally vary by season, with the largest number of departures from May through October.

Ferries are the only form of public transportation to Sapelo and Cumberland islands in Georgia. The Georgia Department of Natural Resources operates a ferry between Meridian and Sapelo.

Advance reservations are required, and can be made by phone or at the Sapelo Island Visitor Center in Meridian. From March to November a privately run passenger ferry runs daily between St. Marys and Cumberland Island. The rest of the year the ferry does not operate on Tuesday and Wednesday. Reservations are essential, especially in March and April.

In North Carolina the Cedar Island–Ocracoke and Swan Quarter–Ocracoke ferries cost $1 for pedestrians, $3 for bicycles, $10 for motorcycles, and $15 for cars and up to $45 for other vehicles (trailers, boats, motor homes). The Southport–Fort Fisher ferry costs $1 for pedestrians, $2 for bicycles, $3 for motorcycles, and $5 to $15 for vehicles. Tickets can be purchased with cash or traveler's checks. Personal checks and and credit cards are not accepted. The other North Carolina ferries are free.

In Georgia the pedestrian ferry to Sapelo Island costs $1 each way. The pedestrian ferry to Cumberland Island costs $17 round-trip, plus a $4 national park fee.

Boat Information Cumberland Island National Seashore (Box 806, St. Marys 31558 912/882–4335 or 877/860–6787 www.nps.gov/cuis). **North Carolina Department of Transportation Ferry Division** (8550 Shipyard Rd., Manns Harbor, NC 27953 800/293–3779 www.ncferry.org). **Sapelo Island Visitor Center** (Route 1, Box 1500, Darien, GA 31305 912/437–3224 www.sapelonerr.org).

▌BY BUS

Regional bus service, provided by Greyhound, is abundant throughout the Carolinas and Georgia. It's an affordable means of getting around; if it's a simple matter of getting from one city to another, consider this option. Buses sometimes make frequent stops, which make the trip much longer but also let passengers see towns they might otherwise bypass. Purchase tickets in advance online, by phone, at a

bus terminal, or the same day at the ticket counter. Check the Web site for discounts and deals, such as the North America Discovery Pass.

Bus Information Greyhound (800/231–2222 www.greyhound.com). **Greyhound Discovery Pass** (800/231–2222 www.discoverypass.com).

▌BY CAR

A car is the most practical and economical means of traveling around the Carolinas and Georgia. Atlanta, Savannah, Charleston, Myrtle Beach, and Asheville can also be explored fairly easily on foot or by using public transit and cabs, but a car is helpful to reach many of the most intriguing attractions, which are not always downtown. ▌TIP→**When returning rental cars to airports, always allow extra time to check in vehicles.**

Although drivers make the best time traveling along the South's extensive network of interstate highways, keep in mind that U.S. and state highways offer some delightful scenery and the opportunity to stumble on funky roadside diners, leafy state parks, and historic town squares. Although the area is rural, it's still densely populated, so travelers rarely drive for more than 20 or 30 mi without passing roadside services, such as gas stations, restaurants, and ATMs.

Among the most scenic highways in the Carolinas and Georgia are U.S. 78, running east–west across Georgia; U.S. 25, 19, 74, and 64, traveling through the Great Smoky Mountains of western North Carolina; U.S. 17 from Brunswick, Georgia, along the coast through South Carolina and North Carolina; and the **Blue Ridge Parkway** from the eastern fringes of the Great Smoky Mountains through western North Carolina into Virginia.

Unlike some other areas of the United States, the Carolinas and Georgia have

TRAVEL TIMES AROUND THE CAROLINAS & GEORGIA BY CAR		
From	To	Time/Distance
Atlanta, GA	Savannah, GA	4 hours / 248 mi
Asheville, TN	Great Smoky Mountains National Park	2 hours / 83 mi
Charlotte, NC	Atlanta, GA	4 hours / 244 mi
Charleston, SC	Raleigh, NC	4½ hours/ 279 mi
Durham, NC	Asheville, NC	3½ hours/ 224 mi
Hilton Head, SC	Columbia, SC	2¾ hours / 167 mi
Winston-Salem, NC	Charlotte, NC	1½ hours / 84 mi

very few toll roads. Currently, only Georgia State Route 400 in Atlanta, the Cross Island Parkway on Hilton Head, South Carolina, and the Southern Connector in Greenville, South Carolina, are toll roads.

RENTAL CARS

It's important to reserve a car well in advance of your expected arrival. Rental rates vary from city to city, but are generally lowest in larger cities where there's a lot of competition. Economy cars cost between $27 and $61 per day, and luxury cars go for $70 to $198. Weekend rates are generally much lower than those on weekdays, and weekly rates usually offer big discounts. Rates are also seasonal, with the highest rates coming during peak travel times, including Thanksgiving and Christmas holiday seasons. Local factors can also affect rates; for example, a big convention can absorb most of the rental-car inventory and boost rates for those remaining.

Don't forget to factor in the taxes and other add-ons when figuring up how much a car will cost. At Atlanta's Hartsfield-Jackson International Airport, add the 7% sales tax, 11.11% concession-recovery fee, 3% city rental car tax, $4 daily customer facility charge, and 70¢ to $1.30 vehicle license-recovery charge. These "miscellaneous charges" mean that a a weekly rental can jump in price far higher than the rental agency cost.

Some off-airport locations offer lower rates, and their lots are only minutes from the terminal via complimentary shuttle. Also ask whether certain frequent-flyer, American Automobile Association (AAA), corporate, or other such promotions are accepted and whether the rates might be lower for other arrival and departure dates. In addition to the national agencies, Triangle Rent A Car serves Georgia and the Carolinas.

CAR RENTAL RESOURCES

Local Agencies Triangle Rent A Car (☎919/840–3400 ⊕www.trianglerentacar.com).

Major Agencies Alamo (☎800/462–5266 ⊕www.alamo.com). Avis (☎800/331–1212 ⊕www.avis.com). Budget (☎800/527–0700 ⊕www.budget.com). Enterprise (☎800/261-7331 ⊕www.enterprise.com). Hertz (☎800/654–3131 ⊕www.hertz.com). National Car Rental (☎800/227–7368 ⊕www.nationalcar.com).

ROADSIDE EMERGENCIES

Travelers in Georgia and the Carolinas have help as close as their cell phones in case of emergencies on roadways. The Georgia Department of Transportation's Intelligent Transportation System works on three levels. First, drivers statewide can call 511 to report problems, get directions, information on traffic, MARTA information, and information on Hartsfield airport. Next, on the 300 miles of metro Atlanta interstate highways, Highway Emergency Response Operators (HEROs) help motorists with everything from empty gas tanks to medical emergencies. Finally, the Georgia Navigator system provides statewide information on the Internet on roadway conditions and, in Atlanta, everything from drive times to incident locations to roadway conditions. Welcome centers statewide can also access that information.

In an emergency, drivers in North Carolina should call 911. In metro areas such as Raleigh, Durham, Burlington, Greensboro, Winston-Salem, Charlotte, and Asheville, and in the Pigeon River Gorge area, drivers on major U.S. highways and interstates receive roadside assistance through the Department of Transportation's Incident Management Assistance Patrols (IMAPs). The IMAP staff remove road debris, change tires, clear stalled vehicles, and can call a private tow truck. Motorists should dial *HP to reach the highway patrol and have an IMAP truck dispatched. In North Carolina's congested metro and construction areas, use the NCDOT Traveler Information Management System (TIMS) on the Internet or via cell phone. Go to ⊕*www.ncdot. org* and click on the link for "Travel Information." Search for travel updates by region, roadway, or county. Both the Great Smoky Mountains National Park and the Blue Ridge Parkway lure travelers to the state. The state's western area has many narrow, steep and winding roads near such towns as Asheville, Boone, Sylva and Waynesville. Use extra caution there, and pay extra attention to winter weather reports for snow and ice when roads may be closed.

South Carolina's Incident Response program operates on interstate highways in urban areas and the constantly busy Myrtle Beach area (specifically the Hwy 17 bypass and US 501). Stranded motorists can call *HP for help and reach the local highway patrol dispatch system. The state operates hundreds of traffic cameras to monitor traffic flow and identify accident sites on all five interstate and in the Myrtle Beach area. They also have a camera at I–95 and I–26, in case of hurricane evacuations. For more information see: ⊕*www.dot.state.sc.us/getting/ incident_response.shtml.*

Roadside Assistance Contacts Georgia Department of Transportation's Intelligent Transportation System (☎511 ⊕www. georgia-navigator.com). **Department of Transportation's Incident Management Assistance Patrols (IMAPs)** (☎*HP ⊕www.ncdot. org/traffictravel). **South Carolina Incident Response Program** (☎*HP ⊕www.dot.state. sc.us/getting/Incident_response.shtml).

RULES OF THE ROAD

Currently there are no restrictions on the use of hand-held cell phones by adults while driving in South Carolina and Georgia. North Carolina drivers must have wireless headsets to use a cell phone on the road, and drivers under 18 cannot use cell phones except to answer calls from parents or report an emergency.

Unless otherwise indicated, motorists may turn right at a red light after stopping if there's no oncoming traffic. When in doubt, wait for the green. In Atlanta, Asheville, Charleston, Columbia, Charlotte, Savannah, and the Triangle and Triad cities of North Carolina, be alert for one-way streets, "no left turn" intersections, and blocks closed to vehicle traffic.

In Georgia, always strap children under age six or under 40 pounds (regardless of age) into approved child-safety seats or booster seats appropriate for their height and weight in the backseat. Children younger than age 8 and weighing less than 80 pounds must be properly secured in child restraints or booster seats in North Carolina. Child safety seats or booster seats are required for children younger than six and weighing less than 80 pounds in South Carolina.

▌ BY CRUISE SHIP

Charleston is the only city in the region where cruises embark. Carnival and Norwegian Cruise Line have ships to Bermuda, the Bahamas, and the Caribbean that depart from Charleston in the spring and fall. Charleston and Savannah are the only cities in the Carolinas and Georgia that are regular ports of call for cruise lines, and they attract only a handful of ships. Princess Cruises, Royal Caribbean International, and Crystal Cruises each have one ship that calls occasionally at Charleston, typically in the fall. Charleston and Savannah are spring destinations for a small cruise ship, the *Spirit of Nantucket,* operated by Cruise West.

Cruise Lines **Carnival Cruise Line** (☎305/599–2600 or 800/227–6482 ⊕www.carnival.com). **Crystal Cruises** (☎310/785–9300 or 800/446–6620 ⊕www.crystalcruises.com). **Norwegian Cruise Line** (☎305/436–4000 or 800/327–7030 ⊕www.ncl.com). **Princess Cruises** (☎661/753–0000 or 800/774–6237 ⊕www.princess.com). **Regent Seven Seas Cruises** (☎954/776–6123 or 800/477–7500 ⊕www.rssc.com). **Royal Caribbean International** (☎305/539–6000 or 800/327–6700 ⊕www.royalcaribbean.com). **Seabourn Cruise Line** (☎305/463–3000 or 800/929–9391 ⊕www.seabourn.com). Silversea

▌ BY TRAIN

Several Amtrak routes pass through the Carolinas and Georgia; however, many areas are not served by train, and those cities that do have service usually only have one or two arrivals and departures each day. The *Crescent* runs daily through Greensboro, Charlotte, and Atlanta as it travels between New York and New Orleans. Three trains, the *Palmetto,* the *Silver Meteor,* and the *Silver Star* make the daily run between New York and Miami via Raleigh, Charleston, Columbia, and Savannah. The *Carolinian* runs daily from New York to Charlotte, via Raleigh.

Amtrak offers rail passes that allow for travel within certain regions, which can save a lot over the posted fare. Amtrak has several kinds of USA Rail Passes, offering unlimited travel for 15 or 30 days, with rates of $299 to $599, depending on the area traveled, the time of year, and the number of days. Amtrak has discounts for students, seniors, and people with disabilities.

Train Information **Amtrak** (☎800/872–7245 ⊕www.amtrak.com).

ESSENTIALS

■ ACCOMMODATIONS

With the exception of Atlanta, Savannah, Charleston, Asheville, and Charlotte, most lodging rates in the region fall at or below the national average. They do vary a great deal seasonally, however—coastal resorts and mountainous areas tend to have significantly higher rates in summer. Fall color creates demand for lodging in the mountains. Expect high-season rates. All major chains are well represented in this part of the country, both in cities and suburbs, and interstates are lined with inexpensive to moderate chains.

In many places consider forgoing a modern hotel in favor of a historic property. There are dozens of fine old hotels and mansions that have been converted into inns, many of them lovingly restored. Many offer better rates than chain hotels. Bed-and-breakfasts are big in some cities, notably Charleston, Savannah, and Asheville. Each of these cities has two dozen or more B&Bs. There also are loads of B&Bs in many small towns along the coast and in the north Georgia and western North Carolina Mountains.

In many coastal resort areas, vacation home and condo rentals dominate the lodging scene. The North Carolina Outer Banks and Hilton Head are two major rental areas, each with several thousand rental properties. Rental prices vary by season, with peak summer rental rates that can double or more over off-season rates.

In the North Carolina and Georgia mountains, cabins are popular. These are usually owner-operated businesses with only a few cabins. In Georgia many state parks rent cabins as well as lodges, and they're often excellent values. In the mountains a number of lodges are available. These vary from simple accommodations to deluxe properties with spas, golf courses,

and tennis courts. Many attract families that come back year after year. Mountain lodges are closed for several months in winter.

Thousands of families camp in the Carolinas and Georgia. The North Carolina Outer Banks, the Sea Islands of Georgia, and the Great Smoky Mountains National Park and Pisgah and Nantahala national forests in western North Carolina are especially popular with campers.

The lodgings listed are the cream of the crop in each price category. Facilities that are available are listed—but not any extra costs associated with those facilities. When pricing accommodations, always ask what's included and what costs extra.

APARTMENT & HOUSE RENTALS

The far-flung resort areas of the Carolinas and Georgia are filled with rental properties—everything from cabins to luxury homes. Most often these properties, whether part of a huge corporation or individually owned, are professionally managed; such businesses have become an industry unto themselves.

Carolina Mornings, Carolina Mountain Vacations, and Flannery Fork Rentals rent cabins in the high country of North Carolina. Homestead Log Cabins has properties in the Pine Mountain area of Georgia. Intracoastal Realty has long-term as well as off-season rentals on the coast of Cape Fear. Hatteras Realty, Midgett Realty, and Sun Realty handle properties on North Carolina's Outer Banks. Island Realty focuses on the Charleston and Isle of Palms area in South Carolina. Hilton Head Rentals and Resort Rentals of Hilton Head Island offer rentals on Hilton Head. Sandy's by the Shore handles properties on Georgia's tiny Tybee island.

Apartment & House Contacts Carolina Mornings (☎828/398-0712 ⊕www. asheville-cabins.com). **Carolina Mountain Vacations** (☎877/488-8500 ⊕www. carolinamountainvacations.com). **Flannery Fork Rentals** (☎828/262-1908 ⊕www. flanneryfork.com). **Hatteras Realty** (☎800/ 428-8372 ⊕www.hatterasrealty.com). **Hilton Head Rentals** (☎800/368-5975 ⊕www. hiltonheadrentals.com). **Homestead Log Cabins** (☎706/663-4951 or 866/652-2246 ⊕www.homesteadcabins.com). **Intracoastal Realty** (☎910/256-3780 or 800/346-2463 ⊕www.intracoastalrentals.com). **Island Realty** (☎843/886-8144 or 800/707-6421 ⊕www.islandrealty.com). **Midgett Realty** (☎252/986-2841 or 800/527-2903 ⊕www. midgettrealty.com). **Resort Rentals of Hilton Head Island** (☎800/845-7017 or 843/686-6008 ⊕www.hhivacations.com). **Sun Realty, Outer Banks** (☎800/334-4745, 888/853-7770 ⊕www.sunrealtync.com). **Sandy's by the Shore** (☎866/512-0531 or 912/786-0531 ⊕www.sandysbytheshore.com).

BED & BREAKFASTS

Historic B&Bs and inns are found in just about every region in the Carolinas and Georgia and include quite a few former plantation houses and lavish Southern estates. In many rural or less touristy areas, B&Bs offer an affordable and homey alternative to chain properties, but in tourism-dependent destinations expect to pay about the same as or more than for a full-service hotel. Many of the South's finest restaurants are also found in country inns.

Reservation Services Asheville Bed & Breakfast Association (☎877/262-6867 ⊕www.ashevillebba.com). **Association of Historic Inns of Savannah** (⊕www.historicinnsofsavannah.com). **Bed & Breakfast.com** (☎512/322-2710 or 800/462-2632 ⊕www. bedandbreakfast.com) also sends out an online newsletter. **Bed & Breakfast Inns Online** (☎800/215-7365 ⊕www.bbonline.com). **BnB Finder.com** (☎212/432-7693 or 888/469-6663 ⊕www.bnbfinder.com). **Romantic Inns of Savannah** (☎No phone ⊕www.romanticinnsofsavannah.com). **South Carolina Bed & Breakfast Association** (☎No phone ⊕www.southcarolinabedandbreakfast.com).

CAMPING

The Carolinas and Georgia are popular for trailer and tent camping, especially in state and national parks. Georgia offers camping sites at more than 40 state parks, including three along its Atlantic coastline: Skidaway Island, Fort McAllister, and Crooked River. In South Carolina a similar number of state parks offer campsites. Hammocks Beach State Park offers primitive beach camping on Bear Island in North Carolina and 29 other state parks offer campsites. For detailed information on the state parks and and to reserve a site, visit the state parks' Web site.

A variety of camping experiences are available at the Great Smoky Mountains National Park, including backcountry and horse camping. Reservations for Elkmont, Smokemont, Cades Cove, and Cosby, the park's most popular developed campgrounds (with flush toilets and running water) are required from May 15–Oct. 31. Camping outside those dates or at the parks other campgrounds is first-come, first-served.

Camping Contacts Georgia State Parks (⊕gastateparks.org). **Great Smoky Mountains National Park** (☎877/444-6777 ⊕www. nps.gov/grsm). **North Carolina State Parks** (⊕www.ncparks.gov). **South Carolina State Parks** (⊕www.southcarolinaparks.com).

HOME EXCHANGES

With a direct home exchange you stay in someone else's home while they stay in yours. Some outfits also deal with vacation homes, so you're not actually staying in someone's full-time residence, just their vacant weekend place.

Exchange Clubs Home Exchange.com (📧800/877–8723 ⊕www.homeexchange. com); $99.95 for a one-year online listing. **HomeLink International** (📧800/638–3841 ⊕www.homelink.org); $110 yearly.

HOSTELS

North Carolina has hostels in Asheville, Greensboro, and Pembroke, as well as in Kitty Hawk on the Outer Banks. In South Carolina, hostels are found in two historic properties in Charleston and in Georgetown. Georgia's offerings include hostels in Atlanta and Savannah. To find U.S. hostels, check out ⊕*hostelhandbook.com*; for hostel listings around the world visit ⊕*hostel.com*.

General Hostel Contacts Hostels.com (⊕www.hostels.com). **The Hostel Handbook** (⊕hostelhandbook.com).

Georgia Hostel Contacts Atlanta International Hostel (✉223 Ponce De Leon Ave. Atlanta, GA 📧404/875–9449 or 800/473–9449 ⊕www.hostel-atlanta.com). **Hostel in the Forest** (✉3901 US Hwy. 82, Brunswick, GA 📧912/264–9738 ⊕www.foresthostel. com). **Savannah Pensione** (✉304 E. Hall St., Savannah, GA 📧912/236–7744 ⊕www. savannahpensione.com).

North Carolina Hostel Contacts Bon Paul & Sharky's Hostel (✉816 Haywood Rd., Asheville, NC 📧828/350–9929 ⊕www. bonpaulandsharkys.com). **Hi-Pembroke Baptist Student Union House** (✉300 N. Odum Rd., Pembroke, NC 📧910/521–8777). **OK Outer Banks International Hostel** (✉1004 West Kitty Hawk Rd., Kitty Hawk, NC 📧252/261–2294).

South Carolina Hostel Contacts OKNotso Hostel (✉156 Spring St., Charleston, SC 📧843/722–8383 ⊕www.notsohostel.com).

HOTELS

In summer, especially July and August, hotel rooms in coastal areas and the mountains can be hard to come by unless you book well in advance. In the mountains, the autumn leaf-peeping season, typically early October to early November, is the busiest time of the year, and on weekends nearly every room is booked. Lodging in North Carolina's Triad area is difficult during the twice-yearly international furniture shows: in April and October all rooms are booked within a 30-mi radius of the show's location in High Point. Lodging in downtown Atlanta, despite its density of hotels, can be problematic during trade shows at the Georgia World Congress Center and the AmericasMart complex.

All hotels listed in this book have private baths unless otherwise noted.

▌ EATING OUT

The increase of international flavors in the region reflects the tastes and backgrounds of the people who have flooded into the Carolinas and Georgia over the past couple of decades. Bagels are as common nowadays as biscuits, and, especially in urban areas it can be harder to find country cooking than a plate of hummus. For the most part, though, plenty of traditional Southern staples—barbecue, fried chicken, greens, and the like—are available.

Atlanta now has a big-city mix of neighborhood bistros, ethnic eateries, and expense-account restaurants. A new wave of restaurants in Charleston and Savannah serve innovative versions of Lowcountry cooking, with lighter takes on traditional dishes. In North Carolina you can find some nationally recognized restaurants in Charlotte, Asheville, and elsewhere. Outside of the many resort areas along the coast and in the mountains, dining costs in the region are often lower than those in the North.

Vegetarians will have no trouble finding attractive places to eat in any of the larger metropolitan areas, although in small towns they may have to stick with pizza. Asheville is a haven for vegetarians; it has been named to many lists of the top vegetarian cities, including being named the most vegetarian-friendly city in the United States by People for the Ethical Treatment of Animals.

MEALS & MEALTIMES

The Southern tradition of Sunday dinner—usually a midday meal—has morphed to some degree, at least in urban areas, to Sunday brunch. For many this meal follows midmorning church services, so be advised that restaurants will often be very busy through the middle of the day. In smaller towns many restaurants are closed on Sunday. On weekdays in larger cities, restaurants will be packed with nearby workers from before noon until well after 1:30 PM. On Saturday, eateries in cities can be packed from morning through night. In small towns and big cities, weekday nights—when crowds are less likely and the staff can offer diners more time—can be the most pleasant for fine dining.

Southerners tend to eat on the early side, with lunch crowds beginning to appear before noon. The peak time for dinner is around 7. However, late-evening dining is not unusual in big cities, college towns, and tourist destinations.

Unless otherwise noted, the restaurants listed in this guide are open daily for lunch and dinner.

RESERVATIONS & DRESS

For the most part, restaurants in the Carolinas and Georgia tend to be informal. A coat and tie are rarely required, except in a few of the fanciest places. Business-casual clothes are safe almost anywhere.

Reservation Contacts OpenTable (⊕www.opentable.com). **DinnerBroker** (⊕www.dinnerbroker.com).

WINES, BEER & SPIRITS

Blue laws—legislation forbidding sales on Sunday—have a history in this region dating to the 1600s. These bans are still observed in many rural areas, particularly with regard to alcohol sales. Liquor stores are closed on Sunday in the Carolinas and Georgia. ■TIP→In Georgia, the law prohibits Sunday sales of beer, wine, or liquor except for consumption on premise in restaurants, entertainment districts, and public venues in certain jurisdictions. Beer and wine can't be sold anywhere before 12 noon in North Carolina and South Carolina on Sundays. There are entire counties in the Carolinas and Georgia that prohibit the sale of alcoholic beverages in restaurants. Some cities and towns allow the sale of beer and wine in restaurants, but not mixed drinks. In North Carolina, bottled distilled spirits are only sold through "ABC" (Alcoholic Beverage Control) outlets; beer and wine, however, are available in most grocery and convenience stores.

Although the Carolinas and Georgia will never be the Napa Valley, the last decade has seen a huge increase in the number of vineyards. North Carolina now has more than 60 wineries, and the Yadkin Valley is the state's first federally recognized American Viticultural Area, with more than 400 acres of vineyards in production. Asheville Biltmore Estate Wine Company is the most popular winery in the United States, with about 1 million visitors each year. Georgia's Wine Highway, which guides visitors to a number of wineries, runs from just north of Atlanta up through the north Georgia mountains. Muscadine and scuppernong grapes are native to warmer parts of the region; the sweetish wine from these grapes may not impress, but traditional wine grapes are also widely grown.

Microbreweries are common all over the region, with hot spots being Asheville, Wilmington, Charlotte, and Charleston, as well as the Triangle of Raleigh, Durham, and Chapel Hill. There are more than 40 microbreweries in North Carolina, some two dozen in South Carolina, and about a half-dozen in Georgia, where state laws on alcohol distribution have crimped the growth of microbreweries.

I HEALTH

With the exception of the mountains of north Georgia and western North Carolina, in the Carolinas and Georgia it's hot and humid for at least six months of the year. Away from the coast, midsummer temperatures can reach the high 90s, making heat exhaustion and heatstroke real possibilities. Heat exhaustion is marked by muscle cramps, dizziness, nausea, and profuse sweating. To counter its effects, lie down in a cool place with the head slightly lower than the rest of the body. Sip cool, not cold, fluids. Life-threatening heatstroke is caused by a failure of the body to effectively regulate its temperature. In the early stages, heatstroke causes fatigue, dizziness, and headache. Later the skin becomes hot, red, and dry (due to lack of sweating), and body temperatures rise to as high as 106°F. Heatstroke requires immediate medical care.

At the beach or anywhere in the sun, slather on the sunscreen. Reapply it every two hours, or more frequently after swimming or perspiring. Remember that many sunscreens block only the ultraviolet light called UVB, and not UVA, which may be a big factor in skin cancer. Even with sunscreen it's important to wear a hat and protective clothing and to avoid prolonged exposure to the sun.

The coastal areas of the Carolinas and Georgia, especially the swamps and marshes of the Lowcountry, are home to a variety of noxious bugs: mosquitoes, sandflies, biting midges, black flies, chiggers, and no-see-ums. Most are not a problem when the wind is blowing, but when the breezes die down—watch out! Experts agree that DEET is the most effective mosquito repellent, but this chemical is so powerful that strong concentrations can melt plastic. Repellents with 100% DEET are available, but those containing less than 30% should work fine for adults; children should not use products with more than 10%. Products containing the chemical icaridin are effective against many insects, and don't have the strong odor or skin-irritating qualities of those with DEET. The plant-based oil of lemon eucalyptus, used in some natural repellents, performed well in some studies. Mosquito coils and citronella candles will also help ward off mosquitoes.

For sandflies or other tiny biting bugs, repellents with DEET alone are often not effective. What may help is dousing feet, ankles, and other exposed areas with an oily lotion, such as baby oil, which effectively drowns them.

The mountains of western North Carolina and north Georgia generally have few mosquitoes or other biting bugs, but in warm weather hikers may pick up chiggers or ticks. Use repellents with DEET on exposed skin. Wasps, bees, and small but ferocious yellow jackets are common throughout the region.

Feel free to drink tap water everywhere in the region, although in coastal areas it may have a sulfur smell. Many visitors to the beaches prefer to buy bottled water.

MONEY

Although the cost of living remains fairly low in most parts of the South, travel-related costs (such as dining, lodging, and transportation) have become increasingly steep in Atlanta. And tourist attractions are pricey, too. For example, a tour of CNN Center is $12, admission to the High Museum of Art in Atlanta is $18, and getting into Georgia Aquarium is a steep $26. Costs can also be dear in resort communities throughout the Carolinas and Georgia.

Prices throughout this guide are given for adults. Substantially reduced fees are almost always available for children, students, and senior citizens.

PACKING

Except for some high-elevation mountain areas, the Carolinas and Georgia are hot and humid in summer and sunny and mild in winter. Smart but casual attire works fine almost everywhere. A few chic restaurants in the cities prefer more elegant dress, and tradition-minded lodges in the mountains and resorts along the coast still require jackets and ties for men for dinner. For colder months pack a lightweight coat, slacks, and sweaters; bring along heavier clothing in some mountainous areas, where cold, damp weather prevails and snow is not unusual. Keeping summer's humidity in mind, pack absorbent natural fabrics that breathe; bring an umbrella, but leave the plastic raincoat at home. A jacket or sweater is useful for summer evenings and for too-cool air-conditioning. And don't forget insect repellent and sunscreen.

SAFETY

In general, the Carolinas and Georgia are safe destinations for travelers. Most rural and suburban areas have low crime rates. However, some of the region's larger cities, such as Atlanta, have high crime rates.

In urban areas, follow proven traveler's precautions: don't wander onto deserted streets after dark, avoid flashing large sums of money or fancy jewelry, and keep an eye on purses and backpacks. If walking, even around the historic district, ask about areas to avoid at a hotel or a tourist information center; if in doubt, take a taxi.

In the Smoky Mountains the greatest concerns are driving on some of the curving and narrow roads—sometimes in heavy traffic—and theft of property and credit cards from vehicles in parking lots. Sometimes thieves will watch for motorists locking valuables in their trunks before leaving their cars. Single-car accidents, with motorists hitting trees or rocky outcroppings are the cause of most accidents. Stolen property is rare in campsites. Drivers should also keep in mind that cell phones don't often work in the park. If visitors encounter bears, they are advised not to move suddenly, but to back away slowly.

Contact Transportation Security Administration (TSA; ⊕ www.tsa.gov)

TAXES

Sales taxes are: Georgia 4%, North Carolina 4.25%, and South Carolina 6%. Some counties or cities may impose an additional sales tax of 1% to 3%. Most municipalities also levy a lodging tax (usually exempting small inns) and sometimes a restaurant tax. The hotel taxes in the South can be rather steep: as much as 8 % in some places in Georgia and many counties in North Carolina. Taxes and fees on car rentals, especially if rented from an airport, can easily add 30% or more to the bill.

▮ TIME

Georgia and the Carolinas fall in the eastern standard time (EST) zone, which is the same as New York and Florida, making it three hours ahead of California.

Time Zones Timeanddate.com (⊕www. timeanddate.com/worldclock) can provide the correct time anywhere.

▮ TIPPING

Tipping in the Carolinas and Georgia is essentially the same as tipping anywhere else in the United States. A bartender typically receives from $1 to $5 per round of drinks, depending on the number of drinks. Tipping at hotels varies with the level of the hotel, but here are some general guidelines: bellhops should be tipped $1 to $5 per bag; if doormen help to hail a cab tip $1 to $2; maids should receive $1 to $3 in cash daily; room-service waiters get $1 to $2 even if a service charge has been added; and tip concierges $5 or more depending on what service they perform.

Taxi drivers should be tipped 15%–20% of the fare, rounded up to the next dollar amount. Tour guides receive 10% the cost of the tour. Valet parking attendants receive $1 to $2 when you get your car back. Tipping at restaurants varies from 15% to 20% by level of service and level of restaurant, with 20% being the norm at high-end restaurants.

▮ TOURS

The Carolinas and Georgia predominantly attract visitors traveling independently, usually by car. But some areas—notably Savannah, Charleston, Asheville, and the Great Smoky Mountains—get a number of escorted bus tours. Collette Tours, whose reservations are booked through Atlas Travel, has eight-day tours of Atlanta, Savannah, Charleston, and the Georgia Sea Islands. The escorted tour prices start at $1,099 per person. Prices

are subject to change. You stay at first-class hotels, such as the Jekyll Island Club, and the price includes most breakfasts and some dinners. Collette Tours also has an eight-day Great Smoky Mountains and Kentucky tour, price starting at $1,249, which stops in Tennessee and Kentucky. A large tour company called Tauck has an eight-day tour of Charleston, Savannah, Jekyll Island, and Hilton Head, staying at such high-end hotels as the Westin Resort on Hilton Head. The cost is $2,250 per person.

Recommended Companies Collette Tours (☎800/942-3301 ⊕www.escortedcollette-tours.com). **Tauck** (☎800/788-7885 ⊕www. tauck.com).

▮ VISITOR INFORMATION

Going online is the fastest way to get visitor information. All of the state tourism offices listed below have excellent Web sites, with maps and other travel information.

Contacts Georgia Department of Economic Development (⊠75 Fifth St., Technology Square, Suite 1200, Atlanta, GA ☎404/962-4000 or 800/847-4842 ⊕www.exploregeorgia. org). **North Carolina Travel & Tourism Division** (⊠301 N. Wilmington St., Raleigh, NC ☎919/715-5900 or 800/847-4862 ⊕www. visitnc.com). **South Carolina Department of Parks, Recreation, and Tourism** (⊠1205 Pendleton St., Room 248, Columbia, SC ☎803/734-1700 or 888/727-6453 ⊕www. travelsc.com).

ONLINE TRAVEL TOOLS

ALL ABOUT THE CAROLINAS & GEORGIA

Civil War Traveler (⊕*www.civilwartrav-eler.com*) has information about Civil War sites in the Carolinas and Georgia, as well as in other states. **Doc South** (⊕*docsouth.unc.edu*) is a vast collection of historical documents and archives on Southern history, culture, and literature. **Dr. Beach** (⊕*www.drbeach*.org) is Dr. Stephen Leatherman's take on the best beaches nationwide. In 2008, two Carolina beaches made his top 10 beaches list. Cape Hatteras, on the Outer Banks in North Carolina, was No. 8. In South Carolina, Kiawah Island's Beachwalker Park was No. 10. The online edition of **Southern Living** (⊕*www.southernliving. com*) has many articles on travel, attractions, gardens, and people in the region.

ART & CULTURE

Gullah Culture (⊕*www.pbs.org/now/arts/ gullah.html*), from the PBS program with Bill Moyers, is a good introduction to Gullah life and culture. **Handmade in America** (⊕*www.handmadeinamerica.org*) is a community organization whose goal is to establish western North Carolina as the nation's center of handmade objects. **Penland School of Crafts** (⊕*www.penland.org*) is devoted to the famous crafts school in the North Carolina Mountains, but it also has a wealth of information on crafts in the region. **Southern High Craft Guild** (⊕*www.southernhighlandguild.org*) represents more than 900 craftspeople in the Southeast.

GOLF

Georgia State Park Golf Courses (⊕*www. georgiagolf.com*) has detailed information on Georgia's public golf courses. **Golf Guide** (⊕*www.golfguideweb.com*) has links to most golf courses in the Carolinas and Georgia. **Golf Link** (⊕*www.golflink. com*) offers information on nearly all the golf courses in the region. **Golf North Carolina** (⊕*www.golfnorthcarolina.com*) offers a database search of North Carolina's 600 golf courses. In addition to the usual course information, this site has sections on golf humor and golf trivia. Public golf courses in South Carolina can be researched on **South Carolina Golf Trail** (⊕*www.scgolftrail.com*).

OUTDOORS

The **Appalachian Trail Conservancy** (⊕*www. appalachiantrail.org*) is dedicated to preserving the nation's longest footpath, which runs from Georgia all the way to

---

FODORS.COM CONNECTION

Before your trip, be sure to check out what other travelers are saying in Talk on ⊕ *www.fodors.com.*

Maine. The **Blue Ridge Parkway Association Guide** (⊕*www.blueridgeparkway.org*) has detailed information on one of the most beautiful roads in America. **Georgia State Parks** (⊕*www.gastateparks.org*) covers accommodations, recreational activities, and special activities at one of the best state park systems in the United States. **National Forests in North Carolina** (⊕*www.cs.unca.edu/nfsnc*) is a comprehensive guide to the state's national forests. The **National Park Service** (⊕*www. nps.gov/grsm*) has information on all of the national parks in the region, including the Great Smoky Mountains, the country's most popular national park. **North Carolina State Parks** (⊕*www.ils.unc.edu/ parkproject/main/visit.html*) has basic information on state parks. **South Carolina State Parks** (⊕*www.southcarolinaparks. com*) is a colorful site with information on accommodations, outdoor activities, and even discounts offered at the parks.

WINE

The excellent site for **Georgia Wine Country** (⊕*www.georgiawinecountry.com*) has information on more than two dozen wineries in Georgia. **North Carolina Wines** (⊕*www.visitncwine.com*) is a comprehensive site with facts on almost 70 wineries in North Carolina. **Winegrowers Association of Georgia** (⊕*www.georgia wine.com*) is a guide to touring and tasting Georgia's wineries.

INDEX

NOTES

NOTES

NOTES

NOTES

NOTES

NOTES

NOTES

NOTES

ABOUT OUR WRITERS

Christine Anderson is a freelance writer and photographer who loves to travel. Her favorite discoveries are those found closest to home. A native of the South Carolina Lowcountry, she now resides with her husband and two sons in Columbia, where she writes for newspapers and magazines around the state. She updated the Midlands & Upstate chapter.

Like nearly everyone else on the North Carolina coast, **Liz Biro** and her family came for the expansive beaches, friendly atmosphere, and fresh seafood. A journalist for 25 years, she's covered everything from local fisheries to capital politics. Liz left it all behind for a while to become a chef, and today writes about food and dining for various publications, including the *Star-News* in Wilmington, N.C., and the statewide *North Carolina Signature* magazine. She updated this guide's chapter on the North Carolina coast.

Born and raised in the Shenandoah Valley of Virginia, **Mary Erskine** left the lovely mountains for the humidity, beaches, and palmetto bugs of South Carolina in 2000. Her work has been featured along the South Carolina coast as a writer, designer, and editor for a number of state newspapers. For this guide, she focused on the Grand Strand region, including Myrtle Beach, where she resided for three years before moving to Charleston.

After 16 years of editing business, metro, and feature stories and developing projects for the *Atlanta Journal-Constitution* and *www.ajc.com*, **Michele Foust** is now a freelance writer, savoring dogwoods and azaleas in the spring, the colorful foliage of the North Georgia mountains in the fall, and everything about Atlanta, a city that balances international flair with world-famous Southern hospitality. She updated the Experience the Carolinas & Georgia, North Georgia, and Travel Smart.

Amber Nimocks is a North Carolina native who lives in downtown Raleigh with her husband, son, and two dogs. Before becoming a freelance writer and editor, her work in newspapers included a stint as food editor at *The News & Observer* of Raleigh and as features editor at the *Star-News* in Wilmington, N.C. She writes a wine column for *The News & Observer* and is a contributing editor for *Edible Piedmont* magazine. She updated the Piedmont & the Sandhills chapter.

Asheville native and former New Orleans newspaper editor **Lan Sluder** has written a half-dozen books, including travel guides to Belize and the coast of the Carolinas and Georgia. His articles have appeared in *Caribbean Travel & Life*, the *Chicago Tribune*, the *New York Times*, *Where to Retire* and other publications around the world. He has also contributed to other Fodor's guides, including *Fodor's Belize* and *InFocus Great Smoky Mountains National Park*. Lan's home base in North Carolina is a mountain farm near Asheville settled by his forebears in the early 1800s.

Her family's move from Connecticut to South Carolina earned **Eileen Robinson Smith** the distinction of being Yankee-born and Southern-raised. Waving good-bye to her apartment in New York City's Park Avenue, she moved into a lakefront home in Charleston in 1982. A former editor of *Charleston* magazine, she has written for local, regional, and national publications such as *Latitudes* and *Sky*. She has been a contributor to *Fodor's Caribbean* for more than a decade. For this guide she returned to her beloved Lowcountry, updating the chapters for Charleston, Savannah, and Hilton Head.

Christine Van Dusen may be a Yankee by birth, but she's a Southerner at heart, living in the Inman Park neighborhood of Atlanta for almost eight years with her husband and two dogs. The founder of Linchpin Media, she's an award-winning journalist whose work has appeared in numerous publications, including the *Atlanta Journal-Constitution*, *Atlanta Magazine*, *Creative Loafing Atlanta*, *Charlotte Magazine*, *US Weekly*, *Paste*, and *The Progressive*. She updated the Atlanta, Southwest Georgia, and Central Georgia chapters.

Fodor's

The Carolinas and Georgia Maps

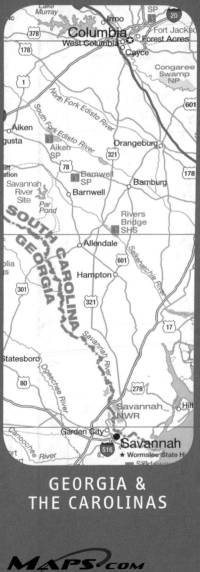

GEORGIA & THE CAROLINAS

ATLANTA & CHARLESTON

MAPS.COM